D0161873

68HC12 Microcontroller
Theory and Applications

Daniel J. Pack
United States Air Force Academy

Steven F. Barrett
University of Wyoming

Prentice Hall
Upper Saddle River, New Jersey 07458

Library of Congress Cataloging-in-Publication Data

CIP data on file.

Vice President and Editorial Director, ECS: *Marcia J. Horton*
Publisher: *Tom Robbins*
Acquisitions Editor: *Eric Frank*
Editorial Assistant: *Jessica Romeo*
Vice President and Director of Production and Manufacturing, ESM: *David W. Riccardi*
Executive Managing Editor: *Vince O'Brien*
Managing Editor: *David A. George*
Production Editor: *Leslie Galen*
Director of Creative Services: *Paul Belfanti*
Creative Director: *Carole Anson*
Art Director: *Jayne Conte*
Art Editor: *Greg Dulles*
Manufacturing Manager: *Trudy Pisciotti*
Manufacturing Buyer: *Lynda Castillo*
Marketing Manager: *Holly Stark*

Cover photograph supplied Courtesy of Motorola, Inc.

Prentice-Hall, Inc.
Upper Saddle River, NJ 07458

Printed in the United States of America

10 9 8 7 6 5 4

ISBN 0-13-033776-5

Pearson Education Ltd., *London*
Pearson Education Australia Pty. Ltd., *Sydney*
Pearson Education Singapore, Pte. Ltd.
Pearson Education North Asia Ltd., *Hong Kong*
Pearson Education Canada, Inc., *Toronto*
Pearson Educacíon de Mexico, S.A. de C.V.
Pearson Education–Japan, *Tokyo*
Pearson Education Malaysia, Pte. Ltd.
Pearson Education, *Upper Saddle River, New Jersey*

Contents

Preface

During the summer of 1992, the first author (D.P.) was first introduced to the family of Motorola 68HC11 Microcontrollers as he was constructing an interface module between a Puma robot arm robot controller and a force-torque sensor. Since then, he has become aware of the *power* of microcontrollers and their unlimited applications. Fortunately, as a professor of electrical engineering at the U.S. Air Force Academy, he has had ample opportunities to share his microcontroller experience with students. In the fall of 1995 at the Academy, he met the second author (S.B.), a friend, mentor, and, at that time, his immediate boss. Soon after the first author's arrival at the Academy, S.B. started to share his expert knowledge on digital systems with D.P., and D.P. has benefited tremendously to this point. Over time, we decided to share our work in a more concrete form. That is when we decided to write a book on the 68HC12.

MOTIVATION

One of the most compelling reasons to write 68HC12 book is that Motorola is slowly phasing out the popular 68HC11 microcontroller-based evaluation boards and replacing them with the 68HC12. The 68HC11 family of microcontrollers have been the preferred choice of educators due to their built-in input and output (I/O) capabilities, a variety of timer functions, and platforms for easy programming and interfacing. The 68HC12 retained all the favorable features of the 68HC11 (in fact, one can run any 68HC11 code on the 68HC12 with minor modifications) and increased the computational power while enhancing hardware and software components. Compared to its predecessor, the 68HC12 has reduced the interrupt latency time, increased the I/O capacity, added complex math operations, incorporated fuzzy logic functions, and improved the overall system performance by adapting a mechanism called *instruction queuing*, which is similar to the pipelining scheme found in more powerful microprocessors. This book is about the 68HC12; we show how to program and uncover the possibilities of 68HC12 applications.

INTENDED READERS

This book is written for undergraduate students taking a microcontroller or microprocessor course, frequently found in electrical engineering and computer engineering curricula. These courses aim to teach students the fundamental knowledge of microcontrollers/microprocessors and techniques to interface them with external devices, pointing out the important role of embedded microcontroller systems in our modern society. The book is designed to assist instructors to fulfill such course objectives by combining both the theory and applications of microcontrollers. In particular, we chose the 68HC12 microcontroller since it is becoming the industry standard.

We expect students to have taken an introductory logic course and a freshmen programming language course. For a quick review of digital logic, we included Appendix D. Having taken a computer language course will help students understand how assembly language programs are related to high-level language programs, but we expect students with a minimal exposure to computer programming will follow the text subjects without too much trouble.

We must also address one other category of readers. Although the book is mainly designed for students learning the subject in an academic setting, it can be easily adopted by engineers who want to learn the subject on their own. Since the underlying concepts and functional components of two different types of microcontrollers are very similar to each other, the acquired knowledge of the 68HC12 can naturally be applied to other microprocessors and microcontrollers. Such knowledge is essential for electrical and computer engineering students as we live in a society where more and more engineering problems are solved by embedded microcontrollers. In fact, we find the scope of actual applications of microcontrollers expanding as new problems are encountered and solved by the engineering community.

OBJECTIVES

We have three objectives for writing this book; we want you to learn (1) fundamental assembly language programming skills, (2) functional hardware components of a microcontroller, and (3) skills to interface a variety of external devices with microcontrollers. The entire book is designed with those three objectives in mind. As you already know, skills cannot be mastered without practice, and we encourage you to program and try the examples as you read. The enclosed software on the back of the book provides a convenient means to write, edit, assemble, and execute your programs. We have included lots of examples and applications to introduce you to some of the important uses of the 68HC12 controller.

Among the many examples, you will find a set of mobile robot applications throughout the book. We included these applications for their pedagogical advantages learned from our own experience for using them in our microcontroller courses. In fact, the mobile robot applications not only made students appreciate the range of tasks the controller can perform, but also helped the students to understand and integrate multiple subject topics in a single project.

Each year, the student response has been nothing short of enthusiastic. The students consistently pointed out the value of the mobile robot applications that provided students with an experience to develop a hands-on working knowledge of the microcontroller. We hope you will take full advantage of the text by creating and developing your own mobile robots. Appendix E contains the information necessary for you to acquire parts to construct your own robot. The applications are, however, not limited to the robot applications. You will find an ample amount of nonrobot applications throughout the book.

ORGANIZATION

In organizing each chapter, we gave a great deal of consideration to the order and means of subject presentations. The assembly language programming techniques are studied in the first portion of the book, whereas the rest of the book is dedicated to the controller hardware and how to program the hardware components to interface the controller with external devices. Each chapter starts with a list of chapter objectives to give you a clear purpose for reading the entire chapter. Following the objectives, you will also find an introductory subsection for each chapter, informing you of the section contents. After the main body of a chapter is presented, starting in Chapter 3, you will find an application section, where a particular application is chosen to illustrate the subjects contained in the chapter. We study the chapter subjects once again in the laboratory application section, which follows the application section.

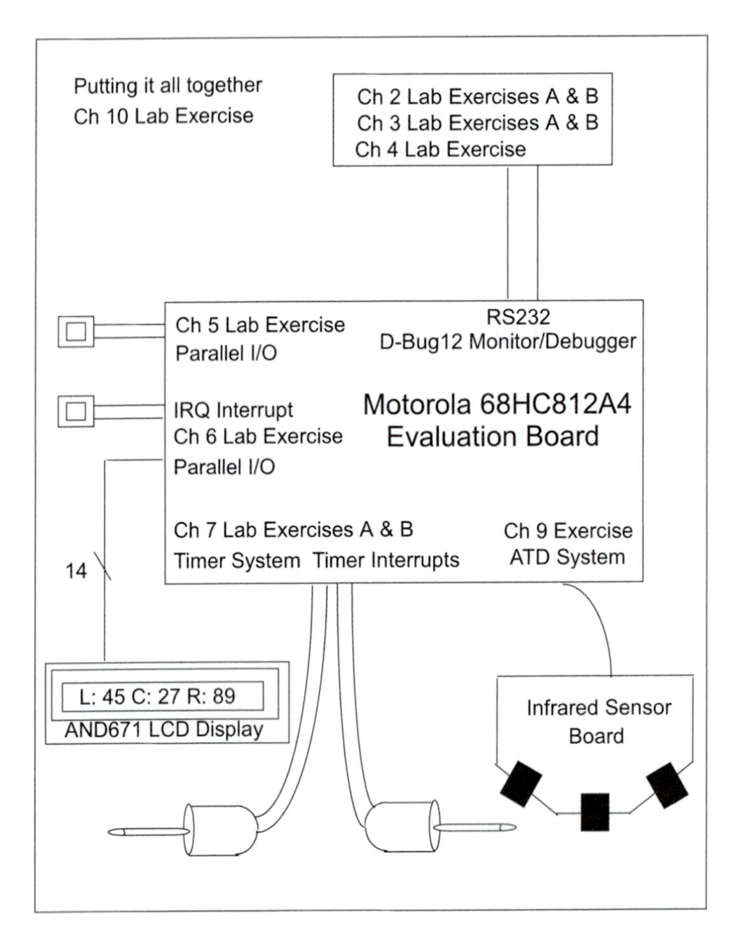

Figure 1 Lab Sequence Block Diagram.

A laboratory application section contains the mobile robot laboratory exercises associated with the chapter subject. The 11 exercises can be used as a set of optional, fun activities as you read this book or as a part of a course requirement. Figure 1 provides an overview of where each laboratory exercise fits in the development of the overall mobile robot control program.

The first five labs found in Chapters 2 through 4 will provide you with opportunities to exercise fundamental assembly language programming skills. Chapter 2 laboratory exercise A teaches you how to use the enclosed software editor, assembler, loader, and the 68HC12 built-in monitor commands. Chapter 2 laboratory exercise B is designed for you to write a simple assembly language program using some basic instructions as well as if-then-else programming constructs (branch instructions). This laboratory exercise is later modified to make navigational decisions for the mobile robot based on infrared sensor values. In Chapter 3 laboratory exercise A, you will write a program with two subroutines, applying two parameter passing methods to generate simulated motor speed profiles. Continuing the subroutine theme, Chapter 3 laboratory exercise B will show you how to access built-in D-bug12 I/O subroutines: You will write a program to display the motor speed profiles on a PC screen using appropriate I/O subroutines. The skills learned in this laboratory exercise are later used to debug other programs. Chapter 4 laboratory exercise gives you the first chance to program a fuzzy logic controller using special 68HC12 fuzzy logic instructions. The fuzzy controller uses a set of three IR sensor inputs and computes a navigational decision, simulating robot motions in a maze. By the end of this lab, we expect you to be comfortable with writing, assembling, running, and debugging small assembly language programs. In addition, you will have a library of routines that form the basis of the final robot control program.

The next six exercises in Chapters 5 through 9 are hardware intensive while we continue to reinforce learned and introduce new programming techniques; we extend your ability to program the controller's hardware modules. Chapter 5 laboratory exercise lets you interface a basic external switch with the 68HC12. The lab can also be used to practice implementing a technique called *polling*. Chapter 6 laboratory exercise teaches students to write a program that incorporates an external interrupt. In addition, you will continue to build your I/O interface skills by controlling the display of an AND671 8-bit Liquid Crystal Display unit with the 68HC12. Chapter 7 laboratory exercises A and B are designed to teach you to program the timer function modules and the I/O ports of the 68HC12. In these exercises, you will write programs to control the direction and speed of the mobile robot by generating pulse-width-modulated signals and control signals for two DC motors. These lab exercises build on Chapter 5 laboratory exercise and exploit the real-time I/O hardware. Chapter 9 laboratory exercise focuses on the built-in analog-to-digital (ATD) converter. Finally, the last lab exercise found in Chapter 10 gives you an opportunity to combine your accumulated 68HC12 hardware knowledge, assembly language programming skills, and hardware interfacing skills to create a fully operational mobile robot. In this exercise, you will find the rules and information necessary to conduct a mobile robot maze navigation competition, which we hold at the end of our microcontroller course. The competition is held during the last lesson period of the course each year; we invite all students and faculty to have a great time together.

These exercises tie together concepts and skills while reinforcing the objectives of this book. The students at the Academy have thoroughly enjoyed these exercises, and we have received very positive student feedback for using them in our courses. Even if you decide not to actually perform all of the laboratory exercises, you should take time to read the laboratory application sections since you will learn implementation details and find hardware interface techniques that do not appear in other parts of the book.

After the laboratory application section, you will find further reading and reference sections. These sections are for those who wish to pursue the chapter subjects beyond the scope covered in the chapter. Finally, the chapter problems that follow the summary sections are divided into three separate groups based on the estimated time to complete each problem: fundamental problems that should be solved within 10 minutes; advanced problems that should take up to 20 minutes to solve; and challenging problems that should take more than 20 minutes to complete. For instructors, the publisher has an instructor manual that contains answers to all chapter problems and the laboratory exercise programs. For both students and instructors, the textbook website (*http://www.prenhall.com/pack*) includes links to a set of selected chapter problem solutions and links to a variety of resources. The website is of necessity due to the dynamic nature of the microcontroller industry and our desire to keep up with the latest industry changes.

The 10 chapters are organized in the following manner. Chapter 1 presents a brief computer history, principle components of a computer, embedded computers, and applications of embedded computers. In this chapter, we give an overview of the Motorola 68HC12 16-bit microcontroller: software and hardware. Chapter 2 starts with fundamental assembly language programming skills that include the 68HC12 instruction set. We show valid addressing modes for the microcontroller and discuss functions of major instructions: arithmetic and logical operations, load and store operations, bit manipulation operations, and branch operations.

Chapter 3 continues to discuss software issues. We present additional assembly language programming skills that include the concept of stack, loops, subroutines, and if-then-else program structures. Chapter 4 explains how to design and implement fuzzy logic controllers. In this chapter, we explain the 68HC12 instructions associated with fuzzy logic controllers by showing a number of example fuzzy logic controllers.

Chapter 5 is the first chapter where we start to present the hardware components of the 68HC12. In this chapter, we discuss how to set up modes of operation and introduce basic functional hardware components including hardware pin definitions. All I/O ports of the controller and their use are also studied in this chapter. Chapter 6 picks up the important subject of interrupts and resets, explaining how to program the exception handling actions in the forms of interrupt service routines.

Chapter 7 is a detailed description of the timer functions of the 68HC12. We spend some time discussing the output compare, input capture, and pulse accumulator functions. Chapter 8 focuses on the memory system of the 68HC12, where we describe the different types of memory, the memory map, and how to expand a memory system. This discussion leads to the topic of bus expansion and timing analysis. Chapter 9 starts with the theories involved in converting analog signals to digital signals. The chapter introduces different ATD conversion techniques and presents the 68HC12 built-in ATD converter. Finally, Chapter 10 is dedicated to the serial communication hardware features of the 68HC12. Two different systems—a serial communication interface system and a serial peripheral interface system—are presented in detail.

For completeness, you will find five appendixes at the end of the book. Appendix A contains the entire instruction set of the microcontroller in a tabulated format: The table contains the opcode, operand, number of clock cycles for execution, and the effects to the control code register for each instruction. Appendix B lists the control registers of the 68HC12, showing the default contents and the memory addresses. Appendix C provides background information on number systems, converting numbers among number systems. This appendix also studies binary arithmetic and the concept of 2's complement numbers. Appendix D summarizes fundamental digital logic concepts, including some combinational and sequential logic devices. Appendix E lists software and hardware vendors of products available for the 68HC12. In this appendix, you will also find information to obtain parts to build your own mobile robot, including the engineering diagrams of the robot.

ACKNOWLEDGMENT

Writing a book is hard work. The text is the culmination of efforts of many individuals besides the authors. We want to thank Tony Plutino of Motorola for his role in providing necessary hardware/software documentation and his assistance in helping us obtain the permission to use Motorola figures. We thank him for his enthusiastic support to get this book off the ground. Of course no good book can appear on the horizon without a great publisher and their people. We are grateful to Eric Frank, our acquisitions editor at Prentice Hall, the chief editor for this book, for his resourcefulness, insights, and cooperation. Jessica Romeo and Leslie Galen were invaluable to cover all necessary details. We benefited greatly from the initial feedback provided by Harold Stone and anonymous reviewers of the first draft. As a result, the quality of this book improved significantly. The enclosed software was developed by the P & E Microcomputer Inc. We want to thank David Perreault, the president of the company and professor of electrical engineering at Boston University, for his willingness to work with us to provide the excellent software environment for easy use of the 68HC12 controllers. We also acknowledge our department heads for their support. Colonel Alan Klayton (USAF Academy) was thrilled to hear of our work and enthusiastically embraced the project. Professor John Steadmen (University of Wyoming) gave tremendous encouragement for pursuing this project. We also thank numerous students who were enrolled in microcontroller courses at both institutions and provided the authors with many useful feedback and comments. We wish to acknowledge many colleagues at both the U.S. Air Force Academy and the University of Wyoming. Some of the problems we have used in this book were based on problems developed by the past and present instructors in the Department of Electrical Engineering at the Academy. Special thanks go to Pam Neal, George York, Bill Nace, and Anne Clark. A definite acknowledgment must be made to Cameron Wright at the Academy for being a patient and critical reviewer and still managing to remain a great friend, providing significant feedback that improved the quality of the book. We also want to appreciate Michael Milligan and Edward Doskocz for their careful reading of the original manuscript. A special thanks goes to Jon Trudeau and Dick Speakman for hardware support for labs in the EE 382 and the EE383 courses. Without their help, this work would not have been possible. We have made every effort to avoid errors in this book; however, this book may contain errors. The authors assume no liability for any damage caused by errors.

We also acknowledge our parents. Thank you moms, Eleanore and Jackie, and thank you dad, Frank, for always believing in me (S.B). Thank you moms, Young Shin and Rana, and thank you dads, Sung Bok and Chong Kon, for your encouragement and unfailing support (D.P.). Finally, our work could not have come to fruition without the sacrifices of our family members: Cindy, Heidi, Heather, Christine, Jon, Andrew, and Graham. We thank you and thank you.

DANIEL J. PACK
Colorado Springs, CO

STEVEN F. BARRETT
Laramie, WY

1

Introduction to the 68HC12

Objectives: After reading this chapter, you should be able to:

- List four functional components of a computer,
- Provide definitions for the terms *microprocessor*, *microcomputer*, and *microcontroller*,
- Give a brief history of computers and microcontrollers,
- Describe a variety of applications of embedded computers, and
- Illustrate the overall software and hardware components of the 68HC12 microcontroller.

As you see above, at the beginning of each chapter, we include a list of chapter objectives to show, at the outset, the topics you encounter in the chapter. Each chapter is written and designed with these objectives in mind. Since the book is about a special computer, called a *microcontroller*, this chapter starts with a brief history of computers followed by a section describing the four principle computer components. In the same section, we define the terms *microcomputers*, *microprocessors*, and *microcontrollers*, also called embedded computers. We include a variety of applications of embedded controllers in Section 1.3 to show you the important roles microcontrollers play in our modern society. In Section 1.4, we begin our study on the embedded computer of our interest, the Motorola 68HC12 microcontroller, and present the software and hardware overview. A summary followed by a further reading section concludes the chapter.

1.1 BRIEF HISTORY OF COMPUTERS

Computers, born over a half century ago, have had a significant impact on how we live today. We can hardly imagine what our daily lives would be like without computers. Ironically, such dependence was not what inventors of these machines had in their minds when computers were first created as part of World War II technology development efforts in the United States and Europe. In the beginning, the general belief of the public and the scientific community was that computers were only useful for big institutions and companies, not for personal use.

Technically speaking, the Chinese invented the first mechanical, computational device, called the *abacus*, in 500 BC. More recently, history records that Pascal, a Frenchman, was responsible for creating the first mechanical adder and subtractor in 1642. Pascal's invention later influenced the development of Babbage's mechanical computer and led to a mechanical relay computer by Konrad Zuse of Germany in 1941 before electronic computers appeared in human history (Hwang).

It was not until the mid-1940s that relay memories were invented. The relay memories were quickly combined with the vacuum tube technologies to construct the Electronic Numerical Integrator and Computer (ENIAC) by Eckert and Mauchly in 1950. This machine used over 18,000 tubes and 1500 electromagnetic relays to operate. The physical size of the machine was enormous: The computer was several feet wide and over 8 feet high. To program the computer, a set of spaghetti-like cables had to be used and no programming language existed (Patterson and Hennesey).

Computer historians usually give credit to Aiken from Harvard University, sponsored by the International Business Machine (IBM) company, for designing and creating one of the first electromechanical decimal computers, named Harvard Mark I. You can still see the remnants of this first machine in the Science building on the Harvard campus. These early computers, such as the Harvard Mark I, showed the benefits of computers in performing logical and arithmetic operations. Governments and commercial companies became increasingly interested in developing faster and more powerful computers. The invention of discrete transistors (analog transistors were invented in 1948 by Bardeen, Brattain, and Schockley from Bell Laboratory) and core memories during the 1950s accelerated the start of commercial computer companies such as IBM, RCA, Honeywell, and UNIVAC. The commercial computers were quickly purchased and put to use by governments and large business firms. During the 1960s, engineers and scientists began to cram in an ever-increasing number of transistors in a single chip, which allowed the creation of large-scale integrated and very large-scale integrated chips. In fact, the semiconductor industry doubled the number of transistors packed into a single chip every $1\frac{1}{2}$ to 2 years: This phenomenon is known as the Moore's Law in the industry. By the early 1970s, the advancement of semiconductor technology and the demands from the industry spurred the development of two quite different computers.

The first type of computers was created for general-purpose applications. These general-purpose computers typically executed complex computations and often processed a large body of data. Typical examples of such computers of today are servers and routers. Servers are computers that provide a variety of services for network computers. Routers are responsible for accurately transferring data to multiple locations in a computer network. The most prominent example of general-purpose computers is your personal computer at home. These computers allow you to execute sophisticated math software programs, write reports, play games, and communicate with friends via electronic mail (e-mail). The goal of general-purpose computers is to accommodate a variety of programs selected by users and execute them quickly. To meet this goal, engineers and scientists have been developing powerful computing units, sophisticated memories, complex input and output (I/O) devices, and efficient connections (buses) among these components. The most visible advancement in this branch of technology is in the personal computer (PC) industry. You may recall how quickly the name of a popular PC changed: IBM PCs, Apple Computers, 286, 386, 486, Pentium, Pentium II, Power PC, AMD K6, Pentium III, Pentium 4, AMD K7, Athlon, and Itanium. The breathtaking improvement of the computer performance was possible by the advancements in computing units, memories, I/O devices, and bus technologies.

During the same period of the general-purpose computer advancement, the second type of computers also emerged. In the mid 1970s, the automobile industry executives saw the benefits of including computers in their cars. They wanted to use the capabilities of computers to make their cars reliable, safe, fuel efficient, and attractive. Such computers did not require the "bells and whistles" or the speed of the general-purpose computers, but they needed to be compact and inexpensive. The compactness is necessary to embed computers in cars, and the computer cost was important to keep down the price of the automobiles. The initial designs of these computers were heavily influenced by the industry's desires and demands. These demands were met by the computer industry with the creation of embedded computers. Soon others saw the same benefits the automobile executives observed and participated in the success of the second type of computer industry. These computers, unlike their general-purpose computer cousins, contained all the necessary parts of a computer, including memory and I/O ports within a single chip. The size of memory within a single chip was varied based on the application of a user. These computers usually run with a much slower system clock[1] and have a small memory. Yet they are designed to meet the specific needs of an application and are not intended for general-purpose use. For example, the auto industry has been using embedded computers in suspension systems, antilock brakes, fuel injection systems, and panel display systems. You can also find this type of computer in your washing machine, microwave oven, camcorder, video cassette recorder, camera, cellular phone, and many other home appliances. You will be surprised to know that the number of microcontrollers sold each year is far greater than the number of general-purpose computers being sold. A typical example of this type of computer is the subject of this book—the 68HC12 microcontroller.

That is enough history. If you are interested in finding out more about computer history, you can read about it by looking up the pointers found in the further reading section at the end of this chapter. Computers now play important roles in every facet of our lives. We close this section with the following interesting fact. In the late 1940s, computers did not have any memory to store programs. In the 1960s, you could not buy a computer with today's desktop capabilities, which currently costs under $1000, even if you were willing to pay over $1 million. What will people say about today's computers in 50 years?

1.2 COMPUTERS AND EMBEDDED CONTROLLERS

In this section, we identify and describe the key components of a computer. We then define and differentiate the following terms: *microprocessors*, *microcontrollers*, and *microcomputers*.

You may have had an opportunity to open up a computer case and wondered how all the variety of electronic and some mechanical pieces within the case work together to make the computer function. To help us understand how a computer operates, let us consider each functional unit one at a time. All computers, whether we are considering the general-purpose computers or the microcontrollers, contain the following four hardware modules as shown in Figure 1.1: central processing unit (CPU), memory, input/output (I/O) devices, and buses.

The CPU governs the order of instruction execution, controls the access to memory and I/O devices, performs arithmetic and logical operations, and handles interrupt services. The CPU contains an arithmetic and logical unit (ALU), a con-

[1]The clock speed is usually used as a benchmark to evaluate the speed of a computer. Although this is not strictly correct, the clock speed of a computer generally gives a good indication of how fast a computer executes programs.

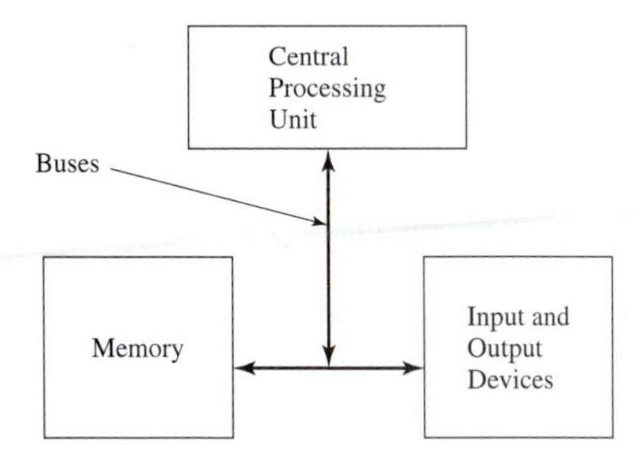

Figure 1.1 Four components of a computer.

trol unit, internal registers (for temporary storage), timer-related components, and internal and external connections (buses). The speed of a CPU is based on its clock, the format of an instruction, the parallel nature of instruction execution, and the access time to its memory and I/O devices. When you hear of an 850 MHz or a 1 GHz machine, you are only being told the clock speed. Although the clock speed gives a good indication of the machine speed, it is equally important to consider other mentioned factors to measure the overall performance of a computer.

If a CPU manages the activities of a computer, the memory is the storage area for instructions and data used by the CPU. As you learn in Chapter 8, the computer memory can be made out of a variety of technologies. We restrict this chapter's coverage to only the function of a memory, postponing our discussion of the memory technologies to Chapter 8. There are two different types of information stored in memory: instructions, specifying types of operations a computer executes, and data, the actual numerical values necessary to carry out instructions. For example, activities such as accessing an I/O device, adding two numbers, and finding out if a statement is true or false are instructions. In adding two numbers, the addition operation is an instruction and the actual numbers being added are data. Some computers store both instructions and data in a single memory. Such machines are known to use the von Neumann memory architecture. Other computers store instructions in an instruction memory and data in a separate data memory. This configuration is called the Harvard memory architecture.

You have probably heard of the term *cache*. It has the same pronunciation as cash. A cache is a type of memory created to reduce the memory access latency by reorganizing the memory. Suppose you have several gigabytes of memory. It naturally takes time to search through the memory to access what the CPU needs. Suppose your memory was only one kilobyte. It will take less time to search the same information if the information resides in both the large and small memories. The current computer industry trend is that the size of a typical application program increases, which results in a computer requiring a large memory space to store data and program. However, a large storage area means slowing down the memory access time, crippling the computer performance. The solution developed by the computer industry is the creation of a layered memory system as shown in Figure 1.2. A large memory, which contains all data and programs, lives on the bottom layer of a memory hierarchy. The size of a memory decreases as its distance to the CPU reduces, moving up the memory hierarchy. As the size of a memory decreases, a memory management algorithm tries to maximize the functionality of each particular memory unit by organizing the memory contents such that the memory access time is minimized. Thus, the goal of a smart memory system is to provide minimum access time while creating an illusion for the CPU that it has an unlimited amount of memory. Therefore, a smaller size of memory is placed closer to the CPU. This small memory component with a fast access time is called the cache.

The second-level cache is an extension of the same idea by creating a memory module that is a bit larger than the first cache but contains more information. The purpose of the second-level cache is to reduce the memory access time when necessary information for the current CPU execution cannot be found in the first-level cache. Instead of going all the way down to the main memory and searching, the CPU can find necessary information quickly and improve the overall system performance with the help of the second-level cache. In most modern-day high-performance computers, one finds the first- and second-level instruction and data caches. Before we move on to the next component, we must mention that the memory units in the hierarchy are created using different memory technologies, and the cost to create the same amount of memory goes down as you move from the top to the bottom of the hierarchy.

We now briefly discuss the third functional component of a computer: the I/O devices. We identify these devices with examples. For a personal computer, the keyboard, mouse, microphone, scanner, and camera are input devices. The pur-

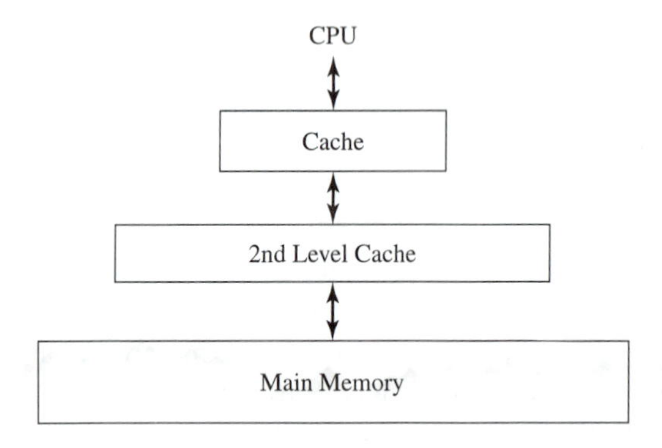

Figure 1.2 Memory hierarchy.

pose of an input device is to transfer outside information into the computer. The output devices, such as your computer monitors, speakers, and printers, are devices that allow the computers to inform their internal states and data to the outside world.

We have described the CPU, the memory, and the I/O devices. The last functional component of a computer is buses. These are not large vehicles that carry people from one place to another; you can think of them as roads that connect different parts of a computer. Buses are physical connections or pathways among the CPU, the memory, and the I/O devices. There are three types of buses: the address bus, the data bus, and the control bus.

The address bus is used to specify address locations where data and instructions reside in memory for the purpose of accessing them. The CPU puts an address on this bus when it needs to fetch particular information from its memory or when it needs to store information to a specific memory location. The data bus is used to carry actual instructions and data to and from memory locations, CPU, and I/O devices. The last bus, the control bus, is necessary to send and receive control commands such as read/write signals among a CPU, a memory, and I/O devices.

So far, we have discussed the hardware components of a computer. For the remainder of this section, we briefly describe the software. There are three different types of software: kernel, operating system, and application programs.

First, a kernel is a program responsible for making the computer hardware perform an instruction a programmer wrote. To carry out a programmer's instruction, all operations first need to be converted to forms understood by a kernel before being executed by the hardware. Kernels are written by system designers who understand the hardware operations of computers. The second type of software, the operating software, is responsible for memory management, exception services, and program execution control. Examples of operating software are BSD, SunOS, IRIX, MacOS, Windows 95,98, 2000, or ME, UNIX, Linux, and Windows NT. The third type of software, the application programs, is the one you are most familiar with (i.e., if you are not a system developer). The programs you write and use daily fall under this category. For example, word processors, spreadsheets, mail handlers, and text editors are all examples of application software.

We discussed the basic software and hardware units of a typical computer. We are now in a position to define the terms *microprocessor*, *microcontroller*, and *microcomputers*. Microprocessors are CPU units packaged in a single chip. Examples are the Intel Pentium family of chips, AMD K series, and the Athlon. A computer that uses the microprocessor as its CPU is called a microcomputer. A personal computer is a good example of a microcomputer. On the other hand, microcontrollers are created by packaging all computer components, the CPU, the memory, the I/O parts, and buses in a single, very large-scale integrated (VLSI) chip. As mentioned in the previous section, the motivation is to create a compact computer.

1.3 APPLICATIONS OF EMBEDDED CONTROLLERS

To name all applications that use embedded microcontrollers would take an entire chapter or even a book. Embedded microcontroller systems are ubiquitous in our modern society. In this section, we mention only a portion of existing embedded microcontroller systems to show the scope of the microcontroller usage.

We start with ones that can be easily found in our homes. Let us start with your family room or living room. You can find microcontrollers in your cable TV box, VCR, and music stereo system. Your personal computer has microcontrollers too: The one in the keyboard scans the keys and transmits codes to your computer, the one in your printer communicates with your computer to make sure a document or picture is printed correctly, and the one inside your modem allows you to surf the Internet using a telephone line.

If you walk into the kitchen, you find microcontrollers in the dishwasher, microwave oven, range, coffee maker, mixer, and telephone. When you wash your clothes, the microcontrollers in your washer and dryer work to make sure the job is done right. In your basement, you find a microcontroller in your temperature-controlling system working diligently to maintain a pleasant indoor temperature. If you step into your garage, you also find microcontrollers in the garage opener and the water sprinkler control box. If you have a house security system, that system, too, is operated by microcontrollers.

In your school, you readily find a list of microcontrollers. We already mentioned the controllers inside of computers. Each time you use a copier, a microcontroller inside the copier controls the copying process. When you walk into your laboratory, you encounter digital oscilloscopes, spectrum analyzers, and universal circuit identifiers and testers. All these devices contain microcontrollers to carry out their functions. Did we mention your calculator?

Microcontrollers are found in every part of our society. Fishermen use them in sonar transducers to locate schools of fish, amateur star gazers rely on them in their telescopes to balance and track stars, travelers receive help from them in navigation systems to find places, moms and dads count on them in their cameras and camcorders to capture their childrens' pictures (making memories last), hobbyists use them to create fun robots, and ever-increasing numbers of people communicate with each other with the help of microcontroller-embedded cellular phones.

One of the most influential embedded microcontroller producers is the Motorola company. Motorola developed and marketed the 68HC11 family of microcontrollers starting in the mid-1980s. Since then, many 68HC microcontroller families followed. The microcontrollers from Motorola have been used in a variety of applications over the years. The biggest buyers of these controllers come from the automobile industry. If you drove a General Motor's car during the past 10 to 15 years, chances are that the car you drove had 68HC11 microcontrollers in it: controlling the suspension system to give you a smooth ride; increasing the fuel economy in the fuel injection system by controlling air-fuel mixture, spark timing, and idle speed; keeping you safe with the antilock brake system that monitors the tire traction; and informing the status of your automobile with the panel display system.

The 68HC microcontrollers are also widely used in the medical community. In particular, the controllers are embedded in medical monitoring systems that store and transfer the vital signs of patients such as blood pressure, sugar levels, and heart rates to doctors. Such monitoring systems are used extensively in nursing homes and for patients who are at home and do not need extensive care of physicians but require constant monitoring. The collected data are is usually sent to a doctor's office or a hospital periodically to inform the status and progress of patients to doctors.

Although the 68HC11 is continually used, an increasing number of embedded computer applications has been seeking microcontrollers with more speed and capabilities. Motorola responded with a barrage of microcontrollers with varying speed, memory capacity, math functions, and I/O capabilities. One of these is the 68HC12 microcontroller family. The 68HC12 provides much needed speed, which is made possible by expanding the width of the data bus from 8 to 16 bits and implementing an instruction-queuing mechanism. In addition, the 68HC12 expanded its math capability by adding complex math operations and distinguished itself from other microcontrollers by being the first microcontroller with a built-in fuzzy controller functions. The new GM and Ford cars are now equipped with the 68HC12 microcontrollers. Motorola also started to use the 68HC12 in some of their cellular phones. We expect that the 68HC12 will replace the 68HC11 in most of the current 68HC11 applications in the near future.

We now shift gears to the 68HC12 exclusively. In the next section, we provide a quick overview of the hardware and software of the controller. The following chapters discuss each component in detail.

1.4 OVERVIEW OF THE 68HC12

The 68HC12 was first introduced in 1997 by Motorola as one of the more powerful next-generation microcontrollers. The new controller increased the 68HC11 system performance by expanding hardware capabilities and software tools. In this section, we briefly consider the software and hardware features of the 68HC12.

1.4.1 Software Instruction Set

There are 209 different instructions, called the *instruction set*, that can be performed on the 68HC12. The instructions range from a simple data transfer operation to a complex fuzzy logic operation. The instruction set includes all instructions of its parent microcontroller, the 68HC11. One of the prominent changes of the 68HC12 compared with the previous versions of the Motorola microcontrollers is the flexible data-accessing methods (a multiple number of new addressing modes). In addition, sophisticated math instructions as well as the fuzzy logic instructions are included in the instruction set. The instruction set contains data transfer instructions, arithmetic and logic instructions, data test instructions, branch instructions, function call instructions, and fuzzy logic instructions. The use and format of these instructions are fully discussed in Chapter 2.

1.4.2 Hardware

The Motorola 68HC12, also referred to as the CPU12, is a 16-bit processing unit consisting of a series of modules connected by an intermodule bus. There are two different versions of the 68HC12: the MC68HC812A4 and the MC68HC912B32. The MC68HC812A4 is designed to run in an expanded mode (some resources exist outside of the chip), whereas the MC68HC912B32 is ideal to be operated in a single-chip mode (all resources reside inside the chip). Figures 1.3 and 1.4 show the overall block diagrams of the MC68HC812A4 and MC68HC912B32, respectively.

Both of the 16-bit microcontrollers contain a low-power, high-speed central processing unit (CPU12), one (MC68HC912B32) or two (MC68HC812A4) asynchronous serial communications interfaces, a serial peripheral interface, a flexible 8-channel timer, a 16-bit pulse accumulator module, an 8-channel, 8-bit analog-to-digital converter, 1 Kbyte RAM, 768 Bytes (MC68HC912B32) or 4 Kbytes (MC68HC812A4) of EEPROM, and a single-wire Background Debug Mode (BDM) module.

In addition to the different modules described before, the MC68HC812A4 contains the following unique features:

- Capability to expand to over 5 Mbytes of memory using paging techniques
- Nonmultiplexed address and data buses
- Phase-locked loop, and
- 24-key wakeup lines with interrupt capabilities.

The 68HC912B32 offers the following unique features:

- 32 Kbyte Flash EEPROM, and
- A built-in pulse-width modulator.

If you are familiar with the 68HC11, you will first notice the increased number of I/O ports on the 68HC12. You will also notice a number of modules you

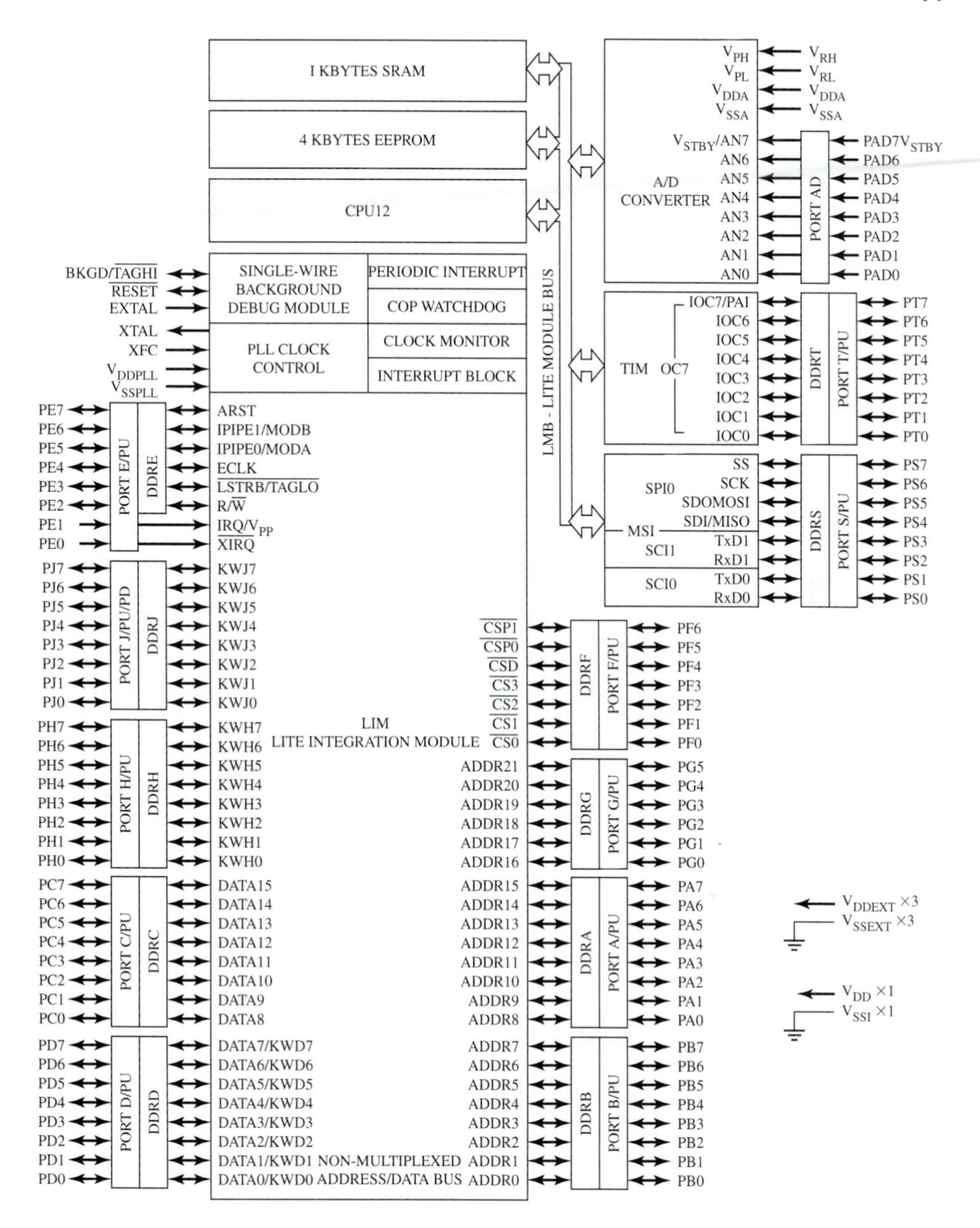

Figure 1.3 The block diagram of the MC68HC812A4 (Motorola).

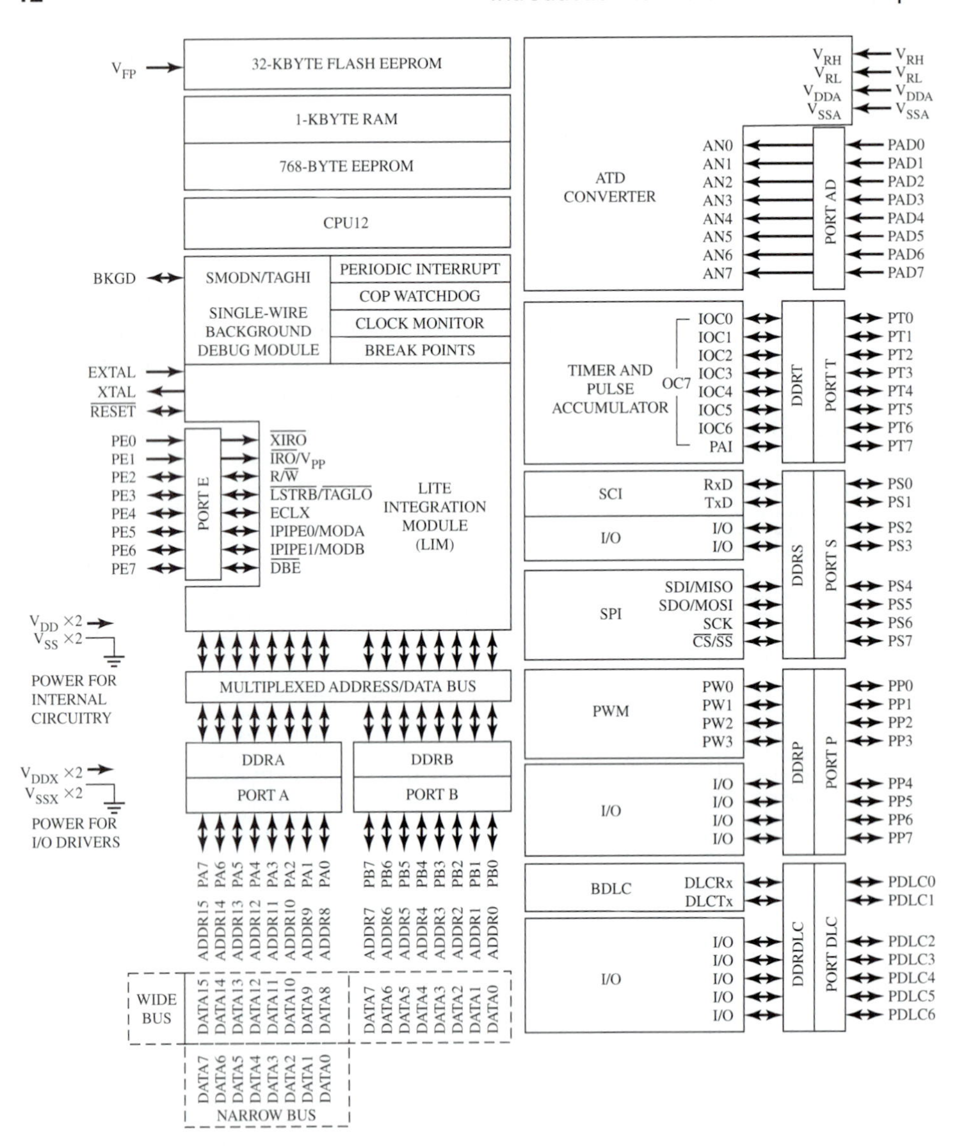

Figure 1.4 The block diagram of the MC68HC912B32 (Motorola).

did not see in the 68HC11, such as the lite integration module, the single-wire background debug module, and the phase-loop-lock clock control module. Do not be overwhelmed by the information contained in the Figures 1.3 and 1.4. Each 68HC12 module shown in these figures is studied one at a time throughout this book using examples and applications. Most of the topics we discuss in the rest of the book apply to both versions of the 68HC12. The mobile robot applications, however, use the MC68HC812A4 microcontroller exclusively.

1.5 SUMMARY

In this chapter, we gave a brief history of computers, starting with the use of purely mechanical computing devices to modern-day high-performance machines. We illustrated that all modern computers have four functional units: CPU, memory, I/O devices, and buses. We described the purpose of each unit and defined *microprocessors*, *microcomputers*, and *microcontrollers*. We also gave a brief overview of the 68HC12 microcontroller software and hardware.

1.6 FURTHER READING

John Hennessy and David Patterson, *Computer Architecture: A Quantitative Approach*, 2nd ed., Morgan Kaufmann, 1996.

David Patterson and John Hennessy, *Computer Organization and Design: The Hardware/Software Interface*, Morgan Kaufmann, 1994.

Kai Hwang, *Advanced Computer Architecture*, McGraw-Hill, 1993.

Marvin Davis, *Engines of Logic: Mathematicians and the Origin of the Computer*, W.W. Norton, 2001.

2

68HC12 Assembly Language Programming

Objectives: After reading this chapter, you should be able to:

- List the contents of the 68HC12 microcontroller programming model and explain how each programming model register is used,
- Identify the common attributes of good programs,
- Illustrate the clock-by-clock execution of a typical 68HC12 instruction,
- State the purpose of an instruction set,
- Categorize the 68HC12 instructions by their functions,
- Use six different 68HC12 addressing modes in simple programs,
- Write 68HC12 program segments performing arithmetic and logical operations,
- Explain the purpose for the 68HC12 fuzzy logic instructions, and
- Use directives in simple programs.

In this chapter, we study the fundamental concepts associated with programming the 68HC12 microcontroller. As noted in the objective list, this chapter covers topics that are essential for learning assembly language programming skills.

We start with the microcontroller programming model in Section 2.1. The programming model is a tool to view the inner workings of the 68HC12 as it executes instructions. In Section 2.2, we explain the proper format of Motorola 68HC12 instructions, followed by a clock-by-clock execution process of the 68HC12 as it operates on example instructions in Section 2.3. Section 2.4 introduces the 68HC12 instruction set and groups the instructions into seven distinct categories. Both the arithmetic and logical instructions are covered in this section. In Section 2.5, we discuss the subject of addressing modes, which are different ways instructions obtain necessary data for execution. We consider each of the six addressing modes of the 68HC12. Section 2.6 explains branch instructions, which are used to implement if-then-else program constructs. Finally, Section 2.7 describes directives, sometimes called *pseudo-op-codes*, which are instructions for an assembler to process programs and data. This section also introduces some skills for writing good programs. Section 2.8 contains two laboratory exercises: The first introduces you to the programming environment of the enclosed software and the 68HC12 monitor program commands; the second provides you with an opportunity to write your first complete 68HC12 assembly language program.

2.1 PROGRAMMING MODEL

The programming model of the 68HC12, depicted in Figure 2.1, succinctly shows the current status of the microcontroller. As the name implies, what we describe in this section is a model of the microcontroller rather than a physical entity. Although the model components physically exist in the microcontroller, they are only parts of a complex implementation necessary for the workings of the controller.

The model has two 8-bit accumulators, two 16-bit index registers, one 16-bit stack pointer, one 16-bit program counter, and one 8-bit condition code register (CCR). The two 8-bit accumulators can be combined and used by a programmer as a one 16-bit accumulator. A bit is the smallest unit to represent information in memory. Physically, a capacitor or flip-flop is used to store the information of a single bit. A single bit can take the state of 1 or 0. A set of four bits forms a *nibble*, two consecutive nibbles together are called a *byte*, and two consecutive bytes are named a *word*.

We begin by defining the terms in the figure. An accumulator was used in early computers to constantly update or accumulate results for a sequence of computer operations. If the operations happen to add a set of numbers, the accumulator term fits the description perfectly. However, the term was used for general purposes and the name stuck.

You should think of accumulators as general-purpose registers used by the microcontroller. What are registers? Remember from your digital logic class? (Appendix D can refresh your memory if you need to brush up on the subject.) Regis-

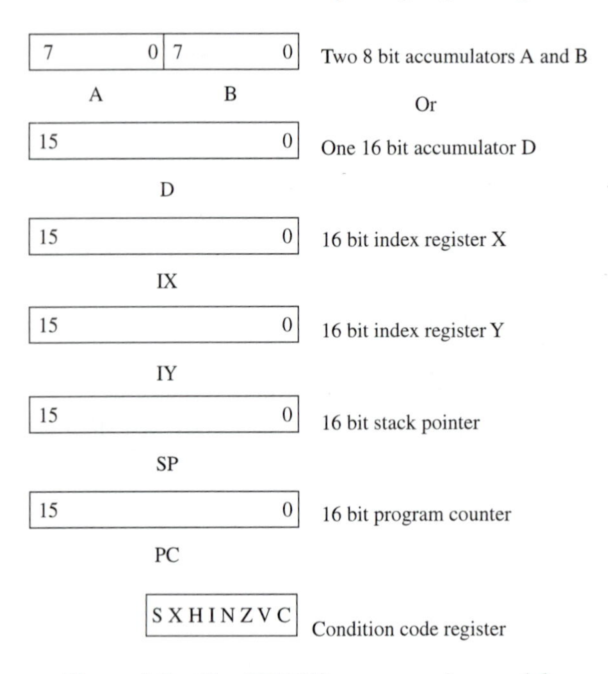

Figure 2.1 The 68HC12 programming model.

ters are storage spaces to maintain computational results, like memories. We give registers special names since values in these locations change rather often compared with traditional memory spaces. Because of this reason, these registers are made using special technologies and placed physically in the CPU such that the register access time is faster compared with accessing other memory locations. Thus, a CPU uses accumulators as locations where the most of its operations are performed.

Index registers are the ones used by the CPU to keep track of a list of data or to identify a data element with respect to a reference location. Traditionally, index registers are used, along with an offset, to process each element of a list. For example, your program can use an index register to keep track of locations in a list while it adds, negates, or manipulates each element of the list.

We explain the program counter next. At all times, a mechanism within a computer that governs the orderly execution of instructions is necessary. This responsibility belongs to the program counter. The program counter always contains a 16-bit address of the next instruction to be executed. This is possible since each memory location is referred to by a unique number, called the *memory address*, and a value representing an instruction or data is stored in a memory location. For example, if the program counter holds decimal value 549, the instruction stored at memory location 549 is executed next. How? When the CPU places the memory address of the next instruction on the address bus, the instruction in the memory location is placed on the data bus for the CPU to read, interpret, and execute. Thus, the CPU uses the contents of the program counter to figure out the memory address for the next instruction. Once the program counter is initialized, it is automatically updated by the CPU such that it always contains the address of the instruction that follows the current instruction being executed. Here is another example of how the program counter helps a CPU. When you turn on your computer, the initial value for the program counter is fixed such that your computer starts to execute a set of initialization instructions pointed to by the program counter before the computer hands over its control to you. Without the program counter, the CPU would not be able to keep track of executing instructions in an orderly manner.

Continuing with our definitions, we now consider stacks. A *stack*, which we discuss further in Chapter 3, is a temporary storage space in memory. The stack pointer holds the address of the last used memory location within the stack.[1] The stack pointer is necessary to safely store and retrieve information from the stack.

The last component of the programming model, the condition code register, is comprised of 8 bit flags where each flag indicates a specific condition of the microcontroller. At all times, each flag in the register is either set (logic 1) or reset (logic 0) based on the current computational results or status of the microcontroller. We consider each flag from the left to the right of the register shown in the figure.

S flag This bit disables the STOP instruction. If this bit is set (you set this bit), the 68HC12 ignores the STOP instruction and treats it as the No Operation (NOP) instruction. The STOP instruction allows the controller to conserve energy by shutting off most of its activities, moving the controller into an inactive mode.

X flag This bit enables the nonmaskable external interrupts of the 68HC12. Interrupts are requests made to the CPU for special services. Maskable means the CPU has a choice to acknowledge or ignore an interrupt. External interrupts are requests coming from the outside of the microcontroller asking for a special service of the CPU. A nonmaskable external interrupt means the CPU must service the request. For example, a reset button of a microcontroller is a nonmaskable request coming from the outside of the controller that must be serviced. The service for this particular interrupt consists of initializing the controller.

H flag This bit is set when an arithmetic operation produced a carry from a lower nibble (4 bits) to an upper nibble. What is an arithmetic operation? Addition, subtraction, multiplication, and division are arithmetic opera-

[1]For the 68HC11 users, notice the change. In the 68HC11, the stack pointer contained the memory address of the next available location, not the memory address of the last used location.

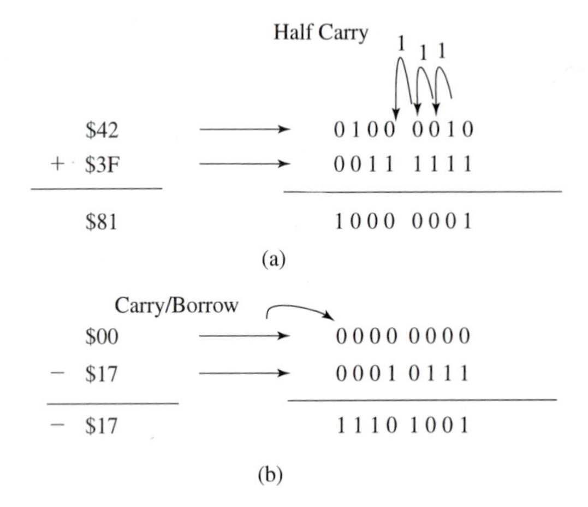

Figure 2.2 An example of a situation where the H bit and the C bit of the condition code register is set.

tions. Now let us see an example where this carry occurs. Suppose we are adding two numbers as shown in Figure 2.2. To perform the addition in the 68HC12, the decimal numbers must first be converted to two binary numbers. (If you do not remember how to do this, see Appendix C.) We have chosen this example so that there is a carry from the lower nibble to the upper nibble. When a situation such as the example in the figure occurs, the H bit (use Half carry for easy memorization) gets set.

I flag This bit is used to enable maskable interrupts. If you want the CPU to service special requests, referred to as *enabling interrupts*, this bit must be cleared (set to 0).

N flag This bit is set when the result of an operation is a negative number in the 2's complement representation (see Appendix C)—that is, the most significant bit, bit 7, of the result is 1.

Z flag This bit is set when the result of an operation is 0.

V flag This bit is set when an overflow occurs as a result of an operation. An overflow occurs when the result of an operation does not fit in the resulting register, causing an erroneous value. For example, if you are adding two positive numbers and the result cannot be represented correctly within a register because the sum is too big, this bit is set.

C flag This bit is set when a carry or borrow occurs for the most significant bit. For example, suppose we want to subtract decimal 23 from 0. To perform this operation, we first convert the two numbers into two binary numbers and then perform the subtraction operation as shown in Figure 2.2 (b). When this operation is complete, the carry/borrow bit is set.

As you have seen, each bit of the CCR contains unique status information about the microcontroller and the result of the current operation, which is often used by the microcontroller to determine its next action. For example, if the I bit is cleared and an interrupt is detected, the next action of the 68HC12 is to take care of (service) the interrupt.

We have learned that the program model allows us to see the internal status of the controller. We close this section with a brief summary, describing the purpose for each programming model component.

- General-purpose accumulators A & B—8-bit registers where all arithmetic and logic operations are performed. Consider these as the work areas of the microcontroller.
- General-purpose accumulator D—The two accumulators A & B are cascaded to form a single 16-bit accumulator, which can be used for operations involving 16 bits.
- Index registers X & Y—16-bit registers used in the index addressing mode, where an effective address[2] is formulated by adding/subtracting an offset value to the contents of an index register.
- Stack Pointer (SP)—A stack is a first-in-and-last-out data structure in memory. The stack pointer (16-bit register) holds the address of the top of this data structure.
- Program Counter (PC)—The address of the memory location where the next instruction for execution is stored in this 16-bit register.
- Condition Code Register (CCR)—This 8-bit register keeps track of the status flags for program execution control.

2.2 MOTOROLA ASSEMBLY LANGUAGE

An instruction is the smallest unit of action a programmer can dictate to a machine to execute. An instruction can range from carrying out simple addition to executing a series of complex computations. In the previous section, we showed that the 68HC12 programming model is a tool to view the internal status of the microcontroller as it executes an instruction. In Section 2.4, we present a variety of 68HC12 instructions. Before you see the various 68HC12 instructions, however, you need to know the universal format each instruction adheres. We describe the 68HC12 instruction format in this section. For each instruction, there are four different fields:

Label Op-Code Operand (s) Comment

[2]An effective address is defined as a memory address used by an instruction to fetch or store data.

An instruction may consist of only one element for a single field, elements for two fields, elements for three fields, or elements for all four fields. Each field is allocated for a special purpose, and you must follow specific rules to place proper elements in each field. We consider each field and its purpose next.

- Label field—An element that occupies this field is created by a programmer to identify a line of code within a program. The most common use of this label field element is to locate a set of instructions to be executed as a result of an if-then-else decision.
- Op-Code field—An op-code, sometimes called *mnemonics*, is the actual action part of an instruction. For example, in an instruction to move data from memory to an accumulator, the moving part is the action part of the instruction or the op-code. You will learn the op-codes of the 68HC12 throughout this book, and those op-codes occupy this field.
- Operand field—This field contains information to obtain data necessary to execute an instruction. The element that occupies this field can be a symbol or an expression. For some instructions, this field is empty. The method identified in this field, along with the op-code field to obtain necessary data, is called an *addressing mode*, which is the topic for Section 2.5.
- Comment field—As the name implies, this field is used by a programmer to include comments. This field must start with a semicolon. If an entire line is a comment, you must start the line with a semicolon in the first column of the line. The primary purpose of this field is to assist programmers to document the functions of instructions and programs for future reference.

2.3 INSTRUCTION EXECUTION CYCLE

In this section, we show a sequence of actions taken by the 68HC12 to carry out a set of example instructions by studying the programming model at each clock cycle. The step-by-step procedure facilitates our understanding of the 68HC12 operation as we observe how the contents of the CPU registers and designated memory locations change. The CPU registers we refer to are the accumulators, the stack pointer, and the CCR found in the programming model. One other CPU register is required for our discussion—the instruction register. The purpose of the instruction register is to accumulate the op-code and the operand of an instruction before it is executed.

There are three steps involved in completing each 68HC12 instruction: fetch, decode, and execute. During the fetch stage, op-codes and operands are loaded from memory to the instruction register. The decode stage interprets each instruction as a predefined CPU action. This decode stage overlaps with the fetch stage:

As soon as the op-code is fetched from the memory, it is decoded. Once the necessary op-code and operand are loaded in the instruction register, the 68HC12 moves into the third stage—the execution stage. During this stage, the decoded instruction is executed.

We now study the three stages using an example. In this section, we show a simplified version of the process; the 68HC12 employs a hardware architecture similar to a pipeline, which can be seen in most modern microprocessors, to facilitate and reduce the actual number of clock cycles required to complete instructions.[3]

The example describes a scenario where the microcontroller loads the contents of memory location $3000 into accumulator A and stores the value to a new memory location—namely, $2000. The symbol $, which proceeds values 3000 and 2000, indicates that the number following the symbol is in a hexadecimal number representation.[4] Figure 2.3 shows the status of the microcontroller registers at the end of each clock cycle. Note that each frame shows the contents of the program counter (PC), instruction register (IR), and accumulators A and B. The actual code for our example is:

$$\begin{array}{ll} LDAA & \$3000 \\ STAA & \$2000 \end{array}$$

The LDAA is the op-code which informs the 68HC12 to load an 8-bit data byte to accumulator A. The $3000 is the operand, indicating the location of the desired data. Similarly, the STAA is the op-code of the instruction for storing the contents of accumulator A, and $2000 is the operand specifying the data location.

We now study the example in detail by referring to the figure. Suppose, initially (at clock cycle 0, not shown in the figure), the contents of the program counter is $4000 and the memory contains instructions LDAA $3000 and STAA $2000 starting at memory address $4000. The LDAA instruction op-code and operand in memory are represented by hexadecimal numbers $86, $30, and $00, whereas the STAA instruction op-code and operand are represented by hexadecimal numbers $7A, $20, and $00.[5] During the first clock cycle, the controller fetches and

[3]Using an advanced logic module with two 16-bit stages (and one 16-bit latch), the 68HC12 instruction queue always makes the next instruction available for the CPU to decode and execute an instruction. This means that the clock cycles to fetch the operands and op-codes no longer apply to the 68HC12 since at least the two following instructions have already been fetched from the memory while the current instruction is executed. Thus, as soon as the 68HC12 completes one instruction, the following instruction is already ready to be processed, removing time to collect the op-codes and operands in the instruction register. The advanced logic module, however, requires additional CPU clocks to align instructions.

[4]A hexadecimal number uses 16 different symbols to represent a number: 0, 1, 2, 3, 4, 5, 6, 7, 8, 9, A, B, C, D, E, and F.

[5]We cover the topic of converting an assembly language instruction to the corresponding hexadecimal machine language representation in Chapter 3.

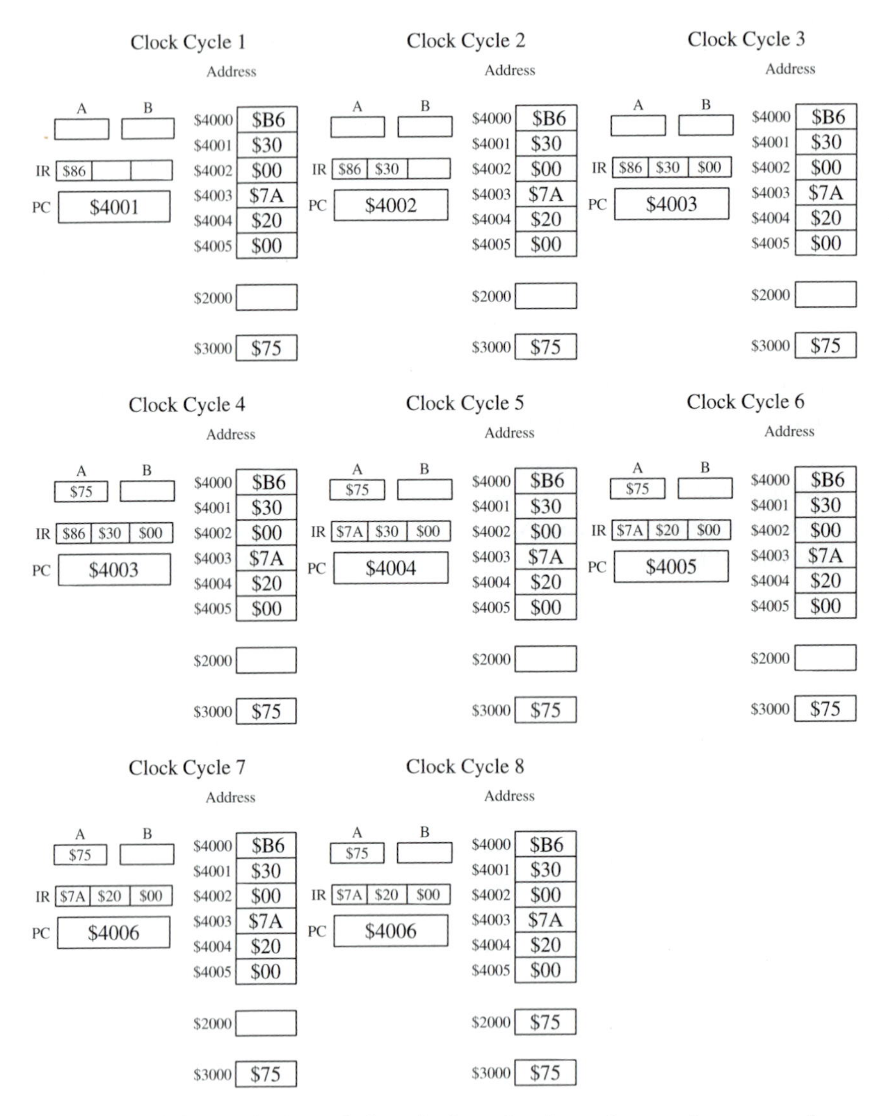

Figure 2.3 A clock cycle by clock cycle view of executing a set of example instructions.

decodes the op-code of instruction Load Data to Accumulator A from memory location $4000 while the program counter value is incremented by 1 as shown in the first frame of Figure **??**.

The decoding of the op-code during the first clock cycle shows that the instruction requires additional data to complete the instruction, and the needed value resides at a memory location whose address immediately follows the op-code. During the second clock cycle, the CPU fetches the high byte of the address ($30)

ing the second clock cycle, the CPU fetches the high byte of the address ($30) from memory location $4001 and stores it to the instruction register. The program counter is again incremented by 1 and the second clock cycle is completed, as shown in the Clock Cycle 2 frame of the figure.

During the third clock cycle, the CPU fetches the last necessary data, the low byte of the address ($00), from the memory. The program counter is incremented again, which is the end of the third clock cycle (Clock Cycle 3 frame of the figure).

At the end of the third clock cycle, the op-code and operand are loaded into the CPU. The instruction is executed during clock cycle four, and value $75 is loaded into accumulator A from memory location $3000. Note that, during the execution stage, the program counter does not increment, as shown in the Clock Cycle 4 frame of the figure.

The fifth clock cycle is used to fetch and decode the next op-code: STore Accumulator A ($7A). The op-code is loaded into the instruction register and the program counter is incremented by one (Clock Cycle 5 frame in the figure). The decoding shows the address of the data must be fetched, and this step is taken during the next two clock cycles as shown in Clock Cycles 6 and 7 frames of Figure 2.3.

Finally, during the final clock cycle, the contents of accumulator A are stored (copied) into the address fetched during the sixth and the seventh clock cycles, completing the desired task. Note the contents of memory location $2000 changes to $75 after the eighth clock cycle.[6]

The previous example shows how the three stages are performed to complete instructions. The complexity of the operation to carry out an instruction determines the number of clock cycles required to complete an instruction. Appendix A shows the actual number of clock cycles required to execute each 68HC12 instruction. The appendix also shows the list of valid op-codes and operands for each instruction.

2.4 INSTRUCTION SET

In this section, we present the various 68HC12 instructions. We call all 68HC12 instructions collectively the instruction set: An *instruction set* is defined as a set of instructions that a microcontroller/microprocessor *understands* to execute.

The 68HC12 has 209 different instructions in its instruction set.[7] We do not want you to be taken back by the sheer number of different instructions. To help

[6]The instruction queue module of the 68HC12 reduces the total clock cycles to perform the two instructions by 2 clock cycles, completing the instructions in 6 clock cycles. In the 68HC12, 16-bit value is fetched at once instead of one shown in the example.

[7]Those readers who are familiar with the 68HC11 microcontroller family will be glad to know that all 68HC11 instructions have been retained in the 68HC12. The instruction set of the 68HC12 is a superset of the one used in the 68HC11 with a variety of enhanced instructions.

you get a handle on the large number of instructions, we show that we can group all the 68HC12 instructions into the following seven categories:

1. Data Transfer and Manipulation Instructions—move and manipulate data. We learn these instructions in Section 2.4.1.

   EXAMPLES

   - MOVB moves a byte of memory from location a to location b
   - LDAA load accumlator A
   - STAA store a memory location with contents of accumulator A
   - PULX retrieve the top two bytes from the stack and load them to index register X
   - PSHA store the contents of accumulator A onto the stack
   - ROL rotate data to its left
   - ASR shift data to its right

2. Arithmetic Instructions—perform arithmetic operations. These instructions are presented in Section 2.4.2.

   EXAMPLES

   - ADDA add contents of accumulator A to a designated value and store the result to accumulator A
   - ABX add the contents of accumulator B with the contents of register X and store the results to register X
   - MUL multiply two 8-bit numbers
   - EMUL multiply two 16-bit numbers
   - IDIV perform integer divide
   - FDIV perform fractional divide

3. Logic and Bit Instructions—perform logical operations. We discuss this group of instructions in Section 2.4.3.

   EXAMPLES

   - ANDA perform a bit-by-bit AND operation with the contents of accumulator A and a designated 8-bit value
   - EORB perform a bit-by-bit exclusive OR operation with the contents of accumulator B and a designated 8-bit value

- ORCC perform a bit-by-bit OR operation with the contents of the condition code register and a designated 8-bit value
- BSET set specified bits of an 8-bit value to ones
- BCLR clear specified bits of an 8-bit value to zeros

4. Data Test Instructions—test the contents of an accumulator or a memory location. These instructions are presented in Section 2.4.4.

EXAMPLES

- CMPA compare the contents of accumulator A with an 8-bit value
- TSTB test the value of accumulator B for a zero

5. Branch Instructions—perform if-then-else operations. We present this category of instructions in Section 2.6.

EXAMPLES

- BEQ branch if the previous operation's result is 0
- BMI branch if the previous operation's result is a negative number
- BNE branch if the previous operation's result is not 0

6. Function Call Instructions—initiate or terminate a subroutine. We present these instructions in Chapter 3.

EXAMPLES

- JSR jump to a subroutine
- RTS return from a subroutine
- RTI return from a service routine
- CALL call a subroutine

7. Fuzzy Logic Instructions—design fuzzy logic controllers. These instructions are introduced in Section 2.4.5 and discussed in depth in Chapter 4.

EXAMPLES

- MEM determine membership values for fuzzy membership functions
- REV evaluate fuzzy rules
- WAV perform a weighted average
- MINA find the minimum between accumulator A contents and an 8-bit value

- MAXA find the maximum between accumulator A contents and an 8-bit value

As you continue to read this book, you will become familiar with these instructions. We emphasize, however, that true learning comes only from practice. The laboratory application section at the end of this chapter is a good place to start. For the remainder of this section, we discuss in depth some of the basic instructions to help you start the journey of mastering 68HC12 assembly language programming. Appendix A provides the complete 68HC12 instruction set.

2.4.1 Data Transfer and Manipulation Instructions

During the first half of this section, we present instructions that move data from one location to another. During the second half, we study the rotate and shift instructions.

Load, Store, Transfer, and Move Instructions A load instruction copies contents of a specified memory location to an accumulator or an index register and affects changes to the N and Z bits of the condition code register (CCR). A store instruction copies the contents of an accumulator or a register to a memory location. The N and Z bits of the CCR are also affected by the store instruction. The op-codes for the 68HC12 load instructions are:

- LDAA Load accumulator A with an 8-bit value
- LDAB Load accmulator B with an 8-bit value
- LDD Load accumulator D with a 16-bit value
- LDX Load index register X with a 16-bit value
- LDY Load index register Y with a 16-bit value
- LDS Load the stack pointer with a 16-bit value
- LEAS Load the stack pointer with a 16-bit effective address
- LEAX Load index register X with a 16-bit effective address
- LEAY Load index register Y with a 16-bit effective address

These instructions are used to load a value or an effective address to accumulators, index registers, and the stack pointer. When we want to save the data in the programming model to memory locations, we use store instructions. The corresponding op-codes for the store instructions are:

- STAA Store the contents of accumulator A in a memory location
- STAB Store the contents of accumulator B in a memory location

- STD Store the contents of accumulator D (16 bits) in two consecutive memory locations
- STX Store the contents of index register X (16 bits) in two consecutive memory locations
- STY Store the contents of index register Y (16 bits) in two consecutive memory locations
- STS Store the contents of the stack pointer in two consecutive memory locations

Besides the load and store instructions, the 68HC12 also provides transfer instructions that copy the contents of a CPU register to another register or accumulator. The TFR is the op-code for the universal transfer instruction that does not affect the CCR flags. On the contrary, op-codes of instructions TBA and TAB move contents of accumulators A and B and do affect the N, Z, and V bits of the CCR. Similar to the transfer instructions, move instructions MOVB and MOVW transfer a byte (8 bits) and a word (16 bits) from one memory location to another, respectively.

Rotate and Shift Operations There are 21 different instructions for 68HC12 that perform some type of shift or rotate operation. We further divide these instructions into the following three different subgroups: rotate, logical shift, and arithmetic shift. The shift operation, whether logical or arithmetic, brings in a zero (for the arithmetic shift right, the seventh bit is repeated) and disregards one original bit after each shift operation. The rotate operations do not alter the original bits, but rotate their positions within a byte: Eight consecutive rotate operations result in the initial value.

The differences among the three subgroup instructions follow next. The rotate instructions should be used to maintain the bit order of the original data. For example, suppose you want to swap the most significant hexadecimal digit with the least significant hexadecimal digit represented by a byte—say $6F. The end desired result is $F5. If we represent this number in a binary form, we have %0110 1111. The % symbol is used to denote binary numbers. To accomplish our original goal, we need to perform the rotate right or rotate left four consecutive times. You can see this by studying the rotate diagram shown in Figure **??**. If you are not familiar with the hexadecimal or binary number representation, we direct you to study Appendix C before moving forward.

The logical shift instructions should be used when each bit in a value needs to be studied. For example, we can test each bit (whether 1 or 0) by continuously performing logical shift left and testing the seventh bit.[8] On the contrary, the arith-

[8]There are other methods in the 68HC12 to test this bit, such as using the BITA instruction.

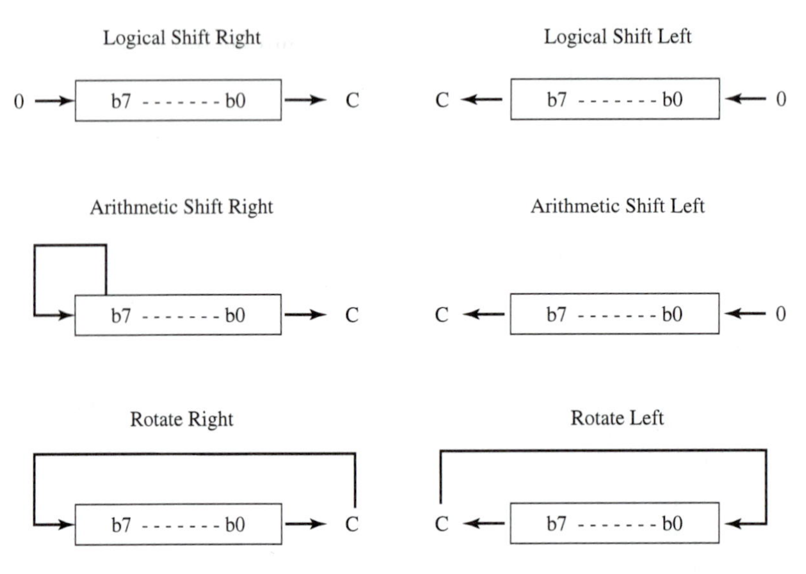

Figure 2.4 Illustrations for the 68HC12 shift and rotate operations.

metic shift instructions should be used to perform arithmetic multiplications or divisions. The arithmetic shift operations are used to multiply or divide a number by a multiple of 2. The shift operation working as a multiplier or divisor can be seen by using a more familiar number system: the decimal number system. Suppose we start with decimal number 2358. If we shift the number to the right by one digit, providing a 0 from the left, we end up with 0235.8, the result of dividing the original number by 10.[9] Similarly, if we shift the original number to the left by one location, providing a 0 from the right, we end up with 23,580. We easily see this is a multiplication by 10 of the original number. Using the same logic, we can equate shifting a binary number to its left or right to multiplying or dividing the original number by decimal number 2.

The logical shift left and the arithmetic shift left perform an identical operation, as shown in Figure 2.4. Yet there is an important difference between the two shift right operations. The logical shift right provides a zero from the left, whereas the arithmetic shift right provides a duplicate of the seventh bit from the left. How can we use these instructions? We answer this question with the following illustration.

[9]Technically, decimal value 8 is no longer a part of the result if we insist on using the four decimal number representation. Such an operation is referred to as an integer division since the result only preserves the integer part of the actual answer. We included decimal number 8 in the result to illustrate the division process using a shift operation.

To test the status of a bit, a logical shift should be used. The operation sets all bits to zero after testing each bit. The logical shift right instruction, however, should be used to divide an unsigned number by a multiple of 2 while the arithmetic shift right must be selected if we desire to divide signed 2's complement numbers by a multiple of 2. (For those unfamiliar with signed and unsigned numbers, see Appendix C.) Basically, the signed number representation allows you to use both positive and negative values while the unsigned number representation considers all data as positive numbers. So why would anyone want to use the unsigned number representation over a signed number representation? Appendix C answers that question.

Either the logical shift left or the arithmetic shift left can be used to multiply a value by 2. In fact, the op-codes for the two operations are identical: The controller has a single operation for both shift instructions. Thus, the shift left instructions apply to both unsigned and signed numbers. The complete 68HC12 shift and rotate instructions are given next.

Rotate

- ROL rotate left the contents of a memory location
- ROLA rotate left the contents of accumulator A
- ROLB rotate left the contents of accumulator B
- ROR rotate right the contents of a memory location
- RORA rotate right the contents of accumulator A
- RORB rotate right the contents of accumulator B

Logical Shift

- LSL logical shift left the contents of a memory location
- LSLA logical shift left the contents of accumulator A
- LSLB logical shift left the contents of accumulator B
- LSLD logical shift left the contents of accumulator D
- LSR logical shift right the contents of a memory location
- LSRA logical shift right the contents of accumulator A
- LSRB logical shift right the contents of accumulator B
- LSRD logical shift right the contents of accumulator D

Arithmetic Shift

- ASL arithmetic shift left the contents of a memory location
- ASLA arithmetic shift left the contents of accumulator A

- ASLB arithmetic shift left the contents of accumulator B
- ASLD arithmetic shift left the contents of accumulator D
- ASR arithemetic shift right the contents of a memory location
- ASRA arithemetic shift right the contents of accumulator A
- ASRB arithemetic shift right the contents of accumulator B
- ASRD arithemetic shift right the contents of accumulator D

We now consider some example question–answer sessions that show how to use the rotate and shift instructions. The sessions deal with multiplication and division of unsigned and signed 2's complement numbers by 2. If you are not familiar with different number representations, you will not understand all of the example sessions. If you are not familiar with the 2's complement number representations, you can skip the second question–answer example and read it later or read Appendix C before proceeding further.

Practice Questions

Question: Given decimal value 42 (equivalent binary value %00101010) in accumulator A, we want to double the value by 2. Which instruction op-code should be used?

Answer: The result of multiplying 42 by 2 gives 84 (binary value %01010100). Clearly, we need to perform an arithmetic/logical shift left to accomplish the desired task: ASLA or LSLA

Question: Given −8 in accumulator A, we want to divide the value by 2. Which instruction op-code should be used?

Answer: ASRA. Representing −8 as a signed 2's complement number gives %1111 1000. Applying the ASRA instruction gives %1111 1000 ⇒ %1111 1100. We can verify the correct result by converting the result to its corresponding decimal number: %00000100 ⇒ −4. Notice that if we chose LSRA, we do not get the correct answer.

The next question–answer example session shows the limitation of the integer division implemented by the arithmetic/logical shift right instructions.

Question: Suppose we start with decimal number 39 and we apply one of the arithmetic shift right instructions to divide the number by 2. What is the resulting value?

Answer: %0010 0111 (39) ⇒ %0001 0011 (19) Instead of getting 19.5, we end up getting 19 since we are performing an integer division.

2.4.2 Arithmetic Operations

Arithmetic operations are additions, subtractions, multiplications, and divisions. In this subsection, we study the 68HC12 arithmetic instructions.

Addition There are eight different addition instructions in the 68HC12: The corresponding op-codes are shown later. The ABA instruction adds the contents of accumulator A to the contents of accumulator B and stores the result to accumulator A (the contents of accumulator B do not change). The ABX and ABY instructions add the contents of accumulator B to index register X and index register Y and store the results to index register X and index register Y, respectively. For multiple precision calculations, the microcontroller has the ADCA and ADCB instructions, where the carry bit of the CCR is used to incorporate a carry from a lower byte addition. These instructions add a memory value to the contents of accumulator A or B along with the carry bit of the CCR. The results are stored back into accumulator A and accumulator B, respectively. The ADDA and ADDB instructions add the contents of an accumulator to the contents of a memory location. The results are then stored in accumulator A and accumulator B, respectively. Finally, the ADDD instruction adds two 16-bit numbers: Accumulators A and B are considered as a single 16-bit accumulator where the contents of accumulator A holds the high byte. The second 16-bit number is extracted from two memory locations (two consecutive bytes) and added to the accumulator D value. The result is again stored in accumulator D.

- ABA Add the contents of accumulator B to the contents of accumulator A and store the result in accumulator A
- ABX Add the contents of accumulator B to the contents of index register X and store the result in index register X
- ABY Add the contents of accumulator B to contents of index register Y and store the result in index register Y
- ADCA Add the contents of a memory location to the contents of accumulator A. Add the C bit of the CCR to the resulting value and store the result in accumulator A.
- ADCB Add the contents of a memory location to the contents of accumulator B. Add the C bit of the CCR to the resulting value and store the result in accumulator B.
- ADDA Add the contents of a memory location to the contents of accumulator A and store the result in accumulator A.
- ADDB Add the contents of a memory location to the contents of accumulator B and store the result in accumulator B.

- ADDD Add a 16-bit value from two consecutive memory locations to the contents of accumulator D (accumulator A and accumulator B). Store the resulting 16-bit value to accumulator D.

We again use some question–answer example sessions to show the use of the instructions.

Practice Questions

Question: Suppose accumulator A and accumulator B contain $23 and $49, respectively. What values will we find in the two accumulators after executing the ABA instruction?

Answer: Accumulator A holds $6C and accumulator B holds $49.

Question: Consider a case of adding two 16-bit values. Suppose we want to add two hexadecimal numbers $3291 and $A275. What are the instructions that will perform the desired task?

Answer: There are two different approaches we can use to perform the task. We illustrate both approaches.

Approach 1: Add the two lower bytes first. Add the two high bytes with a carry bit. We can implement this approach using the following instructions.

```
LDAB    #$91
ADDB    #$75
LDAA    #$32
ADCA    #$A2
```

The # symbol informs an assembler that the number immediately following the symbol must be treated as the actual data, not an address. For example, the first instruction loads $91 to accumulator B, whereas the second instruction adds value $75 to the contents of accumulator B. In this addition, a carry has occurred, which indicates that we must use an add instruction with a carry for adding the high bytes, the ADCA instruction. The prior instructions store the results, $D506, in accumulators A and B: Accumulator A value is $D5 and accumulator B contains $06 when the instructions are performed.

Approach 2: Add the two 16-bit numbers using instructions for 16-bit numbers. See the following instructions and see if you can follow along:

```
LDD     #$3291
ADDD    #$A275
```

The same results found in approach 1 are stored in accumulators A and B when the prior instructions are executed. Which one would you use?

Subtraction We continue this section with the complementary operation of addition: Subtraction. The list of 68HC12 subtraction instruction op-codes are shown later. Notice no equivalent subtract instruction op-codes for the ABX and the ABY exist. You can decipher the meaning of each subtract instruction by observing the letters of the instructions: the SUB or SB represents a subtract instruction op-code; letter C indicates the use of the CCR carry bit; and letters A, B, and D show particular accumulators used for a computation.

- SBA Subtract the contents of accumulator B from the contents of accumulator A and store the result in accumulator A
- SBCA Subtract the contents of a memory location from the contents of accumulator A. Subtract the C bit of the CCR from the resulting value and store it in accumulator A.
- SBCB Subtract the contents of a memory location from the contents of accumulator B. Subtract the C bit of the CCR from the resulting value and store it in accumulator B.
- SUBA Subtract the contents of a memory location from the contents of accumulator A and store the result in accumulator A.
- SUBB Subtract the contents of a memory location from the contents of accumulator B and store the result in accumulator B.
- SUBD Subtract a 16-bit value of two consecutive memory locations from the contents of accumulator D (accumulator A and accumulator B) and store the resulting 16-bit value to accumulator D.

We consider some question–answer example sessions illustrating the use of the 68HC12 subtraction instructions next.

Practice Questions

Question: Suppose we want to subtract $43 from $A9 using accumulator A. What instructions should be used?

Answer: We load accumulator A with $A9 first, then execute the SUBA instruction as shown.

```
LDAA    #$A9
SUBA    #$41
```

After executing the two instructions, accumulator A will have $68.

Question: Suppose you want to subtract $2A75 from $423E. What instructions should be used?

Answer: As was the case for the 16-bit number addition operation, there are two approaches from which we can choose.

Approach 1: Treat a high byte and a low byte separately as shown.

```
LDAB    #$3E
SUBB    #$75
LDAA    #$42
SBCA    #$2A
```

The result of the subtraction is $17C9: Accumulator A contains $17 and accumulator B holds $C9. Notice that we are computing the low-byte subtraction using accumulator B and the high-byte subtraction using accumulator A. What will happen if we swap the use of the two accumulators? We still end up with the correct value, but we must remember now that accumulator B contains the high byte and accumulator A has the low byte.

Approach 2: We can use the SUBD instruction to carry out a 16-bit number computation as shown.

```
LDD     #$423E
SUBD    #$2A75
```

Again the resulting value in accumulator D is $17C9.

Multiplication The 68HC12 has four multiplication instructions. These instructions allow us to multiply 8-bit and 16-bit numbers.

Four multiplication instruction op-codes are listed later. The MUL instruction multiplies two 8-bit numbers, but before the MUL instruction is issued you must load the two 8-bit numbers into accumulator A and accumulator B. The result of executing the multiplication command is stored in accumulator D. The upper half of the result will reside in accumulator A while the lower half of the result will be in accumulator B.

- MUL (MULtiply) Multiply two 8-bit numbers in accumulators A and B and store the result in accumulator D
- EMUL (Extended MULtiply) Multiply two 16-bit numbers in index register Y and accumulator D. The upper 16 bits of the result are stored in index register Y and the lower 16 bits of the result are stored in accumulator D.
- EMULS (Extended MULtiply for Signed numbers) Multiply two 16-bit signed numbers in index register Y and accumulator D. The upper signed 16 bits of the resulting value are stored in index register Y and the lower signed 16 bits of the resulting value are stored in accumulator D.
- EMACS (Extended Multiply and ACcumulate Signed numbers) Multiply two 16-bit signed numbers in two memory locations. The resulting value is then added to a four consecutive memory locations representing a 32-bit signed sum.

For each multiplication instruction, except the EMACS, the two original multiplicands are overwritten by the result. To multiply two 8-bit numbers, use the MUL instruction. For example, the multiplication of $10 and $20 can be coded as

```
LDAA    #$10
LDAB    #$20
MUL
```

To multiply two 16-bit numbers, you must use either the EMUL instruction for two unsigned numbers or the EMULS instruction for two signed numbers. Both instructions assume that the two 16-bit numbers are in index register Y and accumulator D before issuing a multiplication instruction. Either case, the resulting high 16 bits are stored in index register Y while the resulting low 16 bits appear in accumulator D.

The final multiply instruction is specially made for the 68HC12 fuzzy logic operations. In particular, one must multiply a set of two 16-bit numbers and add the results. The EMACS instruction comes in handy to carry out such a task.

Division There are five 68HC12 division instructions: Integer Divide (IDIV), Integer Divide Signed (IDIVS), Fractional Divide (FDIV), Extended Divide Unsigned (EDIV), and Extended Divide Signed (EDIVS). The following list shows the instruction op-codes and how they are used.

- IDIV The instruction performs an **unsigned** integer division of two 16-bit numbers. The dividend should be stored in accumulator D and the divisor should be stored in the X register before the instruction is issued. After the instruction is executed, the quotient and remainder are stored in the X register and the D accumulator, respectively.
- IDIVS The instruction performs a **signed** integer division of two 16-bit numbers. Again, before the instruction is issued, the dividend must be in accumulator D and the divisor in the X register. The resulting quotient is stored in register X while the remainder appears in the D accumulator.
- FDIV The instruction performs an **unsigned** fractional division of two 16-bit numbers. The registers used for the dividend, divisor, quotient, and remainder are the same as the IDIV and IDIVS instructions. If the divisor is not greater than the dividend, the quotient becomes $FFFF and the remainder is indeterminate.
- EDIV The instruction performs an **unsigned** integer division with a 32-bit dividend and a 16-bit divisor. Before this instruction is executed, the dividend must be in register Y and accumulator D, where the high 16 bits are in register and the low 16 bits are in accumulator D. The divisor should

be in register X. The instruction puts the 16-bit quotient in register Y and the 16-bit remainder in accumulator D.

- EDIVS This instruction performs a **signed** integer division of a 32-bit dividend with a 16-bit divisor. The locations for dividend, divisor, quotient, and the remainder are the same as the EDIV instruction.

For all divide instructions, you must be sure not to divide a dividend with a zero. Such instructions are not legal in the 68HC12; if executed, they cause the C bit of the CCR register to be set. We consider a couple of question–answer example sessions showing how some of the divide instructions are used next.

Practice Questions

Question: Suppose you want to divide unsigned number $80 (128 decimal) with $02 (2 decimal) in the 68HC12. Which divide instruction should be used?

Answer: Since we are dealing with unsigned numbers and the original numbers are 8 bits long, we should use the IDIV instruction to perform the task. Before the instruction is issued, we first need to load the dividend and the divisor into accumulator D and register X. We do this using the load instructions as shown.

```
LDD     #$0080
LDX     #$0002
IDIV
```

Once the register and the accumulator are loaded with correct values, we simply issue the IDIV instruction that stores quotient $40 (64 decimal) to register X and remainder $00 to accumulator D.

Question: Suppose you now want to divide 32-bit signed number $000A0000 (655,360 decimal) with 16-bit signed number $2008 (8200 decimal). How can we perform the task?

Answer: The EDIVS instruction should be used. Before the EDIVS instruction is issued, we first need to load the values to appropriate registers and accumulators as shown.

```
LDY     #$000A
LDD     #$0000
LDX     #$2008
EDIVS
```

The EDIVS instruction following the last load instruction produces signed quotient $004F (79 decimal) in register Y and remainder $039A (922 decimal) in accumulator D.

2.4.3 Logical and Bit Operations

In this subsection, we study the 68HC12 instructions associated with logical and bit operations. Logical operations are those performing binary AND, OR, COMPLEMENT, or EXCLUSIVE OR functions. These functions are used in making logic decisions, some of which you see in this subsection. Bit operations are used to turn on and off designated bits in memory locations. As is shown, there are some overlaps between the two types of operations. For those instructions, we can label them as either logic operations or bit operations. Both logic operations and bit operations are accompanied by masks—a bit pattern for testing. We first look at the logical operations.

Logical Operations A logic operation compares two states and produces logic 1 (sometimes you hear people refer it as logic HIGH or logic ON) or logic 0 (similarly referred as logic LOW or logic OFF). For our current discussion, individual data bits are considered as the states. The logic operations you learn in this section compare bits in two separate locations to make a binary decision—logic 1 or logic 0. There are four different types of 68HC12 logic instructions and we consider them next.

AND Logic The logical AND operation compares two bits and subsequently produces a logic 1 if two comparing bits are both 1s or logic 0 if one or both bits are 0s. The AND instruction of the 68HC12 performs the AND operation for two designated bytes from two different locations bit by bit. There are five different 68HC12 AND instructions, as shown in the following list. Each one compares two 8-bit values. For the first three instructions, all 8-bit pairs are examined while one can control the number of pairs to be examined for the last two instructions. The first two instructions alter the contents of the associated accumulator and the status bits of the CCR, the ANDCC instruction op-code changes the CCR, and the last two instructions only affect the status bits of the CCR without changing the contents of accumulators.

- ANDA Compare the contents of accumulator A and a memory location (8 bits) by performing a bit-by-bit AND operation. The bit-by-bit AND results are stored back into accumulator A. This operation always clears the V (overflow) bit of the CCR and sets or clears the N (negative) and the Z (zero) bits of the CCR.
- ANDB Compare the contents of accumulator B and a memory location by performing a bit-by-bit AND operation. The results are stored back into accmulator B. Like the ANDA operation, the ANDB clears the V bit of the CCR while setting or clearing the N and Z bits of the same register.

- ANDCC Perform a bit-by-bit AND operation with the contents of the CCR and a designated 8-bit pattern. This instruction clears the CCR bits.
- BITA Perform the exact same operation as the ANDA instruction except the results of the bit-by-bit AND operation are only used to affect the CCR bits; both the contents of accumulator A and a memory location do not change.
- BITB Perform the exact same operation as the ANDB instruction except the results of the bit-by-bit AND operation only affect the CCR bits.

We now consider some examples using question–answer sessions. The first example shows what happens to the contents of accumulator A after the ANDA instruction is executed.

Practice Questions

Question: Given the two binary values %1000001 and %11011101 in a memory location and accumulator A, respectively, what is the value of accumulator A after the ANDA instruction is performed along with the memory contents?

Answer:

1000 0001 ⇐ contents of a memory location

1101 1101 ⇐ contents of accumulator A

Perform the AND operation

answer 1000 0001 ⇐ contents of the accumulator

As a result of the operation, the N bit of the CCR is set to 1 and the Z bit is cleared. The V bit in the CCR register is also cleared. The N bit is set since the answer as a signed number represents −127. The zero flag and the overflow flag are cleared since the answer is not 0 and the AND instruction did not cause an overflow.

Question: What would be different if we replaced the ANDA instruction with the BITA instruction in the previous example?

Answer: The only difference is that the contents of accumulator A would be %11011101 not %10000001.

Question: Suppose we want to clear the I bit of the CCR without changing other CCR bits. Which AND instruction can we use?

Answer: Recall the eight CCR bits, repeated next for convenience.

S X H I N Z V C

Suppose the contents of the CCR are %01010001. We should choose the ANDCC instruction to accomplish the task as shown.

0101 0001 ⇐ contents of the CCR

1110 1111 ⇐ bit pattern used

Perform the ANDCC operation

answer 0100 0001 ⇐ contents of the CCR

Notice that we chose %11101111 ($EF) to clear the I bit of the CCR that did not affect the rest of the CCR bits. By ANDing the original CCR bits with 1s, we ensured that those bits did not change.

OR Logic An OR operation compares two bits and produces logic 0 if both bits are 0s and logic 1 in all other cases. The 68HC12 OR instructions compare two bytes from two designated locations, bit-by-bit, and generate a byte containing the result of a bit-by-bit OR operation. There are three 68HC12 OR logic instruction op-codes as shown.

- ORAA Compare the contents of accumulator A and a memory location (8 bits) by performing a bit-by-bit OR operation. The results are stored back in accumulator A. This operation always clears the V (overflow) bit of the CCR and sets or clears the N (negative) and the Z (zero) bits of the CCR based on the bit-by-bit OR operation results.
- ORAB Compare the contents of accumulator B and a memory location by performing a bit-by-bit OR operation. The results are stored back in accmulator B. Like the ORAA operation, the ORAB clears the V bit of the CCR register while setting or clearing the N and Z bits of the same register.
- ORCC Performs a bit-by-bit OR operation with the contents of the CCR and a designated mask. This instruction sets the CCR bits.

Unlike the AND instruction op-codes we saw earlier, there is no OR operation equivalent to the BITA instruction op-code or the BITB instruction op-code. Some examples are in order.

Practice Questions

Question: Given two binary values %10000001 and %11011101 in a memory location and accumulator B, respectively, what is the result of executing the ORAB instruction with the designated memory value?

Answer:

1000 0001 ⇐ contents of a memory location

OR 1101 1101 ⇐ contents of accumulator B

Execute the ORAB instruction

answer 1101 1101 ⇐ contents of the accumulator

As a result, the N bit of the CCR is set (1) and both the V and Z bits of the CCR are cleared (0).

Question: We saw how to clear the I bit of the CCR register using the ANDCC instruction earlier. Suppose, now, we want to clear the interrupt bit of the CCR using the ORCC instruction. Can we do this? If so, what should be the contents of a memory location?

Answer: We do not want to disturb other status bits of the CCR, which means we need to choose the corresponding bits to be 0s. What about the bit corresponding to the I bit of the CCR? If we choose 1, the OR operation will set the I bit. If we choose 0, the OR operation will retain the original I bit. Since our goal is to clear the I bit regardless of the original I bit status, the ORCC instruction does not accomplish the desired goal. We need to use the ANDCC instruction or the CLI instruction to clear the I bit of the CCR.

Exclusive OR Instructions The OR operations we saw before are sometimes called inclusive OR operations. The inclusive means the OR operations produce logic 1 if at least one of the two comparing bits is logic 1. There is one other type of OR operation called the exclusive OR. The exclusive OR operation acts similarly to the OR operation, but the difference is that a logic 1 is generated only if two bits are different. That is, the exclusive OR operation will produce logic 0 if two bits considered are both 1s or 0s. Table 2.1 shows the difference between the two OR operations.

There are two 68HC12 exclusive OR instructions whose descriptions are shown later. The EORA op-code and the EORB op-code perform the exclusive OR operation bit by bit with the contents of a memory location designated by an operand and an accumulator.

TABLE 2.1 DIFFERENCE BETWEEN TWO OR OPERATIONS

	Comparing States	Results
Inclusive OR	0 0	0
	0 1	1
	1 0	1
	1 1	1
Exclusive OR	0 0	0
	0 1	1
	1 0	1
	1 1	0

- EORA Compare the contents of accumulator A and a memory location (8 bits) by performing a bit-by-bit exclusive OR operation. The results are stored back in accumulator A. This operation always clears the V (overflow) bit of the CCR and sets or clears the N (negative) and the Z (zero) bits of the CCR based on the bit-by-bit exclusive OR operation.
- EORB Compare the contents of accumulator B and a memory location by performing a bit-by-bit exclusive OR operation. The results are stored back in accumulator B. Like the EORA operation, the EORB clears the V bit of the CCR register while setting or clearing the N and Z bits of the same register.

Practice Questions

Question: Suppose accumulator A contains $45 and a designated memory location has $E9. If we apply the EORA instruction with the memory contents, what is the result in accumulator A? How do the CCR bits change?

Answer: Given the two hexadecimal numbers, represent them as two binary numbers and perform a bit-by-bit exclusive OR operation.

11101001 ⇐ contents of a memory location

01000101 ⇐ contents of accumulator A

Perform the EORA instruction

answer 1010 1100 ⇐ contents of the accumulator

What about the CCR register bits? The V bit is automatically cleared, the Z bit is cleared since the resulting value is not zero, and the N bit is set since the seventh bit of the result is set, which indicates (in the 2's complement number representation) the resulting value is a negative number.

Question: Let us try to clear the I bit of the CCR using one of the exclusive OR instructions. Can we do this? If so, what should be the contents of a memory location?

Answer: Again we only want to change the I bit without changing other CCR bits. Thus, all other bits of the memory location except the one corresponding to the I bit must be 0s. This will ensure that if a CCR status bit is 1, the exclusive operation will retain the 1, and if a CCR status bit is 0, the resulting operation will produce a 0, as desired. Now what about the memory bit corresponding to the I bit? Suppose we chose 1 for this one. This will clear the I bit of the CCR if the I bit were set before an exclusive OR instruction is executed. If the I bit were originally cleared, the instruction will actually set the I bit of the CCR—not a good idea. The answer to the question "Can we do this?" is that it depends. If we know ahead of time that the I bit is set and we need to clear it, we can do so by using memory contents %00010000. If we do not know ahead of time the status of the I bit, this operation is a dangerous one we want to avoid.

Complement Instructions If you are not familiar with the 2's complement number representation, we recommend you study Appendix C before going any further in reading about the 68HC12 complement instructions. It is essential that you have a good understanding of the 2's complement number representation to understand the current topic. If you prefer to move ahead and learn about the different number representations later, skip this part of the section and come back at a later time.

In dealing with both positive and negative (2's complement negative) numbers, there arise situations where the sign of a number must be changed. For those situations, the 68HC12 designers provided us with the NEGA and NEGB instructions, which perform the 2's complement operations to the contents of accumulators A and B, respectively.

To perform the 2's complement, one subtracts the contents of an accumulator from zero. This process generates a number whose magnitude is unchanged, but the sign of the number is reversed. Consider the following example.

Practice Questions

Question: Suppose we have $29 (decimal 41) in accumulator A. The magnitude of this number is decimal 41 and the sign is positive. What is the result of applying the NEGA instruction?

Answer:

	0000 0000	⇐ start with zero
Subtract	0010 1001	⇐ contents of accumulator A
Answer	1101 0111	⇐ result of subtracting accumulator A value from 0

We should get decimal −41. How can we check whether our answer is correct? One quick way is to subtract the answer from 0 again. If the answer is correct, this operation should give us our original number—$29—back. Does it?

The actual 2's complement number conversion is performed by the 68HC12 using one of the 1s complement operations followed by an addition of 1 to the complemented value: The 1s complement operation simply converts each bit to its opposite state. That is, 1 becomes 0 and 0 becomes 1. For example, the 1s complement of %1011 0011 ($B3) is simply %0100 1100 ($4C) by replacing each bit with its opposite state. The sign conversion of a 2's complement number is performed by taking the 1s complement of the number and adding a 1 to the result.[10]

There are two 1s complement instructions in the 68HC12. The instructions COMA and COMB perform the 1s complement operation of accumulator A contents and accumlator B contents, respectively. Let us revisit the example of reversing the sign of \$29. This time we use one of the 1s complement instructions and add 1 to the result to obtain the 2's complement number.

	0010	1001	$\Leftarrow$ start with original value \$29
	1101	0110	$\Leftarrow$ result of taking 1s complement
ADD	0000	0001	$\Leftarrow$ add 1
Answer	1101	0111	$\Leftarrow$ result of adding 1 to 1s complement number

As you can see, we arrived at the same answer we had from the previous example. Does this mean we are correct? Again, we can verify our results by subtracting the result from 0 to check the correctness.

BIT Manipulation Instructions A programmer may need to modify only a limited number of bits in a memory location. For example, suppose a set of eight lights in a house is controlled by the bits of a memory location: If a bit is 1, the corresponding light gets turned on while bit 0 turns the light off. Suppose also that we only want to turn on a single light while others are turned off. Such situations call for an efficient bit manipulation of the memory contents. There are four 68HC12 bit manipulation instructions: Bit CLeaR (BCLR), Bit SET (BSET), Branch if bits specified by a mask is CLeaR (BRCLR), and BRanch if bits specified by a mask is SET (BRSET). A mask is a pattern of bits specified by a programmer. The format for this class of instructions is

Instruction Opcode	Memory Location	Mask	Destination

The Memory Location field specifies the location where an 8-bit value resides. The Mask field shows a pattern of bits designated by you, and the Destination field dictates a location of the next instruction if the result of the current operation requires changing the program flow when the BRCLR or the BRSET instruction is used. We postpone our discussion of the BRCLR and the BRSET instructions until Section 2.6, where we present branch instructions.

For the remainder of this subsection, we focus on the BCLR and BSET instructions. For the two instructions of interest, the Destination field is not used.

[10]For a full explanation on why this is equivalent to the operation of subtracting the original value from 0, see Appendix C.

Only the Instruction Op-code (BCLR or BSET) field, the Memory Location field, and the Mask field are used.

The BCLR instruction clears the memory location bits whose corresponding mask bits are set. Suppose the memory contents and the mask value are %11111111 and %11110000, respectively, before the BCLR instruction is issued. The BCLR instruction clears the memory bits whose corresponding bits in the mask are set, resulting in %0000 1111. Similarly, the BSET instruction uses a mask to set, instead of clear, memory bits whose corresponding bits in the mask are 1s.

Practice Questions

Question: Suppose a memory location holds %0000 0000. The mask we use is the same one we used before—namely, %1111 0000. After the BSET instruction is executed, what is the value in the memory location?

Answer: The memory location will now hold %1111 0000—a new value after setting bits to 1s whose corresponding bits in the mask are 1s.

The following example shows an actual instruction using the BSET op-code. We do not want you to worry about the format of the instruction too much at this point: We cover that topic in the addressing mode section (Section 2.5). Instead, see how the mask is used to turn on only two bits of the memory locations.

Example **BSET $D000, %01100000**

This instruction takes the number in memory location $D000, compares it with mask %01100000, and turns on the fifth and sixth bits (from the right, where the rightmost bit is the 0th bit) to 1s.

2.4.4 Data Test Instructions

The 68HC12 designers created data test instructions to assist in making a variety of decisions within a program. For example, you may want to test a value for zero before selecting one action from another based on the test. In the example of the mobile robot, the robot controller must test sensor values before making appropriate navigational decisions.

There are 10 test instructions in the 68HC12. These instructions affect the CCR bits and, therefore, are usually followed by branch instructions, which actually make decisions based on the CCR status bits. We discuss the topic of branch instructions in Section 2.6. The 10 test instruction op-codes are shown next.

- CMPA Compare the contents of accumulator A and a memory location by subtracting the memory value from the contents of accumulator A. The instruction does not change values in the memory location and the accumulator but only affects the N, Z, V, and C bits of the CCR.

- CMPB Compare the contents of accumulator B and a memory location by subtracting the memory value from the contents of accumulator B. The instruction does not change values in the memory location and the accumulator but only affects the N, Z, V, and C bits of the CCR.
- CBA Compare the contents of accumulators A and B by subtracting the contents of accumulator B from the contents of accumulator A. The instruction does not change values in accumulators but only affects the N, Z, V, and C bits of the CCR.
- CPD Compare the contents of the 16-bit accumulator D with a 16-bit value from two consecutive memory locations. The actual comparison is performed by subtracting the memory value from accumulator D. The instruction does not change either the memory value or the accumulator value. The N, Z, V, and C bits of the CCR are changed accordingly.
- CPS Compare the contents of the 16-bit stack pointer with a 16-bit value from two consecutive memory locations. The actual comparison is performed by subtracting the memory value from the stack pointer value. The instruction does not change the memory value and the stack pointer value. Only the N, Z, V, and C bits of the CCR are changed accordingly.
- CPX Compare the contents of the 16-bit index register X with a 16-bit value from two consecutive memory locations. The actual comparison is performed by subtracting the memory value from the index register. The instruction does not change either the memory value or the register value. Only the N, Z, V, and C bits of the CCR are changed accordingly.
- CPY Compare the contents of the 16-bit index register Y with a 16-bit value from two consecutive memory locations. The actual comparison is performed by subtracting the memory value from the index register. The instruction does not change either the memory value or the register value. Only the N, Z, V, and C bits of the CCR are changed accordingly.
- TST Test the contents of a memory location by subtracting zero from the memory value. The instruction does not change the memory contents. The V and the C bits of the CCR are cleared while the N and the Z bits are changed accordingly.
- TSTA Test the contents of accumulator A by subtracting zero from accumulator A. The accumulator value does not change but the V and the C bits of the CCR are cleared. The N and the Z bits of the CCR also change accordingly.
- TSTB Test the contents of accumulator B by subtracting zero from accumulator B. The accumulator value does not change but the V and the C

bits of the CCR are cleared. The N and the Z bits of the CCR are changed accordingly.

Practice Questions

Question: Suppose we want to see whether a value (8-bit number) in a memory location is a positive number. Which instruction should we use?

Answer: We can certainly load the memory value into an accumulator and perform the task using the CMPA, CMPB, TSTA, or TSTB instruction. The straightforward way, however, is to use the TST instruction with an address specifying the memory location.

2.4.5 Optional*: Fuzzy Logic Instructions

In this section, we introduce fuzzy logic controllers and their associated 68HC12 instructions. An in-depth consideration of this subject is presented in Chapter 4. Since fuzzy logic-based controllers are now fairly commonplace, we only briefly review the various considerations that go into designing such a controller, postponing the detailed discussion to Chapter 4.

Suppose we want to design a system that balances a simple vertical pole using a motor attached at the bottom of the pole. Figure 2.5 shows the system setup. The goal is to balance the pole vertically by adjusting the motor torque. This is similar to a human trying to balance a broom stick on his or her hand.

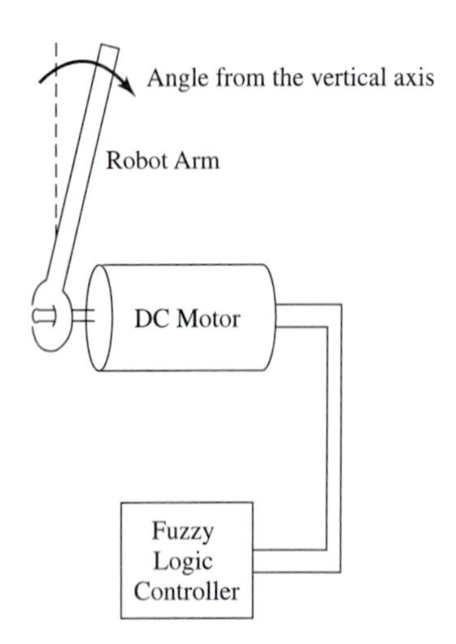

Figure 2.5 The example system with a fuzzy controller.

There are five steps required in the design of a fuzzy logic controller: identification of fuzzy variables and fuzzy membership functions, determination of a method to assign values to input membership functions, derivation of rules connecting input membership functions with output membership functions, determination of a method to assign output membership values, and selection of a method to compute a crisp value from output membership functions.

The initial step is to identify linguistic input and output variables. In the current example, the input variables should be the angular position and the angular velocity of the pole from the vertical axis. The output variable should be chosen as the motor torque. As a part of the initial step, we then must delineate a set of membership functions, also called labels or terms, for each variable. Henceforth, we use the membership functions, labels, and terms interchangeably. For example, we can choose labels such as *right small*, *left large* for the position variable to indicate the position of the pole from the vertical axis. Similarly, we can select labels such as *right medium* and *left high* for the velocity variable depicting the velocity of the pole. The torque output variable can have labels such as *turn right small* and *turn left medium*. These terms are defined using mathematical functions such as the ones shown in Figure 2.6.

Once we have a list of input and output fuzzy membership functions, it is clear that what is needed at the front end of the controller is a process that converts the observations about a state of the link, the position, and the velocity into the linguistic terms. This is the second step called the *fuzzification process*. The purpose of the fuzzification process is to assign a membership value, ranging from 0 to 1, for each input linguistic label. The membership value represents the amount of *belief* we should have for a label. For example, a zero membership value for the *left high* label of the pole position variable indicates that the current pole position does not belong to, or is not a member of, the *left high* label, whereas membership value 1 indicates that the current position is a full member of the label. The unique feature of the fuzzy logic controller is that the designer has the freedom to define the membership labels such that a single pole position can simultaneously belong to more than one label.

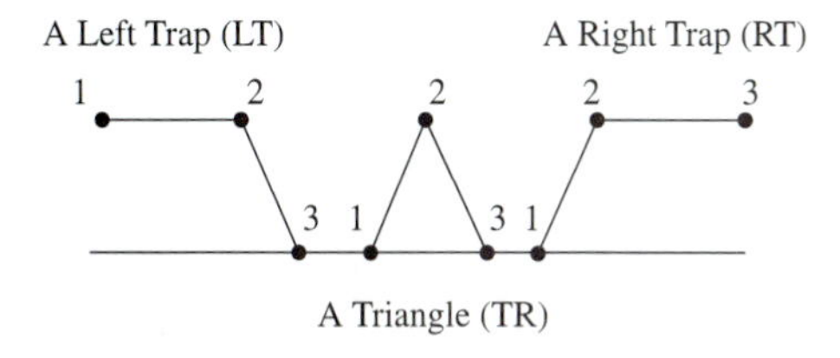

Figure 2.6 Example membership functions.

Once we have a set of input membership labels and the corresponding membership values, the third step is to come up with a set of rules to map the input membership labels with a set of output membership labels. The system control is governed by these rules that are found more on our own intuitive understanding of the problem rather than on some detailed mathematical modeling. In the rules, often stated in the usual IF-THEN form, the input and the output of the system is described by the use of deliberately vague and imprecise labels such as *turn left small*, *very large right*, and so on.

Consider, for example, our intuitive rule such as, "IF the position of the link relative to the goal position is small in the positive direction, AND IF the velocity of the link is small in the negative direction, THEN the motor outputs zero torque." This rule makes intuitive sense since the pole is moving toward the center; the rule matches with one's action to balance the link.

Given a set of variables, their associated labels, and the rules that map input labels to output labels, the next step applies a method to assign output membership values. Determining the method, called fuzzy inferencing, is the fourth step. Fuzzy inferencing involves the manipulations of the fuzzy membership functions defining the fuzzy sets. Since fuzzy sets are generalizations of crisp or Boolean sets, their basic set operations are mathematically consistent with that of crisp sets. Fuzzy inferencing strategies are developed using the basic fuzzy set operations. Among these strategies, the MIN-MAX method is used for the 68HC12, which is the most popular approach in the existing fuzzy controllers. The minimum rule is used to assign input fuzzy membership values, whereas the maximum rule is used to assign output fuzzy membership values.

The final step, called the *defuzzification process*, is used to represent a composite fuzzy subset by a single numerical value by combining contributions made by individual output fuzzy label. The last step is necessary since we need a single control value rather than a set of linguistic labels.

The 68HC12 has instructions that perform the fuzzification, evaluation of rules, and defuzzification processes described earlier. Your responsibility as a designer is to identify variables, generate associated labels, and derive rules that describe the relationships between input and output linguistic terms.

2.5 ADDRESSING MODES

In this section, we present different ways to form effective addresses to acquire data for an instruction, which are called the *addressing modes*. The effective address of an instruction is the actual location of the data, not the address, required to perform the instruction. An addressing mode is then a particular way a microcontroller forms an effective address for an instruction. The more addressing modes mean the more complex instructions a processor can perform; the complexity, however, comes with the price of complex hardware. Six different addressing modes are available in the 68HC12, and we study each one in this section.

2.5.1 Inherent Addressing Mode

Some 68HC12 instructions do not need any data outside of the CPU. These instructions use the inherent addressing mode. You can identify this addressing mode by observing an instruction lacking its operand: the op-code of an instruction contains all the information necessary to execute the instruction. Let us look at a couple of examples.

Example ABA

As we saw earlier, this instruction adds the contents of accumulator B to accumulator A and stores the result back to accumulator A. The data needed for this instruction reside in accumulator A and accumulator B, and no data from memory are used. Note that the operand field is empty.

Example INX

This instruction increments the value in index register X by one. Again the necessary data are in the index register, and the instruction simply does not require any additional data from memory.

2.5.2 Immediate Addressing Mode

The second addressing mode we consider is called the *immediate addressing mode* since the actual data required to complete an instruction follow immediately after the op-code in memory. This addressing mode is used when an actual numerical number (constant data) is desired as the operand of an instruction. The # sign in the operand indicates this particular addressing mode. A couple of examples should help us.

Example LDAA #$22

The instruction loads hexadecimal value $22 to accumulator A. Value $22 is the data needed to complete this instruction. Note the use of the symbol #.

Example LDX #$1000

This instruction loads hexadecimal value $1000 to index register X. Again the instruction employs the immediate addressing mode (use of the # symbol) to acquire necessary data.

2.5.3 Direct Addressing Mode

The direct addressing mode is a means to use data whose address is specified by only a single byte. In particular, the least significant byte of the effective address of the data appears as the operand. This addressing mode assumes that the higher address byte is $00. That is, this addressing mode should only be used if the needed data reside in the address range between $0000 and $00FF. There is an advantage to using this addressing mode: It saves a byte to specify an address, thus producing a compact program.[11] One disadvantage of this addressing mode is of course that the range of addresses that can hold data is limited to $0000 through $00FF. We consider a couple of example instructions using the direct addressing mode next.

Example **ADDA $00**

This instruction takes a value from memory location $0000, adds it to the contents of accumulator A and then stores the result back to accumulator A. Note that the high byte of the effective address is considered to be 0.

Example **SUBA $20**

This instruction takes the value from memory location $0020 and subtracts the value from the contents of accumulator A. It then stores the result back to accumulator A. Again, notice that the data were fetched from memory location $0020 even though the operand only specified $20.

2.5.4 Extended Addressing Mode

Unlike the direct addressing mode we just saw, some instructions use an explicit 16-bit memory address as the effective address. For instructions using this addressing mode, extended addressing mode, the 16-bit address appears in the operand as shown by the following examples.

Example **LDAB $1003**

This instruction loads accumulator B with the value found at address location $1003. The explicit address for the data is given for this instruction.

Example **ADDD $1030**

This instruction adds the 16-bit value stored at memory locations $1030 and $1031 to accumulator D (accumulators A and B) and stores the result in accumulator D. Again, the instruction explicitly specifies the location of the data.

[11]A second advantage exists. It takes fewer clock cycles to execute an instruction using the direct addressing mode compared with the same instruction with the extended addressing mode since the CPU only needs to fetch one byte of the address instead of two. In the 68HC12, however, the instruction queue system erases the second advantage.

2.5.5 Index Addressing Mode

There are cases where we want to go through a list of items one at a time. For example, we may encounter a task to find the location of a 0 from a list of numbers. For such a task involving a list of numbers, the 68HC12 designers included the index addressing mode to formulate effective addresses. This addressing mode allows a programmer to use one of the index registers as the pointer moving along a list, keeping track of the current position in the list. That is, an effective address is formulated by adding the contents of an index register, the stack pointer, or the program counter with an offset value. The advantage of this addressing mode is the flexibility to treat the effective address as a variable. You can modify the contents of the index register and the stack pointer or use the program counter to change the effective address. To reiterate, the effective address is formed by summing two numbers: the contents of a designated register and an offset.

Example ADDA $10,X

> This instruction extracts the value stored at the memory location pointed to by the sum of offset value $10 and the contents of index register X, adds to the contents of accumulator A, and stores the result in accumulator A. Notice the format of the operand. It has two components separated by a comma. Observing such a pattern in the operand allows one to identify instructions that use the index addressing mode. The first number is an offset, and letter X indicates the particular index register being used.

The offset can be a hexadecimal number, decimal number, or binary number. For each number system you choose, the 68HC12 offers three different options for the offset length: 5 bits, 9 bits, or 16 bits. The offsets are **signed** numbers to move the program counter forward as well as backward. These options give programmers flexibility to optimize instructions for minimum code lengths (number of bytes) and minimum execution time (number of clock cycles).

If an index register (X or Y) or the stack pointer is chosen to store a reference value, you can also predecrement, preincrement, postdecrement, and postincrement[12] the reference value as a part of executing an instruction. The amount of increment and decrement can be any number from 1 to 8, and the offset is assumed to be zero.

Unlike the previous versions of the 68HC family, accumulators can also be used as the offset of an index addressing mode instruction. For an 8-bit offset, the contents of accumulator A or B can be used, whereas if a 16-bit offset is desired, the contents of accumulator D can be used. By changing the contents of the index register, we can extract data from any location in memory.

[12]The *pre* and *post* represent an action before and after the execution of an instruction. For example, the predecrement instruction using index register X means to decrement the contents of the index register before executing a specified instruction.

Example SUBA $0,Y

This example instruction extracts the value stored at the memory location pointed to by the sum of 0 and the contents of index register Y, subtracts it from the contents of accumulator A, and stores the result in accumulator A. Again we can change the contents of register Y to extract data from any location in the memory. In particular, we can go through a list of values in memory by incrementing the value in Y by 1 each time we use an instruction using the index addressing mode. A small side note. When you write a program in C that uses pointers to manipulate a list of data, each C commands using a pointer gets converted to assembly instructions using the index addressing mode.

The 68HC12 also provides a new type of index addressing mode called indexed-indirect addressing mode. Here an instruction finds a pointer (address) to its desired data at a location designated by a 16-bit offset (specified by either the contents of D accumulator or a 16-bit number) and one of the following registers: X, Y, SP, or PC. Suppose one is loading an accumulator using the indexed-indirect addressing mode. The contents of the effective address are the address from which the accumulator loads the value. We illustrate this addressing mode using the following example instruction whose function is shown in Figure 2.7.

Example LDAA [D,X]

The example instruction uses the indexed-indirect addressing mode to load a value to accumulator A. First note the brackets surrounding the op-code, which is a syntax rule you must follow to use this addressing mode. Suppose accumulator D has $2035 and index register X contains $3000 before the load instruction is executed. The addressing mode dictates that we must first compute the sum of values in accumulator

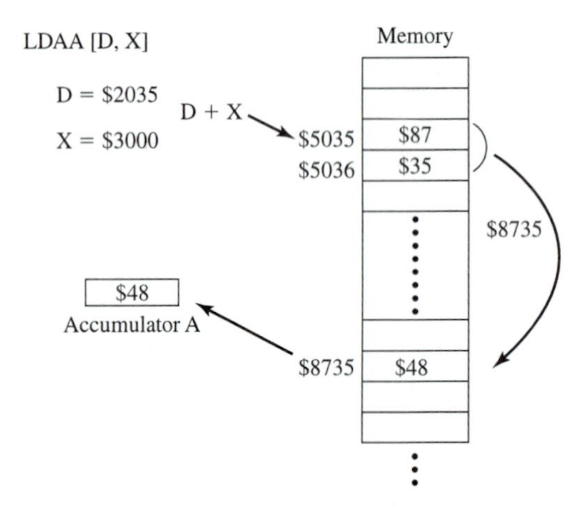

Figure 2.7 An operation using the indexed-indirect addressing mode.

D and index register X to come up with an address. The resulting value is $5035. The contents of the two consecutive locations starting at $5035 are the effective address of the data. From the figure, we see that the value is $8735. This address is then used to fetch $48 from the effective address and load to accumulator A.

2.5.6 Relative Addressing Mode

This type of addressing mode is used only by the 68HC12 branch instructions. The branch instructions are the topic of the next section (Section 2.6). Since branch instructions perform the if-then-else type of instructions, an instruction using this particular addressing mode can change the program counter contents. Instructions using this addressing mode computes the effective address by adding the signed relative offset to the contents of the program counter.

To show how the relative addressing mode works, let us consider an example. In this example, if a branching condition determined by the CCR is true, an effective address is formulated and the branching occurs.

Example

Memory location	Opcode	Operand
\$8000	*BNE*	\$10
\$8002	*STAA*	\$*C*000
...	...	...
\$8012	*INX*	

In the prior example, if the Z bit in the CCR is 1, the branching occurs by adjusting the contents of the PC: The CPU adds the current PC contents ($8002) to the relative offset ($10) and stores the result, $8012, to the program counter. Thus, if the Z bit is 1, the next instruction to be executed after the BNE instruction is the INX instruction in memory location $8012. You may wonder why we are adding $8002 to the offset value when the BNE instruction is located at $8000. Recall from our discussion of a cycle-by-cycle execution of instructions that the program counter increments as we fetch a byte from memory and does not change its value during the execution stage. For a branch instruction, by the time we execute the branch instruction, the program counter is already pointing to the location of the instruction immediately following the branch instruction. Thus, we must incorporate this fact when we assign an offset ($10 instead of $12 for our example).

Note that the relative address $FF is incorrect since it causes the program counter to point to the operand part of the current branch instruction as the next instruction. Similarly, the command BRA $FE creates an infinite loop since the offset value $FE (−2 in decimal) points the program counter to the current instruction on completion of the BRA instruction. Fortunately for us, we can use labels to denote the offset value without explicitly writing down a number when using an editor: An assembler converts labels with appropriate offset values. Thus, we write the following instructions using labels in places of the ones shown in the previous example.

Example

Memory location	Label	Opcode	Operand
$8000		BNE	NEXT
$8002		STAA	$C000
...	...	...	...
$8012	NEXT	INX	

For an in-depth study of the relative addressing mode, we next delve into the 68HC12 branch instructions.

2.6 BRANCH INSTRUCTIONS

Branch instructions are used to implement a loop or if-then-else high-level programming constructs in an assembly language program. That is, a branch instruction can alter the execution order of instructions. The 68HC12 has two types of branch instructions: conditional and unconditional. Both types of branch instructions use the relative addressing mode.

For the unconditional branches, the 68HC12 offers two branch instructions, BRanch Always (BRA) and Long BRanch Always (LBRA), and one non-branch instruction, JuMP (JMP). The BRA instruction always branches to a target location designated by an offset value. The range of the offset value, or the address distance to the next instruction, is -128 to $+127$ (an 8-bit signed value) from the current program counter value. To remove this range limitation, the 68HC12 designers included the JMP and the LBRA instruction to allow the change of the program counter value with any number in the memory ($0000–$FFFF). If instruction JMP can be used to move the program counter value anywhere in the 64K memory, why should one bother with the BRA instruction? The BRA instruction takes up less memory (2 bytes vs. 3 bytes) and saves a clock cycle, resulting in a shorter and faster program. Thus, if the target address lies within the limited range, it is preferred to use the BRA instruction. The format of the three instructions are shown.

(Label)	JMP	extended or indexed address mode operand
(Label)	BRA	relative-address mode operand
(Label)	LBRA	relative-address mode operand

Note that the operand of the JMP instruction can be formulated using the extended addressing mode (explicitly providing a 16-bit address) or the index addressing mode. Yet the BRA and the LBRA instructions, true to their names, uses the relative addressing mode. As alluded to in an earlier section, you should use a label in the operand field instead of formulating an extended address, an indexed address, or a relative address, allowing your assembler to generate a correct operand.

Unlike the unconditional branch instruction, the rest of the 68HC12 branch instructions, called conditional branch instructions, evaluate bits (sometimes called *flags*) of the CCR to determine whether a branch should be taken. The 68HC12 has a variety of conditional instructions as shown. The list explains when each branch instruction should be used. Each branch instruction has the following format, where xx denotes the mnemonics shown in the list.

(Label) Bxx relative-address

For convenience, we included the picture of the CCR again in Figure 2.8.

- BCC (Branch Carry Clear) Branch to a target location if the carry bit (C) in the CCR is cleared (0).
- BCS (Branch Carry Set) Branch to a target location if the carry bit in the CCR is set (1).
- BEQ (Branch EQual) Branch to a target location if the zero bit (Z) in the CCR is set (1).
- BNE (Branch Not Equal)Branch to a target location if the zero bit in the CCR is cleared (0).
- BGE (Branch Greater than or Eqaul) Branch to a target location if the previous computation result immediately preceding the branch instruction is greater than or equal to zero. This branch instruction should be used with a signed number computation.
- BGT (Branch Greater Than) Branch to a target location if the previous computation result immediately preceding the branch instruction is greater

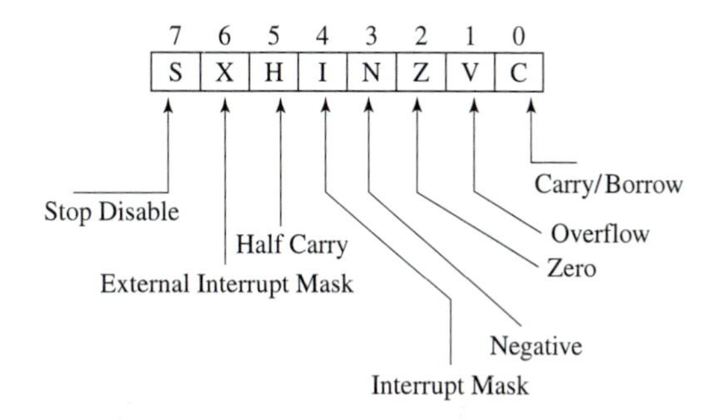

Figure 2.8 The 68HC12 condition coder register.

than zero. This branch instruction should be used with a signed number computation.

- BHS (Branch Higher or Same) Branch to a target location if the previous computation result immediately preceding the branch instruction is higher than or equal to zero. This branch instruction should be used with an unsigned number computation.
- BHI (Branch HIgher) Branch to a target location if the previous computation result immediately preceding the branch instruction is higher than zero. This branch instruction should be used for an unsigned number computation.
- BLE (Branch Less than or Equal) Branch to a target location if the previous computation result immediately preceding the branch instruction is less than or equal to zero. This branch instruction should be used with a signed number computation.
- BLT (Branch Less Than) Branch to a target location if the previous computation result immediately preceding the branch instruction is less than zero. This branch instruction should be used with a signed number computation.
- BLS (Branch Lower than or Same) Branch to a target location if the previous computation result immediately preceding the branch instruction is lower than or equal to zero. This branch instruction should be used with an unsigned number computation.
- BLO (Branch LOwer) Branch to a target location if the previous computation result immediately preceding the branch instruction is lower than zero. This branch instruction should be used for an unsigned number computation.
- BMI (Branch MInus) Branch to a target location if the previous computation result immediately preceding the branch instruction is a negative value. That is, the seventh bit of the result is one.
- BPL (Branch PLus) Branch to a target location if the previous computation result immediately preceding the branch instruction is a positive value. That is, the seventh bit of the result is zero.
- BRN (BRanch Never) Never branches. This instruction is mainly used for debugging purposes.
- BVS (Branch oVerflow Set) Branch to a target location if the overflow bit (V) in the CCR is set (1).
- BVC (Branch oVerflow Clear) Branch to a target location if the overflow bit in the CCR is cleared (0).

For each branch instruction given above, the designers of the 68HC12 also included a corresponding long branch instruction (insert "L" in front of the regular branch instruction mnemonic) in the instruction set. For long branch instructions, the relative offset is no longer limited to a decimal value in the range of -128 to $+127$, but all memory locations can be reached by the offset since signed 16-bit offset values are used in place of 8-bit offsets in regular branch instructions.

One easy way to select the correct branch instruction for a given task is by remembering the convention used by Motorola. Motorola uses terms such as *higher than* and *lower than* for unsigned numbers and terms such as *greater than* and *less than* for signed numbers. You can associate terms *higher*, *lower*, and *same* with unsigned numbers while remembering terms *greater*, *less*, and *equal* for signed numbers.

Since branch instructions entirely base their decisions on the status bits of the CCR, we must ensure those bits are correct before a branch instruction is executed. To do so, you can make a good habit of using one of the test instructions (Section 2.4.4) before a branch instruction. Some examples can help us understand the use of branch instructions.

Practice Questions

Question: Suppose that accumulator B contains decimal value 32 and the next instruction compares the contents with decimal value 12: CMPB #!12. The exclamation mark is used to indicate a decimal number representation. Which of the available branch instructions should be used for a branching to occur?

Answer: We first carry out the compare instruction to study the result, which is used to predict the resulting bits of the CCR bits. The compare instruction performs a subtraction as shown.

$$00100000 - 00001100 = 00010100$$

The resulting bits in the CCR register will be

1. C – 0
2. Z – 0
3. N – 0
4. V – 0
5. H – 0

By observing the CCR register status, we can determine whether each branch instruction will be activated if it is placed right after the compare instruction. Since no borrow occurred for the most significant bit, the carry bit is cleared, thus the **BCC** instruction will take its branch if placed after the compare instruction. The **BGE**, **BGT**, **BHI**, and **BHS** instructions will also take their branches if they immediately follow the compare instruction since the result %00010100 (decimal 20) is bigger than 0. The **BPL** instruction will also branch since the resulting value is a positive value. Finally, the **BNE** instruction will take its branch since the result is not equal to 0.

Some branch instructions check multiple conditions before a branch takes place as shown.

- BGE branch if (N exclusive-or V) = 0
- BGT branch if (Z and (N exclusive-or V)) = 0
- BHI branch if (C and Z) = 0
- BLE branch if (Z and (N exclusive-or V)) = 1
- BLS branch if (C and Z) = 1
- BLT branch if (N exclusive-or V) = 1

We consider the first of the six instructions carefully. You can go through similar steps shown later for the rest of the branch instructions. Recall that the BGE represents **B**ranch if the result of a computation is **G**reater than or **E**qual to 0. To test the condition, we must look at both the negative bit (N) and the overflow bit of the CCR. The prior condition states that we must perform an exclusive OR operation on the two bits and branch if the result is 0. Let us see why.

Recall that an exclusive OR operation generates 0 only if both bits are equal (0 and 0 or 1 and 1). The N bit represents that a result is a negative number (the seventh bit is set), and the V bit is set when the result of a computation cannot be represented correctly (adding two positive numbers results in a negative number or adding two negative numbers results in a positive number). Suppose a test instruction proceeds the BGE, which subtracts a number from another—say A − B for our discussion. There are three possibilities. The result is positive, 0, or negative. If the result is positive and A is bigger than B, the result will clear both the N bit and the V bit of the CCR, as desired. If a positive value resulted due to an overflow, the V bit will be set and the branch will not take a place. If the result is 0, two values must be equal, which clears both the V bit and the N bit of the CCR and the branch will take place. Finally, if the result is negative and B is greater than A, the N bit will be set and the branch will not take a place.

We close this section with a couple of special branch instructions: BRanch SET (BRSET) and BRanch CLeaR (BRCLR). These instructions combine both a test instruction and a branch instruction into a single instruction. The format of the two instructions is as follows.

Format: BRCLR (or BRSET)   memory location   mask   label

The BRSET instruction branches to a target location if the memory bits that correspond to 1 bit in a mask are set. For example, if a designated memory location contains %0011 0000 and the mask is %0110 0000, the branch instruction examines the fifth and sixth bits of the memory location. The fifth bit of the memory is set, which is good, but the sixth bit is cleared. Since the memory contents do not satisfy the condition, the branch does not take a place. What should be the mask to activate the branch instruction?

Similarly, the BRCLR instruction tests the contents of a memory location with respect to bits in a mask and branches to a destination if memory bits, which correspond to bits with ones in the mask are cleared. Here is an example.

Example BRCLR 0,X,%11110000,NEXT

The example instruction compares the contents of a memory location specified by the value in index register X with the mask ($F0). If the upper nibble bits in the memory location are cleared, the branch will take place. If not, the next instruction immediately following the branch instruction is executed. The BRSET and BRCLR instructions use the direct, extended, or indexed addressing mode to formulate the memory location field. Technically, the two instructions use two addressing modes within a single instruction: the relative addressing mode for the label field and the direct, extended, or indexed addressing mode for the memory location field.

2.7 DIRECTIVES (PSEUDO-OP CODE) AND A GOOD PROGRAMMING APPROACH

In the next chapter, we study assemblers and their functions. One of their functions is to facilitate a programmer's task by providing a variety of useful tools. One of those tools is a set of directives. Directives are instructions for assemblers that are used by a programmer to better organize his or her program. In this section, we illustrate various directives and introduce some good programming techniques.

2.7.1 Directives

Directives are instructions that control the operation of an assembler. We discuss only seven essential directives in this chapter. Notice that different assemblers have different numbers of directives, but the following directives are most common ones and should be compatible in most of the available assemblers.

1. *ORG* directive—This directive is used to set the starting address of a program. For example, suppose we want a program to start at memory location $C000 and the first instruction is LDAA #$10. This action can be accomplished using the following example code:

   Example

   ```
   ORG    $C000
   LDAA   #$10
   ```

   The ORG directive forces the LDAA instruction to be stored at the starting memory location $C000

2. *END* directive—This directive informs an assembler the end of a source program. Any assembly statements that follow the directive are disregarded by the assembler.

3. *RMB* directive (Reserve Memory Byte)—This directive reserves a block of specified number of memory bytes for program use. The directive requires a parameter to indicate the actual number of bytes reserved. For example, if we want to reserve $10 bytes of memory, we use the directive as shown.

   Example **TEMP RMB $10**

   The prior statement allocates $10 bytes. Label TEMP is used for the reserved block, and the label can later be used to refer to this block of data.

4. *FCB* directive (Form Constant Byte)—This directive also reserves a block of memory locations, but in addition the directive initializes values for the reserved memory block. For example, if we want to reserve three bytes with initial values $11, $12, and $13, this directive can be used as shown.

   Example **ABC FCB $11, $12, $13**

   The statement tells the assembler that ABC is the symbolic name for the first byte of the block with initial value $11.

5. *FDB* directive (Form Double Byte)—You can reserve double bytes for a number instead of single bytes used in the FCB directive. The FDB directive initializes two consecutive bytes for each argument. For example, let us see what happens if we use the FDB directive in place of the FCB directive in the previous example.

   Example **ABC FDB $11, $12, $13**

   This statement initializes six consecutive bytes in memory whose contents are $00, $11, $00, $12, $00, and $13, respectively.

6. *FCC* directive (Form Constant Character)—This directive also initializes memory contents, but you use this directive for initializing text characters in memory locations. The directive must be used with an expression that must be enclosed within double quotes (some assembler allows you to use single quotes instead of double quotes). For example, if we are writing a program that gives out grades for each student, we must include students' names in the program. The following statement initializes MIKE in memory locations using the FCC directive.

   Example **NAME FCC "MIKE"**

   If you can see inside of the memory, you will find that the statement generated values $4D, $49, $4B, and $45 and stored them in memory with a starting memory location referred by NAME. The numerical values correspond to the

ASCII (American Standard Code for Information Interchange) representations of the characters M, I, K, and E, respectively. Note that NAME refers to the address of the first letter $4D. We discuss the ASCII coding techniques in Chapter 10.

7. *EQU* directive—This directive equates a symbol with a numerical value. The directive is normally used to equate a symbol to an address location or a constant numerical value. The symbols generated by this directive are used only in an assembler and do not appear in memory. The assembler converts symbols into actual numerical values before storing a program into memory. The directive uses a label, the EQU directive, and an expression to define a symbol. For example, if we want to refer to memory location $E000 as the start of a read only memory (ROM) location, we can use the following statement to accomplish the task.

Example **ROM EQU $E000**

During the assembly process, the symbol is substituted with $E000 whenever the symbol ROM appears in the program.

2.7.2 A Good Programming Approach

Now that we covered basic programming tools for the 68HC12 in the forms of the programming model, the instruction set, and the addressing modes, we introduce some good programming techniques. All programmers know that sufficient planning for a program before writing the actual code can save time and energy in the long run. One of the effective methods of planning is called the top–down approach, where a task is divided into smaller subtasks, and the smaller subtasks are tackled, solved, and then combined to solve the original task. This top–down approach is sometimes called the *divide-and-conquer* method. Using this method, a programmer starts with a big picture of what the program is supposed to accomplish. He or she then creates subparts of the program needed. For each subpart, the programmer repeats the same procedure: consider the big picture and divide the task as necessary. This process continues until all the minimal subtasks are identified and proper programming actions are taken.

The approach presents two immediate advantages. First, by breaking a large task into a set of smaller ones, we can concentrate on a simple task at one time instead of trying to figure out one large complex problem with multiple tasks simultaneously. The second advantage is that we can test and evaluate a smaller task at a time that reduces the testing and evaluation time. We revisit this subject again in Chapter 3.

2.8 LABORATORY APPLICATIONS

LABORATORY EXERCISE A

Purpose This lab is designed to familiarize you with the Motorola 68HC12A4 EValuation Board (EVB) and the enclosed software environment. This lab teaches you the basic tools necessary to write, load, execute, and debug programs using the 68HC12A4 Evaluation Board.

Documentation 68HC12A4 EVB User's Manual

Procedure First connect the EVB to a power supply. You need a +5V DC power supply. Connect the EVB serial port to the computer using an RS232 serial cable.

1. The enclosed software is used to write, assemble and load your programs onto the 68HC812EVB and to communicate between a host computer and the EVB. Make sure you loaded the software onto your computer. If you have created a short cut with an icon, just double click the icon. You can also start the software by double clicking the executable file from the directory where you loaded the software.
2. Within the WIN IDE environment, click on the terminal icon (the second radio button on the upper left-hand corner) to establish a communication session between your host computer and the EVB.
3. Push the reset button on the EVB. It is located at the top left-hand corner next to the serial port connecting the board and your host computer. You may have to push it several times until the following message is displayed:

   D-Bug12 v1.0.4
   Copyright 1995-1996 Motorola Semiconductor
   For Commands type "Help"

4. Hit return and the following command prompt will be displayed.

   >

   You are now communicating with the monitor program on the EVB. Typing in HELP <RETURN> will give a list of monitor commands. For the complete commands and their functions, see the user's manual, which comes with the evaluation board, for detailed descriptions.
5. Display and modify a block of memory.

   - To display a block of memory beginning at address XXXX (XXXX is a hexadecimal number specifying a memory address), type in the memory display (MD) command:

MD XXXX

This command allows you to view the contents of memory. Experiment with the command by adding a stop address after the start address.

- Modify RAM memory locations with a starting address XXXX by typing the following memory modify command (MM):

  MM XXXX

  The screen will display:

  XXXX xx

  where xx is the current contents of the memory location. Type in new contents (perhaps the ASCII code for your name). If you type a <RETURN> after the new contents, the current contents of the next memory location will be displayed for modification. Typing a period will terminate the MM operation. There are several subcommands associated with the MM operation. These commands are not used for the labs in which you will be working, but their full descriptions can be found in the manual. Modify a few other memory locations until you feel comfortable with the command.

6. Modify a whole block of memory using the Block Fill command (BF). Type:

BF 4020 4060 yy

where yy is the hexadecimal pattern with which you want to fill the designated memory locations.

Use the MD command to view those memory locations to see that they were filled with your desired pattern.

7. Input a program using the built-in assembler (ASM).

Now you are going to put a simple program into the 68HC12A4EVB using the one-line assembler provided with the monitor program. Type:

ASM 4020

This tells the assembler to put the program starting at address $4020. Now type in the following program:

```
LDAA    $4100
ADDA    $4101
BRA     $4023
```

While you are typing in this program, the assembler will display the current address and the contents at that address. When you type in a new command, the op-code for that command will be displayed and then the next address location and the current contents in that location will be displayed. When you are finished, type a period to exit the assembler. Now type MD 4020 to verify that your instructions are in the memory.

Note that when you entered the BRA instruction you were able to put in the address to which you want to branch. The assembler will calculate the relative offset for you.

8. Run the program.

To run the program, the PC (program counter) register must be set to the starting address of the program. You can do this using the RM (register modify) command. Type:

RM

The monitor program will display the contents of the program counter and wait for you to enter new contents of the PC. At the prompt, type 4020 since that is where the program starts. Enter a period to exit the RM command.

Use the MM command to store two hexadecimal numbers in memory locations 4100 and 4101. You can use any numbers you like, but $FC and $01 are suggested to make it easy to see changes as you run the program.

Normally you can run a program using the GO command (just type G). This program does not display anything and contains an unconditional branch instruction, so typing G will just cause it to run until the RESET button on the EVB is pushed. However, the program does allow us to easily demonstrate another feature of the monitor: the TRACE command.

The TRACE command lets you run a program one instruction at a time. Type:

T

The op-code of the instruction that was executed will be displayed, as well as the contents of the registers after the instruction was executed. Multiple instructions can be traced by entering a number with the T command. Type:

T X

where X is a numerical number. The command will display X instructions on the screen.

Start with command T 2. Now trace one step at a time. Note which registers change and which ones do not. Pay particular attention to the Condition

Code Register (CCR). Continue to trace the instructions until the CCR bits change. Write down the previous and new values contained in the CCR.

Old Value _ _ _ _ Binary Equivalent __ __ __ __ __ __ __ __
New Value _ _ _ _ Binary Equivalent __ __ __ __ __ __ __ __

Why did the CCR bits change?

Experiment with the program and the monitor commands. When you are ready to end the program, press the RESET button on the EVB.

9. Download a program using the loader.

The ASM command is a simple one-line assembler without many features. For the remaining labs, we use the enclosed software to edit, assemble, and download programs.

For practice, write, assemble, and download the previous simple program using the software. First, erase the program in memory by using the Block Fill command to fill memory locations 4020 through 4030 with $FF. Now go to the editor window by closing the communication window. When you are done writing the program, save it. Do not put an extension; the assembler will put the .asm extension for you. Use the ORG directive to tell the assembler to begin at address 4020 (type ORG $4020 <RETURN>), then type the three lines of the program. Remember not to start your directive and commands on column 1. This column is reserved for putting labels. When the program is typed in, assemble it by pushing the first radio button on the left-hand top corner of the screen. If no error appears, open the communication window up and use the pull down menu to load your xxx.s19 program, where xxx is the filename of the program you just assembled. If you do not get the prompt after the program is downloaded, just hit <RETURN> and the prompt should come up.

Now examine memory locations $4020 through $4030, using the MD command, to see if your program was stored there. Put 4020 in the PC using the RM command and then trace through the program to satisfy yourself that your program works.

10. Answer the following questions:

(a) What is the answer to the exercise about the change of contents for the Control Code Register?

(b) What is the monitor command that changes the contents of the program counter?

(c) Assume you want to store the ASCII code for your name in memory. How can you perform the task using the monitor commands?

(d) What does the ASM command do?

(e) Why do we use the programming environment instead of the built-in assembler in the monitor program?
(f) What does the program in this lab do?

Supplementary Information

- Connecting EVB with your PC—Use an RS232 serial cable to connect your EVB station and your PC. Use the male end to connect the cable to your EVB station. The other end of the RS232 serial cable should be connected to the comm1 port on the back of your computer case. There may be two 9-pin ports on the back of your computer case, and you should connect the cable to the comm 1 port. The port number is usually specified next to the port. If you find labels A and B, port A is comm1 port and port B is comm 2 port. If you are already using the comm1 port with some other device (such as your mouse), connect the EVB cable to the comm2 port. If you decide to use the comm 2 port, you need to change the default setting of the enclosed software. To do this, use the pull-down menu in the terminal window. You will find a small subwindow with the communication port specified as "comm 1." Change it to comm 2. The other communication settings should be 9600 baud, 1 stop bit, and no parity. Now you have completed the communication setup between your PC and your EVB station. If you still cannot get it to work, make sure the power supply for the EVB station is plugged in.
- Software—The enclosed software from the P & E company is used as an editor/assembler/loader. The software is also used as a communication tool between a host computer and a 68HC12 EVB board. An assembler translates symbolic representation of instructions (an instruction set along with directives) into binary values for the 68HC12. The assembler performs this conversion. The assembler also generates a list file xxx.lst for your review. Once a converted program is generated (xxx.s19), the communication terminal program can be used to download the binary program onto the 68HC12.

LABORATORY EXERCISE B

Purpose In this lab, you will write your first complete assembly language program. The lab will also provide you an opportunity to review the techniques learned in laboratory A. The lab is designed to facilitate the use of branch instructions in cases that include "if-then-else" situations. You can use the resulting program (with some modifications) as a subroutine in the final lab to create a mobile robot system for a maze navigation. In particular, the subroutine can be used to read a set of Infrared (IR) sensor values to make appropriate robot navigational decisions.

Documentation 68HC12AV EVB User's Manual

Description You must write a program that performs the following tasks:

1. Read a set of three hexadecimal numbers located in memory addresses $4000, $4001, and $4002 and store them to memory locations $0800, $0801, and $0802, respectively. You may consider that the first three memory locations correspond to the three IR sensor output values while the last three are registers to hold the sensor values.
2. Read the three values from the new memory locations and check each one against a threshold value of $55, which one must define using the EQU directive in the beginning of the program. The threshold value will be used to determine the closeness of walls from robot sensors. The sensor output is an unsigned hexadecimal value and indicates the closeness of the robot from surrounding walls.
3. If the value stored in memory location $0800 is greater (unsigned numbers) than the threshold value, compute the sum of five consecutive numbers starting with numerical number 1 ($1 + 2 + 3 + 4 + 5$). Store the number back to the memory location $0800.
4. If the value stored in memory location $0801 is above (unsigned numbers) the threshold value, store $00 to the same memory location.
5. If the value stored in memory location $0802 is greater (unsigned numbers) than the threshold value, subtract $10 from the value stored in the memory location $0802 and store the resulting value back to the same memory location.

The actual program should start at $4100. Once you completed your program, test it by downloading test files, ch2Btest1.s19, ch2Btest2.s19, and ch2Btest3.s19 contained under directory "Examples/labtest" in the CD on the back of this book one at a time and run your program. By studying the corresponding .asm test files found in the same location and performing manual computations, check to see whether your program generates the desired results.

For all programs, you must use assembler directives. A brief explanation for three directives you should use for this laboratory exercise is repeated next.

- ORG: tells the assembler at what memory location a program starts
- END: tells the assembler a program has ended
- EQU: assigns a value to a symbol

Example **ORG $6000**

This directive directs the assembler to start the program segment at memory location $6000. Note that this directive should appear at the top of your main program. Start your program at $4100.

Example **TWO EQU $2**

This directive assigns value $2 to symbol TWO.

Also, recall the format for all Motorola 68HC12 instructions:

```
Label     Opcode     Operand     ;comments
```

where the label starts in column ONE.

For the directives ORG and END, you must leave at least the first column BLANK while the symbol name (a label) for the EQU directive should start at column one.

Your program should have the following structure:

```
;header (This is where you put in the program description, your name,
;and the date on which the program has started or finished.)

;define symbols

Threshold       EQU       $55
(Other values)
;designate the starting address of the main program
                ORG       starting address
                Your Program
;specifies the end of the program
                END
```

Note that a ";" in column 1 indicates a comment line.

2.9 SUMMARY

In this chapter, we introduced the 68HC12 microcontroller programming model and showed how the model displays the status of the microcontroller as the controller executes instructions. After the presentation of the Motorola assembly language instruction format, we studied the 68HC12 instruction set and categorized the instructions according to their functions. We also learned that each instruction forms an effective address using one of six different addressing modes. To complete the basic tools for writing assembly programs, we described a set of directives for a typical assembler and a systematic programming approach for writing organized and structured programs.

2.10 CHAPTER PROBLEMS

Fundamental

1. Write an instruction to load accumulator A with the 8-bit value in memory location $6700.
2. Write two instructions with the same STAB op-code to store the contents of accumulator B to memory location $0023. (Use two different addressing modes.)
3. Suppose you are required to load an 8-bit value in memory location at $7001 into accumulator A using the index addressing mode. Suppose also that you decided to use index register X. What should be the contents of the index register to satisfy the desired task in the following instruction: LDAA $1,X?
4. Write a program segment to compare the contents of register D with immediate value #$1234.
5. Suppose accumulator A contains hexadecimal number $20 and the 68HC12 executes instruction ADDA #$E0. What will be the values for the H, Z, N, and C bits as the result of the instruction? Use Appendix A to answer this question if necessary.
6. Discuss the benefits of the programming approach described in Section 2.7.2.
7. Write a program segment to load an immediate hexadecimal number $30 to accumulator B.
8. What does the following instruction do: LDAA $20,X?
9. Write a program segment that initializes memory locations $0000 and $0001 with $12 and $10 using appropriate directives.
10. Suppose accumulator B has $34. What are the contents of the accumulator if instruction CMPB #$33 is performed? How will the value change if instruction BITB #$33 is performed?
11. What do the following directives do?

```
(a) DATA    FDB    $C200
(b)         FCB    %11110000
(c)         FDB    $11
```

12. What addressing modes are used in the following two instructions: LDD #$2000 and LDD $2000?

Advanced

1. Describe the function of the program counter in the programming model shown in Figure 2.1.
2. Suppose that accumulator A contains $45. If we perform instruction SUBA #$44, which of the following branch instructions will be activated? BHE, BNE, BLT, BHT, BLE, BNZ.

3. What are the advantages of using the direct addressing mode?
4. What are the disadvantages of using the direct addressing mode?
5. What is the benefit of using the extended addressing mode?
6. What is the disadvantage of using the extended addressing mode?
7. When should the auto-increment feature of the index addressing be used?
8. Write a program segment to add $20 and $40 and store the result to memory location $4000.
9. Given the following program segment:

```
        LDAA    #$03
A       DECA
        TSTA
        BNE XX
```

What should be the relative address XX following the BNE op-code to repeat the DECA instruction until the accumulator A value is 0?

Challenging

1. Given the following program segment, compute the number of clock cycles required to complete the instruction sequence: LDAA $20, ADDA #$25, STAA $1000. You need to use Appendix A to accomplish this problem.
2. If you want to copy a table from a memory location to another, which addressing mode should be selected? Why?
3. What is the difference between the RMB and FCB directives?
4. Write a program segment to copy a table with five items from a memory location starting at $5000 to a memory location starting at $6000.
5. Suppose you have the following set of hexadecimal values: $20, $25, $40, $50, $12. Write a segment of program to find the minimum and maximum values of the set.
6. Consider the following program segment:

```
LDD     #$F00D
LDX     #$C100
STD     0,X
BSET    0,X,$44
BCLR    1,X,$11
```

What numbers are in memory locations $C100 and $C101 after the program is executed?
7. Write a program segment starting at $C100 that checks bits 0 and 2 of address $D000 and jumps to $C0CC if both bits are clear.

3

Advanced Assembly Programming

Objectives: After reading this chapter, you should be able to:

- Explain the assembly process and list files generated by an assembler,
- Incorporate loops in programs,
- Describe the purpose of the stack,
- Write subroutines and use the 68HC12 subroutine-related instructions,
- Illustrate the two different methods to call a subroutine,
- Incorporate the D-Bug12 subroutines in your programs,
- Identify bad and good programs, and
- Develop a procedure to write good programs.

This chapter continues to establish the reader's assembly language programming skills by introducing several important programming concepts. In the first section, the assembly process (where assembly code is converted to machine code) is illustrated, followed by the loop construct in Section 3.2. We then study the topic of stack in Section 3.3. In this section, we first define the terms *stack* and *stack pointer*. We then show how to use the stack pointer to access the stack. We continue the discussion of the stack in Section 3.4, where we consider the roles a stack plays in integrating subroutines with a main program. We first study the functions of subroutines in programs and proceed to illustrate how the execution flow is controlled in programs with subroutines. We also discuss two different ways of passing parameters to and from subroutines in this section. The topic for Section 3.5 is the special 68HC12 built-in subroutines: the 68HC12 D-Bug12 subroutines. The special subroutines allow us to display memory contents to a PC monitor, write data to memory, and initialize the starting addresses of routines triggered by exceptions.[1] After considering subroutines, we consider good programming skills in Section 3.6. In particular, we emphasize the value of planning using flowcharts before one writes a single line of his or her program. Starting with this chapter, we include an application section, Section 3.7, where we incorporate the chapter concepts in real applications. Section 3.8 contains two laboratory exercises, providing you with opportunities to write programs with subroutines. We conclude the chapter with a summary section and chapter problems.

3.1 ASSEMBLY PROCESS

In this section, we take you through the 68HC12 assembly process where an assembly language program is converted to a corresponding machine code. As we do so, we explain each file generated during the assembly process. We studied various types of the 68HC12 instructions in the previous chapter. Using the instructions, one writes assembly language programs using a text editor. Before a machine can actually understand what a programmer wrote, programs must first be converted into a form understandable to the machine: a form that consists of ones and zeros. This process of converting assembly program texts to strings of zeros and ones is called the assembly process, which is performed by assemblers. We show the process using the following example program.

```
Line 1                  ORG     $8000
Line 2     BASE         EQU     $8000
Line 3     NUM_ONE      FCB     $23      ; first number
Line 4     NUM_TWO      FCB     $3F      ; second number
Line 5                  ORG     $8100
Line 6                  LDX     #BASE
Line 7                  LDAA    $0,X
Line 8                  LDAB    $1,X
Line 9                  STAB    NUM_ONE
Line 10                 STAA    NUM_TWO
Line 11                 END
```

[1]The exception are events that require a special service from the CPU.

Before reading further, using the knowledge you gained from Chapter 2, see whether you can figure out what the program does. It is a convoluted way to swap two numbers located in memory locations $8000 and $8001. Let us study each line before we move on to assemble the code.

The first line specifies the starting memory location where variables NUM_ONE and NUM_TWO reside using the ORG directive. Line 2 uses directive EQU to equate symbol BASE with $8000. Both the first and second lines use directives and do not directly generate any machine code. The instructions on lines 3 and 4 initialize variables NUM_ONE and NUM_TWO. Using the ORG directive on line 5, the program instructs the assembler that the actual code starts at memory address $8100. The LDX instruction on line 6 loads value $8000 to index register X, and the instructions on lines 7 and 8 load variables NUM_ONE and NUM_TWO to accumulators A and B, respectively. Notice that here the index addressing mode was used to perform the loading tasks. The instructions on lines 9 and 10 then store the contents of the accumulators in the reverse order to swap the two original numbers. After performing the LDAA instruction on line A, variable NUM_ONE contains $3F while variable NUM_TWO holds $23. The END directive tells the assembler the location of the program end. We continue the assembly process using the prior code. Figure 3.1 shows two files generated by a typical assembler.

An assembler converts an assembly language program into a machine language program (1s and 0s). The machine level alphabet of all digital computers is based on the Boolean logic, an event or a state is either true or false. The job of an assembler is to read each instruction of an assembly language program and convert it into a string of ones and zeros that is interpreted by the machine. For Motorola microcontrollers, the machine code file with extension s19 is necessary. An s19 file consists of strings of zeros and ones along with some overhead bits. The overhead bits are used to accurately transfer a machine code file between the host PC and the

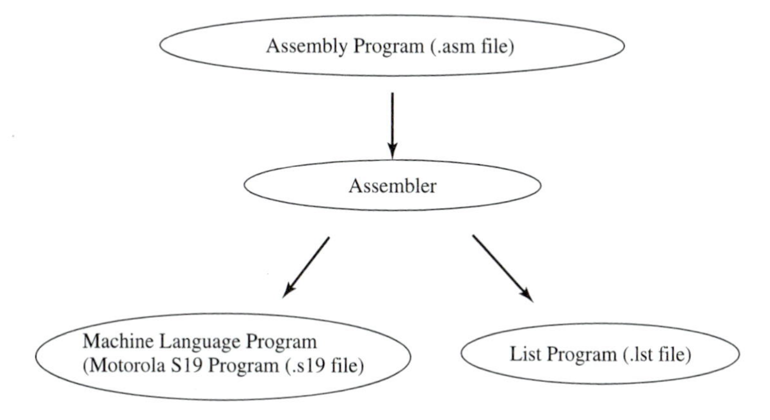

Figure 3.1 Files generated by an assembly process.

68HC12. The s19 files are created using the Motorola 8-bit object code format. The designated file format of s19 files is used by a loader program to send and receive program files between a PC and the 68HC12.

Now let us consider the conversion process using an example. Suppose we want to assemble the following instruction: "LDAA #$25." A 68HC12 assembler converts the instruction to "%1000011000100101." The first eight most significant bits represent the op-code LDAA, whereas the rest of the bits represent the operand. The op-code pattern "10000110" is interpreted by the controller to perform the load accumulator A task. Since it is difficult for humans to distinguish one long string of ones and zeros from another, the engineering community adopted the hexadecimal number representation for the actual display of the machine code. Thus, the instruction in the hexadecimal form is "86 25." You can find the entire listing of machine codes for each 68HC12 instruction in Appendix A.

Now let us get back to our first example program and see whether we can manually assemble it. As mentioned earlier, Lines 1 through 4 contain directives and no instructions are generated. During the loading of the program to the 68HC12 memory, the directive on line 1 instructs the loader to place the data, which follows line 1 to be placed in memory address starting at $8000. The EQU directive on line 2 simply replaces each symbol named BASE appearing in the program with hexadecimal number $8000 during the assembly process. The FCB directives on lines 3 and 4 inform the loader to place $23 and $3F in memory locations $8000 and $8001, respectively. The directive on line 5 dictates the code starts at address $8100. Starting on line 6, we generate the following corresponding machine code for the rest of the assembly program with the help of the instruction set listed in Appendix A.

	Assembly Code		Machine Code
Line 6	LDX	#BASE	CE8000
Line 7	LDAA	$1,X	A601
Line 8	LDAB	$2,X	E602
Line 9	STAB	NUM_ONE	7B8000
Line 10	STAA	NUM_TWO	7A8001

An assembler is a program that performs the exact same task we did earlier—the format conversion. In addition, an assembler uses directives to define variables, specify code locations, and reserve memory locations for use in a program.

Before we move on to the next section, we must discuss one other file associated with the assembly process. As a part of the assembly process, one can generate a list file, as shown in Figure 3.1, corresponding to the assembly source file. An assembler source file, such as the one we wrote in our example, ends with the extension .asm. Once this program is submitted to an assembler, you have an option to create a list file with an extension .lst. This file contains the address for each instruction in the target computer memory, the hexadecimal values that will be put into the designated memory locations, and the source code. At the end of this file, there is a symbol table with all used symbols and the corresponding values. The following figure is the .lst file generated by the P & E software with the example code as the input. The .lst file is useful for debugging purposes since a programmer can see the actual contents of the memory. The hexadecimal representations of instructions can also be used to follow a step-by-step program execution, verifying results at each step, using available debugging tools.

```
CH3A.ASM      Assembled with IASM          07/15/2000 PAGE 1
8000          1                 ORG        $8000
8000          2     BASE        EQU        $8000
8000 23       3     NUM_ONE     FCB        $23
8001 3F       4     NUM_TWO     FCB        $3F
8100          5                 ORG        $8100
8100 CE8000   6                 LDX        #BASE
8103 A601     7                 LDAA       $1,X
8105 E602     8                 LDAB       $2,X
8107 7B8000   9                 STAB       NUM-ONE
810A 7A8001   10                STAB       NUM-TWO
8100          11                END
              12
              13
Symbol Table
BASE          8000
NUM_ONE       8000
NUM_TWO       8001
```

The first column of the list program lists the memory locations, the second column shows the contents of the memory locations, and the rest of the columns contain the assembly language source program. From the list file, you see that the machine code for instruction "LDX #BASE" on line 6 is "CE8000" by reading the corresponding contents in column 2. As can be seen from the illustration, a list file allows a programmer to see assembly instructions (convenient for humans), machine codes (suitable for the microcontroller), and the locations of the codes in a single file: a useful tool for testing and debugging a program. With this introduction to the assembly process, let us examine some advanced assembly language coding techniques starting with the loop construct.

3.2 LOOPS

In this section, we introduce the concept of a loop using an example program. Suppose you want to find the average midterm score for your class with 10 students. The brute force method will add the first student's score to the second student's score. Then add the third student's score to the current sum and add the fourth student's score to the new sum. This process continues until all 10 scores are added. You then divide the sum by 10 to get the average score. Let us focus on the task of adding 10 scores. A pseudocode for summing of the scores using the brute force method is as follows:

```
Initialize Sum = 0;
Sum = Sum + first score;
Sum = Sum + second score;
Sum = Sum + third score;
. . .
Sum = Sum + tenth score;
```

Now compare a scheme with the loop programming construct. Using the loop construct, one writes the program in the concise form as follows:

```
Initialize Sum = 0;
Initialize counter = 0;
While counter < 10
   Sum = Sum + score[counter];
   Increment counter;
```

The term *score[counter]* refers to a member in a score array where the value inside of the bracket is used to single out a particular test score. As we can see, the use of a loop, represented with the "While" statement in the previous pseudocode, reduces the program size, providing for compact coding. To perform the iteration, note that some type of condition must be tested at the beginning or end of each iteration to make a decision to continue a loop or break out of a loop. In the current example, the countervalue was tested to make that decision.

We saw pseudocodes for both the brute force method and a method using the loop construct. Let us go ahead and write the two assembly program segments for the 68HC12 as an exercise. We assume that the 10 midterm scores already reside in memory locations starting at address $1000 and that variable *sum* has also been declared and initialized as zero. The brute force approach generates the following programming segment:

```
LDAA  SUM      ; load variable sum to accumulator A
ADDA  $1000    ; add the first number
ADDA  $1001    ; add the second number
ADDA  $1002    ; add the third number
...            ; add, add, add
ADDA  $1009    ; add the last number
STAA  SUM      ; store the sum
```

Now compare the code with the following program segment using the loop construct. In this program segment, note that we use variable *count* to keep track of the numbers being added at each iteration.

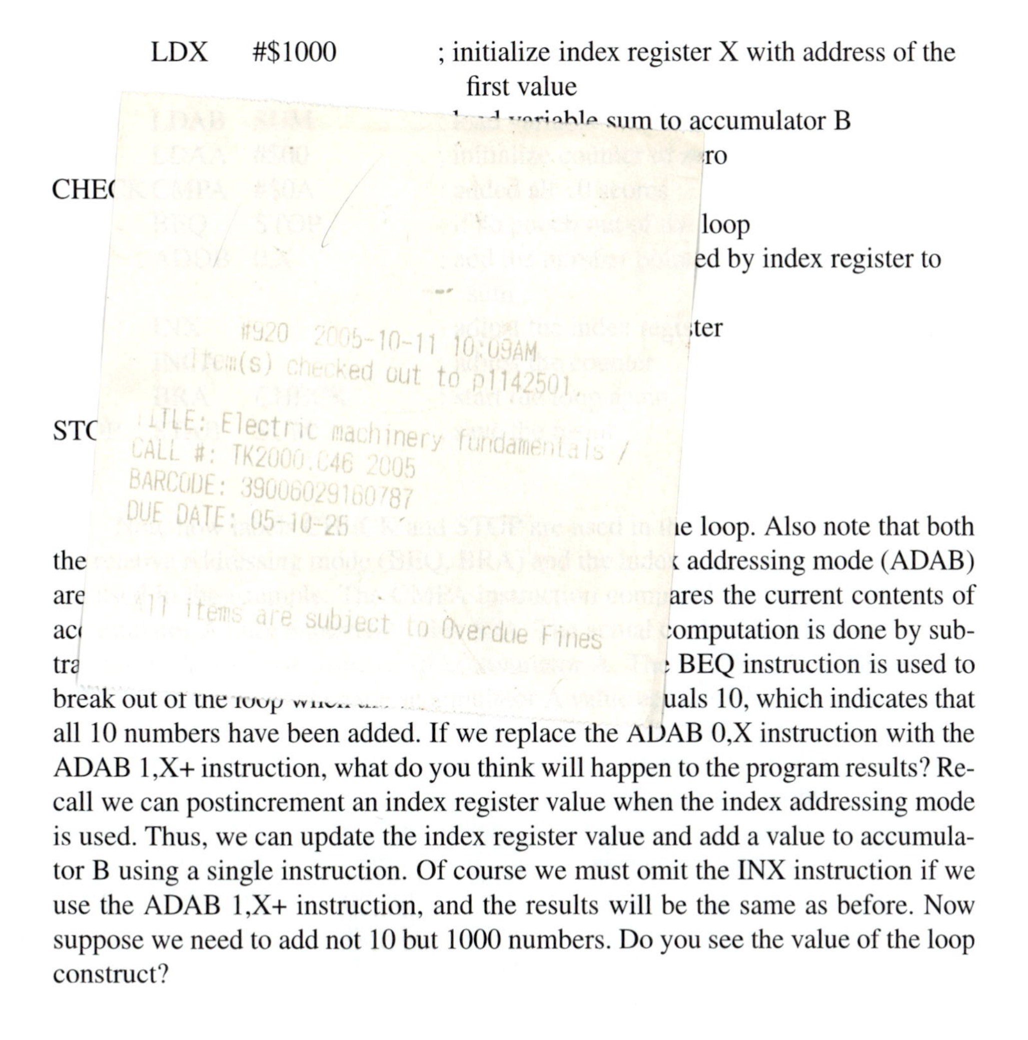


```
        LDX   #$1000   ; initialize index register X with address of the
                         first value
        LDAB  SUM      ; load variable sum to accumulator B
        LDAA  #$00     ; initialize counter to zero
CHECK   CMPA  #$0A     ; [illegible]
        BEQ   STOP     ; [illegible] loop
        ADDB  0,X      ; add the number [illegible]ed by index register to
                         [illegible]
        INX            ; [illegible]ter
        [illegible]
        BRA   CHECK    ; [illegible]
STOP    [illegible]
```

[illegible] the loop. Also note that both the [illegible] addressing mode (ADAB) are [illegible] ares the current contents of ac[illegible] computation is done by subtra[illegible] BEQ instruction is used to break out of the loop [illegible] uals 10, which indicates that all 10 numbers have been added. If we replace the ADAB 0,X instruction with the ADAB 1,X+ instruction, what do you think will happen to the program results? Recall we can postincrement an index register value when the index addressing mode is used. Thus, we can update the index register value and add a value to accumulator B using a single instruction. Of course we must omit the INX instruction if we use the ADAB 1,X+ instruction, and the results will be the same as before. Now suppose we need to add not 10 but 1000 numbers. Do you see the value of the loop construct?

3.3 STACK

In this section, we discuss the important subject of the stack and how it is used during a program execution. We first start with the definition for the stack in the next subsection; we then illustrate the utility of the stack and how to access the contents of a stack in the subsequent subsections.

3.3.1 Definition of Stack

A stack is a set of memory locations where data can be stored temporarily. Such temporary space is critical especially when the 68HC12 CPU executes programs with subroutines (Section 3.4), initiated by software, and programs with interrupt service routines (Chapter 6) triggered by hardware interrupts. The data in a stack can only be accessed from one end. A stack data structure has a top and a bottom, and new data can only enter the structure from the top of the stack. Motorola adopted the convention to assign a lower memory address and a higher memory address for the top and bottom of the structure, respectively, while Intel uses the opposite convention. When the 68HC12 microcontroller is powered on, its stack is empty and the top and bottom addresses of the stack are identical. As new values enter the stack, the bottom address of the stack remains the same while the top address is decreased (increased for Intel machines). Thus, a microcontroller can locate the next available stack memory location to store new data based on the top stack address. For the 68HC12, the top of a stack refers to the address of the last element loaded onto the stack. The job of keeping track of the top of the stack belongs to a special register called the *stack pointer*.

An analogous example follows. Recall the last time you went to a buffet restaurant. As you approached the buffet tables, you probably found a stack of dishes in a plate rack ready to be picked up by customers. When you took out a plate, the one underneath popped up to the top of the dish rack, allowing the next person in line to pick up the plate. When all plates are gone, a bus boy would refill the rack by putting dishes on top of the rack. In our stack analogy, each plate would represent a unit of data. Taking a plate from the rack decreases the number of plates in the rack, which corresponds to decreasing the stack size: The difference between the top and bottom of the stack is reduced. Putting plates back onto the stack corresponds to increasing the stack size, thus widening the difference between the top and bottom of the stack.

Figure 3.2 shows the stack structure and stack pointer of the 68HC12. As you will see, a programmer dictates the initial contents of the stack pointer. Since the stack grows from a higher to a lower address, it is important to leave enough room to grow back. Although one can initialize the stack pointer to be anywhere in the user RAM, the optimal choice is $8000 for the 68HC812A4 evaluation board since

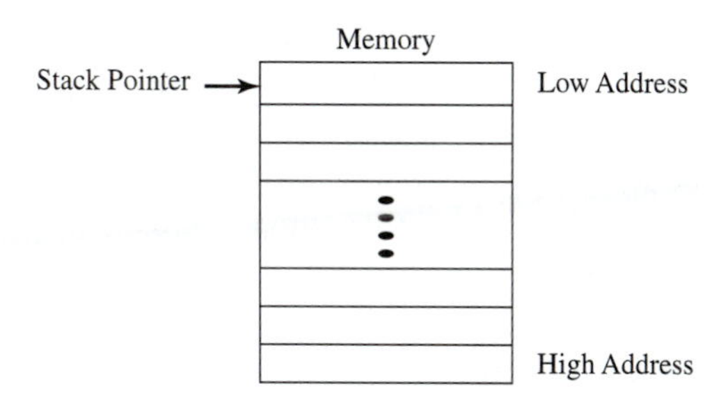

Figure 3.2 A sample stack structure and the use of a stack pointer.

the user RAM memory is located at $4000 through $7FFF, where address $7FFF is the last available RAM memory location.

3.3.2 Use of a Stack

As alluded to in the previous section, the stack is a first-in-last-out data structure. The term *push* represents the process of putting an element onto a stack, whereas the term *pull* signifies the act of taking an element off the stack. Each time a byte of data is pushed onto the stack, the stack pointer is adjusted by subtracting one from the current contents of the stack pointer. The updated stack pointer then holds a memory address of the last data byte pushed onto the stack. In cases of putting two bytes of information (pushing contents of one of the index registers or the D accumulator) onto a stack, the stack pointer value is adjusted by subtracting two from the current pointer value. For the 68HC12 microcontroller, the placement of data on its stack is accomplished using one of the following instructions:

PSHA, PSHB, PSHD, PSHC, PSHX, PSHY

Instructions PSHA, PSHB, and PSHD push the contents of accumulators A, B, and D to the stack, respectively. The contents of the CCR can also be stored in the stack using the PSHC instruction, whereas instructions PSHX and PSHY are used to save the contents of index registers X and Y in the stack. The opposite operation of taking an element out of a stack—the retrieving process—is done using the following instructions:

PULA, PULB, PULD, PULC, PULX, PULY

Again, instructions PULA and PULB take a byte each from the top of a stack and load them into accumulators A and B, whereas instructions PULD and PULC extract two bytes and one byte from the stack and store them into accumulator D and the CCR, respectively. Instructions PULX and PULY load two bytes each from the top of the stack and store them in index registers X and Y. The stack pointer value is changed by 1 for instructions PSHA, PSHB, PSHC, PULA, PULB, and PULC; decremented for the PSHA, PSHB, and PSHC instructions; and incremented for the PULA, PULB, and PULC instructions. The stack pointer value changes by 2 for instructions dealing with an index register and accumulator D; instructions PSHX, PSHY, and PSHD decrement the pointer, whereas instructions PULX, PULY, and PULD increment the pointer.

Remember that before any of the prior instructions are performed, a programmer must first initialize the stack pointer by loading a designated value ($8000) to the stack pointer register. The 68HC12 has other stack-related instructions. We discuss them next.

- INS and DES—increments or decrements the value stored in the stack pointer.
- LDS and STS—loads or stores a value to and from the stack pointer
- TSX, TXS, TSY, TYS—transfers the contents of the stack pointer to the X register, transfers the contents of index register X to the stack pointer, transfers the contents of the stack pointer to the Y register, and transfers the contents of index register Y to the stack pointer, respectively.

3.3.3 Access to a Stack

Now that we have learned the instructions associated with the stack, let us move on to the topic of accessing the stack. We present this topic with the help of the following two examples. The first example illustrates a simple push-and-pull process to access stack elements.

Example

Accessing the stack using two 8-bit values

```
Line 1      NUM1     EQU     $15
Line 2      NUM2     EQU     $2F
Line 3               LDS     #$8000     ; initialize the stack
Line 4               LDAA    #NUM1
Line 5               LDAB    #NUM2
                     :
Line p               PSHA
Line p+1             PSHB
                     :                  ;Do other things
Line q               PULB
Line q+1             PULA
```

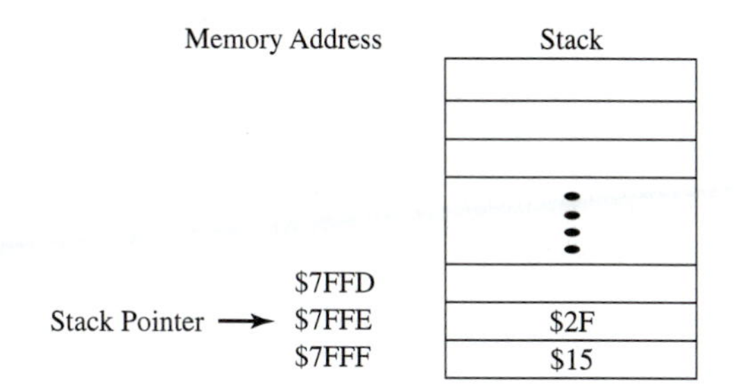

Figure 3.3 Showing the contents of the stack.

In this example code, the first two lines define symbols NUM1 and NUM2 using the EQU directive. As the first step before the stack is used, the stack pointer is initialized on line 3. The instructions on lines 4 and 5 load NUM1 ($15) and NUM2 ($2F) to accumulators A and B, respectively. Commands PSHA and PSHB on lines p and p+1 are used to load values to the stack. Figure 3.3 shows the status of the stack after line p+1 is executed.

Note the contents of the stack pointer. The stack pointer has the address of the last location where a value was stored. Once a number of instructions have been executed between lines p+1 and q, we are ready to restore the accumulator values. To extract values from the stack, commands PULB and PULA on lines q and q+1 are used. The values are loaded from the stack to accumulators B first then A. Now suppose we reverse the order of line q and q+1 in the program segment. The resulting values of accumulators A and B are the original accumulator values of accumulators B and A, respectively. We may want to do so on purpose to swap values stored in the two accumulators.

Let us take a look at another example. Suppose you are not interested in the values on top of the stack and you do not want to pull all components until you reach the one in which you are interested. Suppose you want to load the fourth and the seventh elements from the top of the stack to accumulator A. How would you do it? Consider the following code and try to interpret each line before you read further.

```
Line A    LDS     #$8000 ; initialize the stack pointer
                :
Line B    TSX
Line C    LDAA    3,X
Line D    LDAB    6,X
```

The instruction on line A initializes the stack pointer. The TSX instruction on line B takes the stack pointer contents and stores them to index register X.

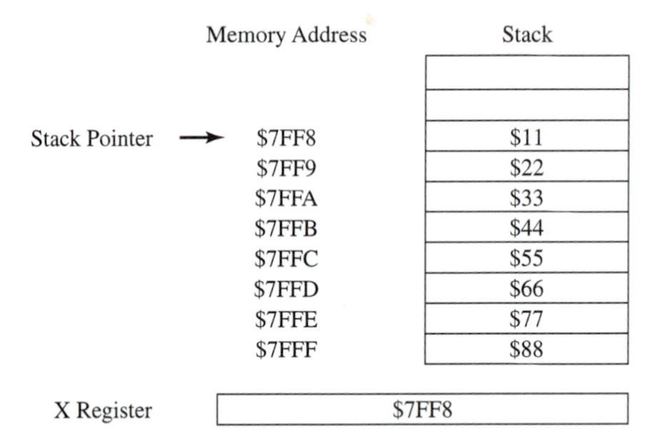

Figure 3.4 Stack and the X register.

Figure 3.4 illustrates the current status of the stack and index register X after line B is executed. We assume that after the stack pointer initialization, the program has pushed data to the stack and the stack pointer is pointing at the top of the stack as shown in the figure. The instruction on line C now uses the updated index X register value to access the fourth element from the top of the stack; the LDAB 6,X on line D extracts the seventh element from the top of the stack. Notice that a stack element is accessed by command LDA- 0,X, where - can be A or B. Since we want to access the fourth element from the top, we need to use LDAA 3,X not LDAA 4,X since index register X already points to the first top number of the stack. After executing the instruction on line D, accumulators A and B will have $44 and $77, respectively, as desired.

3.4 SUBROUTINES

In this section, we study the topic of subroutines and the role of a stack in programs with subroutines. We first define the term *subroutine*. A subroutine is a separate, independent module of a program that is designed to perform a specific task. Usually subroutines are written when the same task needs to be repeated over and over again. A main program or even another subroutine calls a subroutine to carry out the repetitive task. We later show exactly what we mean by *calling a subroutine*.

The first advantage of using subroutines is that we reduce the size of a program when the program repeats a task. The second advantage is that a subroutine can be used by multiple programs that require the subroutine function, saving time not to reinvent the wheel. If you are familiar with high-level programming languages, you already know that a group of subroutines, called a *library*, is available to be included in your program. These subroutines, sometimes referred to as functions, allow you to save time by avoiding re-creation of already existing subroutines.

To write a good subroutine, a programmer must consider the following issues.

- Independence—As mentioned earlier, one writes a subroutine to perform a specific task that can be called by multiple programs. Suppose you are working in a large group where your job is to write a subroutine to perform a task that each member of the group uses. You want to make sure that your subroutine does not depend on other programs. That is not to say that your subroutine cannot call other subroutines, but that your subroutine should be portable to be used on its own.
- Restoration of CPU registers—When a subroutine is called by other program modules, the CPU is at a particular state designated by the contents of the CPU registers, such as the accumulators, index registers, and condition code register. The called subroutine also uses the CPU registers to carry out its own task. Thus, a programmer is responsible to make sure that his or her subroutine restores any changes made to the CPU registers when the subroutine is completed. This step is usually done by storing all CPU registers into a temporary storage space (yes, you guessed it, the stack!) before a subroutine task starts and loading back to the appropriate registers after the completion of the subroutine.
- Data and code location independent—Since one of the goals of writing a subroutine is to accommodate the use by multiple programs, we must be sure that the proper working of your subroutine does not include data with specific addresses or instructions using particular memory locations. You simply do not know where other code lives in a program. To make your subroutine data and code location independent, you must only use variables declared locally and not use the direct and extended addressing modes within your subroutine.

If you conscientiously consider the above three issues as you write your subroutines, you will write good ones that you can use multiple times in different programs. Picture your collection of well-written subroutines as a tool box full of good quality, well-maintained hand tools. Of course the three issues are more important to consider when writing high-level language subroutines as opposed to writing microcontroller subroutines, but a programmer should always try to meet the criteria regardless of the programming language used.

3.4.1 Subroutine Calls and Returns

In this subsection, we show exactly what it means for a main programming module to call a subroutine. Figure 3.5 illustrates the subroutine calling process. Recall

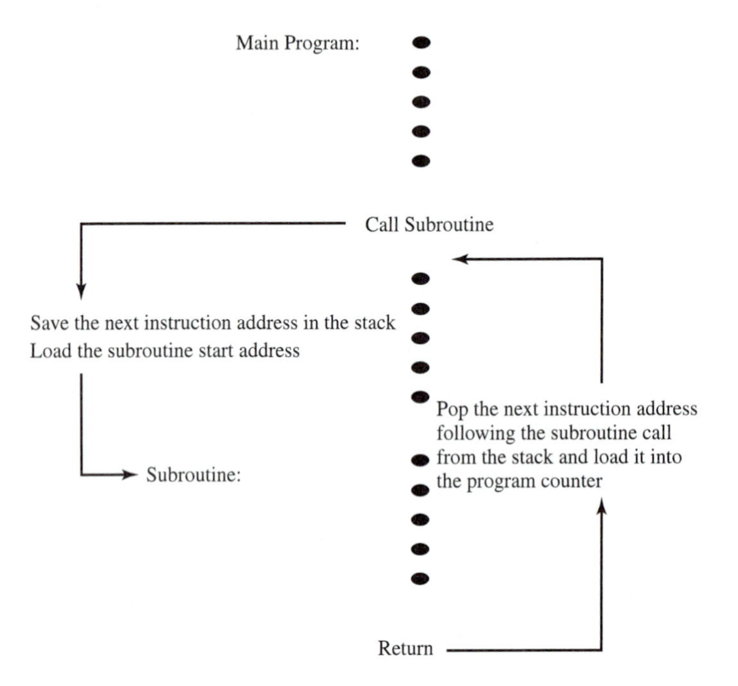

Figure 3.5 The program counter is used to execute a subroutine.

from the previous chapter that the program execution is governed by the contents of a special register—the program counter. The program counter always contains the address of the next instruction the CPU will execute. During normal execution, as each instruction is executed, the program counter value is incremented to point to the next instruction, which follows the current instruction. However, when a main program instruction calls on a subroutine, the main program temporarily relieves its control of the program execution and lets the subroutine take the control of the execution process by changing the contents of the program counter to point to the first instruction in the subroutine. On the completion of the subroutine, the control of program execution is returned back to the main program; the program counter is changed again to hold the address of the instruction following the subroutine call. Thus, a subroutine call instruction simply changes the program counter value.

The process of changing *hands* between a main program and a subroutine, shown in Figure 3.5, is possible by assigning a starting address of the program or a starting address of the subroutine to the program counter when the control changes hands between the two programming modules. Notice that when the main program calls a subroutine, the program counter is pointing to the next instruction that follows a subroutine call. When the subroutine is completed, we want the instruction that immediately follows the subroutine call to be executed. For this to work, the contents of the current program counter, at the time of the subroutine call, must be stored somewhere when a subroutine starts its execution. When the subroutine completes its task, it then knows how to return the control back over to the main program by restoring the program counter value that was saved. Saving and retrieving the contents of the program counter is done using the stack. The last-in-first-out structure of the stack provides a convenient means to carry out the saving and retrieving task. It is comforting to know that the program counter changes related to subroutine operations are handled by the CPU12 automatically.

Now that we understand what a subroutine call means, let us consider how we actually call a subroutine by studying the subroutine associated 68HC12 instructions. We first look at two instructions that call subroutines: Branch SubRoutine (BSR) and Jump SubRoutine (JSR). These instructions are used to call a subroutine. Recall that BSR is a branch instruction, which means that the offset, determining the distance from the instruction following the current instruction, can only be plus 127 bytes or minus 128 bytes. In other words, the start of a subroutine must reside within −128 to +127 bytes from the instruction that immediately follows a subroutine call. On the other hand, the JSR instruction does not have the constraint, and a subroutine can reside anywhere in the accessible memory location. We reiterate the question discussed in the previous chapter: Why bother with the BSR instruction? There are two reasons. The BSR instruction always uses the relative addressing mode that takes up two bytes of memory for storage. To execute the BSR instruction, four clock cycles are needed. The JSR instruction is called with a direct, extended, indexed, or indirect indexed addressing mode. The required memory bytes for storage vary from two to four bytes, and the execution time varies from four to seven cycles. So the answer to the question is that if we are interested in saving storage space and execution time, we should use the BSR instruction while understanding the flexibility the JSR instruction offers.

The instructions BSR and JSR have the following format:

```
[Label]        instruction        operand
```

Note that when one of the BSR and JSR instructions is called, the contents of the current program counter are automatically saved on the stack to *remember* where to return. The counterpart of calling a subroutine is returning from the subroutine back to the calling point when the called subroutine completes its task. The return is accomplished by instruction RTS (ReTurn from Subroutine). This instruction must always appear at the end of each subroutine. Its job is to restore the contents of the program counter such that the instruction that immediately follows the subroutine call instruction in the program can be executed next. The instruction RTS has the following format:

```
[Label]        RTS
```

When the RTS instruction is executed, the address of the next instruction following a subroutine call in the caller program is restored by taking two bytes off the top of the stack and putting the value into the program counter. It is the programmer's responsibility that the top of the stack contains the returning address if the stack were used inside of the called subroutine.

3.4.2 Parameter-Passing Techniques

Although a subroutine performs a specific task, we want to make it as flexible as we can. After all, you want to use your subroutine for many other programs. That brings us to the next subtopic of calling a subroutine with varying parameters. That is, in many cases, subroutines are called with different initial conditions. How does the main program send an initial condition to a subroutine? We answer this question next. Two general different parameter-passing techniques exist. Our coverage of the techniques only deals with main usage of the techniques. For a full list of usage, we refer you to computer science literature.

Call-by-Value The first technique sends actual parameter values to subroutines using CPU registers; accumulators and index registers are used to pass along the parameters and results between a main program and a subroutine. For example, suppose we want to swap two numbers stored in memory locations. We saw this example in the following form before.

```
Line 1                  ORG    $4000
Line 2    BASE          EQU    $4000
Line 3    NUM_ONE       FCB    $23          ; first number
Line 4    NUM_TWO       FCB    $3F          ; second number
Line 5                  ORG    $4100
Line 6                  LDX    #BASE
Line 7                  LDAA   $0,X
Line 8                  LDAB   $1,X
Line 9                  STAB   NUM_ONE
Line 10                 STAA   NUM_TWO
Line 11                 END
```

Suppose in one's line of work, numbers in two memory locations are swapped all the time and we want to write a subroutine that performs the swapping task. Furthermore, suppose that we want to pass along the values to be swapped to the subroutine using the call-by-value technique. The following simple program with a subroutine called SWAP does the job.

```
Line 1                   ORG   $4000
Line 2   BASE            EQU   $4000
Line 3   NUM_ONE         FCB   $23      ; first number
Line 4   NUM_TWO         FCB   $3F      ; second number
Line 5                   ORG   $4100
Line 6                   LDS   #8000
Line 7                   LDX   #BASE
Line 8                   LDAA  $0,X
Line 9                   LDAB  $1,X
Line 10                  BSR   SWAP
Line 11                  STAA  NUM_ONE
Line 12                  STAB  NUM_TWO
Line 13                  END
  :                       :
Line X1                  SWAP  PSHA
Line X2                        PSHB
Line X3                        PULA
Line X4                        PULB
Line X5                        RTS
```

Lines 1 through 5 contain the identical instructions of the program that did not use a subroutine. On line 6, the stack pointer is initialized to hold $8000. The instructions on lines 7 through 9 load the first and second numbers into accumulators A and B. In this example, we assume the subroutine SWAP starts at a location within the $+127$ and -128 range from line 11. When line 10 is executed, the address for line 11 is automatically loaded onto the stack before the program counter obtains the address for Line X1. The status of the stack at this point before executing Line X1 is shown in Figure 3.6. The numerical two-byte value $410C in the stack is the address of the STAA instruction on line 11.

The SWAP subroutine starts at line X1. As the 68HC12 gets ready to execute the instruction on line X1, the accumulators A and B contain two numbers that we want to swap. The subroutine has access to the accumulators at this point, and we consider that the necessary values have been passed down to the subroutine using the accumulators. On line X1, the subroutine stores numerical value $23, the current NUM_ONE value stored in accumulator A, to the stack using the PSHA instruction. On line X2, the subroutine stores numerical value $3F, the current NUM_TWO value stored in accumulator B, to the stack using the PSHB instruction. The contents of the stack and the stack pointer value at this point are shown in Figure 3.7.

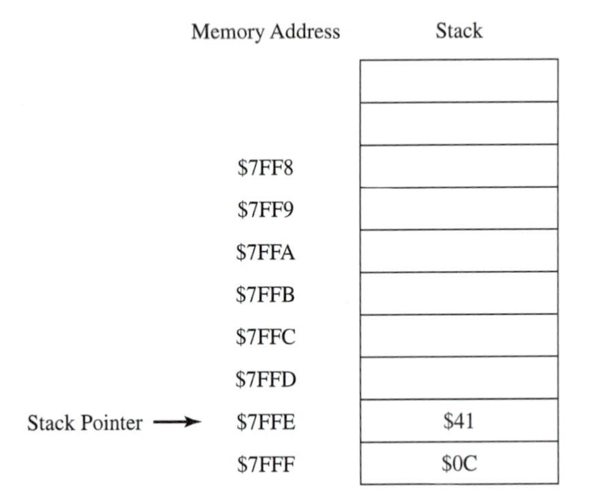

Figure 3.6 Contents of the stack before executing subroutine swap. The stack pointer has been decremented by two, and the address of the instruction, which immediately follows the subroutine call $410C, has been stored in the stack.

The instructions on lines X3 and X4 perform the task of swapping the two numbers. The task is done by restoring accumulator values from the top of the stack but in the reverse order: Accumulator A is restored first followed by accumulator B. After the instruction on line X4 is executed, accumulator A has $3F and accumulator B has $23. Figure 3.6 shows the status of the stack after the instruction on line X4 is executed. Finally, the RTS instruction on line X5 pulls the two bytes from the top of the stack and stores them in the program counter register, returning the program execution to the main program. This enforces that the instruction on line 11 is executed next. The instructions on lines 11 and 12 are used to store the

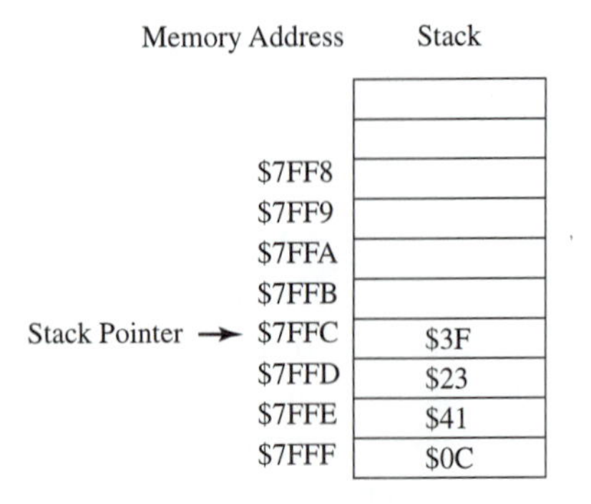

Figure 3.7 Contents of the stack after line X2.

swapped values $3F and $23 to memory locations NUM_ONE and NUM_TWO, respectively.

We wrote the previous program to explain how the stack is used to perform the exchange task. Do you think there is a more direct method to accomplish the job? The answer is yes. We actually did not need a subroutine at all to perform the swapping task. The EXG A,B instruction carries out the exact same task. We simply need to replace line 10 with

EXG A,B

and lines X1 through X5 are not necessary.

Call-by-Reference The second method of passing parameter values between a main program and a subroutine is called the call-by-reference method. For this method, a main program or another subroutine passes along parameter values to a called subroutine by sending the memory address where parameter values reside. Note that this method is used when you intend a subroutine to actually change the contents of memory locations. To implement this method, we use either a CPU register or a program memory location to pass along the memory address of parameters.

Example

Suppose you want to write a program that copies an existing list of 10 values from memory location $5000 to memory location $6000. The 10 values may represent the average number of guests in 10 different hotels in a city during the peak vacation season of the year. Suppose we want to make a copy of the values for record before processing the original numbers. To copy the numbers, we should use a subroutine using the call-by-reference method. To make the program flexible, we use another memory location to indicate the number of data elements to be copied. Thus, the subroutine will copy not just 10 but any number of elements from one location to another. The following program will perform the desired task. Figure 3.8 shows what the program is doing at two different memory locations.

```
Line 1   FIRST      EQU    $5000
Line 2   SECOND     EQU    $6000
Line 3              ORG    $4000
Line 4   NUM_DATA   FCB    $0A          ; number of data to be copied
Line 5              ORG    $4100
Line 6              LDS    #8000
Line 7              LDAA   NUM_DATA
Line 8              LDX    #FIRST
Line 9              LDY    #SECOND
```

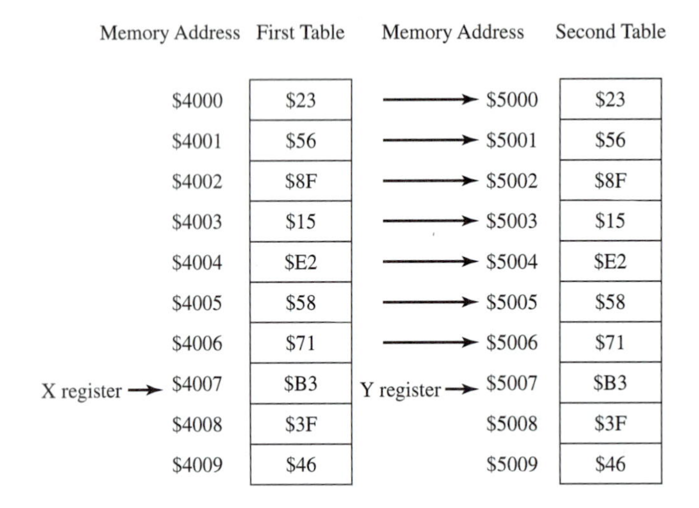

Figure 3.8 Program function illustration.

```
Line 10                 JSR     COPY
Line 11                 END
  :                      :
Line X1   COPY          CMPA    #$00
Line X2                 BEQ     DONE
Line X3                 LDAB    1,X+
Line X4                 STAB    1,Y+
Line X5                 DECA
Line X6                 BRA     COPY
Line X7   DONE          RTS
```

The EQU directives on lines 1 and 2 define constant symbols FIRST and SECOND, representing the start addresses for the original list and the copy list, respectively. The ORG directive on line 3 instructs the assembler that the number of elements in the original list is stored at memory location $4000. The initialization of the number of elements in the list is done on line 4 by the FCB directive. The next ORG directive on line 5 is used to specify where the program will physically reside in memory. The stack pointer is initialized on line 6, and we loaded accumulator A with the table length from memory location $4000 on line 7. The instructions on lines 8 and 9 load the start addresses for the original list and the copy list. In this program, we are assuming that the subroutine COPY, which copies all elements from the first list to the second list, is physically at a distance beyond the range of −128 to +127 from Line 11. Thus, we elected to use the JSR instruction over the BRA instruction on line 10. Notice how the subroutine is called. First, the original list length information is passed to the subroutine in accumulator A—a call-by-value method. If, instead, we store the address of NUM_DATA in accumulator D and call the subroutine, we would be using the call-by-reference method. The original and second lists are passed to the subroutine by sending their starting addresses using the call-by-reference method in the X and Y index registers. Notice we are not sending 10 elements to the subroutine, but only the starting addresses.

Continuing with the program, the instruction on line X1 checks the ending condition for the loop used to copy values from the original list to the copy list. When the accumulator A value reaches zero, it indicates that all elements in the original list have been copied. When that happens, the condition for the branch instruction on line X2 is satisfied and the branch is taken to the end of the subroutine. The instructions on lines X3 and X4 perform the copying task while postincrementing the two index register values for the next iteration. These instructions are identical in functions to instructions LDAB 0,X and STAB 0,Y as we saw in the previous chapter with an exception: After loading and storing a value, the contents of the index register are incremented by one. Thus, the instruction on line X4 stores the value fetched from the original list to a proper location in the copy list and then increments the contents of index register Y to point to the next location in the copy list. The 68HC12 also provides the flexibility to decrement index register contents after an instruction is executed as well as decrement or increment index register values before an instruction is executed.

Back to the program. The instruction on line X5 updates the counter—the number of elements left to be copied. The instruction on line X6 always branches to the beginning of the loop to repeat the process all over again. When all elements in the original list are copied, the subroutine breaks out of the loop and executes the instruction on line X7, which restores program counter with the address of the instruction immediately following the subroutine call.

3.5 68HC12 D-BUG12 UTILITY SUBROUTINES

We continue the topic of subroutines in this section. In particular, we show how to use convenient built-in subroutines of the 68HC12 monitor/debugger program, D-Bug12. The monitor program resides within the read-only memory of the controller and allows us to execute programs, view and alter memory locations, modify CPU register contents, and debug programs by providing a set of useful commands. You have already seen such commands in the laboratory exercise A at the end of Chapter 2. In addition to the convenient commands, the monitor/debugger program contains 18 utility subroutines, with functions ranging from a simple display of messages on a computer screen to the initialization of user-specified interrupt service routine address.[2] These utility subroutines are the focus of this section.

The 18 subroutines are listed in Table 3.1. We first describe the common setup required before any utility routine is called. We then explain how each routine is used. Each utility subroutine requires a set of parameter values. As we learned in this chapter, no parameters, a single parameter, or a set of parameters must be passed to a subroutine when the subroutine is called. Consider a subroutine that requires *n* parameters as shown next.

subroutine (parameter 1, parameter 2, parameter 3, . . . , parameter n)

For the D-Bug12 utility routines, the 68HC12 insists on using the stack as the means to transfer parameter values. In particular, parameters must be pushed onto the stack starting with parameter n to parameter 1. Once all necessary parameter values are stored on the stack, you must load the vector address of the subroutine in index register X. For the D-Bug12 utility routines, you must always treat param-

TABLE 3.1 D-BUG12 UTILITY ROUTINES TABLE.

Routines	Vector Address	Function
main()	$FE00	Starts the D-Bug12 monitor program
getchar()	$FE02	Fetches a character from the keyboard
putchar()	$FE04	Displays a character on the screen
printf()	$FE06	Displays a formatted string on the screen
GetCmdLine()	$FE08	Fetches a command from the keyboard
sscanhex()	$FE0A	Converts a hexadecimal number to an integer
isxdigit()	$FE0C	Checks for a hexadecimal digit
toupper()	$FE0E	Converts a lowercase character to the uppercase character
isalpha()	$FE10	Checks for an alphabet character
strlen()	$FE12	Returns the length of a string
strcpy()	$FE14	Copies a string to another string
out2hex()	$FE16	Outputs a byte of a two hexadecimal number
out4hex()	$FE18	Outputs two bytes of a four hexadecimal number
SetUserVector()	$FE1A	Setup user-specified interrupt service routine address
WriteEEByte()	$FE1C	Write a byte to on-chip EEPROM
EraseEE()	$FE1E	Erase a block of on-chip EEPROM
ReadMem()	$FE20	Read data from memory
WriteMem()	$FE22	Write data to memory

[2] An interrupt service routine is a type of subroutine executed when a special signal, called an *interrupt*, is detected by a controller. The special signal can be initiated by software or hardware. An example of a hardware interrupt is a signal generated by an external device connected to the controller requesting a service of the controller.

eters as 16-bit values; an 8-bit parameter must first be converted to a 16-bit value before being pushed onto the stack. For example, when we use the *out2hex* utility subroutine to display $45 on the computer screen, we must store $0045 to the stack before the subroutine is called as shown in the following code segment.

```
LDD     #$45     ; value for display
PSHD             ; to computer screen
LDX     $FF17    ; 16 bit start address of subroutine
JSR     0,X      ; invoke the subroutine
PULX             ; clean up the stack
```

The instructions on the first and second lines store two bytes, the original hexadecimal value padded with zeros on the left, to the stack. The LDX instruction loads the start address of the subroutine located at memory locations $FF17 and $FE17.[3] At this point, all necessary preliminary steps are performed, and we are ready to call the utility subroutine using the JSR command on the next line.[4] The last line of the PULX instruction adjusts the stack to restore a proper stack pointer value. If more than one parameter was pushed onto the stack, a more convenient way to adjust the stack at this point is to use the Load stack pointer with Effective AddresS (LEAS) instruction. The LEAS instruction changes the stack pointer with one instruction. It is your responsibility to make sure the stack pointer is properly adjusted at the completion of a utility subroutine call.

We now study each utility function in a bit more detail, concentrating on three utility routines that, we feel, are most useful for user interaction and debugging purposes: *printf*, *getchar*, and *putchar*. For detailed descriptions for other utility routines, we refer you to the Motorola literature cited at the end of this chapter. Note that these utility routines are originally designed for high-level programming language C, and the format for the parameters follow the same format of the C programming language parameter specifications. In all possible cases, the names of routines are kept the same as those used in the C program language.

- The *main* utility routine allows a user program as a startup routine in place of the default initialization program of the D-Bug12 routine. For this to occur, you must insert the starting address of the user startup routine in memory locations $FE00 and $FE01. This routine should be used if your application requires an elaborate initialization procedure, such as moving the locations of different memory blocks.

[3]The actual utility subroutine location resides at $FF17.

[4]Some assemblers, including the enclosed software, allow you to use indirect-indexed addressing mode using the program counter instead of the indexed addressing mode we showed here. For those assemblers, you can use command *LDAB #$45* followed by command *JSR [out2hex,pcr]*, where out2hex is the utility vector address.

- The *GetCmdLine* utility subroutine obtains a line of command from a user. It repeatedly applies the *getchar* utility routine until a return character is received. This routine is available for extracting a string of user input.
- The *sscanhex* utility routine converts a string of hexadecimal numbers, terminated by an ASCII space character or an ASCII null character, into an integer number. The main purpose of this routine is to provide a user with a more familiar decimal number representation. One constraint is that the converted number cannot be greater than $2^{16} = 65536$. The start address of an original hexadecimal string and the start address of a result integer number are passed to this subroutine as parameters.
- The *isxdigit* utility routine checks whether an 8-bit ASCII value is one of 16 hexadecimal numbers. The test value must be loaded to accumulator B before calling the subroutine.
- The *toupper* utility routine converts a lowercase ASCII character into its corresponding uppercase character. The lowercase character, an 8-bit value, must first be loaded into accumulator B before the subroutine is called.
- The *isalpha* utility routine checks whether an 8-bit value loaded in accumulator B is an alphabet character. The routine checks for both the lower- and uppercase characters of the alphabet. The routine returns a nonzero value to accumulator B if the tested character is a member of the alphabet. It returns a zero otherwise.
- The *strlen* subroutine counts the number of characters in a string terminated by an ASCII null character ($00) and returns the result to accumulator D. Before this routine is called, the start address of the string must be loaded to accumulator D.
- The *strcpy* utility routine copies a character string from one memory location to another. The starting address for the original string should be pushed onto the stack followed by loading the start address for the destination to accumulator D before this routine is called.
- The *out2hex* routine sends out two hexadecimal digits (an 8-bit value) to a control terminal. The desired hexadecimal number must be loaded to accumulator B before this routine is called.
- The *out4hex* routine sends out four hexadecimal digits (a 16-bit value) to a control terminal. The desired hexadecimal number must be loaded to accumulator D before this routine is called.
- The *SetUserVector* utility routine allows you, a programmer, to specify the starting address of interrupt service routines. We discuss this topic in Chapter 6.
- The *WriteEEByte* utility routine is used to write to a single on-chip EEPROM location. The desired contents must first be loaded into the stack (this

must be done by loading the value to accumulator D and pushing the contents using the PSHD command) and the memory address in accumulator D before the function is called.

- The *EraseEE* routine bulk erases all on-chip EEPROM contents.
- The *ReadMem* routine is used to read the contents of memory locations and place them in a specified buffer. This routine is for internal use by the D-Bug12 program and has limited use for a programmer.
- The *WriteMem* routine is used to write new contents to memory locations. Again, this routine is used internally by the D-Bug12 program and has limited use for a programmer.

We briefly listed 15 of the 18 utility routines earlier. We dedicate the rest of this section to cover three utility routines with some examples that we feel you will use the most. We start with the *getchar* utility routine. The *getchar* utility routine obtains keyboard inputs from a user. The routine takes one keyboard input at a time using the control terminal connected to one of two 68HC12 synchronous communication interface (SCI) systems. It waits until a character is received in a special data register called the SCI Receive Data Register. The routine indefinitely waits for an input if an input is not received. To start the routine, you first need to load the contents of the vector address of the routine, $FE02, into index register X. Once the address is loaded, you can start the routine using the JSR command. The user input is stored in accumulator B as a result of running this subroutine. The following code segment gives you an example of how to use the routine.

```
line 1     GETCHAR    EQU     $FE02      ; vector address of routine
  :           :        :        :
line n                LDX     GETCHAR    ; load vector address to X
line n+1              JSR     0,X        ; invoke the subroutine
line n+2              STAB    TARGET     ; store the input value
  :           :        :        :
```

The EQU directive on line 1 defines the vector address of the subroutine. The instruction on line n loads the vector address and the instruction on line n+1 starts the utility subroutine. Once the subroutine is completed, the instruction on line n+2 stores the user input character into a target location previously defined as TARGET. Once the routine is completed, you can do any task necessary with the user input.

The *putchar* utility routine is the counterpart of the *getchar* routine. The routine is used to display one character at a time to a computer screen through the control terminal. The character must be a printable ASCII character. When the routine is finished, the sent character is stored to accumulator B. To invoke the routine, you must first store the desired character into accumulator B. Recall that a character is an 8-bit value. The following example code shows how you can use the routine.

```
line 1      PUTCHAR      EQU     $FE04
line 2      CHARACTER    FCC     'A'
  :            :          :        :
line n                   LDAB    CHARACTER
line n+1                 LDX     PUTCHAR
line n+2                 JSR     0,X
  :            :          :        :
```

Again, the EQU directive on line 1 defines the vector address of the *putchar* utility routine, and the instruction on line 2 defines a single character using the FCC directive. The instruction on line n loads the ASCII character "A" to accumulator B as the prerequisite step before the utility routine is called. The instruction on line n+1 loads the vector address to index register X and the subroutine is called on line n+2. A string of characters can be displayed on the control terminal using a loop of the prior code segment. For displaying a string of characters of formatted string with numbers and characters, a more convenient utility routine exists—the *printf* routine, which we discuss next.

The *printf* utility routine is a convenient tool for displaying a formatted string of characters. The routine prints all types of numbers with an exception of floating point values. You specify formats using a percentage sign within the character string. Following the percentage sign, you must specify a type of number or character you want to display using one of the characters shown in Table 3.2.

We illustrate the use of routine *printf* with examples next. Suppose we want to display the following message string on the control terminal: *68HC12 Application Result*. Since the character string does not contain any formatted values, we only need to pass the start address of the string to the utility routine via the stack and load the routine's vector address into index register X before invoking the routine as shown next.

```
line 1      PRINTF      EQU     $FE06
line 2                  ORG     $4000
line 3      STRING      FCC     '68HC12 Application Result',
                                $0D,$0A,$00
  :           :          :        :
```

TABLE 3.2 CHARACTERS USED FOR FORMATTING OUTPUTS OF THE *PRINTF* UTILITY ROUTINE.

character	type of number
d or i	signed decimal integer number
o	unsigned octal integer number
x	unsigned hexadecimal integer number
X	unsigned hexadecimal integer number with uppercase ABCDEF
u	unsigned decimal integer number
c	single character
s	character string terminated with a '$0'
p	*implementation dependent representation*
%	percent sign

```
line n      LDD   #STRING
line n+1    LDX   PRINTF
line n+2    JSR   0,X
  :     :     :     :
```

In the prior code, the EQU directive on line 1 specifies the vector address of the utility routine, the ORG directive on line 2 designates the start address of the program, and the FCC directive on line 3 defines the string to be printed. The instructions on lines n and n+1 perform the required preparation before the utility routine is called in line n+2. Note that we padded a return ASCII character ($0D), a linefeed character ($0A), and a NULL ASCII character ($00) at the end of the string on line 2. The return character and the linefeed character force the cursor on a control terminal to appear on the next line; the NULL character is required to inform the utility routine that it has reached the end of the character string. Make sure that you load the starting address of the string into accumulator D, not the first character of the string. Note that the # sign on line n performs the desired task.

Now suppose that we want to display a string with a formatted values. For our illustration, suppose we want to display a set of numerical values on a control terminal as shown next.

```
Computation Result: item <1> 235F
Computation Result: item <2> 12E9
Computation Result: item <3> D02A
:
Computation Result: item <9> ABCF
Computation Result: item <10> 4CB2
```

To display the list, we need to use a loop that displays the result list: $235F, $12E9, $D02A, . . . $ABCF, $4CB2. You will have an opportunity to print a list of items on a control terminal in laboratory exercise B at the end of the chapter. For now, we show how to display one of the result lines. Before writing a code that performs the display, some brief planning is necessary. Notice that the item numbers are decimal numbers, whereas the results are hexadecimal numbers. Therefore, we need the following formatted string.

Computation Result: item <%u> %X

Note that the %u format was chosen to display an unsigned decimal number while the %X is selected for hexadecimal numbers using the uppercase ABCDEF characters. Let us take a closer look at the following code for displaying the first desired line.

```
line 1      PRINTF    EQU     $FE06
line 2                ORG     $4000
line 3      STRING    FCC     'Computation Result: <%u>
                              %X',$0D,$0A,$00
  :           :         :       :
line n                LDD     #$235F
line n+1              PSHD
line n+2              CLRA
line n+3              LDAB    #$01
line n+4              PSHD
line n+5              LDD     #STRING
line n+6              LDX     PRINTF
line n+7              JSR     0,X
  :           :         :       :
```

The prior code displays the first result line. The EQU directive on line 1 designates the vector address of the *printf* utility routine, the ORG directive on line 2 specifies the locations where the formatted string resides in memory, and the FCC directive on line 3 defines the formatted string. Unlike the first *printf* utility example, we need to pass two parameter values to the routine using the stack. Be extra careful on the order shown. We first load the result value $235F to the stack followed by the decimal value $01 on lines n through n+4. Note that the item number is an 8-bit number and the line n+2 CLRA command puts zero into the high byte of the 16-bit number (accumulator D) pushed onto the stack on line n+4. Imagine in your mind the status of the stack at this point. The item number lies on top of the stack. When the utility routine is called, it will take the top value as the argument for the first formatted number and use the next number as the argument for the next formatted number. The order in which you push parameter values into the stack is critical for the correct use of the utility subroutine. The purpose of the instructions on lines n+5 through n+7 is the same as in the first *printf* example.

We showed how to print a single line and used the immediate addressing mode on lines n and n+3. For printing multiple result lines, the index addressing mode should be used for line n. For example, suppose the result list is stored starting at memory location $7000. We can load the starting address of result list into index register X and use the *LDD 2,X+* instruction in place of line n. Recall that numerical value 2 is an offset that is added to the contents of index register X to postincrement the register contents, pointing to the next result. For the item number, you can designate a counter. The contents of the counter should be loaded to accumulator B on line n+3, updating the counter's value for each iteration.

3.6 PROGRAMMING MODULES

In this section, we take a step backward and look at programming in general from a software designer's point of view, considering all program components as one of the three following fundamental programming constructs shown in Figure 3.9. The figure depicts the three constructs using flowchart block diagrams.

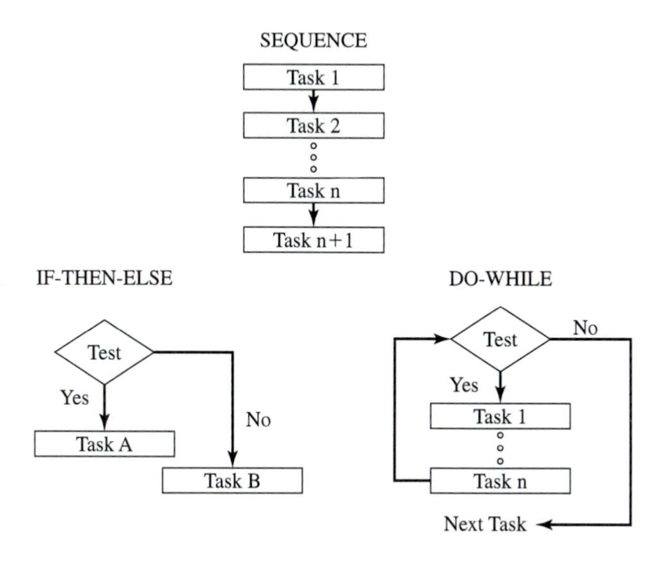

Figure 3.9 Flowcharts of program constructs SEQUENCE, IF-THEN-ELSE, and DO-WHILE.

- SEQUENCE—This construct performs one task after another in a sequence.
- IF-THEN-ELSE—This construct makes a decision out of two choices. For multiple decisions, one iterates the use of this construct.
- DO-WHILE—This construct is for a process that repeats until a condition is satisfied to stop the process.

Amazingly, we can describe functions of any program using only the three programming constructs. The SEQUENCE programming construct is a group of instructions that need to be performed one after another in the order shown in a program. The IF-THEN-ELSE programming construct is used to test a condition before making a decision to perform one of two program segments. This programming construct is used to execute one set of code over another based on a specific condition. The DO-WHILE construct is used to repeat a segment of code over and over until a condition is satisfied.

We stop to mention the value of drawing flowcharts as an important part of developing programs. To this end, we give a simple procedure you can use to create healthy programming habits. At first, following the procedure will seem to you as an overkill and it may seem to take longer to complete a program, but the same procedure has been used time after time by good programmers to complete complex programs quickly. Furthermore, developing these techniques with simple programs now will help you tackle tougher programming assignments later with confidence.

- Procedure 1: Given a program problem statement, write all subtasks necessary to complete the task.
- Procedure 2: Using subtasks as the basic components of the overall task, draw an overall flowchart for the program task.
- Procedure 3: For each subtask module, draw a subflowchart to complete each subtask.
- Procedure 4: Write a program segment for a subtask, proceeding to the next one only after you have thoroughly tested the functionality of the subtask program segment.
- Procedure 5: Integrate subtask program segments one at a time, testing the functions as you proceed until all program segments are integrated and the overall program task is completed.

This step-by-step procedure is commonly referred to as Top–Down Design, Bottom–Up Implementation. We highly encourage you to follow the five steps shown earlier every time you write a program.

3.6.1 Programming Techniques

First, we want to expose you to a proper program layout. That is, you can write an excellent program that is hard to understand by others (or even yourself at some later date), or you can write an excellent program that is easy to understand. All excellent programs have the following features in common: The program is well organized and contains useful comments. Let us consider the format shown in the following program segment as an example of a well-organized program.

```
Line 1    ;;;;;;;;;;;;;;;;;;;;;;;;;;;;;;;;;;;;;;;;;;;;;;;;;;;;;;;
Line 2    ;
Line 3    ; Program Name: EXAMPLE
Line 4    ; Program Description: This program performs ...
Line 5    ; . . . . . . . . . . . . . . . . . . . . . . . . . . ...
Line 6    ;
Line 7    ; Date: 05-23-2000
Line 8    ; Modified: 06-02-2000
Line 9    ; Author: John Smith
Line 10   ;
Line 11   ;;;;;;;;;;;;;;;;;;;;;;;;;;;;;;;;;;;;;;;;;;;;;;;;;;;;;;;
Line 12   ; DATA SECTION
Line 13             ORG      $4000
Line 14   NUM       RMB      $03
Line 15   ARRAY     RMB      $10
Line 16   NAME      FCC      'Wright'
   :                 :
Line X    ; MAIN PROGRAM SECTION
Line X1             ORG      $5000
Line X2             LDS      #$8000
   :                 :

Line Xn              :
Line Y1   ;;;;;;;;;;;;;;;;;;;;;;;;;;;;;;;;;;;;;;;;;;;;;;;;;;;;;;;;;;;;;;;;
Line Y2   ;
Line Y3   ; Subroutine Name:
Line Y4   ; Description: This subroutine is used. . . ...
Line Y5   ; . . . . . . . . ...
Line Y6   ; Date: 05-24-2000
Line Y7   ; Author: Andrew Jones
Line Y8   ;
Line Y9   ; Input Parameters: acc A, acc B, index X
```

```
Line Y10  ; Output Parameters: acc D, index Y
Line Y11  ;
Line Y12  ;;;;;;;;;;;;;;;;;;;;;;;;;;;;;;;;;;;;;;;;;;;;;;;;;;;;;;;;;;;;;;;;;;;;;;;;;;;;;;
   :                   :
```

Note first that the program is organized into blocks. The first block contains line 1 through Xn, and the second block contains the rest of the program segment shown. For each block, we must organize the subcomponents: header, data section, and program section. Each block represents a functional unit that corresponds to a subtask of the program. A natural candidate for a block is a main program and a subroutine as shown in the present example.

The first block of the present example is the main program. Lines 1 through 11 contain header information for the entire program where one writes the program name, program description, creation date, and author information. The program description should be as complete as possible so that when another programmer sees the program heading, he or she would completely understand, albeit at a high level, the function and purpose of the program. You may also want to refer to any key references used in the program in the header. For example, the source for a specific formula used within your program may be included.

Line 12 starts a data section of the program. You want to separate the data section from the program section. When the system requirements change, the separate data section assists a programmer to update the changes quickly without having to go through the entire program. Of course comments for data elements are appropriate to aid readability.

We illustrate the importance of separating data and instructions with the help of another example. The example program multiplies two 8-bit values and stores the 16-bit result to a memory location. We consider three different cases to address the importance of having a separate data section. First, a bad case.

```
BAD
Line 1                    ORG      $C100
Line 2                    LDAA     #$24
Line 3                    LDAB     #$05
Line 4                    MUL
Line 5                    BRA      Continue
Line 6    RESULT          RMB      $02
Line 7    Continue        STD      RESULT
Line 8                    SWI
```

The program simply loads two numbers into accumulators A and B, multiplies them, and stores the result to a memory location. The instruction on line 5 forces the instruction on line 7 to be executed, skipping two bytes of memory that are allocated for storing results. As you can see, we wrote this program mixing data and instructions in the same region of the memory. A better program segment with the same functionality follows.

```
BETTER
Line 1                  ORG      $4200
Line 2    RESULT        RMB      $02
Line 3                  ORG      $4100
Line 4                  LDAA     #$24
Line 5                  LDAB     #$05
Line 6                  MUL
Line 7                  STD      RESULT
Line 8                  SWI
```

In this example program, note that the space for data was allocated at memory address $C200 away from instructions, which reside at memory locations starting at address $C100. We can make the program even better by using assembly directives as shown next.

```
BEST
Line 1                   ORG      $4000
Line 2     NUM1          EQU      $24
Line 3     NUM2          EQU      $05
Line 4     RESULT        RMB      $02
Line 5                   ORG      $4100
Line 6                   LDAA     #NUM1
Line 7                   LDAB     #NUM2
Line 8                   MUL
Line 9                   STD      RESULT
Line 10                  SWI
```

Do you see the differences in the three example programs? The bad program mixes up data with instructions. The second example program is better in that it has a separate data section to store the multiplication result. The difference between the BETTER and BEST programs is the use of the EQU directives to declare the two numbers. In the examples shown earlier, the benefit of using the EQU directive may not be apparent. Yet consider a program that uses the two numbers over and over again throughout the program. Suppose further that you wrote the program similar to the BETTER program. Now consider the work you have to do if you found that the application of the program has changed such that two different numerical values (other than $24 and $05) must be used instead. Compare the work you have to perform if you wrote the program using the EQU directive as in the BEST program. If your program used the directive, simply change the two numbers in the data section. If you did not, go through your entire program and change instructions that use the two new numbers.

We studied the importance of the header and the data section of a block. The third component of a block is the program section. Going back to our original example, line X starts the main body of the program. In general, you want to make your main program as simple as possible, transferring actual work to subroutines. Your main program should only work as a centralized control center where the overall program flow is specified.

Line Y1 starts a new block for a subroutine. Again each block must have a header, data section, and program section. Each subroutine, as we learned, is an independent code that can be used by multiple programs. Thus, it should carry its own title, description, date, and author info, as was the case for the main program. Notice we also added information on the input and output parameters affected by the subroutine on lines Y9 and Y10. Such information is useful to other programmers who might consider incorporating the particular subroutine in their programs.

The objective of our discussion was to address the importance of organizing the program contents properly. You can write an organized program that is easy to understand or a cryptic one that nobody wants to use. The first step toward writing good programs is to organize your program into blocks and organize each block into separate sections. As you continue to write assembly language programs, you can discern good programs from bad ones easily by detecting desirable attributes: A good program is easy to understand and modify because the program is well organized.

3.7 APPLICATIONS

In this section, we present a complete example program incorporating major concepts discussed in this chapter. Namely, we write a program that can be used to navigate a mobile robot through a maze. Recall the components of the mobile robot. Figure 3.10 shows a photo of the robot roaming around a maze. Two round platforms are used to make the robot frame. The circular shape minimizes collisions with the environment while maximizing surface area for electronic components for control. The robot has two DC motors—one on each side of the robot attached to wheels for movement. Three infrared sensor modules are mounted on the platform for gathering navigational information for the robot. Each sensor module consists of a transmitter and receiver that are connected to the 68HC812A4EVB. The sensors are connected to the analog-to-digital (ATD) converter port, which is dis-

Figure 3.10 A photo of the mobile robot navigating through a maze.

cussed in the analog-to-digital chapter (Chapter 9). Periodically, each sensor value, reflecting the distance between a sensor and the maze wall, is sent to the microcontroller through the ATD converter port. The sensor information is then used to make proper navigational decisions for the robot. For example, when the left sensor indicates an obstacle approaching, the robot should turn away from the obstacle to its right. If the right sensor receives a signal indicating an obstacle, of course the robot should turn to its left. If the center sensor receives a signal for an obstacle, the robot should consider both the right and left sensor values and decide to turn toward a direction with a smaller sensor value. Since we did not cover the subject of the 68HC12 ATD converter nor how to control a DC motor, we simplify the example by assuming that signals from the sensors are periodically stored at specified memory locations, and we assume that we control DC motors by storing values to designated memory locations. As discussed before, the first step is to specify requirements for a program which we do next.

Requirements: We assume memory locations $0000, $0001, and $0002 hold unsigned 8-bit numbers indicating infrared sensor values from the robot's left, center, and right sensors, respectively. A high value indicates a wall in front of the sensor, whereas a low value shows a clear path in the direction of the sensor. Let us also assume memory locations $000A and $000B have been reserved for controlling two DC motors. For now, we assume that we can write only two different values to these locations. In later chapters, you see that we continually change output values to DC motors to control their speed. Presently, we assume that an $FF represents the signal for reverse motor motion, and a $7F is used for the forward motor signal. Location $000A corresponds to the right robot motor, whereas address $000B represents the location for the left robot motor; the right and left are from the robot's point of view, not from an observer's point of view.

As mentioned earlier, the program should periodically check sensor values and write appropriate DC motor control values to memory locations corresponding to DC motors. Namely, if a sensor value greater than $E0 is detected on the left sensor, the robot should turn right (send a forward signal to the left motor and a reverse signal to the right motor; the robot makes a tank turn to its right). If the right sensor detects a value greater than $E0, the robot should turn left: Send a forward signal to the right motor and a reverse signal to the left motor. If the center sensor value is greater than $E0, turn toward a direction whose sensor value is the smaller of the two side sensors. We assume the corridor width is greater than a minimum value, causing both the left and right sensors to have values greater than $E0 at the same time. We further assume that the robot will check the center, left, and right sensors in that order.

Now that we have written the problem requirements, we should draw a flowchart before writing the program. To use the ideas from this chapter, we use a subroutine, called MOTOR, for controlling DC motors. Figure 3.11 shows the simple flow charts for the current program. The main program module, shown on the top of the figure, first initializes all necessary parameters before entering into an infinite loop. The first step inside the loop is to check three sensor values and call subroutine MOTOR with a direction information. The subroutine executes its function by storing correct data to designated memory locations and returns the

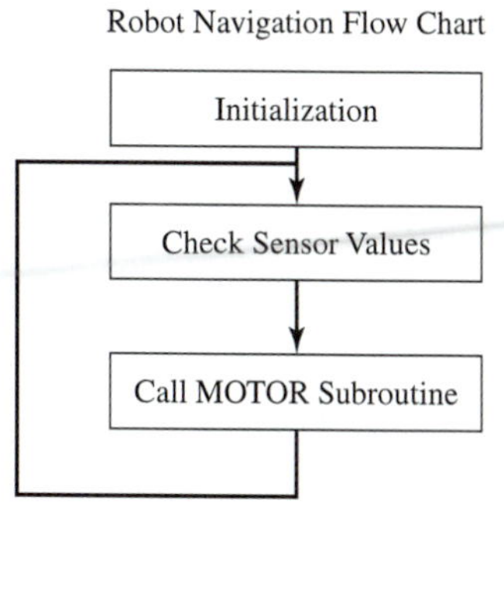

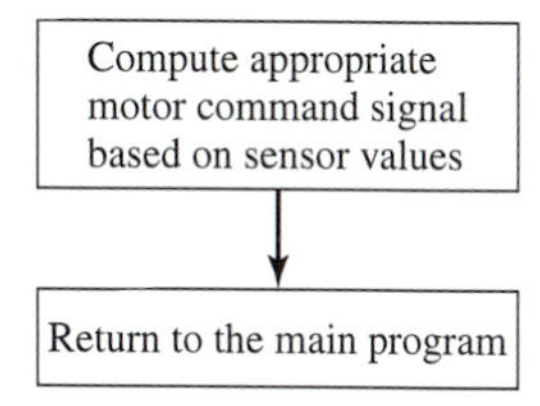

Figure 3.11 Flowcharts for the robot navigation.

control to the main program module that repeats the process all over again. Now that our plan is made and the flowcharts drawn, we are ready to write the actual code.

```
Line 1   ;;;;;;;;;;;;;;;;;;;;;;;;;;;;;;;;;;;;;;;;;;;;;;;;;;;;;;;;;;;;;;;;;;;;;;;;
Line 2   ;
Line 3   ; Program Title: Chapter 3 Application Program
Line 4   ; Description: This program simulates control of a mobile robot by
Line 5   ;              reading in sensor values from memory locations $0000
Line 6   ;              $0001, and $0002 and writing control signal values to
Line 7   ;              memory locations $000A and $000B. We assume the values
Line 8   ;              on memory locations $0000 through $0002 are changed
Line 9   ;              periodically. The program also assumes that values
Line 10  ;              in memory locations $000A and $000B correspond to the
Line 11  ;              right and the left motors of a robot.
Line 12  ;
Line 13  ; Authors: Daniel Pack and Steve Barrett
Line 14  ; Date: 07-29-2000
Line 15  ;
Line 16  ;;;;;;;;;;;;;;;;;;;;;;;;;;;;;;;;;;;;;;;;;;;;;;;;;;;;;;;;;;;;;;;;;;;;;;;;
```

```
Line 17   ; Data Section
Line 18   INITS     EQU    $8000
Line 19   THD       EQU    $E0
Line 20   TR        EQU    $00     ; turn right command
Line 21   TL        EQU    $01     ; turn left command
Line 22   MS        EQU    $02     ; move straight
Line 23   FD        EQU    $7F     ; turn forward
Line 24   BD        EQU    $FF     ; turn backward
Line 25             ORG    $0000
Line 26   LeftS     RMB    $01     ; left sensor value location
Line 27   CentS     RMB    $01     ; center sensor value location
Line 28   RightS    RMB    $01     ; right sensor value location
Line 29             ORG    $000A
Line 30   RIGHT     RMB    $01     ; right motor signal location
Line 31   LEFT      RMB    $01     ; left motor signal location
Line 32   ; Main Program
Line 33             ORG    $4000
Line 34             LDS    #INITS  ; initialize stack
Line 35             LDAA   #MS     ; move straight
Line 36             JSR    MOTOR   ; call by value
Line 37   LOOP      LDAA   CentS   ; load center sensor value for test
Line 38             CMPA   #THD    ; if the center value is lower than
Line 39             BLO    LSEN    ; a threshold value, check next sensor
Line 40             LDAA   LeftS   ; compare LeftS and RightS values
Line 41             LDAB   RightS
Line 42             CBA
Line 43             BLO    TURNL   ; if A > B turn right
Line 44             LDAA   #TR     ; otherwise turn left
Line 45             BRA    CALLS   ; branch to call subroutine
Line 46   TURNL     LDAA   #TL
Line 47   CALLS     BSR    MOTOR   ; calling subroutine (call-by-value)
Line 48   LSEN      LDAA   LeftS   ; check the left sensor value
Line 49             CMPA   #THD
Line 50             BLO    RSEN    ; if value < threshold move on
Line 51             LDAA   #TR     ; otherwise turn right
Line 52             BSR    MOTOR
Line 53   RSEN      LDAA   RightS  ; check the right sensor
Line 54             CMPA   #THD    ; check the value
Line 55             BLO    AGAIN
Line 56             LDAA   #TL     ; turn left
Line 57             BSR    MOTOR
Line 58   AGAIN     BRA    LOOP
Line 59   ;;;;;;;;;;;;;;;;;;;;;;;;;;;;;;;;;;;;;;;;;;;;;;;;;;;;;;;;;;;;;;;;;;;
Line 60   ;
```

```
Line 61   ; Subroutine Title: MOTOR
Line 62   ; Description: This subroutine takes a value stored in accumulator
Line 63   ;              A and sends proper motor control signals:
Line 64   ;              forward, turn left, or turn right.
Line 65   ; Authors: Daniel Pack and Steve Barrett
Line 66   ; Date: 07-29-2000
Line 67   ;
Line 68   ;;;;;;;;;;;;;;;;;;;;;;;;;;;;;;;;;;;;;;;;;;;;;;;;;;;;;;;;;;;;;;;
Line 69   MOTOR    CMPA    #TR       ; turn right?
Line 70            BNE     TLEFT
Line 71            LDAA    #BD       ; right wheel backward
Line 72            STAA    $000A
Line 73            LDAB    #FD       ; left wheel forward
Line 74            STAB    $000B
Line 75            BRA     FIN
Line 76   TLEFT    CMPA    #TL       ; turn left ?
Line 77            BNE     MOVES     ; move straight
Line 78            LDAA    #FD       ; right wheel forward
Line 79            STAA    $000A
Line 80            LDAB    #BD       ; left wheel backward
Line 81            STAB    $000B
Line 82            BRA     FIN
Line 83   MOVES    LDAA    #FD       ; move straight
Line 84            STAA    $000A     ; both wheels forward
Line 85            LDAB    #FD
Line 86            STAB    $000B
Line 87   FIN      RTS
```

Note that we did not strictly follow our discussion of making this subroutine independent since the subroutine is only used for this particular robot navigational program. Lines 1 through 16 are the header information for the main program where a reader can find the title of the program, its description, author information, and date of creation. Lines 17 through 31 contain the data section. The EQU directive on line 18 specifies the initial stack pointer value, the EQU directive on line 19 sets the threshold value for the infrared sensor output. The directives on lines 20, 21, and 22 initialize the navigational command direction values for the mobile robot, whereas the directives on lines 23 and 24 assign actual numerical values to move each wheel to turn forward or backward. The directives on lines 26 through 31 allocate spaces for sensor values and motor commands.

On line 33, directive ORG designates the start location of the main program. The instruction on line 34 initializes the stack pointer. The instructions on lines 35 and 36 are used to initially move the robot forward. On line 35, the value representing the straight move motion is loaded in accumulator A before calling the subroutine. Note that the main program is passing the necessary robot motion information to the subroutine MOTOR using the accumulator. As we learned in this chapter, this type of parameter passing technique is called the call-by-value method. Lines 37 through 57 contain instructions that repeat indefinitely. On line 37, the center sensor value is loaded to accumulator A whose value is compared to a threshold value to determine the existence of an obstacle in front of the robot. If no obstacle is detected, move on to check on the next sensor, the left sensor. The instructions on lines 40 through 47 determine appropriate navigational action for the robot when the robot is facing an obstacle in its front. The instructions on lines 40, 41, and 42 load values from the left and right sensors and compare them to identify direction to which the robot must turn. If the left sensor value is greater than the right sensor value, a signal to turn right is used to call subroutine MOTOR. Otherwise, the instructions on lines 44 and 45 are used to set up accumulator A value to turn left when subroutine MOTOR is called. Lines 48 through 52 contain instructions that check the left sensor for an obstacle, set up accumulator A with proper value, and make the robot turn right if necessary. Similarly, instructions on lines 53 through 56 are dedicated for the action based on the right sensor value: checking the sensor value, setting up appropriate value to accumulator A, and calling subroutine Motor if an obstacle exists in front of the sensor.

Note that lines 59 through 68 are the header information for subroutine MOTOR. The instruction on line 69 checks to see whether the command from the main program module is to have the robot to turn to its right. If accumulator A value indicates that is the case, lines 71 through 74 are used to store correct values to memory locations $000A and $000B. The instruction on line 75 forces the next instruction to be executed, which is the one on line 87, where the RTS instruction returns the control back to the main program. Lines 76 through 82 contain instructions to have the robot to turn right. The instructions on lines 83 through 86 command the robot to move forward. The last line of the subroutine is the RTS command, which must appear at the end of every subroutine.

3.8 LABORATORY APPLICATIONS

LABORATORY EXERCISE A

Purpose This lab provides opportunities to exercise your programming skills using subroutines. As we learned in this chapter, subroutines are useful when you use the same lines of code over and over again. There are two different ways to call subroutines: call-by-value and call-by-reference. In this lab, you write a program with two different subroutines. The main program calls the first subroutine using the call-by-value scheme and the second subroutine using the call-by-reference method. The finished program can (with some modifications) be used in the final lab to control a set of two DC motors.

Documentation 68HC812A4EVB User's Manual

Prelab Prepare a flowchart or pseudocode for your main program and two subroutines.

Description The call-by-value parameter passing technique uses the CPU registers (A, B, X, and Y) to pass parameter values between a main program module and corresponding subroutines. When a main program needs to preserve data before relinquishing the program control to a subroutine, one can either store the values on the stack or in memory locations.

Yet a main program calling a subroutine using the call-by-reference parameter passing technique provides the subroutine with the address (reference) of the memory location (or a starting memory address in the case of a block of data) where the needed parameter value resides. The difference between the two techniques is that the call-by-value technique should be used where subroutines manipulate **copies** of parameter values, whereas the call-by-reference technique is suitable when we want subroutines to work with the **original** parameter values. Also note the number of parameters a program can send to a subroutine is limited by the number of CPU registers for the call-by-value method. In cases where a large block of data needs to be manipulated, the call-by-reference method should be used.

Your assignment for this lab is to write a program to simulate control of two DC motors. To simulate motor control,[5] we assume that storing a two-byte value into the memory locations $xxxx and $xxxx + 1 affects the speed of the left motor of a robot. Similarly, storing a two-byte number into the memory locations $yyyy and $yyyy + 1 controls the speed of the right motor of a robot. Note that the lower memory address byte contains the most significant byte of the motor speed—that is, the most significant bit (MSB) of the 16-bit number is the MSB in the lower memory location. For example, if the desired speed of a motor is $B389, we store the hexadecimal value as shown in Figure 3.12.

Having described how to send a single signal that corresponds to a single-speed signal to the motor, we must now decide how to control the motor speed. One of the most popular ways to control DC motor speed (rotational velocity) is the use of a trapezoidal speed profile. If the speed of a motor follows a trapezoidal profile, the resulting motion of the robot (distance vs. time) can be represented as a smooth trajectory. A sample trapezoidal profile is shown in Figure 3.13.

[5] After learning the 68HC12 parallel I/O ports, we control the actual motors in a later lab.

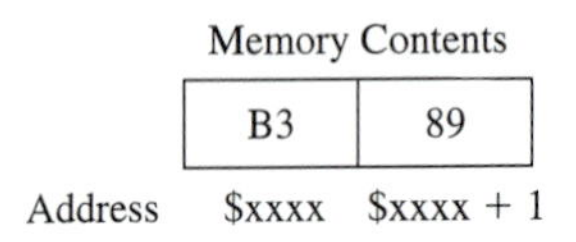

Figure 3.12 An example of specifying motor speed

Your program should control the speed of each motor by following a trapezoidal profile. The main program should call on a subroutine and provide the constant velocity, Vconstant (a 16-bit unsigned hexadecimal number) and the total time, t_{total} (again, a 16-bit hexadecimal unsigned number). The values for these variables should be read from memory locations $080A–$080B (Vconstant) and $080C–$080D (t_{total}). Assume that both motors will be controlled using the same velocity profile. The **call-by-value** technique should be used by the first subroutine that computes the acceleration time interval, P_A, the constant velocity interval, P_C, and the deceleration period, P_D (i.e., solve for t_a and t_c in Figure 3.13). We want the acceleration and deceleration periods to be 20% each of the total time, t_{total}. The subroutine should then store the three 16-bit values t_a, t_c, and t_{total} into memory locations starting at $0800. The subroutine should also compute the delta velocity necessary to accelerate and decelerate linearly as shown in the figure, given that we want 10 chances to adjust the velocity values during each of the three intervals. The delta velocity should be stored in memory locations $0806 and $0807.

The main program should then call on a second subroutine and pass along the delta velocity using the **call-by-reference** technique. Since we have decided to use 10 subintervals for each of the acceleration, deceleration, and constant velocity periods, starting from zero velocity, we can compute 30 different velocity values stretching from time zero to time t_{total}: the first 10 accelerating velocity values, the second 10 constant velocity values, and the last 10 decelerating velocity values. For now, ignore the time values that correspond to instances where the motor speed (velocity) can be changed. In the actual motor control system, the program will be constantly writing velocity values to locations $xxxx$, $xxxx+1$, $yyyy$, and $yyyy+1$. The second subroutine should then carry out the following tasks:

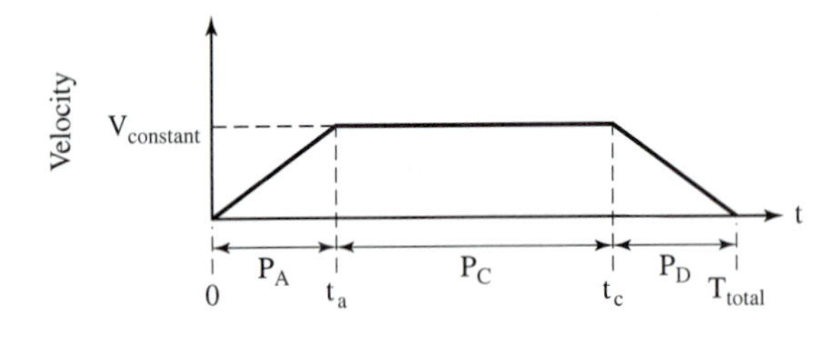

Figure 3.13 A sample trapezoidal velocity profile over time

- Compute and store appropriate velocity values (a set of 30 values) for the right motor starting at memory location $4000 and store the corresponding velocity values (again a set of 30 values) for the left motor starting at memory location $4100. Note that your program should reside at locations with addresses greater than $411E (use $4200) to avoid an overlap with data.
- Once you are finished with the program, download test files ch3Atest1.s19 and ch3Btest2.s19 from the labtest directory on the enclosed diskette to your 68HC12EVB and run your program. Check your answers generated by your program with results manually computed. By studying the corresponding .asm files in the same directory, you can generate a set of correct answers.

LABORATORY EXERCISE B

Purpose In this lab, D-Bug12 subroutines are used to help you to interface the 68HC12EVB with I/O devices using your PC monitor and keyboard. This lab incorporates the built-in 68HC12 D-Bug12 subroutines with your program written in Laboratory Exercise A in this chapter. The lab provides a review on how to use subroutines and teaches how to display the memory and register contents of the controller to a computer screen. This lab is useful for all subsequent laboratory exercises since you can use the D-Bug12 subroutines you learned from this lab to display the status of your program on your computer screen.

Documentation 68HC12A4EVB User's Manual

Prelab Prepare a flowchart and/or pseudocode to complete the lab.

Description Modify your program from Laboratory Exercise A in this chapter such that:

(a) The program asks for a user to insert a constant velocity and a total time using a keyboard. For both the velocity and the total time, your program should ask a user to select one of the following choices: HIGH (1), MEDIUM (2), or LOW (3). In your main program, define the terms HIGH, MEDIUM, and LOW as

HIGH :	$2710	(10k decimal)
MEDIUM:	$03E8	(1k decimal)
LOW:	$0064	(100 decimal)

Use the same numbers for both total time and constant velocity.

(b) Create a third subroutine that displays one of the two velocity profiles (the right or left motor velocity file) on your computer screen using the D-Bug12 subroutines. Your main program from Laboratory Exercise A should call the third subroutine, and the *starting address* for one of the profiles should be passed from your main program to the third subroutine using the **call-by-reference** technique. Finally, print the results of your program on the PC screen. The output of your program on the screen should have the following format. The velocity profile is for the right motor (data in $4000–$403B), and the other values are the results of your program stored in memory locations $0800–$0807. The statements in *italic* represent the output of the program, and the bold numbers are the input of a user.

MOTOR CONTROL SOFTWARE

PLEASE CHOOSE A CONSTANT VELOCITY:
HIGH (1), MEDIUM (2), OR LOW (3)
2
PLEASE CHOOSE A TOTAL TIME PERIOD:
HIGH (1), MEDIUM (2), OR LOW (3)
2

	VELOCITY PROFILE
VELOCITY 1:	*0*
VELOCITY 2:	*64*
VELOCITY 3:	*C8*
...	
...	
VELOCITY 30:	*0*
TA:	*C8*
TC:	*320*
TTOTAL:	*3E8*
DELTAV:	*64*

Use D-Bug12 monitor utility subroutines to send output to your computer screen. Refer to the D-Bug12 utility subroutine section in the chapter to learn how to use the necessary utility subroutines. Suggestion: Use the *printf* and *getchar* utility subroutines.

3.9 SUMMARY

This chapter expands our programming skills of the 68HC12 by illustrating the assembly process, use of the loop construct, stack, and subroutines. We explained the central role the stack plays in program execution and showed how to store and access data to and from the stack. To send and receive parameter values between the main program and subroutines, we explained two different methods: call-by-value and call-by-reference. Both methods use either CPU registers or memory locations to pass parameter values. When multiple parameter values are passed to a subroutine, the call-by-reference method should be preferred over the call-by-value method. To facilitate the interactive nature of our programs, the D-Bug12 utility subroutines are also studied in this chapter. We found that three programming constructs describe the structure of any program. We also illustrated the value of a well-organized program that leads to good programming skills. We emphasized that a good program is easily understood and modified. Finally, we presented a mobile robot application and two laboratory exercises that incorporate the fundamental knowledge of the stack and subroutines.

3.10 FURTHER READING

Gordon Doughman, "Using and Extending D-Bug12 Routines," Motorola Semiconductor Application Note, AN1280/D, 1996.

Gordon Doughman, "Using the Callable Rooutines in D-Bug12," Motorola Semiconductor Application Note, AN1280a/D, 1997.

3.11 CHAPTER PROBLEMS

Fundamental

1. Explain the function of an assembler.
2. What are the files generated by a Motorola 68HC12 assembler?
3. List three programming constructs used to write any program.
4. What advantages do we have for drawing a flowchart before writing a program?
5. Why do the authors insist on initializing the stack pointer with $8000 for the 68HC812A4EVB board?
6. If a subroutine comment says "Destroys A, B, and Y," what instructions must be used before and after the subroutine is executed to preserve the initial values of the accumulators and register?

Advanced

1. What are the differences among a high level language program, an assembly language program, and a machine language program?

2. What criteria should one use to select one of the two parameter passing methods when sending or receiving parameter values from a subroutine?

3. Write a program using a subroutine to copy a table from one location to another. A partially completed program is given next. Write a program by filling in locations where only comments appear.

```
* Copying a table using a subroutine
  Data Section
        ORG     $0000
TAB1    FDB     $D100       ; address of the first table
TAB2    FDB     $D300       ; address of the second table
TABL    FCB     $FF         ; table length
* main program
        ORG     $C100
        LDS     #$8000      ; initialize the stack pointer
                            ; load the table length to acc A
                            ; load table 1 address to X
                            ; load table 2 address to Y
        JSR     COPYT       ; call the subroutine
        SWI                 ; stop subroutine
        ORG     $4500
COPYT                       ; save the CPU registers onto the stack
AGAIN   TSTA                ; check the counter value
        BEQ     DONE        ; if zero jump to the end
        LDAB    1,X+        ; note the use of accumulator B
        STAB    1,Y+
                            ; adjust the counter and target addresses
                            ; continue the loop
DONE                        ; restore the CPU registers
        RTS                 ; IMPORTANT!!!!!!!!
        END
```

4. Suppose you started with the following register contents.

P-C007 Y-7892 X-FF00 A-44 B-70 SP-C04A

What address is in the stack pointer and exactly what is in the stack after the following instruction sequence is executed?

```
PSHA
PSHB
PSHY
```

Challenging

1. Write a subroutine to copy data one byte at a time from memory location $5000 to memory location $6000 until a byte with $FF is detected.
2. For the following assembly language program, hand assemble the program to gain machine language code using the hexadecimal number representation.

```
        ORG     $C200
        LDAB    #COUNT
        LDAA    #NUM1
MORE    ADDA    #NUM1
        STAA    RESULT
        DECB
        BNE     MORE
        SWI
COUNT   EQU     $04
NUM1    EQU     $10
RESULT  RMB     $01
        END
```

3. Is the asterisk legal at the beginning of a program line?
4. Can a semicolon appear in the middle of a program line?
5. Can we use an asterisk in the middle of a program line?
6. If we replace the EQU directives with the FCB directives in the program of Problem 2 (and still have the program perform the same way), what must be changed in the assembly language program? Why might we want to do such a thing?
7. At what address is the RESULT stored for the program in problem 2?
8. Write an instruction sequence to load the contents of the element in the top of the stack onto accumulator A and the third element from the top of the stack onto accumulator B.

4

Fuzzy Logic

Objectives: After reading this chapter, you should be able to:

- Explain the fuzzification, rule application, and defuzzification processes of a fuzzy logic controller,
- Illustrate and use the MEM, REV, WAV, and EDIV instructions of the 68HC12,
- Construct trapezoidal fuzzy membership functions,
- Design and implement a fuzzy logic controller using the 68HC12, and
- Explain the advantages and disadvantages of fuzzy logic controllers compared with classical controllers.

One of the unique features of the 68HC12 compared to other microcontrollers is the built-in instructions to implement fuzzy logic controllers. In this chapter, we present concepts associated with a fuzzy logic control system and how to construct a fuzzy logic-based controller using the 68HC12 instructions. We first discuss the key properties of typical controllers and illustrate how a traditional controller is different from a fuzzy logic controller in Section 4.1. We then explain in detail the components found in a fuzzy logic-based controller in Section 4.2 using a balancing robot example. To illustrate the example, we introduce concepts related to the subject area of robotics where fuzzy logic controllers are used in a variety of applications. In Section 4.3, the 68HC12 instructions for implementing a fuzzy logic-based controller are presented, followed by an application section (Section 4.4), where we take advantage of the fuzzy logic controller to incorporate two infrared (IR) sensor values to generate control commands for mobile robot navigation. Section 4.5 discusses issues involved in designing input membership functions, output membership functions, and fuzzy rules. In Section 4.6, we present a fuzzy logic controller laboratory exercise, where you have an opportunity to implement a fuzzy logic controller for a mobile robot. Finally, in Section 4.7, we summarize the chapter topics, and the chapter problems in Section 4.8 conclude the chapter.

4.1 CONVENTIONAL CONTROLLER VERSUS FUZZY LOGIC CONTROLLER

In a typical day, we encounter numerous control systems around us. When we first get up in the morning and turn on the shower, we adjust knobs to make the water temperature just right, controlling the water temperature system. When you blow dry your hair, you adjust a switch on your blow dryer machine to generate air flow with an appropriate temperature. You turn on the radio to listen to the traffic and weather information while you eat your breakfast. You do so by selecting a channel of your choice using a knob, a switch, or a remote control, controlling the radio. After the meal, you hop in your car to go to work. You move the steering wheel and push the gas and brake pedals to control the movement of your car. The list goes on and on. Any system, whose outputs are controlled by some inputs to the system, is called a *control system*. You can even consider an entire company as a control system; people and resources are inputs, and products of the company are the outputs.

As you can see, understanding how to control systems is an important area of our society. A special branch of engineering, called control systems, is dedicated to examining and improving how we control systems. Of course, there are systems that are controllable, systems whose outputs can match desired outputs, and systems that are not controllable. Our discussion only deals with controllable systems. Do not feel we are limiting ourselves with this constraint. After all, all man-made systems are controllable to an extent.

To fully understand a system's behavior, researchers rely on mathematical models of the system. For example, if a system always produces an output signal that is twice as large as the input to the system, we can simply model the physical system with the following equation: output $= 2\times$ input. Similarly, scientists and

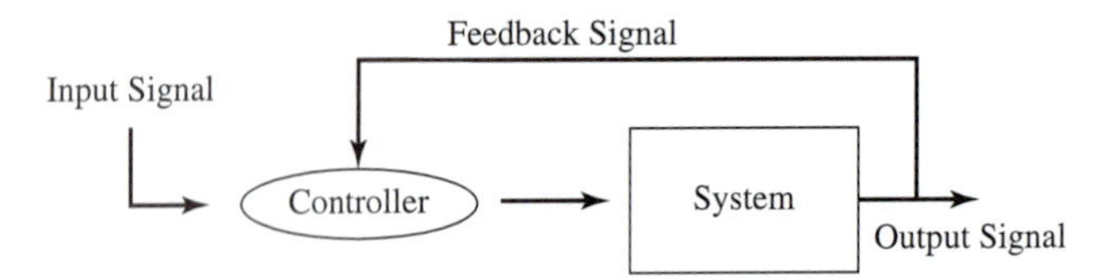

Figure 4.1 A typical control system.

engineers create mathematical models of systems using linear and nonlinear operators to represent behaviors of systems. Once an accurate mathematical model of a system is constructed, we can generate inputs for the model for desired outputs, and we can expect that the same inputs provided to the physical system will generate outputs close to the outputs of the model. The inputs to a control system are usually based on a forcing term[1] and the current state of the system. The information on the current state is usually available through sensors for the control input signal generation. Figure 4.1 shows a block diagram of a typical control system.

A controller contains a mathematical model of a system of interest and uses the model along with the feedback provided by the output of the system to generate a new input to the system. For example, suppose you are driving your car and notice that your car is veering to the left. The actual car movement is the output. You sense the movement (mostly using your visual sensors) and turn your steering wheel (input to the system) based on a model that tells you the appropriate amount of right turn using your steering wheel to correct the direction of your car. We do not know the exact form of the model we have in our brains for driving cars, but we are pretty certain that we do not use complex mathematical models to generate a precise amount to turn steering wheels. This is where fuzzy logic proponents claim that fuzzy systems are much closer to the human control process than conventional systems using precise mathematical models. Let us briefly touch on the history of the fuzzy logic controllers before we start our study of the subject.

Over the past three decades, the control systems society witnessed a new growing field within its community. Before the 1970s, almost all control systems used mathematical models to devise control algorithms. Then came neural networks, fuzzy logic systems, and evolutionary systems. These systems share a common ground: They all advocate for control systems that do not rely on mathematical system descriptions. Advocates of the new systems point to biological systems and argue how complex systems do not use mathematical models to arrive at control decisions. In some cases, the proponents of these systems denounce the conventional approach to describe complex systems mathematically on the bases of practicality

[1] A forcing term is a signal that drives the current state of a system to a desired state.

and accuracy. In return, the traditional camp treats the new approaches with skepticism and criticizes them for lack of mathematical rigor. We are not here to take sides in the debate, but we believe the new approaches have a great deal to offer to the control community. After all, fuzzy logic controllers have been implemented to control public high-speed trains, experimental flying machines, commercial cameras, and home appliances throughout the world. In this chapter, we show how a fuzzy logic controller uses intuitive rules to develop control laws as compared to a mathematical model in a traditional control scheme.

To motivate us for this new subject, we consider a case study: a fuzzy logic controller for a mass-moving balancing robot similar to the one discussed in Chapter 2 (see Figure 4.2). The construction of the fuzzy controller is based on intuitive rules rather than mathematical equations of a conventional system. Such controller

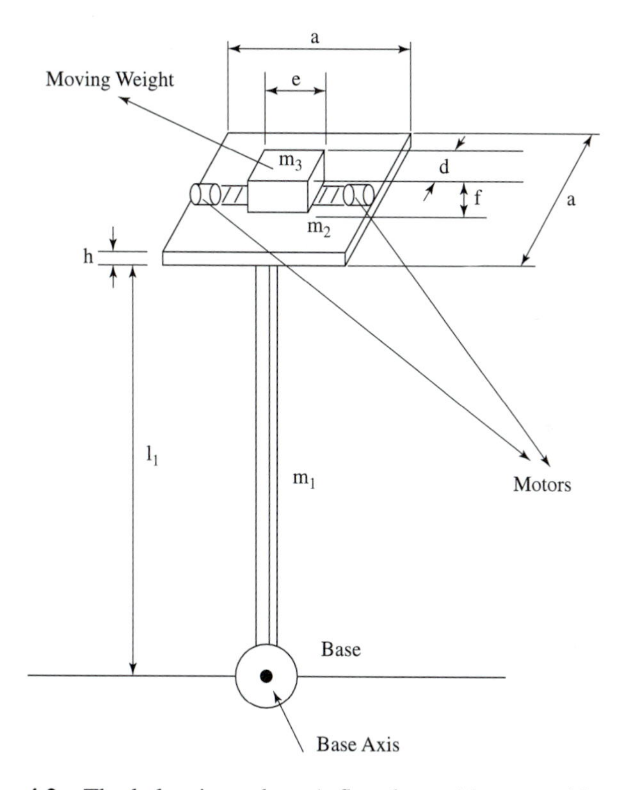

Figure 4.2 The balancing robot: A flat plate with a movable mass is attached to the leg. The leg can freely rotate with respect to the base. The goal of the robot is to remain upright position by moving mass (m_3) using the pair of motors. Symbols a, d, e, f, h, and l_1 represent dimensions of the robot while symbols m_1, m_2, and m_3 denote masses of the leg, the plate plus two motors, and the movable block, respectively.

schemes provide advantages over classical control methods based on mathematical models in the actual process of controller construction. This is especially true if the system we wish to control can only be represented by a set of complex dynamics equations. Motions of complex systems involve second-order differential equations, which introduce a high computational burden to a controller if they are used to generate control system inputs. However, the fuzzy controller allows one to rely on physical rules rather than mathematical equations.

4.2 FUZZY LOGIC CONTROLLER FOR A BALANCING ROBOT

In this section, we take you through each step required to construct a fuzzy logic controller using a case example. The particular example is chosen since it allows us to conveniently illustrate the various issues one must consider while developing a fuzzy controller. The robot controller is suitable as our example since the controller has a limited number of input and output variables, allowing us to study the controller components without getting lost with a large number of operations involved. The example was also chosen to reflect the popular use of fuzzy controllers in the field of robotics. As a necessity, to discuss the example, we must present subjects in robotics and control systems with which you may not be familiar. When the materials become too technical, try to grasp the main points of the particular discussion and move on. Your goal of reading this chapter should not be the comprehension of the technical details associated with the mathematics involved in control systems, but the knowledge to construct fuzzy logic controllers, which offer us an alternative approach to create equivalent and sometimes better controllers.

4.2.1 Background

Consider our example as a simple walking robot trying to maintain its balance or maintain its postural stability while standing straight up. The postural stability of locomotive systems is one of the important issues in the field of walking robotics. The importance is clear since the postural stability is the fundamental basis from which to launch other challenging tasks of locomotive systems. As you can imagine, the more joints and limbs a robot has, the more difficult it is to model the robot's dynamic motions. For our illustration, we study a system that demonstrates the capabilities of a fuzzy logic controller while reducing the complexity of the dynamic equations that we must describe for classical controllers.

Figure 4.2 shows the robot of our interest. The leg, whose mass and length are denoted as m_1 and l_1 in the figure, is attached to the base where it is free to rotate around the base axis perpendicularly (rotate on the page plane), as shown in the figure. The center of a flat square plate is fixed to the top of the leg, with a movable mass (m3) on a rail and two motors fastened on the plate. The dimensions of the movable block and the flat plate are specified by symbols a, d, e, f, and h. The mass of the plate is denoted as m_2. The two motors are used to translate mass m3 back and forth along the rail. The forces generated by these two motors are the only means of control in the system.[2] The goal of a controller for the experiment is to provide the right amount of forces to mass m3 such that the robot will stay balanced in the midst of disturbances or when the initial robot position deviates from the vertical line.

4.2.2 Optional: Dynamic Model for the Robot[3]

The first step for deriving a classical controller is to develop an accurate mathematical model of a system. The process is well established, and we adopt the process to construct the model for the robot. The following dynamic equations for the balancing robot are computed using the *Euler–Lagrange* equation and the corresponding kinematics relations between coordinate frames (Figure 4.3). Actual derivation is done with the help of the symbolic software *Mathematica*.

$$\mathbf{D}\begin{bmatrix} \ddot{\theta}_1 \\ \ddot{d}_2 \end{bmatrix} + \mathbf{C}(\theta_1, d_2, \dot{\theta}_1, \dot{d}_2) + \mathbf{G}(\theta_1, d_2) = \mathbf{F} \tag{4.1}$$

The positive definite (simply means that the matrix determinant is positive and the matrix is invertible) inertia matrix **D** is defined as follows:

$$\mathbf{D} = \begin{bmatrix} d_{11} & -m_3(a_1 + a_2) \\ -m_3(a_1 + a_2) & m_3 \end{bmatrix},$$

where

$$\begin{aligned} d_{11} = {} & m_1\left(\frac{3}{4}l_1^2 - 2l_1 p - hp\right) \\ & + m_2\left(\frac{1}{12}a^2 + l_1^2 + l_1 h + \frac{h^2}{4} - 2l_1 p - hp\right) \\ & + m_3\left(\frac{h^2}{4} + \frac{f^2}{4} + \frac{hf}{2} + d_2^2\right. \\ & \left. + \frac{1}{12}f^2 + \frac{1}{12}e^2 + 2hl_1 + \frac{3h^2}{4} + fl_1 + fh + l_1^2\right). \end{aligned}$$

[2]We could use a single motor to accomplish the task, but the two motors are chosen simply for the purpose of balancing the robot using a movable weight—similar to what we do physically to balance our bodies while standing.

[3]For those who are just interested in learning how to construct fuzzy logic controllers using the 68HC12, you can safely skip this section and move on to Section 4.2.3.

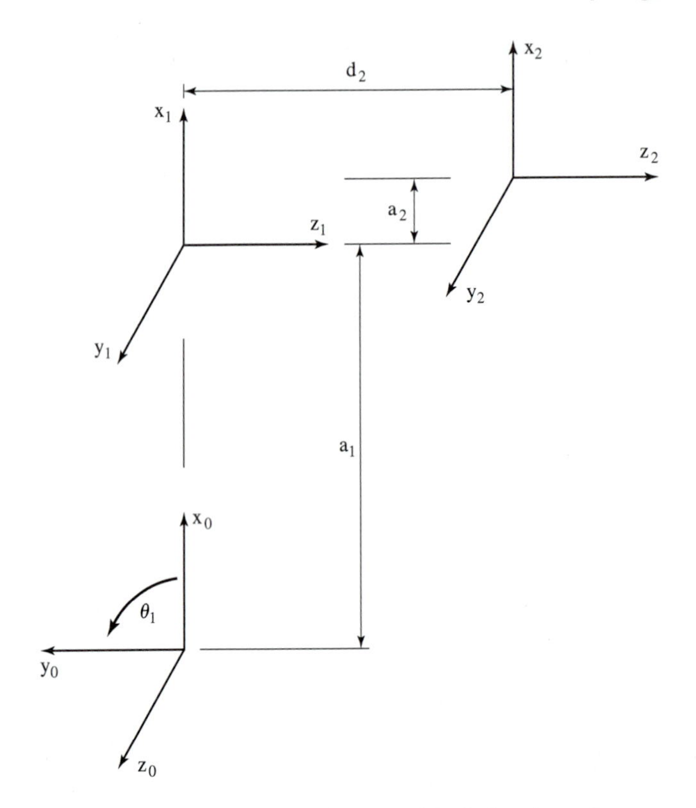

Figure 4.3 Coordinate frames of the balancing robot.

It is useful to see the role of each term for our understanding. The various parameter variables are defined later and shown in Figure 4.2. Variables θ_1 and d_2 are the angle of the leg from the vertical position and the distance of the moving mass from its center position, respectively. The matrix **C**, which contains the Coriolis and Centrifugal terms, can be represented as shown:

$$\mathbf{C}(\theta, \dot{\theta}) = \begin{bmatrix} \dot{\mathbf{s}}^T \mathbf{C}_1 \dot{\mathbf{s}} \\ \dot{\mathbf{s}}^T \mathbf{C}_2 \dot{\mathbf{s}} \end{bmatrix},$$

where the vector **s** is a two element vector with the following components:

$$\mathbf{s} = \begin{bmatrix} \theta_1 \\ d_2 \end{bmatrix}$$

and

$$\mathbf{C}_1 = \begin{bmatrix} 0 & m_3 d_2 \\ m_3 d_2 & 0 \end{bmatrix} \quad \mathbf{C}_2 = \begin{bmatrix} -m_3 d_2 & 0 \\ 0 & 0 \end{bmatrix}.$$

Variable θ_1 represents the revolute joint angle around the base axis, whereas variable d_2 depicts the displacement of mass 3 along the rail. The Coriolis force results from the coupled velocities, $\dot{\theta}_1$ and $\dot{d}_2$, and the Centrifugal force is generated by square terms of individual velocities, $\dot{\theta}_1$ and $\dot{d}_2$. Do you remember these from your dynamics course in college? For example, the element $(1, 1)$ of the $\mathbf{C_2}$ matrix indicates that velocity $\dot{\theta}_1$ generates a Centrifugal force $-m_3 d_2 \dot{\theta}_1^2$, which is exerted on mass 3. Similarly, the $(1, 2)$ element of the matrix $\mathbf{C_1}$ represents a Coriolis term, which along with the coupled velocities $\dot{\theta}_1$ and $\dot{d}_2$ generates a force $m_3 d_2 \dot{\theta}_1 \dot{d}_2$ that is exerted on the leg.

The vector **G** represents the gravitational force:

$$\mathbf{G}(\theta) = \begin{bmatrix} (m_1 + m_2) g \sin\theta_1 (p - l_1 - \frac{h}{2}) + m_3 g (d_2 \cos\theta_1 - l_1 \sin\theta_1 - h \sin\theta_1 - \frac{f}{2} \sin\theta_1) \\ m_3 g \sin\theta_1 \end{bmatrix},$$

and the vector **F** depicts the external force applied to the corresponding generalized coordinate variables. This term affects the dynamic behavior of the robot that we are interested in finding. That is, symbol **f** represents the force generated by the two motors to move mass 3:

$$\mathbf{F} = \begin{bmatrix} 0 \\ \mathbf{f} \end{bmatrix}.$$

The advantage of modeling a robot motion with the Euler–Lagrange method is that the method allows one to write the motion of each coordinate frame (see Figure 4.3) in terms of the acceleration, velocity, and position variables. Remember the mathematical rigor of the classical control approach? Here it is! The coordinate frames are attached to the different parts of the robot using a standard method proposed by Denavit–Hartenberg (DH).

Figure 4.3 shows the coordinate frames of the robot using the DH parameters. The notation allows one to describe a coordinate transformation from one frame to another using four distinct parameters shown in the following table.

	1	2
d	0	d_2
a	$l_1 + \frac{h}{2}$	$\frac{h}{2} + \frac{f}{2}$
α	90^0	0^0
θ	θ_1	0^0

Variables d and a denote distance values between two adjacent coordinate frames, whereas variables α and θ specify angle changes between the same two adjacent coordinate frames. Three coordinate frames describe the system as shown in Figure 4.3: Frame 0 is attached at the base where the leg rotates, frame 1 corresponds to the center of the top plate, and frame 2 is attached to the center of moving block on top of the plate.

Note that Eq. (4.1) is a set of second-order nonlinear coupled differential equations. We can make our lives a bit easier by assigning $x_1 = \theta$, $x_2 = d_2$, $x_3 = \dot{\theta}$, and $x_4 = \dot{d}_2$. We can rewrite Eq. (4.1) into a set of first-order differential equations. This procedure of reducing high-order differential equations to a first-order differential equations is a standard method to solve a set of differential equations. The resulting state equations are

$$\begin{aligned}
\dot{x}_1(t) &= x_3(t) \\
\dot{x}_2(t) &= x_4(t) \\
\dot{x}_3(t) &= \overline{D}_{11}(t) * S_1(t) + \overline{D}_{12}(t) * S_2(t) \\
\dot{x}_4(t) &= \overline{D}_{21}(t) * S_1(t) + \overline{D}_{22}(t) * S_2(t),
\end{aligned} \tag{4.2}$$

where

$$\begin{aligned}
S_1(t) = {} & -2 * m_3(t) * x_2(t) * x_3(t) * x_4(t) - (m_1 + m_2) g \sin x_1(t) \left(p - l_1 - \tfrac{h}{2}\right) \\
& - m_3 g \left(x_2(t) \cos x_1(t) - l_1 \sin x_1(t) - h \sin x_1(t) - \tfrac{f}{2} \sin x_1(t)\right) \\
& - B_{x_1}(x_3(t)) S_2(t) = m_3 * x_2(t) * x_3^2(t) - m_3 g \sin x_1(t) + f - B_{x_2}(x_4(t))
\end{aligned}$$

and $\overline{D}_{ij}$ denotes the ij-th element of the inverse matrix for the inertial matrix D. B_{x_1} and B_{x_2} are the dynamic friction coefficients, where dynamic friction forces are functions of the corresponding joint variable velocities. Symbol p represents the distance between the center of the flat plate to the center of mass 3. Other symbols were defined in Figure 4.2.

This type of analysis is necessary to model the dynamic motion of the robot accurately for the purpose of computing optimal signals to control the system. Now that was just the description of the system. Figure 4.4 shows a diagram of a typical classical controller controlling the system. The figure shows the importance of the mathematical model of system dynamics in constructing control signals. To compute the final control signals using classical control methods for the balancing robot, we now have to go through another mathematically rigorous process, which we do not do since we can see the strain on your facial expression already. Instead, let us start our study of designing a fuzzy logic controller for the same robot. As you can see, this method does not require a mathematical knowledge of the system dynamics to derive control laws, but only the intuitive understanding of the system behavior.

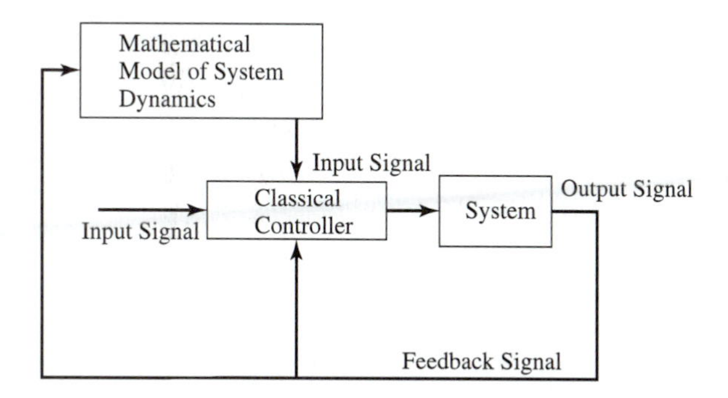

Figure 4.4 A typical classical controller controlling a system.

4.2.3 Fuzzy Logic Controller

The motivation to use a fuzzy logic-based controller comes from the fact that fuzzy logic reasoning is a simple form of an expert system, where the system makes decisions by inferring available data and rules. This simply means that we use an alternative method to generate system control signals and do not use the mathematical expressions of the dynamic robot motions shown in the previous subsection. In place of the mathematical system model, we do need an expert who can develop rules that describe how the system will react to a given input. An expert system is a system that contains all the rules that map input commands to output system responses. A fuzzy logic controller is a simple form of an expert system since the fuzzy logic controller goes through the typical process of an expert system (Match, Select, and Execute) only once to generate a final output.

A fuzzy logic-based controller is also an evidence accumulating system, which uses a certain kind of confidence factor to assign an output of the system according to the confidence measure computed by the following process: fuzzification of the input data, application of rules to a set of fuzzified data, and defuzzification of the output data to generate a crisp numerical output number. The aforementioned single cycle through the expert system modules, instead of multiple cycles used by a typical expert system to compute an end result, is desirable for a real-time robot application such as the one we are currently considering.

First, let us consider the type of data that are available. We can measure the current angular position of the robot and how fast the robot is falling in one of the two possible directions. So a controller with the rules generated by an expert, that is you, can use the angular position and the corresponding angular velocity of the leg as the inputs to your controller. The output of the controller should be the amount of force applied to mass 3. Thus, the controller's task is to use the available input values, which should be sufficient to describe the current status of a system, find appropriate relationships between input state values and output control values, and represent the output control values in suitable forms for the system control. Those processes are called *fuzzification*, *rule applications*, and *defuzzification*, respectively.

The input values (angular position and angular velocity) are first fuzzified by assigning an appropriate value (degree of membership) to each fuzzy membership function: The membership functions are sometimes referred to as *labels* or *terms*. For the remaining discussion, terms, labels, and membership functions are used interchangeably. A fuzzy membership function is defined as an instance of a linguistic variable describing the fuzzy controller input. For example, when we observe the robot falling to its right, we can describe it by saying that the current position of the robot is to its right, halfway between upright and the ground. We can also say that the velocity is medium. The terms such as *right*, *halfway*, and *medium* are fuzzy membership functions. We want to describe the current input data in terms of such membership functions. Why? If we do so, we can now generate intuitive rules that map input fuzzy membership functions with output fuzzy membership functions. For example, if we observe the robot is falling to its right and falling fast, a logical action of the controller is to move the moving weight on the top plate to the robot's left. We can implement this type of rules covering all possible scenarios in a fuzzy logic controller. All fuzzy membership functions have one of the following shapes: a left trap, a trapezoid, a right trap (Figure 4.5).[4] Notice that all three shapes in the figure are special forms of a trapezoid. The 68HC12 implements all of its input membership functions using trapezoids. For our current example, there are seven membership functions for the angular position input and seven membership functions for the angular velocity input, as shown. In this example, we chose triangles as the membership functions and selected a set of three points for the angular position input fuzzy membership functions:

- Negative Large (NL): (−10.0°, −8.0°, −6.0°) (LT)
- Negative Medium (NM): (−7.5°, −5.0°, −2.5°) (TR)

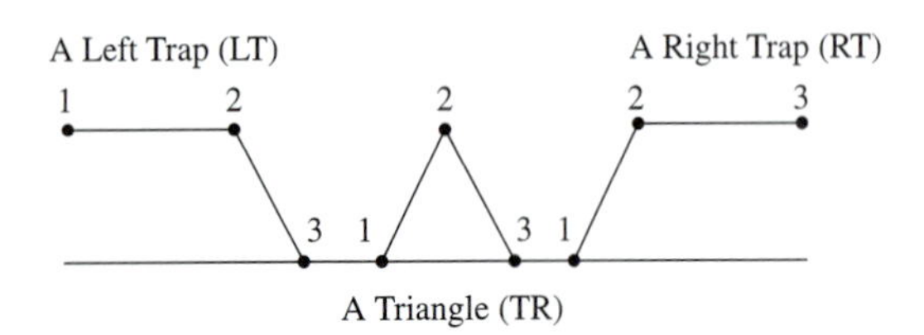

Figure 4.5 Typical fuzzy membership functions.

[4]The membership functions do not have to have the forms in Figure 4.5; a membership function can have any form you think is correct, but it has been shown that trapezoidal shapes are most convenient and effective shapes.

- Negative Small (NS): (−4.0°, −2.0°, 0.0°) (TR)
- Zero (ZR): (−2.0°, 0.0°, 2.0°) (TR)
- Positive Small (PS): (0.0°, 2.0°, 4.0°) (TR)
- Positive Medium (PM): (2.5°, 5.0°, 7.5°) (TR)
- Positive Large (PL): (6.0°, 8.0°, 10.0°) (RT)

Similarly, we chose the corresponding points of the input fuzzy membership functions for the angular velocity (degrees/sec) as shown next.

- Negative Large (NL): ($-60.0°/s$, $-40.0°/s$, $-25.0°/s$) (LT)
- Negative Medium (NM): ($-30.0°/s$, $-20.0°/s$, $-10.0°/s$) (TR)
- Negative Small (NS): ($-14.0°/s$, $-7.0°/s$, $0.0°/s$) (TR)
- Zero (ZR): ($-5.0°/s$, $0.0°/s$, $5.0°/s$) (TR)
- Positive Small (PS): ($0.0°/s$, $7.0°/s$, $14.0°/s$) (TR)
- Positive Medium (PM): ($10.0°/s$, $20.0°/s$, $30.0°/s$) (TR)
- Positive Large (PL): ($25.0°/s$, $40.0°/s$, $60.0°/s$) (RT)

Since the input data are in the form of numerical values, given an input data, the controller must first assign a degree of membership, a value ranging from zero to one, to each fuzzy membership function described above. Figure 4.6 illustrates an example. In this example, the angle between the robot leg and the vertical line is 3° to the right. Thus, we can say that the input belongs to the Positive Small and the Positive Medium position membership functions. Furthermore, we say that the input position is a member of the Positive Small function with 0.5 membership

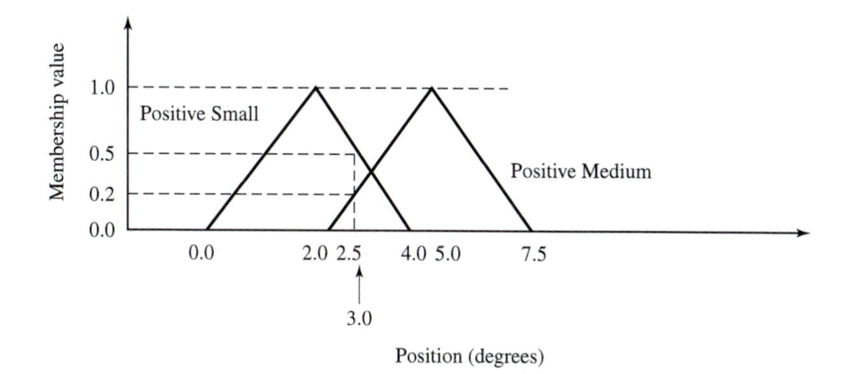

Figure 4.6 An example: mapping numerical values to input membership functions.

TABLE 4.1 FUZZY RULES FOR THE BALANCING ROBOT

vel/pos	NL	NM	NS	ZR	PS	PM	PL
NL	NL	NL	NL	NL	NM	NL	NM
NM	NL	NL	NM	NM	NM	NM	NS
NS	NL	NL	NM	NS	NS	NS	ZR
ZR	NM	NM	NS	ZR	PS	PM	PM
PS	ZR	PS	PS	PS	PM	PL	PL
PM	PS	PM	PM	PM	PM	PL	PL
PL	PM	PL	PM	PL	PL	PL	PL

value, whereas the same input is a member of the Positive Medium function with 0.2 membership value.

We are now ready to apply expert rules to the input membership functions. Table 4.1 displays the 49 rules for the robot. As you see in Table 4.1, we have rules that cover all possible combinations of the input variables: angular position and angular velocity. The first column of the table describes the fuzzy membership functions for the velocity variable, whereas the first row represents the fuzzy membership functions for the angular position variable. The contents of the table are output fuzzy membership functions. For example, the rule table dictates that if the robot's current position is zero (ZR) and the angular velocity is negative medium (NM), then the action is to move the weight to right medium (NM, note the direction definitions). Using our intuition, we can come up with all 49 rules shown in the table.

The 49 rules map all the possible pairs of position and velocity membership functions to output force fuzzy membership functions: The 49 rules completely describe all possible inputs and their corresponding, desired control outputs of the balancing robot controller. In this process of applying rules, the minimum degree of membership among the position membership function and the velocity membership function is assigned to the output force membership function as the confidence factor. The minimum of the two is chosen since it guarantees that both antecedents are true. Theoretically, the AND operator is equivalent to finding the intersection between two fuzzy sets (two antecedents), which is found by computing the minimum of the two membership values. Consider another example. Assume the negative small position membership function has 0.3 degree of membership value while the negative medium velocity membership function has 0.45 degree of membership value. Also assume that there is a rule that says: *If the position is Negative Small and the velocity is Negative Medium, Then the force is Negative Medium.* If we apply this rule, the output negative medium force membership function will attain the degree of membership 0.3, the minimum of the two input fuzzy membership values. This implies that the controller is to believe the lesser of the two—or, in other words, the controller can believe the input information with the confidence factor equaling the minimum degree of membership value among the two input fuzzy input functions. This is known as the minimum rule, which is implemented using a special command in the 68HC12. We now give descriptions for the output membership functions in more detail.

Suppose we choose a set of three points for the output fuzzy membership functions as follows.

- Negative Large (NL): (−5.0 kg-m/s^2, −4.0 kg-m/s^2, −2.0 kg-m/s^2) (LT)
- Negative Medium (NM): (−2.5 kg-m/s^2, −1.5 kg-m/s^2, −0.5 kg-m/s^2) (TR)
- Negative Small (NS): (−1.0 kg-m/s^2, −0.5 kg-m/s^2, 0.0 kg-m/s^2) (TR)
- Zero (ZR): (−0.5 kg-m/s^2, 0.0 kg-m/s^2, 0.5 kg-m/s^2) (TR)
- Positive Small (PS): (0.0 kg-m/s^2, 0.5 kg-m/s^2, 1.0 kg-m/s^2) (TR)
- Positive Medium (PM): (0.5 kg-m/s^2, 1.5 kg-m/s^2, 2.5 kg-m/s^2) (TR)
- Positive Large (PL): (2.0 kg-m/s^2, 4.0 kg-m/s^2, 5.0 kg-m/s^2) (RT)

There can be multiple confidence factors (degrees of membership) for each output fuzzified membership function since more than one rule can assign confidence factors to an output force fuzzy membership function. The controller now takes the **maximum** of those confidence factors as the degree of the membership for the particular fuzzy function. The rationale behind taking the maximum confidence value is to rely on the most dominant rule to assign the output membership value. Theoretically, when multiple rules assign confidence values for an output membership function, it is equivalent to taking the union of output fuzzy membership functions, which corresponds to taking the maximum membership value. Again, for example, if there are three different rules that assign 0.4, 0.5, and 0.7 confidence factors to the Negative Medium force fuzzy membership function, the controller assigns 0.7 as the degree of membership for the Negative Medium force fuzzy function. We say that the process is using the maximum rule, which is also implemented in the 68HC12.

We have performed two tasks: took numerical input values and converted them to fuzzy input membership functions with appropriate membership values using the minimum membership values, mapped input membership functions to output membership functions using the intuitive rules, using the maximum output membership values. The last remaining step is to convert the output membership function values to a form suitable to control the robot. The control value again has to be a numerical one. Thus, we need to do the reverse of the fuzzification process—*defuzzification*.

Among the many methods of defuzzification, the most common one is finding the center of gravity or the centroid of output membership functions. The method combines all the regions of the output fuzzy functions together with an OR operator and computes the center point, thus generating a crisp numerical value. The reason for finding the centroid is to combine contributions made by all output membership functions by giving equal weights to each output membership function. The complete process of the controller is depicted in Figure 4.7.

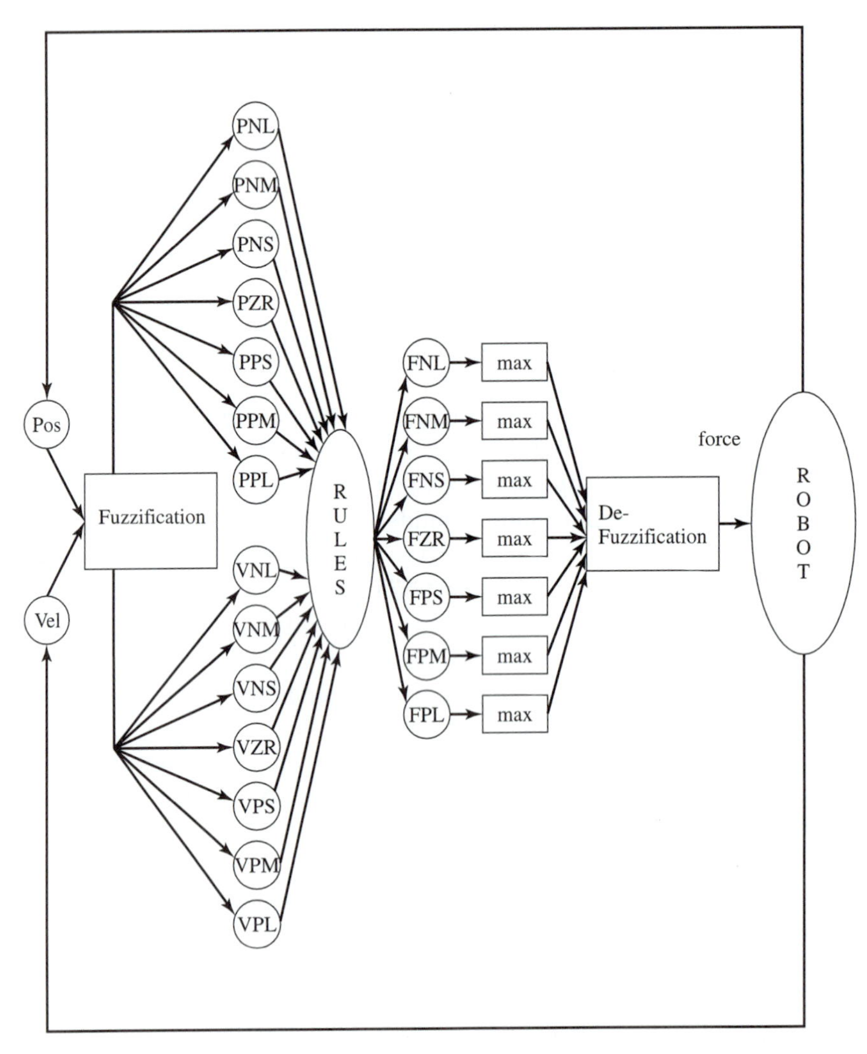

Figure 4.7 The fuzzy logic-based controller for the balancing robot.

4.3 THE 68HC12 FUZZY LOGIC OPERATIONS

In this section, we describe the 68HC12 instructions that enable us to design and implement fuzzy logic controllers. Four 68HC12 instructions are specifically created for fuzzy controllers: MEM, REV, REVW, and WAV. In addition to the four instructions, which are discussed shortly, the 68HC12's instruction set contains others that facilitate the effective implementation and operation of fuzzy logic controllers. These supplementary instructions are ETBL, TBL, EDIV, EDIVS, EMACS, EMAX, EMAXM, EMIND, EMINM, EMUL, and EMULS. We explain the function of these fuzzy logic related instructions also in this section.

Before we dive into the use of each fuzzy logic instruction, let us consider the process of building a fuzzy logic controller using another example: a temperature controller. The first step is to come up with linguistic variables describing the input to the controller. The natural input to the temperature controller is the current temperature of a room. One example of terms for the input variable describing the temperature is *Very Cold*. Other terms that describe the input variable are *Medium Cold, Slightly Cold, Warm*, and so forth. We must do this for all input variables. Each linguistic variable can be defined with a set of membership functions. The 68HC12 insists your definition follows a strict rule; a trapezoidal function is always used to define each linguistic term for an input variable. As mentioned in the previous section, we call these terms (labels) describing the input variable status as membership functions. You can easily remember it by thinking of an input value being a member of each linguistic term defined by a membership function. An input value can be a full member of a membership function (membership value one) or a nonmember (membership value of zero). An input value can also be a pseudomember with any membership value between zero and one. Reconsider the example we used in the previous section. The angle of the leg off the vertical axis is a numerical value. Suppose we define the direction of the angular position, one of the inputs to the controller, as shown in Figure 4.8.

Suppose we newly define position membership functions as shown in Figure 4.9. Also suppose the current position input is 8°. This figure shows that the current input, 8° to the right of the vertical line, is a member of the Positive Small and Positive Medium terms. We want to specify the measure of a membership by assigning a numerical value that corresponds to the input value. Thus, given an input value, we can find the membership value to a membership function by finding a corresponding location on the y-axis of the membership function. This membership value is sometimes referred to as the *confidence value* of a particular membership function for a given input. We can easily find this value by looking for a cross-point along the y-axis of the membership function graph as shown in the figure. Continuing with the example, the current angle is described as Positive Small with membership value 0.4 and Positive Medium with membership value

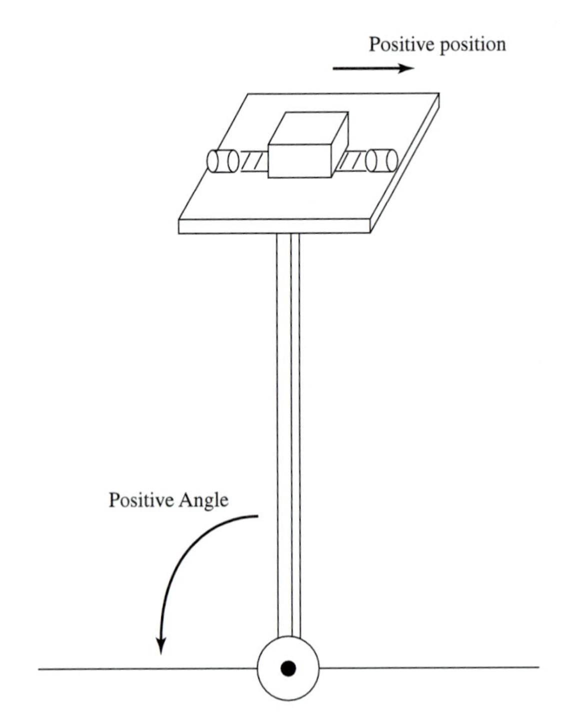

Figure 4.8 Direction specification for the two variables.

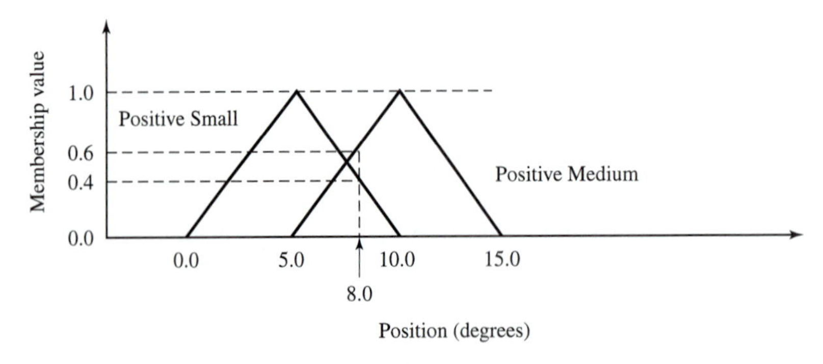

Figure 4.9 Example membership function for the angular position of the balancing robot.

0.6. We can see again why we call these linguistic terms as membership functions; given an input, the membership value is obtained based on the function depicting the linguistic term. This example shows that we need to define the membership functions for the inputs (and outputs) ahead of time before the system receives an input value. Thus, the defining membership functions fall under the category of design process. Once these membership functions are defined, we can compute the membership values for a given input quickly.

We also need to determine membership functions for the fuzzy logic controller outputs. In the example of the balancing robot, the output signal of the controller is the force applied to the mass residing on the plate attached to the leg. We had membership functions such as Negative Medium and Positive Small. We are also responsible for designing the output membership functions. The example in the previous section chose trapezoidal functions for the output variables, but the 68HC12 uses a more simple output function description using singleton functions. The singleton functions simply represent each output linguistic term with a single numerical number as shown in Figure 4.10.

We now have two more steps left to generate an output value: mapping of input membership functions to output membership functions and generation of a numerical output. The mapping is done by a set of rules. We saw such rules in our previous example, such as *If position is Left Medium AND angular velocity is Right Medium, Then apply Zero force*. In this rule, the first part before the word *Then* are two antecedents, and the rest of the sentence is a consequent. Observe that the two inputs, angular position and angular velocity, are connected by the AND operator. This operator is used to select the minimum of the two input membership values as the membership value for the output membership function. Again, it is the designer's responsibility to determine intuitive rules that satisfy the input and output membership function relationships. We discuss how one approaches the process of determining intuitive rules in Section 4.5.

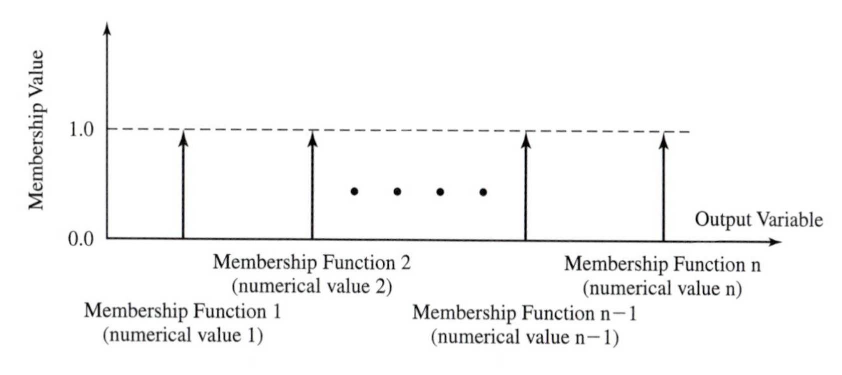

Figure 4.10 Example singleton functions.

The final step is to combine truth values of all output fuzzy membership functions into a single numerical value. This is done by averaging the output function values. This step is equivalent to finding the centroid of arbitrary output membership functions for singleton output membership functions. For example, suppose two output membership functions for the balancing robot are active: Right Medium with 0.3 membership value and Right Small with 0.4 membership value. The resulting output value is obtained by the following equation:

$$Output = \frac{\sum_{i=1}^{n} S_i F_i}{\sum_{i=1}^{n} F_i},$$

where S_i is the singleton value and F_i is the output membership value for fuzzy logic output function i.

Let us summarize the tasks we must perform to design a controller:

- design input membership functions for each input variable,
- design output membership functions for each output variable, and
- devise a set of rules that map input to output membership functions.

4.3.1 Membership Function Design Process

In this section, we show steps you must take to design membership functions; the 68HC12 requires a strict rule to follow when implementing membership functions. First, each function must be a trapezoid. Again notice that right and left traps are special forms of trapezoids. We use Figure 4.11 as we illustrate the design process. Each trapezoid has a left-most point and a right-most point along the x-axis. As can be seen from the figure, each membership function can be uniquely specified if we know the left and right slopes in addition to the two end positions. The slopes are determined by dividing the height (always decimal value 256) by a distance in the horizontal axis. To be more specific, each 68HC12 membership function is defined using four numbers: farthest left point, farthest right point, left slope, and right slope. Notice that the full membership function or degree of one membership corresponds to numerical value $FF. Thus, we have 256 discrete values to represent the degree of membership. Suppose you want to design the input membership function with the representations in Figure 4.11.

As a practice, try to come up with a set of four numbers to describe the three membership functions in the figure. You are probably scratching your head for the one on the far left and the one on the far right. These are special cases where the slope on the left and right are zeros, respectively. Thus, we can specify the three membership functions as:

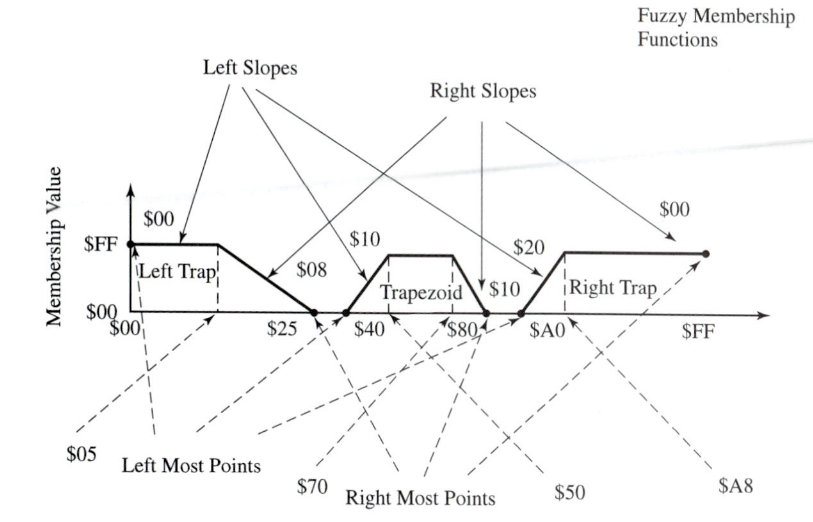

Figure 4.11 Example membership functions for the 68HC12.

Left:	$0	$25	$0	$08
Middle:	$40	$80	$10	$10
Right:	$A0	$FF	$20	$00

Note that, for the left membership function, the leftmost point is $00, the rightmost point is $25, the left slope is $00, and the right slope is $08. The right slope is computed by performing the following computation: $slope = \frac{256}{37-5}$. Recall that $25 and $5 correspond to decimal numbers 37 and 5, respectively. For actual implementation, we store the values usually on read only memory (ROM) locations since we do not change these values once we complete the design of the membership functions. During the test phase, however, say using one of the 68HC12 evaluation boards, we write these values to user random access memory (RAM) space as shown in the following example case:

```
        ORG $8000
LEFT    FCB $00, $25, $00, $08
MIDDLE  FCB $40, $80, $10, $10
RIGHT   FCB $A0, $FF, $20, $00
```

Now that we know the process involved in defining fuzzy input membership functions, let us move on to design output membership functions. Recall that the 68HC12 uses singleton functions for the fuzzy output membership functions in place of the trapezoidal functions. A singleton function simply means each mem-

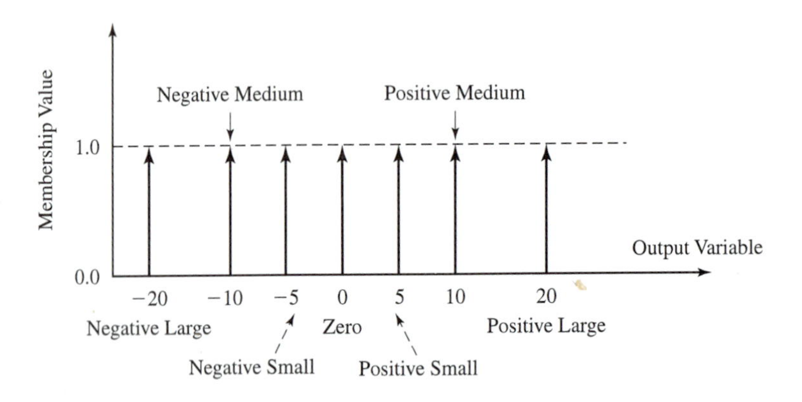

Figure 4.12 Output membership functions: An example.

bership function or label is defined by a single value. Figure 4.12 shows a set of singleton functions, with each corresponding to one of the output membership functions of a fuzzy controller. Return to the balancing robot example, the force output variable of the controller must be implemented using seven singleton functions each corresponding to a term as shown in the figure: Negative Large function is represented by −20, Negative Medium receives −10, Negative Small function corresponds to −5, Zero variable gets 0, Positive Small function is mapped to 5, Positive Medium is shown with 10, and Positive Large is represented with 20.

To implement the output membership functions in the 68HC12, we simply write the following code:

```
Output FCB −20, −10, −5, 0, 5, 10, 20
```

4.3.2 Fuzzy Rule Implementation

Now that we defined both input and output membership functions, we are ready to design fuzzy rules, describing the relationships between the input and output membership functions. In our balancing robot example, we came up with 49 different rules describing the relationships among the two input variables, angular position and angular velocity, and the one output variable—force applied to the mass. Notice that each rule had the following format: IF A AND B THEN C. There are two antecedents and one consequent. Furthermore, notice that the two antecedents are connected using the AND operator. We implement this rule in the 68HC12 using five bytes of data. The first two bytes define antecedents A and B by specifying corresponding membership values: The third byte is designated separator byte \$FE. We shortly explain why we need a separator. The fourth byte describes the consequent using the output membership label. The last byte is again separator byte $FE. For example, to implement rule "IF Angular Position is Positive Small AND Angular Velocity is Negative Small, THEN applied Force is Zero," we need to write the following code segment:

```
RULE1 FCB Positive Small, Negative Small, $FE, Zero, $FE
```

The symbols Positive Small, Negative Small, and Zero are the offset values pointing to locations where the membership values for the Positive Small input membership function for angular position, Negative Small input membership function for angular velocity, and Zero output membership function for applied force, respectively. A rule can have as many antecedents and consequents. The general format for a rule is as follows:

If A AND B AND C AND D AND ..... THEN AA OR BB OR CC .....

The only limitation is the memory space of a system. For the example of the balancing robot, we have two antecedents and one consequent per rule. We define all 49 rules in the same manner as RULE1 shown before. Once all 49 rules are encoded, the 68HC12 expects to see a special value indicating the end of rules. This special value is $FF.

As promised, now we explain the reason for the separator. As is discussed in the hardware interrupt chapter, all microcontrollers have the capability to stop its current operation to take care of an urgent or time-critical request. For example, suppose while a fuzzy logic controller is evaluating a rule, an interrupt request indicating immediate attention of the CPU is detected. The CPU needs convenient locations where it can temporarily halt the current operation and service the interrupt. The separators provide the convenient *break* points for such interrupts.

We have now completed the off-line design process and implementation for actual fuzzy logic controller operation. All input and output membership functions are defined and encoded, and rules have been stored in memory. Once we allocate memory locations to hold values for all membership functions, we can start the fuzzy inference engine. We discuss this fuzzy logic operation in the next three subsections.

4.3.3 68HC12 Fuzzification Process

The first step taken inside of a fuzzy logic controller is finding the fuzzy logic input membership values for the current input variable value in numerical forms. That is, we need to find the membership values for each input membership function for a given input value, which is called the *fuzzification process*. This process is done using the 68HC12 MEM instruction. Let us use an example to illustrate how this process works. Consider using the 68HC12 to implement a fuzzy logic controller for controlling water temperature for your shower. You have a temperature sensor

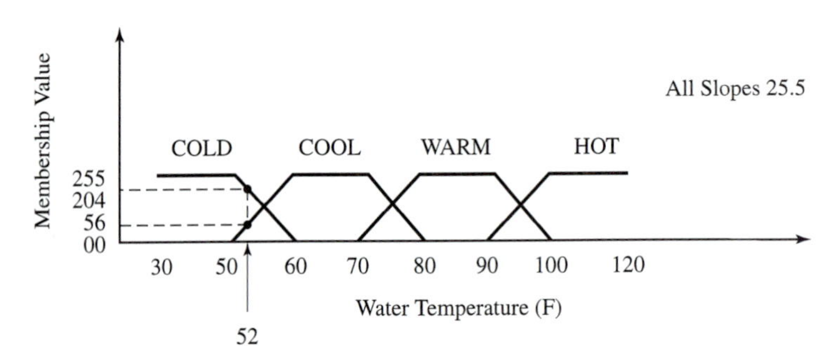

Figure 4.13 Input membership functions for water temperature control.

attached to the shower head whose output is fed to the fuzzy controller. Suppose you defined the input fuzzy membership functions as shown in Figure 4.13.

Also assume the current water temperature is 52° Fahrenheit. As can be seen from the figure, this temperature is represented by membership function Cold with membership value 204/255 and membership function Cool with membership value 56/255. To perform this process using the 68HC12, once the input membership functions are defined as shown before, we need to perform the following task. First, index register X must have the address of the first membership function definition. Second, index register Y must have the starting address for locations where fuzzy membership values will be stored. The actual input value should be stored in accumulator A. Thus, to perform the fuzzification of the example of controlling water temperature, we must write the following code segment:

```
Line 1              ORG    $8000
Line 2   COLD       FCB    !30, !60, !0, !25
Line 3   COOL       FCB    !50, !80, !25, !25
Line 4   WARM       FCB    !70, !100, !25, !25
Line 5   HOT        FCB    !100, !120, !25, !0
Line 6   ;Locations for membership values
Line 7   MCOLD      RMB    1
Line 8   MCOOL      RMB    1
Line 9   MWARM      RMB    1
Line 10  MHOT       RMB    1
Line 11             ORG    $8200
Line 12             LDX    #COLD        ;pointing to the membership
                                        function def
Line 13             LDY    #MCOLD       ;pointing to the results locations
Line 14             LDAA   WATER_TEMP   ;loading the current water
                                        temperature
```

```
Line 15              LDAB    #4        ;number of membership functions
Line 16    Loop      MEM               ;perform fuzzification for the
                                        current mem functions
Line 17              DBNE    B, Loop
```

The directives on lines 2 through 5 define the input membership functions as before. The directive on line 1 dictates the start location where the membership functions will reside. The directives on lines 7 through 10 allocate memory locations to store the membership values for each label. The ORG directive on line 11 specifies the start location of the program. We use the instructions on lines 12 through 15 to set up registers before we use the MEM instruction on line 16. The MEM instruction on line 16 performs the fuzzification process where the membership value for a particular membership function for the current input is determined. The DBNE B, Loop instruction on line 17 decrements the counter stored in accumulator B and checks the completion of the fuzzification process. If the process is not completed, then the instruction on line 16 is executed again. Notice that as a consequence of performing the MEM instruction, index register X is updated by four byte locations, whereas index register Y is updated by one byte pointing to the location to save the next degree of membership function value. Note that the initial accumulator B value corresponds to the number of membership functions for an input variable. Now we have completed the first stage of the fuzzy logic controller. The next step is to connect the input fuzzy membership functions with the output membership functions.

The connections between input and output fuzzy membership functions are performed by applying fuzzy logic rules. There are two different methods to apply a set of rules: Unweighted Rule Evaluation (REV) and Weighted Rule Evaluation (REVW). The main difference is that the Weighted Rule Evaluation allows you to force the controller to assign a variable emphasis to each rule. That is, you may assign greater importance to a rule, if you feel that the particular rule should be valued more than other rules. To accommodate the differences between the two approaches, similar formats but different structures are used for the rule definition and evaluation.

4.3.4 Unweighted Rule Evaluation (REV) and Weighted Rule Evaluation (REVW)

The 68HC12 has a special instruction to perform the unweighted rule evaluation giving each rule an equal weight, called **REV**, acronym for Rule EValuation. This instruction uses CPU registers to process a list of rules, assigning truth values to fuzzy output membership functions based on the truth values of fuzzy input membership functions for a controller. To make our discussion more concrete, we explain the process of evaluation of rules using the example of controlling the water temperature. Recall that the input to your controller is a numerical value of the current water temperature, and the output of the controller is the amount of change of a water temperature control knob. We have already defined the input fuzzy membership functions in the previous section, so let us construct a set of membership functions for the output. For convenience, let us use an 8-bit number representation to specify a particular temperature control knob position. In particular, we assign $00 to denote control for the minimum water temperature while $FF represents the maximum water temperature. For our discussion, we also limit the number of output functions to three, although in real implementation a greater number of input and output fuzzy membership functions yields a superior overall performance. The three output membership functions are defined as shown in Figure 4.14.

These singleton output functions are stored in memory for use during the rule evaluation process. Suppose we came up with the following three rules:

- If water temperature is COLD then turn the knob to Right.
- If water temperature is WARM then leave the knob at the current position.
- If water temperature is HOT then turn the knob to Left.

We have already learned how to encode these rules in memory as shown below.

```
Rule_one     FCB COLD, $FE, RIGHT, $FE
Rule_two     FCB WARM, $FE, ZERO, $FE
Rule_three   FCB HOT, $FE, LEFT, $FF
```

Recall that the hexadecimal value $FE represents the separator, whereas hexadecimal value $FF is used to signal the end of the rule list. Now we are ready to perform the task of rule evaluations. Before performing the task, it is critical to initialize registers used in the evaluation:

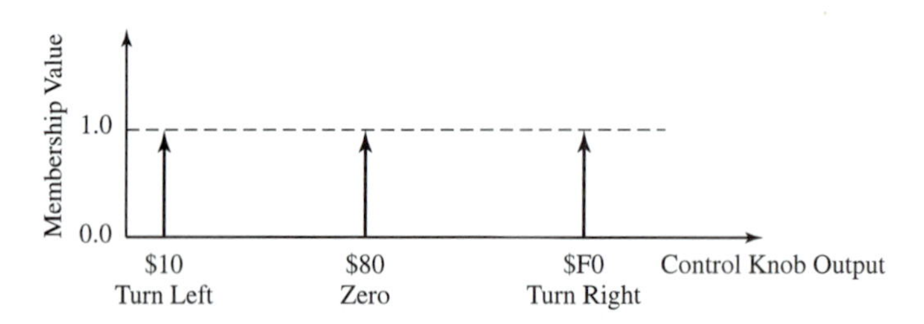

Figure 4.14 Output fuzzy membership functions for controlling water temperature.

- Index register X must be pointing to the beginning of the rule list.
- Index register Y must be pointing to the beginning of the location where the fuzzy input membership values followed by the fuzzy output membership values are stored.
- Accumulator A must be loaded with $FF as the minimum membership truth value and to initialize the V bit of the condition code register.
- Fuzzy output membership values must be cleared to $00.

The first item should be performed since the REV instruction uses the X register to identify each rule for evaluation. The second item is necessary to extract and store input and output fuzzy membership function values. The purpose of the rules is to map truth values of the input fuzzy membership functions to truth values of the output fuzzy membership functions, and this item allows the 68HC12 to know where to get input data and where to write the output data.

Item 3 has two purposes. The first one is to initialize the V bit of the condition code register to zero. This is done by loading value $FF in accumulator A. The reason for initializing the V bit is to accommodate interrupts. As you learn in Chapter 6, interrupts can force the current operation of the microcontroller to stop and take care of the request. When the task is completed, the controller resumes its operation of the instruction before the interrupt occurred. If an interrupt occurs during a rule evaluation, all of the CPU register values along with the condition code register are stored onto the stack. On returning from an interrupt, the CPU will study the V bit of the CCR register to determine whether to execute the antecedent or the consequent of a rule. In all other cases, except performing fuzzy logic-related instructions, an interrupt causes the 68HC12 to store the current CPU data and the program counter value to the stack. When an interrupt is serviced, the program counter register is loaded with the address of the next instruction before the interrupt. So what happens if an interrupt occurs in the middle of executing an instruction? The 68HC12 designers avoid this problem by only looking for an interrupt after the completion of an instruction. This means an interrupt will be serviced after a short delay (usually two to three clock cycles). The situation for fuzzy controller instructions is different since some of these instructions take significant time to complete a single instruction. For example, the execution time for the REV instruction can be high if we have a large number of rules and fuzzy input and output membership functions. This can wreak havoc if a time-critical interrupt is waiting for this instruction to be completed. To avoid this type of problem, the designers of the 68HC12 use the combination of the V bit of the CCR register and the separator ($FE) in the rule definition to periodically stop in the middle of an instruction to service an interrupt.

The second purpose of loading accumulator A with $FF is to initialize the minimum value of the input antecedents. When two or more input variables appear as antecedents, the fuzzy logic dictates that the minimum degree of membership function value should be taken. For example, suppose a rule says *IF air temperature is COLD AND it's WINTER, THEN turn the furnace HIGH.* Suppose further that the membership value for the COLD membership function is $23 and the membership value for the WINTER membership function is $A0. This is a situation when we have unusually warm weather during a winter season. What is the reasonable action of the furnace? Certainly we should not turn the furnace on high since the temperature is warm. That is, the consequent of turning the furnace HIGH should be assigned the minimum of the two input variables. The output membership function HIGH should receive truth value $23, the minimum of the two input membership function values. To execute the prior process, the 68HC12 uses accumulator A to store the minimum input membership function value as the input membership values are compared. As a result, the minimum value is stored as the designated output membership function value. The initial $FF guarantees that the first comparison with an input membership value will cause the input membership value to be the minimum value. The new minimum value is then compared with the next input membership value. This process continues until all rules are processed. What should we use as the initial value of accumulator A if we are looking for the maximum?

If you answered the question correctly ($00), the purpose of item four should be transparent. For the output fuzzy membership functions, we want to take the maximum truth value assigned to a particular membership function. If rules A and B both have the same consequent C, assigning different truth values for the same output membership function, we choose the maximum one. The REV instruction performs this task as a list of rules that are evaluated for each output membership function. After all initialization is completed, we are ready to evaluate. The proper code to perform the rule evaluation for our example of water temperature control is given next:

```
line 1           LDX    #Rule_one
line 2           LDY    #Fuzzy_Output
line 3           LDAA   #$FF
line 4           LDAB   #3
line 5   CLEAR   CLR    1, Y +
line 6           DBNE   B, CLEAR
line 7           LDY    #Fuzzy_Input
line 8           REV
```

The instruction on line 1 loads the address of the rule list. Since rules 2 and 3 immediately follow rule one, we accomplished loading the start address of the rule list block. The instruction on line 2 loads the address where fuzzy output membership values are stored. The instruction on line 2 is performing a preparation work for instructions on lines 4, 5, and 6, where we clear the contents of the output membership function values. Line 3 shows we are initializing accumulator A value to initialize the V bit of the CCR and input fuzzy membership function truth values. The instruction on line 7 loads the starting address of the block containing fuzzy input and output membership function values. Finally, the REV instruction on line 8 goes through each rule and carries out the Min-Max process until $FF is encountered. Recall that the Min-Max process (1) selects the minimum membership value of multiple input membership functions in a single rule and stores it as the output membership value, and (2) finds the maximum membership value among multiple mappings of rules to the same output membership function. As you may have guessed, the REV instruction automatically reinitializes accumulator A to $FF before a new rule is processed, and index registers X and Y are automatically updated as each rule is processed. When all rules are evaluated, each fuzzy output membership function has a truth value assigned by the Min-Max rule.

The weighted rule evaluation process is similar to the unweighted rule evaluation process just described. We only describe the difference between the two. For weighted rule evaluation, we need to use the REVW instruction in place of the REV. In addition, we need to understand the following structural difference. In the unweighted rule evaluation, each rule played an equal role to assign output fuzzy membership truth values. A rule was defined by combining a sequence of 8-bit elements. In particular, we used the offset from the start of the memory locations, specified by the contents of index register Y, where input and output fuzzy membership values reside to specify both antecedents and consequents. For the REVW instruction, however, each rule must be specified with 16-bit number components. Both antecedents and consequents are located by explicit addresses as opposed to an offset used in the unweighted rule evaluation. The addresses for input fuzzy membership function values should hold truth values for corresponding fuzzy input membership functions after performing the MEM instruction. The process of assigning the membership values to a given input is identical for both the REV and REVW instructions.

The REVW instruction also requires the separator within the rule definition, but the separator is now a 16-bit value, $FFFE. Also, the end of fuzzy rule is specified by $FFFF. For each rule evaluation, a minimum truth value from the input fuzzy membership functions are found, multiplied by a weight, and stored as an output fuzzy membership truth value. The 68HC12 uses special internal CPU registers, other than the ones used in the program model, to multiply weights and input fuzzy membership values. By performing the multiplication within the CPU and not accessing memory locations, the 68HC12 can perform the weighted rule evaluation quickly.

For initialization before executing the REVW instruction, you must assign an 8-bit weight for each rule and store it to a designated memory location. These weights must be stored in order; the first weight in the weight block corresponds to the first rule and the last weight is for the last rule. The following requirements for the initialization of the REVW instruction are necessary:

- Index register X must contain the starting address of the rule list.
- Index register Y should hold the starting address of the weight list.
- Accumulator A must be loaded with $FF.
- All output fuzzy membership function values must be $00.
- The C bit of Condition Code Register must be set to 1.

Item one is the same as for the unweighted rule evaluation. The second item is necessary to let the 68HC12 multiply the minimum input fuzzy membership value for a rule with appropriate weights. Item three and four are necessary for the same reason for the unweighted rule evaluation, whereas item five is used to distinguish the REV instruction from the REVW instruction. The 68HC12 studies the C bit of CCR and uses weights during the rule evaluation process only if the bit is set. This bit does not change during the entire process of rule evaluation.

4.3.5 68HC12 Defuzzification Process

So far, we have fuzzified the input to the controller, assigning membership function values, and evaluated rules to map truth values from input membership functions to output membership functions. One more step remains for the fuzzy logic controller. The defuzzificaton process, the topic for this subsection, is presented next.

We need the defuzzification process since we need to have a numerical value as the control signal for a control system. For example, when we control the water temperature for a shower, the temperature control knob must be turned by a specific, numerical amount to a desired direction: Zero amount corresponds to the situation when we do not want to change the knob position. To generate a specific output control signal, the 68HC12 considers all active fuzzy output membership functions whose truth values are greater than zero. It then calculates a single value using the following equation:

$$\textit{Output Signal} = \frac{\sum_{i=1}^{n} S_i F_i}{\sum_{i=1}^{n} F_i}, \tag{4.3}$$

where the S_i represents the ith singleton value preassigned by an expert, the F_i represents ith fuzzy output membership truth value, and n stands for the number of output membership functions. The 68HC12 uses two special internal 16-bit CPU registers to hold the numerator and sum of products, and a single internal 16-bit CPU register to hold the denominator. To perform the process, the 68HC12 uses the WAV (Weighted Average) instruction immediately followed by the EDIV (Extended Division) command. At the completion of the WAV instruction, the sum of products is stored into index register Y and accumulator D where the higher 16 bits reside in register Y and the lower 16 bits are loaded into accumulator D. The denominator value is loaded into index register X, and after the EDIV instruction is performed, the result is stored in register Y and the remainder appears in accumulator D.

Let us look at these two instructions using an example. We return to our water temperature control scenario. Suppose that we have the following truth values for the output fuzzy membership functions as a result of completing a list of rules.

```
RIGHT $25
ZERO  $E0
LEFT  $00
```

Furthermore, let us also suppose that we defined the singleton fuzzy output functions as shown in Figure 4.14. These singleton function definitions are placed in the 68HC12 memory using the following code segment:

```
Knob_Control    FCB $F0 ; TURN RIGHT
                FCB $80 ; ZERO POSITION
                FCB $10 ; TURN LEFT
```

For this example, the output value is then

$$output = \frac{\sum \$F0 \times \$25 + \$80 \times \$E0 + \$10 \times \$00}{\sum \$25 + \$E0 + \$00} = \$8F.$$

Note that this result makes an intuitive sense. We have a small truth value to turn right and a large truth value for leaving the knob at zero position, represented by hexadecimal number $80. The final control signal represents turning to the right by small amount $0F. Now let us actually write the code to perform the defuzzification process. First, we need to know the initialization before the fuzzification process can start.

For the initialization, index register X must hold the starting address of the fuzzy output singleton values. Index register Y must hold the starting address of the fuzzy output fuzzy membership truth values. Finally, accumulator B should be loaded with *n*, the number of output fuzzy membership functions. The actual code segment follows:

```
Line 1    LDX    #Knob_control    ;starting address of the singleton functions.
Line 2    LDY    #RIGHT           ;start address of fuzzy output membership
                                   values
Line 3    LDAB   #$03             ;three membership functions
Line 4    WAV                     ;compute sums for weighted average
Line 5    EDIV                    ;compute the actual average
```

The code segment shown previously will compute the numerical control output value for the water temperature example. Notice that we loaded accumulator B with $03 since three fuzzy output membership functions exist. After the instruction on line 5 is executed, the index register Y will hold the final answer. The actual computation time for the defuzzification process depends on the number of output fuzzy logic membership functions. To accommodate interrupts, the 68HC12 looks for an interrupt after each output membership function is processed. If an interrupt exists, the controller services the interrupt and returns to resume the WAV instruction.

4.3.6 Other Fuzzy Logic Controller-Related Instructions

Some fuzzy logic control purists may object to the particular implementation of the 68HC12. For example, they may argue that input fuzzy membership functions other than trapezoidal functions work better in some control problems. They may also argue that using singleton functions for fuzzy output functions is not the most ideal method to designate output functions and singleton functions should be replaced with Gaussian type functions. To answer to these critics, the 68HC12 designers provide instructions TBL (TaBle Lookup) and ETBL (Extended TaBle Lookup and Interpolate). One can design any desired membership function and implement it using a table lookup scheme. For such a membership function, one can assign varying y-axis values as the truth values (shape of the function) and the x-axis values as the input or output over a range. During the actual fuzzification process, the MEM instruction cannot be used and a custom code segment must be written. Of course this type of implementation will require far more memory than the unique implementation method used by the 68HC12. Nevertheless, if one is so inclined to use a specific input and output fuzzy membership functions, the TBL and ETBL instructions should be used to accomplish the task. Along with the TBL and the ETBL instructions, the 68HC12 controller provides instructions such as EMIND (Extended Minimum for accumulator D), EMAXM (Extended Maximum for Memory Location), EMAXD (Extended Maximum for accumulator D), EMACS (Extended Multiply and Accumulate for Signed Numbers), EDIVS (Extended Divide Signed Numbers), EMUL (Extended Multiply Unsigned Numbers), and EMULS (Extended Multiply Signed Numbers). These instructions provide flexibility to programmers to implement any custom-made fuzzy logic controller.

4.4 APPLICATION

In this section, we design and implement a fuzzy logic controller for navigation of the mobile robot shown in Figure 4.15. In particular, the robot uses two infrared sensors to extract the robot's surrounding information and, based on the sensor values, a 68HC12 fuzzy controller derives control signals for robot navigation. For the current discussion, we assume the robot has only two infrared sensors; we leave

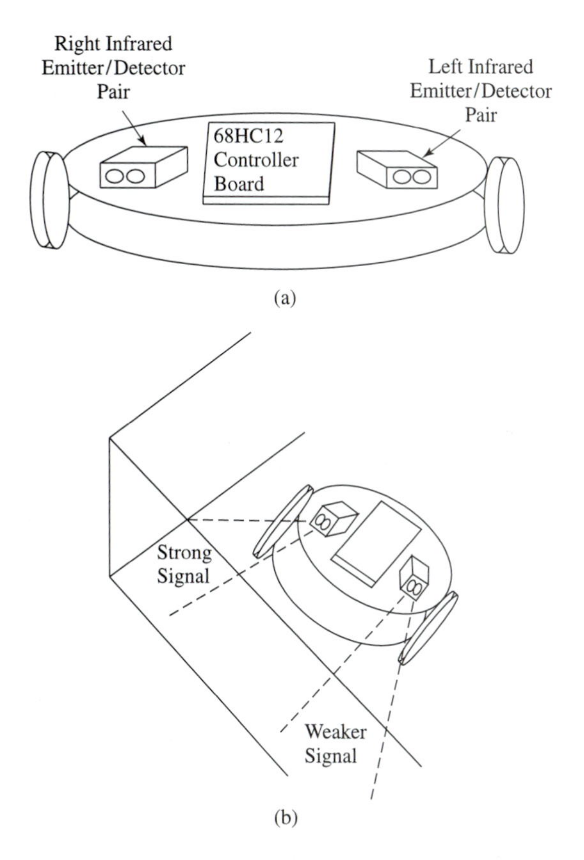

Figure 4.15 Mobile robot navigation example using two infrared sensors: (a) mobile robot diagram, and (b) an example case where the robot is sensing a strong signal from its right sensor and a weaker signal from its left sensor.

the implementation of fuzzy controller using all three sensors as a lab exercise in Section 4.6.

The two infrared sensors are located on top of the robot as shown in Figure 4.15; one on the right and one on the left. These sensors provide information surrounding the robot, indicating the existence of walls. The sensors, working as the robot's *eyes*, continuously provide a pair of numerical values representing the proximities to the surrounding walls from the robot. For example, when the robot is approaching a corner as shown in Figure 4.15(b), the right sensor picks up a strong signal, indicating the approaching wall. The controller is responsible to send a left turn command to the robot to avoid a collision with the wall. The range of each sensor value is $00 to $FF. The sensor values are then used to determine the robot action: go forward, turn left, or turn right.

Our first step is to design fuzzy input and output membership functions. We have two input variables: the left sensor input and the right sensor input. For each input, we decide to use five membership functions. Other numbers can be chosen based on experiments. Since our sensor values, coming from two infrared sensors, are in the range of $00 to $FF, we chose the five membership functions as shown in Figure 4.16: Very Strong, Strong, Medium, Weak, and Very Weak. These variables represent the sensor signal where a large value represents a strong signal indicating that a wall is at a close proximity from the robot and a small value representing a weak signal when a wall is far away from the robot.

The next step is to design the corresponding output fuzzy singleton functions. For the output variable of the robot directional control, we also decide to use five membership functions. The five singleton functions are Medium Left ($40), Small Left ($60), Zero ($80), Small Right ($A0), and Medium Right ($C0) as shown in Figure 4.17.

Note that we are assuming that sending $80 to a motor controller unit will maintain the robot on a straight course while sending other values to the controller will make the robot turn. Now that we have both the input and output fuzzy membership functions, we need to come up with rules that map the two sets of functions.

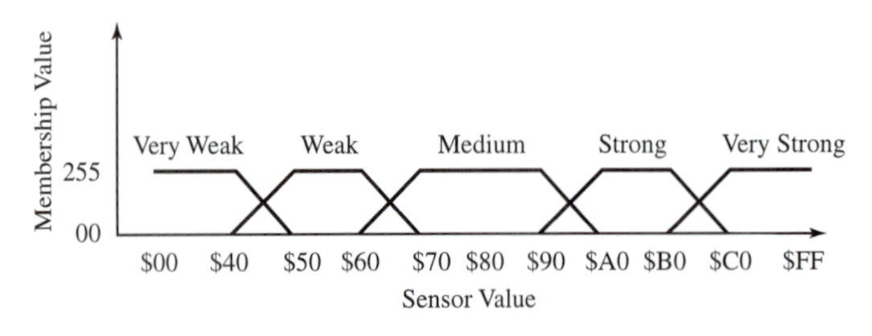

Figure 4.16 Input fuzzy membership function definitions.

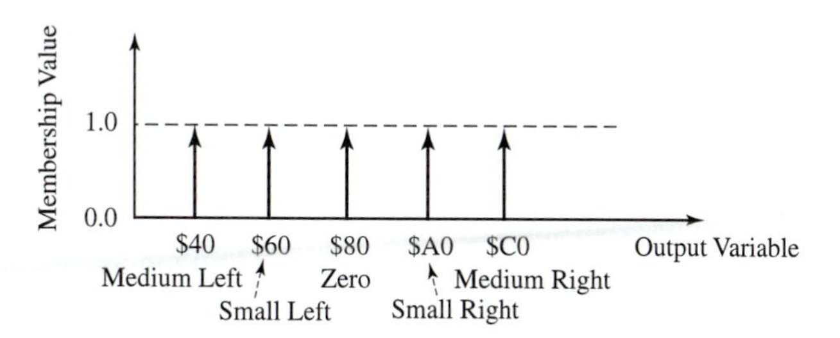

Figure 4.17 Fuzzy output function definitions for the mobile robot controller.

These rules are intuitive rules that we can derive by considering all possible scenarios with input sensor values. For example, if the right sensor detects a strong signal while the left signal detects a weak signal, the logical action for the robot is to take a medium left turn. We write the rule as "IF Right Sensor is Very Strong AND Left Sensor is Weak, THEN Control Signal is Medium Left." Note that variables Right Sensor, Left Sensor, and Control Signal are two inputs and one output for the controller, respectively. A similar train of thought will allow us to come up with the 25 different rules covering all possible fuzzy input states. Table 4.2 shows the 25 rules succinctly. The first column shows symbols for the left sensor fuzzy input membership functions. Symbols VS, ST, MD, WE, and VW stand for Very Strong, Strong, Medium, Weak, and Very Weak, respectively. The first row shows the same membership functions for the right sensor input. The symbols occupying the table are the directional control fuzzy output membership functions: consequents of the 25 rules. Symbols LM, LS, ZR, RS, and RM represent Left Medium, Left Small, Zero, Right Small, and Right Medium, respectively. As can be deduced from the table, if both sensors provide the same input, the robot will maintain its direction (Zero Turn). When a disparity between the two sensor values exists, the rule forces the robot to turn toward the direction of a sensor with a weaker value to move away from a wall. These rules are not the only rules that we must use. Another

TABLE 4.2 FUZZY RULES FOR NAVIGATING ROBOT

LEFT/RIGHT	VS	ST	MD	WE	VW
VS	ZR	RS	RS	RM	RM
ST	LS	ZR	RS	RM	RM
MD	LS	LS	ZR	RS	RS
WE	LM	LM	LS	ZR	RS
VW	LM	LM	LS	LS	ZR

possible control paradigm is to have the robot turn only if one sensor receives a strong or very strong signal, and the robot maintains its direction for all other situations. Since we assume that the robot will constantly move about its environment, the prior rules can be specified as a wall-avoiding rule set for a mobile robot as it roams around its environment without bumping into walls.

Now let us write a program to implement the fuzzy controller. First, since we have not covered the 68HC12 analog-to-digital converter to which our sensors are connected, we assume that the changing sensor values are loaded to two designated memory locations $6000 and $6001. We also assume that writing to memory location $6002 will cause the motor controller to receive a correct signal to control the direction of the mobile robot. When we cover the hardware of the 68HC12 in later chapters, you find out that our assumptions are not much different from the actual implementation using special control registers. The following program accomplishes our goal. Before reading any further, try to make sense of each block of this program. After the trial, you can verify your understanding by reading the next paragraph.

```
Line 1   ;;;;;;;;;;;;;;;;;;;;;;;;;;;;;;;;;;;;;;;;;;;;;;;;;;;;;;;;;;;;;;;;;
Line 2   ; Fuzzy Logic Controller for A Mobile Robot
Line 3   ; Description: This program takes in two infrared
Line 4   ;              sensor values and computes a di-
Line 5   ;              rection control signal to avoid
Line 6   ;              wall collisions. The two sensor
Line 7   ;              values are read from memory
Line 8   ;              locations $6000 and $6001 and
Line 9   ;              the control output value is
Line 10  ;              written to memory location $6002
Line 11  ;
Line 12  ; Authors: Daniel Pack and Steve Barrett
Line 13  ; Date: 8-21-2000
Line 14  ;;;;;;;;;;;;;;;;;;;;;;;;;;;;;;;;;;;;;;;;;;;;;;;;;;;;;;;;;;;;;;;;;
Line 15  ; Data Section
Line 16  O_R_VS   EQU   $00   ; Offset values for input and
                             output mem fns
Line 17  O_R_ST   EQU   $01   ; Right Sensor Strong
Line 18  O_R_ME   EQU   $02   ; Right Sensor Medium
Line 19  O_R_WE   EQU   $03   ; Right Sensor Weak
Line 20  O_R_VW   EQU   $04   ; Right Sensor Very Weak
Line 21  O_L_VS   EQU   $05   ; Left Sensor Very Strong
Line 22  O_L_ST   EQU   $06   ; Left Sensor Strong
Line 23  O_L_ME   EQU   $07   ; Left Sensor Medium
Line 24  O_L_WE   EQU   $08   ; Left Sensor Weak
Line 25  O_L_VW   EQU   $09   ; Left Sensor Very Weak
```

```
Line 26   O_ML           EQU   $0A $00           ; Medium Left
Line 27   O_SL           EQU   $0B               ; Small Left
Line 28   O_ZR           EQU   $0C               ; Zero
Line 29   O_SR           EQU   $0D               ; Small Right
Line 30   O_MR           EQU   $0E               ; Medium Right
Line 31   MARKER         EQU   $FE               ; rule separator
Line 32   ENDR           EQU   $FF               ; end of rule marker
Line 33                  ORG   $6000
Line 34   RSENSOR        RMB   $01               ; Allocating
Line 35   LSENSOR        RMB   $01               ; memory locations
Line 36   CONTROLS       RMB   $01               ; for input/output variables
Line 37   ; Fuzzy Input Membership Function Definitions for Right Sensor
Line 38   R_Very_Strong  FCB   $B0, $FF, $10, $00
Line 39   R_Strong       FCB   $90, $C0, $10, $10
Line 40   R_Medium       FCB   $60, $A0, $10, $10
Line 41   R_Weak         FCB   $40, $70, $10, $10
Line 42   R_Very_Weak    FCB   $00, $50, $00, $10
Line 43   ; Fuzzy Input Membership Function Definitions for Left Sensor
Line 44   L_Very_Strong  FCB   $B0, $FF, $10, $00
Line 45   L_Strong       FCB   $90, $C0, $10, $10
Line 46   L_Medium       FCB   $60, $A0, $10, $10
Line 47   L_Weak         FCB   $40, $70, $10, $10
Line 48   L_Very_Weak    FCB   $00, $50, $00, $10
Line 49   ;Fuzzy Output Membership Function Definitions
Line 50   Medium_Left    FCB   $40
Line 51   Small_Left     FCB   $60
Line 52   Zero           FCB   $80
Line 53   Small_Right    FCB   $A0
Line 54   Medium_Right   FCB   $C0
Line 55   ; Locations for fuzzy membership values
Line 56   R_VS           RMB   $01
Line 57   R_ST           RMB   $01
Line 58   R_ME           RMB   $01
Line 59   R_WE           RMB   $01
Line 60   R_VW           RMB   $01
Line 61   L_VS           RMB   $01
Line 62   L_ST           RMB   $01
Line 63   L_ME           RMB   $01
Line 64   L_WE           RMB   $01
Line 65   L_VW           RMB   $01
Line 66   ; Output Fuzzy Logic Membership Values - initialize them to zero
Line 67   ML             FCB   $00
Line 68   SL             FCB   $00
Line 69   ZR             FCB   $00
```

```
Line 70   SR          FCB    $00
Line 71   MR          FCB    $00
Line 72   ; Rule Definitions
Line 73   Rule_Start  FCB    O_R_VS, O_L_VS, MARKER, O_ZR, MARKER
Line 74               FCB    O_R_VS, O_L_ST, MARKER, O_SL, MARKER
Line 75               FCB    O_R_VS, O_L_ME, MARKER, O_SL, MARKER
Line 76               FCB    O_R_VS, O_L_WE, MARKER, O_ML, MARKER
Line 77               FCB    O_R_VS, O_L_VW, MARKER, O_ML, MARKER
Line 78               FCB    O_R_ST, O_L_VS, MARKER, O_SR, MARKER
Line 79               FCB    O_R_ST, O_L_ST, MARKER, O_ZR, MARKER
Line 80               FCB    O_R_ST, O_L_ME, MARKER, O_SL, MARKER
Line 81               FCB    O_R_ST, O_L_WE, MARKER, O_ML, MARKER
Line 82               FCB    O_R_ST, O_L_VW, MARKER, O_ML, MARKER
Line 83               FCB    O_R_MD, O_L_VS, MARKER, O_SR, MARKER
Line 84               FCB    O_R_MD, O_L_ST, MARKER, O_SR, MARKER
Line 85               FCB    O_R_MD, O_L_ME, MARKER, O_ZR, MARKER
Line 86               FCB    O_R_MD, O_L_WE, MARKER, O_SL, MARKER
Line 87               FCB    O_R_MD, O_L_VW, MARKER, O_SL, MARKER
Line 88               FCB    O_R_WE, O_L_VS, MARKER, O_MR, MARKER
Line 89               FCB    O_R_WE, O_L_ST, MARKER, O_MR, MARKER
Line 90               FCB    O_R_WE, O_L_ME, MARKER, O_SR, MARKER
Line 91               FCB    O_R_WE, O_L_WE, MARKER, O_ZR, MARKER
Line 92               FCB    O_R_WE, O_L_VW, MARKER, O_SL, MARKER
Line 93               FCB    O_R_VW, O_L_VS, MARKER, O_MR, MARKER
Line 94               FCB    O_R_VW, O_L_ST, MARKER, O_MR, MARKER
Line 95               FCB    O_R_VW, O_L_ME, MARKER, O_SR, MARKER
Line 96               FCB    O_R_VW, O_L_WE, MARKER, O_SR, MARKER
Line 97               FCB    O_R_VW, O_L_WE, MARKER, O_ZR, ENDR
Line 98   ; Main Program
Line 99   ;           ORG    $4000
Line 100  ; Fuzzification
Line 101              LDX    #R_Very_Strong    ; Start of Input Mem func
Line 102              LDY    #R_VS             ; Start of Fuzzy Mem values
Line 103              LDAA   RSENSOR           ; Right Sensor Value
Line 104              LDAB   #5                ; Number of iterations
Line 105  Loopr       MEM                      ; Assign mem value
Line 106              DBNE   B, Loopr          ; Do all five iterations
Line 107              LDAA   LSENSOR           ; Left Sensor Value
Line 108              LDAB   #5                ; Number of iterations
Line 109  Loopl       MEM                      ; Assign mem value
Line 110              DBNE   B, Loopl          ; Do all five iterations
Line 111              LDY    #R_VS             ; Process rules
Line 112              LDX    #Rule_Start       ; Point X to the start of the
                                               address
```

```
Line 113          LDAA    #$FF         ; Initialize min and V bit
Line 114          REV                  ; Evaluate rules
Line 115    ; Defuzzification Process
Line 116          LDX     #Medium_Left; Start of output mem func
Line 117          LDY     #ML          ; Start of mem values
Line 118          LDAB    #$05         ; Five elements sum
Line 119          WAV                  ; Computing a crisp value
Line 120          EDIV
Line 121          TFR     Y, D         ; Store answer to D
Line 122          STAB    CONTROLS     ; Save the answer
Line 123          END
```

The directives on lines 16 through 30 define offset values for fuzzy membership functions for the fuzzy rule definitions. The EQU directives on lines 31 and 32 assign symbols Marker and ENDR to designate values as the rule separator and the end of rule marker. Using the RMB directives, memory locations $6000, $6001, and $6002 are reserved for the input and output variables on lines 33 through 36. The directives on lines 37 through 54 define the right and left sensor input fuzzy membership functions and the control signal output fuzzy membership functions. The RMB directives on lines 55 through 71 allocate memory locations for fuzzy membership truth values for the five right sensor input fuzzy membership functions, the five left sensor input fuzzy membership functions, and the five output control fuzzy membership functions.

The 25 fuzzy rules mapping the input to the output fuzzy membership functions are defined on lines 73 through 97. At this point, we completed the initialization process and are ready for the main program to start. The first step is to fuzzify two input variable values, assigning truth values to input fuzzy membership functions based on the membership function definitions. Lines 101 through 104 contain instructions to initialize index registers and accumulators before performing the MEM instruction. Recall that the MEM instruction finds the truth value for a single membership function, and we need to repeat the process five times in the current case since we have five input fuzzy logic membership functions for each input variable. Accumulator A has the input value while accumulator B holds numerical value five for the iterations. At the end of the iterations on line 106, index register X contains the address of the membership function definitions for the left sensor input, and index register Y contains the start address of the left sensor membership function truth values. On lines 107 and 108, the left sensor input value and the number of iterations are loaded to accumulators A and B, respectively. The process of assigning membership truth values is repeated for the left sensor input membership functions on lines 109 and 110.

By the time we reach line 112, index register X contains the starting address of the fuzzy rule block, and index register Y has the starting address of the fuzzy membership truth values. The LDAA instruction on line 113 initializes the V bit in the CCR and initializes the minimum truth value for antecedents. The REV instruction on line 114 processes all 25 rules and assigns appropriate truth values to the output fuzzy membership functions.

Finally, instructions on lines 116 through 118 initialize index register values such that register X contains the starting address of the fuzzy output singleton function block, register Y holds the starting address of the fuzzy output truth value block, and accumulator B has the number of output fuzzy membership functions. The WAV instruction on line 119 computes the denominator and numerator for the defuzzified output equation (Eq. [4.3]), and the EDIV instruction actually performs to compute the numerical output control value. At the end of performing the EDIV instruction on line 120, the solution resides in index register Y. We simply transfer the contents of Y to accumulator D on line 121. Note that the maximum value for the division is $FF, and the output control value lies in accumulator B after the transfer. We store the result onto the appropriate location on line 122.

The program only performs the wall-avoiding scheme once. For the actual implementation, you need to develop a main program that incorporates a fuzzy controller, similar to the prior program, as a subroutine. Your program needs to repeatedly call the subroutine to obtain the robot decision as the robot moves around its neighborhood. The control command generated by the fuzzy controller must also be processed to generate actual motor control signals. That is, we must set a threshold value of the fuzzy controller output value for a turning motion. Presently, the robot control motion for Move Straight only occurs if and only if the fuzzy controller output is exactly $80, which rarely happens. The consequence of the robot motion is the robot constantly making small turns with respect to a pivot point at the center of the robot. To avoid such implementation, we set threshold values such as $70 and $80 for the move straight motion: Only if the fuzzy output value is less than $70 or greater than $80 will the resulting turning motion be executed.

4.5 SOME COMMENTS ON FUZZY LOGIC CONTROLLER DESIGN

In this section, we present some general guidelines on building fuzzy membership functions, fuzzy rules, and testing the correctness of fuzzy controllers. As discussed earlier, the traditional control methods rely on accurate mathematical models of a system to derive an optimal control law. For a fuzzy logic controller, an expert who understands the system dynamics performs an equivalent task.

The expert is responsible to know how an input generated by a controller will affect the output of a system. The expert must first decide the inputs and outputs of a fuzzy controller. In the example of the balancing robot, an expert must know that he or she needs at least the angular position and the angular velocity as the inputs to the controller. The expert must also know that a force to move the mass on the top plate is the output of the fuzzy controller and understand how the system responds to a given controller output.

For the design of membership functions, an expert needs to decide the granularities of input and output membership function labels to adequately describe the input variables (for the balancing robot example, position and velocity) and the output variable (for the balancing robot example, force applied to the movable mass). For the balancing robot example, the linguistic variable of angular position requires multiple labels within a small range of angles with respect to a vertical position. This knowledge is based on the fact that once the angle from a vertical line exceeds a certain value, say 15 degrees, the system cannot be balanced no matter what the applied force may be. Thus, the expert should put in multiple labels close together to carefully monitor the angular position of the robot.

However, the expert understands that the angular velocity can vary within a large range without losing control of the robot. Depending on the sample time period, the angular velocity does not play a significant role as the angular position variable. Thus, the expert can get away with the same number of labels for the velocity variable for a greater range of values as the position variable with a much smaller range. Similarly, the number of fuzzy output functions and their positions must be determined by the expert after considering the capabilities of motors being used, the sampling time, and amount of torque that the motors can generate.

Once fuzzy input and output membership functions are determined, you are ready to construct fuzzy rules. Developing fuzzy rules simply means finding the relationships between the input and output variables of the controller in terms of their membership functions. You can come up with a set of rules by carefully considering all possible relationships between the input and output variables. For example, the expert should know that if the robot is slowly falling to its right (input variables), the controller must generate a large force (output variable) to move the mass to the left side on the top plate to maintain the robot balance. Thus, in place of the accurate mathematical model, the expert needs to use his or her intuitive understanding of the system dynamics to derive correct fuzzy rules.

The procedure, as you can see, requires an extensive knowledge of the overall system. This knowledge must include the physical parameters of a system to be controlled. If so, how can a novice decide the fuzzy functions and rules of a system? You must gain necessary intuitive understanding of the system behavior. If you do not have the precise understanding, it can be fixed during the tuning stage. Once you have the understanding of a system dynamics, start with a reasonable set of fuzzy functions and rules, tuning them as you observe the system response. Until you actually see how the controller outputs are controlling or not controlling a system appropriately, you cannot tell whether your initial fuzzy functions and rules were correctly chosen. This is similar for classical controllers, where the designer must start with some initial estimate (usually after rigorous computations) of optimal parameters and then adjust those parameters after observing the system response.

The good news about the fuzzy controller is that the controller generously tolerates a nonexpert controller design and allows us to learn the system behavior during the tuning phase of a design. For example, suppose our expert chose only two labels for the fuzzy output functions for the balancing robot. During the testing, he or she will notice the underdamped response of the system and quickly realize the need for finer labels for the output functions. Thus, by studying the system behavior (by connecting the controller to a system model), the expert can design the controller for its best performance.

The usual step is to provide sufficient labels for all input and output variables and adjust their positions and fuzzy rules for optimal system performance. This is similar to adjusting the number of nodes and layers for a neural network controller to obtain a desired system performance. As a matter of fact, neural networks are used to find the optimal positions of fuzzy functions in many research and commercial systems.

Finally, designers of fuzzy logic controllers also use mathematical models of system dynamics, similar to the one shown earlier in the chapter, to tune their fuzzy functions and rules. This simulation allows them to see the system states at all sampling times, giving them insights on how to adjust fuzzy controllers. Note, however, that the creation of a system dynamic model is not a requirement of the fuzzy logic controller design as is the case for the classical controller design. After all, we can tune fuzzy controller parameters by directly connecting controller outputs to a control system provided that the controller outputs will not damage the system. For more in-depth study of this topic, we refer readers to the references at the end of this chapter.

4.6 LABORATORY APPLICATION

LABORATORY EXERCISE

Purpose This lab is designed to provide an opportunity to implement a fuzzy logic controller, studied in this chapter, using the built-in 68HC12 fuzzy-related instructions. This lab can be used as part of an overall mobile robot control program in the final lab.

Documentation 68HC812A4EVB User's manual and 68HC12 CPU12 Reference Manual

Prelab For the prelab, you are required to complete a detailed flowchart or pseudocode for your program.

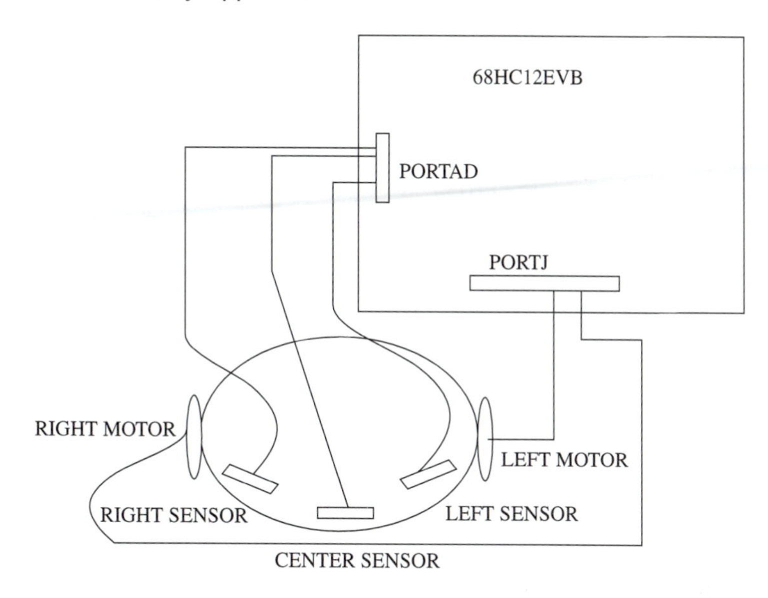

Figure 4.18 Locations of the infrared sensors on the mobile robot.

Description The goal of this lab is to study a fuzzy controller design and implement a fuzzy logic controller on the 68HC12 microcontroller. The fuzzy controller incorporates three infrared (IR) sensor values to determine the next direction of the mobile robot. The three sensors are positioned as shown in Figure 4.18.

The figure shows the sensor outputs and analog signals entering the 68HC12 evaluation board through a special port that converts analog signals to digital signals. Motor direction control signals are sent to the motors using one of the 68HC12 parallel input/output (I/O) ports. You will learn the 68HC12 parallel input and output ports in Chapter 5 and the built-in analog-to-digital (ATD) converter in Chapter 9. For this particular lab, we simulate the process by using a set of designated memory locations. (This process is identical to the actual use of the hardware with an exception: RAM locations are used instead of special memory locations related to the ATD converter and parallel I/O ports.)

Three separate memory locations are used where we assume the three sensor output values are stored. An output sensor value is an 8-bit unsigned value ranging from $00 to $FF. A small value represents that the sensor does not see any object in front of the sensor while a large value indicates the existence of an object in front of the sensor. One other memory location is used to simulate the robot motion.[5] Your

[5]In the actual robot control, as you see at the end of the timer chapter, your program generates two separate robot control signals for two motors (the right and left motors of your robot) to control motor-turning motions.

fuzzy controller will write a value, representing a robot direction, to this memory location as the final output of the fuzzy controller; your controller executes a single iteration using three numerical input values and computes for one numerical output value, representing the desired robot direction. In an actual robot control program, your program for the current lab would be continuously called to generate robot direction commands as new sensor values are obtained.

Procedure In this section, we provide a list of steps you must follow to complete this lab.

1. The first task at hand is to determine the number and types of linguistic variables for the inputs and outputs of the fuzzy controller. The natural candidates for the inputs are Left Sensor, Right Sensor, and Center Sensor. Similarly, the Turning motion of the robot fits well as the output of the controller. For the reason to be clear in the rule formulation stage (item 2), we limit the number of fuzzy membership functions (labels) for each controller input to three: Low, Medium, and High. Furthermore, the membership functions for the three controller inputs are defined identically as shown in Figure 4.19.

   Note that function LOW stretches a wider range of the possible sensor output values compared with the other two functions. We have done this because of the small amount of IR illumination generated from sources other than the sensor emitter in a typical environment. The high cutoff value for function LOW helps us ignore such IR illumination not related to the emitter IR signal.[6]

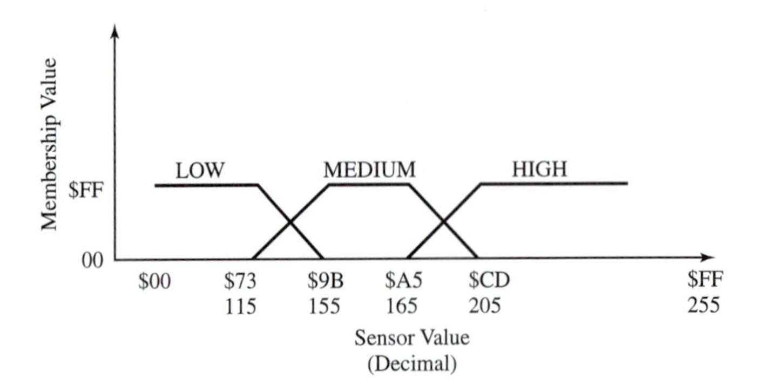

Figure 4.19 Fuzzy Input Membership Function Definitions.

[6]One way to completely remove the dependency on ambient IR lights is to modulate the sensor IR emitter signal and demodulate the reflected signal at the receiver end of the sensor. For both modulation and demodulation, one typically can use the 555 timer chip to carry out the task.

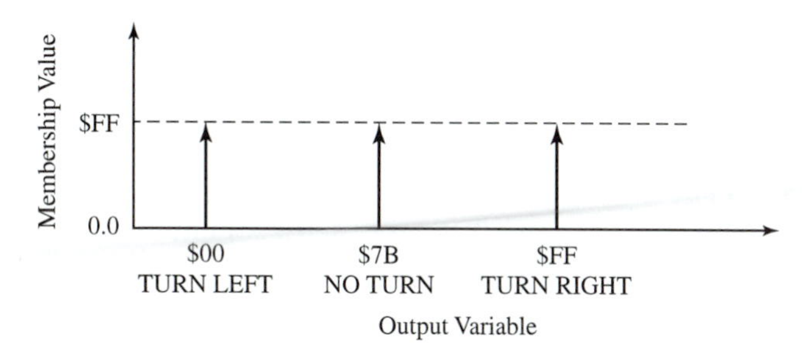

Figure 4.20 Fuzzy controller output membership functions.

As for the fuzzy controller output, the robot direction was chosen, and its membership functions are defined as shown in Figure 4.20.

Note that we assigned values from $00 to $FF to denote a direction of the mobile robot. For example, if the controller output is $80 (128 decimal), then the controller suggests no turn while a value greater than $80 indicates a right turn while a value less than the number indicates a command for a left turn.

2. The second step for the lab is to develop fuzzy rules that relate the fuzzy input membership functions with the fuzzy output membership functions. The reason behind choosing three membership functions for each input sensor variable is to limit the number of the fuzzy rules. This is one of the important considerations you must make when you are designing a new fuzzy logic controller. Let us look at the reason behind our choice. We have three controller input values: Right Sensor, Center Sensor, and Left Sensor. For each input, we have three membership functions: Low, Medium, and High. For each different membership function, we must come up with an intuitive rule to map it to one of the output membership functions. For example, "IF the LEFT Sensor is LOW AND the Center Sensor is LOW AND the Right Sensor is HIGH, THEN TURN LEFT." The rule is intuitive since the rule says that when the robot encounters an obstacle to its right and no other objects are found around the robot, it should turn away to its left avoiding the object to its right. Similarly, we can come up with rules for other possible input scenarios. As you can see, the number of input variables and membership functions for each variable determine the number of fuzzy rules that one must generate. For our current lab, you can see there are $3 \times 3 \times 3$ possible input membership combinations. In general, one must come up with n^m rules, where m represents the number of controller inputs and n represents the number of membership functions for each input provided that each input has the same number of membership functions. For this lab, we came up with the following 27 intuitive fuzzy rules.

LEFT SENSOR	CENTER SENSOR	RIGHT SENSOR	ROBOT MOTION
RULE 1: LOW	LOW	LOW	NO TURN
RULE 2: LOW	LOW	MEDIUM	TURN LEFT
RULE 3: LOW	LOW	HIGH	TURN LEFT
RULE 4: LOW	MEDIUM	LOW	TURN RIGHT
RULE 5: LOW	MEDIUM	MEDIUM	TURN LEFT
RULE 6: LOW	MEDIUM	HIGH	TURN LEFT
RULE 7: LOW	HIGH	LOW	TURN RIGHT
RULE 8: LOW	HIGH	MEDIUM	TURN LEFT
RULE 9: LOW	HIGH	HIGH	TURN LEFT
RULE 10: MEDIUM	LOW	LOW	TURN RIGHT
RULE 11: MEDIUM	LOW	MEDIUM	TURN RIGHT
RULE 12: MEDIUM	LOW	HIGH	TURN LEFT
RULE 13: MEDIUM	MEDIUM	LOW	TURN RIGHT
RULE 14: MEDIUM	MEDIUM	MEDIUM	TURN RIGHT
RULE 15: MEDIUM	MEDIUM	HIGH	TURN LEFT
RULE 16: MEDIUM	HIGH	LOW	TURN RIGHT
RULE 17: MEDIUM	HIGH	MEDIUM	TURN RIGHT
RULE 18: MEDIUM	HIGH	HIGH	TURN LEFT
RULE 19: HIGH	LOW	LOW	TURN RIGHT
RULE 20: HIGH	LOW	MEDIUM	TURN RIGHT
RULE 21: HIGH	LOW	HIGH	TURN RIGHT
RULE 22: HIGH	MEDIUM	LOW	TURN RIGHT
RULE 23: HIGH	MEDIUM	MEDIUM	TURN RIGHT
RULE 24: HIGH	MEDIUM	HIGH	TURN RIGHT
RULE 25: HIGH	HIGH	LOW	TURN RIGHT
RULE 26: HIGH	HIGH	MEDIUM	TURN RIGHT
RULE 27: HIGH	HIGH	HIGH	TURN RIGHT

Note that when the right and left sensor values fall into the same membership functions (e.g., MEDIUM and MEDIUM) or when the center sensor value indicates an object while the two side sensor values indicate a same membership function, we arbitrarily chose to have the robot turn RIGHT. One could, of course, have chosen to make the robot turn left when the robot encounters the same conditions.

3. Implement your program and display the controller output on your PC screen using the 68HC12 built-in D-Bug12 subroutines as shown next.

INPUTS- LEFT: XX CENTER: XX RIGHT: XX OUTPUT: XX

where XX represents a numerical number ranging from $00 to $FF. The input sensor value locations are $0800, $0801, and $0802 for the right, center, and left sensors, respectively. The output robot direction value should be stored in $0803.

4. Test your program for proper functionality by varying sensor input values in the memory locations.

4.7 SUMMARY

In this chapter we studied a new control paradigm using fuzzy logic concepts. To design a fuzzy logic controller, we studied how to develop fuzzy input and output membership functions, how to apply the fuzzification process, how to develop and use fuzzy rules, and how to execute the defuzzification process. In the 68HC12, we learned that input fuzzy membership functions are defined by trapezoidal functions, whereas the output fuzzy membership functions are represented by singleton functions. We learned that input values are fuzzified using the definitions of fuzzy input membership functions into a set of truth values for the corresponding input membership functions, which is performed by the MEM instruction in the 68HC12. A set of intuitive rules allowed us to map input fuzzy membership functions to output fuzzy membership functions. When more than one input membership functions form the antecedent, the minimum truth value of the input membership functions is assigned as the output membership truth value, and when more than a single truth value is assigned to an output membership function by multiple rules, the maximum truth value is taken. We learned that this Min-Max process is performed by the REV or REVW instruction in the 68HC12. The final process of the fuzzy logic controller—computing a numerical value from a set of output fuzzy membership functions—was performed by multiplying output fuzzy membership values with the output fuzzy membership values, summing the multiplied values, and dividing the resulting value with the sum of output fuzzy function truth values. The WAV and EDIV instructions are used in the 68HC12 to perform the last task. We also learned that the 68HC12 provides other fuzzy logic-related instructions for custom design of input and output fuzzy membership functions, defuzzification process, and the weighted rule evaluations. The application section provided you with a complete example for the mobile robot navigation.

4.8 FURTHER READING

J. Denavit and R. Hartenberg, "Kinematic Notation for Lower-Pair Mechanisms Based on Matrices," *Journal of Applied Mechnics*, pp. 215–221, June 1965.

C. Lee, "Fuzzy Logic in Control Systems: Fuzzy Logic Controller-Part I," *IEEE Transactions on Systems, Man, and Cybernatics*, vol. 20., no. 2, pp. 404–418, March/April 1990.

C. Lee, "Fuzzy Logic in Control Systems: Fuzzy Logic Controller-Part II," *IEEE Transactions on Systems, Man, and Cybernatics*, vol. 20., no. 2, pp. 419–435, March/April 1990.

4.9 CHAPTER PROBLEMS

Fundamental

1. Name the three operations performed by a fuzzy logic controller to generate a single control output.
2. Suppose you have the following rules: If A and B, then C. Symbols A, B, and C represent fuzzy membership functions. If the truth value for A is 0.7 and the truth value B is 0.5, what is the truth value for C when the particular rule is processed?
3. Suppose you designed seven fuzzy membership functions for a fuzzy input variable. If a system has three input variables and each input variable has seven fuzzy membership functions, how many input fuzzy membership functions in all do you need to define? How many bytes of memory are required to store the membership definitions?
4. If equally weighted 49 rules for the balancing robot are to be implemented in the 68HC12, how many bytes are needed to specify the rules?
5. Suppose we have the following two rules with the same consequent: (1) IF A and B, then C and (2) If D and E, then C. Furthermore the truth values assigned for membership function C are 0.3 and 0.5 by rule (1) and rule (2), respectively. What is the final truth value for C?

Advanced

1. The 68HC12 specifies that all input fuzzy membership functions are trapezoidal functions. This constraint allows a compact representation of the function. Given the membership function shown in Figure 4.21, find the right and left slopes of the function.
2. Use the 68HC12 representation to define the function shown in Figure 4.21.

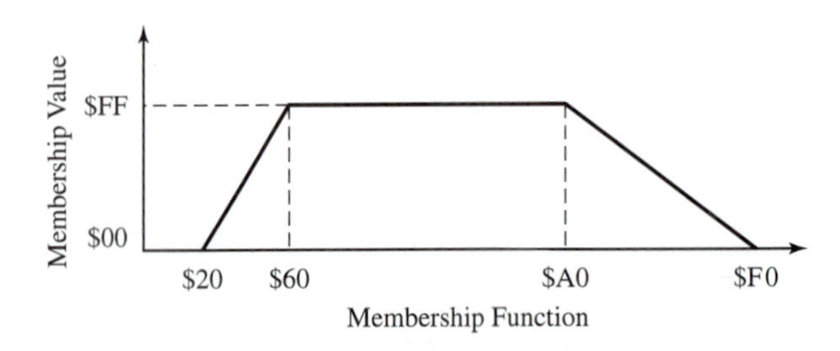

Figure 4.21 Figure for Advanced Problems 1 through 5.

3. If an input to a fuzzy controller whose membership function includes the one shown in Figure 4.21 is $45, what is the corresponding truth value of the function?
4. If an input to a fuzzy controller whose membership function includes the one shown in Figure 4.21 is $70, what is the corresponding truth value of the function?
5. If an input to a fuzzy controller whose membership function includes the one shown in Figure 4.21 is $E0, what is the corresponding truth value of the function?

Challenging

1. What is the consequence of using a nontrapezoidal function for an input fuzzy membership function in terms of the memory use of the 68HC12?
2. What is the difference between the weighted rule evaluation versus the unweighted rule evaluation? Give a situational example where the weighted rule evaluation is beneficial?
3. Design a fuzzy logic controller to control the inside temperature of your house.

5

Hardware Configuration

Objectives: At the completion of this chapter you will be able to:

- Summarize and describe the hardware features of the 68HC12 microcontroller and its subsystems,
- Characterize how different features and subsystems of the 68HC12 microcontroller are employed to satisfy specific application requirements,
- Prescribe a mode of operation for the 68HC12 for a given application, and
- Differentiate between the memory configurations for 68HC12 variants.

This chapter provides a brief introduction to the 68HC12 hardware configuration and its associated subsystems. It is provided as an overview. More detailed information on the different 68HC12 hardware systems is contained in later chapters. In these later chapters, we provide detailed information on the operation of the subsystems, how to program them, and, most important, how to use them in real-world applications.

Rather than launch into a dry "laundry list" of 68HC12 features, functions, and subsystems, we begin by describing in detail the wall following robot project.

We then delineate the requirements for a microcontroller to provide local intelligence for the robot. Then we provide a hardware overview and a discussion of modes of operation of the 68HC12. This is followed by short sections on each of the following hardware systems: timing system, memory system, interrupt and reset systems, serial communication system, port system, and data conversion system.

What you should take away from this chapter is a fundamental understanding of the features of the 68HC12. We test your understanding at the end of the chapter. We give you some new features to add to the wall following robot and ask you to describe the hardware subsystems required to implement these features. We also ask you to design the layout for a remote weather data-collection system and describe what 68HC12 features and subsystems are required to implement the system.

5.1 THE WALL FOLLOWING ROBOT

Throughout this text, we have been learning microcontroller concepts by applying them to a navigable robot system. A picture of the robot is provided in Figure 5.1. The robot is able to move through an unknown maze, detect maze walls, and make decisions to move forward and turn appropriately to make its way through the maze. The robot consists of two lightweight aluminum platforms connected together to form the robot's body. The lower platform is equipped with two direct current (DC) motors that are used to drive the two large wheels. These wheels are mounted on either side of the robot's body. Using this two-wheel configuration, the robot may be steered like a tank. That is, to turn, equal but opposite (clockwise

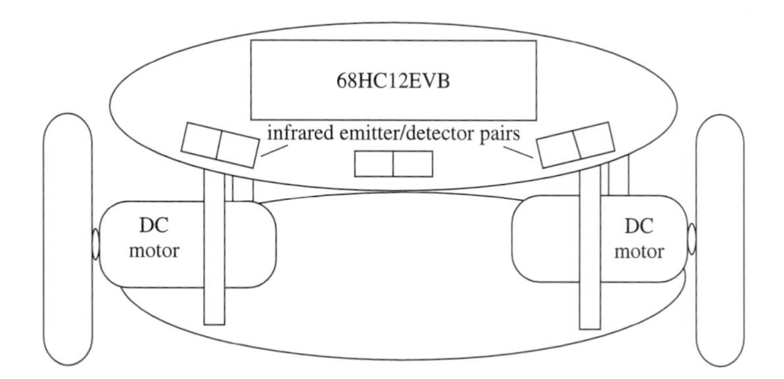

Figure 5.1 The wall following robot. The robot is equipped with two main wheels powered by DC motors. As the robot rolls forward, it constantly monitors for walls using its three sets of IR emitter-detector pairs.

and counterclockwise) signals are issued to the motors to render a turn. Two small round-head screws are used at either end of the robot's body to provide balance and stability. The robot rests on this tail in a tripod configuration. The top platform is equipped with three sets of infrared (IR) emitter and detector pairs to sense walls in front of and to either side of the robot. The top platform also contains the 68HC12 evaluation board (EVB), which is used to input signals, make decisions based on these inputs, and issue signals to control external events.

Suppose a robot is to navigate through an unknown maze. To start, it is placed at an entrance door to the maze. The robot's overall goal is to proceed through the maze while avoiding collisions with the maze walls. The robot rolls forward by issuing identical signals simultaneously to each of its DC motors. As the robot rolls forward powered by its DC motors, it constantly monitors for walls using its three sets of IR emitter-detector pairs.

The maze walls are painted with a highly reflective white paint such that the signals emitting from the IR sources are reflected off the walls back to the detectors. If the robot is within close proximity to a wall, its presence is detected by the appropriate IR emitter-detector pair(s). For example, if the robot approaches a corner on its right side, it senses a wall in front of it with its front IR emitter-detector pair and a wall to its right with its right IR emitter-detector pair. The robot then responds to these inputs by turning left to avoid colliding with the walls.

Let us construct a list of required hardware features and subsystems a microcontroller would need to control a wall following robot. The microcontroller would require:

1. A central processing unit (CPU) to execute the program controlling all robot actions.
2. A memory system to store the control program as well as random access memory (RAM) used to execute the program.
3. An extensive port system to allow signals to be input to and output from the microcontroller such as signals to a liquid crystal display (LCD) panel. A LCD panel is a low-power consumption display device. In the wall following robot project, it is used to provide status information on the robot. For example, it could be used to display the number of wall collisions and robot system fault information.
4. An analog-to-digital (ATD) converter system to convert and process the analog signals provided by the IR detectors.
5. A precision timing system to issue precise control signals to the DC motors controlling the wheels to execute robot movements.
6. A communication system that would allow the robot to communicate with another robot.

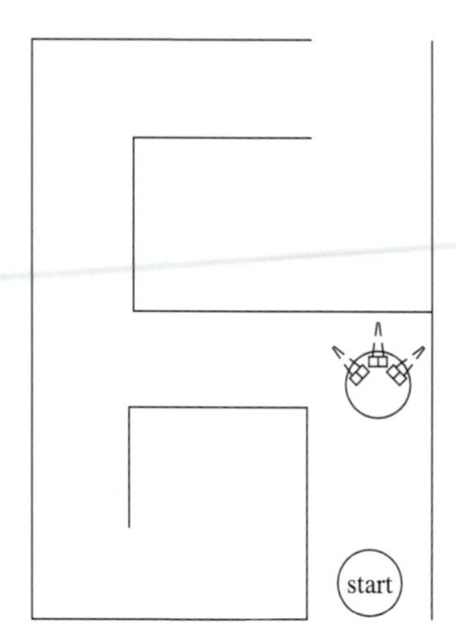

Figure 5.2 A wall following robot executing a left turn to avoid walls to its front and right.

A block diagram of a candidate microcontroller is provided in Section 5.3.

Practice Questions

Question: What should the wall following robot do when: (a) a wall is detected by its right and front IR emitter-detector pairs? (b) a wall is detected to its left and front? and (c) a wall is detected in front of the robot?

Answer: (a) take actions to effect a left turn, (b) take actions to effect a right turn, and (c) turn right or left.

5.2 THE 68HC12 HARDWARE SYSTEM

Figure 5.4 provides the detailed block diagram of the Motorola 68HC12. If you carefully compare this block diagram to the candidate microcontroller block diagram provided in Figure 5.3, you can see it contains all of the necessary subsystems required to control a wall following robot system. It is our intent in the remainder of the chapter to acquaint you with the key features and subsystems of the 68HC12.

Let us get started! The 68HC12 is a 16-bit data bus processing unit with a programming model identical to that of the 68HC11. For those of you familiar with the 68HC11, you may recall that it had an 8-bit data bus. The 68HC11 was and is an industry standard microcontroller. Considerable costs have been expended in developing 68HC11-based applications. It is comforting to know that any M68HC11 source code you have developed from previous applications is readily accepted by

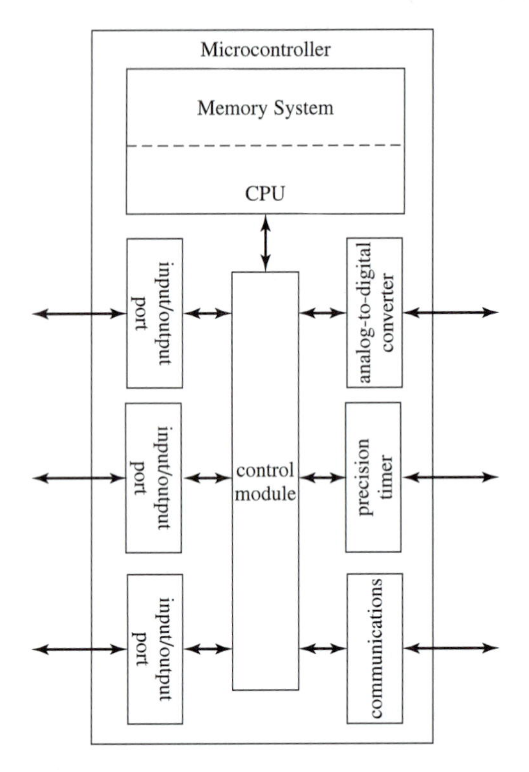

Figure 5.3 A block diagram of a candidate microcontroller to control a wall following robot.

the 68HC12 assemblers with no change. The 68HC12 instruction set is a much larger superset of the 68HC11's instruction set. Therefore, it is more powerful and flexible.

The 68HC12 is currently available in several different variants, including XC68HC12A0 (A0), XC68HC812A4 (or A4), and XC68HC912B32 (or B32). All of these variants are 16-bit devices consisting of a series of modules connected by an intermodule bus called the Lite Integration Module (LIM). Modules within the 68HC12 are detailed later.

The primary differences among the 68HC12 variants is the EEPROM (Electrically Eraseable Programmable Read Only Memory) size, flash EEPROM size, number of input/output (I/O) channels, and the serial communications configuration. Throughout this chapter, we base our hardware discussion on the A4 variant. Realize the hardware configuration of the other variants is quite similar.

Provided next is a list of 68HC12 features. We list the features as provided in the A4 data sheet and then describe the importance of the feature. The 68HC12 features:

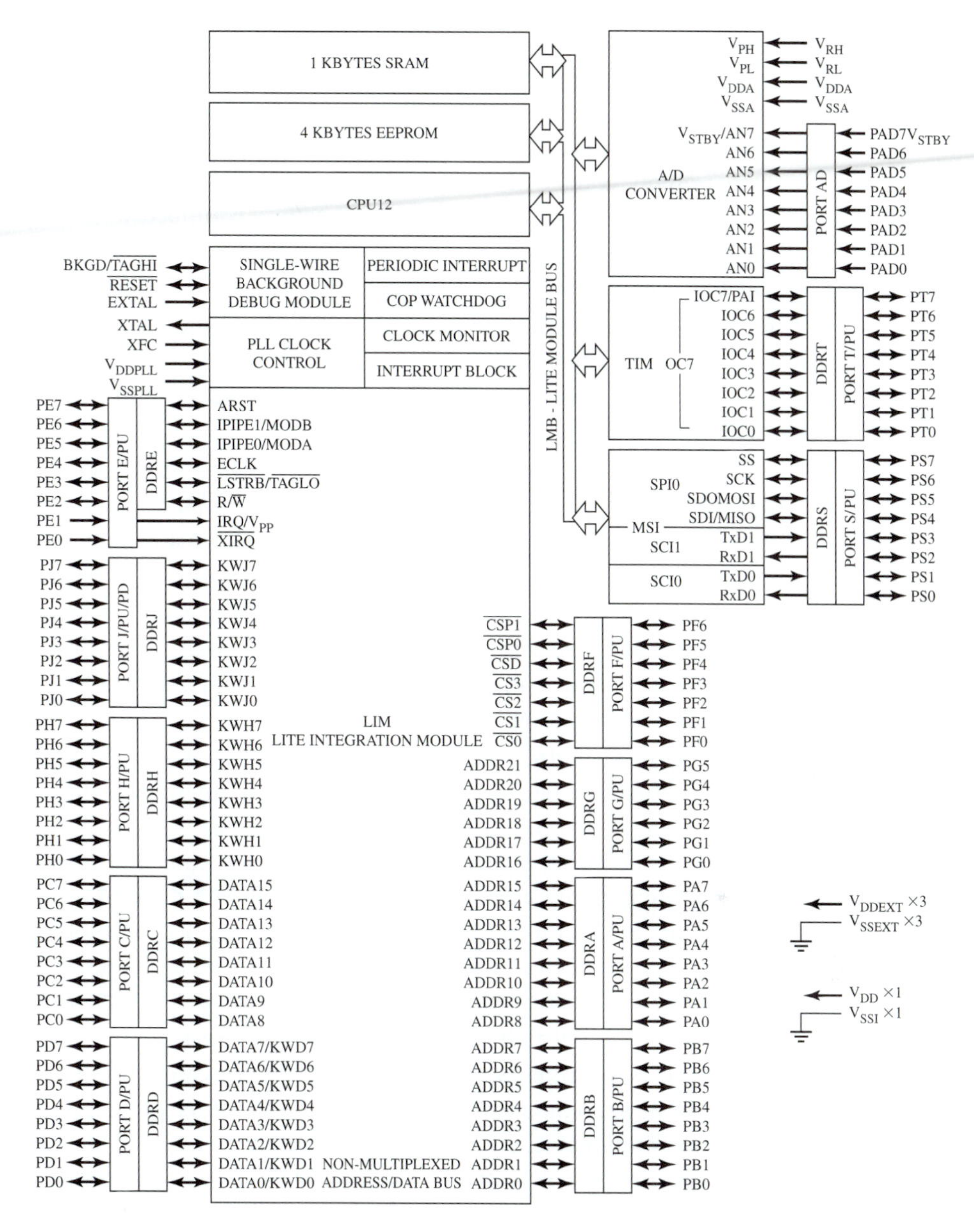

Figure 5.4 MC68HC812A4 block diagram. (Figure used with permission of Motorola, Incorporated.)

- low-power operation—The 68HC12 is manufactured with CMOS technology. CMOS is known for its low-power consumption characteristics. Therefore, the 68HC12 is ideal for remote, battery-operated applications. For example, when the A4 configured 68HC12 is operated in single-chip mode with a supply voltage of 5 volts and operated at 2 MHz, the current drain is only 25 mA. If a typical alkaline 9-volt battery equipped with a 5-volt regulator is used to power the 68HC12, the battery can last for approximately 22 hours (assuming a typical battery capacity of 550 mAH).
- high-speed 16-bit data processing unit—As previously mentioned, the 68HC12's predecessor, the 68HC11, was an eight bit microcontroller. Expansion to a 16-bit data path allows a wider range of allowable operands and two byte operation (op) codes.
- 1024-byte (1K) random access memory (RAM) on all variants—RAM is the type of memory used during program execution to temporarily store variables. A built-in 1K-byte RAM is adequate for many applications.
- electrically erasable programmable read only memory (EEPROM) and on-chip byte-erasable EEPROM–EEPROM is used to store programs on the microcontroller. We discuss PROM technology in great detail later in the book. For now, realize that electrically erasable PROM technology provides for quick and easy program update.
- nonmultiplexed address and data buses (A0 and A4)—Microcontrollers have a limited number of external pins. In some microcontrollers (like the 68HC11), a portion of the address bus and data bus were time multiplexed for efficient use of the pins. Time multiplexing means that the signals on the pins alternate between address information and data information. Although this is an efficient use of microcontroller pins, additional external circuitry is needed to demultiplex the shared information on the pins. This adds to the complexity and cost of a microcontroller system and complicates memory expansion designs and timing analysis.
- 8-channel, 16-bit timer with a programmable prescaler with each channel configurable as an input or output channel—One of the powerful features of a microcontroller is its ability to analyze the characteristics of external signals such as pulse length or the frequency and duty cycle of periodic signals and also issue signals of desired parameters. The timer system aboard the 68HC12 provides this function. It is equipped with eight different channels that can be configured to function as either an input signal analysis channel or an output signal generation channel.
- 16-bit pulse accumulator—The pulse accumulator is used to count external events. For example, we could equip our robot with a wall collision sensor and then use the pulse accumulator system to count how many times the

robot collided with the wall. This feature could be used to score the success of a robot run through the maze.

- real-time interrupt circuit—A real-time interrupt capability allows the microcontroller to suspend normal operations at specified intervals to perform another operation. For example, we could have the wall following robot sense and report its battery supply voltage every 30 seconds to ensure the batteries were not running low.
- serial communication interfaces (SCI) and serial peripheral interface (SPI)—The 68HC12 is equipped with a powerful and flexible serial communications system. This means the 68HC12 can communicate with other devices using a single channel. The primary difference between the SCI and SPI systems is the complexity of the communications interface and speed of data transmission. Aside from communications, the SPI system may be used to extend the features of the 68HC12.
- 8-channel, 8-bit analog-to-digital converters (ADC)—A microcontroller is used extensively to monitor and analyze the external environment. The ADC system allows the 68HC12 to simultaneously monitor eight different analog signals and convert them to an unsigned binary representation using an 8-bit conversion process.

With a brief overview of the 68HC12's features and subsystems complete, let us see how you are doing at applying this system information to the wall following robot requirements.

Practice Questions

Question: Given this list of microcontroller requirements to control a wall following robot, specify which subsystem of the 68HC12 would be a good choice to accomplish the following requirements:

1. A control unit to execute the program controlling all robot actions,
2. A memory system to store the control program as well as RAM used to execute the program,
3. An extensive port system to allow signals to be input to and output from the microcontroller such as signals to an LCD panel,
4. An ATD converter system to convert and process the analog signals provided by the wall sensing IR detectors,
5. A system to issue precise control signals to the DC motors controlling the wheels to execute robot movements, and
6. A communication system that would allow the robot to communicate with another robot.

Answer:
1. The 68HC12's processor and control features.
2. The 68HC12's RAM and EEPROM memory.
3. The CPU'12 port system.
4. The 68HC12's eight-channel ADC system.
5. The 68HC12's eight-channel precision timing system.
6. The 68HC12's serial communication system.

5.3 MODES OF OPERATION

The 68HC12 has eight different operating modes, divided into normal operating modes and special operating modes. In normal operating modes, some registers and bits are protected against accidental changes. Normally we do not use the 68HC12 in a special operating mode. These operating modes are commonly used in factory testing and system development. In the special modes of operation, greater access to protected control registers and bits is possible. Due to the specialized nature of these operating modes, we do not discuss them further. We concentrate on the normal modes of operation.

Each normal mode of operation has an associated memory map and external bus configuration. The specific operating mode of the 68HC12 is determined by the states of the BKGD, MODB, and MODA external pins during a processor reset. Figure 5.5 summarizes the selection and features of each operating mode.

5.3.1 Normal Operating Modes

Typically you use the 68HC12 in a normal operating mode. Three different normal operating modes are available for use. A detailed description of each normal mode

BKGD MODB MODA	Mode	Port A, B	Port C	PortD
0 0 0	special single chip mode	G.P. I/O	G.P. I/O	G.P. I/O
0 0 1	special expanded narrow mode	ADDR	DATA	G.P. I/O
0 1 0	special peripheral	ADDR	DATA	DATA
0 1 1	special expanded wide	ADDR	DATA	DATA
1 0 0	normal single chip mode	G.P. I/O	G.P. I/O	G.P. I/O
1 0 1	normal expanded narrow	ADDR	DATA	G.P. I/O
1 1 0	reserved (forced to peripheral)	—	—	—
1 1 1	normal expanded wide	ADDR	DATA	DATA

Figure 5.5 Mode selection

follows. Realizing that, to allow for a 16-bit data bus and a 16-bit address bus, some microcontroller ports normally used for I/O of signals must be sacrificed.

Normal Single-Chip Mode (BKGD: 1, MODB: 0, MODA: 0) In this mode, there are no external address and data buses. The 68HC12 operates as a stand-alone, self-contained device. That is, all program and data resources are contained on-chip. External port pins normally associated with address and data buses can be used for general-purpose I/O functions.

Normal Expanded Wide Mode (BKGD: 1, MODB: 1, MODA: 1) This is a normal mode of operation in which the expanded bus is present with a 16-bit data bus. Ports A and B are used for the 16-bit address bus. Ports C and D are used for the 16-bit data bus. This mode of operation takes full advantage of the 16-bit wide data bus features of the 68HC12. It allows for a larger range of numerical operands. Furthermore, this mode is used when a program requires more memory resources than what is available in the single-chip mode of operation.

Normal Expanded Narrow Mode (BKGD: 1, MODB: 0, MODA: 1) This is a normal mode of operation in which the expanded bus is present with an 8-bit data bus. Ports A and B are used for the 16-bit address bus. Port C is used as the data bus. In this mode, 16-bit data are presented one byte at a time, the high byte followed by the low byte. The address is automatically incremented on the second cycle. This mode is used when a program requires more memory resources than what is available in the single-chip mode of operation.

5.4 HARDWARE PIN ASSIGNMENTS

As with any integrated circuit, the 68HC12 is available in different configurations. For example, the 68HC12 A4 configuration is available in a 112-pin thin quad flat pack (TQFP). The pin assignments for this specific package are provided in Figure 5.6. The pins of the 68HC12 may be divided into several groups:

- Voltage supply or voltage reference pins. The designator for this group of pins begins with a V. These pins are used to provide power supply voltages to the 68HC12 and reference voltages for different systems within the 68HC12.
- Port pins. The designator for this group of pins begins with a P. Following the P is the designator for the function of the port pin. For example, pin PT0 is the first pin of Port T. Pins for a given port are numbered 0 to 7.

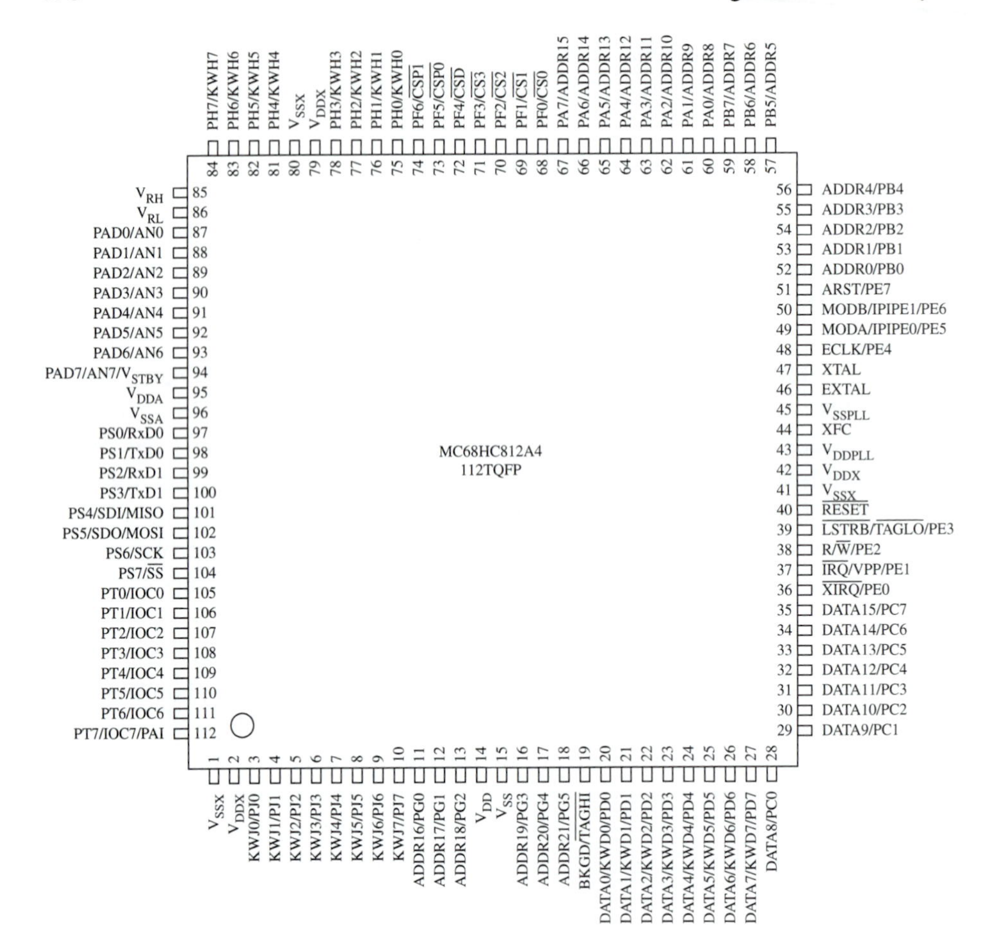

Figure 5.6 A4 pin assignments. Even with 112 pins, most pins will have two or more functions depending on the 68HC12 operating mode selected. (Figure used with permission of Motorola, Incorporated.)

- Miscellaneous pins. These pins are used to provide external signals to the 68HC12. For example, the XTAL pin allows an external crystal time base to be connected to the 68HC12.

Even with 112 pins, most pins will have two or more functions depending on the 68HC12 operating mode selected. We discuss the dual nature of these pins during our discussion of the port configuration and specific systems.

5.5 68HC12 SUBSYSTEMS

In this section, we provide additional technical detail on some of the 68HC12's features and subsystems already described.

5.5.1 Register Block

The 68HC12 is a flexible, versatile processor. It has many diverse and powerful systems. In any given application, we may or may not employ each system. The 68HC12 is equipped with a register block consisting of a 512-byte memory mapped collection of registers. It is through these registers that you configure the 68HC12. Specifically, these registers allow you to turn 68HC12 systems on and off and configure the systems for a specific application.

Memory mapped registers mean that each register has a specific memory address associated with it. This allows the user to configure the registers using memory load (e.g., LDAA) and store type instructions (e.g., STAA). To configure a specific register, the user must examine each and every bit of the register to determine its required setting. With the setting determined, the setting value is sent to the specific register using a memory store type instruction. The user must also communicate to the 68HC12 the address location of each register that is used in a given application. This is accomplished using assembler directives. The directives use an "EQU" to associate a register name label with its memory address.

Example

The ATDCTL2 register is located at memory address $0062. This register is used to power up the analog-to-digital (ATD) conversion system. It is also used to control some of the flags and interrupts associated with the ATD system. Bit 7 of ATDCTL2 is the on/off switch for the ATD system. This bit, called ATD Powerup Bit or ADPU, is reset to 0 after the processor is reset. To power up the ATD system, this bit must be set to "1." To configure the ATDCTL2 register to power up the ATD system, the following code may be used.

```
;------------------------------------
;MAIN PROGRAM ;
;------------------------------------
ATDCTL2   EQU    $0062       ;addr of ATDCTL2
ATD_INI   EQU    $80         ;bit config to power up ATD

          LDAA   #ATD_INI    ;load ATD startup mask to accum A
          STAA   ATDCTL2     ;store ATD startup mask to ATDCTL2
          :
```

The first line of code is an assembler directive equating the register label "ATD-CTL2" to the hexadecimal number $0062. Likewise, the second line of code equates the register content label "ATD_INI" to the hexadecimal number $80. This $80 value represents the individual bit settings (1 0 0 0 0 0 0 0) for the ATDCTL2 register. The "LDAA" step uses an immediate addressing mode technique to load accumulator A with the ATD register mask value. The "STAA" step stores the ATD register mask value to the ATDCTL2 register.

This is one method of initializing registers. We provide other methods throughout the text. Realize we must specify the register location and its initial contents for each and every register that is used in a given application. (An include file may be used within a program to assign register locations.) When the 68HC12 is reset, every register is configured to default setting. These reset settings are provided as we discuss each register.

The register block normally begins at address $0000 and occupies the following 512-byte space. However, the register block can be mapped to any 2-Kbyte space within the standard 64-Kbyte address space by changing the bits in the INITRG register. The register block occupies the first 512 bytes of the 2-Kbyte block. If the register block is moved to a different location in memory, the relative location of a specific register within the block remains fixed. A listing of all registers called the *Register Map* is contained in Appendix B.

5.5.2 Port System

The 68HC12 employs an extensive port system to exchange data and control signals with the external environment. A port is an input register, an output register, or a configurable I/O register that has been assigned a memory address. The port system also has complex hardware that connects a physical pin to a particular control register. The ports are accessed through port registers within the register block. Like the registers just discussed, the port address must be specified to the 68HC12 using the equate (EQU) directive. Data are sent out via a port by first loading it to an accumulator and then storing it to the memory address associated with the given port.

A bidirectional port, such as Port C, may be configured as either an input or output port. To provide complete flexibility, each bit within the port may be separately configured for input or output duties. This is accomplished by setting specific bits within the data direction register associated with the configurable ports. A logic "0" sets a specific port bit as an input, whereas, a "1" configures the specific port pin as an output.

Example

This example shows how to configure Port C with eight output pins and then output a $62.

```
;-------------------------------
;MAIN PROGRAM ;
;-------------------------------
DDRC       EQU     $0006       ;addr of DDRC register
DDRC_INI   EQU     $FF         ;input/output settings
PORTC      EQU     $0004       ;addr of PORTC

           LDAA    #DDRC_INI   ;load DDRC mask to accum A
           STAA    DDRC        ;configure port C with 8 output pins
             :
           LDAA    #62         ;load value to accumulator A
           STAA    PORTC       ;sends 62 data out on PORTC
             :
```

Example

What value must be loaded into the DDRC to configure the odd numbered channels in Port C for input and the even numbered channels for output?

The DDRC must be set for $55.

The 68HC12 is well equipped with an extensive and flexible port system. Provided here is a brief explanation of each port. Realize that most ports have different functions depending on the operating mode of the 68HC12.

- **Port A** Port A is a general-purpose I/O port when the 68HC12 is operating in the Normal Single-Chip Mode. It provides external address lines ADDR[15:8] in the normal expanded modes.
- **Port B** Port B is a general-purpose I/O port when the 68HC12 is operating in the Normal Single-Chip Mode. It provides external address lines ADDR[7:0] in the normal expanded modes.
- **Port C** Port C is a general-purpose I/O port when the 68HC12 is operating in the Normal Single-Chip Mode. It provides external data bus lines DATA[15:8] in the expanded wide modes and external data bus lines DATA[15:8]/DATA[7:0] in expanded narrow modes.
- **Port D** Port D is a general-purpose I/O port when the 68HC12 is operating in the Normal Single-Chip Mode and the Normal Expanded Narrow Mode. It provides external data bus DATA[7:0] in the Normal Expanded Wide Mode. Port D also provides a key wakeup feature. The key wakeup feature of the MCU12 A4 issues a signal that will wake up the CPU when it is in the STOP or WAIT modes. A falling signal edge triggers a wakeup when Port D is used.

- **Port E** Port E pins 1 and 0 are input pins while pins 7 through 2 are configurable as input or output pins. Port E is used for mode selection, bus control signals, interrupt service request signals, or general-purpose I/O pins.
- **Port F** Port F is used for chip select when the memory is expanded and for general-purpose I/O pins.
- **Port G** Port G is used for memory expansion and general-purpose I/O pins.
- **Port H** Like Port D, Port H can be used for key wakeup functions and as a general-purpose I/O port.
- **Port J** Like Ports D and H, Port J can be used for key wakeup functions and as a general-purpose I/O port.
- **Port S** Port S is used with the serial communications interface and serial peripheral interface subsystems and as a general purpose I/O port.
- **Port T** Port T is used with the timing system and as a general-purpose I/O port.
- **Port AD** Port AD is used with the ATD converter system and as a general-purpose input port.

Practice Questions

Question: What ports are "lost" in the normal expanded wide mode?

Answer: In the normal expanded mode, Ports A and B are used for ADDR[15:8] and ADDR[7:0], respectively, Ports C and D are used for DATA[15:8] and DATA[7:0]; and Port E is used for control signals.

Question: What ports are available for general-purpose digital I/O when in the Normal Single-Chip Mode?

Answer: All of them!

Question: When a port is used for general-purpose digital I/O, how are individual pins configured for input or output?

Answer: The direction of the pin, input or output, is set with the corresponding DDRx register. A logic "0" sets a specific port bit as an input, whereas, a logic "1" configures the specific port pin as an output.

A Few More Details on Ports All I/O configurable ports have an associated Data Direction Register (DDRx).

Associated with the port system are specialized configuration registers: the PUCR register, the RDRIV register, and the PEAR register (Figure 5.7).

The Pull-Up Control Register (PUCR) provides the capability to configure the port input pins of the 68HC12 with pull-up resistors. This is an important feature

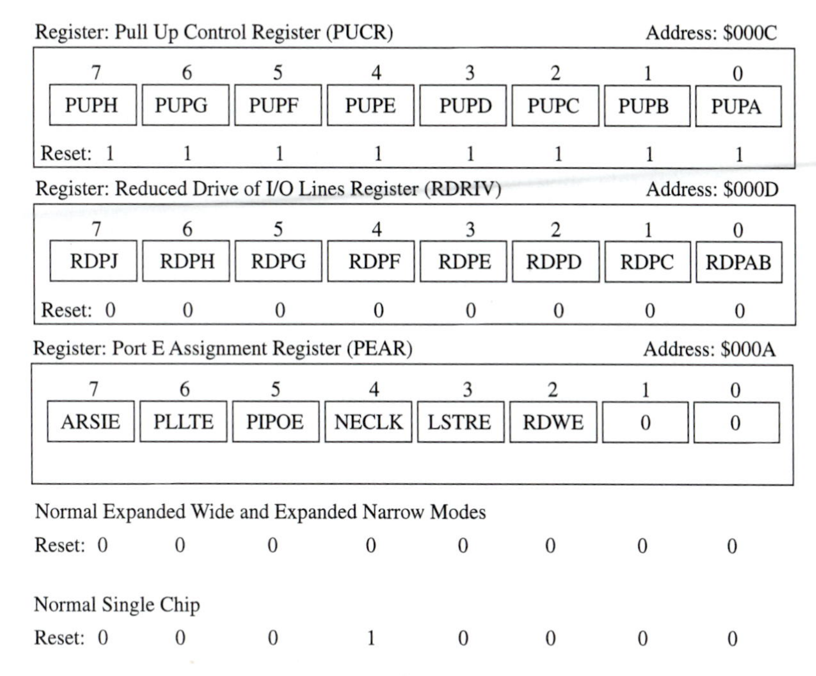

Figure 5.7 The PUCR, RDRIV and REAR registers.

for hardware interfacing. When a specific port's bit is set in the PUCR, all of the pins of that port configured for input are equipped with pull-up pins (Figure 5.7). The PUCR features are deactivated when ports are used in expanded operating modes for data and address lines.

The Reduced Drive of I/O Lines (RDRIV) register is used to reduce the drive capability of the specified port. This feature provides for reduced power consumption. Setting a "1" to the bit associated with a specific port enables the reduced drive features.

The Port E Assignment Register (PEAR) is used to choose between the general purpose I/O functions and the alternate bus control functions of Port E. When external memory is used with the 68HC12, Port E provides the control signals required by the external memory components. We investigate these features of Port E in the memory chapter.

5.5.3 The Timing System—The Standard Timer Module

The standard timer module (TIM) aboard the 68HC12 provides a precision timer system that can be configured to:

- Measure the characteristics of an input signal(s) with the input capture system,
- Generate output signal(s) to given specifications using the output compare system,
- Generate pulse width modulated (PWM) signals, and
- Count events using the 16-bit pulse accumulator.

The standard timer module consists of a 16-bit software-programmable counter driven by a prescalar. This timing system consists of eight complete 16-bit input capture/output compare channels and one 16-bit pulse accumulator. The timer can be simultaneously used for multiple and varied functions. A specific channel is configured as either an input capture or output compare channel by setting the appropriate bit in the TIOS (Timer Input Capture/Output Compare Select) register.

The input capture function is used to find the arrival time of an event external to the controller. The user specifies the type of input event to capture (rising edge, falling edge, or any edge). These input capture features may be used in a variety of ways to measure the parameters of input signals such as frequency, duty, or pulse widths. The output compare function allows the controller to generate a variety of output signals. These user-defined binary output signals may be a single pulse or a repetitive signal with a user-defined frequency and duty cycle.

The timing system also has pulse accumulator features. The pulse accumulator may be used as an event counter or to measure gate time. As an event counter, the pulse accumulator monitors how many user-defined events have occurred on a specific controller input pin. In the gate-time mode, the pulse accumulator uses an internal timing signal to determine how long an input pulse stays high or low. It is termed *gated mode* because the pulse accumulator will count the divide by 64 clock pulses while it is enabled and ceases counting while disabled. However, it maintains the last current count while it is in the disabled mode.

It is important to note that with eight independent configurable I/O channels, the 68HC12 can simultaneously generate multiple precise output signals while measuring the characteristics of multiple input signals.

Practice Questions

Question: The standard timer module consists of a 16-bit bit counter. What is the maximum count of the counter?

Answer: With 16 bits, the counter will count up to 65,535 (hexadecimal $FFFF).

Question: If the counter is incremented every microsecond, how often does the counter roll over?

Answer: The counter will roll over every 65.535 ms.

Question: If an event lasts 15 seconds, how many counts will occur if the counter is incremented every microsecond? How many times will the counter roll over?

Answer: In 15 seconds, the counter will increment 15 million times. It will roll over 228 times.

5.5.4 The Memory System

The memory system of the 68HC12 consists of the register space, RAM, and the electrically erasable programmable read only memory (EEPROM). The memory map for the 68HC12 A4 configuration is provided in Figure 5.8. However, each of these memory components can be remapped to other locations in the memory map.

A memory map is a tool to track how the available memory space is currently configured with different memory components. You can compare the memory map to plans for a new housing development. When a new housing development is planned, the available land is partitioned or platted into different home locations. In other words, the land boundaries of an individual homeowner are carefully sur-

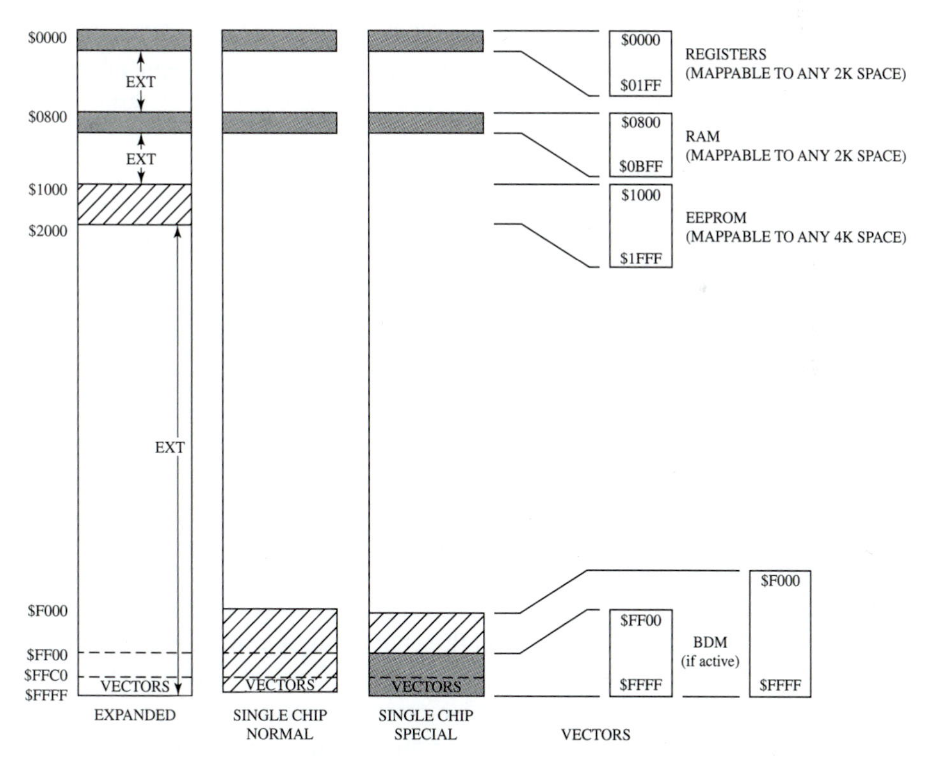

Figure 5.8 A4 memory map. (Figure used with permission of Motorola, Incorporated.)

veyed. Each land parcel within the housing development is then assigned an individual and unique address. As the homes are built, the vacant lots are converted to finished home sites. The land developer maintains a map of addresses to track lots that are currently occupied with a home and those with addresses assigned but without a home present.

The memory map is a similar memory allocation tracking device. The 68HC12 A4 variant is configured with a linearly addressable memory space of 64 Kbytes. This means the 68HC12 can access 1 of 65,536 ($2^{address\ lines}$ = number of memory locations) memory locations at a given time. These 65,536 (commonly referred to as 64-Kbytes) distinct locations may or may not be occupied with memory components. A memory map tracks the current allocation of memory components within the available memory space.

Practice Questions

Question: Reference the A4 memory map in Figure 5.8. Provide the start and stop addresses for the (1) register block, (2) internal RAM, and (3) and Background Debug Mode (BDM).

Answer: (1) $0000 to $01FF, (2) $0800 to $0BFF, and (3) $FF00 to $FFFF.

Question: You are working on an application where the program will require 6K bytes of memory space for storage. Can the 68HC12 A4 variant be used in this application?

Answer: The A4 variant in the single-chip mode does not have enough onboard EEPROM memory resources to support a 6K program. Therefore, external memory components must be used with the A4 in the expanded mode to support this application.

Memory Paging Features The 68HC12's standard, linearly addressable 64K-byte memory space may be significantly expanded using a paging scheme. The paging scheme uses three windows: the program window, the data window, and an extra window. These windows allow access to information in an expanded memory space. The memory window is much smaller than the paged memory space such that only a single page of memory may be viewed through the window at a given time. A page is a portion of memory that is enabled or disabled as a whole. Although it is available to the user as a distinct portion, each specific memory location within the page is separately addressable.

When I was a senior in high school, I took a history course on local community history. As part of the course, each student was required to extensively research and report on a topic of interest. I spent hours in the local library poring over old local newspapers stored on microfiche reels. Although the old newspaper files were voluminous, I could only view the papers through the microfiche window one newspaper page at a time. Memory paging is very similar to this illustration.

5.5.5 Interrupts

If you have ever used a laptop computer running on battery power, I am sure you have been interrupted with the most important message that your battery power is about to expire and you need to save important files immediately. This interrupt was a break in the normal use of your computer to handle a higher priority event. The 68HC12 is equipped with an extensive interrupt system. When an interrupt occurs, the 68HC12 finishes the instruction it is currently executing, stores key register values, and then performs an interrupt service routine (ISR) associated with that specific interrupt. Once the interrupt event has been serviced, the 68HC12 restores its key register values and continues processing where it left off when the interrupt event occurred.

The 68HC12 has a defined set of interrupts. Each interrupt has a 16-bit vector (memory location) associated with it (Figure 5.9). The vector points to the memory

Vector Address	Interrupt Source	CCR Mask	Local Enable	HPRIO Value to Elevate
$FFFE, $FFFF	Reset	none	none	–
$FFFC, $FFFD	COP Clock Monitor Fail Reset	none	CME, FCME	–
$FFFA, $FFFB	COP Failure Reset	none	cop rate selected	–
$FFF8, $FFF9	Unimplemented Instruction Trap	none	none	–
$FFF6, $FFF7	SWI	none	none	–
$FFF4, $FFF5	XIRQ	x bit	none	–
$FFF2, $FFF3	IRQ or Key Wake Up D	1 bit	IRQEN, KWIED(7:0)	$F2
$FFF0, $FFF1	Real Time Interrupt	1 bit	RTIE	$F0
$FFEE, $FFEF	Timer Channel 0	1 bit	TC0	$EE
$FFEC, $FFED	Timer Channel 1	1 bit	TC1	$EC
$FFEA, $FFEB	Timer Channel 2	1 bit	TC2	$EA
$FFE8, $FFE9	Timer Channel 3	1 bit	TC3	$E8
$FFF6, $FFE7	Timer Channel 4	1 bit	TC4	$E6
$FFF4, $FFE5	Timer Channel 5	1 bit	TC5	$E4
$FFF2, $FFE3	Timer Channel 6	1 bit	TC6	$E2
$FFE0, $FFE1	Timer Channel 7	1 bit	TC7	$E0
$FFDE, $FFDF	Timer Overflow	1 bit	TOI	$DE
$FFDC, $FFDD	Pulse Accumulator Overflow	1 bit	PAOVI	$DC
$FFDA, $FFDB	Pulse Accumulator Input Edge	1 bit	PAII	$DA
$FFD8, $FFD9	SPI Serial Transfer Complete	1 bit	SPI0E	$D8
$FFD6, $FFD7	SCI 0	1 bit	TIE0,TCIE0, RIE0,ILIE0	$D6
$FFD4, $FFD5	SCI 1	1 bit	TIE1,TCIE1, RIE1,ILIE1	$D4
$FFD2, $FFD3	ATD	1 bit	ADIE	$D2
$FFD0, $FFD1	Key Wakeup J (stop wakeup)	1 bit	KWIEJ(7:0)	$D0
$FFCE, $FFCF	Key Wakeup H (stop wakeup)	1 bit	KWIEH(7:0)	$CE
$FF80–$FFCD	Reserved	1 bit		$B0–$CC

Figure 5.9 Interrupt vector map. (Figure used with permission of Motorola, Incorporated.)

location where the associated ISR for that specific interrupt is located. These vectors are stored in the upper 128 bytes of the standard 64-Kbyte address map. The six highest vector addresses are used for resets and nonmaskable interrupt sources. A nonmaskable interrupt is one that cannot be turned off by the user. The remainder of the vectors are used for maskable interrupts. A maskable interrupt is under user control. All of the vectors must be initialized to point to the address of the appropriate service routine. We discuss how to write and initialize interrupt service routines later in the text.

The interrupt system of the 68HC12 allows for user-specified interrupts. For example, if you are designing a remote, battery-operated weather station, you could provide a battery voltage sensing feature that would alert the 68HC12 when the battery supply voltage was low. This low-voltage signal could be routed to the 68HC12 hardware interrupt pin ($\overline{IRQ}$). When a low-voltage condition occurred, the low voltage signal would trigger the execution of an associated interrupt service routine within the 68HC12. This interrupt service routine would then execute user-specified actions such as storing key registers and switching the 68HC12 over to a backup battery supply.

Practice Questions

Question: When an $\overline{IRQ}$ interrupt occurs, what will the 68HC12 do?

Answer: Go to memory location $FFF2 and $FFF3 to find the starting address of the associated $\overline{IRQ}$ interrupt service routine.

Question: What is the difference between a nonmaskable and maskable interrupt?

Answer: A nonmaskable interrupt is one that cannot be turned off by the user. A maskable interrupt is under user control.

5.5.6 Clock Functions

The 68HC12 is equipped with clock-generation circuitry to generate the clock signals used by the CPU, on-chip peripherals, and the external peripheral devices. (Figure 5.10). A compatible external clock signal can be applied to the EXTAL pin or the 68HC12 can generate a clock signal using an internal on-chip oscillator circuit with an external crystal or ceramic resonator. The 68HC12 uses four types of internal clock signals derived from the primary clock signal: T clocks, E clock, P clock, and M clock. The T clocks are used by the CPU, whereas, the E and P clocks are used by the bus interfaces, the serial peripheral interface (SPI) system, and the analog-to-digital (ATD) system. The M clock drives on-chip modules such as the Standard Timer Module (TIM), the Serial Communications Interface (SCI) system, and the Real Time Interrupt (RTI) system. The 68HC12 is also equipped with a phase-locked loop (PLL) system. The PLL allows the 68HC12 to run from a different time base than the incoming crystal value.

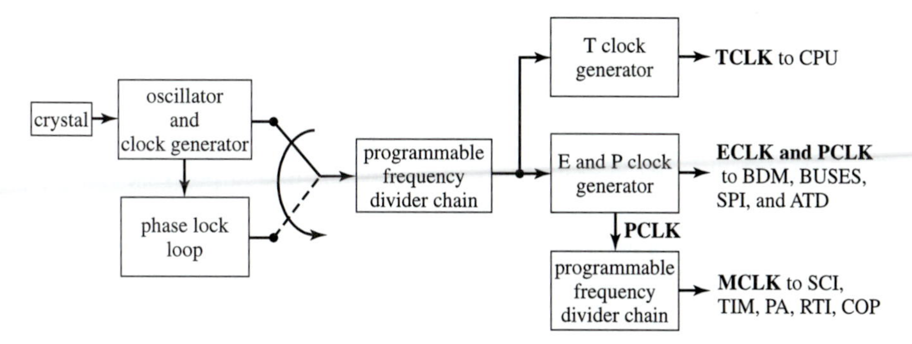

Figure 5.10 Clock module system overview. The 68HC12 uses four types of internal clock signals derived from the primary clock signal: T clocks, E clock, P clock, and M clock.

5.5.7 Serial Communications—The Multiple Serial Interface

Serial communications is an efficient method of communicating between the controller and other devices. A single transmission line is used as a communication link. Data are then sent or received a single bit at a time. Although parallel communication of data is much faster, multiple parallel transmission paths are required. The serial communication features of the 68HC12 allow for serial transmission and reception. Strict communication protocol and timing schemes must be followed to ensure reliable communications.

The 68HC12 serial communication features are provided by the multiple serial interface (MSI) module. This module consists of three independent serial I/O subsystems: two serial communication interfaces (SCIs) and the serial peripheral interface (SPI). Each serial pin shares functions with the general-purpose port pins of port S. The SCI subsystems are nonreturn to zero (NRZ) type systems that are compatible with standard RS-232 systems. The SCI allows easily configurable two-way communications. The SCI system is asynchronous. That is, it does not use a common clock to maintain synchronization between the transmitter and receiver. Synchronization is maintained by using framing bits around each transmitted character. The SPI allows the 68HC12 to communicate synchronously with peripheral devices and other microcontrollers. The SPI requires an additional clock signal to maintain synchronization between the transmitter and receiver. At the expense of the additional clock signal, the SPI may be used at much higher data rates than the SCI system. The 68HC12 SPI system can be configured to act in the master or slave mode. The master mode device controls the timing of the data transfer. The SPI system may also be used to extend the features of the 68HC12. There is a plethora of peripheral devices compatible with the SPI system.

5.5.8 The Data Conversion System—The Analog-to-Digital Converter

Most signals and physical parameters of interest vary continously with time. The 68HC12, like all digital processors, responds to and processes discrete or digital events. To bridge the gap between the analog physical world and the digital processing world, analog-to-digital converters are required.

The 68HC12 contains a powerful and flexible analog-to-digital ATD system. The ATD system is an 8-channel, 8-bit, multiplexed-input successive approximation analog-to-digital converter. The converter is accurate to $\pm$ 1 least significant bit (LSB). What does all of this mean? With an 8-channel capability, the 68HC12 can monitor and convert 8 channels of analog data at a time. A single conversion sequence consists of four or eight conversions as specified by the user. The user may also specify whether a single channel may be read (nonscan mode) or multiple channels will be sequentially scanned (scan type mode) during the ATD conversion process. There is only a single successive approximation type ATD converter within the system. Therefore, the 8 channels must be sequentially fed to the converter using a signal multiplexer. Each analog sample is converted to an 8-bit, unsigned, binary representation. The converter is accurate to $\pm$ 1 least significant bit (LSB) of the 8-bit representation. The ATD module consists of a 16-word (32-byte) memory mapped control register block used for ATD control, testing, and configuration. Like other systems already discussed, we configure the ATD system for operation by writing control words to the memory mapped registers.

5.6 APPLICATION—SWITCHES, KEYPADS, INDICATORS—OH MY!

An embedded controller is used to process data from the outside world, make decisions based on these data, and produce outputs. Often these inputs may be user-activated switches and the outputs are various types of displays. In this section, we provide a brief overview of how to interface switches, keypads, and indicators to the 68HC12. In the laboratory exercises, we provide a detailed example of how to interface a liquid crystal display (LCD) panel to the 68HC12 (Figure 5.11).

5.6.1 Input Switches

Figure 5.11(a) is a switch configuration for a momentary contact pushbutton type switch. This type of switch is used to momentarily introduce a logic "0" to an external pin of the 68HC12. When the switch is in the open position, a logic "1" is provided to the 68HC12. When the switch is depressed, the input to the 68HC12

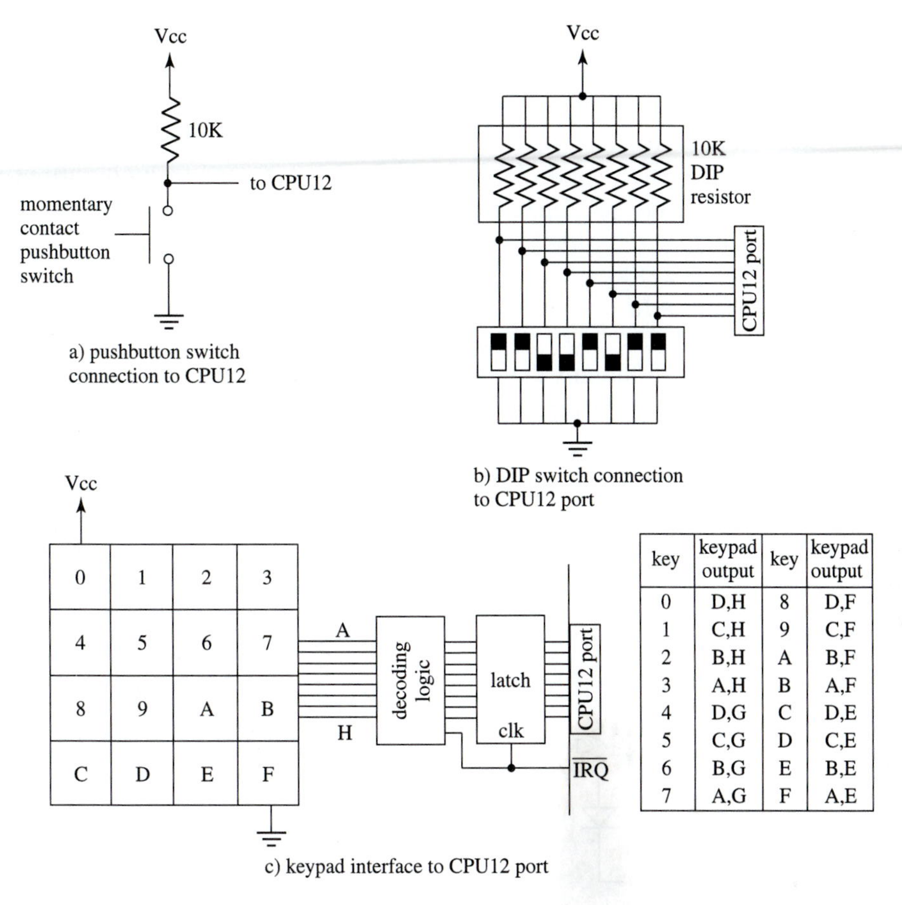

a) pushbutton switch connection to CPU12

b) DIP switch connection to CPU12 port

key	keypad output	key	keypad output
0	D,H	8	D,F
1	C,H	9	C,F
2	B,H	A	B,F
3	A,H	B	A,F
4	D,G	C	D,E
5	C,G	D	C,E
6	B,G	E	B,E
7	A,G	F	A,E

c) keypad interface to CPU12 port

Figure 5.11 Switches, keypads, and indicators.

is grounded through the switch and thus provides a logic "0." The resistor limits current flow when the switch pushbutton is depressed.

Ideally, the switch pushbutton is normally at logic high and transitions to logic low when depressed. In actual switches, the switch has a tendency to bounce. That is, due to the nonideal mechanical characteristics of the switch, the switch makes and breaks contact multiple times. Since the 68HC12 is operating in the range of MHz, it is fast enough to register these switch bounces as multiple switch open and closures. To prevent this phenomenon, switch debouncing techniques may be employed. Switches may be debounced using hardware or software techniques. To debounce a switch in software, the first switch contact is read and then a 100- to 200-ms software delay is inserted. During this short delay, switch bouncing is effectively locked out. Switch debouncing may also be accomplished using additional external hardware.

In Figure 5.11(b), we have extended this idea further to a bank of multiple switches. These switch banks are typically manufactured in a dual inline (DIP) style package. In this case, slide switches are used instead of a pushbutton switch. The individual switch inputs are connected to the individual input lines of a 68HC12 port. As before, a resistor is used to limit current. Resistors are conveniently packaged with eight resistors in a single DIP for this type of application.

5.6.2 Keypads

To introduce different values to the 68HC12, a hexadecimal keypad may be used. An example of this type of switch array is illustrated in Figure 5.11(c). These keypads are available in a wide variety of configurations. These keypads may be equipped with internal limiting resistors such that only a 5-volt supply and a

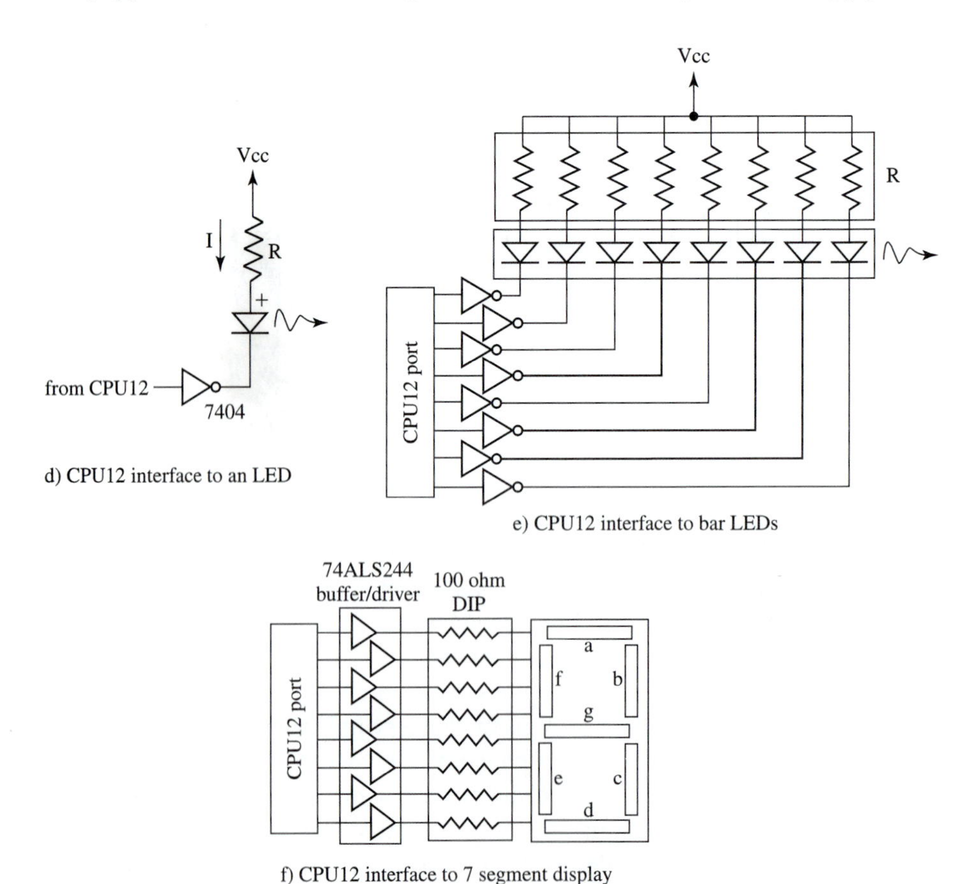

d) CPU12 interface to an LED

e) CPU12 interface to bar LEDs

f) CPU12 interface to 7 segment display

Figure 5.11 (continued)

ground connection are required. The keypad is interfaced to the 68HC12 via pins on the back of the switch panel. These keypad pins are routed to the input pins of a 68HC12 port via decoding logic and also a latch. Figure 5.11(c) indicates which pins of the keypad will be at logic high when the keypad is depressed. These keypad values may be converted to usable (e.g., ASCII [American Standard Code for Information Interchange]) values using combinational logic external to the 68HC12 or they may be converted in software by a user-written program. The combinational logic may be implemented in discrete combinational logic or programmable logic. The output from the keypad is only present when a keypad switch is depressed. Therefore, a latch must be used to capture the keypad value until the 68HC12 has a chance to read its value from the input port. Combinational logic is also used to generate an active low signal when a key is depressed to signal the 68HC12 via the interrupt $\overline{IRQ}$ that a key has been depressed. During the interrupt service routine, the 68HC12 reads the input port. We discuss how to implement interrupts in the next chapter.

5.6.3 Indicators—Light Emitting Diodes

It is often helpful to monitor different signals from the 68HC12 (Figure 5.11[d]). One method of monitoring a 68HC12 output pin is with a light emitting diode (LED). These indicators are now available in a multitude of colors (red, green, yellow, blue, white, and orange) and intensities. These LEDs typically have a low-power requirement coupled with long lifetime characteristics. The LED has two leads: anode (+) and cathode (−). The LED must be forward biased for illumination.

The LED has two specifications: (1) forward voltage drop, and (2) operating current. Both of these specifications must be met to illuminate the LED. A typical value of forward voltage drop for an LED is 1.5 volts, whereas a typical value of operating current is 15 mA. When an LED is connected to the 68HC12, great care must be taken to ensure that a limiting resistor is used to maintain current through the LED to a safe operating level. Furthermore, the device the LED is connected to must also be rated at a current value consistent with the operating current of the LED. To establish a forward bias, the voltage of the anode must be higher than the cathode by the forward voltage parameter of the diode.

We discuss the electrical characteristics of the 68HC12 in great detail in the memory chapter. For now, we are interested in the current specification I_{OL}. This is the current that the 68HC12 can safely sink (current into 68HC12 pin). The electrical specifications provided by Motorola indicate the maximum current per pin is ±25 mA per pin. However, the device is not guaranteed to operate properly at these maximum ratings. Therefore, another logic family (e.g., the 74xx) with sufficient current sink capability is used as an intermediate interface between the 68HC12 and the LED. The 74xx family has an I_{OL} value of 16 mA.

The configuration to equip a 68HC12 with an LED indicator is illustrated in Figure 5.11(d). When a logic high is presented on the 68HC12 output pin, the inverter (7404) inverts the logic high to a logic low. Current flows from the power supply (5 VDC) through the current limiting resistor, R, and the LED to the output pin of the inverter. The LED then illuminates. However, when a logic low is present on the 68HC12 output pin, there is not a sufficient potential difference between the logic high of the inverter and the supply voltage to satisfy the forward voltage drop requirement of the LED, and hence the LED does not illuminate.

Example

> To calculate the value of resistance R to limit the current I to the operating current of the LED, Ohm's Law is employed. Let us assume that the LED we use has a current rating of 15 mA and a forward voltage drop of 1.5 V. The voltage drop across the resistor is 5 V to 1.5 V, whereas the current flowing through the resistor is 15 mA. This provides a resistance value of 233 ohms. We could use a convenient value of 270 ohms as the resistor value.

As we did for switches, the basic circuit for the LED may be extended to eight bits. In fact, LEDs are readily available in a bar type display that consists of eight LEDs provided in the same DIP package (Figure 5.11[e]). We must also duplicate the limiting resistor and inverter configuration hardware. This configuration allows examination of a port's output.

5.6.4 Indicators—Seven-Segment Displays

It is often required to provide some type of an alphanumeric display. One common type of display is a seven-segment LED display. The display consists of seven individual bar LEDs configured to display decimal or even hexadecimal values. The LED segments are labeled "a" through "g" as shown in Figure 5.11(f). As with our previous discussion of LEDs, current through the LEDs must be limited to safe values. To illuminate a "0" on the display, segments "a" through "f" are illuminated. In Figure 5.11(f), we have used an interface chip—the 74ALS244. This chip provides the necessary drive current to illuminate the individual segments. A 100-ohm limiting resistor is used to limit current to a safe value. In this example, we have used a common cathode (CC) display. The "CC" designator indicates that all of the cathodes (negative leads) of all LEDs in the display share a common pin. Seven-segment display are also available in common anode (CA) configurations.

5.6.5 Programming Switches and Indicators

In Figure 5.11, we illustrated various configurations on interfacing input switches and output displays to the 68HC12. In this section, we discuss how to program these interfaces. In Figure 5.11(a), the pushbutton switch is usually interfaced to the 68HC12 via an interrupt input such as the $\overline{IRQ}$. We discuss how to do this in the next chapter. To read the position of the DIP switches connected to a 68HC12 port (Figure 5.11[b]), standard memory reference instructions are used.

Example

An eight-position DIP switch is connected to Port A of the 68HC12. Provide the code to read the position of the DIP switches.

```
PORTA     EQU    $0000      ;Port A address
DDRA      EQU    $0002      ;Data Direction A Register address
INMASK    EQU    $00        ;set port for input

          LDAA   #INMASK    ;configure Port A for input
          STAA   DDRA       ;
            :
          LDAA   PORTA      ;read position of DIP switches
```

An interface for various light emitting diode (LED) interfaces is provided in Figures 5.11 (d)–(f). The assembly code to activate an LED connected to a port is very similar to that provided for reading the DIP switches. We provide the code example to activate a bar LED.

Example

An eight-position bar LED is connected to Port B of the 68HC12. Provide the code to illuminate the LEDs at the odd numbered bit locations in the port.

```
PORTB     EQU    $0001       ;Port B address
DDRB      EQU    $0003       ;Data Direction B Register address
OUTMASK   EQU    $FF         ;set port for output
LITEMASK  EQU    $AA         ;mask to light odd numbered bits

          LDAA   #OUTMASK    ;configure Port B for output
          STAA   DDRB        ;
            :
          LDAA   #LITEMASK   ;load mask to illuminate odd bits
          STAA   PORTB       ;illuminate odd bits Port B
```

5.7 APPLICATION—WALL FOLLOWING ROBOT

At the beginning of this chapter, we introduced the wall following robot project. Throughout the book, we have been using the wall following robot project to illustrate and apply concepts learned in the chapter. On completion of this book, you will be able to construct and program a navigable robot. Different concepts that are covered include:

- program a motor speed profile to start, move, and stop the robot;
- program a right and left turn;
- program forward and reverse movements;
- sense and respond to wall obstacles;
- program pulse width modulation motor speed control;
- interface the 68HC12 to a liquid crystal display (LCD) status monitor;
- interface the 68HC12 to the motor driver integrated circuits; and
- use top–down design techniques to implement an overall navigation system for the robot.

Now that we have learned the necessary software tools in previous chapters and have a background on the 68HC12 hardware systems from this chapter, we learn in upcoming chapters how to program the 68HC12 hardware component subsystems to perform the list of wall following robot functions.

5.8 LABORATORY APPLICATION

LABORATORY EXERCISE: CONNECTING TO THE OUTSIDE WORLD—BASIC EXTERNAL DEVICE INTERFACE

Purpose This lab is designed to assist you in learning how to use the 68HC12 I/O ports along with the polling scheme. The polling technique (a method to wait for an event to occur using a loop programming construct) can be used to interface a microcontroller with external devices. In this lab, you apply the technique to interact with the 68HC12 using a pushbutton switch. The technique you learned in this lab can later be used in the final lab to activate your mobile robot with a pushbutton.

Prelab Draw a flowchart or write a pseudocode for the lab.

Description Modify your program from Laboratory Exercise B in Chapter 3 to:

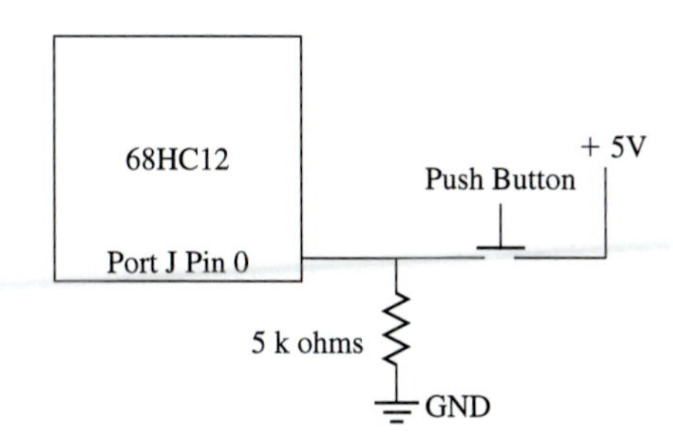

Figure 5.12 Connecting a pushbutton switch with the 68HC12EVB.

1. Wait until the pushbutton is pressed to carry out computations. When the pushbutton is pushed (the switch is closed), the program should display a simple message acknowledging the event (the switch is closed) followed by an audible beep. [Note: Use the D-12Bug subroutines.]
2. Execute Chapter 3 Laboratory Exercise B program (your program).

We now show how to connect the pushbutton to the 68HC12EVB. First, connect the pushbutton switch to port J pin 0 along with a 5K ohms pull-down resistor as shown in Figure 5.12. Note that when the switch is not pushed down, the pin receives a logic low (0) until the logic changes from low to high (0 to 1), which indicates the pushbutton switch is pressed. The port J pin, therefore, should look for an edge that changes from low to high. Your program should poll the port J pin until such an edge appears on the pin. Remember to program the pin as an input using the DDRJ register at $0029 before polling the pin.

5.9 SUMMARY

This chapter provided a brief overview of the 68HC12 hardware configuration. This chapter began with an overview of the wall following robot project to set the stage for required microcontroller hardware features. Short sections described each of the hardware systems: timing system, memory system, interrupts and resets, serial communications, port system, and the data conversion system. The chapter concluded with an overview of the navigable robot projects to follow. More detailed information on the different 68HC12 hardware systems is contained in later chapters. In these chapters, we provide considerable tutorial information, discussions of theory of subsystem operation, instruction on programming the subsystem, and application examples to real-world systems.

5.10 CHAPTER PROBLEMS

Fundamental

1. Sketch a block diagram of the 68HC12 A4 architecture. Briefly describe the function of each A4 subsystem.
2. The 68HC12 consists of several variants. What features distinguish one variant from another?
3. Describe how ports A through D are employed in the Normal Expanded Wide operating mode. How does the user place the 68HC12 in this operating mode?
4. How much memory space does the 68HC12's register block require? Where can the register block be placed in memory?
5. What is the function of Port AD?
6. What is the size of the EEPROM in the 68HC12 A4 configuration?

Advanced

1. What is the difference between a maskable and nonmaskable interrupt? Which has a higher priority?
2. What is an interrupt? Briefly explain how the 68HC12 responds to an interrupt.
3. What is the accuracy of the 68HC12's ATD converter system?
4. Applying the information you have learned in this chapter, draw a block diagram of the navigating robot control system. Your diagram should specify in detail how the 68HC12 will communicate with the robot's motors and wall detection system.
5. What is the purpose of the data direction registers?
6. Design a LED interface for the 68HC12 for a bright white LED that has a forward voltage drop of 2.2 volts and an operating current of 15 mA.
7. The standard timer module consists of a 16-bit bit counter. What is the maximum count of the counter?
8. If the counter is incremented every two microseconds, how often does the counter roll over?
9. If an event lasts 15 seconds, how many counts will occur if the counter is incremented every two microseconds? How many times will the counter roll over? Assuming the counter originally started at $0000, what will be the count on the counter when the 15 seconds has expired?
10. Repeat the question above assuming the counter started at $102F.

Challenging

1. You have been tasked by your employer (Weather Associates International) to develop a remote weather station (Figure 5.13). These remote weather stations are placed

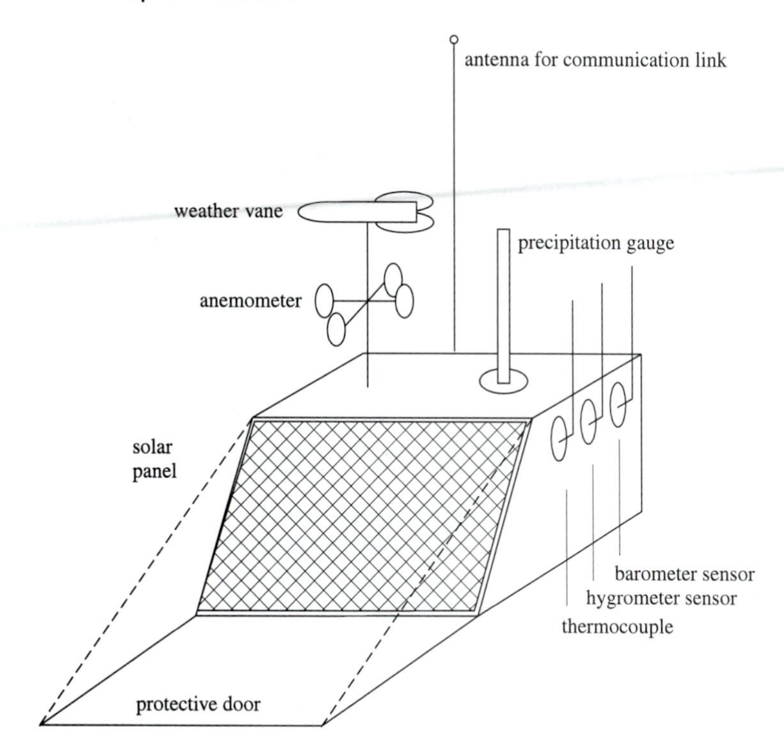

Figure 5.13 Remote weather station.

throughout the region and report back to a central facility. The weather station is equipped with the following weather instruments:

- anemometer—The anemometer provides information on wind velocity. It consists of four wind-catching cups attached to a rotating spindle. The anemometer you will be using provides a 5-volt pulse every time it completes a revolution.
- barometer—The barometer you will be using provides a signal that ranges from 0 to 5 volts depending on the sensed barometric pressure. It provides a 0-volt output for 64 cm of mercury and 5 volts for 81 cm of mercury. For values between these two extremes, there is a linear relationship between output voltage and barometric pressure.
- hygrometer—A hygrometer senses relative humidity. The hygrometer provides a signal that ranges from 0 to 5 volts depending on the sensed atmospheric humidity. It provides a 0-volt output for 0% relative humidity and 5 volts for 100% relative humidity. For values between these two extremes, there is a linear relationship between output voltage and relative humidity.

- rain gauge—The rain gauge measures the amount of precipitation present. The rain gauge you will be using provides 20 millivolts of output for each centimeter of accumulated precipitation.
- thermocouple—A thermocouple is a temperature sensor. The thermocouple you will be using provides a 0-volt output for −50 degrees centigrade and a 5-volt output for +120 degrees centigrade. For values between these two extremes, there is a linear relationship between output voltage and sensed temperature.
- weather vane—A weather vane senses wind direction. The weather vane you will be using provides a 0-volt output when it is pointing north. As the weather vane turns clockwise to the east, south, and west, the voltage increments linearly until it reaches a full-scale value of 5 volts as it completes its rotation back to north.

Further requirements for the system include:

- The remote weather station should forward weather data to the central facility at 15-minute intervals. Another engineer is designing the communication link between the remote station and the central facility. You are required to provide the weather parameters serially to the communication link at regular intervals.
- If wind speed exceeds a critical value (yet to be determined), motor-controlled doors on the remote station will close.
- You must have the ability to periodically empty the rain gauge.
- Aside from providing the weather data to the serial communication link, key weather parameters must be displayed on an LCD panel for troubleshooting purposes.
- The remote weather station must operate 24 hours per day. Normally it will operate on solar power. However, if solar activity is not sufficient, the weather station will switch over to a back up battery supply. Another engineer is designing the solar power system and backup battery supply. However, you are required to provide an interrupt service routine that will respond to low and high levels of solar activity to switch back and forth between solar and battery backup power.

Provide a block diagram of the remote weather station. Indicate which of the 68HC12 subsystems and features are employed to control and collect data for the remote weather station.

6

Exceptions—Resets and Interrupts

Objectives: At the completion of this chapter you will be able to:

- Explain the need for a microcontroller interrupt system,
- Compare and contrast the polling method versus the interrupt service routine method of responding to an exception,
- Describe and apply key terms associated with interrupt and reset features of the 68HC12,
- List the steps accomplished by the 68HC12 in servicing an interrupt,
- Describe the 68HC12 systems configured with interrupt and reset features, and
- Program the 68HC12 to accomplish an interrupt service routine.

In this chapter, we explore the requirement for and importance of interrupt and exception processing mechanisms of the 68HC12. Interrupts and exceptions are unscheduled, usually higher priority events that interrupt the normal flow of a program. Since these events are of higher priority, the processor must transition program flow from the normal program to exception processing-related tasks. Once these tasks are completed, the processor transitions program control back to the main program. We examine how all of these activities take place for a generic processor and then specifically for the 68HC12. We then investigate the exception processing system of the 68HC12 and its response to both resets and interrupts. From there we learn how to program an interrupt service routine.

6.1 OVERVIEW

Recall that our wall following robot is equipped with three infrared (IR) emitter-detector pairs to sense walls in front of and on either side of the robot. The IR emitter provides an IR beam that is projected out from the robot. This beam is reflected off the reflective maze walls and back to the IR detector. The closer the wall is to the robot, the higher the intensity of the reflected IR signal and hence the magnitude of the voltage produced by the IR detector. The analog-to-digital (ATD) converter system was used to convert the analog voltage from the IR detectors into an unsigned binary quantity that could be processed by the 68HC12.

This system worked well for the robot to navigate around an unknown maze. The disadvantage of this approach is that the 68HC12 is busy processing input signals from the three IR emitter-detector (IED) pairs when there is no wall nearby. For example, during the long, straight hallways of the maze, the robot is constantly processing IED information when there are no walls nearby (Figure 6.1). This

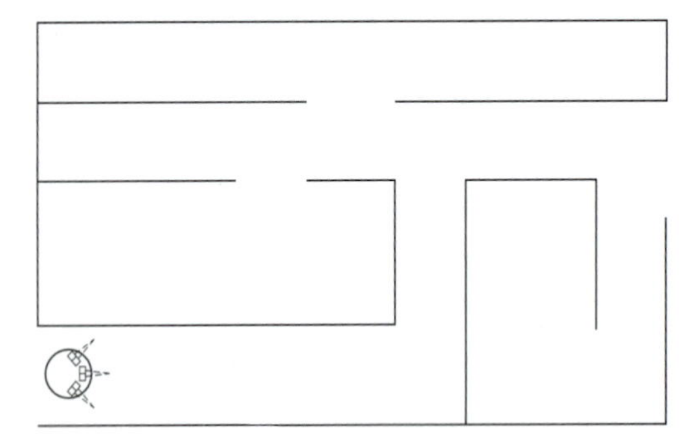

Figure 6.1 Wall sensing using an IR emitter-detector pair. The wall following robot is equipped with three IR emitter-detector pairs to sense walls in front of and on either side of the robot. An IR beam is projected from the emitter. It is reflected off the reflective maze wall and back to the detector. The polling method is used to constantly monitor the return signal from the IR detector. This 68HC12 processing time could be more efficiently used to accomplish other tasks by employing interrupt techniques as opposed to polling techniques to monitor the sensors.

68HC12 processing time could be more efficiently used to accomplish other tasks such as monitoring for the presence of other robots, evaluating the environment, and so on.

An alternative approach might be to provide more external hardware with the IED pairs (Figure 6.2). This hardware would consist of a threshold detector that would provide a logic high signal when a maze wall was at a specified distance from the robot. The threshold would be set using an external reference signal Vth. The output from the threshold detectors could be provided to an OR gate. This gate would provide a logic one signal when a maze wall or walls were in close proximity to the robot. When the threshold detector alerted the robot that a maze wall was nearby, the 68HC12 would interrupt its normal processing and determine which IED pair or pairs sensed a wall. The 68HC12 could then react to the sensed walls with the appropriate wheel turn commands. As part of its actions in response to this interrupt, the 68HC12 would need to determine which IED pair(s) sensed a wall. This could be accomplished by routing the outputs from the threshold detectors to a 68HC12 input port.

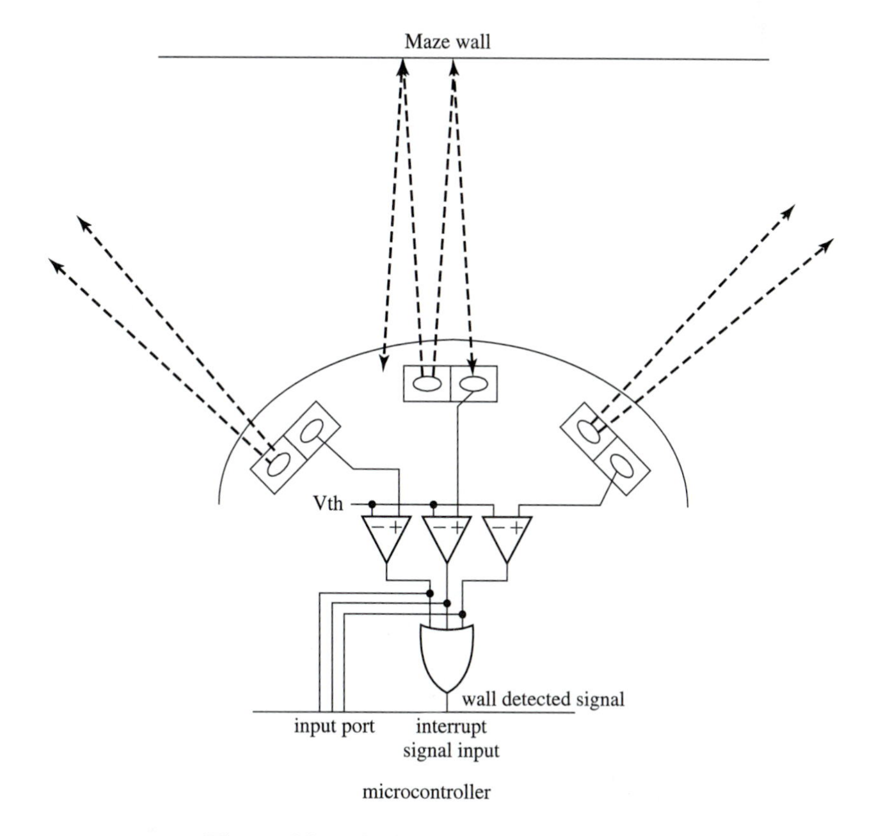

Figure 6.2 Alternative wall sensing scheme.

The remote weather station application processed signals from its multiple sensors into a binary representation suitable for processing by the 68HC12 (Figure 6.3). Recall that the remote weather station processed many analog and digital signals including: barometric pressure, humidity, precipitation, wind direction, and wind velocity. Since weather data does not change second by second, it might be adequate to collect weather data every 15 minutes from the various sensors and transmit the data from the remote site to the central collection facility. To conserve power, it might be advisable to power down the ATD conversion system between data-collection events. Every 15 minutes, the 68HC12 could be alerted (interrupted) to power up the ATD system, collect the data, transmit the data, power down the ATD, and wait for the next data-collection event. If during one of the data-collection events a low battery power condition occurred, the remote weather station could interrupt the data-collection event to respond to this higher priority task (an interrupt within an interrupt). The 68HC12 could activate circuitry to switch over to a back-up battery supply.

Both the wall following robot and the remote weather station microcontroller will be operating in noisy environments. For example, motors are notorious noise

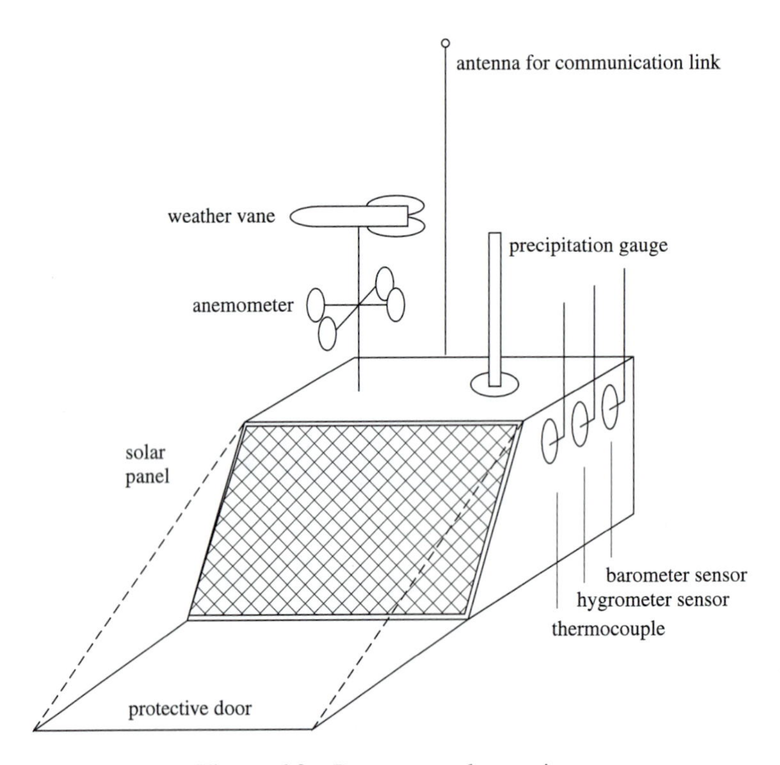

Figure 6.3 Remote weather station.

sources. The motors powering the robot's wheels could possibly inject noise into the microcontroller. Lightning is also a notorious noise source. Lightning in close proximity to our remote weather station could inject noise into the microcontroller. The noise could have spurious effects on program operation. For example, if it threw off the value in the program counter, the program counter could be starting the "fetch-decode-execute" cycle in the middle of an instruction. The 68HC12 has the capability to detect this type of a problem through the "Unimplemented Instruction Trap" interrupt. We could monitor how many of these occur in a specific time period. If too many occur, indicating a noise source is nearby, we could have the 68HC12 trigger a reset event through the external $\overline{RESET}$. This would cause the microcontroller to reset and place the microcontroller in a well-defined, default startup condition.

In this chapter we discuss in detail exactly how to handle such exception events. These exception events are referred to as interrupts and resets.

Practice Questions

Question: Why is an interrupt more efficient than polling?

Answer: In polling, the processor is tied up waiting for an event to occur. In an interrupt environment, the event signals the processor when it occurs.

Question: Discuss the advantages and disadvantages of using hardware versus software threshold detectors as illustrated in Figure 6.2.

Answer: In a software implementation, thresholds are set in software. This provides for an easy method to change the threshold that will set the sensitivity of the wall detecting hardware. In a hardware implementation, an interrupt driven algorithm is easily implemented as illustrated in Figure 6.2. The disadvantage of this implementation is the additional hardware required to implement the threshold detectors.

6.2 WHAT IS AN INTERRUPT?

Recall from our software discussion in chapters 2 and 3, the 68HC12 normally responds to program steps in an orderly fashion as specified by the programmer. The 68HC12 processes instructions in a well-defined "fetch–decode–execute" sequence. The program counter (PC) keeps track in memory of where the next program step is stored. Even when the program deviated from its normal step-by-step sequence in response to a branch or jump instruction, it was always under a controlled sequence of events.

In the real world, exceptions may occur to break out of this orderly flow of events. For example, the 68HC12 may sense high-priority software or hardware malfunctions that it must respond to before continuing lower priority, routine processing. We may also purposely configure and program the 68HC12 systems to respond to random, external events as described earlier in the robot and weather station examples.

We classify a break in normal program flow as an **exception**. Exceptions may be further classified as **interrupts** or **resets**. In this chapter, we discuss in detail the interrupt and reset features of the 68HC12. We begin by discussing a processor's general response to an interrupt. We then discuss the interrupt and reset features of the 68HC12, and provide a detailed step-by-step approach on how to write an **interrupt service routine** (ISR). An ISR is the software routine executed by a processor in response to an interrupt.

6.3 GENERAL INTERRUPT RESPONSE

Before getting into the details of how a processor responds to an exception, let us review alternative software mechanisms for responding to an external event—the polling method. The polling method consists of having the processor continually ask whether an event has occurred. The event of interest is usually signaled by a flag setting indicating the event has occurred. For example, in the timing features of the 68HC12, the input capture system sets a channel flag when a user-specified event occurred. For the input capture system, the event we wait for might be a rising edge, a trailing edge, or any edge of an input signal. If the processor is kept busy checking on the status of various flags, it cannot carry out higher priority tasks. This is an inefficient use of the processor.

We can compare the polling method to teaching. For example, when I teach a new concept it is important that students fully understand the concept before I move on to more complex ideas. It would be an inefficient use of classroom time if, after completing the presentation of a new concept, I sequentially asked each student in the class if he or she understood the concept and had any questions. Instead, I rely on the students to interrupt my lecture anytime they have a question or would like additional clarification of a topic. This is the key difference between how a processor responds to an exception—polling versus interrupts. We already discussed the polling techniques in previous chapters. We now investigate the interrupt technique in great detail.

As we discuss the details of a system's response to an exception, we need to keep a few items in mind:

- Although an exception has occurred, we must provide an orderly exit from normal processing.
- We must store all key data (registers) that were in use by the program at the time of the exception.

- We must provide a smooth transition of control from the main program to the ISR.
- At the completion of the ISR, we must restore the registers to their original values at the time of the initial exception reporting.
- We must provide a smooth transition of control from the ISR back to the main program at the completion of ISR actions.

Figure 6.4 is a flowchart of the actions taken by a processor in response to an exception. Before discussing the flowchart in detail, let us briefly review stack operation. It is a key required component for interrupt processing.

The stack is a user-specified portion of random access memory (RAM) that is set aside to temporarily store variables, register contents, and so on during normal program execution. The stack top is usually defined at the last location of RAM memory. This must be done since the stack grows backward. That is, as an item is placed on the top of the stack, the stack pointer decrements. The user specifies the memory location associated with the stack top using a software command. For example, the 68HC12 uses the Load Stack Pointer (LDS) command to declare the top of the stack. This is usually accomplished at the beginning of a program requiring a stack. As items are placed on the stack using PUSH commands and extracted from the stack using PULL commands, the stack pointer value is automatically adjusted by the processor such that the stack pointer always contains the address of the last item placed on the stack. The stack is often referred to as a last-in-first-out (LIFO) register. You can see how the stack is effectively used by the processor to store key register values during execution of an interrupt service routine.

For the following paragraphs, we use the flowchart in Figure 6.4 for our discussion of exception processing. To begin, a processor that responds to interrupts must provide a stack. In some processors, this is a separate collection of registers specifically set aside to form a stack. In a microcontroller, the stack is a user-specified section of RAM memory designated by the user. After initialization of the stack, the processor's exception processing system must be enabled. This is usually accomplished with a software instruction. At the completion of these two events, the main program is processed in the normal method.

When an exception event occurs, either triggered by an internal software or hardware event or an event external to the processor, a chain of events to respond to the exception are set in motion. First, to provide for an orderly transition from the main program to the ISR, the program step currently under execution within the main program is finished. When we discuss the 68HC12 exception processing system, we see that there are certain exceptions made for an interrupt occurring during the execution of an extremely long instruction. Once the current instruction execution is complete, the interrupt system is normally disabled while the processor responds to the exception event. This prevents the processor from responding to

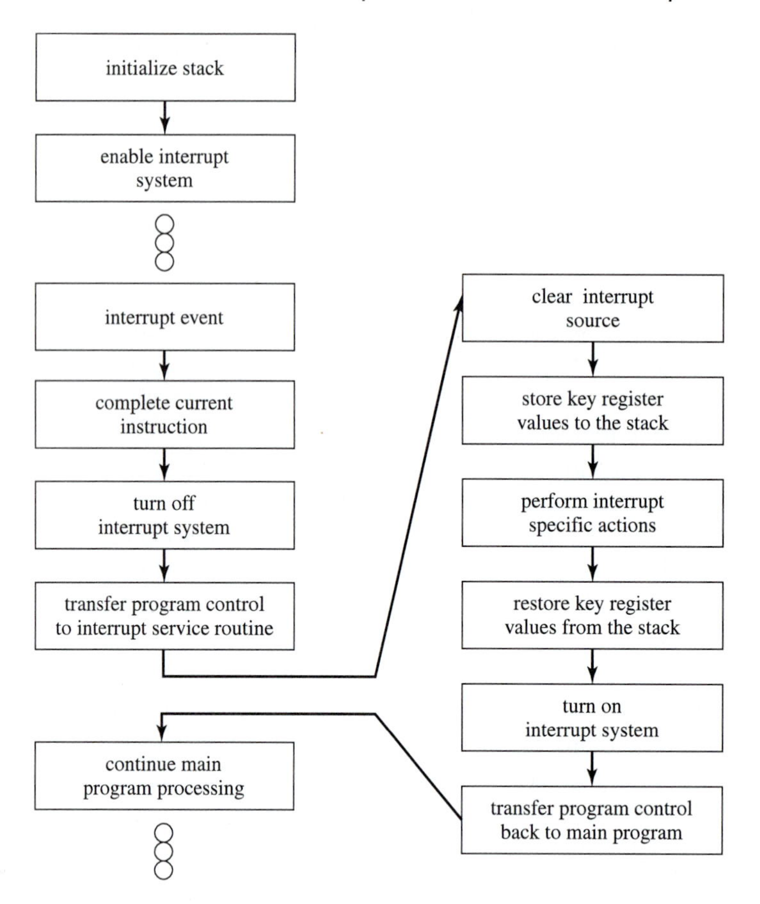

Figure 6.4 Processor response to an exception. When an exception event occurs, either triggered by an internal software or hardware event or an event external to the processor, a chain of events to respond to the exception are set in motion. The processor finishes the instruction it is currently executing, stores key register values, and then performs an interrupt service routine associated with that specific interrupt. Once the interrupt event has been serviced, the processor restores its key register values and continues processing where it left off when the interrupt event occurred.

another exception while processing an exception. The processor transfers program control from the main program to the beginning of the interrupt service routine associated with the exception. It is important to note that most processors have many different types of exception events. Associated with each of these exceptions is a specific interrupt service routine. Therefore, when an exception occurs, program control is transferred to the interrupt service routine specific to the exception event.

Before the interrupt service routine is executed, the key processor register values are automatically stored by the processor onto the stack. Key registers would include such items as accumulator registers, index registers, condition code register, and program counter. The interrupt service routine resets the event that originally caused the exception and performs exception-related tasks.

At the completion of the interrupt service routine, the key register values are pulled from the stack and restored back to the registers. The interrupt system is also enabled to respond to new sources of interrupts. Program control is then returned to the main program. The main program continues processing where it left off prior to the exception event.

With this general understanding of a processor's response to an exception event, let us explore the interrupt and reset features aboard the 68HC12. We begin by describing the interrupts and resets of the 68HC12. We then see how the 68HC12 responds to an exception event.

Practice Questions

Question: What is a stack?

Answer: A stack is a last-in-first-out (LIFO) memory construct. It is usually a portion of RAM that has been set aside for stack purposes.

Question: How is a stack employed during an interrupt event?

Answer: During an ISR, the return address back to the point of interruption and also key registers are stored on the stack.

Question: What is stored on the stack during an ISR?

Answer: Key register values are stored on the stack, such as the return address, the contents of accumulators, the contents of index registers, and the contents of CCR.

6.4 RESET AND EXCEPTION SYSTEMS ABOARD THE 68HC12

The 68HC12 is equipped with a powerful exception processing system. The exceptions that may occur in normal 68HC12 program processing may be categorized into two different subdivisions: resets and interrupts. The interrupts may be further subdivided into nonmaskable interrupts and maskable interrupts. These different categories of exceptions are illustrated in Figure 6.5. Listed under each category are the specific types of exceptions. In the following sections, we discuss each of these major categories and briefly describe the function of each exception.

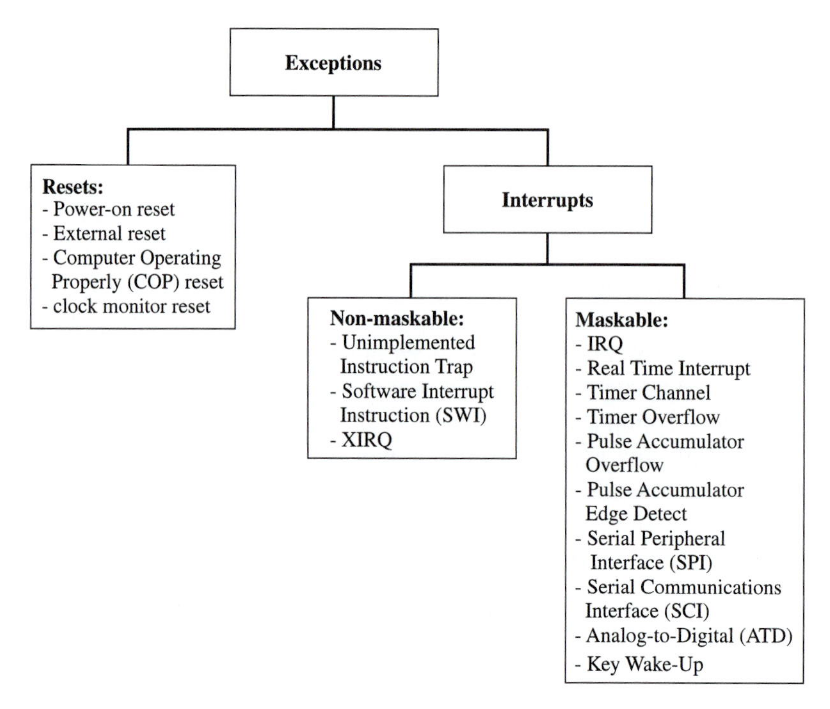

Figure 6.5 The 68HC12 exception processing system.

6.4.1 Resets

The 68HC12 performs a system reset in response to various external events or detected internal system malfunctions. Details of these events and malfunctions are provided later. When the 68HC12 detects a reset condition, it sets registers and control bits to known startup, default values. Throughout this text, we provided the register default values within the diagram for each register. The overall purpose of the system reset is to return the 68HC12 to a known, well-defined state. There are four different events that can trigger a system reset:

- *Power-on reset.* A positive transition on the V_{DD} power pin of the 68HC12 triggers a power-on reset. This feature ensures that when power is applied to the 68HC12, it starts up in a known, well-defined configuration.
- *Computer Operating Properly (COP) reset.* The COP system allows the 68HC12 to detect software execution malfunctions. Normally during software development the COP is disabled. However, it is an important safety feature once a 68HC12-based system is in full operation. Basically, the COP system consists of a user-configurable countdown timer. If the timer expires, a system reset is triggered. To prevent the timer from timing out,

it must be repeatedly reset using a timer reset sequence. Specifically, the program under execution must write a $55 followed by an $AA to the Arm/Reset COP Timer Register (COPRST) before the countdown timer times out. Should a program stall, get caught in a loop, and so forth, it is unable to generate the reset code as required and a COP reset occurs. To implement this feature effectively, the code to write a $55 to the COPRST register should be strategically placed in some major portion of code, whereas the code to write $AA should be placed in another major portion of code. Thus, should the microcontroller get stuck in one major code portion or the other, the required code sequence is not generated and the COP reset is triggered. Multiple $55 and $AA pairs may be used in a given program.

- *Clock Monitor reset.* The clock monitor reset occurs when the system clock frequency falls below a prescribed value or when it is stopped.
- *External reset.* The 68HC12 is equipped with an active low reset pin designated RESET. When this pin is driven low, a reset is triggered. On the evaluation boards (EVBs), the reset pin is handily connected to a pushbutton to allow for easy system reset during system development. This feature is similar to the CTRL-ALT-DEL key sequence in a personal computer.

When a reset is triggered by any of these events, the 68HC12 puts a reset vector (memory address) in the program counter and the processor executes a startup routine. The COP reset and clock monitor reset have their own associated reset vectors.

Clock Monitor and COP Reset Registers Two registers are associated with the Clock Monitor and Computer Operating Properly (COP) resets: the COP Control Register (COPCTL) and the Arm/Reset COP Timer Register (COPRST). These two registers are shown in Figure 6.6.

The COPCTL is used to enable/disable the clock monitor and the COP system. This register can also be used to force one of these two types of resets. Let us take a closer look by examining each bit in the COPCTL register.

- The Clock Monitor Enable (CME) bit. This bit is the on/off switch for the clock monitor system. When this bit is 0, the clock monitor reset is disabled. When set to 1, a slow or stopped clock causes a reset to occur.
- The Force Clock Monitor Enable (FCME) bit. This bit controls how the clock monitor reset function can be disabled. When set to 1, a slow or stopped clock will cause a clock reset sequence.
- The Force Clock Monitor Reset (FCM) bit. As its name implies, this bit can be used to force the 68HC12 into a clock monitor reset by setting this

Register: Computer Operating Properly Control Register (COPCTL) Address: $0016

	7	6	5	4	3	2	1	0
	CME	FCME	FCM	FCOP	DISR	CR2	CR1	CR0
Reset: (Normal)	0	0	0	0	0	1	1	1
Reset: (Special)	0	0	0	0	1	1	1	1

Register: Arm/Reset COP Timer Register (COPRST) Address: $0017

	7	6	5	4	3	2	1	0
	bit 7	bit 6	bit 5	bit 4	bit 3	bit 2	bit 1	bit 0
Reset:	0	0	0	0	0	0	0	0

CR[2:0]	Divide M by:	M = 4.0 MHz Time-out	M = 8.0 MHz Time-out
000	off	off	off
001	2^{13}	2.048 ms	1.024 ms
010	2^{15}	8.192 ms	4.096 ms
011	2^{17}	32.768 ms	16.384 ms
100	2^{19}	131.072 ms	65.536 ms
101	2^{21}	524.288 ms	262.144 ms
110	2^{22}	1.048 s	524.288 ms
111	2^{23}	2.097 s	1.048576 s

Figure 6.6 COP reset registers. These registers are used to configure the Clock Monitor and Computer Operating Correctly (COP) resets. The CR[2:0] bits are used to specify the timeout interval for the watchdog timer. The timer is reset by sending a $55 and $AA sequence to the COPRST register at regular intervals. The $55 and $AA sequence must occur repetitively at an interval shorter than the timeout interval specified by the CR[2:0] bits or a COP reset will occur.

bit to 1 (as long as the clock monitor system is not currently disabled; see DISR bit).

- Force COP Watchdog Reset (FCOP). This bit is similar in operation to the FCM bit except that it can force the 68HC12 into a COP reset (as long as the clock monitor system is not currently disabled; see DISR bit).
- The Disable Resets from COP Watchdog and Clock Monitor (DISR) bit. This bit turns off the COP and Clock Monitor reset features of the 68HC12.

- CR2, CR1, CR0 bits. The COP Watchdog Timer Rate select bits CR[2:0] are used to specify the timeout interval for the watchdog timer. Recall that the timer is reset by sending $55 and $AA sequences to the COPRST register at regular intervals. The sequence must occur repetitively at an interval shorter than the timeout interval specified by the CR[2:0] bits or a COP reset occurs.

The Arm/Reset COP Timer Register (COPRST) is used to reset the COP timeout register. As previously described, it is a two-step sequence: (1) write $55 to the COPRST register, and (2) write $AA to the COPRST register. Other instructions may be executed between these writes, but both steps must be completed in order prior to timeout. Writing any other value besides $55 or $AA causes a COP reset to occur.

Practice Questions

Question: What is the purpose of the COP reset?

Answer: The COP reset is used to detect a software lockup or malfunction. If a software error prevents the COP timer from being reset periodically, it generates a 68HC12 reset.

Question: Provide a code sequence that illustrates how the $55 and $AA reset sequence may be incorporated into a program.

Answer:

```
COPCTL   EQU   $0016      ;location of COP Control Register
COPRST   EQU   $0017      ;location of COP Timer Register
TIMEOUT  EQU   $01        ;set COP timeout for 1.024 ms

         ORG   $8000
         LDAA  #TIMEOUT   ;load timeout value
         STAA  COPCTL     ;set COP timeout value
           :
         LDAA  #$55       ;first step of reset sequence
         STAA  COPRST     ;
           :              ;
           :              ;intervening code
           :              ;
         LDAA  #$AA       ;second step of reset sequence
         STAA  COPRST     ;
```

Question: Suppose a 68HC12 based system is powered by a battery. The battery system also has the capability to automatically switch to a back-up battery when the primary battery source expires. Suppose that the power provided to the V_{DD} pin "glitches" low when the 68HC12 transitions from the primary to the back-up battery. What will happen?

Answer: The 68HC12 will experience a Power-on reset.

Question: How do you choose an appropriate COP watchdog timeout rate?

Answer: The $55 and $AA writes to the COPRST register must be strategically placed in a program to insure that the COPRST register receives the $55 $AA sequence before the timeout expires.

6.4.2 Interrupts

The other major category of exceptions in the 68HC12 is interrupts. Interrupts may be further categorized as nonmaskable and maskable. Before discussing these two types of interrupts, let us review the Condition Code Register (CCR).

In Chapter 2, we presented the programming model for the 68HC12. This programming model contained the Condition Code Register (CCR). Two of the bits in the CCR—the X and I bits—are associated with interrupts. The X controls the nonmaskable interrupts, whereas the I bit controls the maskable interrupts. These interrupt masking bits are both set to a logic 1 during system reset, which turns **off** the corresponding interrupt subsystem.

Nonmaskable Interrupts A nonmaskable interrupt as its name implies may not be turned off by the user. As mentioned earlier, the nonmaskable interrupt system is controlled by the X bit in the CCR. This bit is set to 1, turning this interrupt system off during normal system reset. However, shortly into the system initialization sequence, the X bit is set to 0, which reenables the interrupt system. There are three different types of nonmaskable interrupts:

- *Unimplemented Instruction Trap.* Every instruction in the 68HC12 has an associated numerical operation code (op-code) designator. Due to the coding scheme used for the op-codes, there are 202 unused numerical op-codes. In the event the 68HC12 tries to execute one of these unspecified op-codes, an Unimplemented Instruction Trap interrupt is triggered.
- *Software Interrupt Instruction (SWI).* The use of the SWI instruction causes a software-initiated interrupt to occur.
- *Nonmaskable Interrupt Request ($\overline{XIRQ}$).* The 68HC12 is equipped with an external pin designated $\overline{XIRQ}$. This active low pin when taken to logic low generates an interrupt event.

Maskable Interrupts Maskable interrupts may be turned on and off by the user under program control. As previously mentioned, the maskable interrupt system is normally turned off during system reset and remains off until enabled by the user within a program. The maskable interrupt system's on/off switch is the I bit in the CCR. It is turned on (by setting to logic 0) with the Clear Interrupt Mask (CLI) instruction. The system is turned off using the Set Interrupt Mask (SEI) instruction. The 68HC12 is equipped with an extensive maskable interrupt system. These interrupts are associated with the different hardware subsystems of the 68HC12. As you read over these interrupts, reflect on how each of the associated hardware subsystems may be programmed to run more efficiently with an interrupt event as opposed to a polling event. These interrupt features are discussed individually in other chapters. We provide a consolidated list with a brief description of each interrupt here for convenience. These maskable interrupts include:

- *Maskable Interrupt Request ($\overline{IRQ}$).* The 68HC12 is equipped with an external pin designated $\overline{IRQ}$. This active low pin when taken to logic low generates an interrupt event. This is the main interrupt pin used to signal an interrupt event to the 68HC12 from the outside world. Although it is only one pin, it can be used to signal multiple external exception events. This can be accomplished by tying the interrupt signals together through combinational logic. When an interrupt event occurs, the 68HC12 as part of the interrupt service routine could poll the external hardware through an input port to determine the specific source of the interrupt event. The interrupt event could then be reset through an output port.
- *Real-Time Interrupt (RTI).* The RTI generates an interrupt at a user-specified interval. This interrupt is very useful in reminding the 68HC12 to perform a regular, repetitive task such as collecting weather data every 15 minutes for our remote weather station application.
- *Timer Channel.* The Timer Channel interrupts are associated with the eight input capture/output compare timer channels. An interrupt is initiated when the user-specified event occurs on the channel. For example, if IOC channel 3 is configured to monitor for a rising edge, an interrupt is triggered when this event occurs.
- *Timer Overflow.* The heart of the Timer System is a 16-bit free-running counter. This counter rolls over for every 65,536 counts of the timer clock. The Timer Overflow interrupt may be configured to occur every time this counter rolls over. This interrupt feature is especially useful for timing long events. Rather than keep track of individual pulses with the free-running counter, we could keep track of how many times the counter rolled over. The total elapsed time of the event would be the rollover time of the counter

times the number of interrupt overflow events that had occurred plus the elapsed counts on the free running counter.

- *Pulse Accumulator Overflow.* Much like the free-running counter, the Pulse Accumulator counter has an interrupt associated with its overflow.
- *Pulse Accumulator Input Edge.* This interrupt is generated every time the user-specified pulse accumulator event occurs.
- *Serial Peripheral Interface and Serial Communications Interface.* The 68HC12 is equipped with an extensive communications system including the Serial Peripheral Interface (SPI) and the Serial Communications Interface (SCI). Associated with these communication subsystems are several interrupt events.
- *Analog-to-Digital System.* The analog-to-digital (ATD) subsystem is equipped with an interrupt to indicate when a specified ATD conversion sequence is complete.
- *Key Wake Up.* The Key Wake Up feature of the 68HC12 issues an interrupt that will *wake up* the CPU when it has been placed in the STOP or WAIT mode.

Practice Questions

Question: What is the difference between an interrupt and a reset?

Answer: Both interrupts and resets are considered exceptions. That is, they cause a break in normal program flow. A reset is usually caused by a hardware or software malfunction. When a reset occurs, the processor is restarted into a known state. An interrupt is a break in normal program flow. An interrupt may be caused by a software malfunction, an internally generated hardware or software event, or an external hardware or software event. In response to an interrupt, the processor performs an interrupt service routine specific for the interrupt that occurred.

Question: What is the difference between a nonmaskable interrupt and a maskable interrupt?

Answer: A nonmaskable interrupt may not be turned off by the user, whereas a maskable interrupt may be turned on and off by the user under program control.

Question: What is the difference between the $\overline{XIRQ}$ interrupt and the $\overline{IRQ}$ interrupt?

Answer: Both the $\overline{XIRQ}$ and $\overline{IRQ}$ interrupt systems are connected to external pins on the 68HC12. Both may be used to initiate an interrupt. The $\overline{XIRQ}$ interrupt is nonmaskable, whereas the $\overline{IRQ}$ interrupt is maskable.

Question: How is the $\overline{XIRQ}$ interrupt system enabled?

Answer: The nonmaskable interrupt system is controlled by the X bit in the CCR. This bit is set to 1, turning this interrupt system off during normal system reset. However, shortly into the system initialization sequence, the X bit is set to 0 which reenables the interrupt system.

6.4.3 Exception Vector

When an exception event occurs, the 68HC12 must be told where to begin processing the associated reset sequence for a reset or the associated interrupt service routine for an interrupt. In other words, the 68HC12 needs to know where to go in memory for the required actions in response to the exception event. This information is contained in the Interrupt Vector Map. The Interrupt Vector Map for the 68HC12 A4 variant is shown in Figure 6.7. This map is stored in the upper 128 bytes of the standard 64-Kbyte address map. This map contains useful information about the entire exception processing system. The first column provides the vector address for the interrupt. In other words, this is where the 68HC12 begins process-

Vector Address	Interrupt Source	CCR Mask	Local Enable	HPRIO Value to Elevate
$FFFE, $FFFF	Reset	none	none	–
$FFFC, $FFFD	COP Clock Monitor Fail Reset	none	CME, FCME	–
$FFFA, $FFFB	COP Fail Reset	none	cop rate selected	–
$FFF8, $FFF9	Unimplemented Instruction Trap	none	none	–
$FFF6, $FFF7	SWI	none	none	–
$FFF4, $FFF5	XIRQ	x bit	none	–
$FFF2, $FFF3	IRQ or Key Wake Up D	I bit	IRQEN, KWIED[7:0]	$F2
$FFF0, $FFF1	Real Time Interrupt	I bit	RTIE	$F0
$FFEE, $FFEF	Timer Channel 0	I bit	TC0	$EE
$FFEC, $FFED	Timer Channel 1	I bit	TC1	$EC
$FFEA, $FFEB	Timer Channel 2	I bit	TC2	$EA
$FFE8, $FFE9	Timer Channel 3	I bit	TC3	$E8
$FFE6, $FFE7	Timer Channel 4	I bit	TC4	$E6
$FFE4, $FFE5	Timer Channel 5	I bit	TC5	$E4
$FFE2, $FFE3	Timer Channel 6	I bit	TC6	$E2
$FFE0, $FFE1	Timer Channel 7	I bit	TC7	$E0
$FFDE, $FFDF	Timer Overflow	I bit	TOI	$DE
$FFDC, $FFDD	Pulse Accumulator Overflow	I bit	PAOVI	$DC
$FFDA, $FFDB	Pulse Accumulator Input Edge	I bit	PAII	$DA
$FFD8, $FFD9	SPI Serial Transfer Complete	I bit	SPI0E	$D8
$FFD6, $FFD7	SCI 0	I bit	TIE0, TCIE0, RIE0, ILIE0	$D6
$FFD4, $FFD5	SCI 1	I bit	TIE1, TCIE1, RIE1, ILIE1	$D4
$FFD2, $FFD3	ATD	I bit	ADIE	$D2
$FFD0, $FFD1	Key Wakeup J (stop wakeup)	I bit	KWIEJ[7:0]	$D0
$FFCE, $FFCF	Key Wakeup H (stop wakeup)	I bit	KWIEH[7:0]	$CE
$FF80–$FFCD	Reserved	I bit		$B0–$CC

Figure 6.7 MC68HC812A4 Interrupt vector map. When an exception event occurs, the 68HC12 must be told where to begin processing the associated reset sequence for a reset or the associated interrupt service routine for an interrupt. This information is contained in the Interrupt Vector Map. The interrupt vector map also provides the priority of a specific interrupt. (Figure used with permission of Motorola, Incorporated.)

ing the interrupt service routine for a specific interrupt event. For example, if the $\overline{IRQ}$ pin goes low, indicating that an external interrupt has occurred, the 68HC12 will go to memory location $FFF2 and $FFF3 to find the address of the beginning of the interrupt service routine associated with the $\overline{IRQ}$ interrupt. The second column indicates the source of the interrupt. The third column indicates whether the interrupt is maskable. We find out shortly that, besides enabling the overall maskable interrupt system with the I bit, we must also turn on the individual interrupt hardware with its associated enable pin. For example, to enable the $\overline{IRQ}$ interrupt, we must accomplish two tasks: (1) set the I bit in the condition code register to 0 using the CLI command, and (2) enable the $\overline{IRQ}$ by setting the IRQEN bit to a logic 1 in the Interrupt Control Register (INTCR) at memory location $001E (Figure 6.8). A similar discussion can be made for each of the maskable interrupt systems. The fourth column indicates which bit is needed to turn on the specific interrupt feature of the 68HC12.

6.4.4 Exception Priority

As you might imagine, some of the exception events are more important than others. In general, the nonmaskable interrupts are of higher priority than the maskable events. In fact, the nonmaskable interrupts are hard-wired with the following priorities:

1. Power on reset or $\overline{RESET}$ pin
2. Clock monitor reset
3. COP watchdog reset
4. Unimplemented instruction trap
5. Software Interrupt Instruction (SWI)
6. $\overline{XIRQ}$

The maskable interrupts have a priority as shown in the Interrupt Vector Map. Those higher on the map have higher priority than those appearing lower on the map. However, the priority of a maskable interrupt may be elevated by writing a specific bit sequence to the Highest Priority I Interrupt Register (HPRIO) register.

Register: Interrupt Control Register (INTCR) Address: $001E

	7	6	5	4	3	2	1	0
	IRQE	IRQEN	DLY	0	0	0	0	0
Reset:	0	1	1	0	0	0	0	0

Figure 6.8 Interrupt Control Register—INTCR ($001E).

The value that must be written to this register for a specific interrupt is reflected in the last column of the Interrupt Vector Map. The HPRIO register can only be changed when the I bit is set to logic 1, which disables the maskable interrupt system. When a maskable interrupt is elevated in priority, the remaining interrupts retain their original relative interrupt priority.

This is an important feature. For example, in our Remote Weather Station, it is very important to "batten down the hatches" in a severe weather environment to protect the station's equipment. Recall that the remote weather station is equipped with a motor-controlled door that closes under microcontroller control when severe weather threatens. This protects the solar array from damage due to blowing debris, adverse weather, and so on. Suppose we have a high-wind advisory sensor connected to Timer Channel 0. This interrupt is lower in priority than the IRQ or the RTI interrupts. Due to the critical nature of this interrupt, we could boost its priority using the procedures discussed earlier. In this specific example, we would write an $EE to the HPRIO register to give the Timer Channel 0 interrupt the highest priority of the maskable interrupt types.

Practice Questions

Question: What value must be written to the Highest Priority I Interrupt Register (HPRIO) to boost the priority of the Serial Communication Interface (SCI) 0 interrupt?

Answer: The value $D6 must be loaded into the HPRIO register.

Question: Provide the assembly code to accomplish this.

Answer:

```
HPRIO   EQU     $001F   ;Highest Priority I Interrupt register

        LDAA    #$D6    ;interrupt boost code for SCI0
        STAA    HPRIO   ;
```

Question: Referring to the previous question, what effect will this action have on the nonmaskable interrupt priorities? the maskable interrupt priorities?

Answer: This will have no effect on the nonmaskable interrupt priorities. However, the maskable interrupts are shifted down one level of priority.

Question: What actions are required after a reset event to place the $\overline{IRQ}$ maskable interrupt at the highest possible maskable interrupt level?

Answer: None. After a reset, the $\overline{IRQ}$ maskable interrupt is placed at the highest possible maskable interrupt level.

6.4.5 Interrupt System-Associated Registers

There are two 68HC12 registers associated with the 68HC12 interrupt system: the Interrupt Control Register (INTCR) and the Highest Priority I Interrupt Register (HPRIO). The INTCR is used to enable the maskable interrupt $\overline{IRQ}$ (Figure 6.8). This is a two-step process. Maskable interrupts must first be enabled using the Clear Interrupt Mask (CLI) command and then the individual maskable interrupt system must be enabled. For the $\overline{IRQ}$ interrupt, this is accomplished by setting bit 6, the External $\overline{IRQ}$ Enable (IRQEN) bit to a logic 1. Bit 7 of the INTCR register is the $\overline{IRQ}$ Select Edge Sensitive Only (IRQE) bit. When this bit is set to logic 0, the $\overline{IRQ}$ pin is configured for low-level recognition. When this bit is set to logic 1, the $\overline{IRQ}$ pin responds only to falling edges.

As mentioned previously, the Highest Priority I Interrupt Register (HPRIO) is used to boost the priority of a maskable interrupt to the highest possible interrupt available for maskable types (Figure 6.9). The register is configured with values from the right column of Figure 6.7 to boost the priority of the corresponding interrupt. For example, to boost the priority of the Timer Overflow register, the value $DE is written to the HPRIO register. Note that the reset value for this register is $F2. As expected, this gives the $\overline{IRQ}$ interrupt the highest priority for maskable interrupts.

6.5 HOW DOES 68HC12 RESPOND TO AN INTERRUPT?

Figure 6.10 is a chart detailing the 68HC12's actions in responding to an interrupt. Take a few minutes and study the chart in detail. If the chart seems familiar to you, it is because it is almost identical to the flowchart provided earlier in Figure 6.4. Let us work our way through the diagram to gain an understanding of how the 68HC12 responds and processes an interrupt. Pay close attention to the steps that you the user must accomplish versus those that are automatically accomplished by the 68HC12. (We will quiz you on this shortly!)

To begin, the interrupt vector table must be initiated with the memory address of the first location of the associated interrupt service routine (ISR). Rather than use

Register: Highest Priority I Interrupt (HPRIO) Address: $001F

	7	6	5	4	3	2	1	0
	1	1	PSEL5	PSEL4	PSEL3	PSEL2	PSEL1	0
Reset:	1	1	1	1	0	0	1	0

Figure 6.9 Highest Priority I Interrupt Register—HPRIO ($001F).

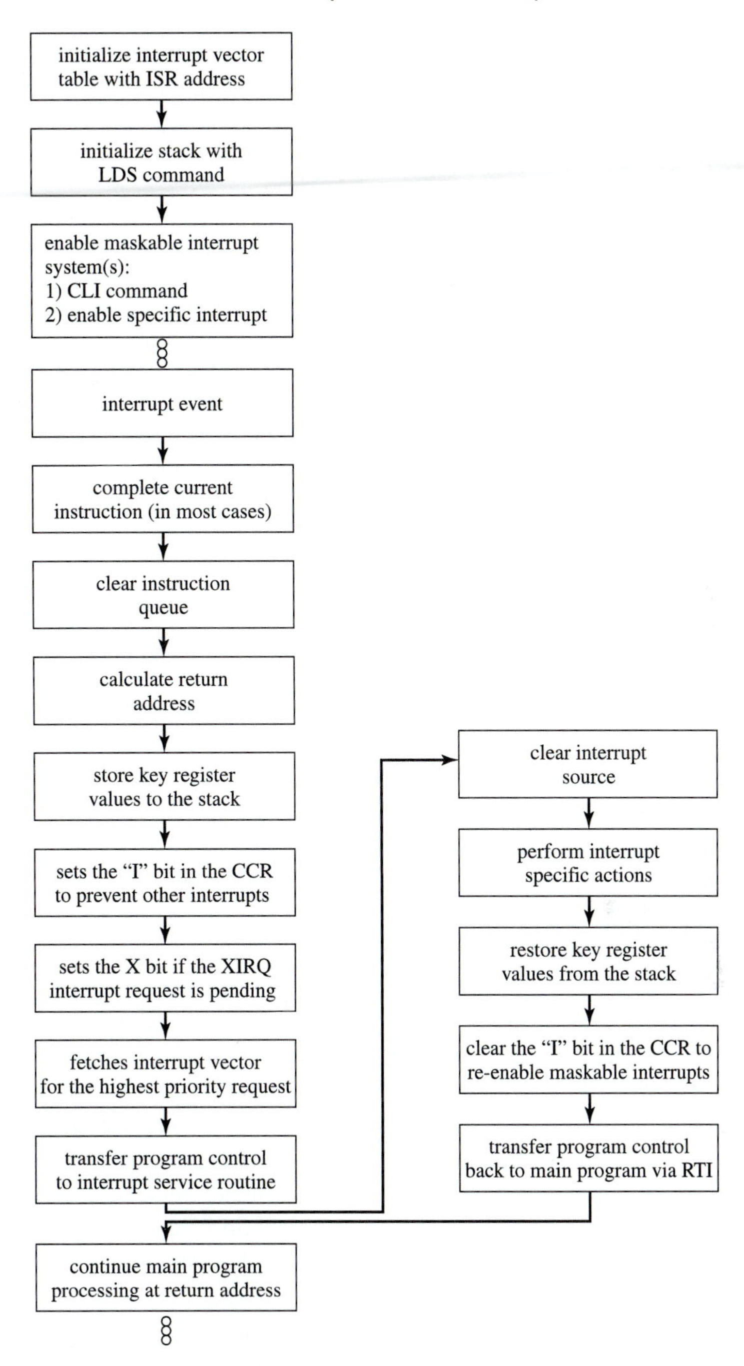

Figure 6.10 68HC12 response to an interrupt.

numerical memory addresses, memory labels are used to specify the beginning of the ISR. This is usually accomplished using assembler directives. For example, the following code fragment associates the label "IRQ_INT" with the dedicated vector for the $\overline{IRQ}$ interrupt.

```
ORG    $FFF2          ;address of IRQ vector
FDB    IRQ_INT        ;name of IRQ ISR
```

A program containing an interrupt must have the stack pointer initialized. As mentioned earlier in this chapter, the stack is where the 68HC12 stores key register values while an interrupt service routine is being processed. The stack pointer is initialized using the Load Stack Pointer (LDS) command.

Next the maskable interrupt system (if it is to be used) must be enabled. This is a two-step process. First, the overall maskable interrupt system must be enabled by setting the I bit in the Condition Code Register to a logic 0. This is accomplished with the CLI command. Second, the enable bit associated with the specific interrupt system must be enabled. Recall that the enable bits associated with each hardware interrupt system was provided in Figure 6.7.

With the stack declared and the maskable interrupt system enabled, the main program may be written as normal. When the interrupt event occurs, a chain reaction of events is initiated. However, if the interrupt event occurs in the middle of an instruction, the current program step in most cases is completed. This provides for an orderly transition of control from the main program to the interrupt service routine. Some of the 68HC12 commands are quite lengthy. In particular, the Fuzzy Logic Rule Evaluation (REV), the Fuzzy Logic Rule Evaluation–Weighted (REVW), and the Weighted Average (WAV) can require many clock cycles to execute. Rather than wait for these to finish, the 68HC12 has special provisions to interrupt these instructions for an interrupt event. The processing of these instructions are finished after the interrupt service routine is completed.

The 68HC12 is equipped with an instruction queue. The queue normally contains the next two instructions that are executed during normal program flow. When an interrupt occurs, the normal flow of events is no longer valid. Therefore, the instructions in the queue are useless and the queue must be emptied. After the queue is emptied, the return address back to the main program is calculated. This is usually the address of the program step after the step that was executing when the interrupt occurred. With the return address calculated, the 68HC12 stores all key register values on the stack. Accumulator A and B, Index Register X and Y, the Condition Code Register, and the return address back to the main program are stored on the stack in a specific order. Figure 6.11 illustrates how these registers are placed on the stack. It is important to note that the 68HC12 accomplishes this

Memory Location	Stacked Values
Stack Pointer - 2	Return address High: Return Address Low
Stack Pointer - 4	Index Register Y High: Index Register Y Low
Stack Pointer - 6	Index Register X High: Index Register X Low
Stack Pointer - 8	Accumulator B : Accumulator A
Stack Pointer - 9	Condition Code Register

Figure 6.11 Interrupt stacking order. The 68HC12 stores all key register values on the stack. Accumulator A and B, Index Registers X and Y, the Condition Code Register, and the return address back to the main program are stored on the stack in the specific order.

register stacking **automatically**. No code is required by the user to accomplish this task.

With the key register values stored on the stack, the 68HC12 disables the maskable interrupt system by placing a logic 1 in the Condition Code Register I bit. This prevents the 68HC12 from responding to additional interrupts that may occur during the processing of the interrupt service routine. The X bit is also set, disabling the XIRQ interrupt if an XIRQ interrupt is pending.

The 68HC12 then fetches the address associated with the specific interrupt that is active. This address, or interrupt vector, specifies the location of the beginning address of the associated interrupt service routine. Program control is now transferred to the first program step in the interrupt service routine.

In the next section, we discuss in detail how to write an interrupt service routine. In general, the interrupt service routine contains specific commands to respond to the interrupt that caused the exception. When the interrupt specific actions are complete, the 68HC12 automatically restores the key register values from the stack, clears the I bit in the Condition Code Register to reenable the maskable interrupt system, and provide for a smooth transition of control from the interrupt service routine back to the main program. These events are triggered by the Return From Interrupt (RTI) instruction, which concludes a user-written interrupt service routine. Again, no code is required by the user to accomplish this task other than placing the RTI instruction as the last instruction of the interrupt service routine.

Practice Questions

Question: Figure 6.12 shows the contents of the stack. Identify the return address to the main program if:

Question: The 68HC12 is in a subroutine called by another subroutine.
Answer: $2236.

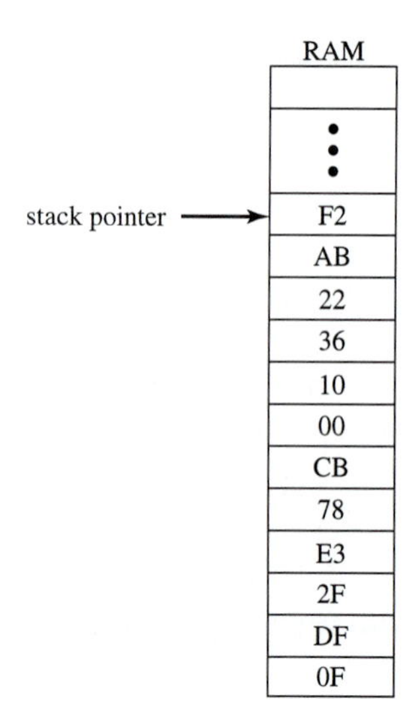

Figure 6.12 Interrupt stacking order example.

Question: The 68HC12 is in an interrupt service routine that interrupted the main program. What was the value in the X register at the time of the ISR?

Answer: $F2AB, $1000.

Question: The 68HC12 is in a subroutine that pushed both X and Y onto the stack.

Answer: $1000.

Question: The 68HC12 is in a subroutine that, prior to its call, the main program pushed two 16-bit numbers onto the stack.

Answer: $F2AB.

Question: Listed next are the 68HC12's response to an interrupt. Indicate which actions are performed automatically by the 68HC12 and which actions must be programmed by the user.

Answer:

- initialize interrupt vector table with ISR address—user
- initialize stack pointer with LDS command—user
- enable maskable interrupt system—user
- complete current instruction—68HC12
- clear instruction queue—68HC12
- calculate return address—68HC12
- store key register values on stack—68HC12
- set I bit in CCR—68HC12

- fetch interrupt vector for highest priority active interrupt—68HC12
- transfer program control to ISR—68HC12
- clear interrupt source–user/68HC12—depends on specific application
- restore key register values—68HC12
- clear the I bit in the CCR—68HC12
- transfer program control back to the main program—68HC12

Question: How does the 68HC12 determine the priority of the pending interrupt events?

Answer: The interrupt vector table sets the priority of the interrupt events.

Question: Often the Set Interrupt Mask "SEI" command is used at the beginning of a program containing interrupts. Why?

Answer: It is good practice to turn off the maskable interrupt features with the "SEI" command while the interrupt is being configured. Once configured, the maskable interrupt system is enabled with the Clear Interrupt Mask "CLI" command.

Question: Why does the 68HC12 flush the instruction queue when an interrupt occurs?

Answer: The instructions awaiting execution in the queue are no longer valid.

6.6 WRITING INTERRUPT SERVICE ROUTINES FOR THE 68HC812A4EVB

As we saw in this chapter, the vector jump table provides convenient locations to store starting addresses of interrupt service routines (ISR). The problem for a developer who uses one of the 68HC12 evaluation boards is that the vector jump table resides in an EPROM and it requires a special EPROM programmer to change the contents of the table. This can cause significant inconvenience since the system developer may find multiple occasions to change the table contents. To remedy this situation, the Motorola company implemented a special utility subroutine as a part of the D-Bug12 monitor/debugger program. This special utility subroutine, called the SetUserVector, is the focus of this section.

The SetUserVector utility routine allows a user to assign the starting address of an interrupt service routine, located in a RAM segment of the memory, in place of a default starting address. Thus, this gives a developer the ability to replace his or her own interrupt service routines in place of the D-Bug12 default interrupt service routines. To this end, the 68HC12EVB allocates a set of RAM memory locations, starting from \$0B0E, as the RAM-based interrupt vector table that corresponds to the interrupt vector table located in EPROM locations starting at \$FFCE. The RAM locations are referred to as the interrupt vector jump table or the user vector addresses—thus, the name of the subroutine is SetUserVector.

The SetUserVector is used to store the starting addresses of user interrupt service routines in the appropriate RAM locations. We illustrate the use of the subroutine with an example. Suppose we want to assign the starting address of an interrupt service routine associated with interrupts triggered by external signals on the $\overline{IRQ}$ pin.

To assign any ISR starting address, the subroutine requires two parameters: an offset value and an ISR starting address. Table 6.1 shows the offset values for all 68HC12 interrupts. The offset values for both the MC68HC812A4 and MC68HC912B32 versions are listed.

TABLE 6.1 D-BUG12 INTERRUPT OFFSETS

Offset (decimal)	MC68HC812A4	MC68HC912B32
7	Port H Key Wakeup	Not Used
8	Port J Key Wakeup	BDLC
9	A/D Converter	A/D Converter
10	SCI System 1	Not Used
11	SCI System 0	SCI System 0
12	SPI	SPI
13	Pulse Accumulator Edge	Pulse Accumulator Edge
14	Pulse Accumulator Overflow	Pulse Accumulator Overflow
15	Time Overflow	Time Overflow
16	Timer Channel 7	Timer Channel 7
17	Timer Channel 6	Timer Channel 6
18	Timer Channel 5	Timer Channel 5
19	Timer Channel 4	Timer Channel 4
20	Timer Channel 3	Timer Channel 3
21	Timer Channel 2	Timer Channel 2
22	Timer Channel 1	Timer Channel 1
23	Timer Channel 0	Timer Channel 0
24	Real-Time Interrupt	Real-Time Interrupt
25	IRQ	IRQ
26	XIRQ	XIRQ
27	Software Interrupt	Software Interrupt
28	Illegal Op-code	Illegal Op-code

Suppose further that the starting address of your interrupt service routine is at $6000. We can now change the contents of the interrupt jump vector table as shown next:

```
line 1      LDD     #$6000
line 2      PSHD
line 3      LDD     #!25
line 4      LDX     $FE1A
line 5      JSR     0,X
line 6      PULX
            ⋮
```

The first parameter, the starting address of the interrupt service routine, is passed to the subroutine by pushing the data on the stack (lines 1 and 2). The interrupt offset, !25, is passed to the subroutine as the second parameter using accumulator D in line 3. The instructions on lines 4 and 5 are used to initiate the SetUserVector subroutine, whereas the PULX instruction on line 6 adjusts the stack pointer to restore the stack condition before the subroutine was called. The assignment of user-defined starting addresses for any other interrupts is a straightforward application of the prior procedure. That is, one only needs to change the starting address (line 1 of the example) and the offset (line 3 of the example) and use the exact same code segment shown before.

When an interrupt is detected, the 68HC12 executes a D-BUG12 code to determine whether a user-assigned address appears in the interrupt vector jump table located in the RAM locations (checks the contents for $0000). If there is a user-assigned value (not $0000), then the specified starting address is loaded into the program counter and the interrupt service routine is executed. The SetUserVector subroutine provides a convenient means, especially when programs are written in C, to assign user interrupt service routine starting addresses during a system development period. Once you have completed testing, starting addresses are burned into the original EPROM locations using an EPROM programmer.

6.7 HOW TO PROGRAM AN ISR—AN EXAMPLE

The interrupt system of the 68HC12 allows for user-specified interrupts. For example, if you are designing a remote, battery-operated weather station, you could provide a battery voltage sensing feature that would alert the 68HC12 when the battery supply voltage was low. A block diagram of such a system is provided in Figure 6.13. This low-voltage signal could be routed to the 68HC12 hardware interrupt pin ($\overline{IRQ}$). When a low-voltage condition occurs the low-voltage signal

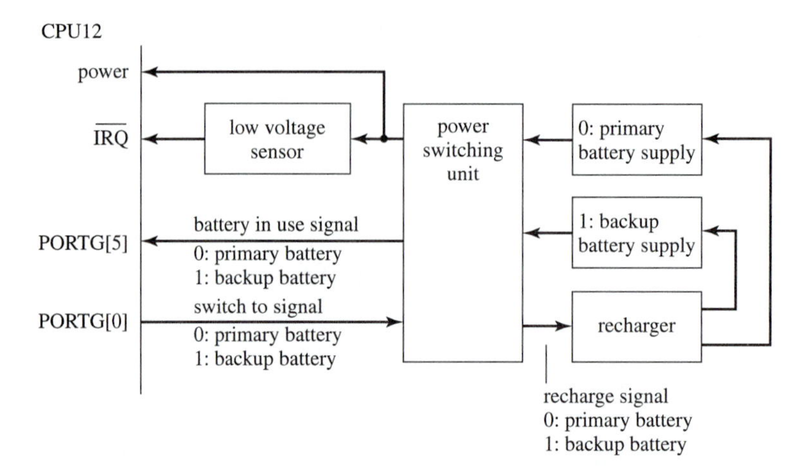

Figure 6.13 Backup power system for remote weather station.

would trigger the execution of an associated interrupt service routine within the 68HC12. This interrupt service routine would then execute user-specified actions to switch the 68HC12 over to a backup battery supply.

A low-voltage sensor is connected to the $\overline{IRQ}$ pin of the 68HC12. The $\overline{IRQ}$ system is configured to initiate an interrupt when this pin goes low. When a low-voltage condition triggers an interrupt, the $\overline{IRQ}$ interrupt service routine determines which battery is currently in use using PORTG[5] and then sends a control to switch to the alternate battery via PORTG[0]. The Power Switching Unit (PSU) provides for a transition between batteries without disrupting power to the 68HC12. The PSU also connects the battery reporting a low-voltage to the recharger unit.

Let us use this as a case study to illustrate how to write an interrupt service routine (ISR).

1. To write an ISR, you should begin by carefully reviewing the documentation on the specific interrupt that will be used. Pay particular attention to how the interrupt is enabled and reset. In our example, we use the $\overline{IRQ}$ interrupt system.
2. Next, you should initialize the vector table using assembler directives. For our example, to initialize the vector table with the address (using labels) for the $\overline{IRQ}$ maskable interrupt, use:

```
ORG   $FFF2          ;address of IRQ vector
FDB   IRQ_INT        ;name of IRQ ISR
```

3. The stack should be initialized. We recommend using the last available location in user Random Access Memory (RAM). For example, let us assume

you are using the 68HC12 in an expanded (nonpaged) memory mode. Additionally, let us assume that you have provided the expanded mode system 8K-bytes of external RAM from memory locations $2000–$3FFF. Therefore, you could declare the top of the stack with the following combinations of directives and instructions:

```
STACKTOP   EQU   $3FFF        ;equate STACKTOP with $3FFF
           LDS   #STACKTOP    ;declare stack
```

This initializes the stack pointer to $3FFF.

4. Next the maskable interrupt system and the individual interrupt must be enabled. In our example, the $\overline{IRQ}$ interrupt is enabled using two steps: (1) the global enable of all maskable interrupts using the CLI command, and (2) enabling the $\overline{IRQ}$ using the INTCR register. The INTCR register is initially set to $60. This enables the $\overline{IRQ}$ interrupt by setting the IRQEN bit to logic 1 (bit 6 in the INTCR) and sets the IRQE bit to logic 0 (bit 7 in the INTCR). Setting the IRQE bit to 0 causes the $\overline{IRQ}$ system to trigger an interrupt when a logic low signal occurs on the $\overline{IRQ}$ pin. The following code fragment accomplishes these actions:

```
INTCR       EQU   $001E       ;addr of INTCR reg
INTCR_INI   EQU   $60         ;initial value of INTCR

            LDAA  #INTCR_INI  ;load initialization values to A
            STAA  INTCR       ;initialize INTCR
            CLI               ;enable maskable interrupts
```

5. The actual ISR is now written. The ISR is written to respond specifically to the specific interrupt. We provide the ISR code for this example shortly. In general terms, the ISR consists of the ISR label, the interrupt specific code, and the Return From Interrupt (RTI) instruction. The ISR label must match the label used to initiate the vector address.

```
IRQ_INT                       ;ISR label
                              ;interrupt specific actions



            RTI               ;ISR must conclude with RTI
```

Here is the code for our battery backup system interrupt service routine. As mentioned in the problem description, we are using PORTG to determine which battery is in use (PORTG[5]) and to switch to the alternate battery (PORTG[0]). Can we use PORTC?

```
STACKTOP   EQU   $3FFF        ;equate STACKTOP with $3FFF
INTCR      EQU   $001E        ;address of INTCR register
INTCR_INI  EQU   $60          ;initial value of INTCR
DDRG       EQU   $0033        ;location of DDRG register
DDRG_INI   EQU   $01          ;PORTG[5] input, PORTG[0] output
PORTG      EQU   $0031        ;location of PORTG
PRIMARY    EQU   $00          ;test mask for primary battery
BACK_UP    EQU   $01          ;test mask for backup battery

           ORG   $FFF2        ;address of IRQ vector
           FDB   IRQ_INT      ;name of IRQ ISR
           ORG   $2000
           LDS   #STACKTOP    ;declare stack
           LDAA  #INTCR_INI   ;load initialization values to A
           STAA  INTCR        ;initialize INTCR
           LDAA  #DDRG_INI    ;load initialization values to A
           STAA  DDRG         ;initialize DDRG
           CLI                ;enable maskable interrupts



           ORG   $9000        ;interrupt service routine
IRQ_INT    LDAA  PORTG        ;determine battery in use
           ANDA  #BACK_UP     ;results in Z flag if primary
                              ;battery in use
           BNE   SWAP_BU      branch if 0 (primary in use)
           LDAA  #PRIMARY     ;swap to primary batt
           STAA  PORTG
           BRA   DONE         ;branch to DONE
SWAP_BU    LDAA  #BACK_UP     ;swap to backup batt
           STAA  PORTG        ;
DONE       RTI                ;CLI accomplished auto
```

This example may have raised some questions in your mind. For example, what if the backup battery malfunctions before the primary battery is recharged? We are letting you handle this situation as a homework problem! How is the interrupt event reset? When the system switches over successfully to the backup battery the low-voltage sensor will provide a logic high signal to the $\overline{IRQ}$ pin resetting the $\overline{IRQ}$ pin.

6.8 PROGRAMMING THE REAL-TIME INTERRUPT (RTI) SYSTEM

In the timer chapter, we briefly describe the Real-Time Interrupt (RTI) system since it is related to the 68HC12 timer system. We examine this system in detail now because it is also related to the 68HC12 interrupt system. The 68HC12 has built-in features to remind it to perform required actions on a regular basis (Figure 6.14). For example, if we would like to check the battery voltage level of our weather station, we can program the RTI system to remind the 68HC12 to check the voltage level on a regular basis. Also weather does not usually change minute by minute. It might be satisfactory to have our remote weather station collect weather data at 15 minute intervals. This too can be accomplished using the RTI features of the 68HC12.

Register: Real-Time Interrupt Control Register (RTICTL) Address: $0014

	7	6	5	4	3	2	1	0
	RTIE	RSWAI	RSBCK	0	RTBYP	RTR2	RTR1	RTR0
Reset:	0	0	0	0	0	0	0	0

Register: Real Time Interrupt Flag Register Address: $0015

	7	6	5	4	3	2	1	0
	RTIF	0	0	0	0	0	0	0
Reset:	0	0	0	0	0	0	0	0

RTR[2:0]	Divide M by:	M = 4.0 MHz Time-out	M = 8.0 MHz Time-out
000	off	off	off
001	2^{13}	2.048 ms	1.024 ms
010	2^{14}	4.096 ms	2.048 ms
011	2^{15}	8.192 ms	4.096 ms
100	2^{16}	16.384 ms	8.196 ms
101	2^{17}	32.768 ms	16.384 ms
110	2^{18}	65.536 ms	32.768 ms
111	2^{19}	131.072 ms	65.536 ms

Figure 6.14 Real-Time Interrupt (RTI) registers.

The RTI system consists of two registers: (1) the Real-Time Interrupt Control Register (RTICTL) and the Real-Time Interrupt Flag Register (RTIFLG). The RTICTL register is used to enable the RTI and set the interrupt rate of the RTI. The RTI system is enabled by setting the Real-Time Interrupt Enable (RTIE) bit to logic 1, and the interrupt rate is set using bits RTR[2:0]. The RTIFLG register contains the RTI interrupt flag (RTIF) in bit 7. This flag sets when the RTI interrupt occurs. It is cleared by a write to the RTIFLG register (e.g., STAA RTIFLG).

The time base for the RTI system is the MCLK (Figure 6.14). The MCLK is divided by a divisor set with bits RTR[2:0], bits 2-0, of the RTICTL. As you can see in Figure 6.14, different MCLK divisors may be chosen that set the timeout value of the RTI. For example, if the MCLK is operating at 8 MHz and bits RTR[2:0] are

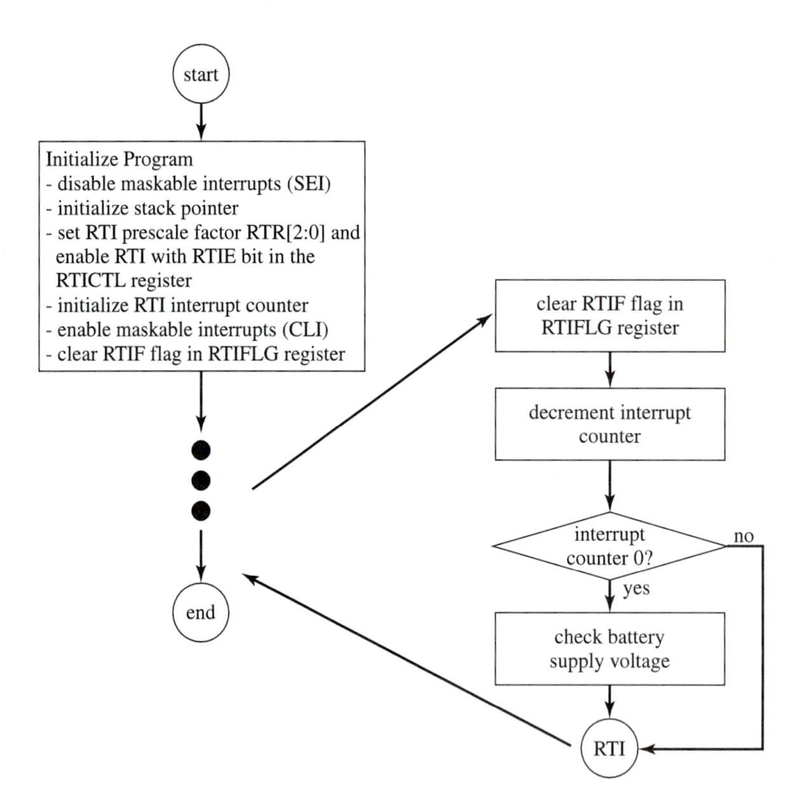

Figure 6.15 Programming the Real-Time Interrupt. Note that the maskable interrupt system is temporarily disabled by the Set Interrupt Mask (SEI) command until the RTI interrupt features are properly configured. Once correctly configured, the RTI is enabled locally with the RTIE bit in the RTICTL register and globally with the Clear Interrupt Mask (CLI) command.

set to "111," the RTI interrupt occurs 65.536 ms after the RTI Flag (RTIF) of the RTIFLG has been cleared.

The flowchart for programming an RTI interrupt is provided in Figure 6.15. The steps are self-explanatory although we illustrate how to apply them in an upcoming example. Before proceeding to the example, let us further explore the use of the RTI interrupt. Rarely does a desired time delay consist of a single RTI interrupt event. Therefore, the desired time delay must be converted to the required number of RTI interrupt events. For example, if a 15-second delay is desired and the MCLK is operating at 8 MHz and the RTR[2:0] bits are set for "111" (timeout = 65.536 ms), then 229 RTI interrupt events must occur to generate the 15-second delay. In the example, we show how to track the RTI interrupt events.

Practice Questions

Question: How many RTI interrupt events must occur to generate a 15 minute delay assuming the MCLK is operating at 8 MHz and the RTR[2:0] bits are set for "111" (timeout = 65.536 ms)?

Answer: Let us perform some unit analysis.

$$15 \text{ min} \times 60 \text{ sec/min} \times 1 \text{ event}/65.536 \text{ ms} = 13{,}733 \text{ events}$$

Example

Program the RTI system to provide a 15-second reminder to check the battery level of the remote weather station. Assume the MCLK is operating at 8 MHz and the RTR[2:0] bits are set for "111" (timeout = 65.536 ms). Let us also assume that this program is being written for the A4 evaluation board (EVB). The memory map for the EVB is provided here for convenience. We also use index addressing techniques in this example.

The M68HC12A4EVB (A4 evaluation board) has the following memory specifications:

- $0000–$01FF, on-chip CPU registers
- $0800–$09FF, on-chip RAM, user code and data
- $0A00–$0BFF, reserved for D-Bug12
- $1000–$1FFF, on-chip EEPROM, user code and data
- $4000–$7FFF, external RAM, user code and data
- $8000–$9FFF, external EPROM, available for user programs*
- $A000–$FD7F, external EPROM, D-Bug12 program
- $FD80–$FDFF, external EPROM, D-Bug12 startup code*
- $FE00–$FE7F, external EPROM, user-accesible functions
- $FE80–$FEFF, external EPROM, D-Bug12 customization data*

- $FF00–$FF7F, external EPROM, available for user programs*
- $FF80–$FFFF, external EPROM, reserved for interrupt and reset vectors

Note: *Code in these areas may be modified. Requires reprogramming of the EPROMs.

To accomplish the programming task, we follow the steps outlined in the flowchart. To begin, let us convert the desired delay to the total number of RTI interrupt events. As previously calculated, 229 RTI interrupts events must occur to generate the 15-second delay.

```
REGBASE    EQU    $0000          ;base addr of A4 EVB register block
RTICTL     EQU    $14            ;offset of RTICTL from REGBASE
RTIFLG     EQU    $15            ;offset of RTIFLG from REGBASE
FIFTEEN    EQU    229            ;number of RTI events for 15s
RTIF       EQU    $80            ;mask for the RTIF flag

           ORG    $4000          ;beginning of A4 EVB RAM
RTICNTR    RMB    2              ;RTI interrupt count
```

Since the A4 EVB is being used in this example, we use EVB interrupt service routines ;initialization techniques for the EVB

```
           ORG    $8000
           LDD    #$6000         ;address of interrupt service routine
           PSHD
           LDD    #24            ;RTI D-BUG12 Interrupt Offset
           LDX    $FE1A          ;Set User Vector Routine
           JSR    0,X
           PULX

           ORG    $5000          ;start address of program
           SEI                   ;disable interrupts
           LDS    $7FFF          ;initialize stack
           LDX    #REGBASE       ;use index addressing
           LDD    #FIFTEEN       ;set RTI interrupt count
           STD    RTICNTR
           BSET   RTICTL,X,$87   ;set RTI prescale and enable RTI
           LDAA   #RTIF          ;load flag mask
           STAA   RTIFLG,X       ;clear the RTI flag
           CLI                   ;enable the interrupt
```

Code for checking battery level would be inserted here:

```
         ORG   $6000        ;location of RTI ISR
RTIservc LDX   #REGBASE     ;use index addressing
         LDAA  #RTIF        ;load RTI flag mask
         STAA  RTIFLG,X     ;reset flag
         LDX   RTICNTR      ;load RTI counter
         DEX                ;decrement RTI intr counter
         CPD   #FIFTEEN     ;are we there yet?
         BNE   NOT_YET      ;not yet
         :
                            ;perform battery level check here
         :
NOT_YET  STX   RTICNTR      ;store result of RTI counter
         RTI                ;return from ISR
```

6.9 A FEW MORE DETAILS

That completes our discussion of the exception system for the 68HC12 except for several more details. It must be emphasized that a separate interrupt service routine must be written for every interrupt the 68HC12 handles in a given application. If more than one interrupt is set at the same time, the 68HC12 responds to the interrupts in priority order. Finally, there is some time processing overhead associated with processing an interrupt. The 68HC12 requires time to stack and unstack the registers during the ISR and the actual processing time of the specific ISR program steps.

6.10 ADVANCED INTERRUPT TOPICS

Interrupts are frequently employed in Real-Time Operating System (RTOS) applications. An RTOS is one that must contend with multiple, often related events in a timely manner. The RTOS must respond to these multiple events, determine the appropriate response to the tasks, and schedule limited resources to accomplish task-related actions in a timely and efficient manner [Miller]. As mentioned, these events are typically interrupt driven. Therefore, great care must be taken in planning the response to these interrupt events. For example, if two event responses attempt to use the same computer resource such as a memory location, unpredictable results may occur. This is known as a concurrency problem. This is just one example of the complex issues involved in programming the RTOS. These concepts are beyond the scope of this book. The interested reader is referred to Miller's text (Chapters 6, 8, and 9).

6.11 LABORATORY APPLICATION

LABORATORY EXERCISE: PARALLEL I/O: LCD INTERFACE AND EXTERNAL INTERRUPTS

Purpose In this lab you will continue to experiment with the parallel I/O capabilities of the 68HC12 as well as the interrupt feature of the 68HC12. The objective of the lab is to program the 68HC12 to accept an external interrupt request and display appropriate messages to an LCD display using the 68HC12 I/O ports. The external interrupt capability can be used as an emergency stop button in the final lab, and the LCD display interface can be used to communicate the mobile robot sensor status to a user.

Documentation 68HC12A4EVB User's manual, AND671/673 LCD display data sheets

Prelab The prelab requirements for this lab are a detailed algorithm and wired hardware (related hardware for a pushbutton switch and the LCD display).

Description Modify your program from Chapter 2 Laboratory Exercise B to do the following tasks.

1. Wait until the pushbutton (the one constructed for Chapter 5 Laboratory Exercise) is pressed to start your program. When the button is pushed (the switch is closed), the program should display a message acknowledging the event. [Note: the initial steps are identical to what you did in Lab 5.]
2. After the start button is pushed (step 1 above), insert a time delay in your program that lasts approximately 2 seconds to allow a user to push the interrupt button. The time delay must precede your executing of Chapter 2 Laboratory Exercise. If an interrupt has occurred (the second button was pushed), display the results of memory locations $0800 through $0802 on the LCD as follows, after the program has completed, showing the contents of the memory addresses.

   L:XX C:YY R:ZZ

   where XX is the value stored in memory location $0800, YY is the value stored in memory location $0801, and ZZ is the value stored in memory location $0802. Since the program has to perform all tasks before you can write the values to the LCD display, your ISR should simply set a flag (using a memory location) that is tested at the end of your program to determine whether the message should be displayed on the LCD.

   Note: In addition to the subroutine for displaying characters on the LCD, you need to write a time delay subroutine (see an example at the end of this laboratory exercise). Such a delay subroutine is necessary since the LCD display cannot respond as fast as the 68HC12 can send out commands. Since the longest delay necessary for the LCD is 40 microseconds, write a time delay routine that lasts 40 microseconds and use it for all delays for LCD commands.

3. If no interrupt has occurred, simply complete the program without any display.

Hardware information First, connect the second pushbutton to the EVB board as shown in Figure 6.16. Note that the IRQ pin is level triggered (logic zero) and the resistor works as a current limiting resistor. The LCD display should be connected to the 68HC12 as shown in Figure 6.17. You connect the LCD to a potentiometer (10K-20K), 5V source, ground, the PJ1 and PJ2 pins, and port H pins. Refer to the following figure on how to hook up the LCD display (AND671/673) to the 68HC12.

The AND671/673 can function as a 16 character x 1 line display. For all practical purposes, it is actually two separate eight-character lines concatenated (linked) together. You must perform the following task.

When power is applied, the display automatically initializes. However, the automatic initialization only brings up the first line (eight characters). To use all 16 characters (the lab requires 14 characters), the display must be manually initialized. For complete information on the LCD, you must refer to the data sheet (*www.purdyelectronics.com*). The following information should be sufficient to send data and commands to the display:

- There are two types of information being sent to the LCD: commands for a microcontroller inside of the LCD and data to be displayed.
- For both commands and data, the enable signal, E, must be logic high while the EVB is sending values on Port H. Connect Port J pin 1 to pin 6 of the LCD as shown in Figure 6.17.

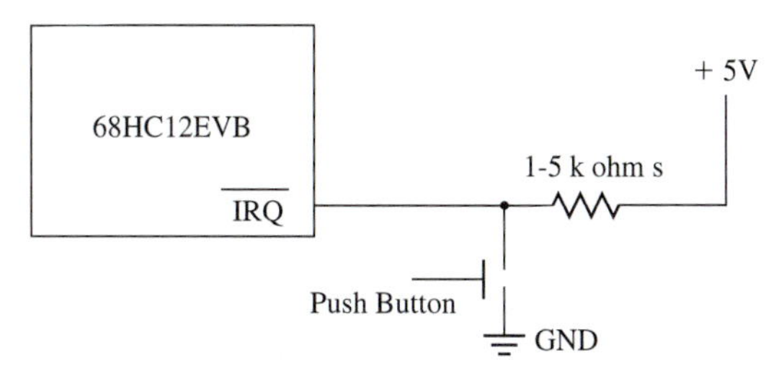

Figure 6.16 Hardware diagram to connect a pushbutton to the IRQ pin.

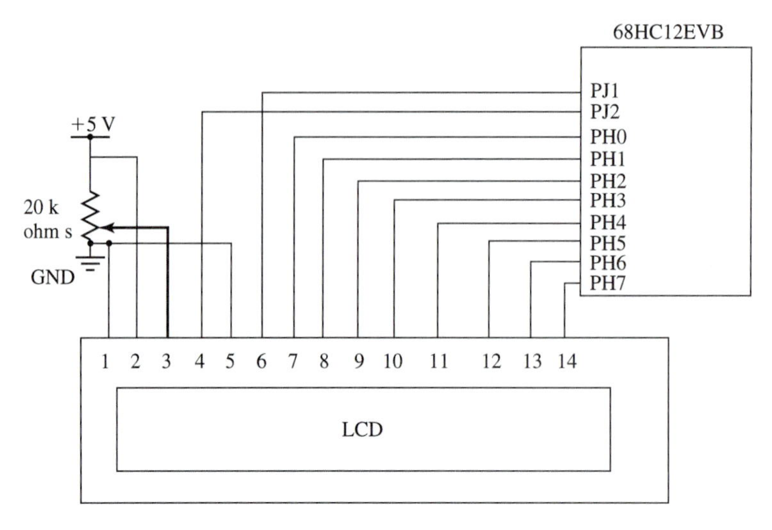

Figure 6.17 Hardware diagram showing the pin connection between the LCD unit with the 68HC12A4EVB.

- Six LCD commands are used in this lab. These commands must be sent to the LCD using the connection through port H while the logic on the E pin of the LCD is high.

  1. Function On: Command %00111000 is used to initialize the LCD.
  2. Entry Mode: Command %000000110 sets up the display mode to increment the cursor after each character is received.
  3. Display On: Command %00001100 turns on the display.
  4. Display Clear: Command %00000001 clears the display.
  5. Character Generator (CG) Memory Location: Command %10000000 sets the display location to be the first character of the first eight-character line. After you set the initial address, an address counter inside the controller (of the display) automatically increments. You do not have to send another address until you want to use another line.
  6. CG Memory Location: Command %11000000 sets the display location to be the first character of the second eight-character line.

- The LCD unit is slow compared with the 68HC12. The MSB of the data lines is also used as a busy flag. If the $R/\overline{W}$ line $= 1$, you can read the flag to see when the display is ready for more data. We could hook that bit up to an input port as well as a pin on Port J and control the $R/\overline{W}$ line, but a simpler solution in this case is to use time delays between commands. Recall that the longest any command takes for the LCD to process is 40 usec. We can tie the R/$\overline{W}$ line low (since we always write to the display) and just wait 40 usec between writes to the display. You can use this feature in the final lab, where you can constantly display the robot status to the LCD unit.

- Once proper commands are sent to the LCD, sending ASCII characters to the display produces the expected result (the proper characters are displayed). To send data to the LCD for display, both the logic on the E pin and the logic on the RS pin of the LCD must be high while data exist on pins 7 through 14 of the LCD. Thus, remember that the RS line (PJ2 logic of Figure 6.17) and E line must contain logic high signals when ASCII values are sent to the LCD, whereas only the E line logic must be high when commands are sent to the LCD.
- Finally, always remember to call your time delay routine in between sending either data or commands to the LCD.

A Time Delay Example This example shows how to write a time delay routine. Suppose you have the following code, which calls a delay subroutine named DELAY.

```
                                    Number of cycles required
          LDX        #VALUE         2
          JSR        DELAY          4
```

Suppose you also wrote the delay subroutine as follows:

```
                                    Number of cycles required
DELAY     DEX                       1
          BNE        DELAY          3
          RTS                       5
```

Note that the delaying time is a function of variable VALUE.

$$\text{Delayed Time} = (6 + 5 + 4 \times \text{VALUE}) \times \text{clock period}$$

The total number of cycles is multiplied by 0.125 usec (the 68HC12 uses an 8 MHz clock). Now suppose you want to delay for 10 usec. You simply need to solve for the VALUE variable using the equation above.

$$\text{VALUE} = (10/0.125 - 11)/4 = 17.25 \text{ round up } \rightarrow \$0012$$

Since we use the 40 usec time delay often in a later laboratory exercise, we can create the following special subroutine and call it (JSR DELAY40) using a single instruction rather than two consecutive instructions: LDX #$004B followed by JSR DELAY.

```
DELAY40    LDX    #$004B
           JSR    DELAY
           RTS
```

6.12 SUMMARY

In this chapter, we explored the requirement for and importance of interrupt processing mechanisms. We then examined a generic processor's response to an exception event and took a detailed look at how the 68HC12 responds to an interrupt. It is important to keep in mind the interrupt-related events performed automatically by the 68HC12 and those that you the programmer are responsible for accomplishing. We then learned how to write interrupt service routines for the 68HC12 using several case studies.

6.13 FURTHER READING

"Microcomputer Engineering," edited by Gene H. Miller, Prentice Hall, 2nd ed, 1999.

6.14 CHAPTER PROBLEMS

Fundamental

1. What is the difference between an interrupt and a reset?
2. What is the difference between a nonmaskable interrupt and a maskable interrupt?
3. What is the difference between the $\overline{XIRQ}$ interrupt and the $\overline{IRQ}$ interrupt?
4. How is the $\overline{XIRQ}$ interrupt system enabled?
5. How is the SCI0 interrupt enabled? (Careful! There are two required steps.)
6. What registers are stored during an interrupt event? How is this register storage accomplished? Where are the register values stored?
7. What is the highest possible priority level for a maskable interrupt?

Advanced

1. What value must be written to the Highest Priority I Interrupt Register (HPRIO) to boost the priority of the analog-to-digital (ATD) interrupt?
2. Referring to the previous question, what effect will this action have on the nonmaskable interrupt priorities? the maskable interrupt priorities?

3. What actions are required after a reset event to place the $\overline{IRQ}$ maskable interrupt at the highest possible maskable interrupt level?
4. Figure 6.18 shows the contents of the stack. Identify the return address to the main program if: (1) The 68HC12 is in a subroutine called by another subroutine. (2) The 68HC12 is in an interrupt service routine that interrupted the main program. What was the value in the Y register at the time of the ISR? (3) The 68HC12 is in a subroutine that pushed both X and Y onto the stack. (4) The 68HC12 is in a subroutine that, prior to its call, the main program pushed two 16-bit numbers onto the stack.

Challenging

1. Write the configuration steps in a mainline program and an interrupt service routine to time an event that may last up to 3 minutes. Assume the MCLK is operating at 4 MHz.
2. Extend the battery backup supply example for one primary battery and two backup batteries. Show all initialization steps in the main code and the interrupt service routine.
3. Write a program to check the battery supply voltage at 15 minute intervals. Use the Power Switching Unit described in the chapter.

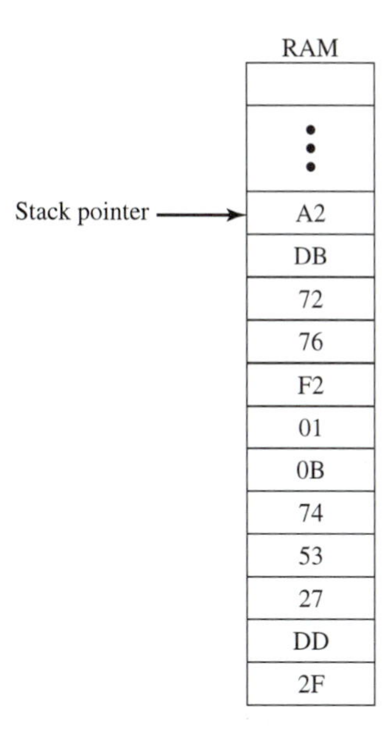

Figure 6.18 Interrupt stacking order.

7

The 68HC12 Clock Module and Standard Timer Module (TIM)

Objectives: At the completion of this chapter you will be able to:

- Describe the operation of the 68HC12 Clock Module,
- Describe the operation of the clock divider chain serving the 68HC12 Standard Timer Module (TIM),
- Explain the operation of the TIM system,
- List and describe in detail the key components of the TIM system,
- Summarize and describe in detail the Input Capture features of the TIM system,
- Summarize and describe in detail the Output Compare features of the TIM system,
- Summarize and describe in detail the Pulse Accumulator features of the TIM system,
- Summarize and describe in detail the Real-Time Interrupt Features of the 68HC12, and
- Summarize and describe in detail the programming of the Input Capture, Output Compare, and the Pulse Accumulator features of the TIM.

In this chapter, we discuss the 68HC12 Clock Module and the Standard Timer Module. Although these are two separate subsystems within the 68HC12, they have related functions. Let us begin with the Clock Module. The 68HC12 is equipped with clock-generation circuitry to generate the internal and external clock signals used by the CPU and the on-chip peripherals. A compatible external clock signal can be applied to the EXTAL pin or the 68HC12 can generate a clock signal using an internal on-chip oscillator circuit with an external crystal or ceramic resonator.

The 68HC12 is also equipped with a powerful and flexible timer module known as the TIM. The TIM is equipped with eight complete 16-bit dual-function input capture/output compare channels. Each of these channels is software configurable for either the input capture or output compare operation. The TIM is also equipped with a single 16-bit pulse accumulator.

As mentioned, the TIM is very flexible. It can be configured to:

- Measure the characteristics of an input signal(s) with the input capture system,
- Generate output signal(s) to given specifications using the output compare system,
- Generate pulse width-modulated (PWM) signals, and
- Count events using the 16-bit pulse accumulator.

In this chapter, we discuss the operation, application, and programming of the Clock and the TIM.

7.1 OVERVIEW

In the hardware overview chapter, we introduced you to the wall following robot project and the design of a remote weather station. Both systems required a microcontroller with features to generate output signals to precise parameters, measure the characteristics of input signals, and count external events (pulses) to the microcontroller. Specifically, the wall following robot required microcontroller features to generate wheel control signals, count the number of wall collisions, and precisely measure the characteristics of an input signal to determine if another robot is a friend or foe. The remote weather station required an output signal to provide drive signals to a motor. The motor opened and closed the doors, which protected the solar array powering the remote weather station. The remote weather station also required a subsystem to count pulses coming from the anemometer, which provided information on wind velocity. All of these requirements are provided by the 68HC12's Standard Timer Module (TIM).

7.2 BACKGROUND THEORY

In the analog-to-digital (ATD) system chapter, we provide a simple subroutine to generate a specified time delay. We use code timing techniques and program loops to consume some desired amount of processor time and hence create a desired time delay. This technique of generating a delay has some obvious disadvantages: (1) the processor cannot perform other operations during the delay, (2) only one delay can be accomplished at a time, (3) timing is imprecise for short delays, and (4) it is inflexible. The powerful yet flexible 68HC12 TIM system solves all of these shortcomings. We begin our discussion with the 68HC12 Clock Module followed by the TIM. Realize that the next section contains considerable technical detail. We recommend that you study the diagrams of the timing systems first, read over the information on the timing system carefully, and then review the diagrams again. It is important that you thoroughly understand how clock signals are generated, divided, and applied within the 68HC12 system.

7.3 THE 68HC12 CLOCK MODULE

The 68HC12 is equipped with clock-generation circuitry to generate the internal and external clock signals used by the CPU and on-chip peripherals. A simplified block diagram is provided in Figure 7.1, whereas a detailed diagram is provided in Figure 7.2. A compatible external clock signal can be applied to the EXTAL pin or the 68HC12 can generate a clock signal using an internal on-chip oscillator circuit with an external crystal or ceramic resonator. The 68HC12 uses four types of internal clock signals derived from the primary clock signal: T clocks, E clock,

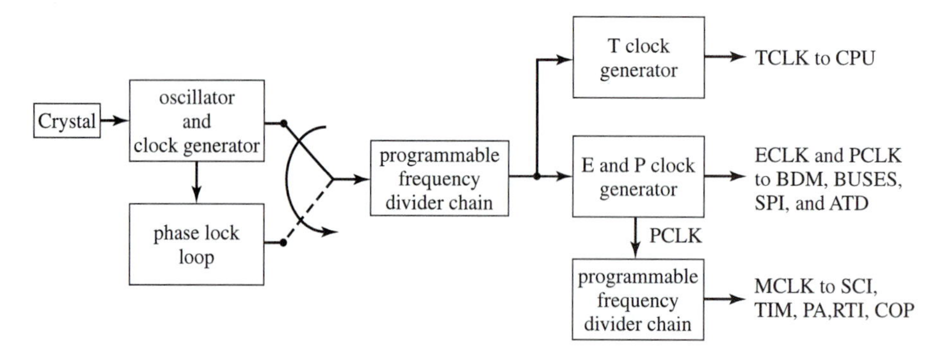

Figure 7.1 Clock module system overview. The 68HC12 uses four types of internal clock signals derived from the primary clock signal: T clocks, E clock, P clock, and M clock.

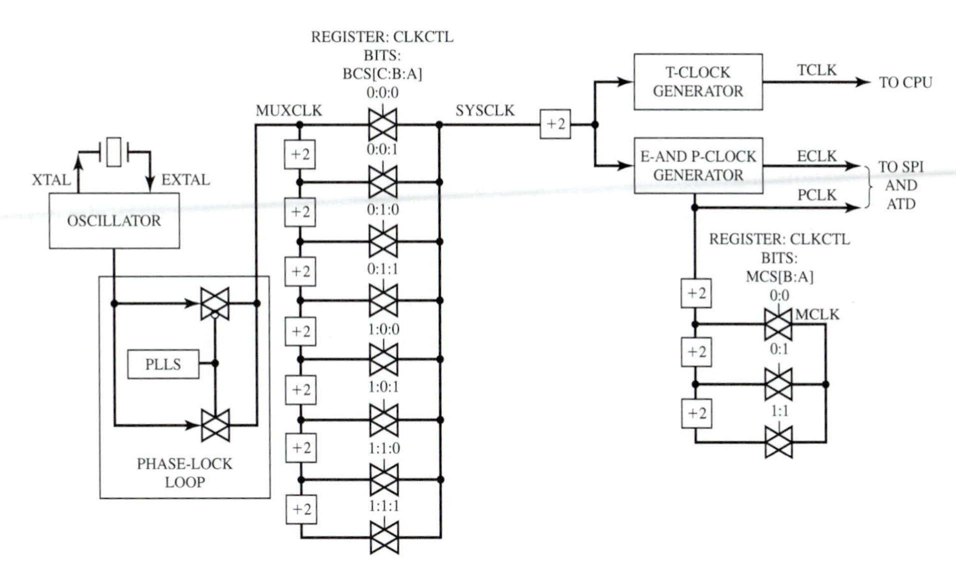

Figure 7.2 Clock Module Block Diagram. The main clock system employs a clock divider chain network to produce the TCLK, ECLK, PCLK, and MCLK signals for the different subsystems of the 68HC12 system. (Figure used with permission of Motorola, Incorporated.)

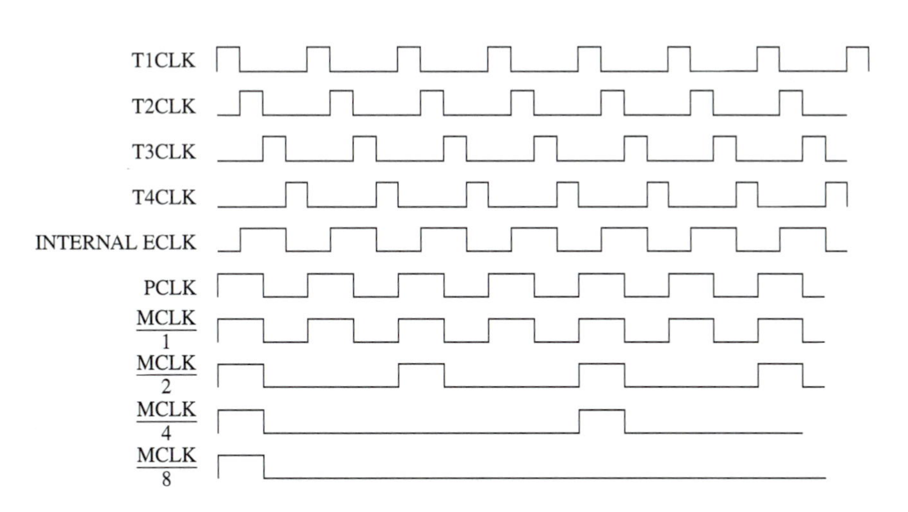

Figure 7.3 Internal Clock Relationships. The 68HC12 uses four types of internal clock signals derived from the primary clock signal: T clocks, E clock, P clock, and M clock. (Figure used with permission of Motorola, Incorporated.)

P clock, and M clock. The T clocks are used by the CPU, whereas the E and P clocks are used by the bus interfaces, the serial peripheral interface (SPI) system, and the analog-to-digital (ATD) system. The M clock drives on-chip modules such as the Standard Timer Module (TIM), the Serial Communications Interface (SCI) system, and the Real-Time Interrupt (RTI) system. The 68HC12 is also equipped with a phase-locked loop (PLL) system. The PLL allows the 68HC12 to run from a different time base than the incoming crystal value.

The main clock system employs a clock divider chain network to produce the TCLK, ECLK, PCLK, and MCLK signals for the different subsystems of the 68HC12 system as shown in Figure 7.3. These individually derived clock signals are routed to other clock divider chains. We discuss these chains as we need them throughout the text.

7.4 CLOCK DIVIDER CHAIN SERVING THE TIM

The TIM system has its own associated clock chain (Figure 7.4). The input to the TIM clock chain is the MCLK signal. As you can see in the clock chain diagram, there are three registers associated with the TIM timing system: the Timer System Control (TSCR) register, the Timer Interrupt Mask 2 (TMSK2) register, and the Pulse Accumulator Control Register (PACTL). The Timer Enable (TEN) bit of the TSCR register must be set to 1 to enable the Timer Module. This is the module's on/off switch. The TMSK2 register has three bits (PR2, PR1, and PR0) that specify how many divide-by-two stages are to be inserted between the MCLK and the timer's free-running counter. This allows the user to control the resolution and the rollover time of the free-running counter. The PACTL register bits PAEN, CLK1, and CLK2 also control features of the TIM clock chain. When the PAEN bit is set to a logic 1, it enables the Pulse Accumulator system, whereas the CLCK1 and CLK0 bits in the PACTL register provide additional time base options for the TIM as shown in Figure 7.5. We discuss the pulse accumulator clock (PACLK) features later in this chapter. For now realize that the output from the pulse accumulator system may be used as an input to the TIM.

7.5 THE 68HC12 TIMER MODULE

The TIM of the 68HC12 was designed to accomplish three main functions:

- **Input Capture.** The input capture feature, as its name implies, allows the characteristics of an input signal to be measured. The 68HC12 can be programmed to measure the length of an input pulse or characteristics of a

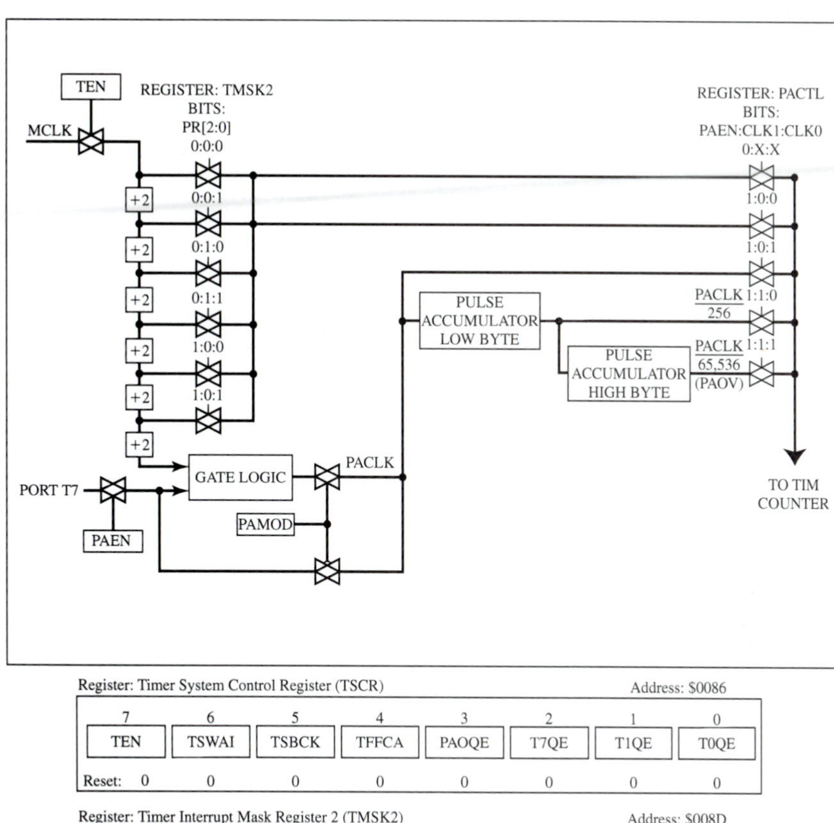

Register: Timer System Control Register (TSCR) Address: $0086

	7	6	5	4	3	2	1	0
	TEN	TSWAI	TSBCK	TFFCA	PAOQE	T7QE	T1QE	T0QE
Reset:	0	0	0	0	0	0	0	0

Register: Timer Interrupt Mask Register 2 (TMSK2) Address: $008D

	7	6	5	4	3	2	1	0
	TOI	0	TPU	TDRB	TCRE	PR2	PR1	PR0
Reset:	0	0	1	1	0	0	0	0

Register: Pulse Accumulator Control Register (PACTL) Address: $00A0

	7	6	5	4	3	2	1	0
	0	PAEN	PAMOD	PEDGE	CLK1	CLK0	PAOVI	PAI
Reset:	0	0	0	0	0	0	0	0

Figure 7.4 Clock Chain for the TIM. The input to the TIM clock chain is the MCLK signal. There are three registers associated with the TIM timing system: the Timer Source Control (TSCR) register, the Timer Interrupt Mask 2 (TMSK2) register, and the Pulse Accumulator Control Register (PACTL). (Figure used with permission of Motorola, Incorporated.)

CLK[1:0]	Timer Counter Clock
00	Timer prescaler clock
01	PACLK
10	PACLK/256
11	PACLK/65,636

Figure 7.5 Clock Selection via CLCK1, CLCK0 of the PACTL register. The Timer Prescaler clock is the Module Clock (MCLK) prescaled by PR2, PR1, PR0.

periodic signal such as period, duty cycle, and frequency. The input capture system may also be used to count pulses (external events). However, the pulse accumulator is specifically designed for this function.

- **Output Compare.** The output compare feature allows the generation of an output signal(s) to user specifications. A single active high or low pulse or a periodic output signal of user-specified frequency and duty cycle may be generated. We also discuss how to generate a pulse width-modulated (PWM) signal in the laboratory exercises using the 68HC12's output compare features.
- **Pulse Accumulator.** The pulse accumulator feature may be used to count pulses (external events) to the 68HC12.

The TIM is equipped with eight complete, individual 16-bit dual-function input capture/output compare channels. That is, each of these channels is software configurable for either the input capture or output compare operation. The input capture/output compare pins are IOC[7:0] of PORT T. The TIM is also equipped with a single 16-bit pulse accumulator. The input for the pulse accumulator is pin IOC7/PAI (Figure 7.6).

Practice Questions

Question: What portion of the Timer Module would you use for the following: (a) timing a race, (b) frequency counter, (c) sending control signals to the motors driving a robot's wheels, (d) counting wall collisions that a robot experiences, (e) generating a "friend or foe" signal for robots within a maze, (f) counting the number of pulses from an anemometer, and (g) generating signals to close the doors to protect the solar array on a remote weather station?

Answer: (a) To time a race the input capture could be used. The input capture system could be programmed to detect the start of the race and when a runner crossed

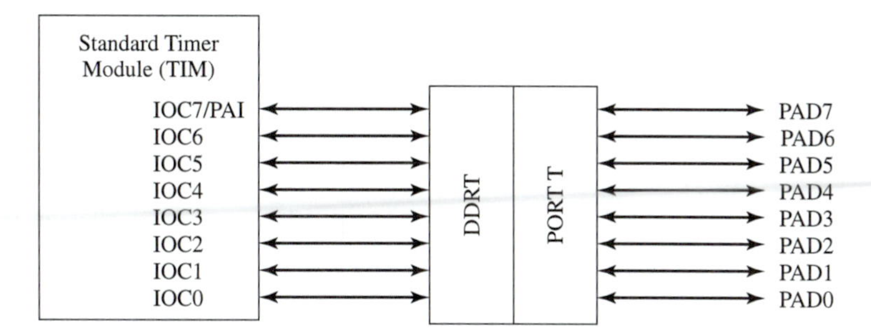

Figure 7.6 Port T. The TIM is equipped with eight complete, individual 16-bit dual-function input capture/output compare channels. Each of these channels is software configurable for either the input capture or output compare operation. The input capture/output compare pins are IOC[7:0] of PORT T. The TIM is also equipped with a single 16-bit pulse accumulator. The input for the pulse accumulator is pin IOC7/PAI.

the finish line. With the start and stop information collected, the elapsed time of the race could be calculated. (b) A frequency counter is a lab bench component to measure unknown frequencies. The input capture system could be used to measure frequencies by detecting the leading and trailing edge of a signal. The period could then be calculated by subtracting the trailing edge from the leading edge time. The frequency of the signal is the reciprocal of the period. (c) The output compare system could be used to send control signals to the motors driving a robot's wheels. We cover this application in great detail later in the chapter. (d) The pulse accumulator could be programmed to count collisions that a robot would encounter while walking through a maze. (e) The output compare system could be used to generate a distinctive "friend or foe" signal. When robots come within close proximity within a maze, they could send a friend or foe signal via their infrared (IR) emitters to determine their relationship with one another. This is easily accomplished by ensuring the friend signal is distinctly different than the foe signal. This is accomplished by sending a train of pulses with different pulse lengths and/or frequency. We ask you to do this as a homework assignment. (f) The pulse accumulator system may be used to count the number of pulses from an anemometer, and (g) the output compare system may be used to generate signals to close the doors to protect the solar array.

7.6 COMPONENTS OF THE TIMER MODULE

The block diagram of the Timer Module is provided in Figure 7.7. At first it appears daunting. Realize that there are really only three main components to the

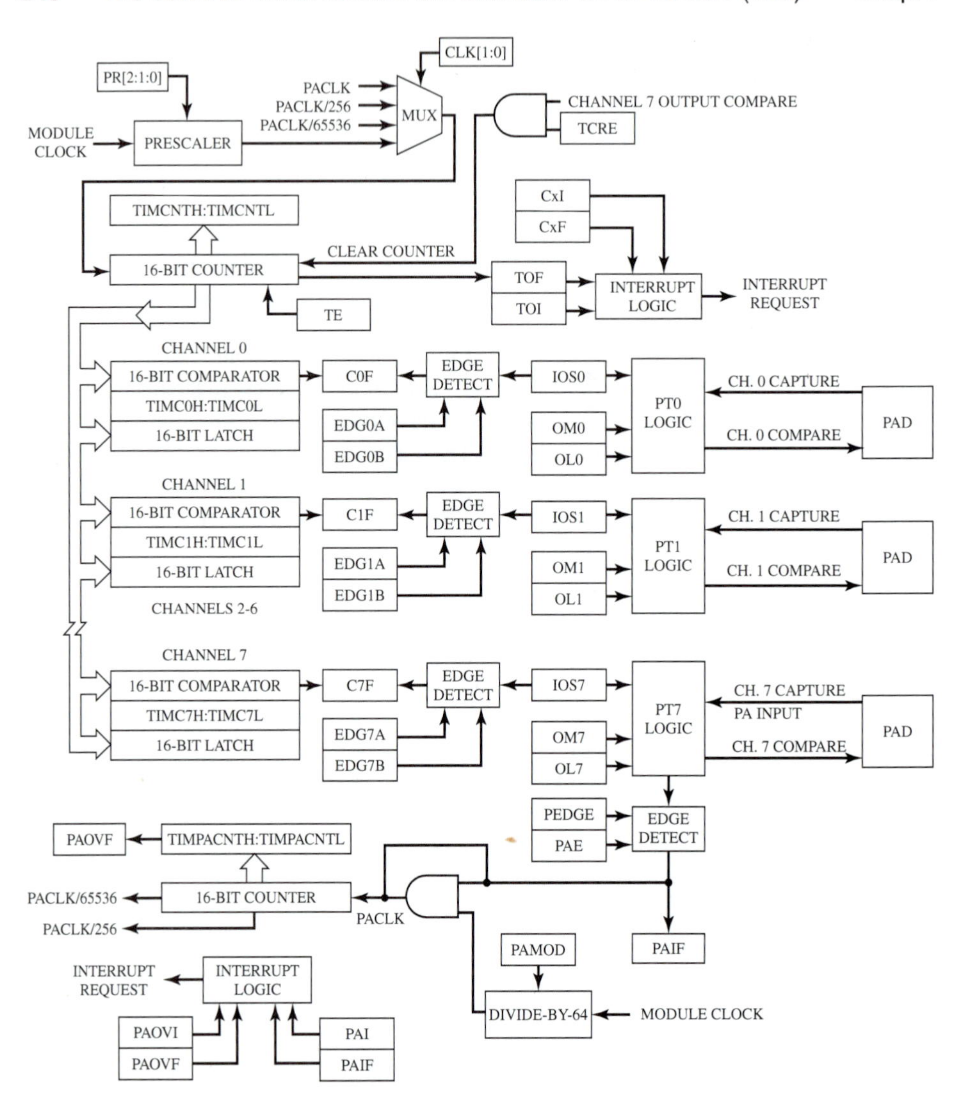

Figure 7.7 Timer Block Diagram. There are three main components to the Timer Module: (1) the 16-bit free-running counter and its associated time scaling hardware, (2) the input capture/output compare channels (eight of them), and (3) the pulse accumulator hardware. (Figure used with permission of Motorola, Incorporated.)

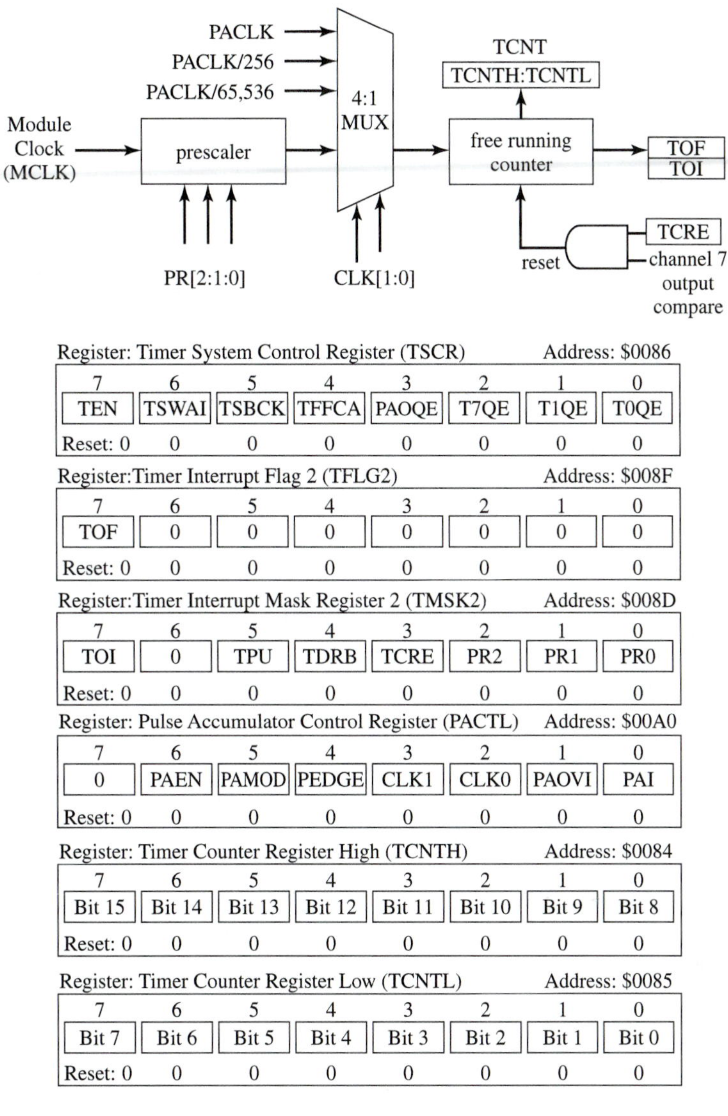

Register: Timer System Control Register (TSCR) Address: $0086

	7	6	5	4	3	2	1	0
	TEN	TSWAI	TSBCK	TFFCA	PAOQE	T7QE	T1QE	T0QE
Reset:	0	0	0	0	0	0	0	0

Register:Timer Interrupt Flag 2 (TFLG2) Address: $008F

	7	6	5	4	3	2	1	0
	TOF	0	0	0	0	0	0	0
Reset:	0	0	0	0	0	0	0	0

Register:Timer Interrupt Mask Register 2 (TMSK2) Address: $008D

	7	6	5	4	3	2	1	0
	TOI	0	TPU	TDRB	TCRE	PR2	PR1	PR0
Reset:	0	0	0	0	0	0	0	0

Register: Pulse Accumulator Control Register (PACTL) Address: $00A0

	7	6	5	4	3	2	1	0
	0	PAEN	PAMOD	PEDGE	CLK1	CLK0	PAOVI	PAI
Reset:	0	0	0	0	0	0	0	0

Register: Timer Counter Register High (TCNTH) Address: $0084

	7	6	5	4	3	2	1	0
	Bit 15	Bit 14	Bit 13	Bit 12	Bit 11	Bit 10	Bit 9	Bit 8
Reset:	0	0	0	0	0	0	0	0

Register: Timer Counter Register Low (TCNTL) Address: $0085

	7	6	5	4	3	2	1	0
	Bit 7	Bit 6	Bit 5	Bit 4	Bit 3	Bit 2	Bit 1	Bit 0
Reset:	0	0	0	0	0	0	0	0

Figure 7.8 Free-Running Counter. The MCLK frequency may be divided (scaled) by different user-programmed divisors. The prescale divisors are set by bits PR[2:1:0], which are located in the Timer Mask Register 2 (TMSK2). The prescale factor controls how long it takes for the free-running counter to roll over. The counter counts from $0000 to $FFFF and automatically rolls over to $0000 and continues to count. Different time bases may be used as the timing source for the free-running counter. The PACLK, PACLK/256, or PACLK/65536 may also be used as the free-running counter's clock source when the pulse accumulator section of the Timer Module is enabled.

Timer Module: (1) the 16-bit free-running counter and its associated time scaling hardware, (2) the input capture/output compare channels (eight of them), and (3) the pulse accumulator hardware. We discuss each of these main components of the Timer Module in turn. For each component we provide a simplified block diagram.

7.6.1 Free-Running Counter

The heart of the 68HC12 Timer Module is a 16-bit free-running counter (Figure 7.8). All input capture and output compare functions derive their timing information from this single counter. When the Timer System is enabled (recall by placing a 1 in the TEN bit of the Timer System Control Register—$0086) the counter starts at $0000 and is normally incremented for each Module Clock (MCLK) pulse. The counter counts from $0000 to $FFFF and automatically rolls over to $0000 and continues to count.

As can be seen in the free-running counter diagram, the frequency of the MCLK may be divided by the prescaler hardware. The MCLK frequency may be divided (scaled) by different user-programmed divisors. The prescale divisors are set by bits PR[2:1:0], which are located in the Timer Mask Register 2 (TMSK2; Figure 7.9). The available prescaler divisors are shown in the chart. For example, if the prescale divisor is set to 32, only one clock pulse is provided to the free-running counter for every 32 MCLK pulses input to the prescaler.

The prescale factor controls how long it takes for the free-running counter to roll over. Since the free-running counter contains 16 bits, it requires 2^{16} or 65,536 pulses to roll over. For example, if the MCLK's frequency is 2 MHz, the free-

PR[2:1:0]	Divisor
000	1
001	2
010	4
011	8
100	16
101	32
110	Reserved
111	Reserved

Figure 7.9 Prescaler Selection. The frequency of the MCLK may be divided by the prescaler hardware. The MCLK frequency may be divided (scaled) by different user-programmed divisors. The prescale divisors are set by bits PR[2:1:0], which are located in the Timer Mask Register 2 (TMSK2).

Register: Timer Interrupt Flag 2 (TFLG2) Address: $008F

	7	6	5	4	3	2	1	0
	TOF	0	0	0	0	0	0	0
Reset:	0	0	0	0	0	0	0	0

Figure 7.10 Timer Flag Register 2—TFLG2 ($008F).

running counter rolls over every 32.768 milliseconds. If the prescale divisor is set for 32, the free-running counter rolls over every 1.048576 seconds.

As you might imagine, if we are timing a long event (an event longer than $FFFF M clock cycles), it is important to monitor how many times the free-running counter rolls over. The 68HC12 sets a timer overflow flag (TOF) every time the counter rolls over. The TOF flag is bit 7 in the Timer Flag Register 2 (TFLG2) register—$008F. Furthermore, a timer overflow interrupt (TOI) can be employed to signal the rollover of the free-running timer. Recall that we discussed how to program the interrupt features in the interrupt chapter. The interrupt approach has a clear advantage over the polling approach. When an interrupt is employed, the 68HC12 issues an interrupt signal indicating that a significant event has occurred. In contrast, with the polling approach, the program must keep polling to see if a significant event has occurred. When teaching a new concept in class, it would be inefficient for a teacher to sequentially ask each student if he or she has a question on the new information (polling). It is much more efficient to have students ask questions as they have them (interrupt).

Different time bases may be used as the timing source for the free-running counter. The PACLK, PACLK/256, or PACLK/65536 may also be used as the free-running counter's clock source when the pulse accumulator section of the Timer Module is enabled. The source is selected via a 4 to 1 multiplexer connected to the input of the free-running counter. The desired clock source is selected using bits CLK[1:0] of the Pulse Accumulator Control Register (PACTL)—$00A0. Later in the chapter, we discuss how the PACLK related signals are generated by the pulse accumulator system.

The current value of the 16-bit free-running counter is contained in two eight-bit registers: Timer Counter Register High (TCNTH) $0084 and Timer Counter Register Low (TCNTL) $0085. Together these two registers form the 16-bit TCNT register. The lower eight bits of the free-running counter (TCNTL) are frozen in the TCNT register when the upper byte (TCNTH) is fetched. The lower byte is accessed during the next bus cycle.

The free-running counter may be reset. To reset the counter, the Timer Counter Reset Enable (TCRE) bit in the Timer Mask Register 2 (TMSK2) must be set. Furthermore, the timer channel 7 registers must contain $0000. When these conditions are met, the timer counter registers remain at $0000. Care must be taken when using this feature. Great caution must be exercised prior to resetting the free-running counter. Recall that all eight input capture/output compare channels derive their timing from the free-running counter.

Practice Questions

Question: Two input capture events occur at counts $0037 and $FB20 of the free-running counter. How many counts (in decimal) have transpired between these two events?

Answer: $FB20 – $0037 = $FAE9 = 64,233 counts

Question: In the preceding question, if the MCLK was 2 MHz and the prescaler bits PR[2:1:0] were set to 000, how much time in seconds transpired between the two input capture events?

Answer: $64{,}233 \times 1/(2\text{ MHz}) = 32.1165$ ms

Question: Repeat the preceding question if PR[2:1:0] were set to 100.

Answer: With the prescaler set for 100, the divisor is 16. Therefore, the counter is incremented every 16 M clock pulses. For this example, 513.864 ms.

7.6.2 Free-Running Counter-Associated Registers

In this section, the registers associated with the free-running counter are discussed. These registers allow the user to tailor the features of the free-running counter to the specific application at hand.

Timer System Control Register—TSCR The Timer System Control Register (TSCR) is located at memory location $0086 (Figure 7.11). The Timer Enable Bit (TEN) when set to 1 enables the timer and disables the timer when set to 0. The other key bit in this register is the Timer Fast Flag Clear-All bit (TFFCA). This bit controls how fast the flags associated with the input capture/output compare channels are cleared. When the TFFCA bit is 0, Timer System flags are cleared using the **standard** method of writing a logic 1 to the flag bit. Writing a logic 0 to the flag bit has no effect. When the TFFCA bit is 1, the fast flag clear features are enabled. The fast flag clear features are slightly different for each portion of the Timer System.

Register: Timer System Control Register (TSCR) Address: $0086

	7	6	5	4	3	2	1	0
	TEN	TSWAI	TSBCK	TFFCA	PAOQE	T7QE	T1QE	T0QE
Reset:	0	0	0	0	0	0	0	0

Figure 7.11 Timer System Control Register—TSCR.

- TFLG1 register: A read from the input capture or write to the output compare channel causes the corresponding channel flag, CnF, to be cleared in the TFLG1 register.
- TFLG2 register: Any access to the TCNT register will clear the Timer Overflow Flag (TOF) in the TFLG2 register.
- PAFLG register: Any access to the PACNT register clears both the PAOVF and PAIF flag bits in the PAFLG register.

Timer Counter Register—TCNTH, TCNTL, TCNT The 16-bit Timer Counter Register (TCNT) is divided into two eight-bit registers: high (TCNTH) and low (TCNTL). These registers are located at memory locations $0084 and $0085, respectively. The TCNT register contains the current value of the free-running counter. It is recommended that a double-byte read instruction be used to read the timer counter such as LDD, LDX, or LDY since the TCNT is a 16-bit register (Figure 7.12).

Timer Mask Register 2—TMSK2 The Timer Mask Register 2 (TMSK2) is located at memory location $008D (Figure 7.13). At this time, we only describe the function of some of the TMSK2 register bits. As previously mentioned, the Timer Counter Reset Enable (TCRE) bit allows the free-running counter to be reset. For this to occur, the TCRE must be set to 1 and the timer channel 7 registers

Register: Timer Counter Register High (TCNTH) Address: $0084

	7	6	5	4	3	2	1	0
	Bit 15	Bit 14	Bit 13	Bit 12	Bit 11	Bit 10	Bit 9	Bit 8
Reset:	0	0	0	0	0	0	0	0

Register: Timer Counter Register Low (TCNTL) Address: $0085

	7	6	5	4	3	2	1	0
	Bit 7	Bit 6	Bit 5	Bit 4	Bit 3	Bit 2	Bit 1	Bit 0
Reset:	0	0	0	0	0	0	0	0

Figure 7.12 Timer Counter Register—TCNTH, TCNTL, TCNT.

Register: Timer Interrupt Mask Register 2 (TMSK2) Address: $008D

	7	6	5	4	3	2	1	0
	TOI	0	TPU	TDRB	TCRE	PR2	PR1	PR0
Reset:	0	0	1	1	0	0	0	0

Figure 7.13 Timer Mask Register 2—TMSK2.

must contain $0000. The TMSK2 register also contains the Timer Prescaler Select (PR[2:1:0]) bits. These bits are used to set the prescale divisor.

The user must communicate to the 68HC12 the address locations of registers. This is usually accomplished via assembler directive statements in the initialization portion of a program.

Example

The following directives would be used to tell the 68HC12 the location of the free-running counter associated registers.

```
;-----------------------------------
;MAIN PROGRAM ;
;-----------------------------------
TSCR    EQU     $0086    ;addr of TSCR
TCNT    EQU     $0084    ;addr of TCNT
TMSK2   EQU     $008D    ;addr of TMSK2
```

Example

If the registers need to be initialized with a specific value, labels and directives may be used to assign initialization parameters to a variable. For example, to enable the Timer Module and configure it for fast flag clearing, the TEN and TFFCA bits in the TSCR register must both be set to 1. This may be accomplished using the following code:

```
;-----------------------------------
;MAIN PROGRAM ;
;-----------------------------------
TSCR       EQU     $0086       ;addr of TSCR
TSCR_INI   EQU     $90         ;initialization mask for TSCR
           :
           LDAA    #TSCR_INI   ;Load A with TSCR mask
           STAA    TSCR        ;Initalize TSCR
```

Practice Questions

Question: If bits PR[2:1:0] in the TMSK2 register are set to 010 and the MCLK frequency is 2 MHz, how often will the free-running counter roll over?

Answer: With PR[2:1:0] set to 010, the prescaler will scale the MCLK by a factor of four. Therefore, the free-running counter will increment every 2.0 μs (MCLK period multiplied by four). The free-running counter rolls over every $2^{16} =$ 65,536 pulses or every 0.131 seconds.

Question: Provide the function and register location of each of the following bits: TEN, TOI, and PR[2:1:0].

Answer: **TEN** The Timer Enable bit in the Timer System Control Register (TSCR—$0086) is the on/off switch for the Timer System.

TOI The Timer Overflow Interrupt Enable (TOI) bit in the Timer Mask Register 2 (TMSK2—$008D) is used to turn on the Timer Overflow Interrupt flag. An interrupt is generated when the free-running counter rolls over.

PR[2:1:0] The prescalar bits are also included in the TMSK2 register. These bits set the prescale divisor value for the Timer System.

7.6.3 Input Capture/Output Compare Channels

The TIM is equipped with eight complete, individual 16-bit dual-function input capture/output compare channels. A block diagram of one of these dual-function channels is provided in Figure 7.14. These eight channels are connected to the outside world via the IOC[7:0] pins (pins PT[7:0]) of PORT T—$00AE. Each specific channel is configured for the input capture or output compare function with the

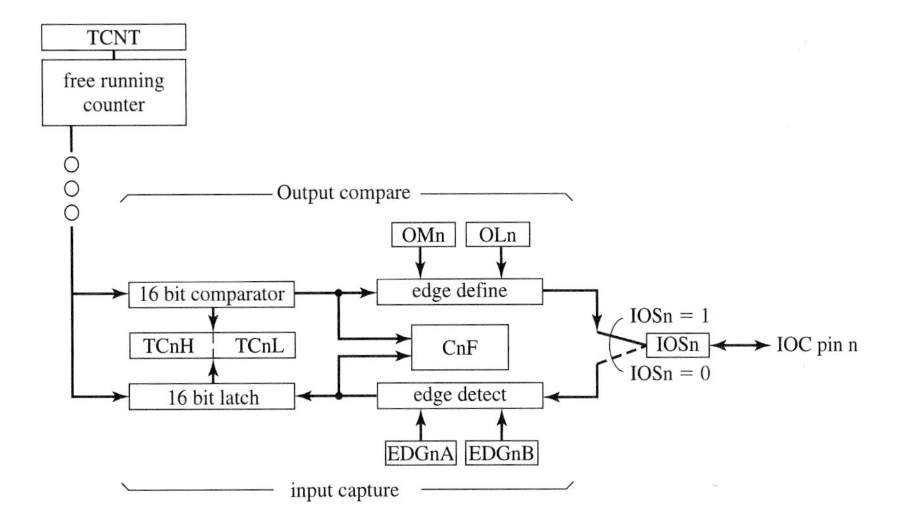

Register: Timer Input Capture/Output Compare Select (TIOS) Address: $0080

7	6	5	4	3	2	1	0
IOS7	IOS6	IOS5	IOS4	IOS3	IOS2	IOS1	IOS0
Reset: 0	0	0	0	0	0	0	0

Figure 7.14 A representative input capture/output compare channel. The TIM is equipped with eight complete, individual 16-bit dual-function input capture/output compare channels. Each specific channel is configured for the input capture or output compare function with the associated bit in the Timer IC/OC Select Register (TIOS)—$0080.

associated bit in the Timer IC/OC Select Register (TIOS)—$0080. When the IOSn bit is set to logic 1, the corresponding channel is configured for the output compare function. When set to logic 0, the corresponding channel functions as an input capture channel. The 16-bit free-running counter provides a reference count to all eight of the input capture/output compare (IC/OC) channels.

Input Capture The input capture system is nothing more than a 16-bit binary stop watch. It can be configured to capture the current count of the free-running timer when a user-specified event occurs. The user-specified event can be a rising edge, falling edge, or any (rising or falling) edge. Since the free-running counter supplies all eight IC/OC channels, it is usually not reset. Instead, elapsed time between key events is used to determine input signal parameters. The input capture system may be used to measure the length of a single pulse or the characteristics of a repetitive signal such as period, duty cycle, or frequency. At first this method of measuring elapsed time between key events may seem cumbersome. However, this method is frequently used to time running events such as hundreds of runners competing in the same marathon. Your time for the marathon would be your stop time minus your start time.

Before proceeding, let us review some basic definitions related to signal timing. The duty cycle of a periodic signal is defined as the *on time* of the signal divided by its total period. The period of a repetitive signal is measured from rising edge to rising edge (or falling edge to falling edge). The frequency of a repetitive signal is simply the reciprocal of the period. These definitions are illustrated in Figure 7.15.

The key components of the input capture channel are illustrated in Figure 7.17. As previously mentioned, the free-running counter provides a 16-bit binary

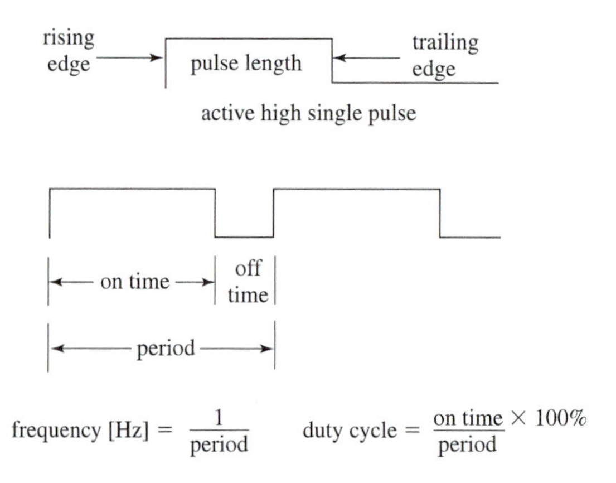

Figure 7.15 Characteristics of signals: duty cycle, period, and frequency.

EDGnB EDGnA	Configuration
00	Capture disabled
01	Rising Edge
10	Falling Edge
11	Any Edge

Figure 7.16 Input capture edge selection. The input channel is configured to wait for a user-specified event. This event can be a rising signal edge, falling signal edge, or any signal edge (rising or falling). The user specifies the desired edge characteristics to the edge-detection logic using the associated EDGnA and EDGnB bits of the Timer Control Registers.

count to the input capture channel. The input channel is configured to wait for a user-specified event. This event can be a rising signal edge, falling signal edge, or any signal edge (rising or falling). The user specifies the desired edge characteristics to the edge-detection logic using the associated EDGnA and EDGnB bits of the Timer Control Registers (TCTL3—$008A and TCTL4—$008B; Figure 7.16).

When the user-specified event occurs on the configured input capture pin, a chain reaction of events is set in motion. First, the current value of the free-running counter is latched into the associated Timer Channel Registers (TCnH/L). To read the 16-bit value from this register, a double-byte read instruction such as LDD or LDX should be used. Second, a desired input capture event on channel "n" sets the associated Channel Flag (CnF). This flag can be reset by writing a logic 1 to it. Finally, the corresponding Channel Interrupt Flag (CnI) is set and generates an interrupt event if it has been previously enabled.

The 16-bit count in the TCnH/L represents the value of the free-running timer clock ticks when the user-specified event occurred. Elapsed time is computed by calculating the difference in clock ticks between the captured time of two key user-specified events. The number of clock ticks may be converted to real time by multiplying the number of clock ticks by the period of the free-running timer.

The input capture system may be configured for many applications. Let us examine one such example—capturing the characteristics of a single pulse. This example assumes the pulse length is less than the rollover time of the free-running counter. To measure the pulse length of a single active low pulse, the following actions are taken:

1. The input capture edge selection is set to wait for a falling edge. This is accomplished by setting the associated EDGnB and EDGnA bits to 1 0 in the Timer Control Register (TCTL3,4).

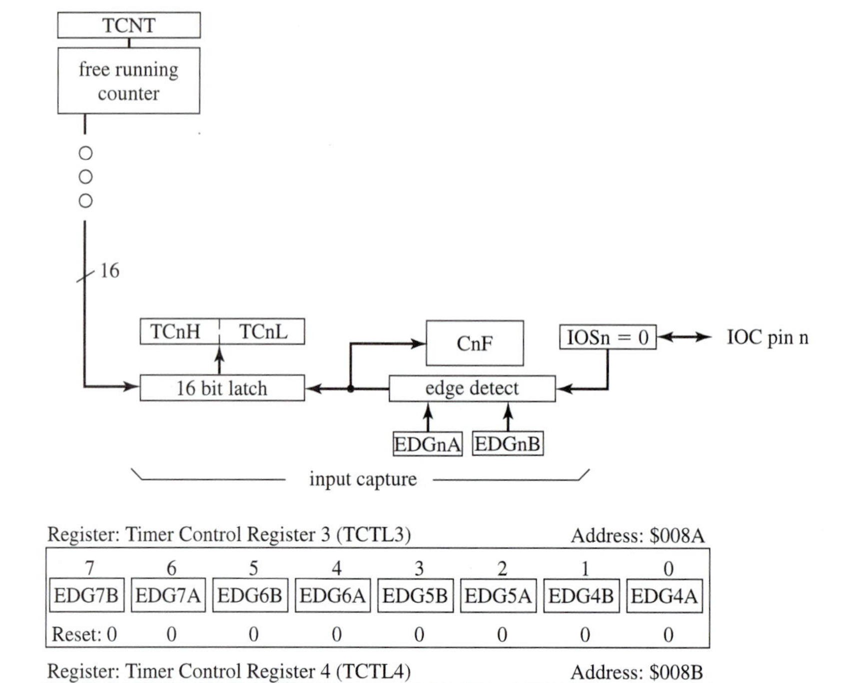

Register: Timer Control Register 3 (TCTL3) Address: $008A

7	6	5	4	3	2	1	0
EDG7B	EDG7A	EDG6B	EDG6A	EDG5B	EDG5A	EDG4B	EDG4A
Reset: 0	0	0	0	0	0	0	0

Register: Timer Control Register 4 (TCTL4) Address: $008B

7	6	5	4	3	2	1	0
EDG3B	EDG3A	EDG2B	EDG2A	EDG1B	EDG1A	EDG0B	EDG0A
Reset: 0	0	0	0	0	0	0	0

Figure 7.17 Key components of the input capture system. The free-running counter provides a 16-bit binary count to the input capture channel.

2. The associated Channel Flag (CnF) is monitored.
3. When the CnF bit sets indicating the desired edge action has occured on the associated input capture pin, the current time in the free-running counter is automatically latched into the Timer Channel Register (TCnH/L).
4. The value in the TCnH/L register is read and stored in a convenient location.
5. The CnF flag is reset by writing a logic 1 to it.
6. The input capture edge selection is set to wait for a rising edge. This is accomplished by setting the associated EDGnB and EDGnA bits to "0 1" in the Timer Control Register (TCTL3,4).
7. The associated Channel Flag (CnF) is monitored.
8. When the CnF bit sets indicating the desired edge action has occured on the associated input capture pin, the current time in the free-running counter is automatically latched into the Timer Channel Register (TCnH/L).

9. The value in the TCnH/L register is read.
10. The difference between the time of the rising edge is subtracted from the time of the falling edge to calculate the elapsed time in clock ticks. **Note:** If the first falling edge and/or the second rising edge count is smaller than the first rising edge count, then $FFFF must be added to the first rising edge count to account for the rollover of the free-running counter.
11. The elapsed time in clock ticks is converted to real time by multiplying the number of clock ticks by the free-running counter's period.

The registers associated with the input capture system are covered after discussing the output compare system.

Practice Questions

Question: How must the prior steps be modified to measure the pulse length of a single active high pulse?

Answer: Step 1 must be modified to capture a rising edge. Step 6 must be modified to capture a falling edge.

Question: How must the prior steps be modified to measure the period of a repetitive signal?

Answer: Step 6 is deleted. This will have the system capture the time of two falling edges. The period is found by taking the free-running count from the second falling edge and subtracting from it the free-running count of the first edge. This assumes the period is shorter than the rollover period of the counter.

Question: How must the steps provided earlier be modified to measure the time between two input capture rising edge events for time increments greater than the rollover time of the counter?

Answer: For time increments greater than the rollover time of the free-running counter, a counter must be implemented in software to count the number of times rollover occurs. We do not ask you to write code for this modification. It is much more efficient to write the code using an interrupt service routine.

Output Compare The output compare function allows the user to generate an output signal to desired specifications. A single active low or high pulse may be generated or a repetitive signal of desired specifications (duty cycle, frequency, etc.) may be generated. Also, a pulse width-modulated signal may be generated. The key components of the output compare system are illustrated in Figure 7.18.

Like the input capture system, the free-running counter provides the time base for the output compare system. A 16-bit value is loaded into the associated 16-bit Timer Channel Registers (TCnH/L). When the 16-bit count in the free-running counter equals the 16-bit value in the TCnH/L, the comparator starts a chain reaction of events. First, the associated Channel Flag (CnF) is set. This flag can be reset

Register: Timer Control Register 1 (TCTL1) Address: $0088

	7	6	5	4	3	2	1	0
	OM7	OL7	OM6	OL6	OM5	OL5	OM4	OL4
Reset:	0	0	0	0	0	0	0	0

Register: Timer Control Register 2 (TCTL2) Address: $0089

	7	6	5	4	3	2	1	0
	OM3	OL3	OM2	OL2	OM1	OL1	OM0	OL0
Reset:	0	0	0	0	0	0	0	0

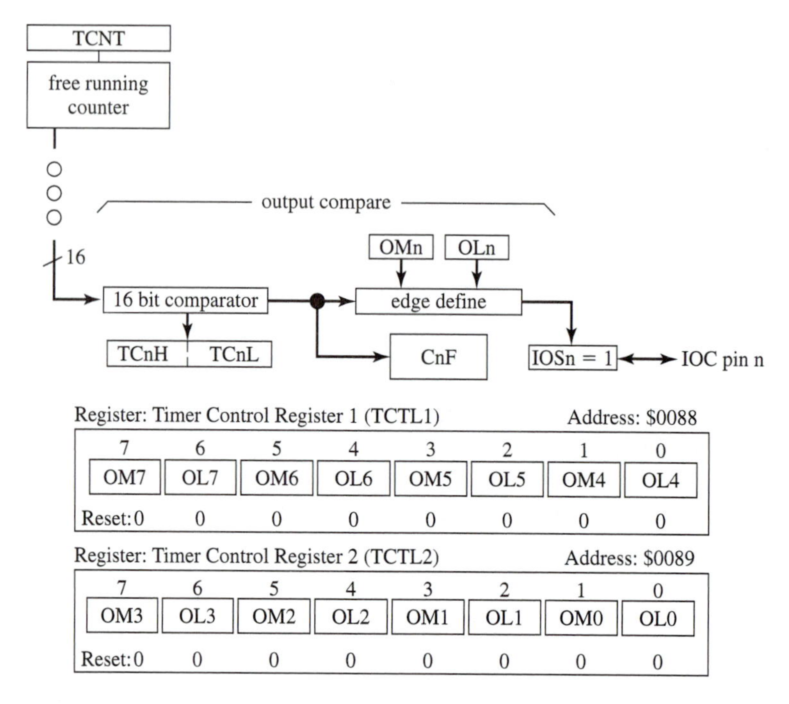

Figure 7.18 Key components of the output compare system.

by writing a logic 1 to it. Second, the corresponding Channel Interrupt Flag (CnI) is set and generates an interrupt event if it has been previously enabled. Finally, the user-specified output event occurs on the associated output pin. The output event is specified by the associated Output Mode/Output Level (OMn/OLn) bits. These bits are located in Timer Control Registers 1 (TCTL1—$0088) and 2 (TCTL2—$0089). The specified output event may be a logic level 1 output, a logic level 0 output, or a toggle (Figure 7.19).

Output capture events are generated in reference to key events. For example, to generate a single active high pulse (assumed to be less than the rollover time of the counter), the following actions are taken:

OMn OLn	Configuration
00	Timer Disconnected
01	Toggle OCn output line
10	OCn output line to 0
11	OCn output line to 1

Figure 7.19 Output compare signal selection.

1. The current value of the free-running counter (TCNT) is obtained.
2. The desired output pin is set to high.
3. The length of the desired pulse duration is calculated in clock ticks. That is, the desired pulse length is divided by the period of the free-running counter. The resulting fraction is multiplied by $FFFF to complete the conversion to clock ticks.
4. The pulse length in clock ticks is added to free-running countervalue obtained in step 1.
5. This sum is stored into the associated Timer Channel Register (TCnH/L).
6. The associated output pin is set to clear the OCn line. This is accomplished by setting the associated OMn/OLn bits in the TCTL1, 2 registers to 10.
7. When the free-running counter value equals the TCnH/L register, the output pin goes low.

Practice Questions

Question: How must the prior steps be modified to generate a single active low pulse?

Answer: In step 2, the desired output pin is set low. In step 6, the associated output pin is configured for logic high.

Question: How must the previous steps be modified for a pulse length lasting longer than the rollover time of the free-running counter?

Answer: There are two different methods that may be employed separately or together: (1) change the prescale divisor using the PR[2:1:0] bits to slow down the rollover time of the counter, and/or (2) monitor the number of Timer Overflows (TOFs) that occur.

Question: What value must be loaded into the Timer Input Capture/Output Compare Select (TIOS) register to set the odd number channels for the output compare function and the even number channels for the input capture function? Provide the code to do this.

Answer:

```
TIOS        EQU     $0080        ;TIOS register address
IOCHMASK    EQU     $AA          ;mask to set odd ch to output, even to input

            ORG     $8000        ;
            LDAA    #IOCHMASK    ;load input/output ch mask
            STAA    TIOS         ;
              :
```

Question: Provide the assembly code to configure input capture/output compare channel 7 for input capture and to capture any edge.

Answer:

```
TIOS       EQU   $0080        ;TIOS register address
TCTL3      EQU   $008A        ;TCTL3 register address
IOCHMASK   EQU   $00          ;mask to set ch 7 to input
EDGEMASK   EQU   $C0          ;mask to capture any edge ch 7

           ORG   $8000        ;
           LDAA  #IOCHMASK    ;load input/output ch mask
           STAA  TIOS         ;
           LDAA  #EDGEMASK    ;load mask for ch 7 edge config
           STAA  TCTL3        ;
             :
```

Question: Provide the assembly code to configure input capture/output compare channel 7 for output compare and to toggle.

Answer:

```
TIOS       EQU   $0080        ;TIOS register address
TCTL1      EQU   $0088        ;TCTL1 register address
IOCHMASK   EQU   $80          ;mask to set ch 7 to output
EDGEMASK   EQU   $20          ;mask to toggle ch 7

           ORG   $4000        ;
           LDAA  #IOCHMASK    ;load input/output ch mask
           STAA  TIOS         ;
           LDAA  #EDGEMASK    ;load mask for ch 7 toggle
           STAA  TCTL1        ;
             :
```

Forced Output Compares The forced output compare feature of the 68HC12 is used to initialize the output compare hardware. The activity associated with an output compare function occurs immediately without waiting for a match between the contents of the free-running counter (TCNT) and the contents of the associated Timer Channel n register. Forcing an output compare action on a given output compare channel is accomplished by writing a logic 1 to the associated bit positions in the Timer Compare Force Register (CFORC—$0081). The forced output compare signal causes the specified output pin actions, but does not set the status flag.

The Input Capture/Output Compare Registers In this section, we discuss the registers associated with the input capture/output compare system. The registers associated with the pulse accumulator system are discussed later.

Timer IC/OC Select Register—TIOS The Timer IC/OC Select Register (TIOS) is located at memory location $0080 (Figure 7.20). The IOSn bits in this register are used to specify whether a given channel is configured for input capture or output compare. When a specific IOSn bit is set to 1, the corresponding channel is configured for output compare operation. When 0, the channel is configured for input capture operations.

Register: Timer Input Capture/Output Compare Select (TIOS) Address: $0080

	7	6	5	4	3	2	1	0
	IOS7	IOS6	IOS5	IOS4	IOS3	IOS2	IOS1	IOS0
Reset:	0	0	0	0	0	0	0	0

Figure 7.20 Timer IC/OC Select Register—TIOS ($0080).

Timer Compare Force Register—CFORC The Timer Compare Force Register (CFORC) is located at memory location $0081 (Figure 7.21). Setting a specific FOCn bit to 1 causes an immediate output compare action on the corresponding channel. This is a useful technique for initializing the output compare channels.

Register: Timer Compare Force Register (CFORC) Address: $0081

	7	6	5	4	3	2	1	0
	FOC7	FOC6	FOC5	FOC4	FOC3	FOC2	FOC1	FOC0
Reset:	0	0	0	0	0	0	0	0

Figure 7.21 Timer Compare Force Register—CFORC ($0081).

Timer Output Compare 7 Mask Register—OC7M The Timer Output Compare 7 Mask Register (OC7M) is located at memory location $0082 (Figure 7.22). The bits of the OC7M register correspond with the bits of the PORT T Timer Port. Setting an OC7Mn bit sets the corresponding port to be an output port regardless of the state of the DDRTn bit when the corresponding TIOSn bit is set for the output compare function.

Register: Output Compare 7 Mask Register (OC7M) Address: $0082

	7	6	5	4	3	2	1	0
	OC7M7	OC7M6	OC7M5	OC7M4	OC7M3	OC7M2	OC7M1	OC7M0
Reset:	0	0	0	0	0	0	0	0

Figure 7.22 Timer Output Compare 7 Mask Register—OC7M ($0082).

Register: Output Compare 7 Data Register (OC7D) Address: $0083

	7	6	5	4	3	2	1	0
	OC7D7	OC7D6	OC7D5	OC7D4	OC7D3	OC7D2	OC7D1	OC7D0
Reset:	0	0	0	0	0	0	0	0

Figure 7.23 Timer Output Compare 7 Data Register—OC7D ($0083).

Timer Output Compare 7 Data Register—OC7D The Timer Output Compare 7 Data Register (OC7D) is located at memory location $0083 (Figure 7.23). The bits of the OC7D register correspond with the bits of the PORT T Timer Port. When a successful OC7 compare action occurs, for each bit set in the OC7M register, the corresponding data bit in OC7D is stored to the corresponding bit of the timer port.

Timer Control Register 1—TCTL1 and Timer Control Register 2—TCTL2 Timer Control Registers 1 and 2 are used to specify the output compare actions for a specific output channel (Figures 7.24 and 7.25). The corresponding OMn and OLn bits specify the output mode and level for a specific channel. The settings for these two bits were provided earlier in the chapter.

Register: Timer Control Register 1 (TCTL1) Address: $0088

	7	6	5	4	3	2	1	0
	OM7	OL7	OM6	OL6	OM5	OL5	OM4	OL4
Reset:	0	0	0	0	0	0	0	0

Figure 7.24 Timer Control Register 1—TCTL1 ($0088).

Register: Timer Control Register 2 (TCTL2) Address: $0089

	7	6	5	4	3	2	1	0
	OM3	OL3	OM2	OL2	OM1	OL1	OM0	OL0
Reset:	0	0	0	0	0	0	0	0

Figure 7.25 Timer Control Register 2—TCTL2 ($0089).

Timer Control Register 3—TCTL3 and Timer Control Register 4—TCTL4 Timer Control Registers 3 and 4 are used to specify the input capture actions for a specific input channel (Figures 7.26 and 7.27). The corresponding EDGnB and EDGnA bits specify the input capture characteristics for a specific channel. The settings for these two bits were provided earlier in the chapter.

Register: Timer Control Register 3 (TCTL3) Address: $008A

7	6	5	4	3	2	1	0
EDG7B	EDG7A	EDG6B	EDG6A	EDG5B	EDG5A	EDG4B	EDG4A
Reset: 0	0	0	0	0	0	0	0

Figure 7.26 Timer Control Register 3—TCTL3 ($008A).

Register: Timer Control Register 4 (TCTL4) Address: $008B

7	6	5	4	3	2	1	0
EDG3B	EDG3A	EDG2B	EDG2A	EDG1B	EDG1A	EDG0B	EDG0A
Reset: 0	0	0	0	0	0	0	0

Figure 7.27 Timer Control Register 4—TCTL4 ($008B).

Timer Mask Register 1—TMSK1 The Timer Mask Register 1 (TMSK1) is located at memory location $008C (Figure 7.28). This register is used to selectively turn on the interrupts associated with the input capture/output compare channels. If cleared, the corresponding flag is disabled from causing a hardware interrupt. If set, the corresponding flag is enabled to cause a hardware interrupt.

Register: Timer Interrupt Mask Register 1 (TMSK1) Address: $008C

7	6	5	4	3	2	1	0
C7I	C6I	C5I	C4I	C3I	C2I	C1I	C0I
Reset: 0	0	0	0	0	0	0	0

Figure 7.28 Timer Mask Register 1—TMSK1 ($008C).

Timer Mask Register 2—TMSK2 The Timer Mask Register 2 (TMSK2) is located at memory location $008D (Figure 7.29). The Timer Counter Reset Enable (TCRE) bit allows the free-running counter to be reset. For this to occur, the TCRE must be set to 1 and the timer channel 7 registers must contain

Register: Timer Interrupt Mask Register 2 (TMSK2) Address: $008D

7	6	5	4	3	2	1	0
TOI	0	TPU	TDRB	TCRE	PR2	PR1	PR0
Reset: 0	0	1	1	0	0	0	0

Figure 7.29 Timer Mask Register 2—TMSK2 ($008D).

$0000. The TMSK2 register also contains the Timer Prescaler Select (PR[2:1:0]) bits. These bits are used to set the prescale divisor. The Timer Overflow Interrupt Enable (TOI) bit is used to turn on the Timer Overflow Interrupt flag. When this bit is set to logic 1, a hardware interrupt is requested when the TOF flag is set.

Timer Flag Register 1—TFLG1 The Timer Flag Register 1 (TFLG1) is located at memory location $008E (Figure 7.30). The bits in the TFLG1 register indicate when an interrupt condition has occurred. A specific flag bit is reset by writing a 1 to the bit. Writing a 0 to a bit does not effect the current status of the bit. When the TFFCA bit in the TSCR register is set, a read from an input capture or a write into an output compare channel causes the corresponding channel flag (CnF) to be cleared.

Register: Timer Interrupt Flag Register 1 (TFLG1) Address: $008E

	7	6	5	4	3	2	1	0
	C7F	C6F	C5F	C4F	C3F	C2F	C1F	C0F
Reset:	0	0	0	0	0	0	0	0

Figure 7.30 Timer Flag Register 1—TFLG1 ($008E).

Timer Flag Register 2—TFLG2 The Timer Flag Register 2 (TFLG2) is located at memory location $008F (Figure 7.31). The Timer Overflow Flag (TOF) bit in the TFLG2 register indicates when the free-running counter rolls over. The TOF flag bit is reset by writing a 1 to the bit.

Register: Timer Interrupt Flag 2 (TFLG2) Address: $008F

	7	6	5	4	3	2	1	0
	TOF	0	0	0	0	0	0	0
Reset:	0	0	0	0	0	0	0	0

Figure 7.31 Timer Flag Register 2—TFLG2 ($008F).

Timer Input Capture/Output Compare Registers High (TCnH) and Low (TCnL) There are eight separate Timer Input Capture/Output Compare Registers (Figure 7.32). Each of these registers contains 16 bits. Depending on the corresponding TIOS channel bit, these registers are used to latch the value of the free-running counter during an input capture event or to trigger an output compare event.

Register: Timer Input Capture/Output Compare Register 0 Address:$0090-0091
Register: Timer Input Capture/Output Compare Register 1 Address:$0092-0093
Register: Timer Input Capture/Output Compare Register 2 Address:$0094-0095
Register: Timer Input Capture/Output Compare Register 3 Address:$0096-0097
Register: Timer Input Capture/Output Compare Register 4 Address:$0098-0099
Register: Timer Input Capture/Output Compare Register 5 Address:$009A-009B
Register: Timer Input Capture/Output Compare Register 6 Address:$009C-009D
Register: Timer Input Capture/Output Compare Register 7 Address:$009E-009F

Register: Timer Input Capture/Output Compare Register n (TCnH) Address:

	7	6	5	4	3	2	1	0
	Bit 15	Bit 14	Bit 13	Bit 12	Bit 11	Bit 10	Bit 9	Bit 8
Reset:	0	0	0	0	0	0	0	0

Register: Timer Input Capture/Output Compare Register n (TCnL) Address:

	7	6	5	4	3	2	1	0
	Bit 7	Bit 6	Bit 5	Bit 4	Bit 3	Bit 2	Bit 1	Bit 0
Reset:	0	0	0	0	0	0	0	0

Figure 7.32 Timer Channel n Register High (TCnH) and Low (TCnL) ($0090—$009F).

Practice Questions

Question: Describe two different methods that an interrupt flag (CnF) may be cleared in register TFLG1.

Answer: A specific flag bit is reset by writing a 1 to the bit. Writing a 0 to a bit does not effect the current status of the bit. When the TFFCA bit in the TSCR register is set, a read from an input capture or a write into an output compare channel causes the corresponding channel flag (CnF) to be cleared.

7.6.4 The Pulse Accumulator

The Pulse Accumulator (PA) portion of the Timer Module, as its name implies, is used to count pulses. The heart of the PA system is a 16-bit counter. This counter can be configured to operate in two different modes of operation:

- Event countermode. This mode is used to count user-specified edges that occur on the pulse accumulator input (PAI) pin.
- Gated time accumulation mode. In this mode, the PA counts pulses from a divide by 64 clock. It is termed *gated mode* because the pulse accumulator counts the divide by 64 clock pulses while it is enabled and ceases counting while it is disabled. However, it maintains the last current count while it is in the disabled mode.

Pulse Accumulator System Description A block diagram of the pulse accumulator system is provided (Figure 7.33). As you can see, the input pin to the PA system (PAI) shares the same external 68HC12 pin as IC/OC channel 7. To use this pin for the PA system, channel 7 must be turned off. This is accomplished by:

- Set the IOS7 bit in the Timer IC/OC Select Register—TIOS ($0080) to 0 to disable output compare channel 7,
- Set bits OM7 and OL7 to 00 in Timer Control Register 1—TCTL1 ($0088) to disconnect the IC/OC channel from the output logic pin, and

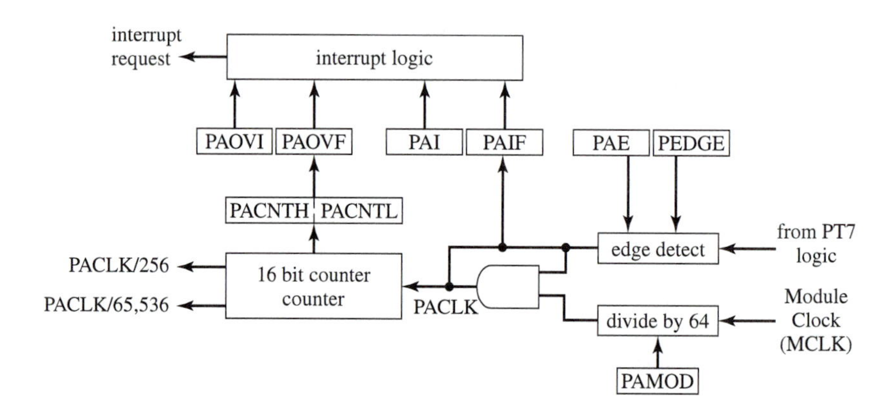

Register: Pulse Accumulator Control Register (PACTL) Address: $00A0

	7	6	5	4	3	2	1	0
	0	PAEN	PAMOD	PEDGE	CLK1	CLK0	PAOVI	PAI
Reset:	0	0	0	0	0	0	0	0

Register: Pulse Accumulator Flag Register (PAFLG) Address: $00A1

	7	6	5	4	3	2	1	0
	0	0	0	0	0	0	PAOVF	PAIF
Reset:	0	0	0	0	0	0	0	0

Register: 16 bit Pulse Accumulator Count Register (PACNTH) Address: $00A2

	7	6	5	4	3	2	1	0
	Bit 15	Bit 14	Bit 13	Bit 12	Bit 11	Bit 10	Bit 9	Bit 8
Reset:	0	0	0	0	0	0	0	0

Register: 16 bit Pulse Accumulator Count Register (PACNTL) Address: $00A3

	7	6	5	4	3	2	1	0
	Bit 7	Bit 6	Bit 5	Bit 4	Bit 3	Bit 2	Bit 1	Bit 0
Reset:	0	0	0	0	0	0	0	0

Figure 7.33 Pulse Accumulator System.

- Set the OC7M7 bit to 0 in the Timer Output Compare 7 Mask Register—OC7M ($0082).

The signal from the input pin of the pulse accumulator is then routed to the edge-detection circuitry. This functions much like the edge-detection circuitry previously described for the input capture system. The edge-detection circuitry is controlled by the Pulse Accumulator Enable (PAEN) bit and the Pulse Accumulator Edge (PEDGE) bit. The PAEN when set to 1 enables the pulse accumulator, whereas the PEDGE bit selects falling or rising edges on the PAI pin to increment the counter. In the event countermode with PEDGE set to 1, the pulse accumulator counts rising edges. With PEDGE set to 0, the pulse accumulator counts falling edges on the PAI pin. The edge-detection circuitry has an associated flag called the Pulse Accumulator Input Flag (PAIF). This flag is set when the user-specified edge is detected on the PAI pin. The PAIF is located in the Pulse Accumulator Flag Register—PAFLG ($00A1).

In the gated time accumulation mode, a PEDGE value of 1 allows a low PAI pin level to enable a MCLK/64 pulse train to be the input to the pulse accumulator's 16-bit counter. A PEDGE value of 0 allows a high PAI pin value to enable the MCLK/64 pulse train.

Once an input source is selected for the 16-bit counter within the pulse accumulator, it increments for each incoming pulse. The value in the 16-bit counter may be read from the 16-bit Pulse Accumulator Counter Register—PACNTH/L ($00A2 and $00A3). The 16-bit count in these registers reflects the number of active input edges on the PAI pin since the last system reset.

The 16-bit pulse accumulator counter has an overflow flag called the Pulse Accumulator Overflow Flag (PAOVF). This flag is located in the Pulse Accumulator Flag Register—PAFLG ($00A1). As with the other Timer Module flags, this flag is cleared by writing a logic 1 to it. The pulse accumulator system has powerful interrupt features. There are two separate interrupts associated with the Pulse Accumulator System: the Pulse Accumulator Overflow Interrupt and the Pulse Accumulator Input Interrupt Enable.

The Pulse Accumulator Overflow Interrupt, when enabled by the PAOVI bit of the PAFLG register, initiates an interrupt event when the 16-bit pulse accumulator overflows from $FFFF to $0000. The Pulse Accumulator Input Interrupt, when enabled by the PAI bit of the PAFLG register, initiates an interrupt event when the selected edge is detected at the pulse accumulator input pin. When set for the event mode, the event edge triggers the PAIF. When set for the gated time accumulation mode, the trailing edge of the gate signal at the pulse accumulator input pin triggers the PAIF.

Pulse Accumulator Registers In this section, we discuss the registers associated with the pulse accumulator system.

Pulse Accumulator Control Register (PACTL) The Pulse Accumulator Control Register (PACTL) is located at memory location $00A0 (Figure 7.34). This register is used to set the operating mode, the edge control, and the timing variables of the pulse accumulator system. The PAEN bit is used to enable the Pulse Accumulator system. When the PAEN bit is set to 1, the PA system is enabled. When 0, it is disabled. The Pulse Accumulator Mode (PAMOD) bit selects either the event countermode (0) or the gate time accumulation mode (1) for the pulse accumulator.

Register: Pulse Accumulator Control Register (PACTL) Address: $00A0

	7	6	5	4	3	2	1	0
	0	PAEN	PAMOD	PEDGE	CLK1	CLK0	PAOVI	PAI
Reset:	0	0	0	0	0	0	0	0

Figure 7.34 Pulse Accumulator Control Register (PACTL) ($00A0).

The Pulse Accumulator Edge Control bit (PEDGE) determines how the PA system responds to an edge. When the PA system is set for the event countermode (PAMOD = 0), the PA system responds to falling edges when the PEDGE bit is set to 0 and to rising edges when set to 1.

When the PA system is set for the gate time accumulation mode (PAMOD=1), the PA system is clocked by the MCLK/64 signal. If the PEDGE pin is 0, the falling edge of the clock signal sets the pulse accumulator interrupt flag (PAIF). Similarly, if the PEDGE pin is 1, the rising edge of the clock signal sets the pulse accumulator interrupt flag (PAIF).

The CLK1 and CLK0 bits of the PACTL select the clock signal for the PA system. The different available configurations for these pins were provided earlier in this chapter.

Pulse Accumulator Flag Register (PAFLG) The Pulse Accumulator Flag Register (PAFLG) located at memory location $00A1 contains the pulse accumulator system flags—PAOVF and PAIF (Figure 7.35). The Pulse Accumulator Overflow Flag is set when the 16-bit pulse accumulator counter rolls over from $FFFF

Register: Pulse Accumulator Flag Register (PAFLG) Address: $00A1

	7	6	5	4	3	2	1	0
	0	0	0	0	0	0	PAOVF	PAIF
Reset:	0	0	0	0	0	0	0	0

Figure 7.35 Pulse Accumulator Flag Register (PAFLG) ($00A1).

to $0000. The Pulse Accumulator Input Edge Flag (PAIF) is set when the selected edge event occurs at the pulse accumulator input pin.

Pulse Accumulator Counter Registers (PACNTH/L) The 16-bit Pulse Accumulator Counter Register (PACNT) contains the current pulse accumulator count value (Figure 7.36). Since it is a 16-bit register, it should be read using the LDD, LDX, or LDY command.

Register: 16 bit Pulse Accumulator Count Register (PACNTH) Address: $00A2

	7	6	5	4	3	2	1	0
	Bit 15	Bit 14	Bit 13	Bit 12	Bit 11	Bit 10	Bit 9	Bit 8
Reset:	0	0	0	0	0	0	0	0

Register: 16 bit Pulse Accumulator Count Register (PACNTL) Address: $00A3

	7	6	5	4	3	2	1	0
	Bit 7	Bit 6	Bit 5	Bit 4	Bit 3	Bit 2	Bit 1	Bit 0
Reset:	0	0	0	0	0	0	0	0

Figure 7.36 Pulse Accumulator Counter Registers (PACNTH/L) ($00A2 and $00A3).

7.7 THE REAL-TIME INTERRUPT (RTI)

The real-time interrupt system was described in the interrupt chapter. However, by function, it is considered part of the timer system. Therefore, a brief review of the RTI is provided here for completeness. The 68HC12 has built-in features to remind it to perform required actions on a regular basis (Figure 7.37). For example, weather does not usually change minute by minute. It might be satisfactory to have our remote weather station collect weather data at 15-minute intervals. This can be accomplished using the real-time interrupt (RTI) features of the 68HC12. We describe how to program an interrupt service routine in the interrupt chapter. In this section, we describe the features of this clock-related system.

The RTI system consists of two registers: (1) the Real-Time Interrupt Control Register (RTICTL) and the Real-Time Interrupt Flag Register (RTIFLG). The RTICTL is used to enable and set the interrupt rate of the RTI. The RTI system is enabled by setting the real-time interrupt Enable (RTIE) bit to logic 1 and the interrupt rate is set using bits RTR[2:0]. The RTIFLG contains the RTI interrupt flag (RTIF) in bit 7. This flag sets when the RTI interrupt occurs. It is cleared by a write to the RTIFLG register. We discuss how to program the RTI features of the 68HC12 in the interrupt chapter.

Register: Real-Time Interrupt Control Register (RTICTL) Address: $0014

	7	6	5	4	3	2	1	0
	RTIE	RSWAI	RSBCK	0	RTBYP	RTR2	RTR1	RTR0
Reset:	0	0	0	0	0	0	0	0

Register: Real Time Interrupt Flag Register Address: $0015

	7	6	5	4	3	2	1	0
	RTIF	0	0	0	0	0	0	0
Reset:	0	0	0	0	0	0	0	0

RTR[2:0]	Divide M by:	M=4.0 MHz Time-out	M=8.0 MHz Time-out
000	off	off	off
001	2^{13}	2.048 ms	1.024 ms
010	2^{14}	4.096 ms	2.048 ms
011	2^{15}	8.192 ms	4.096 ms
100	2^{16}	16.384 ms	8.196 ms
101	2^{17}	32.768 ms	16.384 ms
110	2^{18}	65.536 ms	32.768 ms
111	2^{19}	131.072 ms	65.536 ms

Figure 7.37 Real Time Interrupt (RTI) registers.

7.8 PROGRAMMING INPUT CAPTURE, OUTPUT COMPARE, AND THE PULSE ACCUMULATOR FEATURES OF THE TIM

In this section, we provide representative samples of how to program the different sections of the Timer Module. We illustrate three different methods to initialize the contents of required registers. Recall that a detailed example using the real-time interrupt (RTI) system is provided in the interrupt chapter.

7.8.1 Programming the Input Capture System

As a representative sample of programming the input capture system, we measure the period of a periodic signal connected to input capture channel 2. We configure channel 2 for input capture action. Note that we use directives to specify the base register address and then the offset to the input capture-related registers. This allows us to use an index addressing technique to initialize the input capture-related registers. For this example, we assume an MCLK value of 8 MHz. We set the prescaler to divide by four. This results in a clock signal to the input capture system of 2 MHz or a period of 0.5 μs.

```
;------------------------------------------------------------------
;MAIN PROGRAM: This program measures the period of a signal connected to
;input capture channel 2 by measuring the count difference between two
;consecutive rising edges.
;------------------------------------------------------------------
REG_BASE    EQU     $0000       ;addr of register base
TMSK1       EQU     $8C         ;declare offset of reg from base
TMSK2       EQU     $8D         ;declare offset of reg from base
TCTL4       EQU     $8B         ;declare offset of reg from base
TIOS        EQU     $80         ;declare offset of reg from base
TC2H        EQU     $94         ;declare offset of reg from base
TSCR        EQU     $86         ;declare offset of reg from base
TFLG1       EQU     $8E         ;declare offset of reg from base
TCNT        EQU     $84         ;declare offset of reg from base
TMSK2_IN    EQU     $02         ;disable TOI, prescale=4
TCTL4_IN    EQU     $10         ;config IC2 for rising edge
TIOS_IN     EQU     $00         ;select ch2 for IC
TSCR_IN     EQU     $80         ;enable timer, normal flag clr
CLR_CH2     EQU     $04         ;mask to clr ch 2 flag

            ORG     $7000       ;User RAM at $7000
edge_1      FDB     $0000       ;reserve word for variable
period      FDB     $0000       ;reserve word for variable

            ORG     $8000
            BSR     TIMERINIT   ;timer initialization subr
            BSR     MEAS_PER    ;measure period
DONE        BRA     DONE        ;Branch to self

;--------------------------------------
;Subroutine TIMERINIT: Initialize timer for IC2;
;--------------------------------------

TIMERINIT   CLR     TMSK1           ;disable interrupts
            LDX     #REG_BASE       ;load register base to X
            LDAA    #TMSK2_IN       ;load TMSK2 using index addr
            STAA    TMSK2,X         ;disable ovf, prescale=4
            LDAA    #TCTL4_IN       ;conf IC2 for rising edge
            STAA    TCTL4,X         ;
            LDAA    #TIOS_IN        ;select ch 2 for IC
            STAA    TIOS,X          ;
            LDAA    #TSCR_IN        ;conf IC2 for rising edge
            STAA    TSCR_IN,X       ; enable timer, standard flag clr
            RTS                     ;Return from subroutine
```

```
;-----------------------------------------
;Subroutine MEAS_PER: measures period
;between two input capture events.
;-----------------------------------------

MEAS_PER  LDAA   #CLR_CH2              ;Clear IC2 flag
          STAA   TFLG1,X
WTFLG     BRCLR  TFLG1,X, $04,WTFLG    ;wait for first edge
          LDD    TCNT,X                ;load value from TCNT reg
          STD    EDGE_1                ;store rising edge 1 count
          LDAA   # CLR_CH2             ;Clear IC2 flag
          STAA   TFLG1,X
WTFLG1    BRCLR  TFLG1,X, $04,WTFLG    ;wait for second edge
          LDD    TCNT,X                ;load value from TCNT
          SUBD   EDGE_1                ;calculate period
          STD    PERIOD                ;store period
          RTS
          END                          ;end program
```

The result of finding the count difference between two consecutive rising edges is now at location PERIOD. To convert this count to real time, we simply multiply the value in PERIOD by the length of the input capture period. For this example, we configured the clock for a period of 0.5 μs.

7.8.2 Programming the Input Capture System with an Interrupt

Until now, we have programmed the input capture system using the polling method. As we have discovered, the polling method is an inefficient use of the 68HC12. It is much more efficient to use the 68HC12 in an interrupt driven mode. Earlier in this chapter, we discussed the interrupt features associated with the timer system. In particular, the free-running counter is equipped with a timer overflow flag (TOF) that sets when the counter rolls over from $FFFF to $0000. If the Timer Overflow Interrupt (TOI) enable bit is also set, the TOF flag also generates an interrupt event. The TOI provides an efficient method of tracking input capture events that last longer than the rollover time of the counter. The parameters of the long event are captured as described earlier in this section. In addition, we must also monitor the number of timer overflow events using the TOI.

7.8.3 Programming the Output Compare System

As a representative sample, let us generate a 1000 Hz square wave with a 50% duty cycle on output compare channel 2 (OC2). Using a MCLK value of 8 MHz, we set the prescaler to divide by four. This results in a clock signal to the output compare system of 2 MHz or a period of 0.5 μs. Therefore, the period of a 1000 Hz signal

(1.0 ms) is equivalent to approximately 2000 pulses. The signal is high for 1000 ($3E8) pulses and low for 1000 ($3E8) pulses.

The program to generate this signal is provided next. Note that we use directives to specify the register addresses. We also use these directives to initialize the contents of the registers. The Move Byte (MOVB) and Move Word (MOVW) commands are used to initialize the registers.

```
;------------------------------------------
;MAIN PROGRAM: This program generates a
;1000 Hz square wave with a 50% duty cycle
;on output compare channel 2.
;------------------------------------------
TMSK1       EQU     $008C       ;declare locations of registers
TMSK2       EQU     $008D       ;declare locations of registers
TCTL2       EQU     $0089       ;declare locations of registers
TIOS        EQU     $0080       ;declare locations of registers
TC2H        EQU     $0094       ;declare locations of registers
TSCR        EQU     $0086       ;declare locations of registers
TFLG1       EQU     $008E       ;declare locations of registers
TMSK2_IN    EQU     $02         ;disable TOI, prescale=4
TCTL2_IN    EQU     $10         ;initialize OC2 toggle
TIOS_IN     EQU     $04         ;select ch2 for OC
TSCR_IN     EQU     $80         ;enable timer, normal flag clr

            ORG     $7000       ;User RAM at $7000
            BSR     TIMERINIT   ;timer initialization subr
DONE        BSR     SQ_WAVE     ;square wave gen subr
            BRA     DONE        ;Branch to self

;----------------------------------------------
;Subroutine TIMERINIT: Initialize timer for OC2;
;----------------------------------------------

TIMERINIT   CLR     TMSK1                   ;disable interrupts
            MOVB    #TMSK2_IN,TMSK2         ;disable ovf, prescale=4
            MOVB    #TCTL2_IN,TCTL2         ;OC2 toggle on compare
            MOVB    #TIOS_IN,TIOS           ;select ch 2 for OC
            MOVW    #$03E8,TC2H             ;load TC2 with initial comp
            MOVB    #TSCR_IN,TSCR           ;enable timer, standard flag clr4
            RTS                             ;Return from subroutine

;---------
; CLEARFLG
;---------
```

```
;Clear C2F flag by reading TFLG1 when C2F set and then writing 1 to C2F

CLEARFLG  LDAA   TFLG1                ;To clear OC2 flag, read flag first
          ORAA   #$04                 ;then write 1 to it
          STAA   TFLG1
          RTS

;------------------------------
;Subroutine SQWAVE: ;
;------------------------------
;

SQWAVE    BRCLR  TFLG1,$04,SQWAVE     ;Poll for C2F Flag
          LDD    TC2H                 ;load value from TC2 reg
          ADDD   #$03E8               ;add hex value high count
          STD    TC2H                 ;set up next transition time
          BRA    CLEARFLG             ;generate repetitive signal
          RTS
          END                         ;end program
```

7.8.4 Programming the Output Compare System with Interrupts

Until now, we have ignored output compare events that last longer than the rollover time of the free-running counter. For events lasting longer than the rollover time of the counter, what do we do? We could:

- Slow down the frequency of the MCLK. If the free-running counter is being used to time a mixture of both fast and slow events, decreasing the MCLK frequency may decrease the resolution of the faster timed events to an unacceptable level.
- Change the MCLK prescaler bits PR[2:1:0]. As in the previous suggestion, this may not be acceptable.
- Count timer overflow (TOF) flags. As mentioned previously, the TOF bit may also be equipped to simultaneously generate an interrupt. Every time the free-running counter rolls over, an interrupt occurs. As part of the interrupt service routine, the number of timer overflows may be tabulated.

Let us illustrate these concepts with an example.

Example

Weather balloons are used to gather data in the upper atmosphere. Also many educational agencies use weather balloon projects as a way to develop expertise in placing a satellite in orbit. The idea is that the payload for the satellite may be developed and tested using a low-cost weather balloon prior to sending an actual satellite into orbit aboard an expensive space booster (Figure 7.38).

The payload of such a project is critical. Care must be taken to minimize the weight of the payload as much as possible. Often batteries are used to power the payload. The actual payload is often not powered until sometime after balloon launch in an effort to minimize battery requirements and hence weight. The payload is powered-up when needed. In this example, we use the output compare features with interrupts of the timing system to generate an active high-payload power-up signal 30 minutes after balloon launch. For this example, let us assume the following:

Assumptions:

- The MCLK is running at 8 MHz.
- The prescale values are set to PR[2:1:0] = 010 (an MCLK divisor of 4).
- Use timer channel 0 to serve as the output compare channel.
- Timer channel 0 should be set to logic 0 at launch and transition to logic 1 level 30 minutes later.

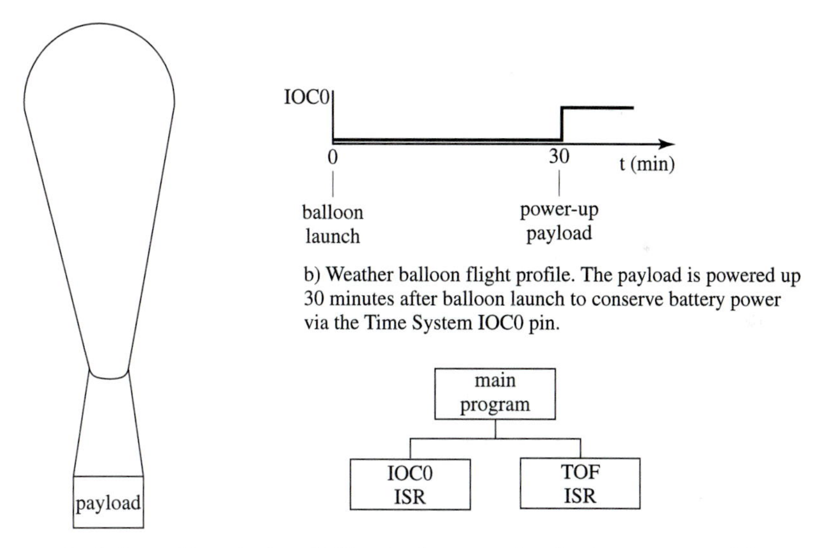

a) weather balloon with payload

b) Weather balloon flight profile. The payload is powered up 30 minutes after balloon launch to conserve battery power via the Time System IOC0 pin.

c) Abbreviated structure chart for the program containing two different interrupt service routines.

Figure 7.38 Balloon Launch. (a) A weather balloon equipped with a payload. (b) The actual payload is often not powered until sometime after balloon launch in an effort to minimize battery requirements and hence weight. (c) The output compare features with interrupts may be used.

Preparation: We need to calculate the number of overflows and the count to add to the initial value of the free-running counter to obtain a 30-minute delay. The total number of pulses in 30 minutes is:

$$30\ min \times 60\ secs/min \times 8 \times 10^6/4\ pulses/sec = 3.6 \times 10^9\ pulses$$

Now convert this total number of pulses to timer overflows and extra counts. Recall that timer overflows occur every 65,536 pulses.

$$3.6 \times 10^9\ pulses \times 1\ overflow/65{,}536\ pulses = 54{,}931\ overflows + 41{,}984\ counts$$

What does all of this mean? At the beginning of the balloon launch, we obtain the count in the free-running counter. We add 41,984 counts to this total. We then monitor for 54,931 free-running counter overflows and set the output compare to go high when the desired free-running count occurs. This corresponds to 30 minutes of elapsed time.

Writing the assembly language program We are not going to provide you with the assembly language code to accomplish this task. We have provided enough examples in the interrupt chapter and earlier in this chapter to guide programming. The program is left as a Challenge homework problem at the end of this chapter. However, we do provide some pointers to guide you to a successful solution.

1. Earlier in this chapter, we provided a step-by-step algorithm to program the output compare system. Go back to these steps and modify them to include interrupt processing events.
2. At the beginning of the algorithm, you need to set Timer Channel 0 to a logic low level.
3. Every time the free-running counter hits the desired value for the output compare event, the output compare could be activated. Therefore, do not set the output compare initially. Wait for the number of overflows to occur and then configure the output compare for a logic high output when the free-running counter reaches the desired value on its next cycle.
4. Use the TOI to keep track of the free-running counter overflows.
5. Draw a good flowchart of the program before writing a single line of assembly code. If you cannot explain the algorithm in the form of a flowchart, you cannot be successful in your coding activities.

7.8.5 Programming the Pulse Accumulator System

The pulse accumulator system is used to count events external to the 68HC12. In this example, we configure the 68HC12 to count trailing edge pulses occurring on the pulse accumulator pin.

```
;--------------------------------------------------------------
;MAIN PROGRAM: This program counts the number of trailing edge pulses
;that occur on the pulse accumulator pin.
;--------------------------------------------------------------
PACTL       EQU     $00A0       ;specify register locations
PAFLG       EQU     $00A1       ;specify register locations
PACNT       EQU     $00A2       ;specify register locations
PACTL_IN    EQU     $44         ;enable PA, event count mode
                                ;rising edge, prescale 00
            ORG     $7000       ;User RAM at $7000


            BSR     PAINIT      ;PA initialization subr
DONE        BRA     DONE        ;Branch to self


;------------------------------------
;Subroutine PAINIT: Initialize PA ;
;------------------------------------
PAINIT:
        LDAA    #PACTL_IN               ;initialize PA variables
        STAA    PACTL                   ;disable ovf, prescale=4
        RTS                             ;Return from subroutine
```

With the pulse accumulator initialized, the number of pulse accumulator events that have occurred may be checked by reading the 16-bit pulse accumulator count in the PACNT register. This is easily accomplished by using this line in your code.

```
        LDD     PACNT                   ;read 16-bit pulse accumulator
```

7.9 APPLICATIONS

The laboratory exercises have been designed to provide you with experience using the input capture and output compare features of the 68HC12. You program the 68HC12 to generate pulse width-modulated waveforms to control the speed of two direct current (DC) motors for both the right and left motors of the mobile robot. Two other output compare channels are used to turn off pulses to the two motors. You control the robot motion (acceleration, constant speed, and deceleration) by modifying the contents of two output compare registers (TCn) using pulse width modulation techniques.

7.10 LABORATORY APPLICATIONS

LABORATORY EXERCISE A: GENERATION OF PULSE WIDTH MODULATION TO CONTROL DC MOTORS FOR MOBILE ROBOT NAVIGATION—PART I

Purpose This lab is designed to provide you with experience using the input capture and output compare features of the 68HC12—valuable tools for time-related tasks. You program the 68HC12 to generate pulse width-modulated waveforms to control the speed of two DC motors for the mobile robot. In this lab, you are only responsible for generating forward robot motions (during the next lab, you work on the backward and turning motions of the robot). To accomplish the objectives in this lab, you must:

(a) Use the output compare function to modify the duty cycle of the rectangular output waveform;
(b) Use the input capture function to monitor the number of pulses arriving at an input capture pin and modify the output waveform accordingly,
(c) Change the speed of the motor by adjusting the duty cycle of the output waveform according to a specified speed profile,
(d) Interface the 68HC12 with two DC motors using a motor driver chip (SN754410NE),
(e) Configure Port T pins, and
(f) Display results on the PC screen.

Documentation

68HC812A4EVB User's manual

SN754410 data sheets

Prelab For the prelab, you must have a flowchart and pseudocode for your program as well as wired hardware which includes the motor driver chip. On completion of your program, hook up your 68HC12 board with motors and demonstrate your working robot.

Note: Before you connect motors to the 68HC12, use an oscilloscope to observe output signals from the output compare pins. Connect motors on your mobile robot **only if** you are convinced that the output signal waveforms are correct.

DESCRIPTION

Introduction One of the most powerful subsystems of the 68HC12 is the timing system. The timing system is usually used for signal generation, measurement, and timing. The programmable Timer System uses port T to communicate with the external world.

The contents of an output compare register can be used by a programmer to set an output pin logic level to high/low and/or to cause an interrupt when the value of the free-running counter matches that of the output compare register. An input capture register can be used for the opposite function. When a signal on an input capture pin goes to either low or high, the input capture register can store the time that the event occurred and can cause an interrupt. We can program the eight channels of port T as inputs or outputs. For the present lab exercise, pins PT0 and PT1 are used to monitor input signals, whereas pins PT2 and PT3 are used to generate output signals. If you are not familiar with port T, you are directed to the hardware chapter for review.

Pulse Width Modulation We start with a brief description of the pulse width-modulated signal-based motor speed-control scheme. Suppose you are controlling a motor by connecting a voltage source to the motor as shown in Figure 7.39. If you close the switch, the motor starts to rotate. Now imagine what would happen if you open and close the switch and repeat this process rapidly. The motor speed is proportional to the time the switch is closed, which is identical to the underlying principle for the pulse width-modulated speed-control scheme. That is, by controlling the time during which the switch is on, the motor speed can be controlled. The amount of fractional time period when the switch is on compared with the total time period is referred to as the *duty cycle*: A 100% duty cycle means that the switch is closed at all times, whereas 0% duty cycle means that the switch is open at all times. Figure 7.40 shows the waveforms with 20% and 80% duty cycles, and Figure 7.41 shows a simplified view of how such a waveform can control a DC motor.

For this lab, you write a motor control program by manipulating the duty cycles of output signals to control motor speeds. The speed-versus-time profile is shown in Figure 7.42—similar to one you worked out in Laboratory Exercise in Chapter 3. Notice that the speed of a DC motor is proportional to the duty cycle of a pulse width-modulated signal; the duty cycle on the y-axis of the graph represents the amount of time we turn on the motor within each cycle period. Naturally, the more time we leave the motor on (higher duty cycle), the higher the motor speed is. We discuss this more shortly.

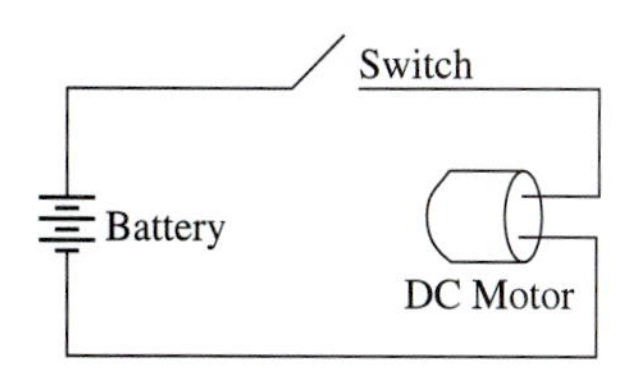

Figure 7.39 A sample setup to control a DC motor.

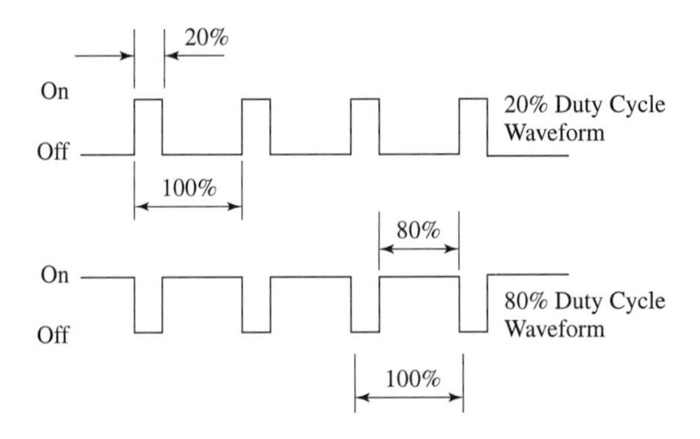

Figure 7.40 Two pulse width-modulated signals.

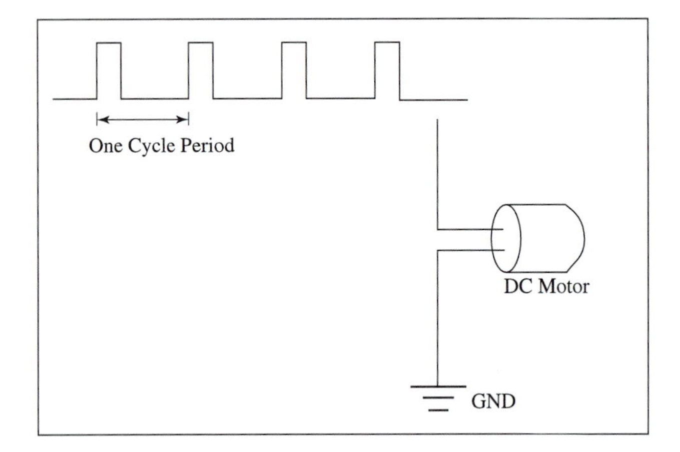

Figure 7.41 A pulse width-modulated signal controlling a DC motor.

The period of the motor voltage waveform should be 8.192 msec. *(This is the default time required for the TCNT counter, the built-in timer, to count from 0 to 65,536, which means you do not have to do anything for this step.)* You must generate the rectangular signal (pulse width-modulated signal) for approximately 15 seconds (1,831 8.192 msec pulses). The built-in timer is a 16-bit register, and it takes 8.192 msec to count from $0000 to $FFFF (we are using the 8MHz clock; you can do the math to come up with 8.192 msec). The duty cycle of the waveform should change according to the speed profile shown in Figure 7.42.

The initial duty cycle starts at 5% and should linearly increase up to 20% as the total running time reaches the 5-second mark, as measured from the time your robot starts to send a signal out to the output compare pins. The same speed profile is used to control both the right and left motors. Use the OC2 and OC3 output compare systems to control the right and the left motors, respectively. (You

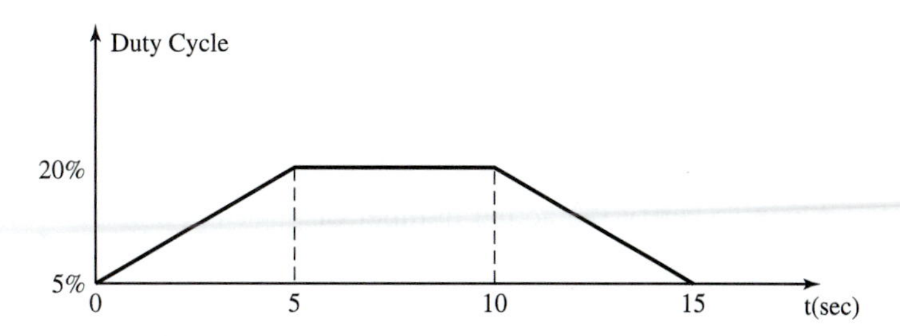

Figure 7.42 The desired duty cycle profile for lab 7.

must also use the OC7 system as we discuss later in this lab.) Note that the 5-second point is represented by $1{,}831/3 = 610$ pulses (1,831 cycles $\simeq$ 15.0 sec). After the 5-second mark, the signal should maintain the duty cycle at 20% until the accumulated running time reaches the 10-second mark (which corresponds to approximately 1,221 pulses from the start of the control process). Starting from this point, the duty cycle should decrease linearly down to 5% again as the accumulated running time of the signal generation reaches the 15-second mark (the number of pulses reaches 1,831). At this time, the output compare pin should go to zero (motor off) before exiting the program to complete the control process. This corresponds to your mobile robot moving straight with the designated acceleration, constant speed, and deceleration periods.

As stated earlier, two pulse width-modulated signals are used to control the right and the left motors of the robot where two output compare pins are used to send out the signals. As the speed-control scheme described in the previous paragraph is carried out, the same two output signals should also be used as inputs to two of the input capture pins (you use two input capture systems specified in the procedure section of this lab). The task of the input capture hardware is to monitor (count) the number of pulses generated by the output compare system to determine where the system is with respect to the speed profile.[1] Your program should also display the status (number of pulses generated so far) to a PC monitor using the D-Bug12 subroutines every second (the time for 122 pulses on the input capture pin). A sample message is shown:

The total running time is 1 sec.
The total running time is 2 sec.

⋮

⋮

The total running time is 15 sec.

[1] In a sophisticated robot, optical encoders attached to the robot wheels generate this type of feedback.

Notice that after the last message is displayed on the PC screen, your program still needs to generate one more pulse to complete the process. (You probably cannot tell the difference between the ending time of the program and the ending time of the pulse generation.)

Again to verify the actual number of pulses generated from the output pins, the generated signals should be connected to the appropriate input capture pins. The number of pulses received by the input capture pins should be used to control the duty cycle of the output waveforms according to the desired speed profile. Although other methods can be used to count the number of pulses generated by the output compare hardware, for this lab you must use the 68HC12 input capture system.

Procedure To generate a pulse width-modulated signal, you can take advantage of the output compare hardware associated with port T pins. Two particular pins must first be programmed to be as output compare pins. For this lab, use PT2 and PT3.

1. Turn on the Timer System by enabling the TEN bit in the TSCR register.
2. Generate pulse width-modulated signals:

   - Use the output compare systems associated with pins PT2 and PT3 to control the right and left motors, respectively. The corresponding output compare registers associated with pin PT2 and pin PT3 are OC2 and OC3. (Notice that you can choose any of the two output compare pins to control the motors. We specify the pins for you to make the debugging process easier and to make the motor control code portable.) Set the logic states on the output pins to be low (off) when successful compares are made by config-

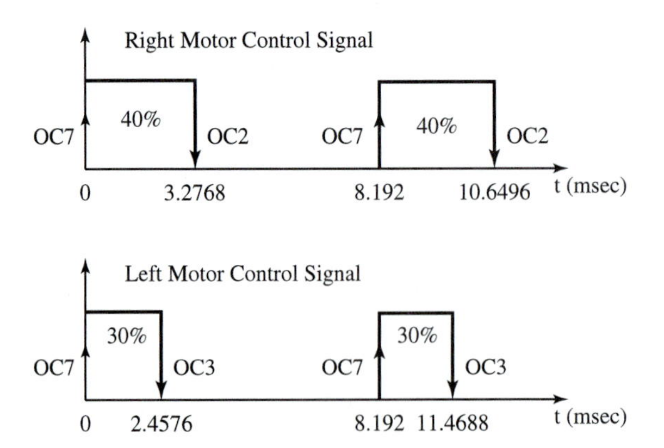

Figure 7.43 A close view of motor control signals for the right and left motors.

uring bits in the TCTL2 register: bits OM2 and OL2 for the OC2 system and bits OM3 and OL3 for the OC3 system.

- Now recall that the OC7 system can control logic states of the any output compare pins. Configure the OC7 system to set (turn on) the logic levels on pins PT2 and PT3 when successful matches are detected between the contents of the TC7 register and the free-running counter. Recall you need to set up the OC7M and OC7D registers to perform this task. Figure 7.43 shows how the varying duty cycle signal can be generated on the PT2 pin logic by using OC2 to turn the pulse off and OC7 to turn it on after the appropriate pulse width time. The same process applies for the PT3 pin logic for the left motor as shown in the figure. (Of course you can switch the functionalities of the two output compare systems. That is, in the example of the right motor, you can configure the system to turn off the signal logic on the PT2 using the OC7 and turn it on using the OC2.)
- Since we want the robot to move forward in a straight line, the pulse waveforms sent to the right and left motors should be the same. In the figure, however, we purposely showed different duty cycle values to illustrate that you can send different pulse width-modulated signals to the two motors.
- Note that the free-running counter and the output compare registers are 16-bit registers. Furthermore, the free-running counter starts at $0000 after a reset and counts up to 2^{16} (65,536 counts). The counter then overflows and starts from $0000 again. Since we are using an 8 MHz M-clock, each clock period is 0.125 microsecond and the period it takes to count up to $FFFF (65,536 counts) is 8.192 milliseconds.

3. Setting up the duty cycle:

- Since we use a period of the square wave as 8.192 msec (or 65,536 counts), we can find the corresponding number of counts for a given duty cycle. For example, if you want the duty cycle to be 10%, you simply need to store $65{,}536/10 = 6,554$ (of course you need to convert values into hexadecimal numbers) in the TCx register, and wait for the contents of the free-running counter to count up to this number before you turn the signal off, assuming that you turned the signal on when the contents of the counter was $0000.
- During the acceleration and deceleration periods of the speed profile, your program needs to constantly (at every pulse period) change the duty cycle to reflect the desired change of the motor speed. To accomplish this task, you need to find the incremental counts to be added from the time the pulse logic is high before the logic is forced to be low again. The overall change of the duty cycle during the acceleration or deceleration period is 15% (20%–5%), which corresponds to a change of approximately 9,830

counts (65,536 × 0.15). The total time period to make this change is 5 seconds, which turns out to be the period to generate about 610 pulses (recall the period of the rectangular wave is 8.192 msec). This means that we have 610 opportunities to modify the duty cycle by making an incremental change to the contents of the TC2 and TC3 registers at each of the 610 opportunities. The incremental change is approximately 9,830/610 = 16 counts. Thus, during the acceleration period, the pulse or time will increase by 16 counts each 8.192 msec.

- Note that by cleverly using the input capture interrupt service routine associated with counting each of the generated pulses, you may not need to use any output compare interrupt service routine.

4. Measuring the number of pulses arriving at an input capture pin:

   - Use the input capture systems IC0 and IC1 with the associated pins PT0 and PT1 for the right and left motors, respectively. To capture an incoming signal, you first need to configure the type of signal change at the input pin you want each system to monitor. This task is done using bits EDG3B and EDG3A for the IC3 system and bits EDG2B and EDG2A for the IC2 system in the TCTL4 register. For an example, if you want the input capture to occur for a rising edge using the IC0 system, you need to put %00000001 into the TCTL4 register.
   - At every instance your program detects a pulse coming into the input capture pins, your program needs to update the number of pulses received so far. To do so you can use the interrupt module associated with the input capture system and update the number of received pulses within the corresponding interrupt service routine. Recall that you also need to use the following registers to perform the desired task: TMSK1 and TFLG1.

5. Displaying the intermediate results on the PC screen. You have already performed this task a couple of times in the previous labs.
6. Interfacing the motor driver chip. The primary purpose of the motor driver chip is to provide the voltage and current required to run the DC motor. For the forward motion, use the diagram in Figure 7.44 to connect the motors to the 68HC12EVB.

LABORATORY EXERCISE B: GENERATION OF PULSE WIDTH MODULATION TO CONTROL DC MOTORS FOR MOBILE ROBOT NAVIGATION—PART II

Purpose In the previous lab, you learned how to use the input capture and output compare features of the 68HC12 to control the forward motion of the mobile

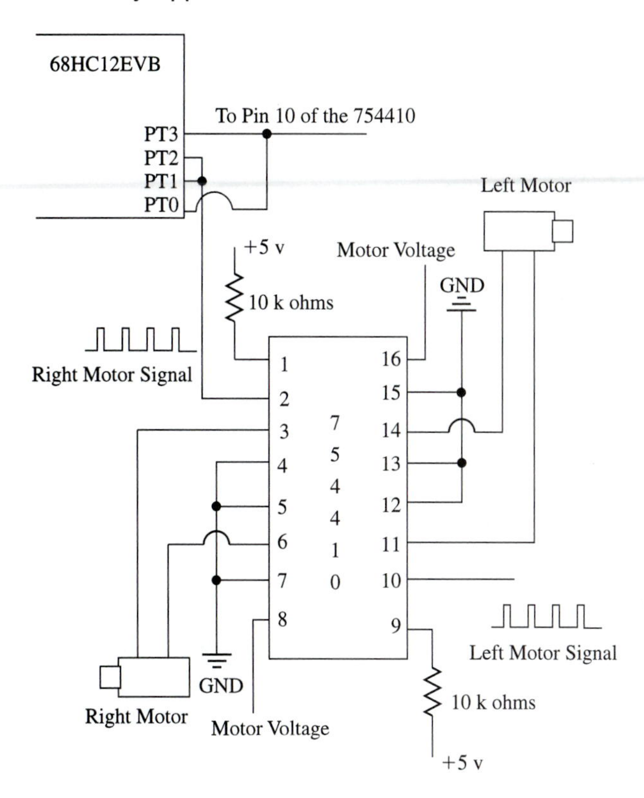

Figure 7.44 A diagram for connecting the motor driver chip, motors, and the 68HC12EVB.

robot. This lab is designed to expand the application of these features for other mobile robot motions—namely, the turning motion. The interface hardware from the previous lab needs a slight modification to accommodate the additional motion. The motion of the robot is still controlled by sending appropriate pulse width-modulated signals to the two DC motors. To accomplish the objectives in this lab, you must:

1. Use the output compare function to modify the duty cycle of the rectangular output waveform.
2. Use the input capture function to monitor the number of pulses arriving at input capture pins and modify the output waveforms accordingly.
3. Change the speed of the motor by adjusting the duty cycle of the output waveform according to a specified speed profile. (For the turning motion, we use a constant duty cycle from the start to the end of the turn.)

4. Interface the 68HC12 with two DC motors using a motor driver chip (SN754410NE) (This part also needs to be modified to accommodate the backward and turning motion. We show how to accomplish this at the end of this section.)
5. Be able to configure Port T pins.

Documentation 68HC12EVB User's manual

Prelab For the prelab, you must have a flowchart and pseudocode for your program as well as wired hardware associated with the motor driver chip.

Description You write a mobile robot motion control program using the timing features of the 68HC12. You have already completed the bulk of the programming in Lab A and this is an extension to your Lab A program to include both the straight motion as well as the turning motion of your mobile robot.

1. Programming turning motion. To generate the mobile robot turning motion, a couple of different strategies need to be developed.
   (a) a 90-degree turn

   - To make the robot turn 90 degrees, you must experiment with your own robot.[2] The value you want to find is the length of time the 68HC12 needs to send out identical pulse width-modulated signals to two motors with a fixed duty cycle. For the fixed duty cycle value, you should use 20% (increase your duty cycle only if your robot cannot overcome the friction to turn with this duty cycle). To find the time it takes to turn 90 degrees, use the input capture signal pulses as a unit of times. For example, it may take 620 pulses for the robot to turn 90 degrees.
   - Note that you want to program your robot such that it turns like a tank. This means the 68HC12 needs to provide signals with opposite polarities to the two motors: While one wheel turns forward, the other wheels turns backward.

   (b) A non-90-degree turn

   - This type of motion can come in handy if you need to change the direction of your robot only slightly. A typical scenario is when a robot tries to move down the hall in a straight line, but it veers off to one side of the hallway and approaches a wall. In this case, the robot needs to make a small compensating turn to correct its direction of motion.

[2]Each robot is made slightly different from the rest, and each robot needs to be calibrated to make a proper turn.

- We could formulate sophisticated control rules for such motion, but for this lab we only concern ourselves with couple of simple turns. Again, the amount of turn depends on how long the 68HC12 provides a pair of opposite pulse width-modulated signals to the two motors. Develop a small turning motion (10–35 degrees).

(c) You may think that you need to write separate subroutines for each turning motion, but you only need to write a single subroutine which takes in to account a couple of parameters. The first parameter tells the subroutine which direction the robot should turn, and the second parameter should provide the time interval (in # of pulses) the turning motion should continue.

2. Modification on the interface with the motor driver chip. You need to modify the circuit you implemented in Lab Exercise A. The key difference is that by using simple logic gaits, you provide capabilities for the forward, backward,

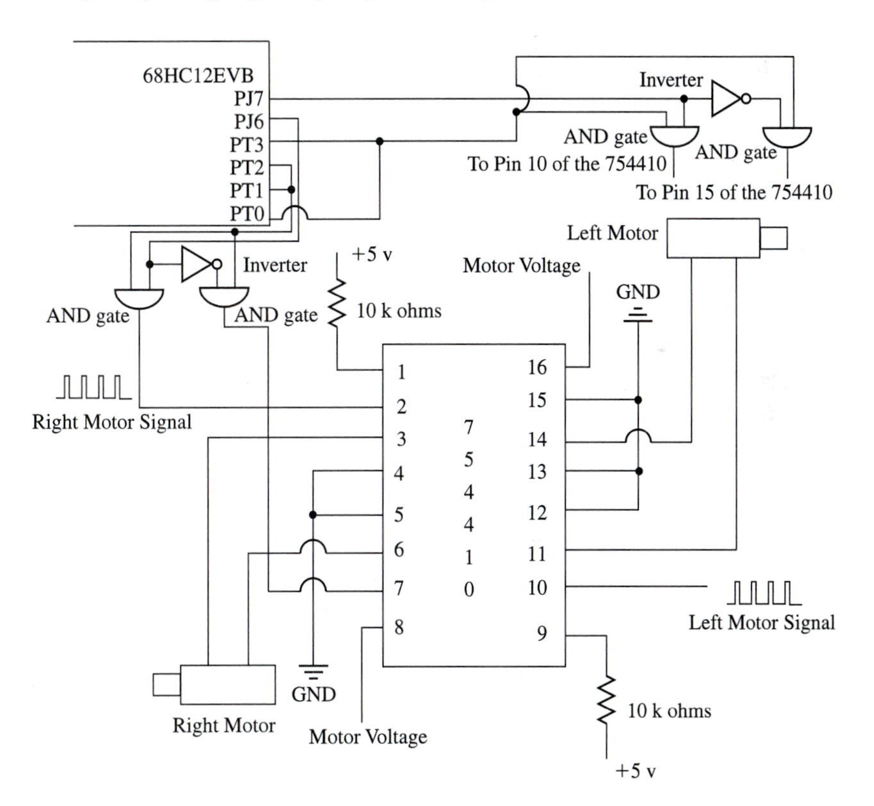

Figure 7.45 A diagram for connecting the motor driver chip, motors, and the 68HC12EVB for a set of robot motions.

and turning motions. Refer to Figure 7.45 for your circuit configuration. Note that, in addition to the output compare pin connections, you need to provide a logic pin for each motor as shown in the figure. You can easily use two of the Port J pins (use PJ6 and PJ7 as shown) for this purpose. The logic pin decides whether the motion of the motor is forward or turning. If you provide opposite logic states to two lines LOGIC 1 and LOGIC 2, shown in the figure, the robot turning motion is obtained. If the logic states for both lines are one, the robot moves forward, whereas logic zero causes the robot to move backward.

7.11 SUMMARY

In this chapter, we described the operation of the 68HC12 Clock Module; described the operation of the clock divider chain serving the 68HC12 Standard Timer Module (TIM); explained the operation of the TIM system; listed and described the key components of the TIM system; summarized and described the Input Capture, Output Compare, and Pulse Accumulator features of the TIM system; and programmed Input Capture, Output Compare, and the Pulse Accumulator features of the TIM.

7.12 REFERENCES

MC68HC812A4 Technical Summary 16-Bit Microcontroller, Motorola, Inc. 1997.
68HC12 Evaluation Board User's Manual, Motorola, Inc. 1996.

7.13 CHAPTER PROBLEMS

Fundamental

1. Two input capture events occur at counts $1037 and $FF20 of the free-running counter. How many counts (in decimal) have transpired between these two events.
2. In the preceding question, if the MCLK was 2 MHz and the prescaler bits PR[2:1:0] were set to 000, how much time in seconds transpired between the two input capture events?
3. Repeat the preceding question if PR[2:1:0] were set to 101.

Advanced

1. How must the input capture algorithm provided in the chapter be modified to measure the duty cycle and frequency of a periodic signal? (Assume that the period of the signal is less than the rollover time of the free-running counter.)

2. Write the assembly language code to implement the algorithm described in the preceding question.
3. How must the output compare algorithm provided in the chapter be modified to generate a periodic signal with a user-specified duty cycle and frequency?
4. The following two counts are captured: $1993 and $07C8. Assume that the prescaler value of the free-running counter is set to 1 and the MCLK is operating at 2 MHz. If you assume the pulse width is less than the rollover time of the free-running counter, what is the pulse length?
5. If you cannot assume the pulse length is less than the rollover time of the free-running counter in the prior question, how would you modify your program to accurately calculate the pulse width? Provide an equation.
6. The anemometer on a remote weather station (reference the hardware chapter) provides a pulse for every revolution of the spindle containing four cups to catch the wind. Write a subroutine to count the pulses using the pulse accumulator system (Figure 7.47).

Challenging

1. Write an assembly language subroutine to generate a repetitive friend signal. The friend signal consists of a 1000 μs pulse train. The signal alternates between high- and low-level 100 μs pulses followed by a 1000 μs low-level signal. The signal then repeats. The signal is sent out on the IR emitter at the front of the robot, which is connected to output compare channel 0 (IOC0). Assume the MCLK is set to 1 MHz (Figure 7.46).
2. Write an assembly language program to discriminate between a friend and foe. The signal is received on the IR detector on the front of the robot and connected to input capture channel 2 (IOC2). The friend signal is described in the preceding question. The foe signal is a repetitive pulse train of 200 μs pulses (Figure 7.46).

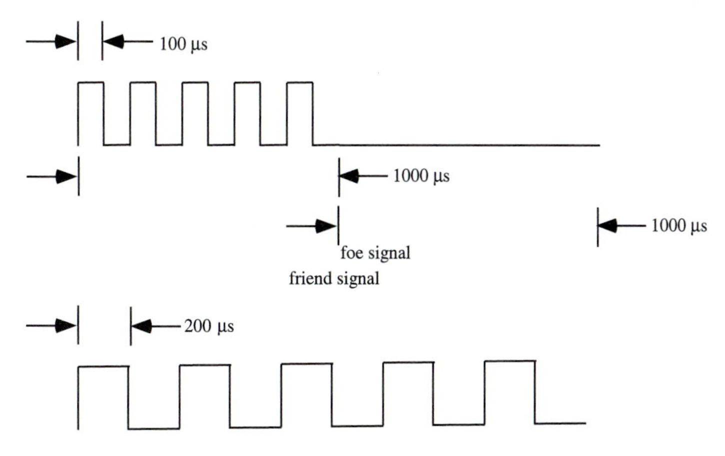

Figure 7.46 Friend or foe signal.

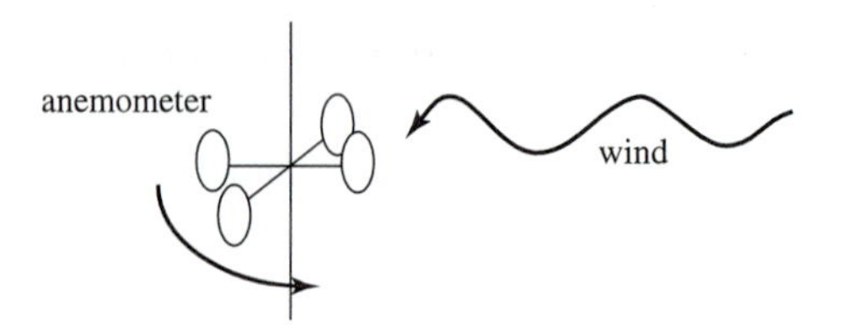

Figure 7.47 Anemometer. The anemometer on a remote weather station (reference the hardware chapter) provides a pulse for every revolution of the spindle containing four cups to catch the wind.

3. A stepper motor is used in applications for precise angular positioning (Figure 7.48). The motor is turned by sending it two to four different pulse trains. To turn the motor clockwise, the pulse train values are provided in forward order. To turn the motor counterclockwise, the pulse train values are provided in reverse order. Stepper motors may be used to open and close the solar array doors on the remote weather station. The control signal for a stepper motor requiring two control signals is shown. All these control signals may be compatible to the 68HC12 from a voltage point of view; they usually must source up to 1 amp (or more) of current. The current amplification is usually pro-

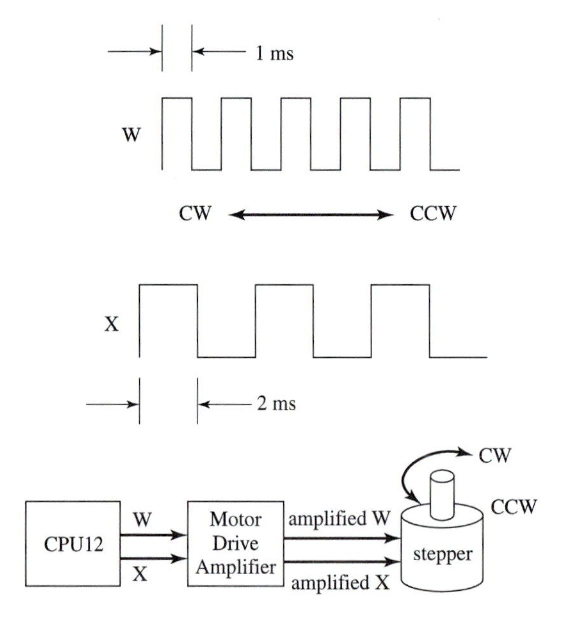

Figure 7.48 A stepper motor is used in applications for precise angular positioning. The motor is turned by sending it two to four different pulse trains.

vided by high-power semiconductor devices between the 68HC12 and stepper motor. Write a program to generate the W and X motor drive signals using the time parameters provided in the diagram. The signals should provide for clockwise and counterclockwise operations. The motors should turn clockwise until the *door closed* signal (logic high, pin 0, PORTC) is received. The motors should turn counterclockwise until the *door fully open* signal (logic high, pin 1, PORTC) is received.

4. Write the assembly language program for the weather balloon example provided in the text.

8

The 68HC12 Memory System

Objectives: At the completion of this chapter you will be able to:

- Discuss the different variants of the 68HC12 with reference to different memory configurations,
- Define the different memory technologies employed by the 68HC12,
- Interpret the memory map for a 68HC12-based system,
- Expand the memory of the 68HC12 to given specifications,
- Analyze the interface requirements for a CPU memory system (electrical, timing, and memory decoding), and
- Employ the memory paging features of the 68HC12.

This chapter begins with a brief overview of the two main variants of the 68HC12. These two variants have different memory configurations since they are intended for two different modes of operation. We review basic memory concepts and technologies employed in memory systems. From there, we discuss the concept of a memory map. A memory map is a useful tool for effective planning and use of the available memory space addressable by a computer. We then discuss basic memory operations: reading from memory and writing to memory. We also look at the timing associated with these operations. We conclude the chapter with a discussion of memory system interfacing, expansion, and paging. We examine two different types of memory expansion: linear expansion and memory paging. Linear expansion allows the addition of external memory components up to the 64K-bytes of the 68HC12 addressable memory space. The 68HC12 memory paging features allow the memory to be expanded well beyond the 64K-bytes of the linearly addressable memory space.

8.1 OVERVIEW

In Chapter 5, we introduced two different applications of the 68HC12: a wall following robot system and a remote weather station. These systems are quite different from one another, but they also have a lot in common. Both systems require an overall software program to control their operation. In one case, we need to control the operation of a robot as it travels through an unknown maze. In the other, we need to collect a wide range of weather data on a regular basis and send it to a central collection site. In this chapter, we find out how to store such a program in memory. We also investigate different types of memory. Usually a microcontroller system needs several different types of memory to accomplish its task. We examine these different memory technologies and specifically see how the 68HC12 is equipped with memory components.

The 68HC12 is an amazing integrated circuit. Within the confines of this single chip are several different memory subsystems. In some applications, these internal memory components are sufficient to accomplish the required task. However, in other applications, we need to add additional memory components to the 68HC12. In other words, we need to transition from the 68HC12 in the single-chip mode to one of the expanded modes. When additional memory is added to the 68HC12, we must be careful to ensure that address lines are decoded properly. That is, we need to ensure that for every address produced by the 68HC12 one and only one memory address is enabled at a time. We must also ensure the memory devices connected to the 68HC12 are configured for proper timing and electrical compatibility. In short, we need to ensure that when the 68HC12 generates control signals to load information from memory (e.g., during an LDAA command) or store information to memory (e.g., during a STAA command), the external memory components respond in sufficient time for correct execution of the memory-related instruction. We also need to ensure that the voltage and current parameters for the 68HC12 are compatible with any external device connected to the 68HC12. All of these concepts are investigated in this chapter.

8.2 BACKGROUND THEORY

The predecessor of the 68HC12 was the Motorola 68HC11. The 68HC11 microcontroller is equipped with a time-multiplexed address data bus when it is operated in the memory expanded mode. What does all of this mean? A microcontroller has a limited number of external pins. To efficiently use these available pins, certain functions of the pins are shared. When the 68HC11 is used in an expanded mode, the lower address lines (0 through 7) and data lines (0 through 7) shared the same eight-chip external pins. Address and data are placed on these pins in precise time slots. The lines are then required to be demultiplexed (de-interleaved) by external hardware to reverse this time-sharing process to yield separate address and data lines. Although this technique provides for an efficient use of 68HC11 external pins, it requires additional external hardware. The 68HC12 does not use this time-sharing scheme. It provides dedicated (separate) address and data lines to interface external memory devices.

The 68HC12 is available in several different variants. We only discuss two: the MC68HC912B32 (B32) and the MC68HC812A4 (A4). The most important distinguishing features of these variants are their memory configurations. The B32 is intended primarily for single-chip applications. It is equipped with a 32K-byte flash electrically erasable programmable read only memory (EEPROM) for program memory, 1K-byte of static RAM (random access memory), and 768 bytes of byte-erasable EEPROM for storing system data. We discuss each of these memory terms in the next section. The A4 variant has 1K-byte of static RAM and 4K-bytes of byte-erasable EEPROM for program and data storage. It is not equipped with a large internal EEPROM program memory like the B32 variant because it is primarily intended for use in applications requiring an expanded memory system. In this chapter, we concentrate primarily on the A4 variant.

8.3 BASIC MEMORY CONCEPTS

Before beginning a detailed discussion of the 68HC12 memory system, let us review some basic memory concepts common to most memory systems. We provide a brief review in the next section. For a full treatment of these concepts, refer to "Digital Design Principles and Practices" by John Wakerly.

8.3.1 Memory Capacity and Control Signals

Let us start by developing a convenient method of viewing memory systems. Memory systems may be thought of as a two-dimensional array of memory elements. (Figure 8.1). Each of these memory elements or cells can store a single bit of information—either a logical 1 or 0. The specific implementation of a memory cell

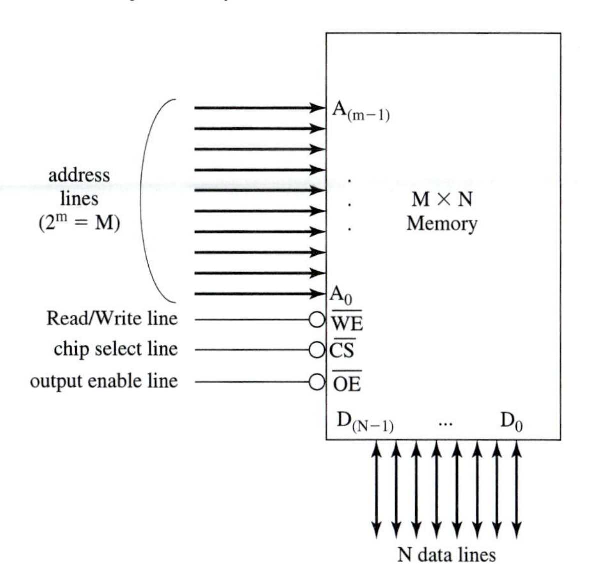

Figure 8.1 Generic memory configuration. Memory may be viewed as a two-dimensional array whose length is the number of separately addressable memory locations (M) and whose width corresponds to the number of bits (N) at each memory location. Memory capacity is usually defined as an M × N bit memory.

depends on the type of memory technology. In more specific terms, memory may be viewed as a two-dimensional array whose length is the number of separately addressable memory locations (M) and whose width corresponds to the number of bits (N) at each memory location. Memory capacity is usually defined as an M × N bit memory. For example, the 68HC12 is said to have a 64K × 8 memory space. This means the 68HC12 has the capability of addressing 64,000 different memory locations (actually 65,536 locations), with each location storing a 8-bit word. Typically, single bits of memory are not individually accessible. Rather, information is read from or written to memory as a byte (8 bits) or a word (16 bits).

Most memory devices have the following associated control pins (although they may have different names or designations):

- The write enable ($\overline{WE}$) is usually an active low signal. When activated during the write cycle, the binary values on the memory chip's data lines are written to the specified memory address.
- The output enable ($\overline{OE}$) is usually an active low signal. When activated during the read cycle, the data at the specified memory location are placed on the data pins of the memory chip and the data lines are connected to the

memory system's data bus using tristate outputs. (We discuss the tristate logic configuration in an upcoming section.)

- The chip select ($\overline{CS}$) is usually an active low-control pin used to select a specific chip in a memory array. We assume in our design exercise that all memory chips are enabled with an active low signal ($\overline{CS}$).

8.3.2 Memory Buses

Memory systems require three separate buses to accomplish memory operations. A bus is a collection of transmission paths (lines) with the same function. Most memory systems require an address bus, data bus, and control bus. The width (the number of individual lines it contains) of a specific bus depends on the function the bus serves. Rather than show the individual lines of the bus, the bus is usually drawn as a single line with a number next to it indicating the number of conductors in the bus. For example, in Figure 8.2, the address bus is shown as an "m" bit bus. We now discuss each of the three common types of buses found in a microcontroller system.

The Memory Address Bus The address bus' function is to provide a memory address that may be decoded such that one and only one memory location is accessed by a processor at a given time. This means that each memory location must have a separate and distinct address. Memory addresses are assigned using binary notation. For example, a processor that has an address bus containing 10 address lines may access 1024 (commonly called 1K-byte) different memory locations. The address of the first memory location is 00 0000 0000, whereas the address of the last location is 11 1111 1111. It becomes quite cumbersome to

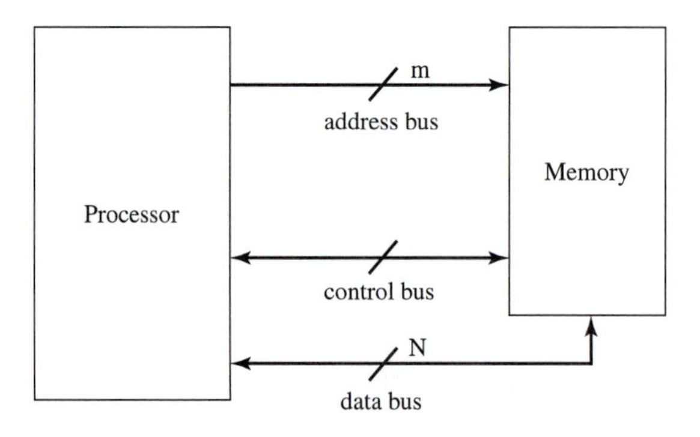

Figure 8.2 Memory buses.

specify memory locations using binary notation. Therefore, memory address locations are usually specified with their hexadecimal equivalents. For a processor with a 10-bit address bus, the address of the first location is $000, whereas the address of the last location is $3FF. We use the $ to precede hexadecimal numbers.

In general, the span of linearly addressable locations for a given processor is specified by:

$$\text{addressable memory locations} = 2^{address\ lines}$$

Earlier we said the 68HC12 is equipped with a 16-bit address bus. This allows the 68HC12 to have a linear memory span of $2^{16} = 65{,}536$ memory locations, which we refer to as 64K-bytes of addressable memory. The first memory location in the 68HC12 has an address of 0000 0000 0000 0000 or $0000, whereas the last memory location addressable by the 68HC12 has an address of 1111 1111 1111 1111 or $FFFF.

The Memory Data Bus The memory data bus is a collection of data lines used to read from or write to memory using parallel transfers. For example, a processor equipped with an 8-bit data bus reads from or writes to memory a byte at a time. The data bus on the 68HC12 is 16 bits wide. Therefore, the 68HC12 normally reads from or writes to memory 16 bits at a time using a parallel transfer.

The Memory Control Bus It is quite straightforward to identify the address and data bus on a processor. The pins associated with these are usually clearly labeled. For example, on the 68HC12, the address lines are designated ADDR0 through ADDR15. You can also note that the 68HC12 has address lines designated ADDR16 through ADDR21. These lines are not used for normal linear addressing. Rather, they are special purpose address lines used for memory paging, which we discuss later in this chapter. The data bus lines for the 68HC12 are designated DATA0 through DATA15. Some of these lines have dual functions. For example, the DATA0 line is labeled DATA0/KWD0 and it is connected to output pin PD0.

Early processors sometimes had an easily distinguishable control bus. These control buses contained the control signal lines required to properly execute a memory read or write operation. Most modern microcontrollers do not have a specifically designated control bus. Instead, they are equipped with different control signals to ensure that the different steps required for the memory read and write operations occur in the correct order and at the correct time. Common control signals in most microcontrollers include: a system clock, memory read/write signal, output enable signal for external memory components, and chip selects for external devices.

Practice Questions

Question: A memory system is equipped with 12 address lines and 8 data lines. Specify: (a) the number of linearly addressable memory locations, (b) the length of the memory, (c) the width of the memory, (d) the size of the memory in bits, and (e) the size of the memory in bytes.

Answer: (a) $2^{address\ lines}$ = *number of linearly addressable memory locations* or 4096 locations, (b) length: 4096 locations, (c) memory width is equal to the number of data lines or 8 bits, (d) memory size is equal to length × width or 4096 locations ×8 bits/location = 32,768 bits, and (e) 4096 bytes.

Question: A memory system is required that has 1 million locations. At each memory location, a 32-bit word must be stored. Specify: (a) the number of required address lines, (b) the number of required data lines, and (c) the size of the memory in bytes.

Answer: (a) With 20 address lines, 1,048,576 memory locations may be separately addressed, (b) 32 data lines are required, and (c) memory size is equal to length × width or 1M locations ×4 bytes/location or 4 Mbytes of memory.

8.3.3 Memory Technologies: ROM versus RAM

As mentioned earlier, most microcontrollers require several different types of memory technologies to accomplish their required tasks. In this section, we review these different memory technologies, the related terminology, and how these different technologies are used in a microcontroller system.

To start with, there are two different major types of memory technology: random access memory (RAM) and read only memory (ROM). The term *random access* is a holdover from the early days of computing, and it may be misleading the way it is used today. Early memory technology consisted of information stored on tape reels. This type of memory was known as *sequential access*. That is, the amount of time to access a given piece of information on a reel was determined by the physical location of the information on the reel. As memory technology improved, the amount of time to access a given piece of memory was no longer related to its physical location in memory. This type of memory was called *random access*. Today the term *random access memory* (RAM) refers to a memory device that can have information written to it or read from it. Yet you can only perform the read operation on read only memory (ROM). Let us take a more detailed look at each of these memory technologies beginning with RAM.

Random access memory has the following features:

- RAM is volatile. That is, when power is removed, it loses its stored information.
- RAM may be written to or read from.

- RAM has shorter access times as compared with other memory technologies.
- In an embedded controller application, RAM is used during program execution to temporarily store data.

RAM memory is manufactured in many different types: dynamic RAM (DRAM—pronounced "D-ram"), static RAM (SRAM—pronounced "S-ram"), synchronous SRAM, and synchronous DRAM. We only discuss the first two types. See Wakerly's text for a complete description of the other RAM variants. Dynamic RAM has a high density. That is, many individual memory cells can be packed into a small area on a semiconductor wafer. This high density is achieved through a simple, single transistor memory cell design. A binary 1 or 0 may be stored in the cell. The 1 is stored as a capacitive charge within the transistor. The capacitive charge has a tendency to bleed off and therefore must be refreshed at regular intervals. Additional hardware and processing time is required to perform the refresh operation.

SRAM technology has a more complex design for the individual memory cell than DRAM. It requires multiple transistors for a single cell. Hence, the density for a SRAM is not as high as that for a DRAM. However, it does not require periodic refresh. Moreover, a SRAM has a much faster access time than a DRAM. However, this faster access time comes at a price—SRAM requires considerably more power than DRAMs.

Read only memory has the following features:

- ROM is nonvolatile memory (NVM). That is, when power is removed, it retains its stored information.
- ROM may be read.
- ROM has a much longer access time as compared with SRAM memory.
- In an embedded controller application, ROM is typically used to store instructions and constants during program execution.

ROMs are available in many different variants, including ROMs, PROMs, EPROMs, byte-erasable EEPROMs, and flash EEPROMs. All of these ROM variants are nonvolatile memory. The differences between the variants are whether they can be reprogrammed and the length of the reprogram cycle.

ROM is programmed with required data during the fabrication process by masks that create and omit connections. This type of memory is used to mass produce ROMs when no further changes in memory contents are anticipated. There is no method to reprogram ROM once it leaves the factory. If a change in ROM contents is required, a new ROM must be fabricated. It could take weeks to obtain a new ROM with updated contents. This type of ROM is useful to mass produce a product containing an embedded controller system.

A programmable read only memory (PROM) is a two-dimensional memory array of fusible links to store logical 1s and 0s. PROMs are purchased with all fusible links intact. PROMs are programmed using a hardware device called a universal programmer. The universal programmer and its associated software are hosted by a personal computer. The user programs the PROM through the software. The software controls the universal programmer which issues signals to blow the fusible link for a logic 0 or leave a fusible link intact for a logical 1. Once programmed, the blown links of a PROM cannot be restored. If a change in PROM contents is required, a new PROM must be used. The advantage of PROM technology over ROM technology is the length of the reprogram cycle. A new PROM may be programmed in a matter of minutes since programming is performed by the user.

The electrically programmable read only memory (EPROM) is programmed with 1s and 0s using a universal programmer just like the PROM technology. However, when a change in memory contents is required, the EPROM is removed from its circuit and exposed to ultraviolet (UV) light. The UV light passes through a quartz window located on the top of the EPROM. The UV light resets the contents of the EPROM so it may be reprogrammed. The EPROM has a clear advantage over the PROM since it may be reused multiple times. This makes it useful when developing a system prototype since the program stored in the EPROM may be changed multiple times before it is finalized.

The electrically erasable programmable read only memory (EEPROM)—as its name implies may be quickly erased electronically while it is still resident within its circuit. There are two different major variants of the EEPROM: the flash EEPROM and the byte-erasable EEPROM. The flash EEPROM, or simply *flash memory*, allows electrical erasure of the entire memory or a major block of memory. The byte-erasable EEPROM, or simply EEPROM, allows single bytes within the memory to be erased and reprogrammed. These two EEPROM technologies are used to debug and quickly modify embedded controller software during the development process. Code may be tested and modified within its intended target system. EEPROMs are used within an embedded controller system as a scratch pad memory, data storage, or for storing end-product characteristics.

8.3.4 Memory Map

Normally we only use a portion of the entire linearly addressable space for a given processor. As mentioned previously, the A4 68HC12 variant has 16 address lines for linearly addressing 64K of memory. However, rarely is the entire memory space in use. A memory map is an effective tool to track the location, size, and technology of memory in use for a given processor configuration.

You can compare the memory map to plans for a new housing development. When a new housing development is planned, the available land is partitioned or platted into different home locations. In other words, the land boundaries of an individual homeowner are carefully surveyed. Each land parcel within the housing development is then assigned an individual and unique address. As the homes are built, the vacant lots are converted to finished home sites. The land developer maintains a map of addresses to track addresses that are currently occupied with a home and those with addresses assigned but without a home present.

The memory map is a similar allocation-tracking device. Figure 8.3 is the memory map for different configurations of the A4 CPU variant. As previously mentioned, the 68HC12 A4 variant is configured with a linearly addressable memory space of 64K-bytes. This means the 68HC12 can access 1 of 65,536 ($2^{address\ lines}$ = number of memory locations) memory locations at a given time.

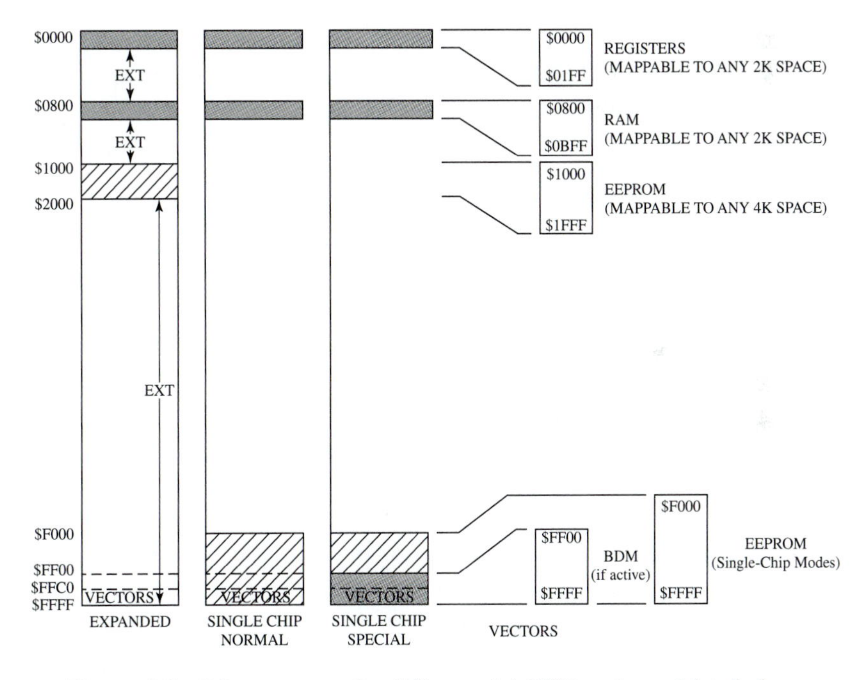

Figure 8.3 Memory map for different A4 CPU variants. Listed along the horizontal axis are the different modes of operation for the 68HC12. Associated with each of these modes of operation is a map of memory usage. Rarely is the entire memory space in use. Therefore, the memory map tracks the current allocation of memory addresses for a specific mode of operation. (Figure used with permission of Motorola, Incorporated.)

These 65,536 (commonly referred to as 64K-bytes) distinct locations may or may not be occupied with memory components. A memory map tracks the current allocation of memory components within the available memory space.

As you can see, the first memory location is $0000, whereas the last location is $FFFF. It is convenient to review several binary to hexadecimal conversions that aid in reading a memory map:

- In general: $2^{address\ lines}$ = addressable memory locations
- 8-bit address bus: $2^8 = 256 = 1\ 0000\ 0000$ binary = $100 hexadecimal locations
- 10-bit address bus: $2^{10} = 1024 = 100\ 0000\ 0000$ binary = $400 hexadecimal locations
- 12-bit address bus: $2^{12} = 4096 = 1\ 0000\ 0000\ 0000$ binary = $1000 hexadecimal locations

Default locations for the 68HC12 register block, RAM, and EEPROM are shown on the map. The register block spans the memory locations from $0000 to $01FF—that is, 512 locations. The 1K-byte static RAM spans the memory locations from $0800 to $0BFF, whereas the 4K-byte EEPROM spans the memory locations from $1000 to $1FFF. Also, interrupt vectors are located at memory locations from $FF80 to $FFFF. The 68HC12's resident debugger, the Background Debug Mode (BDM), has an associated on-chip ROM mapped to addresses $FF20 to $FFFF while the BDM control registers reside at memory locations $FF00 to $FF06. The placement of the BDM results in a memory resource conflict between the BDM system and the interrupt vectors. When the BDM is active, the BDM ROM replaces the interrupt vectors.

Notice that there are gaps or unused locations in the memory map. These memory spaces are available for expanded, external memory components. During expansion, the internal memory components may not be in convenient locations. These internal resources may be mapped to other locations by setting bits in the three mapping registers: the Initialization of Internal Register Position Register (INITRG) at memory location $0011, the Initialization of Internal RAM Position Register (INITRM) at memory location $0010, and the Initialization of Internal EEPROM Position Register (INITEE) at memory location $0012. As their names imply, these registers are used to move the internal register block, the internal RAM memory, and the internal EEPROM memory. These registers are normally configured during the initialization phase of program execution. Let us take a closer look at each of these registers.

Register Block Mapping The 68HC12 is equipped with a 512-byte register block. After reset, the register block is mapped to memory location $0000.

Register: INITRG - Internal Register Position Register Address: $0011

7	6	5	4	3	2	1	0
REG15	REG14	REG13	REG12	REG11	0	0	0
Reset: 0	0	0	0	0	0	0	0

Figure 8.4 Initialization of Internal Register Position Register (INITRG).

However, it may be reassigned to any 2K-byte block within the 64K-byte address space. This is accomplished by specifying the starting address of the desired location with REG[15:11] (bits 7 through 3) of the INITRG register as shown in Figure 8.4. These bits, REG[15:11], specify the upper five bits of the register block's starting address. This requirement only allows for placement within 2K-byte blocks.

RAM Mapping The 1K-byte of static RAM aboard the 68HC12 A4 variant is normally mapped to start at memory location $0800. However, it may be reassigned to any 2K-byte block within the 64K-byte address space. This is accomplished by specifying the starting address of the desired location with RAM[15:11] (bits 7 through 3) of the INITRM register as shown in Figure 8.5. These bits, REG[15:11], specify the upper five bits of the RAM's starting address. This requirement only allows for placement within 2K-byte blocks. For example, to move the starting location of internal RAM to $2000, we would load $20 to the INITRM register.

Register: Initialization of Internal RAM Position Register (INITRM) Address: $0010

7	6	5	4	3	2	1	0
RAM15	RAM14	RAM13	RAM12	RAM11	0	0	0
Reset: 0	0	0	0	0	0	0	0

Figure 8.5 Initialization of Internal RAM Position Register (INITRM).

EEPROM Mapping The 4K-byte of EEPROM aboard the 68HC12 A4 variant is normally mapped to start at memory location $1000. However, it may be reassigned to any 4K-byte block within the 64K-byte address space. This is accomplished by specifying the starting address of the desired location with EE[15:12] (bits 7 through 4) of the INITEE register as shown in Figure 8.6.

Memory Contention Memory resource mapping conflicts occurs if any portion of two memory components are mapped to the same locations. If memory resource mapping conflicts occur, the following mapping precedence is followed:

Register: Initialization of Internal EEPROM Position Register (INITEE) Address: $0012

	7	6	5	4	3	2	1	0
	EE15	EE14	EE13	EE12	0	0	0	EEON
Reset: (expand and peripheral)	0	0	0	0	0	0	0	0
Reset: (single chip)	1	1	1	1	0	0	0	1

Figure 8.6 Initialization of Internal EEPROM Position Register (INITEE).

1. BDM ROM (if active)
2. Register Space
3. Internal RAM
4. Internal EEPROM
5. External Memory

For example, if external RAM overlaps the memory space occupied by internal RAM, the 68HC12 accesses internal memory over the external components.

8.4 THE A4 MEMORY SYSTEM

The 68HC12 A4 variant has the capability of addressing 64K × 8-bit locations in a linearly addressable memory configuration. As previously mentioned, it is internally equipped with 1K bytes of static RAM and 4K bytes of byte-erasable EEPROM. It is not equipped with a large internal program memory like other variants since it is primarily intended for use in applications requiring an expanded memory. The A4 variant also has the ability to enable access to more than 4M bytes of program space and 1M byte of data space via a memory paging system. In the following sections, we detail how to expand the memory via the 64K linear address space, modify the EEPROM memory, and expand the memory via paging techniques.

8.5 LINEAR MEMORY EXPANSION

In this section, we discuss how to properly expand the 68HC12 within the confines of the 64K linearly addressable space. Realize that, depending on what expanded mode of the A4 is used, certain I/O ports are lost during the memory expansion process.

- **Normal Expanded Wide Mode:** In this expanded mode, the A4 has a 16-bit data bus and a 16-bit address bus. Ports C and D are used for the 16-bit data bus, and ports A and B are used for the 16-bit address bus.
- **Normal Expanded Narrow Mode:** In this expanded mode, the A4 has an 8-bit data bus and a 16-bit address bus. Port C is used for the 8-bit data bus, and ports A and B are used for the 16-bit address bus.

Recall from the hardware configuration chapter that the operating mode of the processor is set by the configuration of the BKGD, MODB, and MODA pins during reset. For our examples, we concentrate on the Normal Expanded Wide Mode. The memory system addressable by a processor often consists of many different memory chips, frequently of different technologies (RAMs, ROMs, etc.). As memory is expanded, we need to ensure the following:

1. Unique addresses are maintained for each memory location.
2. The data bus is connected properly to all memory chips in the system.
3. The control lines are routed to the appropriate pins on the individual memory chips.
4. The control signals from the 68HC12 are compatible with the external memory chips from a timing point of view.
5. The external memory chips are electrically compatible with the 68HC12.

A word of caution: It needs to be emphasized that a logical and methodical approach to memory design must be followed. We provide a step-by-step approach. Do not skip over material because all of it is critical. Some details early in our discussion are deferred to provide for a detailed discussion of these items. These items are clearly identified in the text and figures.

In the upcoming sections, we explore the expansion of memory in detail. We begin by discussing the overall layout of a memory system. Specifically, we discuss how to expand memory length and width. In this section, we defer details on memory timing. After we discuss memory layout design, we examine memory timing constraints in great detail. We then discuss electrical compatibility issues that must be considered when connecting any device (such as memory) to the 68HC12.

8.5.1 Memory Layout Design

Dr. Jerry Cupal of the University of Wyoming developed a straightforward, step-by-step approach to correctly design a memory layout. His technique can be summarized with these four simple steps:

1. From the needs of the system, determine the amount of external memory devices needed (RAM, ROM, I/O).
2. Draw the desired memory table and design the address decoding and control logic.
3. Draw the schematic of the circuit.
4. Verify the design.

Note: All control signal and timing analysis details are deferred until the next two sections. These deferred items are clearly marked on all memory layout diagrams in this section.

To accomplish **step 1** of the memory layout design, you must determine the size of external memory required and the type of each memory component. Moreover, actual chips that are used must be determined so that the memory system layout may be designed. To accomplish this task, memory must often be expanded by its length, width, or both. We discuss each of these concepts in turn. For simplicity, we assume that the memory system contains all of the same type of chips.

Expanding Memory Length To expand memory length, enough memory chips must be used to obtain the desired memory span. For example, let us design an 8K × 8 RAM memory array using 1K × 8 RAM memory chips equipped with tristate outputs.

A tristate output may be a logic 1, logic 0, or a high impedance (Z) state (Figure 8.7). A memory chip is placed in the high Z mode when its output enable ($\overline{OE}$) pin is deactivated. When in the high Z state, the memory chip is not electrically connected to the bus, although it retains its physical bus connection. This allows multiple chips to be connected to the bus simultaneously. Since only one memory chip is allowed to be output enabled at a time, only one memory chip is **electrically** connected to the bus at any instant of time. This prevents simultaneous data bus access by more than one memory chip. Without a tristate output, memory chips could not be connected simultaneously to the bus. If multiple memory

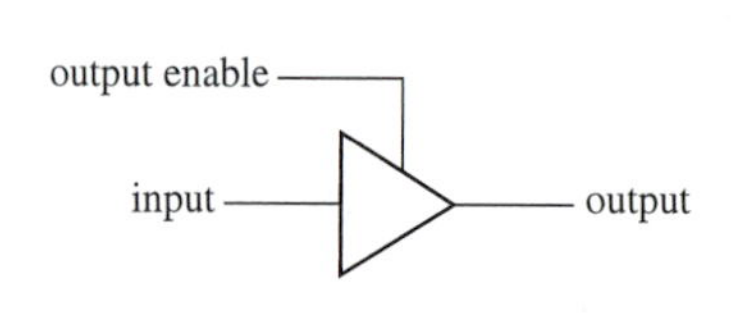

output enable	input	output
L	L	High-Z
L	H	High-Z
H	L	L
H	H	H

Figure 8.7 Tristate logic.

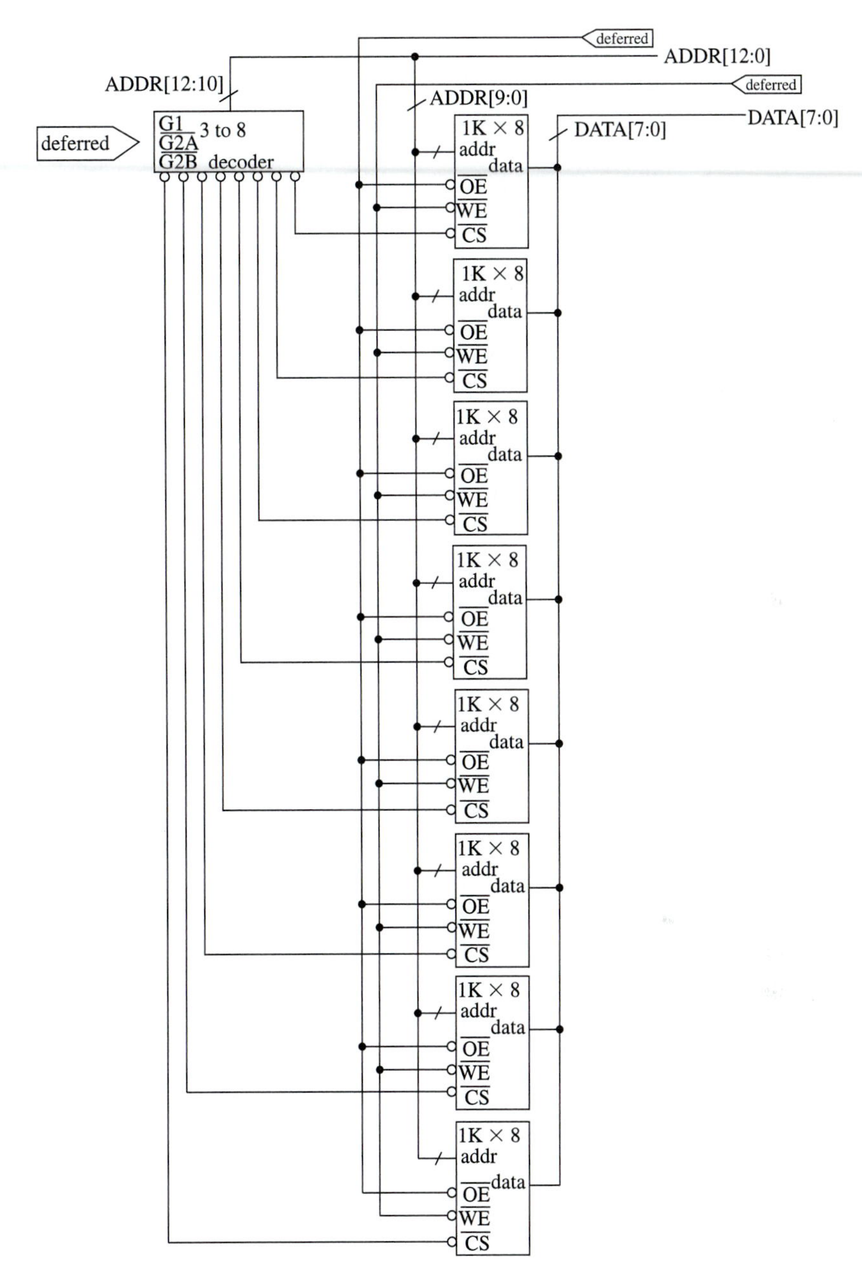

Figure 8.8 Expanding memory length. An 8K × 8 RAM memory constructed from eight 1K × 8 RAM chips.

chips are connected without the benefit of the tristate output configuration, **severe damage** to the bus and memory components would result.

Eight 1K × 8 RAM chips will be required to construct the 8K × 8 memory array (see Figure 8.8). The 8K memory array requires 13 address lines ($2^{13} = 8192$ memory locations). Each 1K memory chip in the array has 10 address lines ($2^{10} =$ 1,024 memory locations). The 13 address lines are labeled A12–A0, with A12 being the most significant bit. The 10 lower order bits A9–A0 are routed and connected to the 10 address lines on each 1K × 8 RAM chip. The remaining address lines A12–A10 are routed to a decoder to generate chip select (CS) signals to activate the appropriate 1K × 8 RAM chip via its chip select pins. For this example, we assume each RAM is equipped with an active low-chip select pin ($\overline{CS}$). Recall that a decoder has a vector of binary inputs and outputs. When a binary vector is placed on the input pins, the single output corresponding to the binary input is activated. Only one of the decoder's outputs is active at any given time. In this example, we require a 3:8 decoder with active low-outputs. This decoder has three inputs and eight outputs. Most decoders are equipped with a combination of active high and active low-chip enables. These are designated $G1$, $\overline{G2A}$, and $\overline{G2B}$. Control signals from the 68HC12 are connected to these chip enables.

Expanding Memory Width Let us now investigate how to expand memory width. Let us design a 1K × 16 RAM memory array using 1K × 8 RAM memory chips equipped with tristate outputs (see Figure 8.9). Two 1K × 8 RAM chips are required to construct the 1K x 16 memory array. The 1K memory array requires 10 address lines ($2^{10} = 1024$ memory locations) and 16 data lines (D15 through D0). The address lines A9–A0 are routed and connected to the ten address lines on each 1K × 8 RAM chip. The chip select pin ($\overline{CS}$) on each RAM chip is connected to control signals from the 68HC12. The tristate outputs allow the data lines (D7–D0) from each RAM chip to be connected to the corresponding data lines of the data bus. Data lines (D7–D0) from RAM chip 1 are connected to D15 to D8,

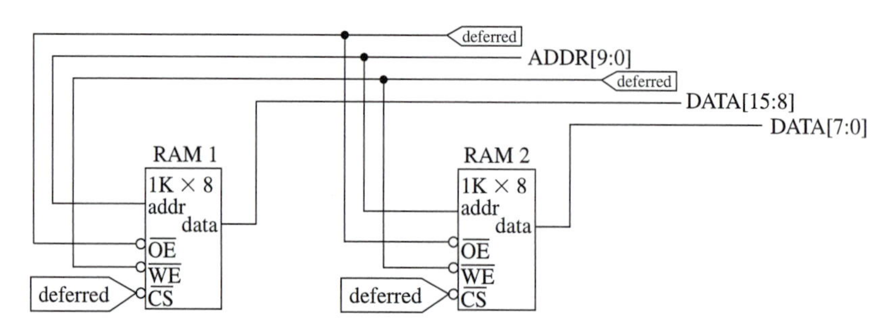

Figure 8.9 Expanding memory width.

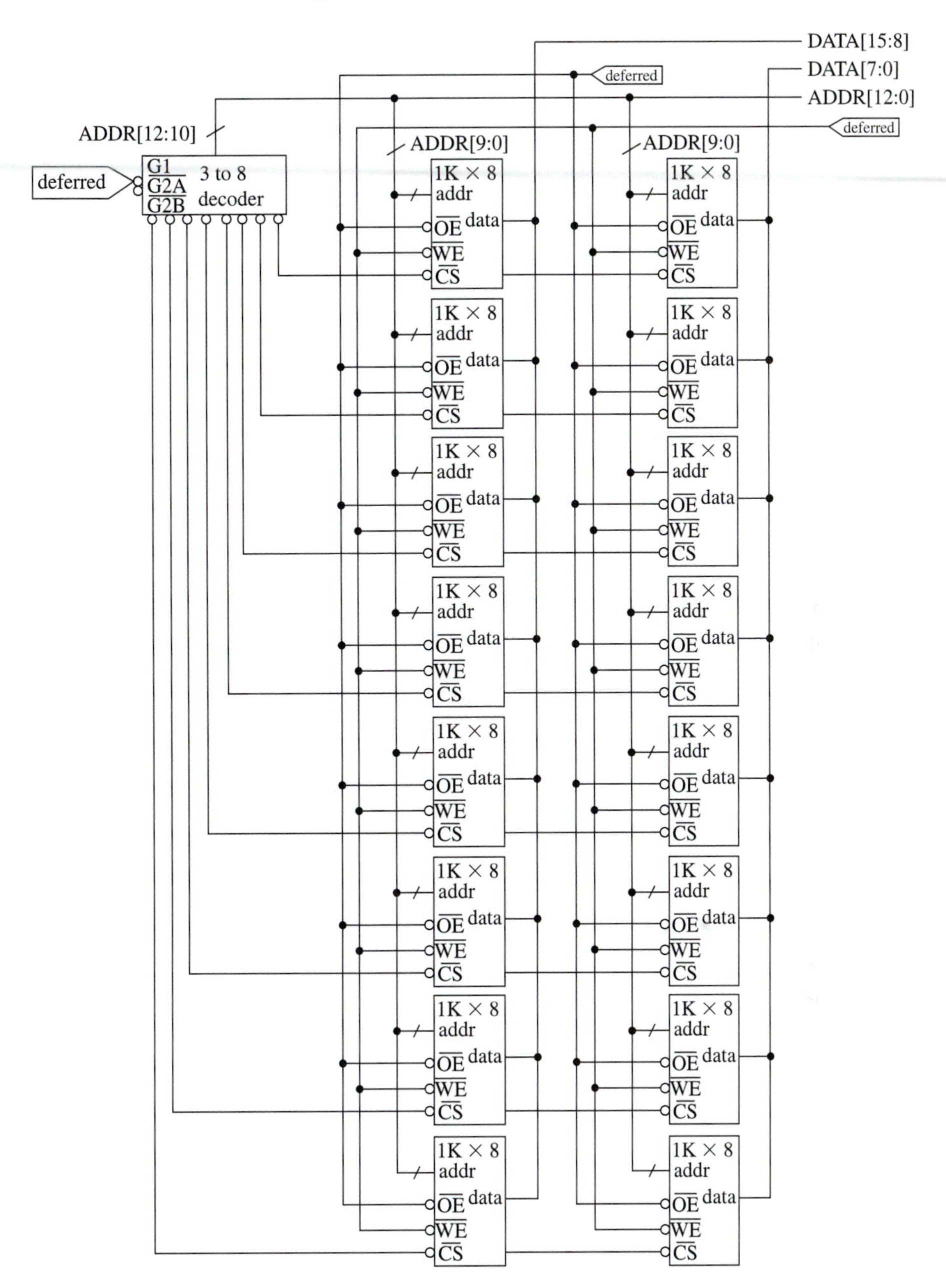

Figure 8.10 Expanding memory length and width.

respectively, of the data bus. Data lines (D7–D0) from RAM chip 2 are connected to D7–D0, respectively, of the data bus.

Expanding Memory Length and Width To expand both memory length and width, the concepts discussed before must be combined (see Figure 8.10). Let us design an 8K × 16 RAM memory array using 1K × 8 RAM memory chips equipped with tristate outputs. Sixteen 1K × 8 RAM chips are required to construct the 8K × 16 memory array. The 8K memory array requires 13 address lines ($2^{13} = 8192$ memory locations). Each 1K memory chip in the array has 10 address lines ($2^{10} = 1024$ memory locations). The 13 address lines will be labeled A12–A0, with A12 being the most significant bit. The 10 lower order bits A9–A0 will be routed and connected to the 10 address lines on each 1K × 8 RAM chip. As before, the remaining address lines A12–A10 are routed to a decoder to generate active low-chip select ($\overline{CS}$) signals to activate the appropriate 1K × 8 RAM chip. However, to obtain a 16-bit data width, each activation signal from the decoder must be routed to the appropriate chip select pins ($\overline{CS}$) on two RAM chips. As before, the tristate outputs allow the data lines (D7–D0) from each RAM chip to be connected to the corresponding data lines of the data bus. Data lines (D7–D0) from the left column of RAM chips are connected to D15 to D8, respectively, of the data bus. Data lines (D7–D0) from the right column of RAM chips are connected to D7–D0, respectively, of the data bus. As before, the decoders are equipped with a combination of active high and active low-chip enables. These are designated $G1$, $\overline{G2A}$, and $\overline{G2B}$. Control signals from the 68HC12 are connected to these chip enables.

Once the number of required memory chips have been determined to obtain the correct memory length and width, we may proceed to **Step 2**. **Step 2** of the memory layout design requires that we construct a memory table. A memory table illustrates the required binary values to put on each address line to properly place the memory device at the desired locations in memory. It also illustrates the required direct connection to the address lines of the memory device. We use a "·" to designate these direct connections. As an example, Figure 8.11 is the memory table for the 8K × 16 RAM memory array. Let us assign this 8K × 16 RAM to start at memory location $2000. Based on our previous discussion of memory maps, an 8K length memory starting at $2000 spans memory locations up to $3FFF.

For each RAM chip in the array, the start and stop addresses are calculated. The individual address line values (A[15:0]) are then determined. Address line values common to both the start and stop addresses are recorded in the memory table as fixed values while noncommon values are shown as "·." For example, in Figure 8.11, address lines A[15:10] are common for the start and stop addresses of RAM0 and are therefore set to 0010 00. The remaining address lines A[9:0] are not common and are designated "·."

Device	A_{15}	A_{14}	A_{13}	A_{12}	A_{11}	A_{10}	A_9	A_8	A_7	A_6	A_5	A_4	A_3	A_2	A_1	A_0	Useable Locations
RAM0	0	0	1	0	0	0	•	•	•	•	•	•	•	•	•	•	$2000 - $23FF
RAM1	0	0	1	0	0	1	•	•	•	•	•	•	•	•	•	•	$2400 - $27FF
RAM2	0	0	1	0	1	0	•	•	•	•	•	•	•	•	•	•	$2800 - $2BFF
RAM3	0	0	1	0	1	1	•	•	•	•	•	•	•	•	•	•	$2C00 - $2FFF
RAM4	0	0	1	1	0	0	•	•	•	•	•	•	•	•	•	•	$3000 - $33FF
RAM5	0	0	1	1	0	1	•	•	•	•	•	•	•	•	•	•	$3400 - $37FF
RAM6	0	0	1	1	1	0	•	•	•	•	•	•	•	•	•	•	$3800 - $3BFF
RAM7	0	0	1	1	1	1	•	•	•	•	•	•	•	•	•	•	$3C00 - $3FFF

Figure 8.11 Memory table for 8K × 16 RAM system constructed of 1K memory chips placed at memory locations $2000 to $3FFF.

For **Step 3** of the memory layout design, we need to draw the schematic. This has already been illustrated in Figure 8.8 for expanding memory length, Figure 8.9 for expanding memory width, and Figure 8.10 for expanding memory length and width. For the specific example of placing an 8K × 16 RAM system at memory location $2000 to $3FFF, see Figure 8.12. Note that we have included control signal information in Figure 8.12. We explain how to obtain control signal connections in the next section.

The final step, **Step 4** requires verification of the design. In this step, we ensure that the first address, the last address, and several test addresses between the two extremes activate the correct memory locations on the correct memory chips. At this step, you must also ensure that one and only one memory location is activated for a given address.

8.5.2 68HC12 and Memory Chip Control Signal Connections

The third item of concern while expanding memory is to ensure that the control signals from the 68HC12 are compatible with the external memory chips. To fully investigate these connections, we (1) define the control signals provided by the 68HC12, (2) define the control signals required by the external memory chips, and (3) demonstrate how to connect the control signals from the 68HC12 to the external memory devices.

68HC12 Control Signals During single-chip modes of operation, the control signals are internal to the 68HC12. When the 68HC12 is used in an expanded mode, the 68HC12 control signals must be provided to the external memory devices. You may recall from our discussions in the hardware chapter that Port E provides the control signals when the 68HC12 is in expanded modes. Of particular importance in memory expansion operations are the E Clock (ECLK) and the

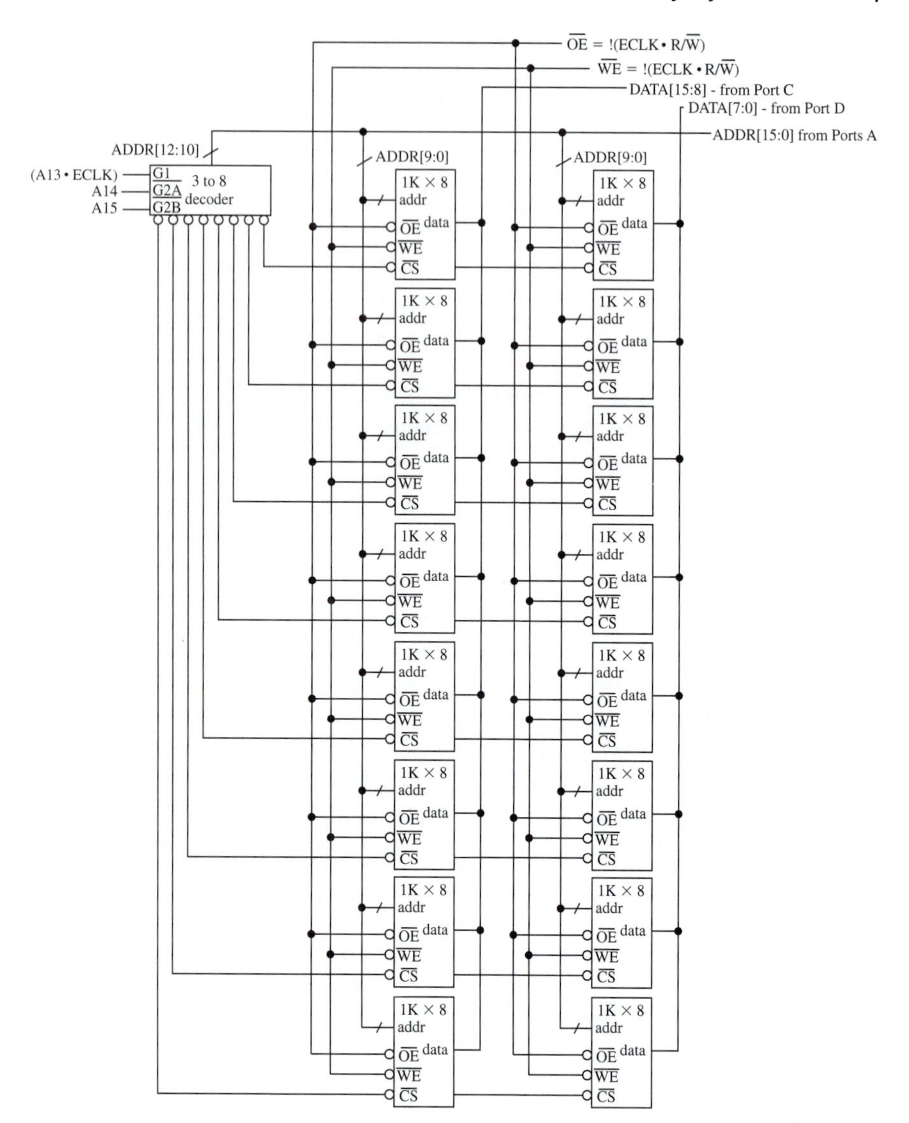

Figure 8.12 Schematic of an 8K × 16 RAM memory at $2000 to $3FFF.

read/write ($R/\overline{W}$) control lines. Here are some additional details on each of these control lines:

- **ECLK**: The ECLK is the basic bus clock. The 68HC12 ECLK signal is half the frequency of the external timing crystal. Bus cycles begin on the falling edge of the ECLK and run to the next falling edge. The ECLK indicates when address and data are valid during memory reference instructions. Addresses become valid when the ECLK is high. The data lines are considered (and must be) valid on the falling edge of the ECLK.
- $R/\overline{W}$: The *read*/$\overline{\text{write}}$ control line indicates data direction.

Control Signals Required by the Memory Chips Most memory devices have the following associated control signals (although different manufacturers may use different names or designations):

- The write enable ($\overline{\text{WE}}$) is usually an active low signal. When activated during the write cycle, the binary values on the memory chip's data lines are written to the specified memory address. Note ROM chips do not have this control signal.
- The output enable ($\overline{\text{OE}}$) is usually an active low signal. When activated during the read cycle, the data at the specified memory location are placed on the data pins of the memory chip and the data lines are connected to the memory system's data bus using tristate outputs.
- The chip select ($\overline{\text{CS}}$) is usually an active low input used to select a specific chip in a memory array.

Connecting Control Lines from the 68HC12 to External Memory With the control signals provided by the 68HC12 and those required by the external memory components defined, let us see how to connect these control signals together. These connections are shown in Figure 8.13. Let us discuss each of these connections in turn.

- The address lines of the 68HC12 are connected to the address lines of the external memory components. In the expanded mode of operation, the 68HC12 address lines are provided by Ports A and B. Port A provides address lines ADDR[15:8], and Port B provides address lines ADDR[7:0]. These address lines ADDR[15:0] are connected to the address lines of the external memory components as discussed in previous sections. Also note that some of the address lines may be routed to a decoder to generate chip select signals for memory address decoding as discussed.

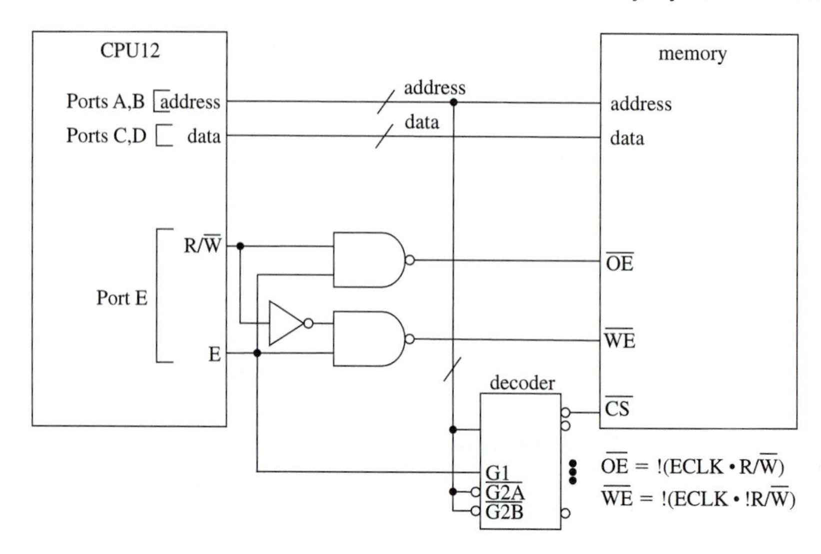

Figure 8.13 Control signal connections from the 68HC12 to external memory. The address lines of the 68HC12 are connected to the address lines of the external memory components.

- The data lines of 68HC12 are connected to the data lines of the external memory components. In the expanded mode of operation, the 68HC12 data lines are provided by Ports C and D. Port C provides data lines DATA[15:8], and Port D provides data lines DATA[7:0]. These data lines DATA[15:0] are connected to the data lines of the external memory components as discussed in previous sections. Because the memory components are equipped with tristate outputs, the data lines from multiple memory chips may be connected to the data bus simultaneously.
- We see in the next section that the ECLK is logic high when the address bus contains a valid address. Therefore, to generate an active low-output enable ($\overline{OE}$) during a memory read cycle, the ECLK signal is "NANDed" with the $R/\overline{W}$ signal.
- To generate an active low-write enable ($\overline{WE}$) during a memory write cycle, the ECLK is "NANDed" with the inverted $R/\overline{W}$ signal.
- The active low-chip select ($\overline{CS}$) signal is generated using a combination of address lines (as previously discussed) and the ECLK. Remember the ECLK is logic high when a valid address is present. Therefore, the ECLK needs to be connected to an active high enable pin (G1) of the decoder. This ensures that memory components are only selected when a valid address is present.

8.5.3 Timing Analysis of Basic Memory Operations

The fourth concern item while expanding memory is to ensure the timing associated with control signals from the 68HC12 to external memory chips are compatible. Timing of memory is critical! If memory timing analysis is not accomplished correctly, the memory system may fail even if all of the other memory design steps have been accomplished correctly.

To perform memory timing analysis, the read cycle must be analyzed for ROM memory components, and both the read and write cycles must be analyzed for the RAM memory. The read cycle analysis for ROM and RAM follows the same procedures. Therefore, we only discuss RAM read cycle analysis. The RAM write cycle is also investigated. We limit our discussion to static RAM (SRAM) timing analysis.

To investigate timing analysis in a logical and methodical manner, we: (1) investigate the internal diagram of a RAM memory cell, (2) define timing signal definitions associated with the memory read and write cycles, (3) examine the timing diagrams for the 68HC12, (4) discuss the required steps for the memory read and write cycle, and (5) perform a detailed timing analysis for both the read and write cycles.

The Static RAM (SRAM) Memory Cell Figure 8.14 is a representative memory cell contained within a SRAM memory. Each cell can store a single bit in the D type latch. Additional combinational circuitry is provided to read from or write to the cell. It is important to have a general understanding of the internal

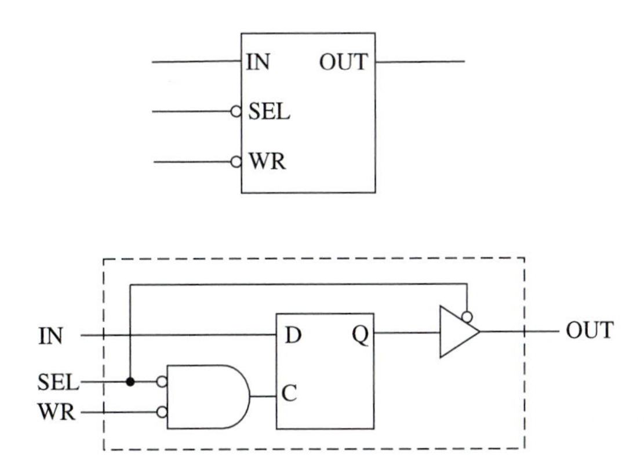

Figure 8.14 The static RAM memory cell. Each cell can store a single bit in the D-type latch. Adapted from "Digital Design Principles and Practices" by J.F. Wakerly.

configuration of the cell to appreciate some of the timing constraints of SRAM memory components we discuss.

As you can see in Figure 8.14, during a read operation, the "SEL" line goes low, which activates the active low tristate equipped output. This places the value of the D latch output Q on the output line. For the write operation, the value to be stored (either a logic 1 or 0) is placed on the "IN" line. For this value to be stored in the D latch, both the "SEL" and "WR" lines must be set low.

Associated with the D latch (as with most flip-flops) there are certain timing constraints. These constraints ensure that data provided to the circuit are stable for a period of time before the latch is activated (set up time), and a period of time the data must remain stable after the latch is activated (hold time) to ensure proper operation. Due to these timing constraints, we have both setup and hold-time requirements for SRAM memory components.

68HC12 Timing Diagrams Figures 8.15 and 8.16 provide the critical timing data for the 68HC12 A4 variant. These were extracted directly from Motorola technical data sheets. The timing diagrams illustrate the logical behavior of signals as a function of elapsed time. The timing diagram shows signals in time from left to right. Each signal (or signal group) is on a time line by itself, with the name of the signal(s) on the extreme left. If the actions shown on the timing diagram are synchronized by a signal, that signal is shown on the top of the diagram. Transitions from one logic level to another are shown as slanted lines since transitions do not occur instantaneously. As you can see on the bus timing diagram, actual 68HC12 timing values are determined in reference to ECLK signal edges. Figure 8.15 provides the definitions and timing values for the timing signals illustrated in Figure 8.16. Great care must be exercised in reading these diagrams because they are not drawn to scale. We simplify these diagrams in an upcoming section.

68HC12 Read Cycle There are two main memory operations typically performed on external memory components: read from memory and write to memory. We analyze each of these operations in turn beginning with the memory read operation. To correctly perform a memory read operation, the following steps are executed by the 68HC12 in response to a memory reference instruction:

1. A valid address is placed on address lines ADDR[15:0].
2. Control signals are issued by the 68HC12 (ECLK and $R/\overline{W}$) to provide control inputs to the memory components ($\overline{\text{CS}}$, $\overline{\text{OE}}$) to control the transfer of data from the external memory to the 68HC12 during a read operation.
3. Data are read from the external memory by the 68HC12.

Num	Characteristic(1), (2)		Delay	Symbol	5 MHz		Unit
					Min	Max	
	Frequency of operation (E-clock frequency)		—	f_0	dc	8.0	MHz
1	Cycle time	$t_{cyc} = 1/f_0$		t_{cyc}	125	—	ns
2	Pulse width, E low	$PW_{EL} = t_{cyc}/2 + delay$	−2	PW_{EL}	60	—	ns
3	Pulse width, E high(3)	$PW_{EH} = t_{cyc}/2 + delay$	−2	PW_{EH}	60	—	ns
5	Address delay time	$t_{AD} = t_{cyc}/4 + delay$	29	t_{AD}	—	60	ns
6	Address hold time		—	t_{AH}	20	—	ns
7	Address valid time to E rise	$t_{AV} = PW_{EL} - t_{AD}$	—	t_{AV}	0	—	ns
11	Read data setup time		—	t_{DSR}	30	—	ns
12	Read data hold time		—	t_{DHR}	0	—	ns
13	Write data delay time	$t_{DDW} = t_{cyc}/4 + delay$	25	t_{DDW}	—	46	ns
14	Write data hold time		—	t_{DHW}	20	—	ns
15	Write data setup time(3)	$t_{DSW} = PW_{EH} - t_{DDW}$	—	t_{DSW}	30	—	ns
16	Read/write delay time	$t_{RWD} = t_{cyc}/4 + delay$	18	t_{RWD}	—	49	ns
17	Read/write valid time to E rise	$t_{RWV} = PW_{EL} - t_{RWD}$	—	t_{RWV}	20	—	ns
18	Read/write hold time		—	t_{RWH}	20	—	ns
19	Low strobe delay time	$t_{LSD} = t_{cyc}/4 + delay$	18	t_{LSD}	—	49	ns
20	Low strobe valid time to E rise	$t_{LSV} = PW_{EL} - t_{LSD}$	—	t_{LSV}	11	—	ns
21	Low strobe hold time		—	t_{LSH}	20	—	ns
22	Address access time(3)	$t_{ACCA} = t_{cyc} - t_{AD} - t_{DSR}$	—	t_{ACCA}	—	35	ns
23	Access time from E rise(3)	$t_{ACCE} = PW_{EH} - t_{DSR}$	—	t_{ACCE}	—	30	ns
26	Chip-select delay time	$t_{CSD} = t_{cyc}/4 + delay$	29	t_{CSD}	—	60	ns
27	Chip-select access time(3)	$t_{ACCS} = t_{cyc} - t_{CSD} - t_{DSR}$	—	t_{ACCS}	—		ns
28	Chip-select hold time		—	t_{CSH}			ns
29	Chip-select negated time	$t_{CSN} = t_{cyc}/4 + delay$	5	t_{CSN}			ns

1. $V_{DD} = 5.0$ Vdc ± 10%, $V_{SS} = 0$ Vdc, $T_A = T_L$ to T_H, unless otherwise noted.
2. All timings are calculated for normal port drives.
3. This characteristic is affected by clock stretch.
   Add $N \times t_{cyc}$ where N = 0, 1, 2, or 3, depending on the number of clock stretches.

Figure 8.15 Nonmultiplexed expansion bus timing definitions. (Figure used with permission of Motorola, Incorporated.)

We need to examine these steps in much closer detail to ensure the timing between the 68HC12 and external memory is correct. To properly analyze the timing interface for the 68HC12 with external memory components, the timing diagram of both the 68HC12 and the external components must be examined for compatibility during the read cycle. We continue our example of the 68HC12 connected to an 8K × 16 SRAM module located at memory location $2000 to $3FFF (Figure 8.12). During this discussion, reference the simplified timing diagram for the

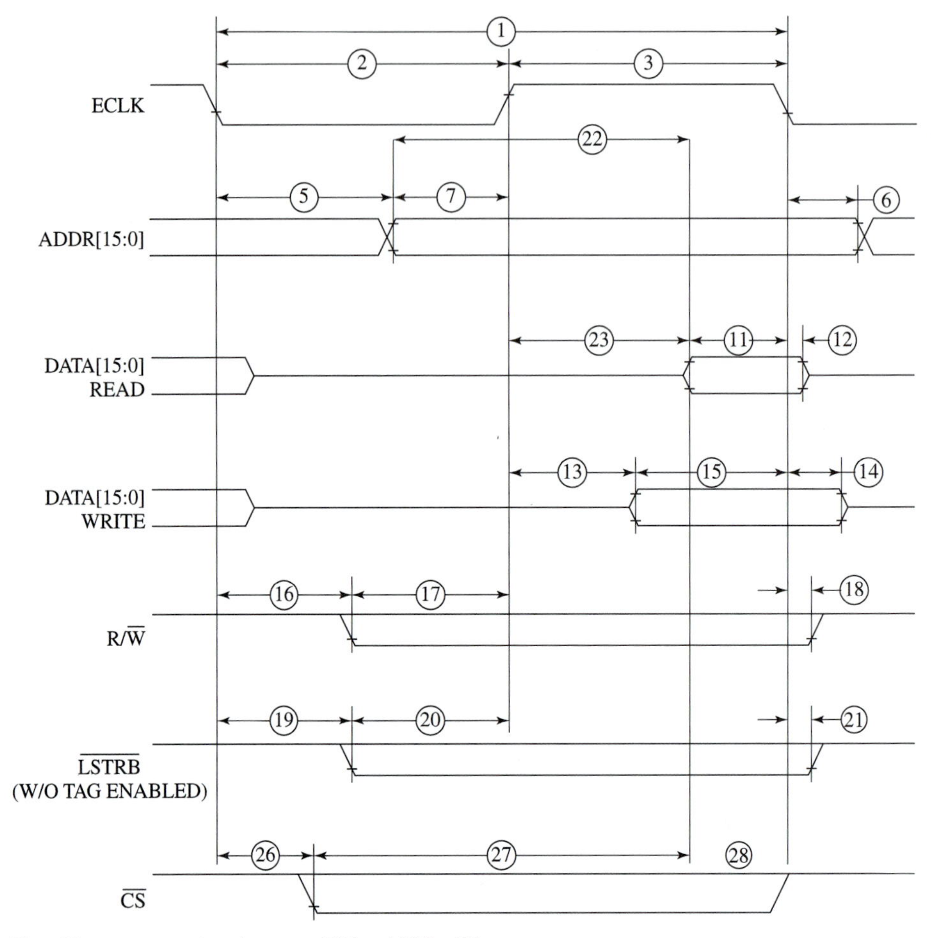

Figure 8.16 Nonmultiplexed expansion bus timing diagram. (Figure used with permission of Motorola, Incorporated.)

68HC12 read cycle provided at Figure 8.17. This diagram was developed from the information provided in Figures 8.15 and 8.16.

During the 68HC12 read cycle, the following timing protocol is followed:

1. *Chip select signal timing*: The 68HC12 provides an address on lines ADDR [15:0]. The address becomes valid on the rising edge of the ECLK. We use ECLK = 1 to indicate a valid address is present on the address lines. Aside from providing the address to the memory components, the address lines are also used to select the proper chip in the memory array via the decoder out-

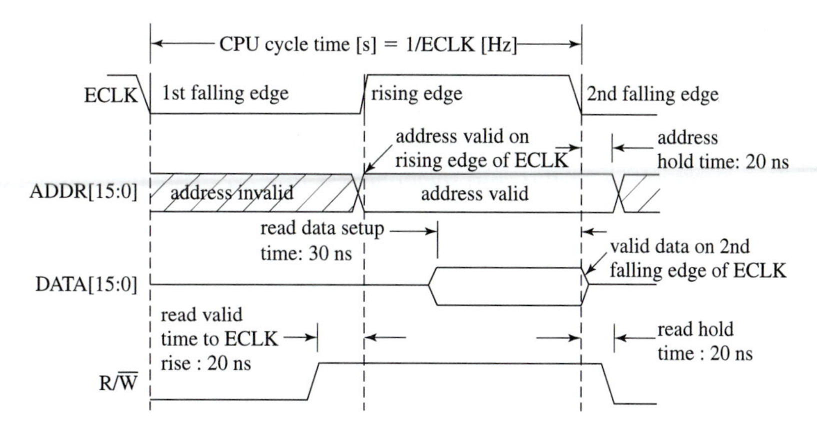

Figure 8.17 Simplified timing diagram for the 68HC12 read cycle. (Figure used with permission of Motorola, Incorporated.)

puts. Address lines ADDR [15:13] are used to enable the decoder. Most decoders are equipped with a series of active high (G1) and active low ($\overline{\text{G1A}}$, $\overline{\text{G2A}}$) enable pins. To ensure that the decoder is activated only when a valid address is present, we "AND" the ECLK signal with ADDR[13] and feed the result to the G1 enable pin on the decoder. The active low-outputs of the decoder are routed to the active low-chip select ($\overline{\text{CS}}$) pins of each SRAM memory component. The address lines ADDR[9:0] select the proper location within the enabled chip using the chips' address lines as described in the previous section (Figure 8.12).

2. *Output enable signal timing*: The $R/\overline{W}$ control line goes high (logic 1) for the read cycle. As you can see in Figure 8.17, this occurs 20 ns before the rising edge of the ECLK. To ensure that the memory components are not provided a read signal before a valid address is provided to the memory components, we "NAND" the $R/\overline{W}$ signal with a high ECLK (valid address) signal to provide an active low signal for the output enable ($\overline{\text{OE}}$) control of the RAM chip. Recall most memory chips have an active low-output enable control. The output enable pin must remain low until the 68HC12 successfully retrieves data from the RAM memory. Data are read from memory by the 68HC12 on the second falling edge of the ECLK. Therefore, the output enable signal must remain present beyond the falling edge of the ECLK. As you can see in Figure 8.17, both the address lines and the $R/\overline{W}$ signal remain valid until 20 ns after the falling edge of the ECLK. When the output enable ($\overline{\text{OE}}$) control signal is no longer present, the SRAM enters the high-impedance state since the tristate configured data outputs are no longer enabled.

3. *Read data setup time*: Once these control signals are provided to the RAM chip, valid data are available on the output data pins of the RAM chip after the specified access time of the memory chip has transpired. Memory chips have three different types of access times (defined below): the address access time (t_{ADDR}), the chip select access time (t_{CS}), and the output enable access time (t_{OE}). Typically, t_{ADDR} and t_{CS} for a memory chip are the same value. The t_{OE} value is approximately one half of the other two access times. When we refer to a "10 ns" SRAM memory, we mean that the address access time of the SRAM is 10 ns.
4. *Data read*: The 68HC12 then reads the data from the memory system during the second falling edge of the ECLK. For the 68HC12 to properly read the data, the read data setup time (t_{DSR}) and the read data hold time (t_{DHR}) must be satisfied. These times specify how long the data must be present before the falling edge of the ECLK (setup time) and how long it must remain valid after (hold time) the falling edge of the ECLK. For the 68HC12, the read data setup time is 30 ns while the read data hold time is 0 ns.

There are other timing constraints associated with memory design during the read cycle. These include the chip select access time, output enable access time, and address access time. These are illustrated in Figure 8.18.

- *Chip select access time* (t_{CS}): The chip select access time is defined as the time delay between when a memory component is provided a valid

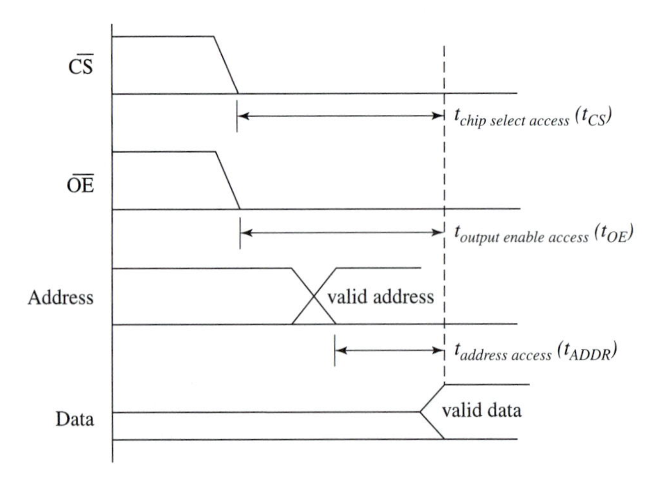

Figure 8.18 Generic timing signals.

chip select control signal and when valid data are provided by the memory component.

- *Address access time* (t_{ADDR}): The address access time is defined as the time delay between when a memory component is provided a valid address and when valid data are provided by the memory component.
- *Output enable access time* (t_{OE}): The output enable access time is defined as the time delay between when a memory component is provided a valid output enable control signal and when valid data are provided by the memory component.

From this word description of the read cycle, precise timing constraints for the memory interface may be determined. We have to examine the timing constraints provided by each signal requirement described before and choose the worst-case scenario to specify the required access time for the chips in our memory system. Let us examine each of the timing constraints provided earlier in further detail. We examine these timing constraints as a series of questions.

1. **Question 1**: How soon can valid data be provided by the SRAM memory chip after a chip select signal is provided by the 68HC12 under worst-case conditions?

   Let us make the following assumptions:

   - **Assumption**: Let us assume that the ECLK frequency in this example is 4.0 MHz. Therefore, the CPU cycle time is 250 ns (1/ECLK frequency).
   - **Assumption**: We reference all of our timing to the first falling edge of the ECLK.
   - **Assumption**: Recall that a valid address is not available from the 68HC12 until the ECLK goes high. This occurs 125 ns after the first falling edge of the ECLK for a 4 MHz ECLK frequency.

   Analysis: As mentioned, some of the address lines are routed directly to the address lines of the memory chips (ADDR[9:0]), whereas the remaining lines (ADDR[15:10]) are routed through a decoder and through an AND gate for address line A13 on its way to the active low-chip select pin ($\overline{CS}$). Reference the 16K x 16 RAM memory layout diagram in Figure 8.12. Once the memory chip receives the chip select signal, the memory chip provides valid data after the chip select access time has expired. This must occur 30 ns before the second falling edge of the ECLK to satisfy the read data setup time t_{DSR} requirement. With an ECLK of 4 MHz, all of these actions must occur

(250 ns–30 ns) or 220 ns after the first falling edge of the ECLK. This time constraint can be stated as:

$$\text{CPU cycle time} - t_{DSR} = (\text{CPU cycle time}/2) + t_{decoder} + t_{AND} + t_{CS}$$

The propagation delay of the decoder ($t_{decoder}$) and the "AND" gate (t_{AND}) can be found in a data book. For this example, we use a 74HC138 decoder and a 74HC08 "AND" gate. The propagation delays for these components are 22 ns and 15 ns, respectively. This information was found in Motorola's "High-Speed CMOS Logic Data" book.

Substituting in known values, our constraint equation becomes:

$$250\ ns - 30\ ns = 125\ ns + 22\ ns + 15\ ns + t_{CS}$$

This yields a chip select access time of:

$$t_{CS} = 58\ ns$$

2. **Question 2**: How soon can valid data be provided by the memory chip after a valid address is provided under worst-case conditions?

   Analysis: Using similar reasoning, we can develop the following equation:

$$\text{CPU cycle time} - t_{DSR} = (\text{CPU cycle time}/2) + t_{ADDR}$$

Substituting in known values, our constraint equation becomes:

$$250\ ns - 30\ ns = 125\ ns + t_{ADDR}$$

This yields an address access time of:

$$t_{ADDR} = 95\ ns$$

Recall that typically the address and chip select access times for a memory chip are the same value. Therefore, the first equation provides the more stressing case.

3. **Question 3**: How soon can valid data be provided to the 68HC12 once the memory chip has received a valid output enable signal?

   Analysis: As previously described, the active low-output enable signal is formed by "NANDing" the $R/\overline{W}$ control line with the ECLK signal. The $R/\overline{W}$ control line goes logic high 20 ns before the rising edge of the ECLK. The ECLK goes high 125 ns after the first falling edge of the ECLK. So both signals required for the NAND are available 125 ns after the first falling edge of the ECLK. The propagation delay of the NAND must also be considered. Once the memory chip receives a valid output enable signal, valid data are provided once the output enable access t_{OE} time has expired. We can calculate how long this step takes using the following:

$$\text{CPU cycle time} - t_{DSR} = (\text{CPU clock cycle}/2) + t_{NAND} + t_{OE}$$

Substituting in known values (propagation delay for 74HC00A is 15 ns), our constraint equation becomes:

$$250\ ns - 30\ ns = 125\ ns + 15\ ns + t_{OE}$$

This yields an output enable access time of:

$$t_{OE} = 80\ ns$$

Recall that typically the output enable access time is approximately one half the value of the chip enable access time and the address access time. Therefore, again, the first equation provides the more stressing case.

4. **Final Analysis**: As mentioned previously, the 68HC12 then reads the data from the memory system during the second falling edge of the ECLK. For the 68HC12 to properly read the data, the read data setup time (t_{DSR}) and the read data hold time (t_{DHR}) must be satisfied as previously discussed. We have included these constraints in the equations developed earlier. Based on the worst-case equation developed before, we can determine the required access time of our memory chip. For this example, we need to choose a SRAM memory component with at least a 58 ns access time to satisfy timing constraints during the memory read cycle. Typically, we round this value down to an available SRAM memory component with the required access time.

This completes our analysis of the read cycle. Next we accomplish a similar analysis for the SRAM write cycle.

68HC12 Write Cycle To correctly perform a memory write operation, the following steps are executed by the 68HC12 in response to a memory reference instruction:

1. A valid address is placed on address lines ADDR[15:0].
2. A data word is placed on data lines DATA [15:0].
3. Control signals are issued by the 68HC12 (ECLK and $R/\overline{W}$) to provide control inputs to the memory components ($\overline{WE}$ and $\overline{CS}$) to control the transfer of data from the 68HC12 to memory during the write operation.
4. The latches in the selected memory location open and the input word is stored.

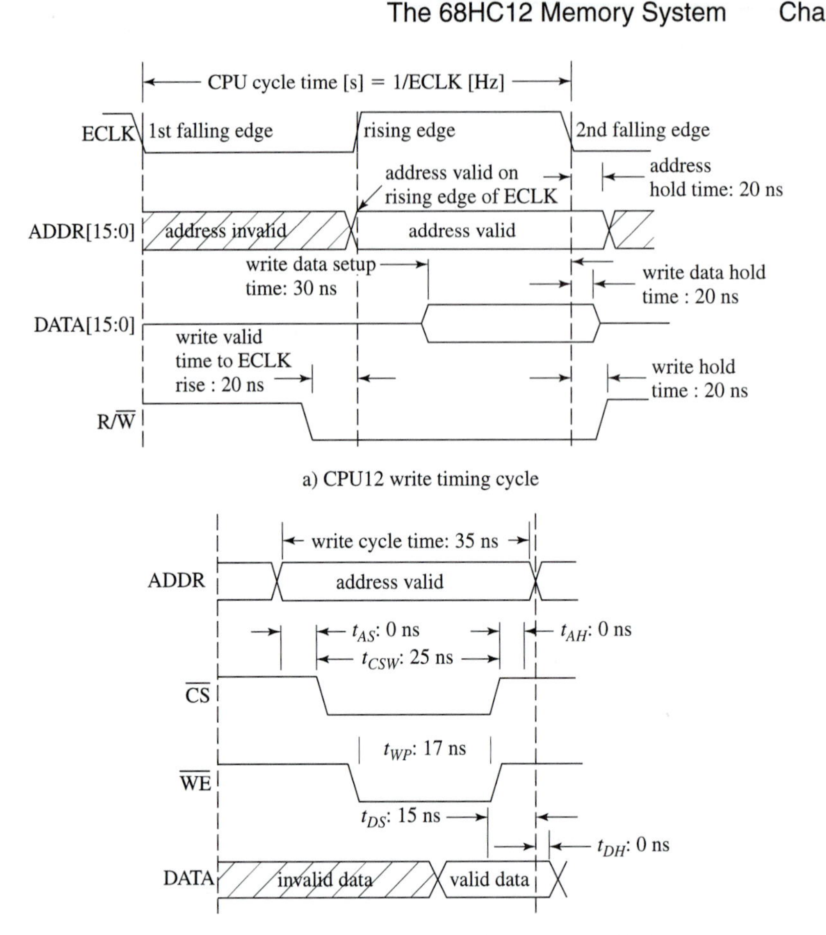

Figure 8.19 Simplified timing diagram for the 68HC12 read cycle: (a) 68HC12 write timing cycle, and (b) "35 ns" SRAM write timing cycle when used in a chip select controlled write cycle.

A simplified timing diagram for the 68HC12 write cycle is provided in Figure 8.19(b). This figure also includes the timing constraints levied by the SRAM component for the memory write cycle. These timing constraints are due to the timing requirements of the individual memory cells discussed earlier. Provided here is a brief definition of each of the SRAM timing constraints. Different memory component manufacturers may use slightly different names for these timing definitions. These definitions were adapted from Wakerly in "Digital Design Principles and Practices."

- t_{AS}: address setup time before write. The address lines must be stable at this time before the control signals $\overline{\text{WE}}$ and $\overline{\text{CS}}$ are activated.
- t_{AH}: address hold time after write. All address lines must be held stable until this time after the control lines $\overline{\text{WE}}$ and $\overline{\text{CS}}$ are deactivated.
- t_{CSW}: chip select setup before end of write. The chip select ($\overline{\text{CS}}$) control line must be asserted at least this long before the end of the write cycle to select a cell.
- t_{WP}: write-pulse width. The write enable control signal ($\overline{\text{WE}}$) must be asserted at least this long to reliably latch data from the 68HC12 into the selected cell in SRAM memory.
- t_{DS}: data setup time before the end of write. All of the data input lines from the 68HC12 must be stable at this time before the write cycle ends. If this constraint is not met, the data may not be properly latched into the memory cells.
- t_{DH}: data hold time after the end of write. All data inputs from the 68HC12 must be held stable until this time after the write cycle ends.

Manufacturers of SRAM components provide this write cycle timing constraint information in two different memory variants: write enabled controlled memory and chip select controlled memory. The only difference between these two variants is whether the write enable ($\overline{\text{WE}}$) control line or the chip select ($\overline{\text{CS}}$) control line is the last to be asserted and the first to be negated when enabling the SRAM's write operation [Wakerly]. For example, if the chip select line of the SRAM is activated after the write enable control line, we must use the chip select write cycle information.

How do we choose which timing data to use for a specific memory design? The hardware diagram of the memory layout must be carefully analyzed to determine which of the control lines is activated last. In our example (Figure 8.12), we must examine the combinational logic used to generate $\overline{\text{WE}}$ and the $\overline{\text{CS}}$ control signals to determine which one is activated last.

Earlier in the chapter, we developed the equation for the $\overline{\text{WE}}$ control signal as: $\overline{WE} = !(ECLK \cdot !R/\overline{W})$. (The symbol "!" indicates logic inversion.) From this equation, we can determine how soon after the first falling edge of the ECLK that the $\overline{\text{WE}}$ is asserted. For a 4 MHz ECLK, the ECLK becomes logic high 125 ns into the CPU cycle. As you can see in Figure 8.19, the R/ $\overline{\text{W}}$ was asserted 20 ns earlier. The R/ $\overline{\text{W}}$ signal is passed through an inverter (74HC04, propagation delay 15 ns) and then "NANDed" (74HC00, propagation delay 15 ns) with the ECLK to generate the $\overline{\text{WE}}$ signal. Therefore, the $\overline{\text{WE}}$ signal is asserted 140 ns (125 ns + 15 ns) after the first rising edge of the ECLK. What happened to the propagation delay of the inverter? Since the $R/\overline{W}$ was asserted 20 ns before the ECLK, the $R/\overline{W}$ was inverted while waiting for the ECLK to become a logic 1.

We now need to perform a similar analysis for the chip select signal. In our example, the chip select signals are provided by the decoder. The decoder is activated by a combination of address lines and the ECLK. Recall that the G1 enable pin of the decoder was activated with the "ANDed" result of the ECLK and address line A13. Therefore, the $\overline{\text{CS}}$ control signal is asserted 162 ns after the first rising edge of the ECLK. We arrived at this assertion time by adding 125 ns (when ECLK becomes high) with 15 ns (propagation delay of the "AND" gate) and 22 ns (the propagation delay of the decoder).

From this analysis, it is clear that we have a chip select controlled write cycle and therefore use the chip select controlled memory write timing information in the analysis that follows. Provided in Figure 8.19(b) are the timing constraints for a chip select controlled write cycle. We have also provided the actual timing constraints for a generic "35 ns" SRAM. Recall from our read cycle analysis in the previous section that we needed to use at least a 58 ns SRAM (or faster) to satisfy timing constraints. Therefore, the "35 ns" SRAM satisfies the read cycle timing constraint.

Let us now examine the 68HC12 write cycle in detail. We continue our example of the 68HC12 connected to an 8K $\times$ 16 SRAM module located at memory location \$2000 to \$3FFF. During this discussion, reference the simplified timing diagram for the 68HC12 read cycle provided in Figure 8.19. As mentioned, we use actual numbers from a "35 ns" SRAM memory component.

As described, during the 68HC12 write cycle, the following timing protocol is followed:

1. *Address timing*: The 68HC12 provides an address on lines ADDR [15:0]. The address becomes valid on the rising edge of the ECLK. We use ECLK $= 1$ to indicate valid data are present on the address lines. This occurs 125 ns after the first falling edge of the ECLK for a 4 MHz ECLK value.
2. *Data timing*: Data are then provided by the 68HC12 on DATA [15:0]. As you can see in Figure 8.19, this occurs 30 ns before the second falling edge of the ECLK, which occurs 220 ns (250 ns -30 ns) after the first rising edge of the ECLK.
3. *Control signal—write enable signal timing*: We just finished analyzing the write enable control signal. Our previous analysis is repeated here for completeness. The equation for generating the $\overline{\text{WE}}$ control signal is $\overline{\text{WE}} =!(ECLK \cdot !R/\overline{W})$. From this equation, we can determine how soon after the first falling edge of the ECLK that the $\overline{\text{WE}}$ is asserted. For a 4 MHz ECLK, the ECLK becomes logic high 125 ns into the CPU cycle. As you can see in Figure 8.19, the $R/\overline{W}$ was asserted 20 ns earlier. The $R/\overline{W}$ signal

is passed through an inverter (74HC04, propagation delay 15 ns) and then "NANDed" (74HC00, propagation delay 15 ns) with the ECLK to generate the $\overline{WE}$ signal. Therefore, the $\overline{WE}$ signal is asserted 140 ns (125 ns + 15 ns) after the first rising edge of the ECLK.

4. *Control signal—chip select signal timing*: The chip select timing analysis is also provided here for completeness. In our example, the chip select signals are provided by the decoder. The decoder is activated by a combination of address lines and the ECLK. Recall that the G1 enable pin of the decoder was activated with the "ANDed" result of the ECLK and address line A13. Therefore, the $\overline{CS}$ control signal is asserted 162 ns after the first rising edge of the ECLK. We arrived at this assertion time by adding 125 ns (when ECLK becomes high) with 15 ns (propagation delay of the "AND" gate) and 22 ns (the propagation delay of the decoder).

5. *SRAM timing constraints*: In the previous section, we defined each of the timing constraints levied by the SRAM component. As previously mentioned, we use actual values for a "35 ns" SRAM.

    - t_{AS}: address setup time before write—"35 ns" SRAM value: 0 ns. The address lines must be stable at this time before the control signals $\overline{WE}$ and $\overline{CS}$ are activated. Recall from the read cycle analysis that we combined a logic high ECLK to ensure the address lines were stable. Since both $\overline{WE}$ and $\overline{CS}$ are formed from combinational logic using the logic high ECLK, we can deduce that the address lines are stable before the control lines are activated.
    - t_{AH}: address hold time after write—"35 ns" SRAM value: 0 ns. All address lines must be held stable until this time after the control lines $\overline{WE}$ and $\overline{CS}$ are deactivated. The actual requirement is 0 ns.
    - t_{CSW}: chip select setup before end of write—"35 ns" SRAM value: 25 ns. The chip select ($\overline{CS}$) control line must be asserted at least this long before the end of the write cycle to select a cell. From our previous analysis, we know that the chip select line is asserted 162 ns after the first falling edge of the ECLK. It remains active until the ECLK is no longer valid. Without even taking the propagation delay into account, we can see the $\overline{CS}$ line is present through the second falling edge of the ECLK at 250 ns. The difference between the assertion of the $\overline{CS}$ control signal and a rough estimate of the deactivation of this signal yields an active signal time of 88 ns (250 ns −162 ns). Clearly, this constraint is met.
    - t_{WP}: write-pulse width—"35 ns" SRAM value: 17 ns. The write enable control signal ($\overline{WE}$) must be asserted at least this long to reliably

latch data from the 68HC12 into the selected cell in SRAM memory. From our previous analysis, we know that the write enable line is asserted 142 ns after the first falling edge of the ECLK. It remains active until the ECLK is no longer valid. Without even taking the propagation delay into account, we can see the $\overline{WE}$ line is present through the second falling edge of the ECLK at 250 ns. The difference between the assertion of the $\overline{WE}$ control signal and a rough estimate of the deactivation of this signal yields an active signal time of 108 ns (250 ns−142 ns). Clearly, this constraint is met.

- t_{DS}: data setup time before the end of write—"35 ns" SRAM value: 15 ns. All of the data input lines from the 68HC12 must be stable at this time before the write cycle ends. If this constraint is not met, the data may not be properly latched into the memory cells. From the timing diagram of the 68HC12 write cycle provided in Figure 8.19, you can see the data are stable 30 ns before the second falling edge of the ECLK and remains stable 20 ns after the falling edge of the ECLK. Therefore, this constraint is also met.
- t_{DH}: data hold time after the end of write—35 ns SRAM value: 0 ns. All data inputs from the 68HC12 must be held stable until this time after the write cycle ends. Since this value is 0 ns, we have also met this constraint.

Closing Remarks on Memory Timing Analysis That completes our timing analysis for a 8K × 16 RAM array located at memory location $2000 to $3FFF. We have shown that when this memory array is implemented with "35 ns" SRAM components, all memory read and write timing constraints are met. If our memory system contains external ROM components, memory timing analysis for the ROM read cycle must be accomplished. It follows the same procedure as the SRAM timing analysis for the read cycle.

In certain situations, timing analysis may yield an impossible memory access time. For example, re-accomplish the previous timing analysis when the ECLK frequency is 8 MHz. For our 8K × 16 SRAM example, you obtain a negative memory access time requirement. To remedy this situation, we could do the following:

- Choose different memory chips such that a decoder is not required for memory decoding,
- Employ the chip select features of the 68HC12,
- Employ the ECLK cycle stretching features of the 68HC12, or
- Choose a slower operating frequency for the 68HC12. Choosing a slower 68HC12 operating frequency may not be the best solution since the

68HC12 has built-in features to interface to slower memory systems. We discuss these features later in the chapter.

In closing, the timing analysis process detailed in this section may be adapted and used for any external device. For example, when a liquid crystal display (LCD) is connected to the 68HC12, several ports are used. A similar timing analysis exercise must be followed to ensure compatibility between the LCD and the 68HC12.

8.5.4 Electrical Compatibility

The fifth item of concern while expanding memory is to ensure that the external memory chips are electrically compatible with the 68HC12. The 68HC12 is a member of Motorola's "HC," or high-speed CMOS, family of chips. As long as all components in our system are also of the HC family, electrical compatibility issues are minimal. If the 68HC12 is connected to some component not in the HC family, electrical compatibility analysis must be completed.

Manufacturers readily provide the electrical characteristic data necessary to complete this analysis. There are eight different electrical specifications required for electrical compatibility analysis. These parameters are illustrated in Figure 8.20. The parameters are:

- V_{OH}: the lowest guaranteed output voltage for a logic high,
- V_{OL}: the highest guaranteed output voltage for a logic low,
- I_{OH}: the output current for a V_{OH} logic high,
- I_{OL}: the output current for a V_{OL} logic low,
- V_{IH}: the lowest input voltage guaranteed to be recognized as a logic high,
- V_{IL}: the highest input voltage guaranteed to be recognized as a logic low,
- I_{IH}: the input current for a V_{IH} logic high, and
- I_{IL}: the output current for a V_{IL} logic low.

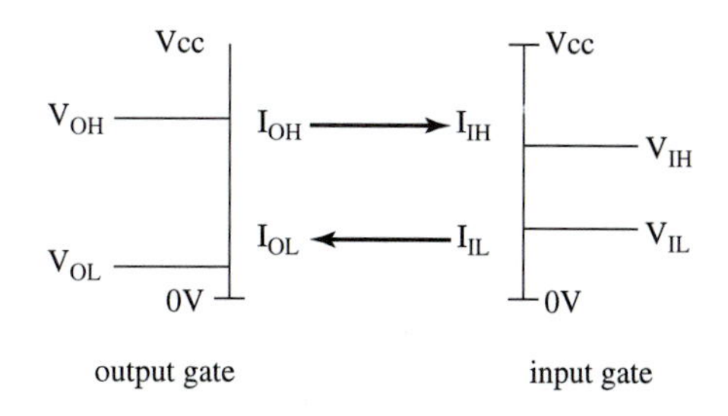

Figure 8.20 Electrical compatibility. There are eight different electrical specifications required for electrical compatibility analysis. The arrows indicate the direction of current flow.

These electrical characteristics are required for both the 68HC12 and external components. The 68HC12 values for these characteristics are (assuming $V_{DD} = 5.0$ volts and $V_{SS} = 0$ volts):

- $V_{OH} = 4.2$ volts,
- $V_{OL} = 0.4$ volts,
- $I_{OH} = -0.8$ milliamps,
- $I_{OL} = 1.6$ milliamps,
- $V_{IH} = 3.5$ volts,
- $V_{IL} = 1.0$ volts,
- $I_{IH} = 10$ microamps, and
- $I_{IL} = -10$ microamps.

Note: The minus sign on several of the currents indicates a current flow out of the device. A positive current indicates current flow into the device. How will you remember this sign convention? Money coming into your bank account is a positive event, whereas money going out of your bank account is a negative event.

Analysis To complete a thorough electrical analysis, the following items must be checked:

- Insure that the output voltages, both logic high and low, are compatible with the input voltages;
- Insure that the output currents, both logic high and low, are compatible with the input currents; and
- Fanout. The fanout is the maximum number of devices that can be connected to a chip's pin. As before, two cases must be analyzed: (1) output logic high, and (2) output logic low.

Let us illustrate the electrical analysis process with an example.

Example

Two new logic families (DP1 and SB2) have been developed. Key parameters for each logic family are provided:

DP1:

$V_{IH} = 2.0$ V, $V_{IL} = 0.8$ V, $I_{OH} = -0.4$ mA, $I_{OL} = 16$ mA

$V_{OH} = 3.4$ V, $V_{OL} = 0.2$ V, $I_{IH} = 40$ uA, $I_{IL} = -1.6$ mA

$$\text{SB2:} V_{IH} = 2.0 \text{ V}, \quad V_{IL} = 0.8 \text{ V}, \quad I_{OH} = -0.4 \text{ mA}, \quad I_{OL} = 8 \text{ mA}$$

$$V_{OH} = 2.7 \text{ V}, \quad V_{OL} = 0.4 \text{ V}, \quad I_{IH} = 20 \text{ uA}, \quad I_{IL} = -0.4 \text{ mA}$$

Can the DP1 logic family drive SB2 logic family? If so, what is the fanout? To correctly answer this question, you must compare voltage levels for compatibility and current for fanout calculations. The fanout must be calculated for both the logic high and logic low level case. The worst-case value is then chosen.

- The high voltage levels must be compared. The V_{OH} value of DP1 must be compared to the V_{IH} of SB2 for compatibility. DP1's V_{OH} is 3.4 volts while SB2's V_{IH} = 2.0 V. These levels are compatible since by definition V_{OH} is the lowest guaranteed output voltage for a logic one while V_{IH} sets the lower threshold for interpreting an input voltage as being a logic high.
- The low voltage levels must be compared. The V_{OL} value of DP1 must be compared to the V_{IL} of SB2 for compatibility. DP1's V_{OL} is 0.2 volts while SB2's V_{IL} = 0.8 V. These levels are compatible since by definition V_{OL} is the highest guaranteed output voltage for a logic zero while V_{IL} sets the upper threshold for interpreting an input voltage as being a logic low.
- Fanout must now be calculated for the logic high level case:

$$\text{fanout} = I_{OH}/I_{IH} = -400\ uA/20\ uA = 20 \text{ chips}$$

- Fan out must now be calculated for the logic low level case:

$$\text{fanout} = I_{OL}/I_{IL} = 16\ mA/-0.4\ mA = 40 \text{ chips}$$

- The worst-case fanout is then chosen: fanout = 20 chips

Example

Let us determine the fanout for an HC series component connected to another HC series component. Recall that:

$$V_{IH} = 3.5V, V_{IL} = 1.0V, I_{OH} = -0.8mA, I_{OL} = 1.6mA$$

$$V_{OH} = 4.2V, V_{OL} = 0.4V, I_{IH} = 10 \text{ uA}, I_{IL} = -10 \text{ uA}$$

To correctly answer this question, you must compare voltage levels for compatibility and current for fanout calculations. The fanout must be calculated for both the logic high and logic low level case. The worst-case value is then chosen.

- The high voltage levels must be compared. The V_{OH} value of HC must be compared to the V_{IH} of HC for compatibility. HC's V_{OH} is 4.2 volts while HC's V_{IH} = 3.5 V. These levels are compatible since by definition V_{OH}

is the lowest guaranteed output voltage for a logic one while V_{IH} sets the lower threshold for interpreting an input voltage as being a logic high.

- The low voltage levels must be compared. The V_{OL} value of HC must be compared to the V_{IL} of HC for compatibility. HC's V_{OL} is 0.4 volts while HC's $V_{IL} = 1.0$ V. These levels are compatible since by definition V_{OL} is the highest guaranteed output voltage for a logic zero while V_{IL} sets the upper threshold for interpreting an input voltage as being a logic low.
- Fanout must now be calculated for the logic high level case:

$$\text{fanout} = I_{OH}/I_{IH} = -0.8\,mA/10\,uA = 80 \text{ chips}$$

- Fanout must now be calculated for the logic low level case:

$$\text{fanout} = I_{OL}/I_{IL} = 1.6\,mA/-10\,uA = 160 \text{ chips}$$

- The worst-case fanout is then chosen: fanout = 80 chips

This section provided a brief introduction to connecting the 68HC12 to an external device. For an exhaustive treatment of this topic, see "The Art of Electronics" by P. Horowitz and W. Hill.

This section detailed how to expand the 68HC12 to its linear 64K addressable space. An exciting feature of the 68HC12 is the capability to expand the memory addressable far beyond the 64K linear space. This topic is covered in the next section.

8.5.5 Memory Paging

The external memory of the 68HC12 A4 variant may be expanded dramatically beyond the linear 64K addressable space. The memory paging scheme allows different designated portions of memory to be expanded: A program designated portion of memory may be expanded to 4M bytes, a data-designated portion of memory expanded to 1M bytes of memory, and the 68HC12 allows an extra designated portion to be expanded up to 256K bytes of additional memory. As mentioned before, the 68HC12 must be configured in one of the expanded modes to use these expanded memory features.

Memory paging is a concept in which a large portion of memory may be viewed from a fixed sized memory window. The memory window is much smaller than the paged memory space, such that only a single page of memory may be viewed through the window at a given time.

When I was a senior in high school, I took a history course on local community history. As part of the course, each student was required to extensively research and report on a topic of interest. I spent hours of time in the local library poring over old local newspapers stored on microfiche reels. Even though the old newspaper files were voluminous, I could only view the papers through the microfiche window a newspaper page at a time. Memory paging is similar to this illustration.

The 68HC12 is equipped with three different types of memory expansion windows: the **program** window, the **data** window, and the **extra** window (Figure 8.21).

The Program Window The program window as its name implies allows expansion of external memory space for storing larger programs. The program window occupies a 16K-byte address space from memory locations $8000 to $BFFF. One of 256 different 16K-byte pages may be viewed through the window at a given time. Therefore, the total addressable space through this window is (256 pages) $\cdot$ ($16K-$ byte/page) $= 4M-$ bytes of memory.

A specific memory page is selected by the eight-bit PPAGE register. Since this register contains eight bits, 256 different pages may be specified using binary encoding.

Internal circuitry automatically keeps track of whether a given address falls within the $8000 to $BFFF program window. If the address falls within the window and the program window is enabled (PWEN $= 1$), then the 68HC12 automatically builds a 22-bit external address using contents of the PPAGE register (PPAGE[7:0]) and a portion of the normal external address lines (CPU_ADDR[13 : 0]). This may be summarized in pseudocode as:

If CPU_ADDR[15:0] = $8000-$BFFF and PWEN = 1
Then EXT_ADDR[21:0] = PPAGE[7:0]:CPU_ADDR[13:0]

If the CPU address is not in the enabled window:

EXT_ADDR[21:0] = 1:1:1:1:1:1:CPU_ADDR[15:0]

The Program Window Enable Bit (PWEN) is bit 5 of the Window Definition Register (WINDEF) located at address $0037. When this bit is set to 1, paging of the program space is enabled (Figure 8.29).

The Data Window As its name implies, the data window allows expansion of external memory space for storing data. The data window occupies a 4K-byte address space from memory locations $7000 to $7FFF. One of 256 different 4K-byte pages may be viewed through the window at a given time. Therefore, the total addressable space through this window is (256 pages) $\cdot$ ($4K-$ byte/page) $= 1M-$ bytes of memory.

A specific memory page is selected by the eight-bit DPAGE register. Since this register contains eight bits, 256 different pages may be specified using binary encoding.

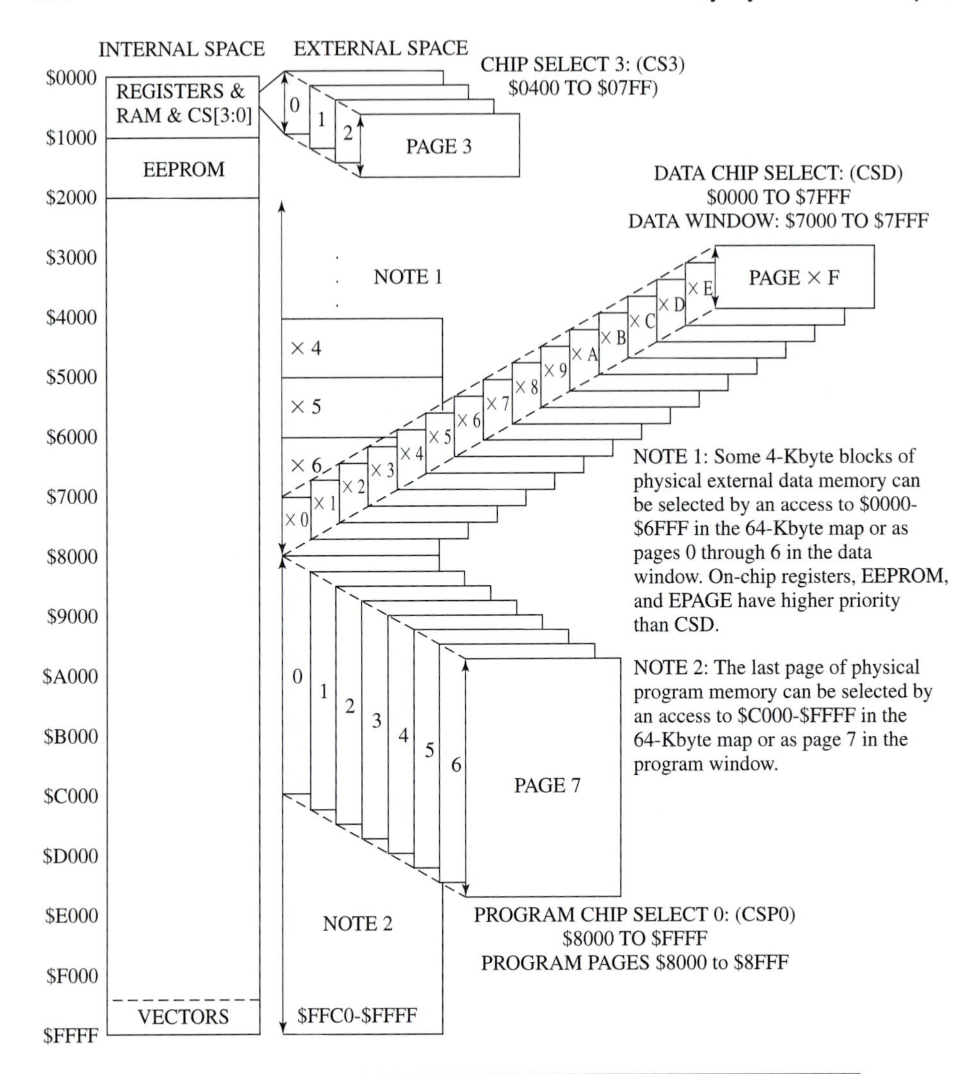

Register	Value	Meaning
WINDEF	$E0	Enable EPAGE, DPAGE, EPAGE
MXAR	$01	Port G bit 0 assigned as extended address ADDR16
CSCTL0	%00111xxx	Enables CSP0, CSD, and CS3
CSCTL1	$18	Makes CSD follow $0000-$7FFF and CS3 select EPAGE
MISC	%0xxxxxxx	Puts EPAGE at $0400-$09FF

Figure 8.21 Memory expansion windows. (Figure used with permission of Motorola, Incorporated.)

Internal circuitry automatically keeps track of whether a given address falls within the $7000 to $7FFF data window. If the address falls within the window and the data window is enabled (DWEN = 1), then the 68HC12 automatically builds a 22-bit external address using contents of the DPAGE register (DPAGE[7:0]) and a portion of the normal external address lines (CPU_ADDR[11:0]). This may be summarized in pseudocode as:

If CPU_ADDR[15:0] = $7000-$7FFF and DWEN = 1
Then EXT_ADDR[21:0] = 1:1:DPAGE[7:0]:CPU_ADDR[11:0]

If the CPU address is not in the enabled window:

EXT_ADDR[21:0] = 1:1:1:1:1:1:CPU_ADDR[15:0]

The Data Window Enable Bit (DWEN) is bit 7 of the Window Definition Register (WINDEF) located at address $0037. When this bit is set to 1, paging of the data space is enabled (Figure 8.29).

The Extra Window The extra window expands access to special types of memory such as EEPROM. The extra window occupies a 1K-byte address space. The window may be located at $0400 to $07FF or at locations $0000 to $03FF as determined by the Extra Window Positioned in Direct Space (EWDIR) bit in the Miscellaneous Mapping Control Register (MISC) located at $0013. If the EWDIR bit is set to 1, the extra window is located at $0000 to $03FF. If it is 0, the extra window is located at $0400 to $07FF. One of 256 different 1K-byte pages may be viewed through the window at a given time. Therefore, the total addressable space through this window is (256 pages) $\cdot(1K-$ byte/page$) = 256K-$ bytes of memory.

A specific memory page is selected by the eight-bit EPAGE register. Since this register contains eight bits, 256 different pages may be specified using binary encoding.

Internal circuitry automatically keeps track of whether a given address falls within the specified window. If the address falls within the window and the window is enabled (EWEN = 1), then the 68HC12 automatically builds a 22-bit external address using contents of the EPAGE register (EPAGE[7:0]) and a portion of the normal external address lines (CPU_ADDR[11:0]). This may be summarized in pseudocode as:

If CPU_ADDR[15:0] = $0000-$03FF and EWDIR = 1 and EWEN = 1
or CPU_ADDR[15:0] = $0400-$07FF and EWDIR = 0 and EWEN = 1
Then EXT_ADDR[21:0] = 1:1:1:1:EPAGE[7:0]:CPU_ADDR[9:0]

If the CPU address is not in the enabled window:

EXT_ADDR[21:0] = 1:1:1:1:1:1:CPU_ADDR[15:0]

The Extra Window Enable Bit (EWEN) is bit 5 of the Window Definition Register (WINDEF) located at address $0037. When this bit is set to 1, paging of the extra space is enabled (Figure 8.29).

Expanded Memory Port Requirements As mentioned previously, to employ these expansion windows, the 68HC12 must be configured for one of the expanded modes. For our discussion, we assume the A4 variant has been configured for the Normal Expanded Wide Mode. In this expanded mode, the A4 has a 16-bit data bus and a 16-bit address bus. Ports C and D are used for the 16-bit data bus, and Ports G, A, and B are used for the 21-bit address bus. Furthermore, chip selects (to be discussed shortly) use Port F. Some of the these ports may be replaced with an additional chip called a *port replacement unit* (PRU).

Building an Expanded Memory Address Each window has an associated page select register: PPAGE register for the program window, DPAGE register for the data window, and the EPAGE register for the extra window. This xPAGE registers select which page of external memory is currently in view by the respective windows. For the data and extra windows page switching is accomplished by the user placing the correct page address in the DPAGE and the EPAGE registers, respectively. The effective 21-bit address is then assembled by the 68HC12.

The 68HC12 CALL and RTC instructions automatically manipulate the program page select (PPAGE) register for the program window.

The CALL and RTC instructions are similar to the JSR (jump to subroutine) and the RTS (return from subroutine) instructions. Recall that the JSR and RTS instructions are used to jump to and return from a subroutine. When the JSR instruction was executed, the memory address of the next instruction following the JSR instruction was placed on the STACK so that when the RTS instruction was executed at the end of the subroutine, the 68HC12 would know where to find the address to continue processing after completion of subroutine operation.

The CALL instruction is much like the JSR. However, the CALL instruction may be used to call a subroutine located anywhere in the 64K-byte linear address space or in the program expansion memory. Much like the JSR, when CALL is executed, a return address is calculated and placed on the STACK. The return address stored on the STACK includes the value of the PPAGE register.

The RTC instruction is much like the RTS instruction. The RTC instruction terminates subroutines originally called with the CALL instruction. When RTC is executed, the address to resume processing is pulled from the STACK and placed in the Program Counter for continued execution. Although it appears the CALL/RTC instruction pair replaces the JSR/RTS instruction pair, this is not the case. The JSR/RTS combination should continue to be used when operating within the 64K linearly addressable space since their execution time is less than the CALL/RTC combination.

Memory Expansion Registers In this section, we discuss the registers required to configure the expanded memory features of the 68HC12.

Port F Data Register—PORTF The Port F Data Register is located at memory location $0030. Seven of the PORTF pins are associated with the chip selects (to be discussed in the next section). Any pin not configured to work as a chip select can be used as a general purpose input/output (I/O) pin. Enabling a pin as a chip select overrides the associated data direction bit and port data bit.

Register: Port F Data Register (PORTF) Address: $0030

	7	6	5	4	3	2	1	0
	0	Bit 6	Bit 5	Bit 4	Bit 3	Bit 2	Bit 1	Bit 0
Reset:	0	0	0	0	0	0	0	0
Alternate pin function:	0	CSP1	CSP0	CSD	CS3	CS2	CS1	CS0

Figure 8.22 Port F Data Register—PORTF, $0030.

Port G Data Register—PORTG The Port G Data Register is located at memory location $0031. Six of the PORTG pins PG[5:0] are associated with memory expansion. Any pin not configured for memory expansion can be used as a general purpose I/O pin. Enabling a pin in a memory expansion role overrides the associated data direction bit and port data bit.

Register: Port G Data Register (PORTG) Address: $0031

	7	6	5	4	3	2	1	0
	0	0	Bit 5	Bit 4	Bit 3	Bit 2	Bit 1	Bit 0
Reset:	0	0	0	0	0	0	0	0
Alternate pin function:	0	0	ADDR21	ADDR20	ADDR19	ADDR18	ADDR17	ADDR16

Figure 8.23 Port G Data Register—PORTG, $0031.

Port F Data Direction Register—DDRF The Port F Data Direction Register is located at memory location $0032. When Port F is active, the bits in DDRF determine the direction of the associated I/O pin. When a DDRFx bit is set to 1, the associated Port F pin is an output. When a DDRFx bit is set to 0, the associated Port F pin is an input.

Port G Data Direction Register—DDRG The Port G Data Direction Register is located at memory location $0033. When Port G is active, the bits in DDRG

Register: Port F Data Direction Register (DDRF) Address: $0032

7	6	5	4	3	2	1	0
0	Bit 6	Bit 5	Bit 4	Bit 3	Bit 2	Bit 1	Bit 0
Reset: 0	0	0	0	0	0	0	0

Figure 8.24 Port F Data Direction Register—DDRF, $0032.

Register: Port G Data Direction Register (DDRG) Address: $0033

7	6	5	4	3	2	1	0
0	0	Bit 5	Bit 4	Bit 3	Bit 2	Bit 1	Bit 0
Reset: 0	0	0	0	0	0	0	0

Figure 8.25 Port G Data Direction Register—DDRG, $0033.

determine the direction of the associated I/O pin. When a DDRGx bit is set to 1, the associated Port G pin is an output. When a DDRGx bit is set to 0, the associated Port G pin is an input.

Data Page Register—DPAGE The DPAGE register is located at memory location $0034. When the Data Window Enable Bit (DWEN) in the Window Definition Register (WINDEF) is enabled (DWEN = 1), the value in the DPAGE register determines which of the 256-Kbyte pages is active in the data window. An access to a memory location within the data page memory area ($7000–$7FFF) transfers the contents of DPAGE to address pins ADDR[15:12] and expansion address pins ADDR[19:16] as discussed previously. The ADDR[21:20] bits are forced to 1 if they are enabled by the Memory Expansion Assignment Register (MXAR). The data chip select (CSD) must be used in conjunction with this memory expansion window.

Register: Data Page Register (DPAGE) Address: $0034

7	6	5	4	3	2	1	0
PDA19	PDA18	PDA17	PDA16	PDA15	PDA14	PDA13	PDA12
Reset: 0	0	0	0	0	0	0	0

Figure 8.26 Data Page Register—DPAGE, $0034.

Program Page Register—PPAGE The PPAGE register is located at memory location $0035. When the Program Window Enable Bit (PWEN) in the Window Definition Register (WINDEF) is enabled (PWEN = 1), the value in the PPAGE register determines which of the 256 16-Kbyte pages is active in

Register: Program Page Register (PPAGE) Address: $0035

	7	6	5	4	3	2	1	0
	PPA21	PPA20	PPA19	PPA18	PPA17	PPA16	PPA15	PPA14
Reset:	0	0	0	0	0	0	0	0

Figure 8.27 Program Page Register—PPAGE, $0035.

the program window. An access to a memory location within the program page memory area ($8000 to $8FFF) transfers the contents of PPAGE to address pins ADDR[15:14] and expansion address pins ADDR[21:16] as discussed previously. At least one of the program chip selects (CSP0 and/or CSP1) must be used in conjunction with the memory expansion window. This register is used along with the CALL and RTC instructions to automate program flow changes between pages of program memory.

Extra Page Register—EPAGE The EPAGE register is located at memory location $0036. When the Extra Window Enable Bit (EWEN) in the Window Definition Register (WINDEF) is enabled (EWEN = 1), the value in the EPAGE register determines which of the 256-Kbyte pages is active in the extra window. An access to a memory location within the extra page memory area transfers the contents of EPAGE to address pins ADDR[15:10] and expansion address pins ADDR[17:16] as discussed previously. The ADDR[21:18] bits are forced to 1 if they are enabled by the Memory Expansion Assignment Register (MXAR). Chip select 3 (CS3) must be used in conjunction with this memory expansion window.

Register: Extra Page Register (EPAGE) Address: $0036

	7	6	5	4	3	2	1	0
	PEA17	PEA16	PEA15	PEA14	PEA13	PEA12	PEA11	PEA10
Reset:	0	0	0	0	0	0	0	0

Figure 8.28 Extra Page Register—EPAGE, $0036.

Window Definition Register—WINDEF The WINDEF register is located at memory location $0037. This register is used to enable the three different expan-

Register: Window Definition Register (WINDEF) Address: $0037

	7	6	5	4	3	2	1	0
	DWEN	PWEN	EWEN	0	0	0	0	0
Reset:	0	0	0	0	0	0	0	0

Figure 8.29 Window Definition Register—WINDEF, $0037.

sion windows (Data, Program, and Extra) using the DWEN, PWEN, and EWEN bits, respectively. A 1 enables paging of the specified window space, whereas a 0 disables the respective page.

Memory Expansion Assignment Register—MXAR The MXAR register is located at memory location $0038. The bits A21E through A16E select the memory expansion pins ADDR 31 through ADDR16. A1 in a respective bit location selects memory expansion for the associated bit, whereas a 0 selects general purpose I/O for the associated bit.

Register: Memory Expansion Assignment Register (MXAR) Address: $0038

	7	6	5	4	3	2	1	0
	0	0	A21E	A20E	A19E	A18E	A17E	A16E
Reset:	0	0	0	0	0	0	0	0

Figure 8.30 Memory Expansion Assignment Register—MXAR, $0038.

Chip Selects To use the chip select features, the A4 must be in one of the expanded modes. Each of the seven chip selects has an associated address space for which it is active. When the current address is in the range of addresses spanned by the chip select, the chip select becomes active. Chip select pins are an effective way to reduce or altogether eliminate the need for external address decode logic.

The 68HC12 chip select pins are active low. This is consistent with the active low-chip select pins on most memory devices. All of the pins in the associated port are pulled up when they are inputs and the Pull-Up Port F Enable—PUPF (pin 5) of the Pull Up Control Register—PUCR ($000C) is set to a 1 as discussed in the 68HC12 hardware chapter. When memory expansion is employed in a system, the chip select pins recommended before should also be used. This prevents confusion within memory addressing. There are three different chip select registers.

Chip Select Control Register 0—CSCTLO The CSCTLO register is located at memory location $003C. The bits in this register provide a chip select

Register: Chip Select Control Register 0 (CSCTL0) Address: $003C

	7	6	5	4	3	2	1	0
	0	CSP1E	CSP0E	CSDE	CS3E	CS2E	CS1E	CS0E
Reset:	0	0	0	0	0	0	0	0

Figure 8.31 Chip Select Control Register 0—CSCTLO, $003C.

for different portions of memory. A 1 in the bit location enables the chip select, whereas a 0 disables the associated chip select.

- Chip Select Program 1 Enable Bit (CSP1E): enables the chip select that covers the space $8000 to $FFFF or full map $0000 to $FFFF.
- Chip Select Program 0 Enable Bit (CSP0E): enables the chip select that covers the program space $8000 to $FFFF or full map $0000 to $FFFF.
- Chip Select Data Enable Bit (CSDE): enables the chip select that covers either $0000 to $7FFF if CSDHF = 1 or $7000 to $7FFF if CSDHF = 0.
- Chip Select 3 Enable Bit (CS3E): enables the chip select that covers a 128-byte space following the register space ($x280 to $x2FF or $xA80 to $xAFF).
- Chip Select 2 Enable Bit (CS2E): enables the chip select that covers a 128-byte space following the register space ($x380 to $x3FF or $xB80 to $xBFF).
- Chip Select 1 Enable Bit (CS1E): enables the chip select that covers a 256-byte space following the register space ($x300 to $x3FF or $xB00 to $xBFF). Note that the space controlled by this chip select overlaps the memory areas of CS3E and CS2E. Both of these chip selects can override CS1E.
- Chip Select 0 Enable Bit (CS0E): enables the chip select that covers a 512-byte space following the register space ($x200 to $x3FF or $xA00 to $xBFF). Note that the space controlled by this chip select overlaps the memory areas of CS3E, CS2E, and CS1E. These chip selects can override CS0E.

Chip Select Control Register 1—CSCTL1 The CSCTL1 register is located at memory location $003D. The bits in this register provide a chip select for different portions of memory. A 1 in the bit location enables the chip select, whereas a 0 disables the associated chip select.

Register: Chip Select Control Register 1 (CSCTL1) Address: $003D

	7	6	5	4	3	2	1	0
	0	CSP1FL	CSPA21	CSDHF	CS3EP	0	0	0
Reset:	0	0	0	0	0	0	0	0

Figure 8.32 Chip Select Control Register 1—CSCTL1, $003D.

- Program Chip Select 1 Covers Full Map (CSP1FL): If CSP1FL is zero and CSPA21 (described later) is also zero, chip select program 1 covers half the map, $8000 to $FFFF. If CSP1FL is set to 1 and CSPA21 is zero, chip select program 1 covers the entire memory map.
- Program Chip Select Split Based on ADDR21 (CSPA21): If this bit is zero, CSP0 and CSP1 do not rely on the status of ADDR21. If CSPA21 is 1, program chip selects are both active (if they have been enabled) for space $8000 to $FFFF.
- Data Chip Select Covers Half the Map (CSDHF): If the CSDHF bit is zero, the data chip select covers only $7000 to $7FFFF, whereas if CSDHF is one, the data chip select covers half the memory map ($0000 to $7FFF) including the optional data page window ($7000 to $7FFF).
- Chip Select 3 Follows Extra Page (CS3EP): When this bit is zero, chip select 3 includes only accesses to a 128-byte space following the register space. When 1, chip select 3 follows accesses to the 1-Kbyte extra page ($0400 to $07FF or $0000 to $03FF). Any accesses to this window cause the chip select to go active (EWEN must be set to a logic 1).

Chip Select Stretch Registers 0 and 1—CSSTR0 and CSSTR1

The CSSTR0 and CSSTR1 registers are located at memory locations $003E and $003F. The bits in these registers allow the chip selects described earlier to be stretched by some number of E clock cycles. This stretching allows the A4 to be used with slower memory components without slowing down the entire system. Each of the seven chip selects has a two-bit field in these registers, which determines the amount of clock stretch for accesses in that chip select space.

Register: Chip Select Stretch Register 0 (CSSTR0) Address: $003E

	7	6	5	4	3	2	1	0
	0	0	SRP1A	SRP1B	SRP0A	SRP0B	STRDA	STRDB
Reset:	0	0	1	1	1	1	1	1

Figure 8.33 Chip Select Stretch Register 0—CSSTR0.

Register: Chip Select Stretch Register 1 (CSSTR1) Address: $003F

	7	6	5	4	3	2	1	0
	STR3A	STR3B	STR2A	STR2B	STR1A	STR1B	STR0A	STR0B
Reset:	1	1	1	1	1	1	1	1

Figure 8.34 Chip Select Stretch Register 1—CSSTR1.

Stretch Bit SxxxA	Stretch Bit SxxxB	Number of E Clocks Stretched
0	0	0
0	1	1
1	0	2
1	1	3

Figure 8.35 Stretch bit definition.

8.5.6 EEPROM Modification

The 68HC12 A4 variant is equipped with a 4-Kbyte (4096-byte) nonvolative EEPROM memory. This memory may be used for data constants, program code, operating system kernels, or standard subroutines. The EEPROM requires that each memory word be erased (set to 1s) before it is programmed.

The EEPROM consists of two separate sections: (1) a four-byte memory mapped control register block, and (2) the actual EEPROM memory space. The four-byte register starts at location $00F0 and the EEPROM from $1000 to $1FFF. The "EEON" bit (bit 0 in the Inititialization of Internal EEPROM Position Register—INITEE) when zero, removes the EEPROM from the memory map. When "EEON" is 1, the on-chip EEPROM is accessible in the memory map at the address specified by EE[15:12] bits of the INITEE register.

EEPROM Control Register—EEPROG The EEPROM Control register ($00F3) is the main register used to program and erase the EEPROM.

The key bits in this register are:

- The EEPGM bit is the Program and Erase Enable bit. If 1 the program voltage is on, whereas if 0, the program voltage is off.
- The EELAT bit is the EEPROM Latch Control. If 1 the EEPROM is placed in the latch mode for erasure and programming. When this bit is 0, the EEPROM is in the normal read mode.

Register: EEPROM Programming Register (EEPROG) Address: $00F3

	7	6	5	4	3	2	1	0
	BULKP	0	0	BYTE	ROW	ERASE	EELAT	EEPGM
Reset:	1	0	0	0	0	0	0	0

Figure 8.36 EEPROM control register—EEPROG.

Byte	Row	Block Size
0	0	Bulk erase entire EEPROM array
0	1	Row erase 32 bytes
1	0	Byte or aligned word erase
1	1	Byte or aligned word erase

Figure 8.37 Erase selection.

- The ERASE bit is the Erase Control bit. When 0, the EEPROM is configured for programming. When 1, the EEPROM is configured for erasure.
- The BYTE and ROW bits select the various erase modes as shown in Figure 8.37.

Erasing and Programming the EEPROM To erase a byte of EEPROM, follow these steps:

1. Set EELAT, ERASE, and BYTE.
2. Write anything to the location.
3. Set EEPGM.
4. Wait 10 ms.
5. Clear all bits in the EEPROG register.

To program a byte of EEPROM, follow these steps:

1. Set EELAT.
2. Write desired data to the location.
3. Set EEPGM.
4. Wait 10 ms.
5. Clear all bits in the EEPROG register.

EEPROM Protection Registers Other registers associated with EEPROM control are the EEPROT register and the EEMCR register. The EEPROM Block Protect register (EEPROT) is located at $00F1. The register prevents accidental writes to EEPROM. The bits BPROT[6:0] in the EEPROT register allows the associated EEPROM block to be programmed and erased. When 1, the associated EEPROM block is protected from accidental programming or erasure.

The EEPROM Module Configuration Register (EEMCR) at location $00F0 provides further protection. In particular, the Block Protect Write Lock bit (PROT-

Register: EEPROM Block Protect Register (EEPROT) Address: $00F1

7	6	5	4	3	2	1	0
1	BPROT6	BPROT5	BPROT4	BPROT3	BPROT2	BPROT1	BPROT0
Reset: 1	1	1	1	1	1	1	1

Figure 8.38 EEPROM block protect—EEPROT.

Bit Name	Block Protected	Block Size
BPROT6	$1000 to $17FF	2048 Bytes
BPROT5	$1800 to $1BFF	1024 Bytes
BPROT4	$1C00 to $1DFF	512 Bytes
BPROT3	$1E00 to $1EFF	256 Bytes
BPROT2	$1F00 to $1F7F	128 Bytes
BPROT1	$1F80 to $1FBF	64 Bytes
BPROT0	$1FC0 to $1FFF	64 Bytes

Figure 8.39 4-Kbyte EEPROM block protection.

LCK) when 0, allows the Block Protect Bits described earlier to be modified. When 1, the Block Protect Bits are locked.

8.6 APPLICATIONS

For the robot implementation, we use the Motorola M68HC12A4EVB (A4 evaluation board).

Practice Question

Question: The M68HC12A4EVB (A4 evaluation board) has the following memory specifications:

- $0000–$01FF, on-chip CPU registers
- $0800–$0BFF, on-chip RAM
- $1000–$1FFF, on-chip EEPROM
- $4000–$7FFF, external RAM
- $8000–$FFFF, external EPROM

Specify the size of each memory component and draw the memory map for the M68HC12A4EVB.

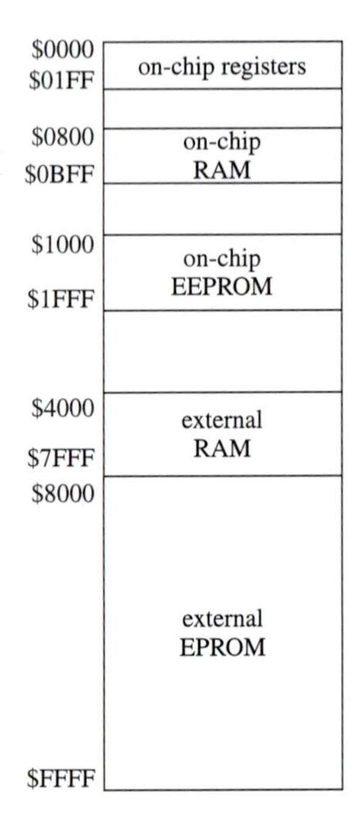

Figure 8.40 Memory map.

Answer:

- $0000–$01FF, on-chip CPU registers, $200 = 512 locations
- $0800–$0BFF, on-chip RAM, $400 = 1024 locations
- $1000–$1FFF, on-chip EEPROM, $1000 = 4,096 locations
- $4000–$7FFF, external RAM, $4000 = 16K locations
- $8000–$FFFF, external EPROM, $8000 = 32K locations

Memory Map: Figure 8.40.

8.7 FURTHER READING

"Digital Design Principles and Practices," John F. Wakerly, Prentice-Hall Inc, 3rd ed, 2000.

"The Art of Electronics," P. Horowitz and W. Hill, Cambridge University Press, 2nd ed., 1989.

"A Technique for the Design of Microprocessor Memory Systems," J.J. Cupal, IEEE Transactions on Education, Volume 37, No. 3, August 1994, pages 237–242.

"MC68HC812A4 Technical Summary 16-Bit Microcontroller," Motorola, Inc., 1997

"68HC12 Evaluation Board User's Manual," Motorola, Inc. 1996.

8.8 SUMMARY

In this chapter, we provided a thorough introduction to memory components, memory expansion techniques, and memory timing analysis. We started the chapter by investigating different variants of the 68HC12 with reference to different memory configurations. We then explored different memory technologies employed by the 68HC12. We then saw how the memory map is an effective tool for tracking memory usage in a computer and specifically interpreted the memory map for the 68HC12. We then covered the design of expanded memory in great detail for both RAM and ROM components examining layout procedures, control signal connections, and timing analysis. We also examined the paging memory features of the 68HC12.

8.9 CHAPTER PROBLEMS

Fundamental

1. What is the last location of a 12K-byte memory starting at location $2000?
2. A beefed-up version of the 68HC12 has become available. It has the following memory specifications:

   - $0000–$01FF, on-chip CPU registers
   - $0800–$09FF, on-chip RAM, user code and data
   - $0A00–$0BFF, reserved for D-Bug12
   - $1000–$3FFF, on-chip EEPROM, user code and data
   - $4000–$7FFF, external RAM, user code and data
   - $8000–$9FFF, external EPROM, available for user programs*
   - $A000–$FD7F, external EPROM, D-Bug12 program
   - $FD80–$FDFF, external EPROM, D-Bug12 startup code*
   - $FE00–$FE7F, external EPROM, user-accessible functions
   - $FE80–$FEFF, external EPROM, D-Bug12 customization data*
   - $FF00–$FF7F, external EPROM, available for user programs*
   - $FF80–$FFFF, external EPROM, reserved for interrupt and reset vectors

   Note: *Code in these areas may be modified. Requires reprogramming of the EPROMs. Specify the size of each memory component and draw the memory map for the M68HC12A4EVB.
3. In the prior question, memory locations from $8000 to $9FFF have been designated for user programs. Explain how you would load a program into this memory space.

4. Design a 32K × 16 SRAM array from 8K × 8 SRAM chips beginning at memory location $2000. Your design should include a detailed memory diagram. Do not perform memory timing analysis.
5. Explain the difference between SRAM, DRAM, EPROM, and EEPROMs. Explain how each may be employed in an embedded controller system. List these memory technologies in order from fastest to slowest access times. List these memory technologies in order from fastest to slowest memory write cycle times.

Advanced

1. A memory system is equipped with 18 address lines and 16 data lines. Specify: (a) the number of linearly addressable memory locations, (b) the length of the memory, (c) the width of the memory, (d) the size of the memory in bits, and (e) the size of the memory in bytes.
2. A memory system is required that has 4 million locations. At each memory location a 16-bit word must be stored. Specify: (a) the number of required address lines, (b) the number of required data lines, and (c) the size of the memory in bytes.
3. Two new logic families (DP1 and SB2) have been developed. Key parameters for each logic family are provided:

   DP1:

   $$V_{IH} = 2.0\text{ V}, \quad V_{IL} = 0.8\text{ V}, \quad I_{OH} = -0.4\text{ mA}, \quad I_{OL} = 16\text{ mA}$$

   $$V_{OH} = 3.4\text{ V}, \quad V_{OL} = 0.2\text{ V}, \quad I_{IH} = 40\text{ uA}, \quad I_{IL} = -1.6\text{ mA}$$

   SB2:

   $$V_{IH} = 2.0\text{ V}, \quad V_{IL} = 0.8\text{ V}, \quad I_{OH} = -0.4\text{ mA}, \quad I_{OL} = 8\text{ mA}$$

   $$V_{OH} = 2.7\text{ V}, \quad V_{OL} = 0.4\text{ V}, \quad I_{IH} = 20\text{ uA}, \quad I_{IL} = -0.4\text{ mA}$$

   Can the SB2 logic family drive DP1 logic family? If so, what is the fanout?
4. Describe in detail the memory paging features of the 68HC12 A4 variant.
5. Can the HC system drive the DP1 logic family?
6. Can the HC system drive the SB2 logic family?

Challenging

1. Perform the memory interface timing analysis for the SRAM memory system described in the timing analysis section of the text with an ECLK frequency of 6 MHz. Use the same "35 ns" SRAM used in the example for your timing analysis. Is the "35 ns" SRAM fast enough for use with the 6 Mhz clock?
2. Perform a complete memory analysis for a 32K-byte external EPROM beginning at location $8000. Assume that a 32K-byte EPROM is available in a single chip. Specify the required access times of the EPROM chip. Assume an ECLK frequency of 4 MHz.

9

Analog-to-Digital (ATD) Converter

Objectives: At the completion of this chapter you will be able to:

- Define the need for a transducer subsystem to convert a physical variable to an electrical signal compatible with an embedded controller system,
- Describe and apply key terms associated with an analog-to-digital (ATD) conversion process such as sampling frequency, quantizing, resolution, and encoding,
- Summarize the operation of different ATD converter technologies with their associated advantages and disadvantages,
- Calculate different ATD parameters for a given scenario,
- Describe the ATD conversion system used aboard the 68HC12,
- List and describe the key registers associated with the 68HC12 ATD conversion system, and
- Program the 68HC12 to accomplish ATD conversions for a given situation.

In this chapter we examine the need for a transducer subsystem to convert a physical variable to an electrical signal compatible with an embedded controller system. We then describe and apply key terms associated with an analog-to-digital (ATD) conversion process such as sampling frequency, quantizing, resolution, and encoding. We examine different ATD converter technologies with their associated advantages and disadvantages and calculate different conversion parameters for a given scenario. We investigate the ATD conversion system used aboard the 68HC12 in detail and describe the key registers associated with the 68HC12 ATD conversion system. Finally, we complete the chapter by learning how to program the 68HC12 to accomplish ATD conversions for a given situation.

9.1 OVERVIEW

We live in an analog world. Virtually every physical variable that an embedded controller might measure, such as temperature, pressure, weight, displacement, chemical parameters, or light intensity, needs to first be converted to an electrical signal such as a voltage. The conversion from a physical variable to an electrical variable is accomplished by a transducer. Once the conversion is accomplished, the resulting signal may need to be scaled (amplified or attenuated), filtered, or even provided a direct current (DC) voltage offset such that it is compatible with an embedded controller system. The purpose of this chapter is not to review the fundamentals of transducer subsystems, but to describe how an embedded controller converts a suitable voltage into a corresponding binary value. However, we provide a brief review of transducer interface concepts. Several excellent references on instrumentation and signal conditioning topics are provided at the end of this chapter.

Recall that our wall following robot required an ATD conversion system to sense the presence of walls in a maze. The wall following robot is equipped with three infrared (IR) emitter-detector pairs to sense walls in front of and on either side of the robot (Figure 9.1). The IR emitter provides an IR beam that is projected out from the robot. This beam is reflected off the reflective maze walls and back to the IR detector. The closer the wall is to the robot, the higher the intensity of the reflected IR signal and hence the magnitude of the voltage produced by the IR detector. An ATD converter may be used to convert the analog voltage from the IR detector into an unsigned binary quantity that can be processed by the 68HC12.

The remote weather station introduced in the previous chapter also required an ATD converter system to convert analog signals from its multiple sensors into a binary representation suitable for processing by the 68HC12. Recall that the remote weather station processed many analog signals. Here is a summary of these signals:

- barometer—The barometer here provides a signal that ranges from 0 to 5 volts depending on the sensed barometric pressure. It provides a 0-volt out-

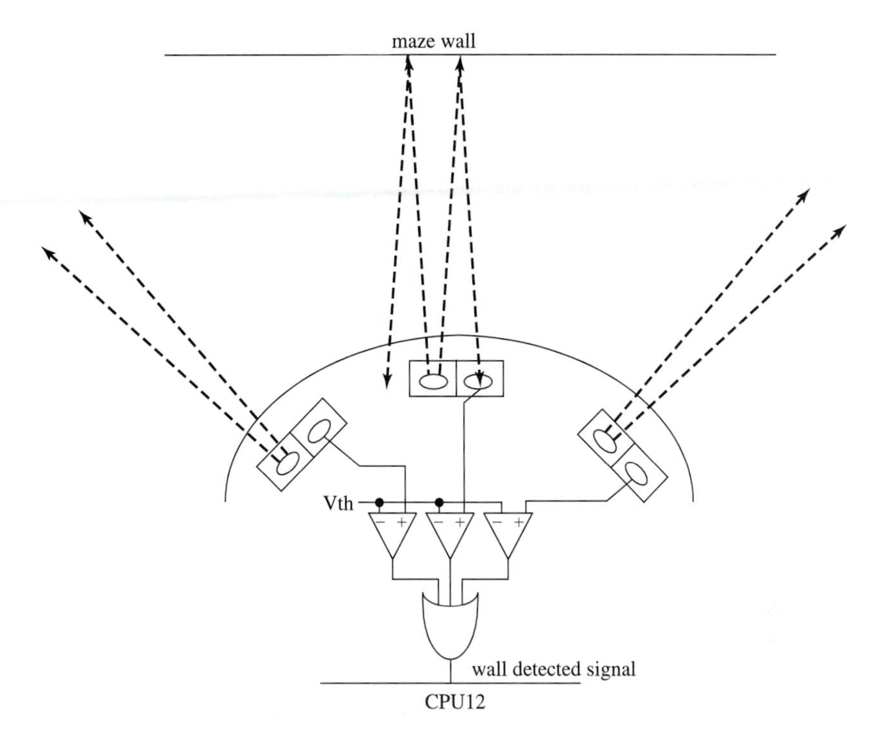

Figure 9.1 Wall sensing using an IR emitter-detector pair. The wall following robot is equipped with IR emitter-detector pairs to sense walls.

put for 64 cm of mercury and 5 volts for 81 cm of mercury (the normal range for barometric pressure). For values between these two extremes, there is a linear relationship between output voltage and barometric pressure.

- hygrometer—A hygrometer senses relative humidity. The hygrometer here provides a signal that ranges from 0 to 5 volts depending on the sensed atmospheric humidity. It provides a 0-volt output for 0% relative humidity and 5 volts for 100% relative humidity. For values between these two extremes, there is a linear relationship between output voltage and relative humidity.
- rain gauge—The rain gauge measures the amount of precipitation present. The rain gauge here provides 20 millivolts of output for each centimeter of accumulated precipitation.
- thermocouple—A thermocouple is a temperature sensor. The thermocouple here provides a 0-volt output for −50 degrees centigrade and provides a 5-volt output for +120 degrees centigrade. For values between these two

extremes, there is a linear relationship between output voltage and sensed temperature.

- weather vane—A weather vane senses wind direction. The weather vane here provides a 0-volt output when it is pointing north. As the weather vane turns clockwise to the east, south, and west, the voltage increments linearly until it reaches a full-scale value of 5 volts as it just completes its rotation back to north.

In this chapter, we explore the theory behind the ATD conversion process, different methods of performing an ATD conversion, the ATD features of the 68HC12, and how to program the 68HC12 to perform ATD conversions.

9.2 TRANSDUCER INTERFACE DESIGN

A transducer is a mechanical and/or electronic component that converts a physical variable such as temperature, pressure, displacement, and so on into an electrical signal. In the weather station example provided in the previous section, the weather parameter transducers conveniently transduced the physical phenomena into an electronic signal compatible with the 68HC12. In this ideal example, we did not have to concern ourselves with conditioning the signal. Often this is not the case. The output signal from the transducer may require scaling (amplification or attenuation), filtering of undesired frequency components, and/or addition of a DC bias signal. It is beyond the scope of this book to cover the myriad details of signal conditioning. Several excellent references are provided at the end of the chapter. In this section, we provide the basic concept of transducer interface design at a block diagram level.

A block diagram of a basic transducer interface design is provided in Figure 9.2. The transducer converts a physical variable X into an electronic signal. Generally speaking, the transducer output X is scaled by a factor K and then has a DC bias (B) applied. In our discussion, we assume that the output from the transducer is linear. That is, when the physical variable X_1 is provided to the transducer, the

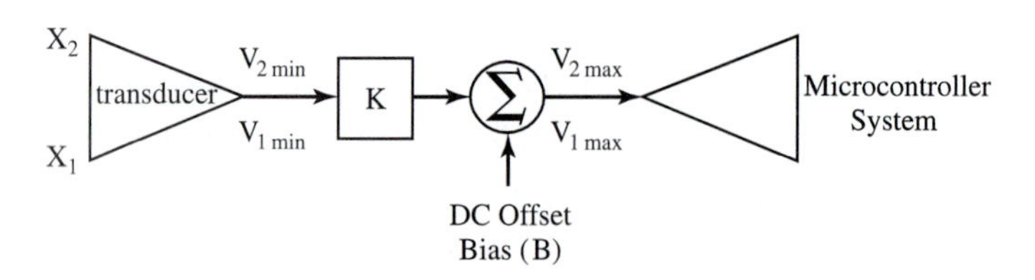

Figure 9.2 Transducer interface design.

transducer provides an output voltage of V_{1min}. Likewise, when the physical variable X_2 is provided to the transducer, the transducer will provide an output voltage of V_{2min}. When physical variables between the extremes of X_1 and X_2 are provided to the transducer, a corresponding linearly related value is provided at the transducer's output.

Ideally, we would like our transducer to provide a voltage of 5 VDC to the microcontroller's ATD converter's input when X_2 is applied to the transducer and 0 VDC to the microcontroller's ATD converter's input when X_1 is applied to the transducer. To accomplish this conversion, the output from the transducer V_{2min} and V_{1min} may require scaling and the addition of a DC offset bias. In our block diagram, we have designated the scaling operation with a K and the addition of the bias with a summation.

In general, we can develop two equations with two unknowns to describe the operation of our transducer interface design. These equations are given as:

$$V_{2max} = V_{2min} * K + B$$

and

$$V_{1max} = V_{1min} * K + B$$

Usually the specifications of our transducer provides the values of V_{2min} and V_{1min} while the specifications of the 68HC12s ATD converter provides the values of V_{2max} and V_{1max}. Substitution of these values results in a set of two equations and two unknowns (K and B). Therefore, the desired values of scaling (K) and the DC offset bias (B) may be determined for a specific interface. The scaling and addition of DC offset bias is easily implemented with basic operational amplifier (op amp) circuitry. Reference the sources provided at the end of this chapter for implementation details. Let us illustrate the approach to transducer interface design with an example.

Example

In the previous section, we indicated that the barometer on our weather station provided a signal that ranged from 0 to 5 volts depending on the sensed barometric pressure. It provides a 0-volt output for 64 cm of mercury and 5 volts for 81 cm of mercury (the normal range for barometric pressure). For values between these two extremes, there was a linear relationship between output voltage and barometric pressure.

Let us suppose instead that the barometer we used provided a −100 mV output for 64 cm of mercury and 300 mV output for 81 cm of mercury. As before, for values between these two extremes, there is a linear relationship between output voltage and barometric pressure. We would like to interface the barometric sensor to the

68HC12s ATD converter such that 0 volts is provided for 64 cm of mercury and 5 volts for 81 cm of mercury.

By interpreting these specifications, we can determine that V_{1min} is -100 mV and V_{2min} is 300 mV while V_{1max} is 0 volts and V_{2max} is 5 volts. Substituting these values into our two equations provide the following:

$$5 \text{ volts} = 300 \text{ mV} \ * K + B$$

and

$$0 \text{ volts} = -100 \text{ mV} * K + B$$

Simultaneously solving these equations provides a scale factor (K) of 12.5 volt/volt and a DC offset bias (B) of 1.25 volts. Check these values. Do you agree? As previously mentioned, it is easy to implement an op amp circuit to scale the transducer's output by a factor of 12.5 volt/volt and add an offset of 1.25 volts.

This transducer interface procedure may be used for a wide variety of transducers. Realize that the signal may require further conditioning, such as using a filter circuit to remove undesired frequency components. In the next section, we examine the time-related considerations of sampling a signal and the need for signal filtering.

9.3 ANALOG-TO-DIGITAL CONVERSION BACKGROUND THEORY

The ATD conversion process is simply sampling an analog (continuous) signal at regular intervals and then converting each of these analog samples into a corresponding binary code. The sampling process may be compared to using a strobe light to photograph a quickly changing event. A strobe light is a bright light that flashes at user-specified intervals. If we synchronize the strobe light to a camera shutter, we can capture the movement of a quickly moving object at regular time intervals on film. The sequence of resulting pictures provides a record of object movement. If the strobe is flashed too slowly, we do not obtain an accurate record of the object's movement. If the strobe is flashed too quickly, we obtain an accurate record of object movement, but we do not see much change in object movement from camera image to image and hence waste a lot of film. The optimal rate at which the strobe should be pulsed is somewhere between the two extremes. This strobe light example provides insight to selecting the required sampling rate for an ATD conversion. If we sample too slow, we do not adequately capture the changing details of the signal. If we sample too fast, we capture the details, but generate excess data. The correct sampling rate for the ATD conversions is between the two extremes.

There are many different types of ATD converter designs. We discuss several of these designs in this chapter along with their inherent advantages and disadvantages. We concentrate on the successive approximation converter design since this

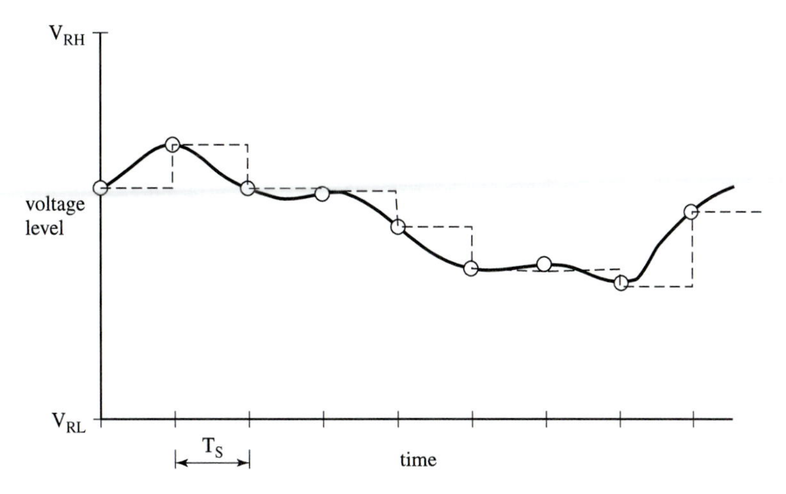

Figure 9.3 Analog-to-digital conversion process. The ATD conversion process is simply sampling an analog signal at regular intervals and then converting each of these analog samples into a corresponding binary code.

is the type implemented within the 68HC12. The ATD conversion process consists of three steps:

1. Determining the sampling rate,
2. Encoding the different analog voltage levels into a corresponding binary code, and
3. Determining the required resolution of the converter.

We discuss each of these concepts in turn.

9.3.1 Sampling Rate

Capturing an analog electronic signal using an ATD conversion system is similar to the strobed camera example. To adequately reconstruct a continuous analog signal from discrete (or digital) snap shots requires an adequate sampling rate. Considerable analysis has been accomplished to determine just what is an adequate sampling rate. In the 1920s, Harry Nyquist at Bell Laboratories was able to quantify the minimum sampling rate required for adequate reconstruction. His work led to the Nyquist criterion, which stipulates that we must sample a signal at a minimum frequency of twice the highest frequency component contained in the signal to be sampled. This can be concisely stated as:

$$f_s \geq 2f_h$$

where f_s is the sampling frequency and f_h is the highest expected frequency component in the sampled signal.

The sampling frequency chosen provides a discrete sample of the signal at regular time intervals given by:

$$T_s = 1/f_s$$

where T_s is the time interval between samples.

For a simple sinusoidal signal containing a single frequency, the sampling frequency f_s is twice the frequency of the sinusoid. For a more complex signal, harmonic analysis must be used to estimate the highest expected frequency component of the signal.

Example

The human voice spectrum has an upper frequency bound of approximately 4 KHz. The telephone company digitizes the analog human voice using a sampling frequency of 8 KHz.

Frequently a low pass filter (LPF) is employed to condition the signal prior to conversion. The LPF reduces unwanted electrical interference noise, electronic noise from the signal, and unwanted high-frequency components. If unwanted frequency components cause the Nyquist criterion to be violated, frequency folding or aliasing occurs. In the process of recovering the signal, the folded part of the spectrum causes distortion in the recovered signal, which cannot be removed by filtering from the recovered signal. Frequency folding is eliminated by using an LPF that has a cutoff frequency corresponding to f_h, the expected frequency content of the signal.

9.3.2 Encoding

The overall purpose of the ATD conversion process is to convert each of the voltage samples provided at regular time intervals into a corresponding unsigned binary value. The step referred to as *encoding* provides a unique binary code for each and every voltage step between the two reference voltages, which we describe later. Since a binary code is used, the following equation describes how many binary bits (b) are required to uniquely specify (n) different voltage levels:

$$n = 2^b$$

where n equals the number of discrete encoded events and b is the number of bits used for encoding. The number of bits in the binary code used to specify each converted value is a design parameter of the ATD converter.

Example

The 68HC12 has an eight-bit ATD converter system. This means that each analog sample provided to the 68HC12 ATD system is converted to an unsigned, eight-bit

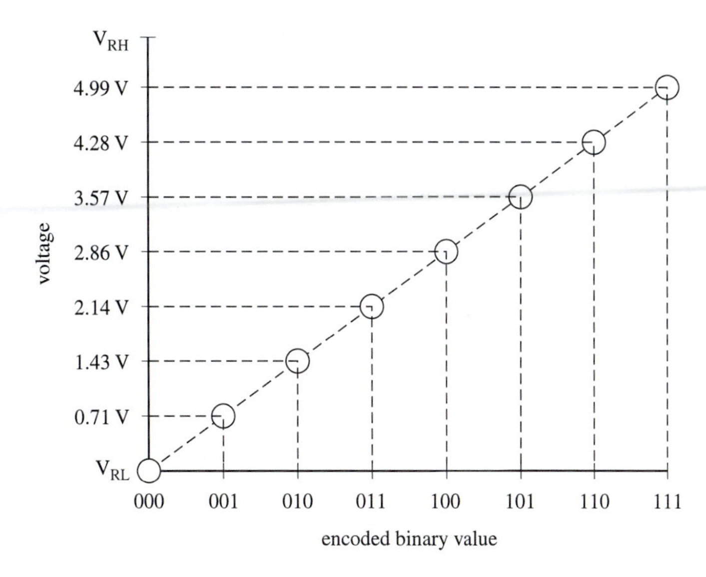

Figure 9.4 Encoding. The encoding step provides a unique binary code for each and every voltage step between the two reference voltages. This figure illustrates the encoding for a three-bit ATD converter. With three bits $2^3 = 8$ different voltage levels may be encoded.

binary representation. Therefore, these eight bits generate $2^8 = 256$ different voltage levels.

9.3.3 Quantizing and Resolution

After the proper sampling frequency and the number of bits available for encoding are determined, the quantization levels must be established for the ATD conversion process. Quantization is nothing more than establishing how many discrete levels the analog signal is divided into between its two reference voltage levels. An ATD converter must have an established lower voltage reference level V_{RL} and a higher voltage reference level V_{RH}. These references are applied to the 68HC12 via external hardware pins. All signals applied to the ATD converter must fall between these two extremes. Quantization provides multiple levels between the two references. If more levels are provided, a better representation of the sampled voltage results.

For illustration purposes, let us assume that the two reference levels chosen for our ATD converter is 5.0 volts for V_{RH} and 0 volts for V_{RL}. If we divide the voltage span between these two references into 256 identically spaced levels, the voltage difference (quantum) represented by each step is:

$$(5\text{ V} - 0\text{ V})/(256\text{ steps}) = 19.53\text{ millivolts/step}$$

Furthermore, the 1st step corresponds to 0 volts, the 10th step to 175.78 millivolts, and the 256th step to 4.980 volts (5.0 volts − 19.53 mV). Intuitively, if we increase the number of steps between the two voltage references, the individual voltage steps become smaller or the converter resolution improves. In general, resolution may be described by:

$$Resolution = (V_{RH} - V_{RL})/(\text{number of steps})$$

We can tie together all of these concepts with:

$$Resolution = (V_{RH} - V_{RL})/2^b$$

Another helpful expression that ties these concepts together is:

$$V_x = V_{RL} + x(V_{RH} - V_{RL})/2^b$$

where V_x is the sample voltage, x is its converted digital value, and b is the number of bits in x.

Another related specification of a converter is the dynamic range in decibels (dB). The dynamic range is given by:

$$DR(dB) = 20\log 2^b = 20b\log 2 = 20b(0.301) = 6.02b$$

where the DR is the dynamic range and b is the number of bits produced by the converter.

Example

What is the dynamic range of a 12-bit converter? 72.2 dB

9.3.4 Data Rate

The amount of data generated by an ATD converter, the data rate (d), may be calculated by multiplying the sampling frequency by the number of bits required to represent each sample. This is given by:

$$d = f_s b$$

Practice Questions

Question: An analog signal has a spectrum (frequency content) that varies from 200 Hz to 3.9 KHz. It is to be sampled at a rate of 10,000 samples per second. Is the sampling rate adequate to allow reconstruction of the signal?

Answer: The minimum sampling rate as determined by

$$f_s \geq 2f_h$$

is 7.8 KHz. Therefore, the sampling rate of 10,000 samples per second or 10 KHz is adequate.

Question: The 68HC12 ATD converter system converts each analog sample to an eight-bit unsigned binary value. What is the resolution of the converter? Assume that the reference voltages for the 68HC12 designated as V_{RH} and V_{RL} are 5 volts and 0 volts, respectively.

Answer: The resolution is given by:

$$Resolution = (V_{RH} - V_{RL})/2^b = (5-0)/(256) = 19.53 \text{ mV}$$

Question: If the 68HC12 is modified such that each analog conversion yields an unsigned, 10-bit binary value, what is the resolution of the converter? Assume that the reference voltages for the 68HC12 designated as V_{RH} and V_{RL} are 5 volts and 0 volts, respectively.

Answer: The resolution is given by:

$$Resolution = (V_{RH} - V_{RL})/(2^b) = (5-0)/(1024) = 4.88 \text{ mV}$$

Question: A 1 KHz square wave is to be sampled using an ATD conversion system. Harmonic analysis of the signal indicates that harmonic content up to 10 Khz should be sampled. What should the sampling frequency be?

Answer:

$$f_s \geq 2f_h \geq 2(10 \cdot 10^3) \geq 20\text{KHz}$$

Question: In the prior question, how many bits of binary data are generated per second assuming an eight-bit ATD converter?

Answer: In the prior example, 20,000 analog samples are converted per second. Each sample requires eight bits for an unsigned, binary representation. Therefore, the total number of bits generated per second is

$$20,000 \; samples/second \cdot 8 \; bits/sample = 160,000 \text{ bits/second}$$

Question: Assume that music consists of frequencies from 20 Hz to 20 KHz. A compact disc converts stereo analog music signal using a 16-bit analog converter at a sampling frequency of 44 KHz. Is the Nyquist criterion maintained? What is the data rate of an audio compact disc?

Answer: Yes, the Nyquist criterion is maintained. The music is sampled at a frequency of 44 KHz, which is more than double the highest expected frequency (20 Khz) of the music signal. If a 16-bit analog converter is used to digitize the left and right (stereo) channels, the bit rate is given by:

$$bit\ rate = sample\ rate * bits/sample * number\ of\ channels$$

$$bit\ rate = 44\ Khz * 16\ bits/sample * 2\ channels = 1.41\ Mbps$$

Note: In an actual compact disk storage protocol, additional bits are used for error-correcting procedures.

9.4 ANALOG-TO-DIGITAL CONVERTER TECHNOLOGIES

There are several different types of technologies used to convert an analog sample into a corresponding digital representation. Most of the converter types require a sample and hold circuit at the input to keep the analog sample under conversion constant during the conversion process. Some of the more common techniques include:

- Successive-approximation converters
- Integration-based converters
- Counter-type converters
- Parallel converters

9.4.1 Successive-Approximation Converters

I had a close friend who appeared on the "Price is Right" show several years ago. I had not seen him in quite awhile, so I was quite surprised when my wife called me at work and told me Mark (we preserve his privacy) was on the show. Mark had the tough task of guessing how much money Bob Barker, the game show's host, had stowed in his pocket. The amount was somewhere between 0 and $10,000. If you were in Mark's place, what would you do?

A sound engineering approach would be to guess halfway between the two extremes. This guessing strategy is illustrated in Figure 9.5. In Mark's case, applying our engineering approach, his first guess should have been $5000. Bob Barker would then quickly tell him whether the unknown amount was either higher or lower than Mark's guess. If Bob said "lower," then Mark should guess $2500 as his second guess. If Bob said "higher," then Mark should guess $7500 as his second guess. Based on Bob Barker's continued "higher/lower" promptings, Mark should continue to halve the remaining distance of the unknown dollar amount region. Using this technique, he could quickly close in on the unknown amount.

This is exactly how a successive-approximation ATD converter system works. This method approximates an unknown analog sample using an n-bit code in "n" guesses. The operation of this converter is best illustrated with an example.

Example

Again, let us assume our converter has V_{RH} set at 5.0 v and V_{RL} set to 0 v. Each analog sample is converted to an eight-bit binary representation. These eight bits provide 256 distinct conversion levels and a corresponding resolution of:

$$Resolution = (5.0 - 0.0)/256 = 19.53 \text{ millivolts}$$

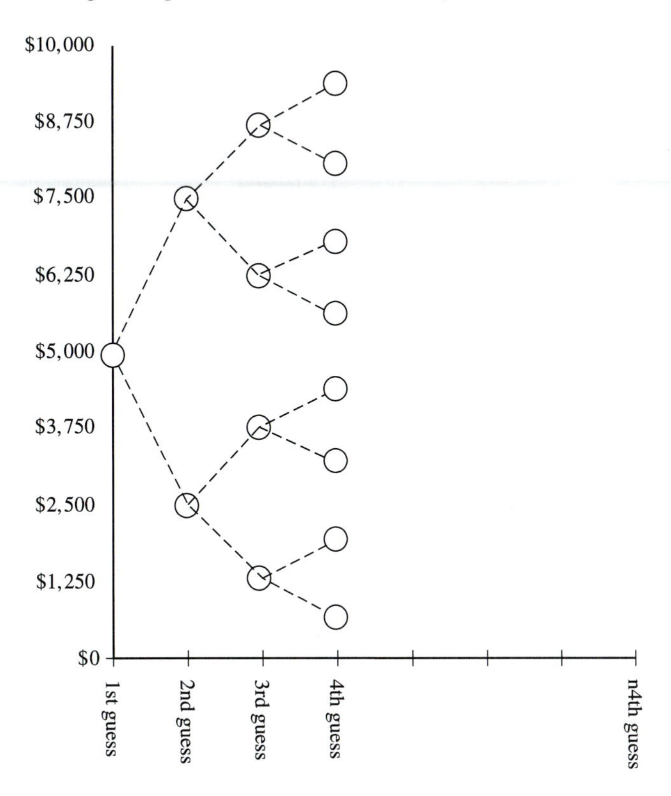

Figure 9.5 A scientific guessing strategy. If you need to efficiently guess an unknown amount between two extremes, start by guessing a value halfway between the two extremes. If the unknown amount is lower than the first guess, your second guess would be halfway between the first guess and the lower extreme. Repetitively using this technique, you can quickly close in on the unknown amount.

As a first guess, the converter sets the most significant bit (MSB) of the result register to 1 and the rest of the bits to 0 (Figure 9.6). This corresponds to a binary value of 128 or 128/256 or 1/2 full-scale or 2.5 volts. The comparator indicates whether the unknown analog sample is higher or lower. A comparator is an analog component that compares an unknown input signal to a known voltage reference. If the unknown signal is higher than the reference voltage, the comparator's output is a logic high. If the unknown signal is lower than the reference voltage, the comparator's output is a logic low. If the unknown sample is higher than 2.5 volts, the next guess is 11000000, which corresponds to 192/256 or 3/4 full-scale or 3.75 volts. If the unknown sample is lower than 2.5 volts, the next guess is 01000000, which corresponds to 64/256 or 1/4 full-scale or 1.25 volts. This process continues for six more guesses. That is, one guess for each bit.

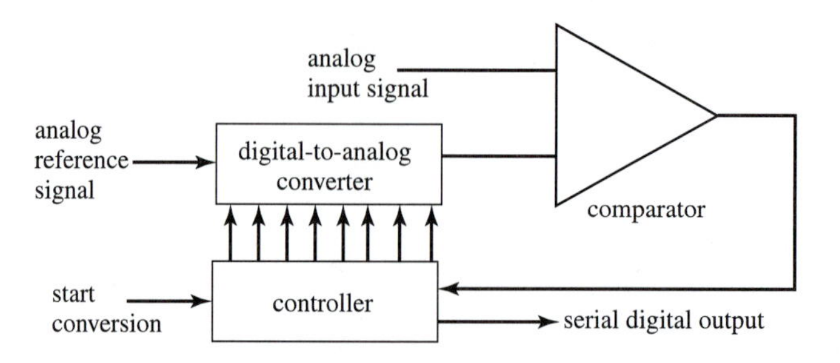

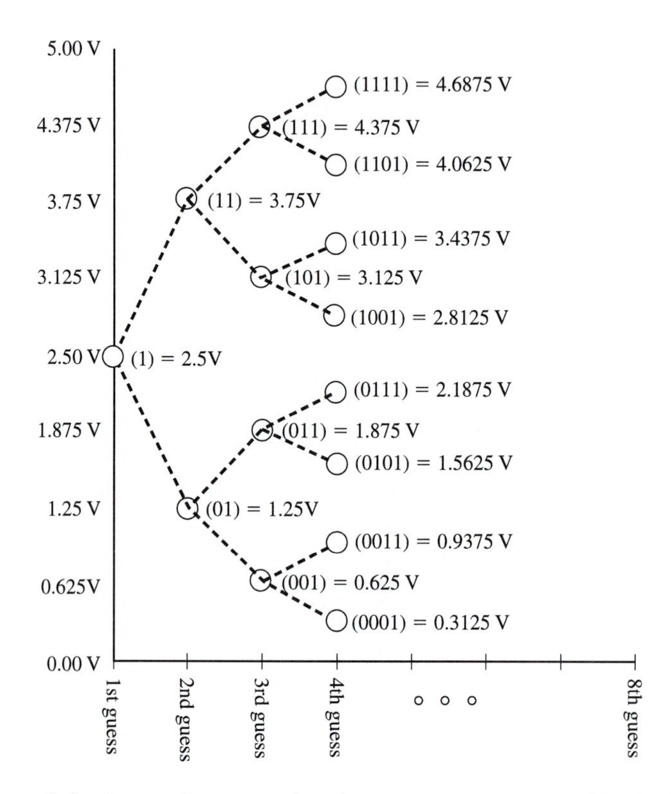

Figure 9.6 Successive-approximation converter process. This method approximates an unknown analog sample using an n-bit code in “n” guesses.

The successive-approximation converter has a number of distinct advantages and disadvantages:

- Advantage. The conversion time is fixed and independent of the magnitude of the unknown analog sample. This is an especially important advantage in a synchronous machine such as the 68HC12 since the time of the conversion process is fixed and precisely known.

- Advantage. Since the internal logic clears at the end of each conversion, each conversion is independent and unique of the results of previous conversions.
- Disadvantage. The hardware implementation of this converter is quite complex.

I do not know if Mark used our sound engineering appoach; however, he won the unknown amount and the final showcase.

9.4.2 Integration-Based Converters

There are several different types of integration-based ATD converters. One of the most common types is called a dual-slope converter. The heart of the dual-slope converter is an integrator. An integrator may be implemented with an operational amplifier circuit that consists of an input resistor and a feedback capacitor (C) as shown in Figure 9.7. To start the conversion process, the unknown analog sample is applied to the input of the integrator. The integrator integrates the unknown signal for a predetermined length of time—some fixed number of clock pulses. For purposes of illustration, let us say that an eight-bit binary counter keeps track of these clock pulses. At the end of the fixed integration time, the integrated unknown analog sample voltage is present on the capacitor of the integrator circuit.

After the integration of the unknown voltage is complete, a known reference voltage of opposite polarity is applied to the input of the integrator. The integrator will now integrate the reference signal until the integrator's capacitor voltage reaches 0 V. The time to integrate, or the number of clock pulses, to get back to 0 V is proportional to the unknown analog sample voltage. If we monitor the number of clock pulses to reach 0 V with an eight-bit binary counter, we have an eight-bit binary representation of the unknown voltage.

The primary advantage of the dual slope converter is noise immunity. Any high-frequency noise present in the unknown analog sample will be integrated or filtered. However, it has several distinct disadvantages. First, the time to provide a conversion is not constant. Larger magnitude inputs require a longer conversion time. Second, errors occur when measuring signals close to zero volts due to noise.

9.4.3 Counter-Type Converters

The counter-type ATD converter employs a straightforward conversion process (Figure 9.8). A comparator is used to compare an unknown analog input sample with a reference input generated by a binary counter (assume an eight bit counter) applied to a digital-to-analog converter (DAC). The counter starts at a count of 0 and a corresponding voltage is generated by the DAC. The counter is incremented

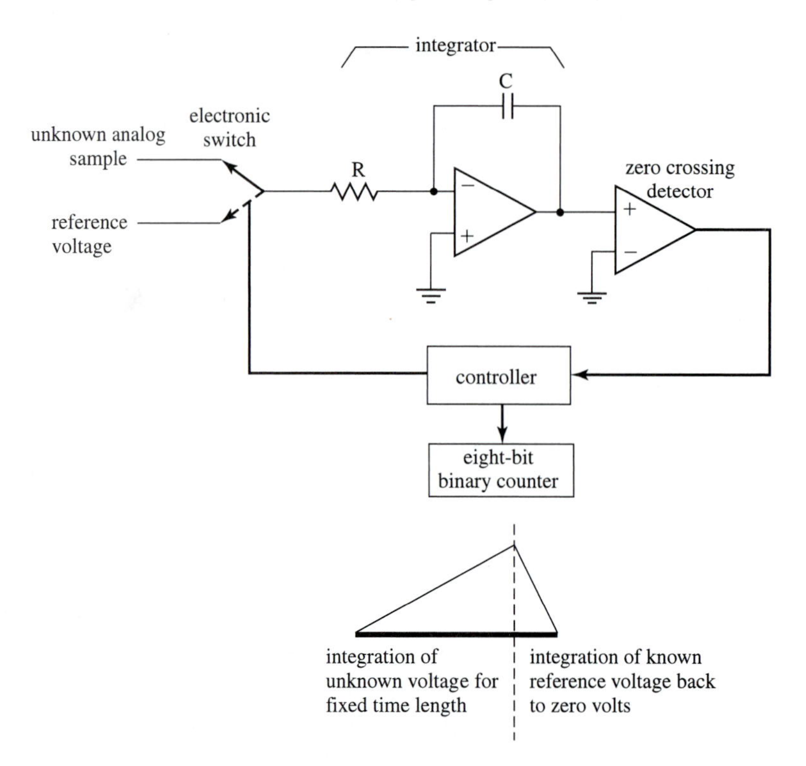

Figure 9.7 Dual-slope converter. The unknown analog sample is applied to the input of the integrator which integrates the unknown signal for a predetermined length of time. At the end of the fixed integration time, the integrated unknown analog sample voltage is present on the capacitor of the integrator circuit. A known reference voltage of opposite polarity is applied to the input of the integrator. The integrator now integrates the reference signal until the integrator's capacitor voltage reaches 0 V. The time to integrate to get back to 0 V is proportional to the unknown analog sample voltage.

at each clock pulse, and hence the DAC output is incremented by a corresponding analog voltage. This process continues until the analog voltage provided by the DAC equals the unknown analog sample voltage. At this point, the comparator trips and stops the counter from incrementing. The number of clock pulses registered in the counter corresponds to the eight-bit binary representation of the unknown analog input signal.

The advantage of this type of converter is its simplicity. However, it has a distinct disadvantage of nonuniform ATD conversion time. That is, the conversion time is directly related to the magnitude of the unknown sample voltage.

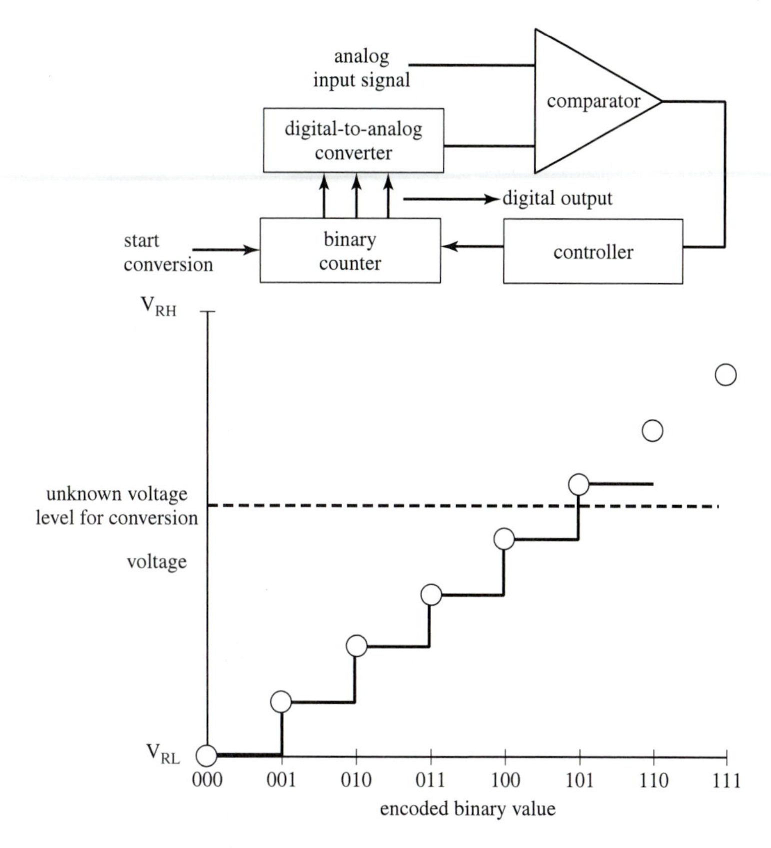

Figure 9.8 Counter-type converter.

9.4.4 Parallel Converters

A parallel type ATD converter functions much like a rain gauge (Figure 9.9). As rain falls and fills the gauge, the amount of rain is indicated as a level. A parallel ATD type converter indicates the voltage level of the unknown analog signal. It is constructed of a parallel bank of comparators, to determine the level of the unknown analog input sample. It consists of $2^n - 1$ comparators, each with a different analog reference input. The analog reference inputs are biased at a voltage corresponding to the LSB of the converter using a precision resistive network. The unknown analog input sample is provided to the input of the converter. As the magnitude of the unknown analog input sample increases, more of the comparators are switched on. The number of comparators that are switched to the on position by the input signal indicates the level of the input signal. However, the level does not correspond directly to a binary equivalent value. Combinational circuitry following the bank of analog comparators converts the level to a binary equivalent signal.

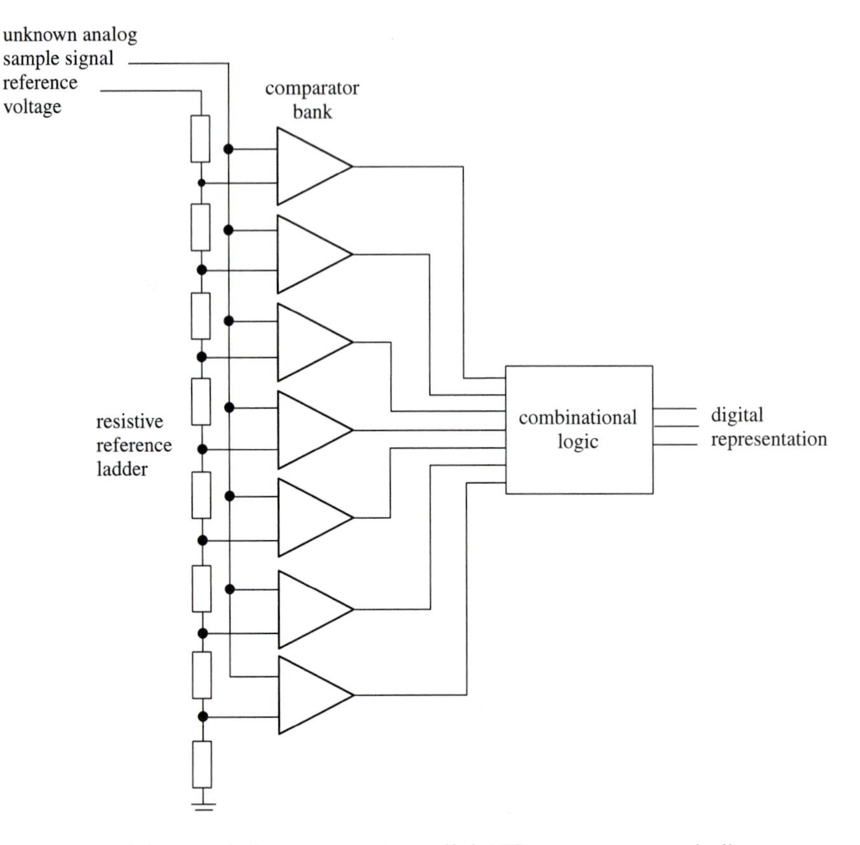

Figure 9.9 Parallel converter. A parallel ATD type converter indicates the voltage level of the unknown analog signal. It is constructed of a parallel bank of comparators to determine the level of the unknown analog input sample.

The advantage of this type of converter is its extreme speed of conversion since the conversion occurs in parallel. However, it has a significant disadvantage: The number of required comparators increases exponentially as the number of required bits increases. For example, an eight-bit converter requires 255 analog comparators, whereas a 10-bit converter requires 1023 analog comparators.

Practice Questions

Question: Does the maximum value of a converter's digital output (all 1s) correspond to the maximum analog full-scale (FS) of the converter?

Answer: The maximum value of the digital code (all 1s) does not correspond with the analog full-scale value, but rather with one LSB less than full-scale or

$FS(1 - 2^{-n})$. Therefore, a 12-bit converter with a 0 to +10V analog range has a maximum digital code of 1111 1111 1111 and a maximum analog value of $10(1 - 2^{-12}) = 9.99756\ V$. In other words, the maximum analog value of the converter corresponding to all 1s in a code never quite reaches the point defined as analog full scale.

9.5 THE 68HC12 ANALOG-TO-DIGITAL (ATD) CONVERSION SYSTEM

In this section, we discuss the 68HC12 ATD conversion system in detail. The block diagram of the ATD system is shown in Figure 9.10. We begin by providing a brief overview of the system, followed by a discussion of the system block diagram. We then discuss the ATD associated registers and conclude by discussing how to program the ATD for proper configuration and operation.

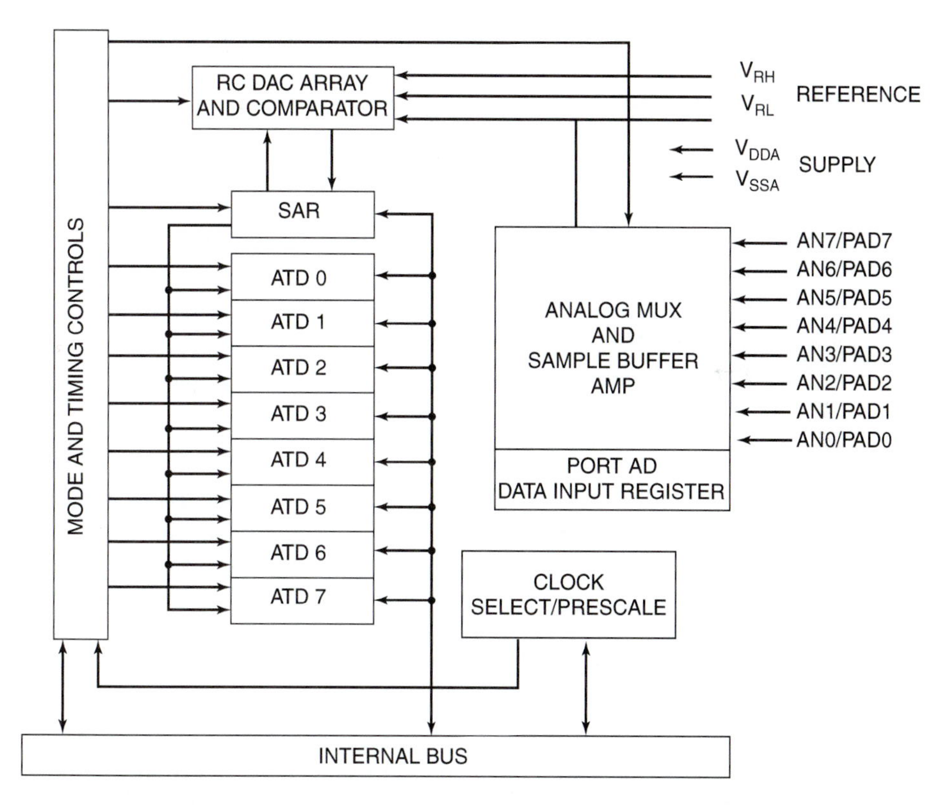

Figure 9.10 Analog-to-digital (ATD) block diagram. The eight ATD system analog inputs are located on pins AN0/PAD0 to AN7/PAD7. (Figure used with permission of Motorola, Incorporated.)

The 68HC12s analog-to-digital (ATD) system contains 8-channels. Each channel converts its input into an unsigned, 8-bit binary representation. The 8 inputs are multiplexed such that only a single input signal is fed to the input of the successive approximation analog to digital converter at a time. This converter is accurate to ± 1 least significant bit (LSB).

The ATD system may be configured for a single conversion sequence or continuous conversions. Additionally, the user has the flexibility to configure the ATD to perform conversions on a single channel or multiple sequential channels. The user tailors the ATD system operation for a specific application using a 16 word (32 byte) memory mapped control register bank and by proper selection of the high V_{RH} and low V_{RL} reference voltages.

9.5.1 68HC12 ATD System

The eight ATD system analog inputs from the outside world are located on pins AN0/PAD0 through AN7/PAD7. The analog input signals are fed into an analog multiplexer. The multiplexer selects which signals are routed to the successive-approximation ATD converter as specified by the ATD control registers. An ATD conversion sequence is initiated by writing to one of the ATD control registers. At the completion of the ATD conversion process, the results are placed in the corresponding ATD Converter Result Register (ADR0H through ADR7H), and the corresponding flags are set in the ATD Status Register (ATDSTAT). Timing for the conversion process is provided by the P clock.

Two dedicated lines V_{RH} and V_{RL} are used as reference voltage levels for the high voltage and low voltage, respectively. If an input voltage value is equal to V_{RL}, it is converted to $00, whereas if the input voltage is equal to V_{RH}, it is represented as $FF. The results are represented as unsigned binary values.

9.5.2 68HC12 ATD System Control Registers

As mentioned previously, the user tailors ATD system operation for a specific application using a 16-word (32-byte) memory mapped control register bank. Listed next are the different types of registers found in the control bank. We discuss each of these register types in turn.

- Control registers—The ATD control registers are used to tailor an ATD conversion sequence to user specifications.
- Status register—The ATD status register is a two-byte register containing a series of flags that indicate the status of the ATD system.
- Result registers—After the specified conversion(s) take place in the ATD system, the results are placed into the corresponding result register (ADR0H through ADR7H). These are eight identical eight-bit result registers.

- Test registers—The ATD test register (ATDTEST) is a two-byte register. It can only be read from or written to in special modes. In normal operating modes, reads and writes have no effect. Due to the special nature of this register, we do not discuss it any further.

Each register is eight bits wide and has an associated memory address. This means that registers may be written to or read from using memory reference-type instructions. In the next several subsections, we review each of the 16 registers associated with the ATD system.

ATD Control Registers The ATD control registers are used to tailor an ATD conversion sequence to user specifications. There are six ATD control registers named ATDCTL0 through ATDCTL5. These registers allow you to turn the ATD system on since it is shut off after processor reset to conserve power. Once the ATD system is powered up, you must wait 100 microseconds for the ATD system to stabilize prior to starting a conversion. You also use these control registers to specify whether you perform a single conversion or perform continuous conversions. Finally, these registers are used to specify which of the ATD channels will be used to perform the conversion. You may configure the ATD converter to perform conversions on a single channel or scan through multiple channels. Control registers 0, 1, and 3 are used infrequently and are mentioned only briefly. Control registers 2, 4, and 5 allow the user to completely tailor the operation of the ATD system to a specific application.

ATD Control Registers 0 (ATDCTL0) and 1 (ATDCTL1) The ATDCTL0 is located at memory address $0060. This register is used to abort a conversion sequence. This is accomplished by writing a value to the register. In normal operation you do not use this register. The ATDCTL1 is located at memory address $0061. It is only used in special test cases, so we do not discuss it further.

ATD Control Register 2 (ATDCTL2) The ATDCTL2 is located at memory address $0062. This register is used to power up the ATD conversion system. It is also used to control some of the flags and interrupts associated with the ATD system. The function of each bit is:

Register: Analog-to-Digital Converter Control Register 2 (ATDCTL2) Address: $0062

	7	6	5	4	3	2	1	0
	ADPU	AFFC	AWAI	0	0	0	ASCIE	ASCIF
Reset:	0	0	0	0	0	0	0	0

Figure 9.11 ATD Control Register 2 (ATDCTL2).

- ADPU: Bit 7 of ATDCTL2 is the on/off switch for the ATD system. This bit, called ATD Powerup Bit or ADPU, is reset to 0 after the processor is reset. To power up the ATD system, this bit must be set to 1. Once the ADPU is set, you must wait 100 microseconds for the ATD system to become stable.
- AFFC: The ATD Fast Flag Clear All bit controls how the ATD system-related flags are cleared. When the AFFC bit is set to 0, the ATD system flags are cleared in the normal manner. When the AFFC bit is set to 1, all of the ATD conversion complete flags are set for a fast, clear sequence. Both the normal and fast clear mode of flag-clearing are discussed later.
- AWAI: The ATD Wait Mode bit determines whether the ATD continues to operate when the 68HC12 is in the wait mode. If AWAI is set to 0, the ATD continues to operate while the 68HC12 is in the wait mode. However, if the AWAI is set to 1, ATD system operation is halted while the 68HC12 is in the wait mode to conserve power.
- ASCIE: Bit 1 contains the ATD Sequence Complete Interrupt Enable bit (ASCIE). When this bit is set to 1, interrupt requests generated by the ATD sequence complete interrupt flag (ASCIF) are enabled.
- ASCIF: Bit 0 contains the ATD Sequence Complete Interrupt Flag (ASCIF). This flag is set when a conversion sequence is finished. If the ASCIE bit described before is set, the ASCIF also generates an interrupt.

The interrupt features allow the CPU to continue to process other tasks while waiting for a significant event—the interrupt—to occur. For example, when the ATD interrupt features are enabled (by setting the ATD Sequence Complete Interrupt Enable [ASCIE] bit to a logic 1), the 68HC12 can initiate an ATD conversion sequence and then continue to process other program steps. When the specified conversion is complete, an interrupt is generated and the 68HC12 can then process interrupt-related events. The alternative to using an interrupt is to initiate an ATD conversion sequence and then poll the Conversion Complete Flag(s) (CCF), which signals conversion completion. While polling the CCF flags, the 68HC12 cannot perform other operations.

ATD Control Register 3 (ATDCTL3) The ATDCTL3 is located at memory address $0063. This register contains two freeze bits: FRZ1 and FRZ0. As their names imply, these bits are used to suspend ATD operation for background debugging. Like control registers 0 and 1, control register 3 is not used in normal operation and therefore is not discussed further.

ATD Control Register 4 (ATDCTL4) The ATDCTL4 is located at memory address $0064. This register is used to control the sample timing for the ATD system. The total conversion time for an eight-bit conversion consists of four com-

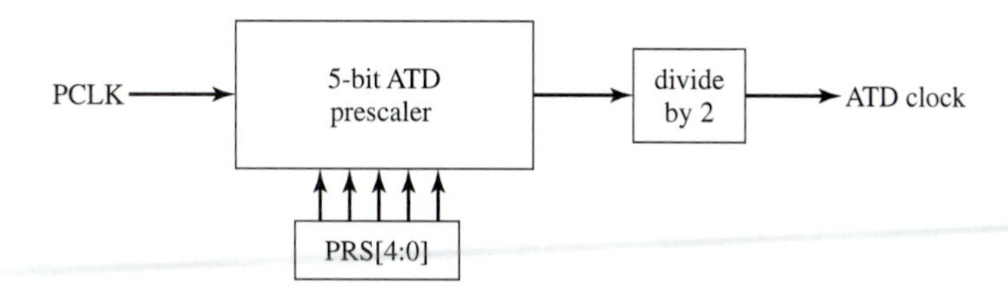

Figure 9.12 The time base for the ATD system is the P clock. A prescalar value is used to further divide the P clock frequency. The P clock goes through two different divider stages. The first stage divide factor is set by the binary value written to PRS[4:0] (bits 4 to 0 of the ATDCTL4 register) plus one. The second divide stage is always two.

ponents. Three of these components are fixed while one may be set by the user. These components include:

- initial sample time, which consists of two ATD clock periods,
- transfer time, which consists of four ATD clock periods,
- final sample time, which is programmable by setting bits 6 (SMP1) and 5 (SMP0) in the ATDCTL4 register to a desired value, and
- resolution time consisting of 10 ATD clock periods.

The time base for the ATD system is the P clock. A prescalar value is used to further divide the P clock frequency. The P clock goes through two different divider stages. The first stage divide factor is set by the binary value written to PRS[4:0] (bits 4 to 0 of the ATDCTL4 register) plus one. For example, if you set PRS[4:0] to 00101, the first divider stage divides the P clock by 6 (that is $5 + 1$). The second divide stage is always two. Therefore, the total division factor when PRS[4:0] is set to 00101 is 12.

The Select Sample Time bits (SMP1 and SMP0) are used to select one of four sample times. As previously mentioned, three of the four time components of the ATD conversion are fixed and total 16 ATD clock periods. The final sample time is

Register: Analog-to-Digital Converter Control Register 4 (ATDCTL4) Address: $0064

	7	6	5	4	3	2	1	0
	0	SMP1	SMP0	PRS4	PRS3	PRS2	PRS1	PRS0
Reset:	0	0	0	0	0	0	0	0

Figure 9.13 ATD Control Register 4 (ATDCTL4).

SMP1 SMP0	Final Sample Time	Total 8-bit Conversion Time
0 0	2 ATD clock periods	18 ATD clock periods
0 1	4 ATD clock periods	20 ATD clock periods
1 0	8 ATD clock periods	24 ATD clock periods
1 1	16 ATD clock periods	32 ATD clock periods

Figure 9.14 Sample time selection.

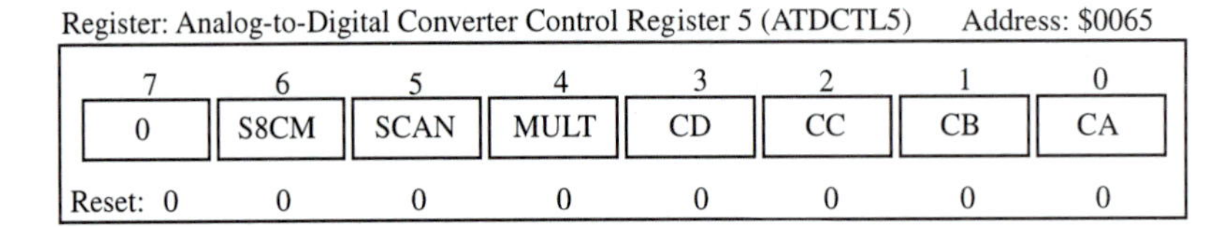

Figure 9.15 ATD Control Register 5 (ATDCTL5).

variable and is set by the user. Figure 9.14 lists the different settings for these two bits.

ATD Control Register 5 (ATDCTL5) The ATDCTL5 control register is used to select the conversion mode of the ATD system, specify the channels for conversion, and initiate the actual conversion process. It is located at memory address $0065.

Conversions are completely specified by the user by the following bit settings:

- The S8CM (Select 8 Channel Mode) bit is used to select a conversion sequence of four conversions (0) or eight conversions (1).
- The SCAN (Enable Continuous Channel Scan) bit allows the user to choose between a single conversion sequence (0) or a continuous conversion sequence (1). In a single conversion sequence, the ATD performs a single conversion and stops.
- The MULT (Enable Multichannel Conversion) bit when set to 0 specifies that the ATD system performs all specified conversions on a single input channel. When the MULT bit is set to 1, the ATD system performs conversions on sequential channels as specified by the CD, CC, CB, and the CA bits.
- The CD, CC, CB, and CA bits are used to specify the channels for conversion to the ATD system.

Figure 9.16 shows how to properly set the S8CM and the CD, CC, CB, and CA bits for proper multichannel mode operation. Note that when S8CM and the

S8CM	CD	CC	CB	CA	Channel Signal	Result in ADRx if MULT = 1
0	0	0	0	0	AN0	ADR0
			0	1	AN1	ADR1
			1	0	AN2	ADR2
			1	1	AN3	ADR3
0	0	1	0	0	AN4	ADR0
			0	1	AN5	ADR1
			1	0	AN6	ADR2
			1	1	AN7	ADR3
0	1	0	0	0	Reserved	ADR0
			0	1	Reserved	ADR1
			1	0	Reserved	ADR2
			1	1	Reserved	ADR3
0	1	1	0	0	V_{RH}	ADR0
			0	1	V_{RL}	ADR1
			1	0	$(V_{RH}+V_{RL})/2$	ADR2
			1	1	TEST/Reserved	ADR3
1	0	0	0	0	AN0	ADR0
		0	0	1	AN1	ADR1
		0	1	0	AN2	ADR2
		0	1	1	AN3	ADR3
		1	0	0	AN4	ADR4
		1	0	1	AN5	ADR5
		1	1	0	AN6	ADR6
		1	1	1	AN7	ADR7
1	1	0	0	0	Reserved	ADR0
		0	0	1	Reserved	ADR1
		0	1	0	Reserved	ADR2
		0	1	1	Reserved	ADR3
		1	0	0	V_{RH}	ADR4
		1	0	1	V_{RL}	ADR5
		1	1	0	$(V_{RH}+V_{RL})/2$	ADR6
		1	1	1	TEST/Reserved	ADR7

Figure 9.16 Multichannel mode result register assignment. (Figure used with permission of Motorola, Incorporated.)

CD bits are both set to 1, reference signals associated with the ATD system, V_{RH} and V_{RL}, may be converted and analyzed. Before proceeding to the other ATD registers, let us do a few examples to illustrate the proper use of the ATD control registers.

Practice Questions

Question: Specify the contents of the ATDCTL2 register to power up the ATD system and set the ATD for normal flag-clearing operations.

Answer: Recall the ADPU (ATD Power Up) bit is Bit 7 of the ATDCTL2 register and the flag-clearing parameters are set by the AFFC (ATD Fast Flag Clear All) bit, bit 6 of the ATDCTL2 register. To power up the ATD, the ADPU bit should be set to 1. On 68HC12 reset, the AFFC bit is reset to 0. This is the same setting required for normal flag-clearing operations. Therefore, to configure the ATDCTL2 register, a 1000 0000 or $80 must be sent to memory location $0062.

Question: Specify the code to accomplish the actions of question 1.

Answer: ATDCTL2 EQU $0062; addr of ATDCTL2

```
LDAA   #$80        ;config word to turn on ADPU,
STAA   ATDCTL2     ;flags clr normal, disable interrupts
```

Question: Specify the contents of the ATDCTL5 register to configure the ATD system for a continuous sequence of conversions with eight conversions per sequence.

Answer: To properly configure the ATD to these specifications the S8CM bit (bit 6) should be set to 1, the SCAN bit (bit 5) to 1, and the MULT bit (bit 4) to 1. According to the previous figure, the CD bit (bit 3) should also be set to 1 while the CC,CB, and CA bits are *don't care*. Therefore, to configure the ATDCTL5 register, a 0111 1000 or $78 must be sent to memory location $0065.

Question: Specify the code to accomplish the actions of question 3.

Answer: ATDCTL5 EQU $0065; addr of ATDCTL5

```
LDAA   #$78        ;config word for specified actions
STAA   ATDCTL5     ;store config values to register
```

ATD Status Register The ATD status register (ATDSTAT) is a two-byte register located at memory locations $0066 and $0067. It contains a series of flags that indicate the status of the ATD system.

Register: Analog-to-Digital Converter Status Register (ATDSTAT) Address: $0066

	7	6	5	4	3	2	1	0
	SCF	0	0	0	0	CC2	CC1	CC0
Reset:	0	0	0	0	0	0	0	0

Register: Analog-to-Digital Converter Status Register (ATDSTAT) Address: $0067

	7	6	5	4	3	2	1	0
	CCF7	CCF6	CCF5	CCF4	CCF3	CCF2	CCF1	CCF0
Reset:	0	0	0	0	0	0	0	0

Figure 9.17 The ATD status register (ATDSTAT).

The Sequence Complete Flag (SCF) bit indicates when the ATD system has completed the specified conversion. If a single conversion sequence was specified by the user, the SCF bit is set at the end of the conversion sequence. If the ATD system is configured for continuous mode, the SCF bit is set at the end of the first conversion sequence. As discussed earlier, the AFFC bit in ATD Control Register 2 specifies how the flags are reset. If the AFFC bit is 0, the SCF is cleared when a write is performed to ATDCL5 to initiate a new conversion sequence. In contrast, if the AFFC bit is 1, the SCF flag is cleared after the first result register is read.

The CCx bits CC[2:0] form a three-bit conversion counter. This counter indicates which channel is currently undergoing conversion and hence which result register is written to next in a four- or eight-channel conversion sequence.

There are eight Conversion Complete Flags, CCF[7:0] in the ATDSTAT register, each associated with an individual ATD result register. This bit is set on completion of the conversion associated with a given channel. Each of the individual flags remain set until the associated result register for that channel is read. It is cleared when the register is read, if the AFFC bit (previously discussed) is set. If the AFFC bit is not set, the status register must be read to clear the flag. The Conversion Complete Flags may be continuously polled to see if a specific channel conversion is complete. The code to accomplish this is shown in the following fragment:

```
WTCONV    BRCLR   ATDSTAT2,#$80, WTCONV       ;wait Seq Comp Flag
```

This program fragment causes the program to continually loop back to itself, the location designated "WTCONV," until the Conversion Complete Flag (CCF) associated with ATD channel 7 sets indicating the result of the conversion has been loaded into ATD Result register 7.

ATD Input Register Input signals are provided to the ATD conversion system via the Port AD Data Input Register (PORTAD). PORTAD may also be used as a general-purpose digital input port. When PORTAD is read, the digital signal levels currently connected to each of the PORTAD pins are sensed. The PORTAD register is mapped to memory location $006F.

Register: Port AD Data Input Register (PORTAD) Address: $006F

	7	6	5	4	3	2	1	0
	PAD7	PAD6	PAD5	PAD4	PAD3	PAD2	PAD1	PAD0
Reset:	0	0	0	0	0	0	0	0

Figure 9.18 Port AD Data Input Register (PORTAD).

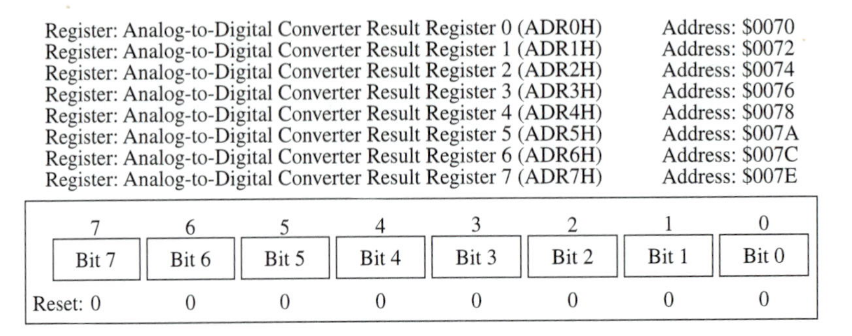

Figure 9.19 ATD result registers.

ATD Result Registers After the specified conversion(s) take place in the ATD system, the results are placed into the corresponding result register (ADR0H through ADR7H). These are eight identical eight-bit result registers located at memory locations $0070 through $007E. The results of the conversion are an eight-bit, unsigned binary value between 0 and 255. To interpret the result as a decimal voltage, the binary value must be scaled by the highest conversion value (255) and then multiplied by the difference of the two ATD system reference voltages V_{RH} and V_{RL}.

Example

Question: An eight-bit analog converter with $V_{RH} = 5$ V and $V_{RL} = 0$ V converts an unknown voltage to an unsigned binary representation of 1000 1010. What is the unknown voltage?

Answer: The decimal equivalent of 1000 1010 is 138. This value must be scaled by the highest conversion value and then multiplied by the difference of the reference voltages.

$$(138/255) \cdot 5.0 = 2.71 \text{ volts}$$

ATD Test Registers The ATD test register (ATDTEST) is a two-byte register at memory locations $0068 and $0069. It can only be read from or written to in special modes. In normal operating modes, reads and writes have no effect.

9.5.3 Programming the 68HC12 ATD System

To successfully configure and program the ATD for proper operation, follow these simple steps:

1. Connect the appropriate reference voltage sources to 68HC12 external pins V_{RH} and V_{RL}. The reference voltage for pin V_{RH} cannot exceed 5 volts and the reference voltage for pin V_{RL} cannot be less than 0 V.

2. Connect the analog signal(s) for conversion to the appropriate A/D input pin(s): PAD0 through PAD7.
3. Write 1 to the ADPU bit in the ATDCTL2 register located at memory address $0062.
4. After the ADPU bit is set, you must wait 100 microseconds before using the ATD system. In the examples, we show how to provide a 100-microsecond software delay.
5. Configure the ATD for proper operation using the ATD control registers.
6. Initialize the ATD conversion process by writing to ATD Control Register 5 (ATDCTL5).
7. Monitor for ATD conversion completion using the ATD status registers.
8. Use the results of the conversion which are located in the corresponding result register (ADR0H through ADR7H).
9. If processor power consumption is an issue, the ATD system may be powered down after conversion completion using the ADPU bit in the ATDCTL2 register.

Example

Write an assembly language program to measure an unknown analog signal connected to 68HC12 pin PAD6.

The problem statement for this programming exercise is rather concise. However, there is much work to be done. Let us process our checklist to ensure proper ATD configuration and initiation. The subroutines provided in this example were adapted from Motorola literature.

1. Connect the appropriate reference voltage sources to 68HC12 external pins V_{RH} and V_{RL}. The reference voltage for pin V_{RH} cannot exceed 5 volts and the reference voltage for pin V_{RL} cannot be less than 0 V. For this example, let us set V_{RH} to 5 V and V_{RL} to 0 V.
2. Connect the analog signal(s) for conversion to the appropriate A/D input pin(s): PAD0 through PAD7. For this example, the unknown analog voltage is connected to 68HC12 pin PAD6.
3. Write 1 to the ADPU bit in the ATDCTL2 register located at memory address $0062.
4. After the ADPU bit is set, you must wait 100 microseconds before using the ATD system. In the examples, we show how to provide a 100-microsecond software delay.
5. Configure the ATD for proper operation using the ATD control registers.

Let us write a subroutine to accomplish these initialization steps. We will call it INIT. This subroutine also calls another subroutine called DELAY. The DELAY subroutine provides the 100-microseconds of delay required by the ATD system to stabilize after being powered up.

```
            ORG     $4000
;-------------------------------
;Subroutine INIT: Initialize ATD ;
;-------------------------------
INIT        LDAA    #$80            ;config word to turn on ADPU,
            STAA    ATDCTL2         ;flags clr normal, disable interrupts
            BSR     DELAY           ;branch to subroutine DELAY
            LDAA    #$00            ;select continue conversions in
            STAA    ATDCTL3         ;active background mode
            LDAA    #$01            ;select final sample time = 2 ATD clocks,
            STAA    ATDCTL4         ;prescalar = 4 (PRS4:0 = 1)
            RTS                     ;Return from subroutine
```

The code for subroutine delay is:

```
;-------------------------------
;Subroutine DELAY: delays 100 uS ;
;-------------------------------
DELAY       LDAA    #$C8            ;load accumulator with 100 uS delay
LOOP        DECA                    ;Decrement ACC
            BNE     LOOP            ;Branch if not equal to zero
            RTS
```

How does this subroutine generate a 100-microsecond delay? The $C8 value corresponds to a decimal number of 200. This means that the delay loop within the DELAY subroutine is executed 200 times. The delay consists of only two instructions: DECA and BNE. The DECA instruction requires one clock cycle to execute, whereas the BNE requires three clock cycles to execute if the branch is taken. Therefore, each pass through the loop requires 4 clock cycles or 800 clock cycles for 200 passes. At an ATD clock rate of 8 MHz, 800 cycles consume 100 microseconds.

6. Initialize the ATD conversion process by writing to ATD Control Register 5 (ATDCTL5).
7. Monitor for ATD conversion completion using the ATD status registers.
8. Use the results of the conversion, which are located in the appropriate result register (ADR0H through ADR7H).

   Again we write a subroutine to accomplish these steps. We call this subroutine CONVERT.

```
;-------------------------------
;Subroutine CONVERT ;
;-------------------------------
;Set-up ATD, make single conversion and store the result to a memory location
```

```
;Configure and start ATD conversion
;Analog input signal on PAD6
;Convert: using single channel, non-continuous mode
;The result will be located in ADR2H
CONVERT   LDAA    #$06              ;ATD SCAN=0,
                                    MULT=0, PAD6
                                    ;write clears flag
          STAA    ATDCTL5           ;4 conversions on single
                                    sequence
WTCNV     BRCLR   ATDSTAT2, $40, WTCNV
                                    ;wait Seq Comp Flag
          LDD     ADR2H             ;Loads result (ADR2H)
                                    to ACC D
          RTS
```

9. If processor power consumption is an issue, the ATD system may be powered down after conversion completion using the ADPU bit in the ATDCTL2 register. In this example, we leave the ATD power on.

With our subroutines written, let us write the main program to call the subroutines. We assume that equate directives have been used to assign register names to appropriate 68HC12 addresses. This allows the user to refer to registers by name. We also assume that user onboard RAM is available at memory location $7000. We also assume you have properly declared the STACK.

```
;-------------------------------
;MAIN PROGRAM ;
;-------------------------------
        ORG   $7000      ;User RAM at $7000
        BSR   INIT       ;Branch to INIT for initialization
        BSR   CONVERT    ;Branch to CONVERT for conversion
DONE    BRA   DONE       ;Branch to self
```

9.5.4 Programming the ATD System Using Interrupts

In the previous programming examples, the ATD system has been used in a polling mode. That is, the ATD was configured for an analog conversion event, and the completion of the event was signaled by either the setting of the Sequence Complete Flag (SCF bit) in the ATD Status Register or the Conversion Complete Flags (within the ATD Status Register) associated with each channel of the ATD.

The ATD system is equipped with an interrupt that sets when the ATD sequence is complete. The ATD Sequence Complete Interrupt is enabled with the ASCIE bit in ATD Control Register 2 (ATDCTL2). When enabled, the ASCIF

(ATD Sequence Complete Interrupt bit) in the ATDCTL2 register sets and causes an interrupt event.

9.6 APPLICATION

In this section, we present a 68HC12 analog-to-digital (ATD) application. The application deals with the mobile robot navigation. In the laboratory applications section found at the end of this chapter, you are asked to program three channels of the ATD system to convert three infrared (IR) light sensor signal values. The three sensors should be mounted on top of your mobile robot. In the lab, the converted sensor values are then used to determine a robot action to avoid walls surrounding the robot in a maze. In this section, we consider a simplified version of the lab, where only two IR sensor values are converted and continuously stored in specified

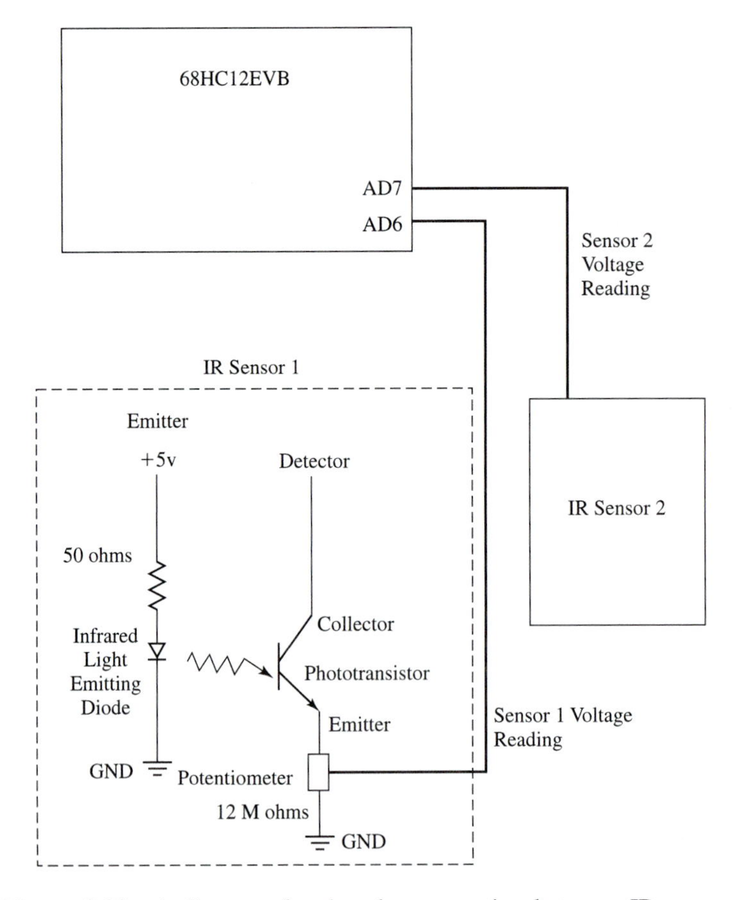

Figure 9.20 A diagram showing the connection between IR sensors and the 68HC12EVB.

memory locations. The two sensors feed signals that represent distances between the robot and walls surrounding the robot. We use channels six and seven of the 68HC12 ATD system for our application.

Figure 9.20 shows how the sensors are connected to the 68HC12 evaluation board. As shown in this figure, pins PAD6 and PAD7 are used to bring in sensor analog values to the 68HC12EVB.

The circuit for sensor one is shown within the sensor one box in Figure 9.20. The more reflection of the emitting light the detector receives, the higher the sensor output voltage signal is transmitted to the ATD converter. As can be seen, the range of the analog voltage values as the output of a sensor is from 0 to 5 volts. The sensor two circuit is identical to the one for sensor one.

Now that the hardware is all ready, let us write the software that uses the hardware to perform the desired task. The goal of this application is to continuously monitor the two sensor values to detect any approaching objects or walls. The following program accomplishes our desired goal. Let us consider the program line by line.

```
line 1  ***********************************************************
line 2  *                                                         *
line 3  * Description: This program is used to continually         *
line 4  * monitor two IR sensor values using the                  *
line 5  * built-in 68HC12EVB analog-to-digital                    *
line 6  * convert.                                                *
line 7  *                                                         *
line 8  * Authors: Daniel Pack and Steve Barrett                   *
line 9  *                                                         *
line 10 *                                                         *
line 11 * Date: 1-2-2000                                          *
line 12 *                                                         *
line 13 ***********************************************************
line 14 * Symbol Definitions                                      *
line 15 ***********************************************************
line 16 REGBAS   EQU  $0000      ; base addresses
line 17 ATDCTL2  EQU  $62        ; AD control register with ADPU bit
line 18 ATDCTL5  EQU  $65        ; AD mode control register
line 19 ATDSTAT  EQU  $66        ;sequence complete flag register
line 20 ADR2H    EQU  $74        ;sensor one value
line 21 ADR3H    EQU  $76        ; sensor two value
line 22 MMSB     EQU  %10000000  ; mask for ATD
line 23 MADCTL   EQU  %00010100  ; mask to choose multiple channels
                                 converting once
line 24 STACK    EQU  $8000
line 25 ***********************************************************
```

```
line 26 * Data Section                                               *
line 27 *******************************************************
line 28 ORG        $4000
line 29 SEN1       RMB    $01            ;sensor one
line 30 SEN2       RMB    $01            ; sensor two
line 31 *******************************************************
line 32 * Main Program                                          *
line 33 *******************************************************
line 34            ORG    $4100
line 35            LDS    #STACK         ;setup stack pointer
line 36            LDX    #REGBAS
line 37            LDAA   #MMSB          ; turn on ATD converter
line 38            STAA   ATDCTL2,X
line 39            LDY    #$C8           ; stabilize the ATD converter by delaying
                                         100 usec
line 40 STALL      DEY
line 41            BNE    STALL
line 42 START      LDAB   #MADCTL        ;start the AD converter
line 43            STAB   ATDCTL5,X
line 44 DONE       LDAB   ATDSTAT,X      ; wait until all sensor values are gathered
line 45            BPL    DONE
line 46            LDAB   ADR2H,X        ; read and store sensor one value
line 47            STAB   SEN1
line 48            LDAB   ADR3H,X        ; read and store sensor two value
line 49            STAB   SEN2
line 50            BRA    START
line 51            END
```

The symbol definition section defines numerical values for all symbols used in the program: The REGBAS on line 16 specifies the base address, lines 17 through 21 declare the ATD converter register names, lines 22 and 23 define values for two different masks, and the STACK symbol on line 24 is later used to initialize the stack pointer. The two memory locations at $4000 and $4001 are reserved for sensor storage values in the data section in lines 28 through 30.

The main program starts at line 34, which specifies the start of the main program as $4100 with the ORG directive. The instruction on line 35 initializes the stack pointer, whereas the LDX instruction on line 36 loads the base register value to index register X (the instructions on lines 38, 43, 44, 46, and 48 use the index addressing mode with the value loaded in the index register X). The instructions on lines 37 and 38 turn on the 68HC12 ATD converter by setting the ADPU bit to 1 using the MMSB mask. The instructions on lines 39, 40, and 41 are used to implement 100-microsecond delay time to stabilize the system. Can you explain why we chose $C8 on line 39? The instructions on lines 42 and 43 start the ATD process by dictating the type of conversion and the channels to be used. The mask MADCTL specifies to carry out a sequence of four conversions on channels AD4, AD5, AD6, and AD7. The instructions on lines 44 and 45 wait for the end of the sequence conversion by polling the Sequence Complete Flag (SCF) of the ATDSTAT register. Once the conversions are finished, the converted sensor values are stored to reserved memory locations by instructions on lines 46 through 49. Since we connected the two sensors to pins AD6 and AD7, the resulting converted values are stored in registers ADR2H and ADR3H, respectively. The instruction shown on line 50 directs the program counter to perform the conversion process all over again by jumping back to line 42. The program repeats the process and updates the sensor values to memory locations SEN1 and SEN2. These values are used by a mobile robot navigation control engine to determine desired robot actions.

9.7 LABORATORY APPLICATION

LABORATORY EXERCISE: EXTRACTING IR SENSOR VALUES USING THE A-TO-D CONVERTERS

Purpose This lab is designed to assist you in learning concepts associated with the built-in 68HC12 analog-to-digital (ATD) converter. You practice what you have learned in this chapter by programming the 68HC12 to accept analog data and convert it to digital format using the ATD converter. A set of three IR emitter and detector pairs is used to bring in analog voltage values into the 68HC12. You program the 68HC12 to interpret these incoming voltages to determine whether your mobile robot is approaching a wall in front or on one of its sides. The skills you learn from this lab come in handy in the future since many design projects require you to interface analog systems with digital systems.

Documentation 68HC12EVB User's Manual

Prelab For the prelab, you must have a flowchart and pseudo-code for your program as well as the circuit board with three IR sensor pairs mounted on your mobile robot.

Description Write a program using the ATD converter of the 68HC12. In the final laboratory exercise, this lab is combined with motor control labs (labs from Chapter 7) to navigate your mobile robot through a maze.

Background Information The 68HC12 uses the successive-approximation technique to convert an analog signal into a digital one. You should use the built-in P clock signal for the approximation process (to select a sample time, you put an appropriate value in the ATDCTL4 register). The reference voltages for the ATD converter are provided by voltages connected to the V_{RH} and V_{RL} pins. The V_{RH} line represents the high-reference voltage and the V_{RL} line corresponds to the low reference voltage. Note that the voltage provided to the V_{RH} cannot be greater than the source voltage VDD (+5V), and the low-reference voltage connected to the V_{RL} cannot be lower than the source ground VSS (0V). In addition, the difference between the two voltages connected to pins V_{RH} and V_{RL} cannot be smaller than 2.5 V (i.e., $V_{RH} - V_{RL}$ must be $\geq$ 2.5V).

The ATD converter is enabled by setting the ADPU bit in the ATDCTL2 register. You must wait at least 100 microseconds after the system is enabled before taking in analog signals. The time is necessary to stabilize the charge pump circuit used in the successive-approximation method in the 68HC12.

There are four different ATD modes of operations:

1. single channel (nonscan mode)
2. single channel (scan mode)
3. multiple channels (nonscan mode)
4. multiple channels (scan mode)

In this lab, we use option number 3, the nonscan mode for multiple channels. We now describe how this option works.

Nonscan multiple channel mode In this mode of operation, the signals coming into the four selected channels (pins PAD0 through PAD3 or pins PAD4 through PAD7) are converted one by one and stored into registers ADR0H through ADR3H. After the four conversions, the conversion process stops until the system is enabled again by writing an appropriate value to the ADCTL5 register.

There are eight different registers that are required for this lab. The first one is the ADCTL2 register where the enable bit for the ATD converter resides as shown in Figure 9.21. The ADPU bit enables the ATD converter system. The second register associated with the 68HC12 ATD converter system is the ATDCTL4 register. This register allows you to choose the sample time of the ATD process. For this lab, use the default value ($01) for this register. The third register involved with the ATD converter system is the ADCTL5 register shown in Figure 9.22.

The S8CM bit is used to select a sequence of four consecutive ATD conversions (0) versus a sequence of eight consecutive ATD conversions (1). For this lab, use S8CM = 0. The SCAN bit determines whether the system should continuously scan and perform the ATD process or do a set of four or eight conversions and stop. In this lab, we set this bit to 0 since we do not desire a continuous scan. The MULT

Register: ATDCTL2 - Analog-to-Digital Control Register 2 Address: $0062

	7	6	5	4	3	2	1	0
	ADPU	AFFC	AWAI	0	0	0	ASCIE	ASCIF
Reset:	0	0	0	0	0	0	0	0

Figure 9.21 The ATDCTL2 register.

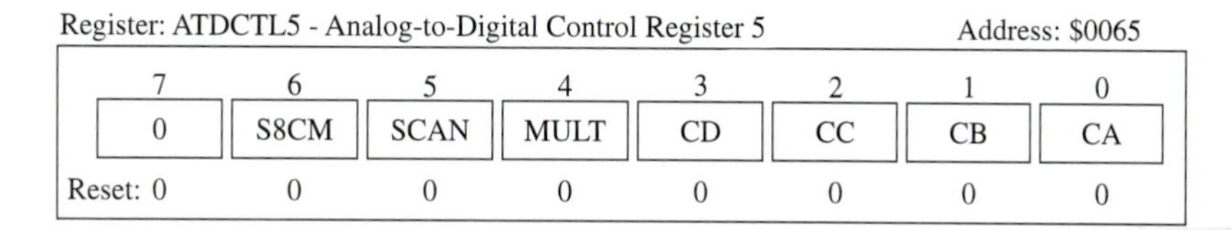

Figure 9.22 The ATDCTL5 register.

bit is used to specify a single or multiple channel mode. In this lab, we set this bit 1 to select multiple channels. The bits CD, CC, CB, and CA are used to select which channels (PAD0 through PAD7) are used as input pins to the ATD converter. Refer to Section 8.5.2 for all possible combinations of these four bits, but we use the following values for this lab:

$$CD = 0 \qquad CC = 1 \qquad CB = N/A \qquad CA = N/A$$

The prior selection forces the ATD converter system to read channels 4 through 7 or pins PAD4 through PAD7 (you only use three of the four channels).

The fourth register is the ATDSTAT register. For this lab, we are only concerned with bit 7 of this register—the SCF bit. The SCF bit is a conversion complete flag, which indicates that the conversions are completed. In this lab, you poll for this bit before getting the converted values from registers ADR0H through ADR3, where the ATD converted values are stored. That brings us to the other four registers associated with the ATD converter: ADR0H through ADR3H. These registers are the storage places where the resulting converted values reside. In this lab, once you have set up the ADCTL2, ADCTL4, and ADCTL5 registers as we discussed, the resulting converted values for signals coming through pins PE4, PE5, PE6, and PE7 are stored in registers ADR0H, ADR1H, ADR2H, and ADR3H, respectively.

IR Emitter/Detector Infrared light lies outside of the visible spectrum with slightly longer wavelength. Over the years, such a light source (LED) and a corresponding detector (phototransistor) have been used extensively in the optoelectronics industry. The pair can also be used to provide proximity detection for the purpose of avoiding collision of our mobile robot with maze walls. You can get a pair of emitter and detector from any electronic store. For this lab, you need three pairs. The sensors are used by your mobile robot to *look for* obstacles (walls).

Procedure

1. Connect +5V to pin V_{RH} and the ground to pin V_{RL}. Next, connect the sensor board to the 68HC12 using an extended cable. There are five cables you need to connect between the I/R circuits to the 68HC12 (we show you this connection shortly): a +5v line, a ground line, a line between the PAD4 pin and your left sensor output, a line between the center sensor and the PAD5 pin, and a

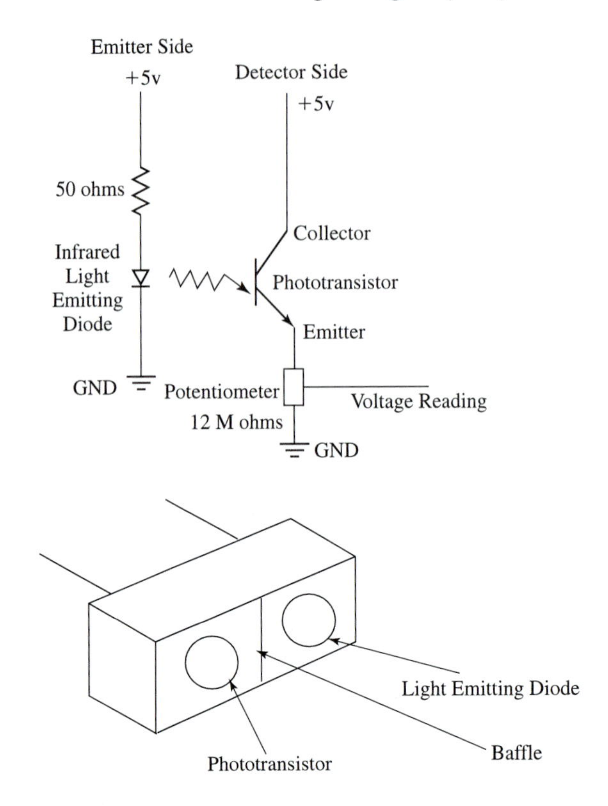

Figure 9.23 The operation of an IR emitter and detector pair and a housing case for the pair. The baffle provides isolation between the IR emitter and detector.

line between the right sensor and the PAD6 pin. The directions left and right are relative to a person sitting on the robot facing robot's front. Figure 9.23 shows one IR emitter/sensor pair. To interface the IR sensor/detector pairs with the 68HC12, refer to Figure 9.24.

2. Start the conversion process.
   (a) enable the ATD converter by setting the ADPU bit in the ATDCTL2 register,
   (b) wait for 100 microseconds,
   (c) set up the mode of operation by writing #%00010100 to the ADCTL5 register,
   (d) check the SCF flag for completion of a sequence of ATD conversion,
   (e) read values stored in registers ADR0 through ADR2 (only three of them are used) and display the results on the PC screen (read part 3 below),

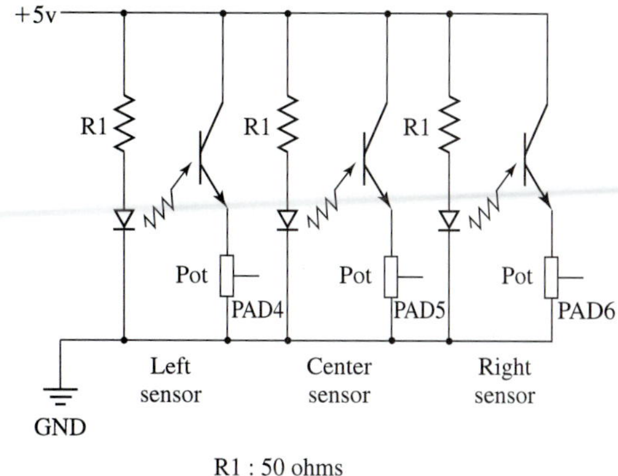

Figure 9.24 A diagram showing the connections between a set of IR emitter/detector pairs and the 68HC12EVB.

and

(f) repeat the process starting on step c.

3. Display the converted voltages on the PC screen using the DBUG-12 subroutines. The message on the screen should display once every second showing the voltage values measured by the right, center, and left IR sensors. Here is a sample message.

```
LEFT:XX    CENTER:XX    RIGHT:XX
LEFT:XX    CENTER:XX    RIGHT:XX
   ⋮           ⋮            ⋮
```

9.8 SUMMARY

That completes our introduction to the 68HC12s ATD conversion features. We began this chapter by examining the need for a transducer subsystem to convert a physical variable to an electrical signal compatible with an embedded controller system. We then described and applied key terms associated with an ATD conversion process such as sampling frequency, quantizing, resolution, and encoding. We then examined different ATD converter technologies with their associated advantages and disadvantages and calculated different conversion parameters for a given scenario. We then examined the ATD conversion system used aboard the 68HC12 in detail, described the key registers associated with the 68HC12 ATD conversion system, and learned how to program the 68HC12 to accomplish ATD conversions for a given situation.

9.9 FURTHER READING

"Analog-Digital Conversion Handbook," edited by Daniel H. Sheingold, Analog Devices, Norwood, MA, 1976.

"Transducers," Omega Engineering Inc., 1 Omega Drive, Stamford, CT, 06907.

"Handbook of Operational Amplifier Circuit Design," David F. Stout and Milton Kaufman, McGraw-Hill Inc., 1976.

"The Art of Electronics," P. Horowitz and W. Hill, Cambridge University Press, 2nd ed, 1995.

"Electrical Signals and Systems," Department of Electrical Engineering, United States Air Force Academy, 4th ed, 2001.

9.10 CHAPTER PROBLEMS

Fundamental

1. An analog signal has a spectrum (frequency content) that varies from 400 Hz to 5.9 KHz. It is to be sampled at a rate of 10,000 samples per second. Is the sampling rate adequate to allow reconstruction of the signal?
2. The 68HC12 ATD converter system converts each analog sample to an eight-bit,unsigned binary value. What is the resolution of the converter? Assume that the reference voltages for the 68HC12 designated as V_{RH} and V_{RL} are 4 volts and 1 volt, respectively.
3. If the 68HC12 is improved such that each analog conversion yields an unsigned, 10-bit binary value, what is the resolution of the converter?
4. A 2 KHz square wave is to be sampled using an ATD conversion system. What should the sampling frequency be?
5. In the previous question, how many bits of binary data are generated per second assuming an eight-bit ATD converter?
6. What is the dynamic range of the ATD system aboard the 68HC12? Explain.
7. What is aliasing? Describe two methods to avoid aliasing.

Advanced

1. Specify the contents of the ATDCTL2 register to power up the ATD system and set the ATD for fast flag-clearing operations.
2. What is meant by fast flag-clearing operations?

3. Specify the contents of the ATDCTL5 register to configure the ATD system for a continuous sequence of conversions with four conversions per sequence on ATD channels 4 through 7. Where are the results of these conversions placed?
4. If $V_{RH} = 5.0$ V and $V_{RL} = 0$ V, what digital value is returned when the ATD system converts the following voltage assuming an 8-bit conversion?
   - 5.0 volts
   - 0.0 volts
   - 2.7 volts
   - 3.2 volts
   - 1.2 volts
5. In the previous question, what is the dynamic range of the converter in dB?
6. The 68HC12 ATD system is configured with $V_{RH} = 5.0$ volts and $V_{RH} = 0$ volts. Write a subroutine that when called from the main program performs 15 conversions on channels 0 to 3 and stores the results in a buffer starting at location $3000. Initialization of the ATD should take place in a different subroutine.
7. In Figure 9.6, we provided the voltage levels for the first several guesses of the successive-approximation converter. Complete this diagram through the fifth guess. Provide the analog voltage and the corresponding binary value for each guess.
8. A transducer produces a signal of 30 mV corresponding to 0 RPM and 500 mV at 5000 RPM. Provide a design to interface this transducer to the 68HC12.
9. Repeat the problem with a transducer that provides 500 mV at 0 RPM and −30 mV at 5000 RPM.
10. Assume that music consists of frequencies from 20 Hz to 20 KHz. A compact disc (CD) converts stereo analog music signal using a 16-bit analog converter at a sampling frequency of 44 KHz. You have been tasked by your chief engineer to develop a quadraphonic (4-channel) CD system. What is the data rate of the quadraphonic audio CD? What is its dynamic range?
11. What analog value corresponds to the 68HC12s converter's maximum digital output (all 1s) when $V_{RH} = 5.0$ V and $V_{RL} = 0$ V?

Challenging

1. Write a subroutine that reads channel 1 of the ATD, calculates the average value of the last eight data points, and outputs the value to PORT B of the 68HC12.
2. Write a subroutine that continuously senses the voltage at PAD3. If the voltage is between 0 and 1 volts, bit 0 on PORT B is set high. If the voltage is between 1 and 2 volts, bit 1 on PORT B is set high. If the voltage is between 2 and 3 volts, bit 2 on PORT B is set high. If the voltage is between 3 and 4 volts, bit 3 on PORT B is set high. If the voltage is between 4 and 5 volts, bit 4 on PORT B is set high.

10

68HC12 Communications System—Multiple Serial Interface

Objectives: At the completion of this chapter you will be able to:

- Recognize the need for serial communication features within a microcontroller system,
- Compare and contrast the differences between parallel and serial communication techniques,
- Define terms related to serial communications,
- Describe the Serial Communication Interface (SCI) features of the 68HC12,
- Program the Serial Communication Interface (SCI) system to a given specification,
- Describe the Serial Peripheral Interface (SPI) features of the 68HC12,
- Program the Serial Peripheral Interface (SPI) system to a given specification, and
- Extend the hardware features of the 68HC12 via the Serial Peripheral Interface (SPI) system.

In this chapter we discuss the serial communication features of the 68HC12. Specifically, we see how the 68HC12 (A4 version) is configured with two separate and distinct asynchronous Serial Communication Interface (SCI) channels and a single synchronous Serial Peripheral Interface (SPI) channel. The synchronous SPI channel provides for faster data transmission at the expense of an additional synchronous serial clock control signal (SCK). For both the SCI and SPI systems we examine the hardware operation in detail, look at the registers associated with each system, and discuss how to program each system. We then examine applications for both the SCI and SPI systems.

10.1 NEED FOR COMMUNICATION FEATURES

A microcontroller is frequently used in stand-alone or remote applications. For example, throughout this book, we have been examining a mobile robot application. The 68HC12 in this robot application is a stand-alone device. That is, it is providing all of the required computer power for the robot. In our remote weather station example, we have both stand-alone and remote applications. That is, the remote weather station is geographically separated.

In these types of applications, it sometimes becomes necessary to communicate with other devices or processors. For example, in the mobile robot application, we examined a "friend or foe" signal exchange, where two robots could exchange signals to determine if they were friends. Also, as robotics become more advanced, we may want robots to communicate back and forth with one another to exchange information that is of interest to both robots. For example, if we placed two mobile robots in the opposite ends of the same maze, they could map different portions of the maze. When they met within the maze they could exchange information on maze layout (Figure 10.1).

In the remote weather station example, the remote weather station must periodically report its collected data to a central, possibly distant facility. This could be accomplished by using a modulator/demodulator (modem) link between the 68HC12 and the central facility if phone lines are available or accomplished with a radio frequency link if phone lines are not available.

Finally, you have probably already realized that, although the 68HC12 is a powerful and flexible processor, it may lack desired hardware in certain applications. What should we do in such situations? We find out in this chapter that the communication system aboard the 68HC12 allows direct interface to a plethora of different peripheral components. For example, the communication system may be interfaced to additional ports, liquid crystal displays, digital-to-analog converters, analog-to-digital converters, real-time clocks, phase locked loops, and many other devices. In this chapter, we find out how to accomplish these different desired tasks.

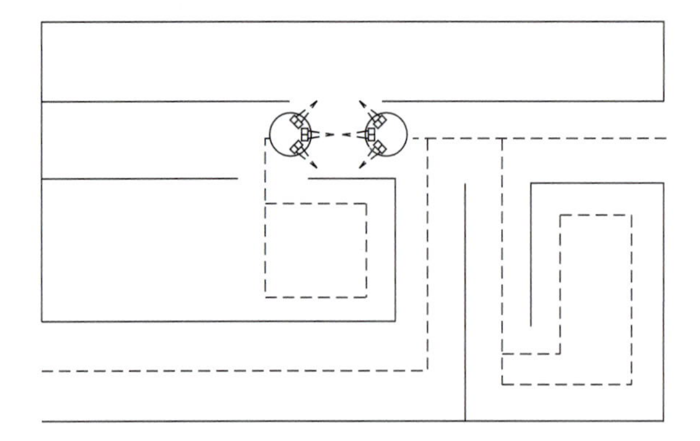

Figure 10.1 Robot information exchange. If we placed two mobile robots in the opposite ends of the same maze, they could map different portions of the maze. When they met within the maze, they could exchange information on maze layout.

10.2 FUNDAMENTALS OF SERIAL COMMUNICATION

Before we launch into the intricacies of the SCI and SPI communications systems, let us review some basic terminology associated with serial communications. First, serial communications is an efficient method of communicating between the controller and other devices. A single transmission line is used as a communication link. Data are then sent or received a single bit at a time. Strict communication protocol and timing schemes must be followed to ensure reliable communications.

In parallel communication systems, multiple bits are sent and received simultaneously. A separate line is provided for each bit of a data word. This type of connection is used when the fast exchange of information is required. Recall that all of the memory components we examined in the memory chapter were all written to or read from in parallel. Although parallel communication of data are much faster, multiple parallel transmission paths and associated hardware for each transmission line is required to achieve this faster speed.

10.2.1 Serial Communication Terminology

Figure 10.2 provides an illustration of some of the key terms associated with serial communication. These terms are briefly described here:

clock The clock signal establishes the rate of data transfer. As you can see in the figure, a single bit is sent on each clock pulse.

bit rate The bit rate is the number of bits transmitted per second (bps). The bit rate in bps is numerically equal to the clock signal in Hertz.

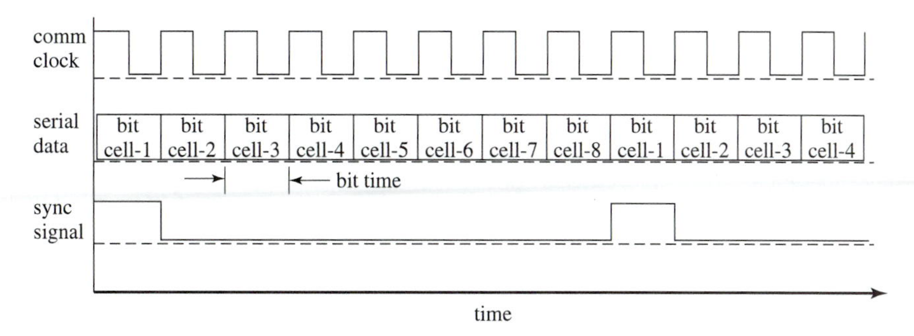

Figure 10.2 Serial communication terminology (adapted from Wakerly).

bit time The bit time is the reciprocal of the bit rate. This term describes the time increment required to transmit a single bit. (*bit time* $[s] = 1/$*bit rate* $[Hz]$)

bit cell The time required to transmit a single bit is also referred to as the bit cell.

BAUD rate The BAUD rate (pronounced "bod") is used to describe the number of bits transmitted per second. For example, if a serial channel is transmitting at 9600 BAUD, it is transmitting 9600 bits per second.

NRZ line code The term line code describes the format used to transmit each information bit. There are many different types of line codes that are used. The 68HC12 communication system employs the Nonreturn-to-Zero (NRZ) line code format. To transmit a 1, a 1 is placed on the transmission line for the entire bit cell, whereas to transmit a 0, a 0 fills the entire bit cell (Figure 10.3).

ASCII coding ASCII stands for American Standard Code for Information Interchange. It is a character code used to encode uppercase letters, lowercase letters, punctuation, numbers, and control characters into a seven-bit binary code representation. A table of the ASCII code is provided in Figure 10.4.

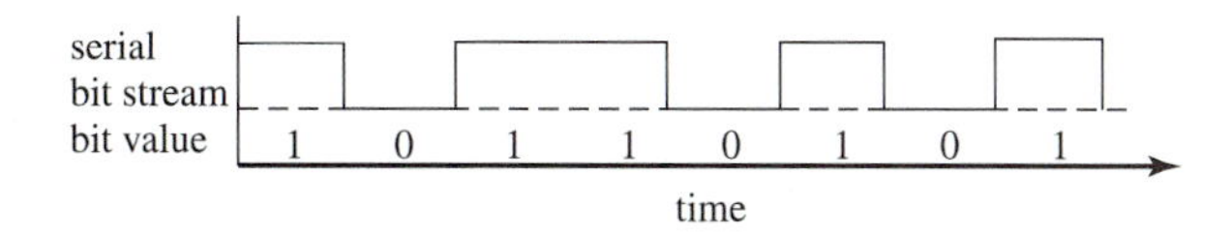

Figure 10.3 Nonreturn to zero serial communications format. The 68HC12 communication system employs the Nonreturn-to-Zero (NRZ) line code format. To transmit a 1, a 1 is placed on the transmission line for the entire bit cell. To transmit a 0, a 0 fills the entire bit cell. In this figure, a 1 0 1 1 0 1 0 1 is being transmitted using NRZ code.

ASCII CHARACTER SET (7-Bit Code)								
LS Dig. \ MS Dig.	0	1	2	3	4	5	6	7
0	NUL	DLE	!	0	@	P	`	p
1	SOH	DC1	1	1	A	Q	a	q
2	STX	DC2	"	2	B	R	b	r
3	ETX	DC3	#	3	C	S	c	s
4	EOT	DC4	$	4	D	T	d	t
5	ENQ	NAK	%	5	E	U	e	u
6	ACK	SYN	&	6	F	V	f	v
7	BEL	ETB	'	7	G	W	g	w
8	BS	CAN	(	8	H	X	h	x
9	HT	EM	)	9	I	Y	i	y
A	LF	SUB	*	:	J	Z	j	z
B	VT	ESC	+	;	K	[	k	{
C	FF	FS	,	<	L	\	l	|
D	CR	GS	–	=	M	]	m	}
E	SO	RS	.	>	N	^	n	~
F	SI	US	/	?	O	_	o	DEL

Figure 10.4 American Standard Code for Information Interchange (ASCII) is a character code used to encode uppercase letters, lowercase letters, punctuation, and control characters into a seven-bit binary code representation. (Figure used with permission of Motorola, Incorporated.)

parity bit The parity bit is used to detect a single error in a character transmission. When odd parity is employed, the parity bit is set to a value (either 1 or 0) such that there is an odd number of bits at logic 1 in the character code. Conversely, when a system employs even parity, the parity bit is set to a value such that there is an even number of bits at logic 1 in the character code.

simplex communication A simplex communication link is one that at any one time can either transmit or receive data (Figure 10.5).

duplex communication A duplex communication link provides a simultaneous two-way communication path (Figure 10.5).

Before moving forward, let us stop and review some key terms and concepts using the following questions.

Practice Questions

Question: What is the ASCII coding for 68HC12? (Assume a 7-bit ASCII character code is used as illustrated in Figure 10.4.)

Answer: $36 $38 $48 $43 $31 $32.

Question: In the prior question, if the most significant bit (MSB) was used as an odd parity bit, what would the ASCII coding be for 68HC12?

Answer: $B6 $38 $C8 $43 $31 $32.

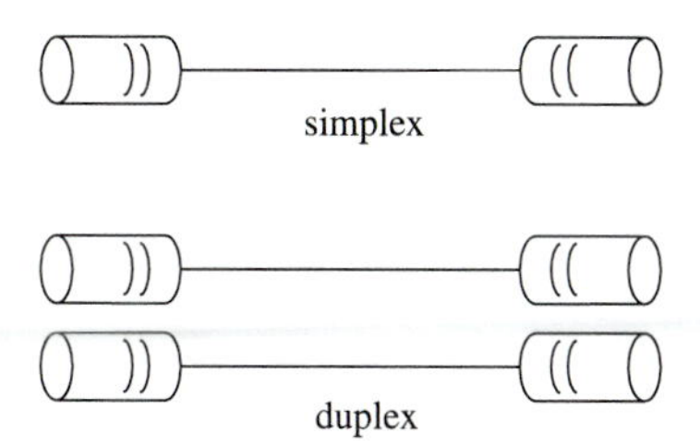

Figure 10.5 Simplex versus duplex communications. A simplex communication link is one that at any one time can be either transmission or reception, but not both. A duplex communication link provides both a transmission and a reception transmission link. When you were a child, you probably made a simplex communication system by using two empty cans with a string stretched between them. When one person spoke, the other person was required to listen. For a duplex system, you would require two of the "tin-can telephones." This would allow you to listen and speak at the same time.

Question: Assuming the MSB is used as an even parity bit, what character stream is represented by the following ASCII code $47, $6F, $6F, $E4, $A0, $6A, $6F, $D2, $21?

Answer: Good job!

Question: How long would it take to transmit this ASCII code stream assuming a transmission rate of 1200 BAUD?

Answer: At 1200 BAUD, a bit is sent every 833.3 microseconds. Since each character consists of eight bits each, 60 ms are required.

10.2.2 Serial Communication Signals

To ensure correct synchronization between a serial transmitter and receiver, a number of different methods are employed. In an **asynchronous** system, such as the 68HC12's Serial Communication Interface (SCI), information is transmitted using ASCII code. Also a parity bit may or may not be used. To synchronize the transmitter to the receiver, a start bit and two stop bits are used to frame the ASCII coded character as shown in Figure 10.6. The 68HC12 may also be configured to set the transmit (TxD) pin to logic 1, an idle signal, when the transmitter is not transmitting a character frame.

On the receiving end, the receiver looks for a falling edge on the receive (RxD) line. When one is detected, it samples the bit several times to ensure it is truly a logic low. If a valid low bit is received, it is interpreted as the start bit and the system begins sampling the incoming bits. The data bits are sampled at three different points on the incoming bit, and a majority vote system is used to

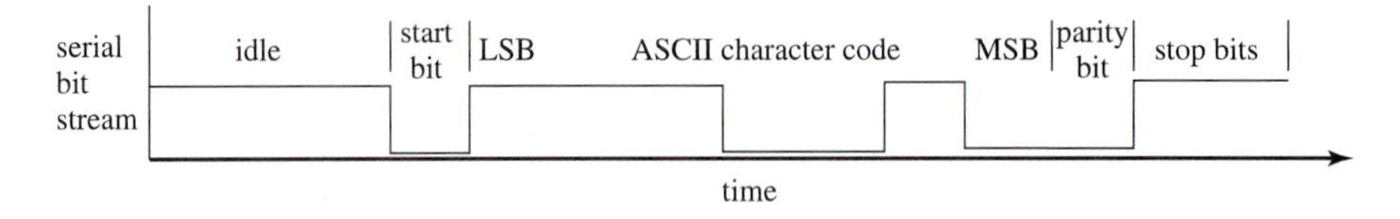

Figure 10.6 Synchronizing an asynchronous transmitter/receiver.

determine if the incoming bit is a logic 1 or a logic 0. This technique allows the information bits to be extracted from some level of noise.

A **synchronous** serial communication system, such as the 68HC12's Serial Peripheral Interface (SPI), may use two different methods of synchronizing the transmitter and receiver. The first method uses a unique code word as a sync pulse. When the receiver receives this unique word, it synchronizes itself to the incoming data. An alternative method is to provide a separate shift clock (SCK) signal. As data are output on the serial output line by the transmitter, the SCK signal pulses once for each bit output on the serial line. Although this technique requires an extra signal line, data may be transmitted and received at a much greater rate than the **asynchronous** technique. The 68HC12's SPI system uses the SCK signal technique.

With this basic review of serial communications terminology and concepts, let us take a closer look at the serial communication features of the 68HC12. First, look at some review questions.

Practice Questions

Question: Describe the key similarities and differences between the SCI and SPI communication systems.

Answer: Both the SCI and SPI systems are serial systems. That is, they transmit a single bit at a time. The SCI system is an asynchronous system in that a common clock signal is not used to maintain synchronization between the transmitter and receiver. Instead, distinctive framing bits (start and stop bits) are used to maintain synchronization. Fewer control signals are required in the SCI system at the expense of the transmission of these additional overhead bits. The SPI system uses a separate clock synchronization signal to maintain sync between the transmitter and receiver and is therefore designated a synchronous system. An extra control signal line is required between the transmitter and receiver. However, the transmission rate may be significantly higher in a synchronous configured system.

Question: Sketch the NRZ ASCII code character for SCI transmission using one start bit, two stop bits, and even parity for a comma.

Answer: Figure 10.6 illustrates the SCI transmission of a comma.

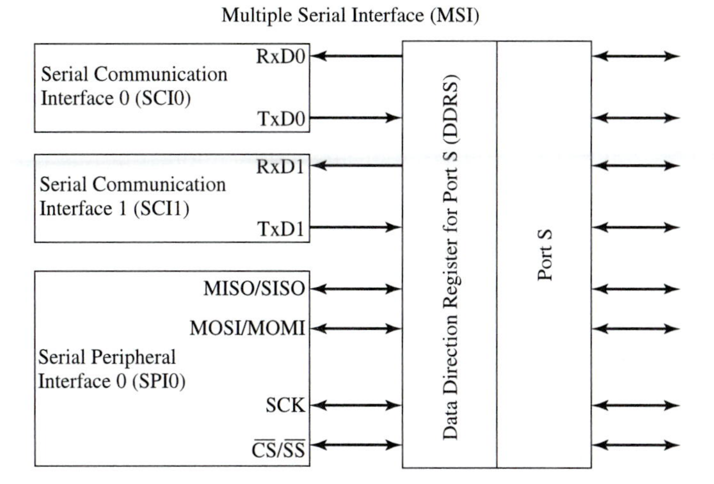

Figure 10.7 The Multiple Serial Interface (MSI) System. This MSI module consists of three independent serial I/O subsystems: two SCIs and the SPI. The communication system uses the pins of Port S for signal input and output.

10.3 MULTIPLE SERIAL INTERFACE

The communication system aboard the 68HC12 is called the Multiple Serial Interface (MSI) module. As its name implies, this is a serial format communication system. The MSI module consists of three (A4-variant) independent serial input/output (I/O) subsystems: two SCIs and the SPI (Figure 10.7). As you can see in the figure, the communication system uses the pins of Port S for signal input and output.

The MSI consists of two distinctly different types of serial communication systems. The SCI subsystems are considered asynchronous communications system. That is, the SCI system does not use a common clock signal to keep the transmitter and receiver in synchronizaion with another. Yet, the SPI system uses an additional clock signal (SCK) that is shared by both the transmitter and receiver to maintain synchronization. This allows for a relatively fast exchange of information between the transmitter and receiver. We now take an in-depth view of both systems beginning with the SCI.

10.4 THE SERIAL COMMUNICATIONS INTERFACE

The Serial Communications Interface (SCI) is an **asynchronous** serial communications system. As previously discussed, the asynchronous system does not use a separate shift clock line to maintain synchronization between the transmitter and receiver. Instead, it employs a start bit and two stop bits to frame each transmitted character. The 68HC12 is equipped with two complete, independent SCI systems designated SCI0 and SCI1. Provided next is a list of characteristics for the SCI system. Several SCI-related registers are mentioned in this list. We discuss these registers in detail in an upcoming section.

Full-duplex operation Full-duplex operation provides for simultaneous transmission and reception.

Nonreturn-to-zero (NRZ) format The NRZ format, as previously described, fills the entire bit cell with either a logic 1 or 0 for the entire bit time.

Baud rate selection The 68HC12 SCI system allows for the selection of many different Baud rates. The Baud rate is set by configuring the SCI Baud Rate Control Registers (SC0BDH/SC1BDH and SC0BDL/SC1BDL).

Programmable eight-bit or nine-bit data format The SCI system may be configured for either an eight-bit or nine-bit data word. The specific format is configured using the Mode ("M") bit in SCI Control Register 1.

Two receiver wake-up methods: idle line and address mark This feature is important for systems that may contain multiple receivers. The SCI receiver evaluates the first characters of each message. If the message is not addressed for that specific receiver, the receiver is placed in a sleep mode. A receiver may be put "asleep" by setting the Receiver Wake-Up Control (RWU) bit in the SCI Status Register to logic 1. The receiver can be woken up using one of two methods: (1) wake up by IDLE line recognition, or (2) wake up by address mark. In the wake-up by idle line method, a sleeping receiver wakes up as soon as its receive (RxD) line becomes idle. When wake-up by address mark is selected, the SCI system uses the most significant bit signal to wake up the receiver. When the wake-up condition is detected, the 68HC12 resets the RWU bit back to logic 0, which wakes the receiver.

Interrupt-generation capability As discussed in the interrupt and reset chapter, the interrupt concept is a powerful technique to efficiently use the processor. The SCI system has two associated interrupt sets; one set for SCI0 and another set for SCI1. Associated with each of these interrupts are four separate interrupts. We discuss the meanings of each of these flags in an upcoming section.

- Transmit Interrupt Enable (TIE): SCI interrupt is requested whenever the Transmit Data Register Empty (TDRE) flag is set.
- Transmit Complete Interrupt Enable (TCIE): SCI interrupt is requested whenever the Transmit Complete (TC) flag is set.

- Receiver Interrupt Enable (RIE): SCI interrupt is requested whenever the Receive Data Register Full (RDRF) flag is set.
- Idle Line Interrupt Enable (ILIE): SCI interrupt is requested whenever the IDLE status flag is set.

Receiver noise error detection As mentioned previously, the 68HC12 uses a majority vote system to determine if a received bit is a logic 1 or 0. This is accomplished by sampling the received bit at three different locations. If the majority vote is not unanimous (3 for 3), the Noise Error Flag (NF) is set in the SCI Status Register 1.

Framing error detection We already established how important it is to maintain synchronization between a serial transmitter and receiver. If synchronization is lost, it is important to detect this condition as soon as possible. The 68HC12 monitors for a logic 1 stop bit at the end of a character frame. If a stop bit is not detected as expected, the 68HC12 sets the Framing Error (FE) bit in the SCI Status Register 1.

Receiver parity error detection The 68HC12 is equipped with a user-configured parity checking system. The user may elect to use the system and also elect whether to use even or odd parity. If a parity error is detected by the receiver, the Parity Error Flag (PF) is set in the SCI Status Register 1.

Now that we have covered the features of the SCI, let us take a closer look at the SCI transmitter and receiver hardware. Due to the complexity of the hardware, we discuss the transmitter and receiver separately. First, a few questions.

Practice Questions

Question: When any SCI interrupt occurs, what is the vector address for the interrupt service routine? (You may have to go to the interrupt chapter for this information.)

Answer: The 68HC12 is equipped with a single interrupt for each SCI channel. Channel SCI0's interrupt vector is $FFD6, $FFD7. Channel SCI1's interrupt vector is $FFD4, $FFD5.

Question: What is the SPI-related interrupt? What is its vector address?

Answer: The SPI interrupt is serial transfer complete with an associated vector address of $FFD8, $FFD9.

10.4.1 Hardware Description—The SCI Transmitter

Transmit Shift Register. The SCI transmitter is illustrated in Figure 10.8. The main component of the SCI transmitter is the 11-bit Transmit Shift Register. As you can see in the diagram, the actual data are bits 0–6 (recall that the ASCII code only requires seven bits). The transmit shift register is preconfigured with a logic low START bit and a logic high STOP bit. The Mode bit ("M") is user-configured to select either an eight-bit or nine-bit data word. A detailed description of each register is provided in an upcoming section. The 68HC12 is equipped with automatic parity generation hardware. If the parity hardware is enabled (PE bit = 1), a parity bit is generated and inserted into bit 7 of the Transmit Shift Register. Either even or odd parity may be selected by the user.

Transmitter Control. The Transmitter Control hardware generates all of the required signals to control SCI transmission. The user controls this hardware using

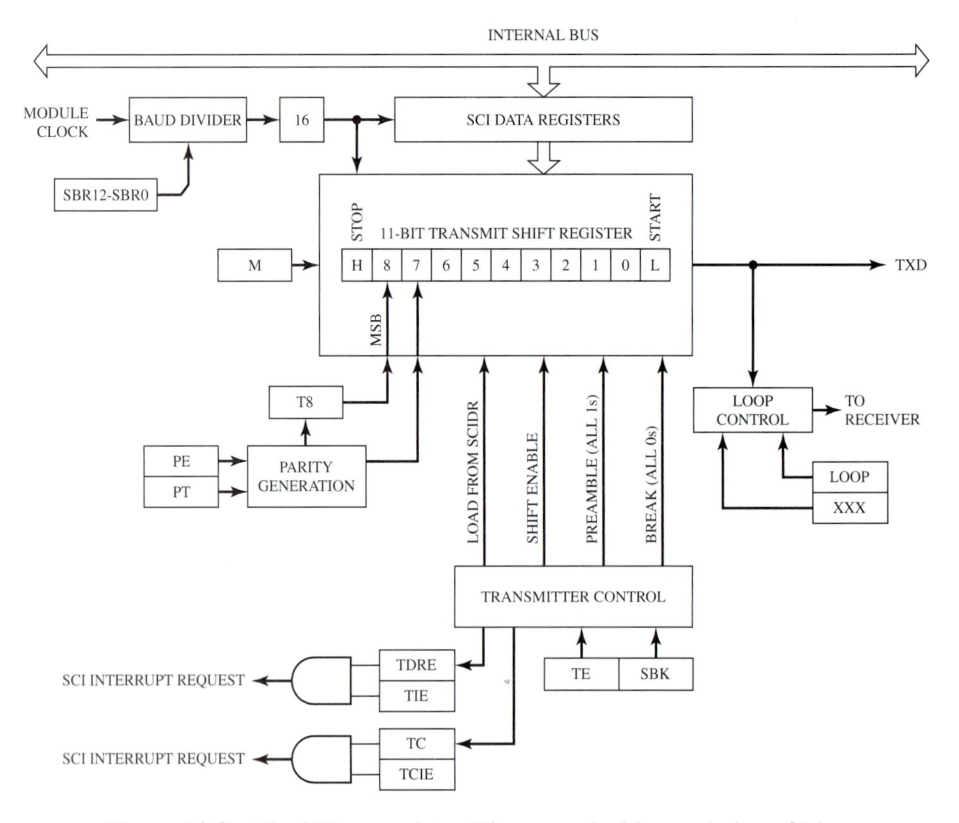

Figure 10.8 The SCI transmitter. (Figure used with permission of Motorola, Incorporated.)

the Transmitter Enable (TE) and the Send Break (SBK) bits. When the TE bit is set to logic 1, the SCI transmit logic is enabled and the TxD pin is set for transmitter use. The Transmitter Control logic also generates SCI-associated interrupts.

Baud Divider. The transmission Baud rate is set by the SBR[12:0] bits in the SCI Baud Rate Control Registers. The time base for the SCI transmitter is derived from the Module Clock (MCLK).

SCI Data Register. The SCI Data Register is the portal through which the user accesses the Transmit Shift Register. When using a standard seven- or eight-bit data word, the user sends the character to be transmitted to the SCI Data Register Low. The 68HC12 transfers the contents of the SCI Data Register to the Transmit Shift Register for transmission.

Loop Control. The loop control hardware allows the output of the transmitter to be connected to the input of the receiver. This is accomplished by setting the LOOPS bit and the Receiver Source (RSRC) bit to logic 1.

10.4.2 Hardware Description—The SCI Receiver

The SCI Receiver hardware is illustrated in Figure 10.9. It contains much of the same hardware already discussed for the SCI Transmitter. Furthermore, we have

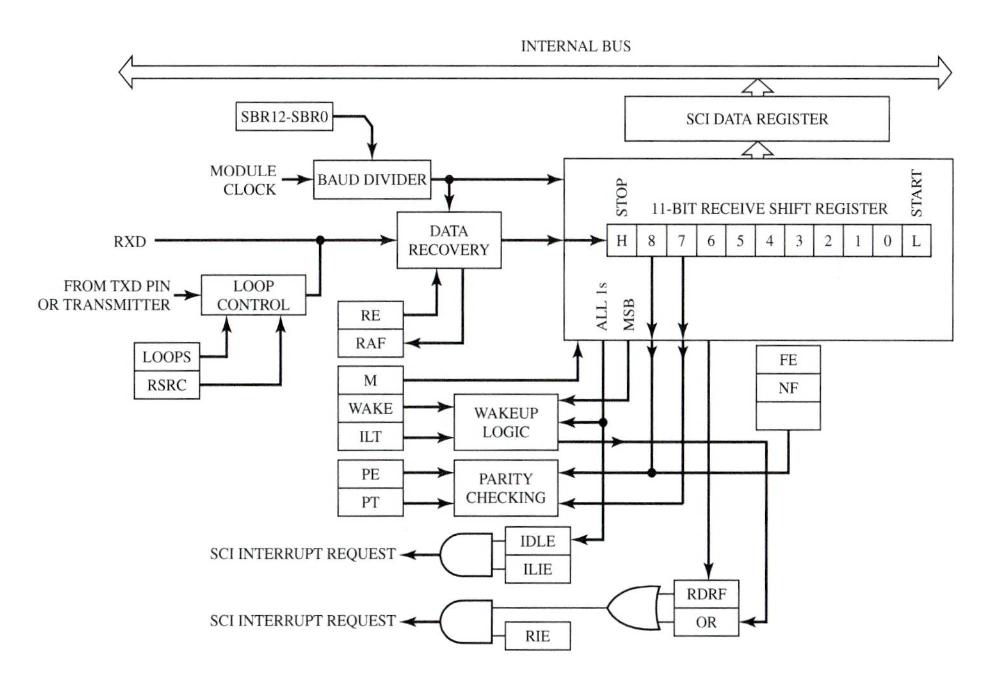

Figure 10.9 The SCI receiver. (Figure used with permission of Motorola, Incorporated.)

discussed many of the flags and hardware associated with the SCI Transmitter. The primary difference between the transmitter and receiver is the direction of the data flow. We only discuss the hardware not previously discussed.

Data Recovery. The Data Recovery hardware contains the majority vote generator to determine if a received bit is either a logic 1 or 0. If a unanimous vote is received (3 for 3), the received bit is determined to be a logic 1 or 0. If the vote is not unanimous (2 for 3), the received bit is determined to be a logic 1 or 0, and the noise flag (NF) bit in the SCI Status Register 1 (SCxSR1) is set.

RDRF Flag. The Receive Data Register Full (RDRF) flag is set when a received character is ready to be read from the Serial Communications Data Register (SCxDR).

The remaining registers and their associated bits are discussed in the next section.

10.4.3 SCI Registers

The SCI has a dedicated set of registers to control the operation of the SCI system. We discuss each of these registers in turn. We then discuss how to program these registers for SCI transmission and reception.

SCI Baud Rate Control Registers The SCI Baud Rate Control Registers are used to set the rate of SCI transmission and reception. The SCI Baud Rate is set using bits SBR[12:0]. These values are determined using the following relationship:

$$SBR = MCLK/(16 \cdot SCI\ Baud\ Rate)$$

The SBR value for different desired SCI Baud Rates are shown in Figure 10.10. It is important to note that SBR[12:0] bits are distributed between the two SCI Baud Rate Control Registers: SCxBDH and SCxBDL. The SCI Baud rate settings, BR Divisor, in Figure 10.10 are provided in decimal. To configure the SCI system for a desired Baud rate, the appropriate value from Figure 10.10 is loaded to the SCxBDH and SCxBDL registers.

Example

If the MCLK is 8 MHz and it is desired to set the SCI 1 (SCI1) to 9600 Baud, a 52 ($34) must be loaded into SCxBDH and SCxBDL. The following code fragment accomplishes this baud rate setting. (We assume the location of the registers were declared earlier in the program with EQU directives.)

```
MOVB   #$34,SC1BDL          ;Set Baud rate to 9600 for SCI 1
MOVB   #$00,SC1BDH
```

Desired SCI Baud Rate	BR Divisor for M = 4.0 MHz	BR Divisor for M = 8.0 MHz
110	2273	4545
300	833	1667
600	417	833
1200	208	417
2400	104	208
4800	52	104
9600	26	52
14400	17	35
19200	13	26
38400	--	13

Figure 10.10 SCI Baud Rate Generation. The SCI Baud Rate Control Registers are used to set the rate of SCI transmission and reception using bits SBR[12:0].

Register: SCI Baud Rate Control Register (SC0BDH/SC1BDH) Address: $00C0/$00C8

	7	6	5	4	3	2	1	0
	BTST	BSPL	BRLD	SBR12	SBR11	SBR10	SBR9	SBR8
Reset:	0	0	0	0	0	0	0	0

Register: SCI Baud Rate Control Register (SC0BDL/ SC1BDL) Address: $00C1/$00C9

	7	6	5	4	3	2	1	0
	SBR7	SBR6	SBR5	SBR4	SBR3	SBR2	SBR1	SBR0
Reset:	0	0	0	0	0	1	0	0

Figure 10.11 SCI Baud Rate Control Register—SCxBDH/SCxBDL ($00C0/$00C8, $00C1/$00C9)

SCI Control Register 1 The SCI Control Register 1 (SCxCR1) is used to set different features for the SCI communications system.

LOOPS The SCI LOOP Mode/Single Wire Mode Enable bit configures the SCI system for loop operation when set to 1. In LOOP operation, the RxD pin is disconnected from the SCI system and the transmitter output is routed internally to the receiver input. Since both the receiver and transmitter is used in LOOP mode, both the receiver and transmitter must be enabled.

WOMS The wired-OR mode for serial pins bit allows the TxD and RxD pins to operate in an open drain-configuration when set to logic 1. Open drain config-

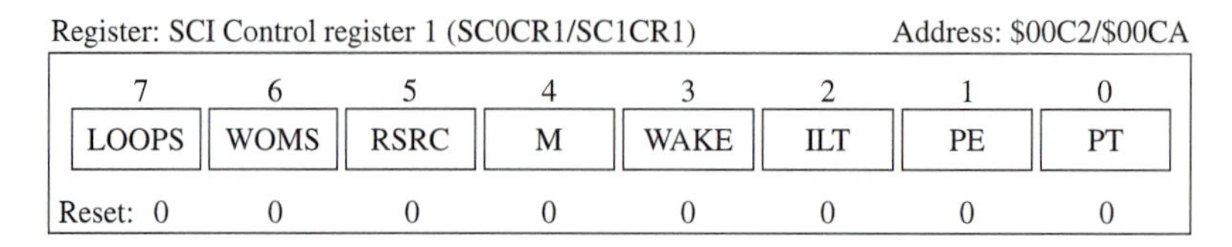

Figure 10.12 SCI Control Register 1—SCxCR1 ($00C2, $00CA)

ured gates allow the outputs from several gates to be tied directly together and then connected to an external pullup resistor (this is usually forbidden in other gate configurations). When the TxD and RxD pins are configured for WOMS operation, the TxD pins may be tied together in a multiple-transmitter system. The TxD pins of nonactive transmitters follow the logic level of an active logic one.

RSRC The receiver source bit determines the internal feedback path for the receiver when used in conjunction with the LOOPS bit. When the LOOPS bit is set to logic 1, a RSRC bit set to 1 connects the receiver output to the transmitter input pin (TxD).

M The mode bit is used to select the character format. When M = 0, the character format is one start, eight data, and one stop bit. When M = 1, the character format is one start, nine data, and one stop bit.

WAKE As previously discussed, the SCI system can be woken up once put to sleep. When WAKE = 0, the 68HC12 is woken up using the IDLE line method. When WAKE = 1, the 68HC12 is woken up by the address mark method.

ILT The idle line type (ILT) bit determines when the SCI receiver starts counting logic 1s as idle character bits. Recall that an idle character contains all logic 1s and has no start, stop, or parity bit. The idle line character counting begins after either the start bit or the stop bit. If the count begins after the start bit, then a string of logic 1s preceding the stop bit may cause false recognition of an idle character. Beginning the count after the stop bit avoids false recognition of an idle character. When ILT = 1, the idle character bit count starts after the stop bit, whereas if ILT = 0, the idle character bit count begins after the start bit.

PE This bit is the on/off switch for the parity generation system. A logic 1 turns the parity system on.

PT The parity type bit is used to select even (0) or odd (1) parity.

SCI Control Register 2 The SCI Control Register 2 (SCxCR2) is used to set different features for the SCI communications system. The first four bits of this register (TIE, TCIE, RIE, and ILIE) are used to enable different maskable interrupts associated with the SCI system. Recall from our discussion in the interrupt and

Register: SCI Control register 2 (SC0CR2/SC1CR2) Address: $00C3/$00CB

	7	6	5	4	3	2	1	0
	TIE	TCIE	RIE	ILIE	TE	RE	RWU	SBK
Reset:	0	0	0	0	0	0	0	0

Figure 10.13 SCI Control Register 2—SCxCR2 ($00C3, $00CB)

reset chapter that maskable interrupts must be turned on by (1) enabling the I bit in the Condition Code Register, and (2) locally enabling the interrupts using their respective enable bits. The first four bits of the SCxCR2 registers (TIE, TCIE, RIE, and ILIE) are the local enable bits for different SCI-associated interrupts.

Transmit Interrupt Enable (TIE): This interrupt is requested whenever the Transmit Data Register Empty (TDRE) flag is set.

Transmit Complete Interrupt Enable (TCIE): This interrupt is requested whenever the Transmit Complete (TC) flag is set.

Receiver Interrupt Enable (RIE): This interrupt is requested whenever the Receive Data Register Full (RDRF) flag is set.

Idle Line Interrupt Enable (ILIE): This interrupt is requested whenever the IDLE status flag is set.

TE: Transmitter Enable—This is the on/off switch for the SCI transmitter. A logic 1 turns the SCI transmitter on.

RE: Receiver Enable—This is the on/off switch for the SCI receiver. A logic 1 turns the SCI receiver on.

RWU: Receiver Wake-Up Control—When the RWU bit is set to logic 1, the SCI receiver is placed in the sleep mode. It is woken up by hardware as previously described.

SBK: Send Break—When the SBK bit is set to logic 1, the transmitter sends zeros to the receiver.

SCI Status Register 1 As its name implies, SCI Status Register 1 provides detailed status on the SCI system. These flags within this register are set in

Register: SCI Status register 1 (SC0SR1/SC1SR1) Address: $00C4/$00CC

	7	6	5	4	3	2	1	0
	TDRE	TC	RDRF	IDLE	OR	NF	FE	PF
Reset:	1	1	0	0	0	0	0	0

Figure 10.14 SCI Status Register 1—SCxSR1 ($00C4, $00CC)

response to different events that occur in the SCI system. The receive-related flag bits are cleared by a read of the SCxSR register followed by a read of the transmit/receive data register low byte.

TDRE: Transmit Data Register Empty Flag—The TDRE flag is set to a logic 1 when the data register associated with the SCI transmission system is empty.

TC: Transmit Complete Flag—The TC flag is set to logic 1 when the transmitter is idle.

RDRF: Receive Data Register Full Flag—The RDRF flag is set to logic 1 when a received character is ready to be read from the SCI data register (SCxDR).

IDLE: Idle Line Detected Flag—The IDLE flag is set to logic 1 when 10 consecutive logic 1s appear on the receiver input (recall that an idle character contains all logic 1s and has no start, stop, or parity bit) when the Mode (M) bit is set to zero. When M = 0, the SCI is configured for eight-bit data words. The IDLE flag is also set to logic 1 when 11 consecutive logic 1s are received for M = 1 (SCI configured for nine-bit data words).

OR: Overrun Error Flag—The OR is set to logic 1 when the SCI data register is not read before the receive shift register receives the next frame. As its name implies, the new received character has overrun the preceding character.

NF: Noise Error Flag—As previously discussed, the SCI system uses a majority vote system to detect reception of a logic 1 or 0. If a unanimous vote (3 of 3) is not received, the NF is set to a logic 1 indicating that noise is present.

FE: Framing Error Flag—The FE flag is set when a logic 0 is accepted as the stop bit. Recall that the stop bit should be a logic 1. A framing error indicates that the transmitter and receiver are out of synchronization with one another. Therefore, when the FE bit is set, data reception is inhibited until the FE bit is cleared.

PF: Parity Error Flag—The PF bit is set when a parity error is detected. Recall that no, even, or odd parity may be used with the SCI system. A parity error indicates an error has occurred in transmission of a character.

SCI Status Register 2 The SCI Status Register 2 contains only a single flag—the Receiver Active Flag (RAF). This flag is active (logic 1) when a character is being received.

SCI Data Registers The SCI Data Registers (SCxDRH and SCxDRL) contain the transmitted/received data. The SCxDRL register contains bits [7:0], whereas the eighth bit is contained in SCxRDH. The SCxDRL register is used for the eight-bit data format. Both SCxDRH and SCxDRL are used for the nine-bit data format. This completes our discussion of the transmitter and receiver hardware and

Register: SCI Status register 2 (SC0SR2/SC1SR2) Address: $00C5/$00CD

	7	6	5	4	3	2	1	0
	0	0	0	0	0	0	0	RAF
Reset:	0	0	0	0	0	0	0	0

Figure 10.15 SCI Status Register 2—SCxSR2 ($00C5, $00CD)

Register: SCI Data Register High (SC0DRH/SC1DRH) Address: $00C6/$00CE

	7	6	5	4	3	2	1	0
	R8	T8	0	0	0	0	0	0
Reset:	-	-	0	0	0	0	0	0

Register: SCI Data Register Low (SC0DRL/SC1DRL) Address: $00C7/$00CF

	7	6	5	4	3	2	1	0
	R7T7	R6T6	R5T5	R4T4	R3T3	R2T2	R1T1	R0T0
Reset:	-	-	-	-	-	-	-	-

Figure 10.16 SCI Data Register High/Low—SCxDRH/SCxDRL ($00C6/$00CE, $00C7/$00CF)

the SCI-associated registers. We now discuss how information is transmitted and received by this hardware. We then discuss how to program the SCI for transmission and reception. First, some review questions.

Practice Questions

Question: What is the difference between the TDRE and RDRF bit?

Answer: Both bits are flags that indicate the status of the SCI system. The TDRE bit, Transmit Data Register Empty Flag, is set to logic 1 when the SCI Data Registers are empty. This indicates transmission of a character. The RDRF bit, Receive Data Register Full Flag, is set to logic 1 when the SCI Data Registers are full. This indicates reception of a character.

Question: What is the purpose of the PF flag? Why is it important?

Answer: The PF, Parity Error Flag, is set to indicate that a parity error has occurred. A parity indicates that the character received is not correct.

Question: Are there any interrupts associated with the SCI system? If so, describe them.

Answer: There are actually four interrupts associated with the SCI system. The enable bits for each of these interrupts are located in SCI Control Register 2. These bits are:

Transmit Interrupt Enable (TIE): This interrupt is requested whenever the Transmit Data Register Empty (TDRE) flag is set.

Transmit Complete Interrupt Enable (TCIE): This interrupt is requested whenever the Transmit Complete (TC) flag is set.

Receiver Interrupt Enable (RIE): This interrupt is requested whenever the Receive Data Register Full (RDRF) flag is set.

Idle Line Interrupt Enable (ILIE): This interrupt is requested whenever the IDLE status flag is set.

10.4.4 SCI Transmitter and Receiver Operation

There are three distinct operations used by the SCI communications system: SCI system initialization, SCI transmission, and SCI reception. The required steps for these operations are illustrated via flowcharts provided in Figure 10.17.

SCI System Initialization To properly initialize the SCI system, the following actions must be completed: (1) set the SCI system Baud rate, (2) initialize the SCI system for the data format (eight- or nine-bit data format), (3) configure SC control registers (SCxCR1 and SCxCR2) for desired parameters, (4) clear the TDRE flag using the two-step process of first reading the SCxSR1 register and then writing to the SCxDR register. It goes without saying, but we will say it anyway.

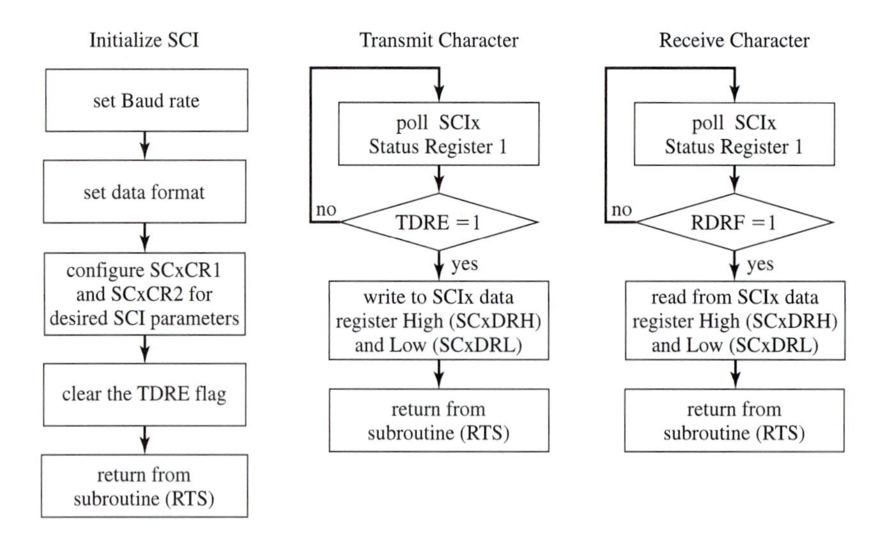

Figure 10.17 SCI transmitter and receiver operation. There are three distinct operations used by the SCI communications system: (left) SCI system initialization, (middle) SCI transmission, and (right) SCI reception.

The SCI transmitter and the intended SCI receiver must be initialized identically for proper reception. That is, they must both (transmitter and receiver) be configured for the same Baud rate, parity, and so on.

SCI Transmission To transmit a character, you must wait for the TDRE flag to set indicating that the transmit data register is empty and is therefore ready for another character. Once the flag sets, the character to be sent is transferred to the serial communications data register (SCxDRH and L). This transfer of data sets the TDRE bit and may generate an interrupt if the transmit interrupt is enabled. All data are transmitted least significant bit (LSB) first. On completion of data transmission, the transmission complete (TC) bit of the SCSR is set and an interrupt may be generated if the transmit complete interrupt is enabled.

SCI Reception To receive a character, the Receive Data Register Full (RDRF) flag is monitored. It sets to logic 1 when the receive data register is full, which can cause an interrupt if the receiver interrupt is enabled. The received character can then be read from the serial communications data register (SCxDRH and L).

10.4.5 Programming the Serial Communication Interface

Example

In this example, we provide the assembly code to initialize the SCI system and transmit characters via subroutines. We have named these subroutines SCI_ini and SCI_trans. We have left the subroutine to receive characters (SCI_rx) via the SCI as a homework exercise.

Requirement: Initialize the SCI1 system for 9600 Baud and eight-bit data mode. No parity features or interrupts are used in this example.

Note: Let us assume that all 68HC12 related registers have been defined with EQU directives in a header file designated "68HC12REG.ASM." The main program serves as a base of operations. From the main program, we call the subroutines to initialize the SCI system using the subroutine "SCI_ini" and then transmit characters using the subroutine "SCI_trans."

```
INCLUDE 68HC12REG.ASM'
;------------------------------
;MAIN PROGRAM ;
;------------------------------
        ORG     $7000       ;User RAM at $7000

        BSR     SCI_ini     ;Subroutine to initialize SCI1
        BSR     SCI_trans   ;Subroutine to start transmission
DONE    BRA     DONE        ;Branch to self
```

The subroutine "SCI_ini" initializes the SCI system to user-desired parameters. Reference the flowchart in Figure 10.17 to see that all initialization actions are completed.

```
;-----------------------------------
```

```
        MOVB    #$34,SC1BDL          ;Set Baud to 9600
        MOVB    #$00,SC1CR1          ;eight-bit data, disable LOOP and
                                     parity
        MOVB    #$08,SC1CR2          ;no interrupts, transmitter enabled
        LDAA    SC1SR1               ;1st step to clear TDRE: Read
                                     SC1SR1
        STD     SC1DRH               ;2nd step to clear TDRE:Write
                                     SC1DR
        LDX     #DATA                ;use X register as pointer to DATA
        RTS                          ;return from subroutine
```

The subroutine "SCI_trans" provides for character transmission. Again reference the flowchart in Figure 10.17 for proper SCI character transmission actions. The TDRE bit, which indicates the data register, is first polled before loading in a character for transmission. When a data character is then loaded to the SCI data register (SC1DRL), the SCI system automatically initiates actions to transmit the character a bit at a time with the user-specified start- and stop-bit configurations framing each bit.

The FCB designator is an assembler director to form a character byte. It allows the declaration of ASCII string character and control variables.

```
;-----------------------------------
;Transmit Subroutine ;
;-----------------------------------
SCI_trans   BRCLR   SC1SR1,$80,SCI_trans    ;wait for TDRE flag
            LDAA    0,X                     ;load character to accumulator
                                            A
            STAA    SC1DRL                  ;load character to SCI data
                                            register
            INX                             ;increment X
            CPX     #EOT                    ;detect if last character
                                            transmitted
```

```
        BNE     SCI_trans                 ;if last character not equal to
                                          "EOT"
                                          ;branch to SCI_trans else
                                          transmission
                                          ;complete
        RTS                               ;return from subroutine



;------------------------------
;Data for transmission ;
;------------------------------
DATA    FCB     "CPU 12"                  ;
        FCB     $0D,$0A                   ;carriage return, line feed
EOT     FCB     $04                       ;end of data marker
        END                               ;end of program
```

That completes our discussion of the asynchronous SCI system of the 68HC12. In the next portion of this chapter, we discuss the synchronous serial peripheral interface (SPI).

10.5 SPI—SERIAL PERIPHERAL INTERFACE

The serial peripheral interface (SPI) is a synchronous serial communication system. That is, a common clock signal is shared between the transmitter and receiver for data synchronization purposes. Before we begin a detailed discussion of the SPI system, let us review concepts related to the SPI system.

10.5.1 SPI Concepts

Figure 10.18 can be used to develop the concept of SPI communications. Figure 10.18(a) illustrates an edge-triggered D flip-flop. On the rising edge of the clock (CLK), the value on the D input is transferred to the Q output. The value is held on the Q output until the next positive clock edge, when the D input is again transferred to the Q output. The D input is said to be a synchronous input since it is under clock control.

The flip-flop is also equipped with asynchronous inputs designated S for set and R for reset. Asynchronous inputs do not require a clock signal for activation. (Recall that the prefix "a-" means without.) The asynchronous inputs produce their required action when asserted. When a logic 1 is placed on the data input line, the S input is asserted and the output Q is set to logic 1. Yet when a logic 0 is placed

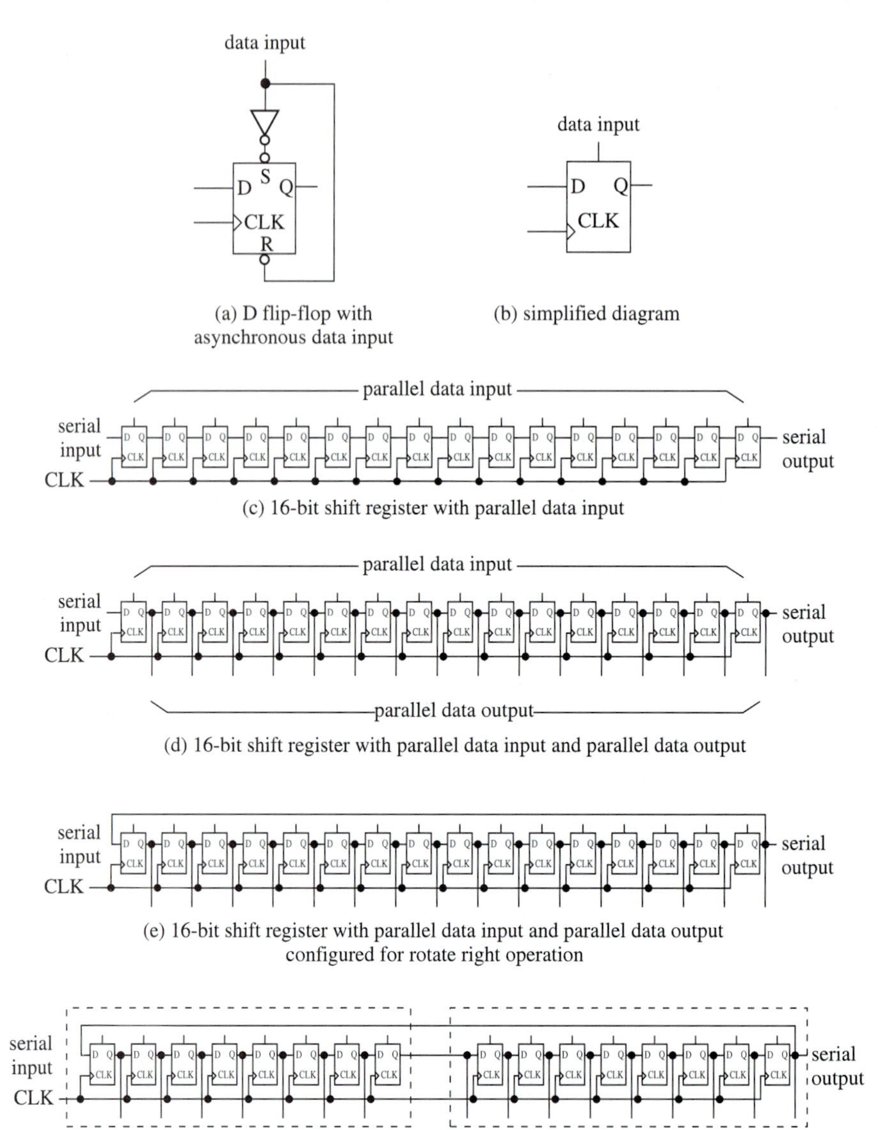

(a) D flip-flop with asynchronous data input

(b) simplified diagram

(c) 16-bit shift register with parallel data input

(d) 16-bit shift register with parallel data input and parallel data output

(e) 16-bit shift register with parallel data input and parallel data output configured for rotate right operation

(f) 16-bit shift register configured for rotate right operation and split into two separate 8-bit shift registers

Figure 10.18 Serial peripheral interface (SPI) concept.

on the data input line, the R input is asserted and the output Q is reset to logic 0. A simplified diagram of this D flip-flop is provided in Figure 10.18(b).

This generic D flip-flop may be configured into a shift register by connecting the Q output from a flip-flop to the input of a subsequent D flip-flop. In Figure 10.18(c), we have connected 16 D flip-flops in sequence to form a 16-bit shift register. We have also provided each flip-flop with a data input, which we collectively refer to as the *parallel data input*.

In Figure 10.18(d), we have added additional output lines to provide for parallel data output for each flip-flip. If the serial output from the last flip-flop in the shift register is connected to the serial input of the first flip-flop in the register, as illustrated in Figure 10.18(e), the output of the last flip-flop rotates to the input of the first flip-flop. In this configuration, data may be loaded in parallel asynchronously and then serially shifted synchronously. With each clock pulse, the contents from each D flip-flop is shifted to the flip-flop to the right. This shifting operation is illustrated in Figure 10.19.

Finally, in Figure 10.18(f), we have separated the 16-bit shift register into two eight-bit halves. The first eight-bit half we could designate as the transmitter and the second eight-bit half as the receiver. We could separate these two halves into two different instruments and effectively have a two-way synchronous, serial transmission system. This is exactly how the SPI in the 68HC12 system operates.

Figure 10.18(f) contains more detail than we need to discuss the operation of the SPI system. Figure 10.20 is a block diagram of the SPI system. This figure provides some new terminology associated with SPI communications. Let us discuss these terms:

Master Mode A 68HC12 configured for master mode generates the serial shift clock (SCK) and initiates data transmission actions. Basically, it is in charge of all slave-configured peripheral components.

Slave Mode A 68HC12 configured in slave mode depends on a master-configured component (another 68HC12 or a peripheral component) to synchro-

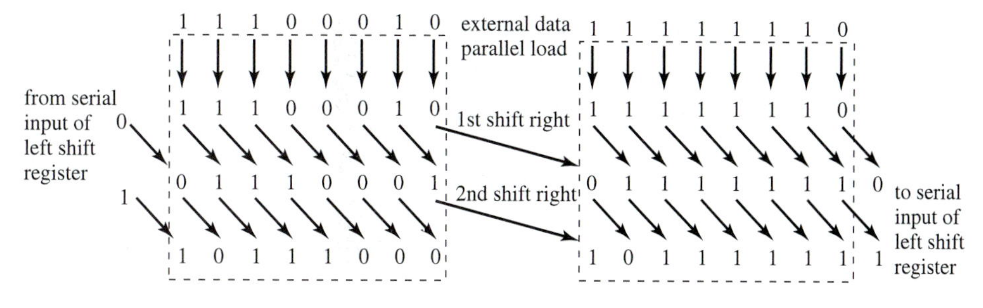

Figure 10.19 Serial shifting with a 16 bit shift register.

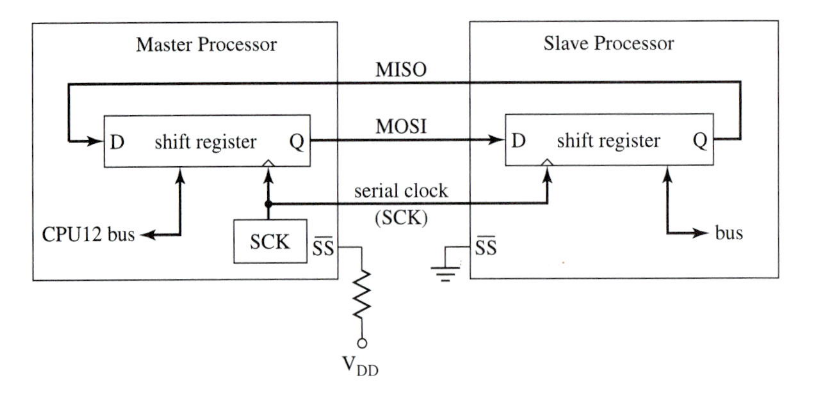

Figure 10.20 Serial peripheral interface block diagram. There are two data connections between the master and slave components. Both of these are defined from the point of view of the master component.

nize and initiate transmission. As the name implies, the slave mode-configured component is submissive to the master mode-configured component.

SCK The serial shift clock (SCK) signal is the synchronization clock between the master and slave components. It controls the rate of data transmission. A single bit is transmitted for each cycle of the SCK. As we see in a later section, the SCK's polarity and phase are fully programmable by the user.

MOSI and MISO There are two data connections between the master and slave components. Both of these are defined from the point of view of the master component. The "Master Out Slave In" (MOSI) line, as its name describes, is the output data line from the master component, which is connected to the input data line of the slave component. Similarly, the "Master In Slave Out" (MISO) line is the output data line from the slave component to the input data line to the master component.

Slave Select The 68HC12 is equipped with a slave select input pin ($\overline{SS}$). The configuration of this pin determines if the 68HC12 is configured for master mode ($\overline{SS} = 1$) or slave mode ($\overline{SS} = 0$) in a system containing a single slave-configured device. Later in this chapter, we discuss how to configure the $\overline{SS}$ pin to select from a number of slave-configured peripheral devices.

10.5.2 SPI General Description

In this section, we provide a general description of an SPI data transfer and some of the features related to the SPI system. We also introduce the function of the SPI-associated registers. In the following section, we discuss these registers in detail describing the function of each register bit. After becoming comfortable with the SPI system hardware, we discuss how to program the SPI system.

The block diagram of the SPI is provided in Figure 10.21. Let us start with the clock source for the SPI system illustrated in the upper left corner of the diagram. The clock source for the SPI system is the P clock. The P clock has the same frequency as the E clock. The P clock is divided by a set of dividers. The output from each of these dividers may be selected by the SPI Baud rate register bits SPR[2:1:0] to establish the clock source for the SPI. The main component of the SPI system is the SPI data register (SP0DR). The SP0DR is configured for SPI operation by SPI control registers 1 and 2 (SP0CR1 and SP0CR2). The SPI status register (SP0SR) sets flags to indicate the status of the SPI system. Finally, the SPI system is interfaced to other peripheral devices via the pins or Port S (MISO, MOSI, SCK, and $\overline{SS}$).

In the SPI system, the 8-bit data register (SP0DR) in the master component and the 8-bit data register (SP0DR) in the slave component are linked to form a distributed 16-bit shift register. We introduced this concept in Figures 10.18 and 10.20. When a data transfer operation is performed, this 16-bit register is serially

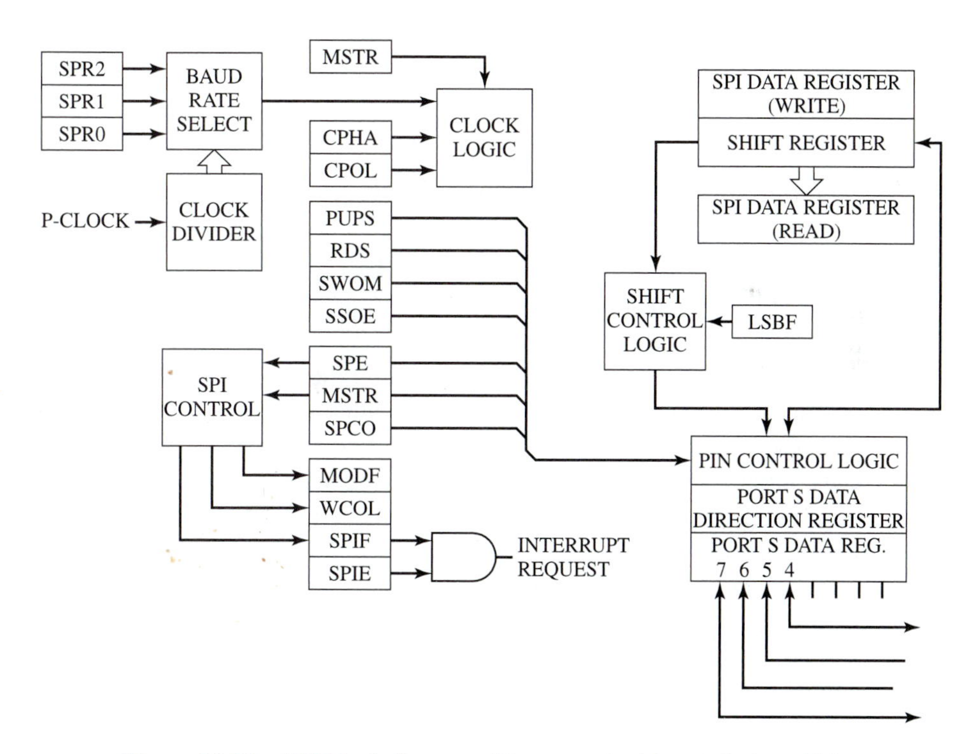

Figure 10.21 SPI block diagram. (Figure used with permission of Motorola, Incorporated.)

shifted by the common SCK clock. For each SCK clock cycle, a single bit is shifted from the master component to the slave component. Simultaneously, as each bit is transferred from master to slave, a bit is also transferred from slave to master. After eight SCK clock cycles have occurred, the data in the master component are effectively exchanged with the data in the slave component. With this general description of the data transfer complete, let us take a closer look at some of the required actions to initiate and complete a data transfer.

To initialize an SPI data transfer, there are a series of initialization steps that must be completed. First, Port S must be configured for SPI operation by setting the appropriate bits in the Data Direction for Port S (DDRS) register. In Figure 10.7, we illustrated how Port S provides the input and output pins for SPI operation. We discuss the details of this configuration step in the next section. Next, the Baud rate and phase of the SCK clock signal must be set. The SCK clock source is derived from the P-clock. We discussed the P-clock in the timer chapter. A clock divider in the SPI hardware produces eight divided P-clock signals. The P-clock divisors are 2, 4, 8, 16, 32, 64, 128, and 256. The SPI Clock Rate Select Bits, SPR[2:1:0], in the SPI Baud Rate Register (SPOBR) select one of the divided P-clock signals to serve as the SCK signal. The SCK signal controls the rate of the shifting from master to slave. The SCK clock can be tailored with four different combinations of serial clock phase and polarity combinations. We discuss these combinations when we discuss the details of the SPI registers.

After setting the baud rate, the SPI control registers (SP0CR1 and SP0CR2) must be configured for desired SPI parameters. For example, both the master and slave components must be properly configured for SPI transmission. The SPI operates in the master mode when the master mode bit (MSTR) in the SPI control register 1 (SP0CR1) is set to logic 1. However, when the MSTR bit is set to logic 0, the SPI component is set for slave operation. Therefore, these bits must be properly configured by the user in both the master and slave SPI components. In addition to properly setting the MSTR bit, the Slave Select pin ($\overline{SS}$) must also be configured on both the master and slave components. Recall, the configuration of this pin determines if the 68HC12 is configured for master mode ($\overline{SS} = 1$) or slave mode ($\overline{SS} = 0$) in a system containing a single master-configured component and a single slave-configured component. The $\overline{SS}$ pin may be controlled via register settings as discussed in the next section for systems containing more than one slave-configured component. Once the $\overline{SS}$ pins are configured for proper operation, the SPI flag in register SP0CR1 must be cleared.

Once both SPI modules have been properly configured as a master or slave component, they must be enabled. The master component must be enabled before the slave-configured component. Components are enabled for SPI operation using the SPI Enable (SPE) bit in the SP0CR1 register. When SPI actions are complete, the slave component should be disabled before disabling the master component.

When initialization actions are complete, SPI data transmission can commence. An SPI data transmission from the master component to the slave component is initiated by writing the character to be transmitted to the SPI data register (SP0DR) in the master component. If the master shift register is empty, the data byte is immediately transferred to the shift register. The byte begins shifting out on the master out, slave in (MOSI) pin under the control of the serial clock (SCK). As the data byte shifts out on the MOSI pin a bit at a time, a byte shifts in from the slave on the master in, slave out (MISO) pin a bit at a time. On the eighth serial clock cycle, the transmission ends and sets the SPI flag (SPIF) in the SPI status register (SP0SR) indicating that transmission is complete. At the same time that the SPIF becomes set, the byte from the slave transfers from the shift register to the slave's SPI data register (SP0DR). If the $\overline{SS}$ pin is under software control, the $\overline{SS}$ must be de-asserted to stop transmission. This two-way communication between the master and slave components provides for a full-duplex serial communication system.

In the slave-configured device, the SPI flag (SPIF) sets to indicate receipt of a character. When the flag is set, the character may be read from the SPI data register (SP0DR). The 68HC12's SPI system is also equipped with several interrupts. The SPIF generates an interrupt request if the SPI interrupt enable (SPIE) bit in the SPI control register 1 is set to logic 1. Like the SPIF flag, the interrupt indicates transmission complete. The other interrupt is related to mode fault detection. It is also enabled by the SPIE bit. The mode fault interrupt flag (MODF) is set and an interrupt occurs when a mode fault is detected. Mode fault conditions occur when contention occurs between master and slave mode settings.

With this general description of the SPI complete, let us take a detailed look at the SPI-related registers.

Practice Questions

Question: What is the difference between the SPI Master and Slave Modes?

Answer: A 68HC12 configured for Master Mode generates the serial shift clock (SCK) and initiates data transmission actions. Basically, it is in charge of all slave-configured peripheral components. A 68HC12 configured in Slave Mode depends on a master-configured component (another 68HC12 or a peripheral component) to synchronize and initiate transmission. As the name implies, the Slave Mode configured component is submissive to the Master Mode configured component.

Question: What is the purpose of the SCK signal?

Answer: The serial shift clock (SCK) signal is the synchronization clock between the master and slave component. It controls the rate of data transmission. A single bit is transmitted for each cycle of the SCK. As we shall see in a later section, the SCK's polarity and phase are fully programmable by the user.

Register: SPI Baud Rate Register (SP0BR) Address: $00D2

7	6	5	4	3	2	1	0
0	0	0	0	0	SPR2	SPR1	SPR0
Reset: 0	0	0	0	0	0	0	0

Figure 10.22 SPI Baud rate register—SP0BR ($00D2).

10.5.3 SPI Registers

The SPI is controlled and configured with associated registers. In this section, we discuss these registers and describe the function of each bit. In the next section, we discuss how to configure these registers for proper SPI operation.

SPI Baud Rate Control Registers The SPI Baud rate register is used to select the frequency of the SPI clock (SCK) and hence the rate of SPI data transmission. Recall that a single bit is transmitted with each clock cycle of the SCK. The SPI Baud rate is set by configuring the SPR[2:1:0] bits as shown in Figure 10.23. The most important thing to note from this figure is how much faster SPI transmission rates are compared with SCI transmission rates discussed earlier in the chapter. Recall that the maximum Baud rate possible with the SCI system was 38,400 Baud. Compare this to the maximum Baud rate of the SPI system illustrated in Figure 10.23.

SPI Control Register 1 The SPI system contains two control registers designated SP0CR1 and SP0CR2 to configure the system for a specific application. SPI control register 1 (SP0CR1) contains the following configuration bits:

SPR[2:1:0]	E Clock Divisor	Frequency at E Clock=4.0 MHz	Frequency at E Clock=8.0 MHz
[0:0:0]	2	2.0 MHz	4.0 MHz
[0:0:1]	4	1.0 MHz	2.0 MHz
[0:1:0]	8	500 KHz	1.0 MHz
[0:1:1]	16	250 KHz	500 KHz
[1:0:0]	32	125 KHz	250 KHz
[1:0:1]	64	62.5 KHz	125 KHz
[1:1:0]	128	31.3 KHz	62.5 KHz
[1:1:1]	256	15.6 KHz	31.3 KHz

Figure 10.23 SPI Clock Rate Selection.

Register: SPI Control Register 1 (SP0CR1) Address: $00D0

	7	6	5	4	3	2	1	0
	SPIE	SPE	SWOM	MSTR	CPOL	CPHA	SSOE	LSBF
Reset:	0	0	0	0	0	1	0	0

Figure 10.24 SPI Control Register 1—SP0CR1 ($00D0).

SPIE The SPI interrupt enable bit allows a hardware interrupt sequence (described in the interrupt and reset chapter) to occur each time the SPIF (SPI interrupt request) and the MODF (SPI mode error interrupt status flag) in the SPI status register (described later) are set.

SPE The SPI system enable bit is the on/off switch for the SPI system. When this bit is logic 0, the SPI system is placed in a low-power disabled state. When the SPE bit is set to logic 1, bits 4 to 7 of Port S are dedicated to the SPI function.

SWOM Port S Wired-OR Mode. The Wired-OR Mode for Port S bit allows Port S[4:7] pins to operate in an open drain configuration when set to logic 1. Open drain-configured gates allow the outputs from several gates to be tied directly together and then connected to an external pullup resistor. (Again, this is usually forbidden in other gate configurations!)

MSTR The SPI Master/Slave Mode Select bit configures the SPI hardware for master mode (MSTR = 1) or Slave Mode (MSTR = 0).

CPOL The SPI clock (SCK) may be configured in several different variations using the SPI clock polarity (CPOL) bit and the SPI clock phase (CPHA) bit. Together these two bits are used to specify the clock format to be used in SPI operations. To transmit between SPI modules, both modules must have identical CPOL and CPHA values. When the clock polarity bit (CPOL) is cleared and data are not being transferred, the SCK pin of the master device is low. When CPOL is set, the SCK idles high.

CPHA The SPI clock phase bit determines whether a falling $\overline{SS}$ edge or the first SCK edge begins the transmission. When CPHA = 0, a falling edge $\overline{SS}$ signals the slave to begin transmission. After transmission of all eight bits, the slave $\overline{SS}$ pin must toggle from low to high to low again to begin another character transmission. This format is preferable in systems having more than one slave-configured device. When CPHA = 1, the master begins driving its MOSI pin and the slave begins driving its MISO pin on the first serial clock edge. The $\overline{SS}$ pin can remain low

Register: SPI Control Register 2 (SP0CR2) Address: $00D1

	7	6	5	4	3	2	1	0
	0	0	0	0	PUPS	RDS	0	SPC0
Reset:	0	0	0	0	1	0	0	0

Figure 10.25 SPI Control Register 2—SP0CR2 ($00D1).

between transmissions. This format may be preferable in systems having only one slave driving the master MISO line.

SSOE The slave select output enable ($\overline{SS}$) output feature is enabled only in the master mode by asserting the SSOE bit and DDRS7 bit.

LSBF The SPI least significant bit first enable bit controls the direction that data are shifted out of the SPI system. When the LSBF bit is set to 0, data are shifted out of the SPI system most significant bit first. Yet, when the LSBF bit is set to 1, data are shifted out of the SPI system least significant bit first. Normally data are transferred most significant bit first.

SPI Control Register 2 SPI control register 2 (SP0CR2) has three configurable bits. They are:

PUPS The Pull-Up Port S Enable bit when set to logic 1, all Port S input pins are configured with active pull-up devices.

RDS The Reduce Drive of Port S bit when set to logic 1, configures Port S output pins for reduced drive capability. This configuration reduces power consumption.

SPC0 The Serial Pin Control 0 bit in conjunction with the MSTR control bit (previously described) determines serial pin configurations as illustrated in Figure 10.26.

As mentioned previously, bits within the SPI control registers (SP0CR1 and SP0CR2) specify the operation of the SPI hardware. Specifically, the SPC0 bit in register SP0CR2 and the MSTR bit in SP0CR1 specify the operational configuration of the SPI as illustrated in Figure 10.26. For example, if the SPC0 is set to 0 and the MSTR to 1, the MISO pin is configured as the master input pin and the MOSI pin as the master output pin. Furthermore, the SCK pin is configured as the SCK output signal and the $\overline{SS}$ pin is configured for input or output. The notes (1–5) in Figure 10.26 provide further guidance on using additional DDRS pins for enabling the signals. We illustrate the use of these features in the upcoming programming examples.

	Pin Mode	SPCO[1]	MSTR	MISO[2]	MOSI[3]	SCK[4]	$\overline{SS}$[5]
#1	Normal	0	0	Slave Out	Slave In	SCK In	$\overline{SS}$ In
#2	Normal	0	1	Master In	Master Out	SCK Out	$\overline{SS}$ I/O
#3	Bidirectional	1	0	Slave I/O	GPI/O	SCK In	$\overline{SS}$ In
#4	Bidirectional	1	1	GPI/O	Master I/O	SCK Out	$\overline{SS}$ I/O

1. The serial pin control 0 bit enables bidirectional configurations.
2. Slave output is enabled if DDRS4=1, SS=0, and MSTR=0. (#1, #3)
3. Master output is enabled if DDRS5=1 and MSTR=1. (#2, #4)
4. SCK output is enabled if DDRS6=1 and MSTR=1. (#2, #4)
5. $\overline{SS}$ output is enabled if DDRS7=1, SSOE=1 and MSTR=1. (#2, #4)

$\overline{SS}$ Output Selection

DDRS7	SSOE	Master Mode	Slave Mode
0	0	$\overline{SS}$ input with MODF feature	$\overline{SS}$ Input
0	1	Reserved	$\overline{SS}$ Input
1	0	General-Purpose Output	$\overline{SS}$ Input
1	1	$\overline{SS}$ Output	$\overline{SS}$ Input

Normal Mode and Bidirectional Mode

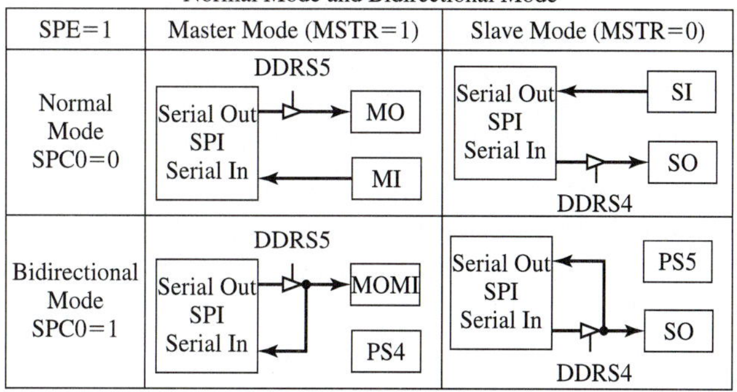

Figure 10.26 SPI mode selection. Bits within the SPI control registers specify the operation of the SPI hardware. Specifically, the SPC0 bit in register SP0CR2 and the MSTR bit in SP0CR1 specify the operational configuration of the SPI.

As can be seen in Figure 10.26, the SPI system may be configured for normal or bidirectional modes. In the bidirectional mode, the SPI system uses only one serial pin for external device interface connections.

SPI Status Register The SPI status register (SP0SR) contains three flag bits: SPIF, WCOL, and MODF.

Register: SPI Baud Rate Register (SP0BR) Address: $00D2

	7	6	5	4	3	2	1	0
	0	0	0	0	0	SPR2	SPR1	SPR0
Reset:	0	0	0	0	0	0	0	0

Figure 10.27 SPI Status Register—SP0SR ($00D3).

SPIF The SPI interrupt request bit is set to indicate the transmission of eight bits of peripheral data transmission. It is set after the eighth clock of the SCK cycle in a data transfer and it is cleared by reading the SP0SR register followed by a read or write to the SPI data register.

WCOL The write collision status flag is set to logic 1 to indicate that a serial transfer was in progress when the 68HC12 tried to write new data into the serial peripheral data register (SP0DR).

MODF The mode error interrupt status flag is set automatically by the SPI hardware if the master control (MSTR) bit is set and the slave select input pin ($\overline{SS}$) becomes zero. Basically, the MSTR bit is trying to place the SPI system in master mode while the $\overline{SS}$ pin is trying to place the SPI system in slave mode.

SPI Data Registers The SPI data register (SP0DR) serves as both the input and output data register for the SPI system. As previously discussed, the data register in the master-configured device is serially linked to the data register in the slave-configured device to form a 16-bit shift register. When a data transfer operation is initiated, this shift register is shifted eight times (once for each pulse of the SCK clock). This results in a data exchange between the master and slave-configured devices. Note that some of the more simple slave-configured peripheral devices either accept data from the master and do not return data or pass data to the master without requiring input data from the master-configured device.

Register: SPI Data Register (SP0DR) Address: $00D5

	7	6	5	4	3	2	1	0
	Bit 7	Bit 6	Bit 5	Bit 4	Bit 3	Bit 2	Bit 1	Bit 0
Reset:	0	0	0	0	0	0	0	0

Figure 10.28 SPI Data Register—SP0DR ($00D5).

Port S Data Register—Port S The Port S data register (called Port S) may be used as a general-purpose input port. However, it also provides the input

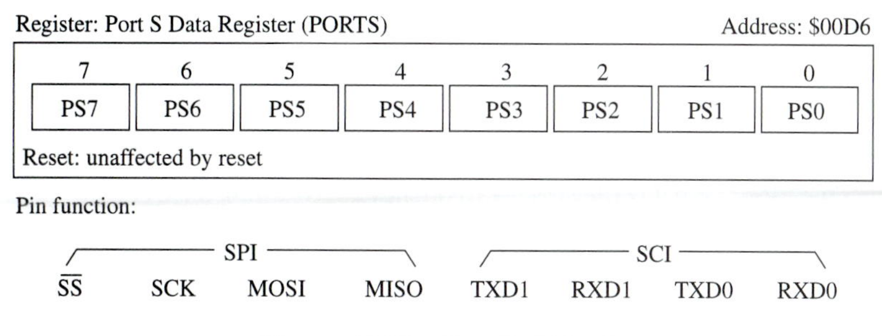

Figure 10.29 Port S ($00D6).

and output pins for the SCI (TXD1, RXD1, TXD0, and RXD0) system and SPI ($\overline{SS}$, SCK, MOSI, and MISO) system as illustrated in Figure 10.29.

Data Direction Register for Port S—DDRS As mentioned previously, Port S may be used as a general-purpose I/O port. The data direction register for Port S (DDRS) configures the different pins on Port S for either an input or output. When a specific bit in the DDRS register is set to logic 0, the corresponding pin in Port S is configured as an input pin. Yet when a specific bit in the DDRS register is set to logic 1, the corresponding pin in Port S is configured as an output pin. When used as SCI and SPI input and output pins, the following restrictions apply:

DDRS2, DDRS0 If the SCI receiver is configured for two-wire SCI operation, corresponding port S pins are input regardless of the state of these bits.

DDRS3, DDRS1 If the SCI receiver is configured for two-wire SCI operation, corresponding port S pins are output regardless of the state of these bits.

DDRS[6:4] If the SPI is enabled and expects the corresponding Port S to be an input, it is an input regardless of the state of the DDRS bit. If the SPI is enabled and expects the bit to be an output, it is an output only if the DDRS bit is set.

DDRS7 In the SPI slave mode, DDRS7 has no meaning or effect; Port S pin 7 is dedicated as the ($\overline{SS}$) input pin. In SPI master mode, DDRS7 determines whether Port S pin 7 is an error-detect input to the SPI, a general-purpose line, or a slave select output line.

Register: Ports S Data Direction Register (DDRS) Address: $00D7

	7	6	5	4	3	2	1	0
	DDRS7	DDRS6	DDRS5	DDRS4	DDRS3	DDRS2	DDRS1	DDRS0
Reset:	0	0	0	0	0	0	0	0

Figure 10.30 DDRS ($00D7).

Practice Questions

Question: What is the maximum frequency for SPI transfer when the ECLK = 8 MHz?

Answer: When SPR[2:1:0] bits are set to 000, the the SPI frequency is 4 MHz.

Question: What is the slowest frequency for SPI transfer when the ECLK = 4 MHz?

Answer: When SPR[2:1:0] bits are set for 111, the the SPI frequency is 15.6 KHz.

Question: Provide the assembly language code to set the SPI to the lowest frequency.

Answer:

```
SP0BR       EQU     $00D2       ;SPI Baud rate register address
SPRMASK     EQU     $07         ;set SPR bits to 111

            LDAA    #SPRMASK    ;load mask
            STAA    SP0BR       ;
              :
```

Question: What is the purpose of the SPIF bit?

Answer: The SPI interrupt request bit is set to indicate the transmission of eight bits of peripheral data transmission. It is set after the eighth clock of the SCK cycle in a data transfer and it is cleared by reading the SP0SR register followed by a read or write to the SPI data register.

10.5.4 Programming the SPI

Earlier in this chapter we discussed required actions to initiate SPI transmission. These actions are summarized in the form of a flowchart provided in Figure 10.31. We illustrate in this section how to program the SPI for initialization and character transmission.

Example

In this example, we provide the assembly code to initialize the SPI system and transmit characters via subroutines. We have named these subroutines: SPI_ini and SPI_trans. We have left the subroutine to receive characters (SPI_rx) via the SPI as a homework exercise.

Requirement: Configure the SPI system as a master-configured device. The slave-configured peripheral device is chip selected with the slave select ($\overline{SS}$) line. Recall this is accomplished by configuring the SPI clock phase (CPHA) bit in the SPI control register 1 (SP0CR1) to a logic 0. In this configuration, the $\overline{SS}$ control line returns to logic high between character transmission, thus providing chip select action. As a further constraint, do not allow the serial clock (SCK) rate to exceed 75

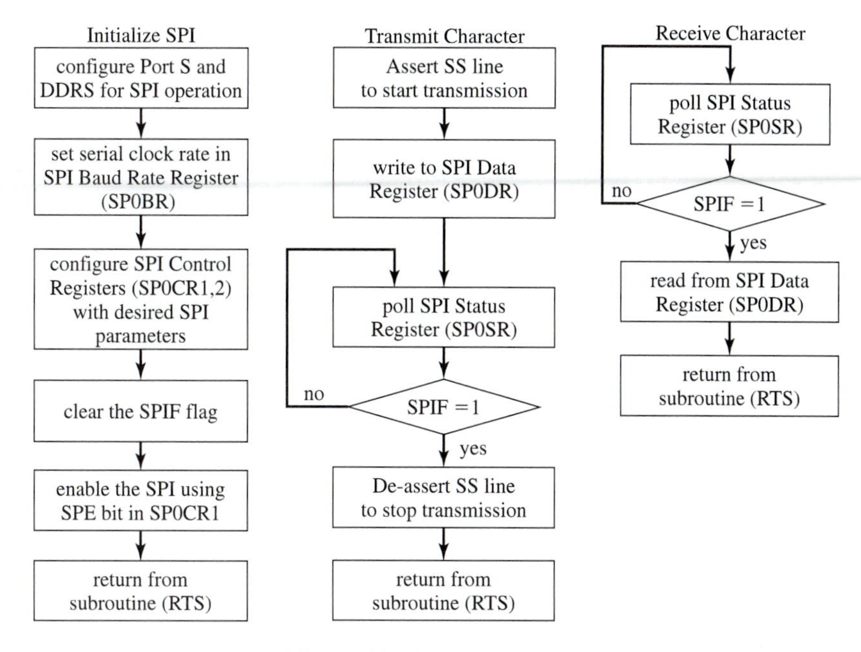

Figure 10.31 SPI activities.

Khz. Assume the ECLK rate is 4 MHz. Note that our programming actions follows the flowcharts of Figure 10.31.

Note: Let us assume that all 68HC12-related registers have been defined with EQU directives in a header file designated "68HC12REG.ASM."

The main program serves as a base of operations. From the main program, we call the subroutines to initialize the SPI system using the subroutine "SPI_ini" and then transmit characters using the subroutine "SPI_trans."

```
INCLUDE '68HC12REG.ASM'
;-------------------------------------
;MAIN PROGRAM ;
;-------------------------------------
        ORG     $7000           ;User RAM at $7000

        BSR     SPI_ini         ;Subroutine to initialize SPI
        BSR     SPI_trans       ;Subroutine to start transmission
DONE:   BRA     DONE            ;Branch to self
```

The "SPI_ini" subroutine follows the SPI initialization actions outlined in Figure 10.31.

```
;-------------------------------------
;Subroutine SPI_ini: Initialize SPI ;
;-------------------------------------

SPI_ini  BSET   PORTS,$80       ;Set SS line to high to disable slave
                                during SPI config
         MOVB   #$E0,DDRS       ;Configure Port S input/output levels
                                for MOSI and SCK,
                                ;SS configured for output, MISO for
                                input
         MOVB   #$05, SP0BR     ;Select serial clock rate of 62.5 KHz
         MOVB   #$12,SP0CR1     ;Configure SP0CR1 for no interrupts,
                                ;MSTR=1, CPOL=0, CPHA=0
         MOVB   #$08,SP0CR2     ;Configure SP0CR2 for normal
                                Port S drive and
                                ;active pull-up devices
         LDX    #DATA           ;use X register as pointer to 1st
                                character
         LDAA   SP0SR           ;1st step to clear SPIF: Read SP0SR
         LDAA   SP0DR           ;2nd step to clear SPIF:Read SP0DR
         BSET   SP0CR1, $40     ;Enable the SPI: SPE bit = 1
         RTS                    ;return from subroutine
```

The "SPI_trans" subroutine sends a single character at a time. The slave-configured peripheral device is chip selected with the slave select ($\overline{SS}$) line. In this configuration, the $\overline{SS}$ control line is returned to logic high between character transmission, thus providing chip select action.

```
;-------------------------------------
;Transmit Subroutine ;
;-------------------------------------
SPI_trans  LDAA   0,X                ;load character to accumulator A
           INX                       ;increment X
           BEQ    DONE               ;Test for last character. If EOT
                                     branch
                                     ;to done, else continue
           BCLR   PORTS, $80         ;Assert SS (active low) to start
           STAA   SP0DR              ;load character to SPI data register
WAIT       BRCLR  SP0SR, $80, WAIT   ; wait for SPIF flag in SP0SR
           BSET   PORTS, $80         ;de-assert SS line
           BRA    SPI_trans          ;continue character transmission
DONE       RTS                       ;return from subroutine
```

```
;-----------------------------------
;Data for transmission ;
;-----------------------------------
DATA    FCB 'CPU 12"                                    ;
        FCB     $0D,$0A         ;carriage return, line feed
EOT     FCB     $00             ;end of data marker
        END                     ;end of program
```

The FCB designator is an assembler directive to form character byte. It allows the declaration of ASCII string character and control variables.

That completes our discussion of programming the synchronous SPI system of the 68HC12. In the programming example, we purposely did not discuss details of the slave device. In this next section, we show the plethora of devices that can be used to extend the features of the 68HC12. We also demonstrate how to configure and program a peripheral device.

10.5.5 SPI Applications

You have probably already realized that, although the 68HC12 is a powerful and flexible processor, it may lack desired hardware in certain applications. What should we do in such situations? It turns out the SPI system may be used to connect many different peripheral devices to the 68HC12. Motorola, along with other manufacturers, have developed many varied peripheral devices to extend the features of the 68HC12. Provided here is a brief (and incomplete) list of SPI comptaible peripherals. These devices include:

- additional memory components,
- additional ports,
- a real-time clock,
- a phase-locked loop,
- a frequency-modulated (FM) transmitter/receiver set,
- a higher resolution (more than eight-bit) analog-to-digital converters,
- a light-emitting diode (LED) and liquid crystal display (LCD) drivers, and
- a multiple channel digital-to-analog converters.

Example

Rather than describe all of these peripherals, we cover one in detail since the connection and programming of the other peripheral devices are similar. As a case study, we discuss how to configure the SPI system with a Motorola MC144111 digital-to-analog converter (DAC) system. To fully discuss the configuration of the MC144111 to the SPI system, we follow this step-by-step design approach:

1. Review the hardware details of the MC144111.
2. Determine the hardware connections between the SPI system and the MC144111.
3. Examine the timing relationship between the SPI system and the MC144111.
4. Program the SPI system.

Digital-to-Analog Converter Before getting into the details of the MC144111 DAC system, let us discuss digital-to-analog converters (DAC) in general. A DAC translates a multibit binary input into a corresponding analog output (Figure 10.32). We do not discuss the different methods of DAC conversions. We simply treat the DAC as a black box and describe its function with a block diagram. The analog output is provided by summing the weighted binary inputs as shown in Figure 10.32.

Example

The full-scale (FS) voltage (where $FS = V_{RH} - V_{RL}$) of an eight-bit DAC is 5 volts with the high- and low-reference voltages of 5 volts and 0 volts. If the binary input is $F0, what is the analog output voltage? This voltage is determined using the following weighted sum for the $F0 input:

$$V_{out} = 5[(1 \cdot 1/2) + (1 \cdot 1/4) + (1 \cdot 1/8) + (1 \cdot 1/16) + (0 \cdot 1/32) + (0 \cdot 1/64) + (0 \cdot 1/128) + (0 \cdot 1/256)]$$

$$V_{out} = 4.6875 \text{ volts}$$

With this general description of the DAC, let us take a detailed look at the Motorola MC144111 DAC.

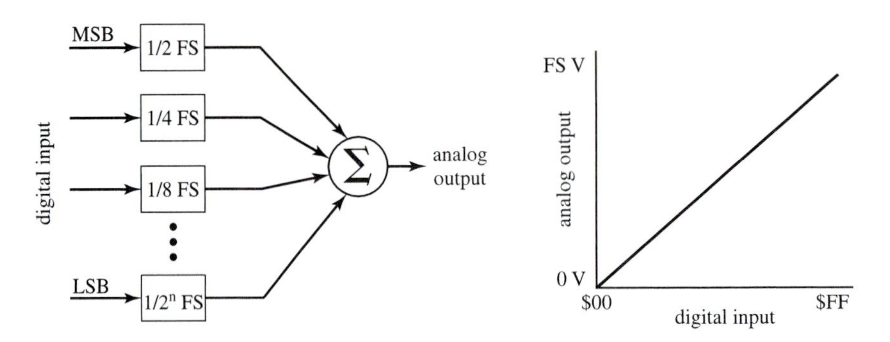

Figure 10.32 A digital-to-analog converter (DAC). A DAC translates a multibit binary input into a corresponding analog output. The analog output is provided by summing the weighted binary inputs.

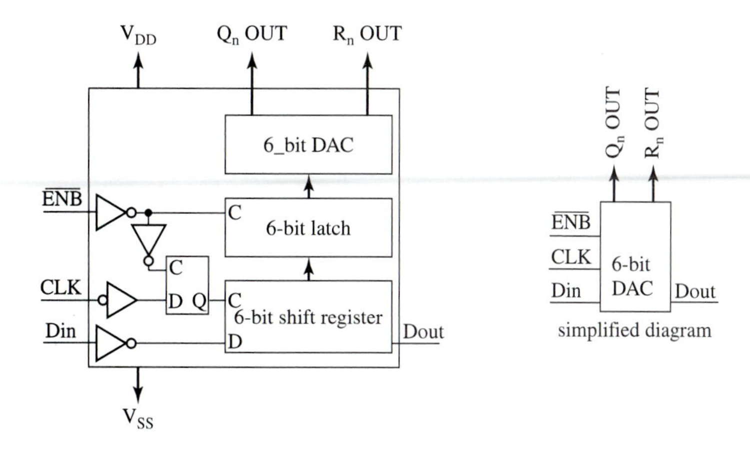

Figure 10.33 The Motorola MC144111 four-channel, six-bit digital-to-analog converter. Each six-bit binary input is converted to a corresponding analog value.

Case Study: The MC144111 Digital-to-Analog Converter The Motorola MC144111 is a four-channel, six-bit DAC. That is, the MC144111 contains four duplicate DAC channels each configured with a six-bit input. Therefore, each six-bit binary input is converted to a corresponding analog value as described in the previous section. The block diagram of the MC144111 is shown in Figure 10.33. The full-scale (FS) range of this DAC is $V_{DD} - V_{SS}$. The voltage V_{SS} is normally grounded while the value of V_{DD} may be set for a value from 4.5 to 15 VDC.

The MC144111 is equipped with three inputs ($\overline{ENB}$, CLK, and D_{in}) and outputs (Q_n OUT, R_n OUT, and D_{out}). A brief definition of each of these pins are:

negative logic enable The negative logic enable ($\overline{ENB}$) must be low during the serial load. On the low-to-high transition of this pin, data contained in the DAC shift register are loaded into the latch and converted to an analog value.

shift register clock The shift register clock (CLK) shifts in a single bit on the data input line (D_{in}) on the high-to-low transition of the CLK. The MC144111 requires 24 clock cycles (four channels at six bits/channel) to load the 24 bits required by the DAC.

data in Six-bit words are entered serially, most significant bit (MSB) first. Four six-bit words are loaded into the MC144111 for each DAC cycle.

Q OUT These analog-buffered outputs were specifically designed for interface to low-impedance circuits.

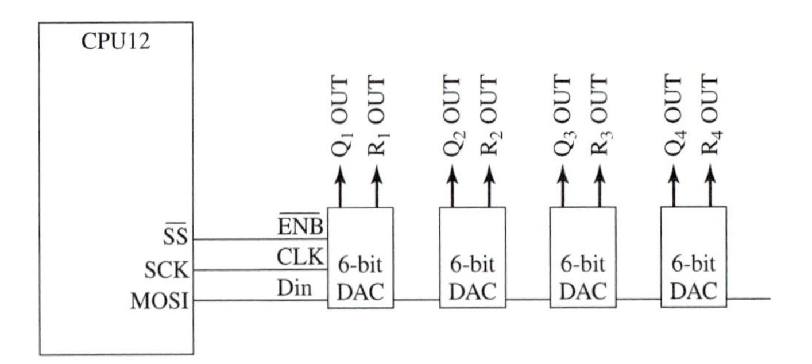

Figure 10.34 The 68HC12 SPI configured with the Motorola MC144111.

R OUT These analog outputs were designed for interface to high-impedance circuits such as a field-effect transistor (FET) input-configured operational amplifier.

data out The digital data output is used for cascading the DACs together for multichannel DAC configurations. The D_{out} pin is connected to D_{in} of the next stage.

Hardware Connections between the SPI System and MC144111 Now that we have examined the hardware input and output pins of the MC144111, can you sketch the connection between the SPI system and the MC144111? Take a moment and sketch the interconnection diagram before looking at Figure 10.34. How did you do? If you did not sketch a correct connection, go back and review the definitions of each of the SPI pins discussed earlier in the chapter.

Timing Relationships—SPI and the MC144111 A detailed timing analysis must be accomplished by examining the timing requirements of the SPI system and the MC144111 much like we did in analyzing memory timing in an earlier chapter. We do not provide a detailed analysis here. Instead let us examine the timing diagram of the MC144111 to determine how to configure the SPI system. The timing diagram for the MC144111 is provided in Figure 10.35. As mentioned previously, the negative logic enable ($\overline{ENB}$) must be low during the serial load. On the low-to-high transition of this pin, data contained in the DAC shift register are loaded into the latch and converted to an analog value. The shift register clock (CLK) shifts in a single bit on the data input line (D_{in}) on the high-to-low clock transition. The MC144111 requires 24 clock cycles (four channels at six bits/channel) to load the 24 bits required by the DAC. Based on your knowledge of the SPI system, how must the SPI's slave select line ($\overline{SS}$) be configured for connection to the MC144111 DAC? The slave select line must be configured for

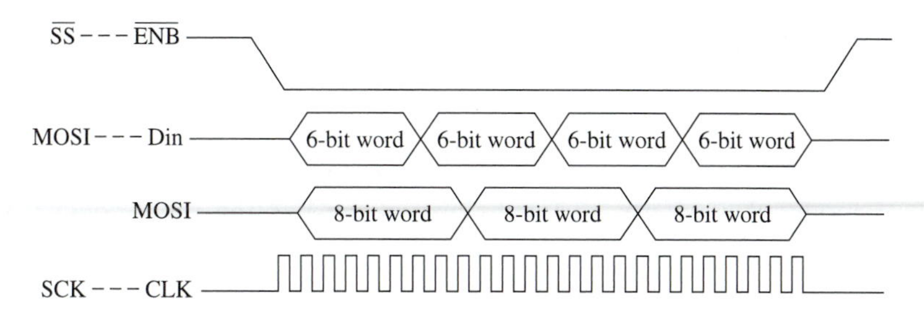

Figure 10.35 Timing for the MC144111 DAC.

output and the clock phase (CPHA) bit must be set to 0 to use the slave select line as a chip select to assert and de-assert the slave through the MC144111's $\overline{ENB}$ control bit.

Programming the SPI System In the previous section, we discussed how to program the SPI for initialization and transmission. How must the code provided in the previous example be modified for this MC144111 application? In the example, we asserted the slave select line, sent an ASCII character, and then de-asserted the slave select line after each character. In this example, we must modify the code to assert the slave select line, transmit 24 bits of data corresponding to the four each six binary inputs for the four DAC channels, and then de-assert the slave select line. This is left as a homework assignment for you. This completes our discussion of the SPI system and our discussion of the serial communication features of the 68HC12.

10.6 LABORATORY APPLICATION

LABORATORY EXERCISE: PUTTING IT ALL TOGETHER: AN OPERATIONAL MOBILE ROBOT

Purpose The lab provides a chance to put together what you have learned from this book by creating your own maze navigating robot. Your goal is to use your assembly programming skills, knowledge of the 68HC12 microcontroller, and I/O interface skills to make your mobile robot (I hope you have named your robot by now) move through a preconstructed maze without bumping into walls. The map for the maze is included at the end of this lab. Your goal is to complete the task of maze navigation (finding an exit and moving out of the maze) as fast as possible. You are free to come up with your own strategy to accomplish this goal: various duty cycles, no acceleration or deceleration for straight motions, different patterns of IR sensing combined with motion control methods, and so on.

Documentation EVB User's manual

Prelab For the prelab, you must have a flow-chart and pseudo code for your robot navigation program.

Description

Maze The dimensions of the maze are given in Figure 10.36. The maze is a modified version used for the annual fire-fighting robot contest held at Trinity College in Hartford, Connecticut. Each maze has three different exits, as shown in the figure, and your score reflects which of the three exits your robot uses to get out of the maze.

Rules

1. Your robot always starts at the position designated by the label "HOME."
2. Initially your robot must be completely within the HOME circle.
3. You inform your referee which one of the three exits your robot has chosen to exit before starting your robot.
4. Your robot is considered to successfully complete the navigation only if it finds the predesignated exit and completely moves out of the maze.
5. There is a time limit of 3 minutes for each robot to complete the task.

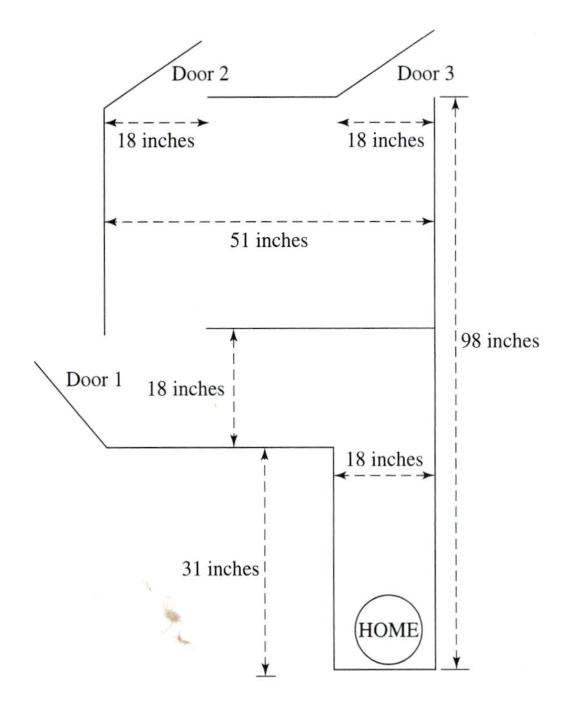

Figure 10.36 The maze used for mobile robot navigation competitions

6. Each robot gets three chances to complete the task, and the two best scores are used to compute the average score.
7. Your robot must exit door number 1 (see the figure) during at least one of the three trials.

Tabulating Your Score Your goal is to move your robot as quickly as possible through a maze exit. The score depends on what exit you choose, the number of collisions your robot had during a run, and whether the robot has successfully completed a selected task. Each run must be completed within 3 minutes or the run is considered incomplete and receives 180 seconds for the run. For each run, only ONE door is opened.

Door #1 If you choose this door as the exit for your robot, the total navigation score is computed by multiplying the navigation time in seconds by 1.x, where $x = 2n$ and n is the number of times your robot comes in contact with any maze wall. If n exceeds numerical number 3, the run is considered incomplete and the run automatically receives 3 minutes.

Door #2 and Door #3 If you choose Door #2 or Door #3 as the exit for your robot, the total navigation score is computed using the following two rules.

(a) The rules specified in part A of Door #1 are applied first, and

(b) the resulting value from part (a) is then multiplied by 0.5 or 0.2, for Door #2 selection or Door #3 selection, respectively.

Your two best scores are used to get an average score, and the average score is your score for the competition. The robot with a minimum score is declared as the winner of the competition. You are encouraged but not required to use a fuzzy logic controller, relating sensor values with robot control signals, to navigate your robot through the maze.

10.7 SUMMARY

In this chapter, we discussed the serial communication features of the 68HC12. Specifically, we saw the 68HC12 (A4 version) is configured with two separate and distinct asynchronous SCI channels and a single synchronous SPI channel. The synchronous SPI channel provides for faster data transmission at the expense of additional synchronous serial clock control signal (SCK). For both the SCI and SPI systems. we examined the hardware operation in detail, looked at the registers associated with each system, and then discussed how to program each system. We then examined applications for both the SCI and SPI systems.

10.8 CHAPTER PROBLEMS

Fundamental

1. What is the ASCII coding for "D. Pack"? (Assume a seven-bit ASCII character code is used as illustrated in Figure 10.4.)
2. In the prior question, if the most significant bit (MSB) was used as an odd parity bit, what would the ASCII coding be for "D. Pack"?
3. Assuming the MSB is used as an odd parity bit, what character stream is represented by the following ASCII code $D3, $E3, $EF, $EF, $62, $79, $AD, $C4, $EF, $EF, $A1?
4. How long would it take to transmit this ASCII code stream assuming a transmission rate of 1200 BAUD?
5. How does the SCI system achieve synchronization between the transmitter and receiver? How about the SPI system?
6. What is the maximum data transmission rate possible with the SCI system? the SPI system? Comment on the relative difference between the two rates.
7. Reference the prior question. Why is the maximum data rate of the SPI system so much faster than the SCI system? What is the cost of this higher data transmission rate?

Advanced

1. Write a subroutine that properly initializes SCI1 for eight data bits, one stop bit to be transmitted at 2400 Baud. The 68HC12 is operated with an MCLK of 8 MHz crystal.
2. An asynchronous SCI serial port configured for eight data bits, even parity, and two stop bits outputs the word "68HC12" at 9600 Baud. Show the timing of the output signal on the serial line if the 68HC12 is operated with an MCLK of 4 MHz crystal.
3. The serial port described in the previous question must output a 3K-byte buffer to another computer system. How much time is required for this data transfer.
4. Write a subroutine called SCI_rx to receive characters via the SCI system. Use the same SCI system parameters provided in the text in section "Programming the SCI."
5. Sketch the output relationship for a six-bit digital-to-analog converter. That is, sketch the relationship between output voltage and the six-bit binary input.

Challenging

1. The Motorola MC144110 is a six-channel digital-to-analog converter. Each channel converts a six-bit binary representation to a corresponding analog voltage. The MC144110 has the same hardware configuration and timing specifications of the MC144111 discussed in the chapter. (1) Design the interface between the SPI system and the MC144110, (2) show the timing relationships between the two devices, and

(3) write an assembly language program to initialize the SPI and transmit data from the SPI to the MC144110.

2. In the chapter, we discussed how to program the SPI for initialization and transmission. In the chapter's SPI example, we asserted the slave select line, sent an ASCII character, and then de-asserted the slave select line after each character. Modify the example code to assert the slave select line, transmit 24 bits of data corresponding to the four each six binary inputs for the four MC144111 DAC channels, and then de-assert the slave select line.

A

68HC12 Instruction Set

(Table used with permission of Motorola, Incorporated)

Notation Used in Instruction Set Summary

Explanation of Italic Expressions in Source Form Column

abc — A or B or CCR

abcdxys — A or B or CCR or D or X or Y or SP. Some assemblers also allow T2 or T3.

abd — A or B or D

abdxys — A or B or D or X or Y or SP

dxys — D or X or Y or SP

msk8 — 8-bit mask, some assemblers require # symbol before value

opr8i — 8-bit immediate value

opr16i — 16-bit immediate value

opr8a — 8-bit address used with direct address mode

opr16a — 16-bit address value

oprx0_xysp — Indexed addressing postbyte code:

- *oprx3,–xys* Predecrement X or Y or SP by 1 . . . 8
- *oprx3,+xys* Preincrement X or Y or SP by 1 . . . 8
- *oprx3,xys–* Postdecrement X or Y or SP by 1 . . . 8
- *oprx3,xys+* Postincrement X or Y or SP by 1 . . . 8
- *oprx5,xysp* 5-bit constant offset from X or Y or SP or PC
- *abd,xysp* Accumulator A or B or D offset from X or Y or SP or PC

oprx3 — Any positive integer 1 . . . 8 for pre/post increment/decrement

oprx5 — Any value in the range –16 . . . +15

oprx9 — Any value in the range –256 . . . +255

oprx16 — Any value in the range –32,768 . . . 65,535

page — 8-bit value for PPAGE, some assemblers require # symbol before this value

rel8 — Label of branch destination within –256 to +255 locations

rel9 — Label of branch destination within –512 to +511 locations

rel16 — Any label within 64K memory space

trapnum — Any 8-bit value in the range $30-$39 or $40-$FF

xys — X or Y or SP

xysp — X or Y or SP or PC

CPU12 REFERENCE GUIDE

Address Modes

IMM — Immediate
IDX — Indexed (no extension bytes) includes:
  5-bit constant offset
  Pre/post increment/decrement by 1 . . . 8
  Accumulator A, B, or D offset
IDX1 — 9-bit signed offset (1 extension byte)
IDX2 — 16-bit signed offset (2 extension bytes)
[D, IDX] — Indexed indirect (accumulator D offset)
[IDX2] — Indexed indirect (16-bit offset)
INH — Inherent (no operands in object code)
REL — 2's complement relative offset (branches)

Machine Coding

`dd` — 8-bit direct address $0000 to $00FF. (High byte assumed to be $00).

`ee` — High-order byte of a 16-bit constant offset for indexed addressing.

`eb` — Exchange/Transfer post-byte.

`ff` — Low-order eight bits of a 9-bit signed constant offset for indexed addressing, or low-order byte of a 16-bit constant offset for indexed addressing.

`hh` — High-order byte of a 16-bit extended address.

`ii` — 8-bit immediate data value.

`jj` — High-order byte of a 16-bit immediate data value.

`kk` — Low-order byte of a 16-bit immediate data value.

`lb` — Loop primitive (DBNE) post-byte.

`ll` — Low-order byte of a 16-bit extended address.

`mm` — 8-bit immediate mask value for bit manipulation instructions. Set bits indicate bits to be affected.

`pg` — Program page (bank) number used in CALL instruction.

`qq` — High-order byte of a 16-bit relative offset for long branches.

`tn` — Trap number $30–$39 or $40–$FF.

`rr` — Signed relative offset $80 (–128) to $7F (+127). Offset relative to the byte following the relative offset byte, or low-order byte of a 16-bit relative offset for long branches.

`xb` — Indexed addressing post-byte.

Access Detail

Each code letter equals one CPU cycle. Uppercase = 16-bit operation and lowercase = 8-bit operation. For complex sequences see the *CPU12 Reference Manual* (CPU12RM/AD).

f — Free cycle, CPU doesn't use bus
g — Read PPAGE internally
I — Read indirect pointer (indexed indirect)
i — Read indirect PPAGE value (call indirect)
n — Write PPAGE internally
O — Optional program word fetch (P) if instruction is misaligned and has an odd number of bytes of object code — otherwise, appears as a free cycle (f)
P — Program word fetch (always an aligned word read)
r — 8-bit data read
R — 16-bit data read
s — 8-bit stack write
S — 16-bit stack write
w — 8-bit data write
W — 16-bit data write
u — 8-bit stack read
U — 16-bit stack read
V — 16-bit vector fetch
t — 8-bit conditional read (or free cycle)
T — 16-bit conditional read (or free cycle)
x — 8-bit conditional write

Special Cases

PPP/P — Short branch, PPP if branch taken, P if not
OPPP/OPO — Long branch, OPPP if branch taken, OPO if not

Condition Codes Columns

– — Status bit not affected by operation.
0 — Status bit cleared by operation.
1 — Status bit set by operation.
Δ — Status bit affected by operation.
⇓ — Status bit may be cleared or remain set, but is not set by operation.
⇑ — Status bit may be set or remain cleared, but is not cleared by operation.
? — Status bit may be changed by operation but the final state is not defined.
! — Status bit used for a special purpose.

Source Form	Operation	Addr. Mode	Machine Coding (hex)	~*	S	X	H	I	N	Z	V	C
ABA	(A) + (B) ⇒ A Add Accumulators A and B	INH	18 06	2	–	–	Δ	–	Δ	Δ	Δ	Δ
ABX	(B) + (X) ⇒ X *Translates to* LEAX B,X	IDX	1A E5	2	–	–	–	–	–	–	–	–
ABY	(B) + (Y) ⇒ Y *Translates to* LEAY B,Y	IDX	19 ED	2	–	–	–	–	–	–	–	–
ADCA *opr*	(A) + (M) + C ⇒ A Add with Carry to A	IMM	89 ii	1	–	–	Δ	–	Δ	Δ	Δ	Δ
		DIR	99 dd	3								
		EXT	B9 hh ll	3								
		IDX	A9 xb	3								
		IDX1	A9 xb ff	3								
		IDX2	A9 xb ee ff	4								
		[D,IDX]	A9 xb	6								
		[IDX2]	A9 xb ee ff	6								
ADCB *opr*	(B) + (M) + C ⇒ B Add with Carry to B	IMM	C9 ii	1	–	–	Δ	–	Δ	Δ	Δ	Δ
		DIR	D9 dd	3								
		EXT	F9 hh ll	3								
		IDX	E9 xb	3								
		IDX1	E9 xb ff	3								
		IDX2	E9 xb ee ff	4								
		[D,IDX]	E9 xb	6								
		[IDX2]	E9 xb ee ff	6								
ADDA *opr*	(A) + (M) ⇒ A Add without Carry to A	IMM	8B ii	1	–	–	Δ	–	Δ	Δ	Δ	Δ
		DIR	9B dd	3								
		EXT	BB hh ll	3								
		IDX	AB xb	3								
		IDX1	AB xb ff	3								
		IDX2	AB xb ee ff	4								
		[D,IDX]	AB xb	6								
		[IDX2]	AB xb ee ff	6								
ADDB *opr*	(B) + (M) ⇒ B Add without Carry to B	IMM	CB ii	1	–	–	Δ	–	Δ	Δ	Δ	Δ
		DIR	DB dd	3								
		EXT	FB hh ll	3								
		IDX	EB xb	3								
		IDX1	EB xb ff	3								
		IDX2	EB xb ee ff	4								
		[D,IDX]	EB xb	6								
		[IDX2]	EB xb ee ff	6								
ADDD *opr*	(A:B) + (M:M+1) ⇒ A:B Add 16-Bit to D (A:B)	IMM	C3 jj kk	2	–	–	–	–	Δ	Δ	Δ	Δ
		DIR	D3 dd	3								
		EXT	F3 hh ll	3								
		IDX	E3 xb	3								
		IDX1	E3 xb ff	3								
		IDX2	E3 xb ee ff	4								
		[D,IDX]	E3 xb	6								
		[IDX2]	E3 xb ee ff	6								

Source Form	Operation	Addr. Mode	Machine Coding (hex)	~*	S	X	H	I	N	Z	V	C
ANDA *opr*	(A) • (M) ⇒ A	IMM	84 ii	1	–	–	–	–	Δ	Δ	0	–
	Logical And A with Memory	DIR	94 dd	3								
		EXT	B4 hh ll	3								
		IDX	A4 xb	3								
		IDX1	A4 xb ff	3								
		IDX2	A4 xb ee ff	4								
		[D,IDX]	A4 xb	6								
		[IDX2]	A4 xb ee ff	6								
ANDB *opr*	(B) • (M) ⇒ B	IMM	C4 ii	1	–	–	–	–	Δ	Δ	0	–
	Logical And B with Memory	DIR	D4 dd	3								
		EXT	F4 hh ll	3								
		IDX	E4 xb	3								
		IDX1	E4 xb ff	3								
		IDX2	E4 xb ee ff	4								
		[D,IDX]	E4 xb	6								
		[IDX2]	E4 xb ee ff	6								
ANDCC *opr*	(CCR) • (M) ⇒ CCR Logical And CCR with Memory	IMM	10 ii	1	⇓	⇓	⇓	⇓	⇓	⇓	⇓	⇓
ASL *opr*	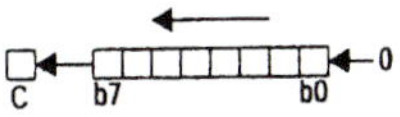	EXT	78 hh ll	4	–	–	–	–	Δ	Δ	Δ	Δ
		IDX	68 xb	3								
		IDX1	68 xb ff	4								
		IDX2	68 xb ee ff	5								
	Arithmetic Shift Left	[D,IDX]	68 xb	6								
		[IDX2]	68 xb ee ff	6								
ASLA	Arithmetic Shift Left Accumulator A	INH	48	1								
ASLB	Arithmetic Shift Left Accumulator B	INH	58	1								
ASLD	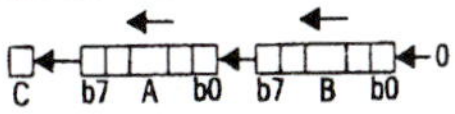 Arithmetic Shift Left Double	INH	59	1	–	–	–	–	Δ	Δ	Δ	Δ
ASR *opr*	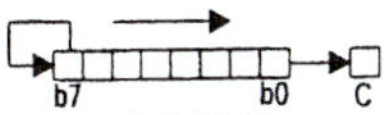	EXT	77 hh ll	4	–	–	–	–	Δ	Δ	Δ	Δ
		IDX	67 xb	3								
		IDX1	67 xb ff	4								
	Arithmetic Shift Right	IDX2	67 xb ee ff	5								
		[D,IDX]	67 xb	6								
		[IDX2]	67 xb ee ff	6								
ASRA	Arithmetic Shift Right Accumulator A	INH	47	1								
ASRB	Arithmetic Shift Right Accumulator B	INH	57	1								
BCC *rel*	Branch if Carry Clear (if C = 0)	REL	24 rr	3/1	–	–	–	–	–	–	–	–
BCLR *opr, msk*	(M) • ($\overline{mm}$) ⇒ M	DIR	4D dd mm	4	–	–	–	–	Δ	Δ	0	–
	Clear Bit(s) in Memory	EXT	1D hh ll mm	4								
		IDX	0D xb mm	4								
		IDX1	0D xb ff mm	4								
		IDX2	0D xb ee ff mm	6								
BCS *rel*	Branch if Carry Set (if C = 1)	REL	25 rr	3/1	–	–	–	–	–	–	–	–
BEQ *rel*	Branch if Equal (if Z = 1)	REL	27 rr	3/1	–	–	–	–	–	–	–	–
BGE *rel*	Branch if Greater Than or Equal (if N ⊕ V = 0) (signed)	REL	2C rr	3/1	–	–	–	–	–	–	–	–
BGND	Place CPU in Background Mode see Background Mode section.	INH	00	5	–	–	–	–	–	–	–	–
BGT *rel*	Branch if Greater Than (if Z + (N ⊕ V) = 0) (signed)	REL	2E rr	3/1	–	–	–	–	–	–	–	–
BHI *rel*	Branch if Higher (if C + Z = 0) (unsigned)	REL	22 rr	3/1	–	–	–	–	–	–	–	–

Source Form	Operation	Addr. Mode	Machine Coding (hex)	~*	S	X	H	I	N	Z	V	C
BHS *rel*	Branch if Higher or Same (if C = 0) (unsigned) same function as BCC	REL	24 rr	3/1	–	–	–	–	–	–	–	–
BITA *opr*	(A) • (M) Logical And A with Memory	IMM DIR EXT IDX IDX1 IDX2 [D,IDX] [IDX2]	85 ii 95 dd B5 hh ll A5 xb A5 xb ff A5 xb ee ff A5 xb A5 xb ee ff	1 3 3 3 3 4 6 6	–	–	–	–	Δ	Δ	0	–
BITB *opr*	(B) • (M) Logical And B with Memory	IMM DIR EXT IDX IDX1 IDX2 [D,IDX] [IDX2]	C5 ii D5 dd F5 hh ll E5 xb E5 xb ff E5 xb ee ff E5 xb E5 xb ee ff	1 3 3 3 3 4 6 6	–	–	–	–	Δ	Δ	0	–
BLE *rel*	Branch if Less Than or Equal (if Z + (N ⊕ V) = 1) (signed)	REL	2F rr	3/1	–	–	–	–	–	–	–	–
BLO *rel*	Branch if Lower (if C = 1) (unsigned) same function as BCS	REL	25 rr	3/1	–	–	–	–	–	–	–	–
BLS *rel*	Branch if Lower or Same (if C + Z = 1) (unsigned)	REL	23 rr	3/1	–	–	–	–	–	–	–	–
BLT *rel*	Branch if Less Than (if N ⊕ V = 1) (signed)	REL	2D rr	3/1	–	–	–	–	–	–	–	–
BMI *rel*	Branch if Minus (if N = 1)	REL	2B rr	3/1	–	–	–	–	–	–	–	–
BNE *rel*	Branch if Not Equal (if Z = 0)	REL	26 rr	3/1	–	–	–	–	–	–	–	–
BPL *rel*	Branch if Plus (if N = 0)	REL	2A rr	3/1	–	–	–	–	–	–	–	–
BRA *rel*	Branch Always (if 1 = 1)	REL	20 rr	3	–	–	–	–	–	–	–	–
BRCLR *opr, msk, rel*	Branch if (M) • (mm) = 0 (if All Selected Bit(s) Clear)	DIR EXT IDX IDX1 IDX2	4F dd mm rr 1F hh ll mm rr 0F xb mm rr 0F xb ff mm rr 0F xb ee ff mm rr	4 5 4 6 8	–	–	–	–	–	–	–	–
BRN *rel*	Branch Never (if 1 = 0)	REL	21 rr	1	–	–	–	–	–	–	–	–
BRSET *opr, msk, rel*	Branch if ($\overline{M}$) • (mm) = 0 (if All Selected Bit(s) Set)	DIR EXT IDX IDX1 IDX2	4E dd mm rr 1E hh ll mm rr 0E xb mm rr 0E xb ff mm rr 0E xb ee ff mm rr	4 5 4 6 8	–	–	–	–	–	–	–	–
BSET *opr, msk*	(M) + (mm) ⇒ M Set Bit(s) in Memory	DIR EXT IDX IDX1 IDX2	4C dd mm 1C hh ll mm 0C xb mm 0C xb ff mm 0C xb ee ff mm	4 4 4 4 6	–	–	–	–	Δ	Δ	0	–
BSR *rel*	(SP) – 2 ⇒ SP; $RTN_H:RTN_L \Rightarrow M_{(SP)}:M_{(SP+1)}$ Subroutine address ⇒ PC Branch to Subroutine	REL	07 rr	4	–	–	–	–	–	–	–	–

Source Form	Operation	Addr. Mode	Machine Coding (hex)	~*	S	X	H	I	N	Z	V	C
BVC *rel*	Branch if Overflow Bit Clear (if V = 0)	REL	28 rr	3/1	–	–	–	–	–	–	–	–
BVS *rel*	Branch if Overflow Bit Set (if V = 1)	REL	29 rr	3/1	–	–	–	–	–	–	–	–
CALL *opr, page*	(SP) – 2 ⇒ SP; $RTN_H:RTN_L \Rightarrow M_{(SP)}:M_{(SP+1)}$ (SP) – 1 ⇒ SP; (PPG) ⇒ $M_{(SP)}$; pg ⇒ PPAGE register; Program address ⇒ PC Call subroutine in extended memory (Program may be located on another expansion memory page.)	EXT IDX IDX1 IDX2	4A hh ll pg 4B xb pg 4B xb ff pg 4B xb ee ff pg	8 8 8 9	–	–	–	–	–	–	–	–
CALL [D,*r*] CALL [*opr,r*]	Indirect modes get program address and new pg value based on pointer. *r* = X, Y, SP, or PC	[D,IDX] [IDX2]	4B xb 4B xb ee ff	10 10	–	–	–	–	–	–	–	–
CBA	(A) – (B) Compare 8-Bit Accumulators	INH	18 17	2	–	–	–	–	Δ	Δ	Δ	Δ
CLC	0 ⇒ C *Translates to* ANDCC #$FE	IMM	10 FE	1	–	–	–	–	–	–	–	0
CLI	0 ⇒ I *Translates to* ANDCC #$EF (enables I-bit interrupts)	IMM	10 EF	1	–	–	–	0	–	–	–	–
CLR *opr* CLRA CLRB	0 ⇒ M Clear Memory Location 0 ⇒ A Clear Accumulator A 0 ⇒ B Clear Accumulator B	EXT IDX IDX1 IDX2 [D,IDX] [IDX2] INH INH	79 hh ll 69 xb 69 xb ff 69 xb ee ff 69 xb 69 xb ee ff 87 C7	3 2 3 3 5 5 1 1	–	–	–	–	0	1	0	0
CLV	0 ⇒ V *Translates to* ANDCC #$FD	IMM	10 FD	1	–	–	–	–	–	–	0	–
CMPA *opr*	(A) – (M) Compare Accumulator A with Memory	IMM DIR EXT IDX IDX1 IDX2 [D,IDX] [IDX2]	81 ii 91 dd B1 hh ll A1 xb A1 xb ff A1 xb ee ff A1 xb A1 xb ee ff	1 3 3 3 3 4 6 6	–	–	–	–	Δ	Δ	Δ	Δ
CMPB *opr*	(B) – (M) Compare Accumulator B with Memory	IMM DIR EXT IDX IDX1 IDX2 [D,IDX] [IDX2]	C1 ii D1 dd F1 hh ll E1 xb E1 xb ff E1 xb ee ff E1 xb E1 xb ee ff	1 3 3 3 3 4 6 6	–	–	–	–	Δ	Δ	Δ	Δ

Source Form	Operation	Addr. Mode	Machine Coding (hex)	~*	S	X	H	I	N	Z	V	C
COM *opr*	$(\overline{M}) \Rightarrow M$ *equivalent to* \$FF – (M) ⇒ M 1's Complement Memory Location	EXT IDX IDX1 IDX2 [D,IDX] [IDX2]	71 hh ll 61 xb 61 xb ff 61 xb ee ff 61 xb 61 xb ee ff	4 3 4 5 6 6	–	–	–	–	Δ	Δ	0	1
COMA	$(\overline{A}) \Rightarrow A$ Complement Accumulator A	INH	41	1								
COMB	$(\overline{B}) \Rightarrow B$ Complement Accumulator B	INH	51	1								
CPD *opr*	(A:B) – (M:M+1) Compare D to Memory (16-Bit)	IMM DIR EXT IDX IDX1 IDX2 [D,IDX] [IDX2]	8C jj kk 9C dd BC hh ll AC xb AC xb ff AC xb ee ff AC xb AC xb ee ff	2 3 3 3 3 4 6 6	–	–	–	–	Δ	Δ	Δ	Δ
CPS *opr*	(SP) – (M:M+1) Compare SP to Memory (16-Bit)	IMM DIR EXT IDX IDX1 IDX2 [D,IDX] [IDX2]	8F jj kk 9F dd BF hh ll AF xb AF xb ff AF xb ee ff AF xb AF xb ee ff	2 3 3 3 3 4 6 6	–	–	–	–	Δ	Δ	Δ	Δ
CPX *opr*	(X) – (M:M+1) Compare X to Memory (16-Bit)	IMM DIR EXT IDX IDX1 IDX2 [D,IDX] [IDX2]	8E jj kk 9E dd BE hh ll AE xb AE xb ff AE xb ee ff AE xb AE xb ee ff	2 3 3 3 3 4 6 6	–	–	–	–	Δ	Δ	Δ	Δ
CPY *opr*	(Y) – (M:M+1) Compare Y to Memory (16-Bit)	IMM DIR EXT IDX IDX1 IDX2 [D,IDX] [IDX2]	8D jj kk 9D dd BD hh ll AD xb AD xb ff AD xb ee ff AD xb AD xb ee ff	2 3 3 3 3 4 6 6	–	–	–	–	Δ	Δ	Δ	Δ
DAA	Adjust Sum to BCD Decimal Adjust Accumulator A	INH	18 07	3	–	–	–	–	Δ	Δ	?	Δ
DBEQ *cntr, rel*	(cntr) – 1⇒ cntr if (cntr) = 0, then Branch else Continue to next instruction Decrement Counter and Branch if = 0 (cntr = A, B, D, X, Y, or SP)	REL (9-bit)	04 lb rr	3	–	–	–	–	–	–	–	–
DBNE *cntr, rel*	(cntr) – 1 ⇒ cntr If (cntr) not = 0, then Branch; else Continue to next instruction Decrement Counter and Branch if ≠ 0 (cntr = A, B, D, X, Y, or SP)	REL (9-bit)	04 lb rr	3	–	–	–	–	–	–	–	–

Source Form	Operation	Addr. Mode	Machine Coding (hex)	~*	S	X	H	I	N	Z	V	C
DEC *opr*	(M) – \$01 ⇒ M Decrement Memory Location	EXT	73 hh ll	4	–	–	–	–	Δ	Δ	Δ	–
		IDX	63 xb	3								
		IDX1	63 xb ff	4								
		IDX2	63 xb ee ff	5								
		[D,IDX]	63 xb	6								
		[IDX2]	63 xb ee ff	6								
DECA	(A) – \$01 ⇒ A Decrement A	INH	43	1								
DECB	(B) – \$01 ⇒ B Decrement B	INH	53	1								
DES	(SP) – \$0001 ⇒ SP *Translates to* LEAS –1,SP	IDX	1B 9F	2	–	–	–	–	–	–	–	–
DEX	(X) – \$0001 ⇒ X Decrement Index Register X	INH	09	1	–	–	–	–	–	Δ	–	–
DEY	(Y) – \$0001 ⇒ Y Decrement Index Register Y	INH	03	1	–	–	–	–	–	Δ	–	–
EDIV	(Y:D) ÷ (X) ⇒ Y Remainder ⇒ D 32 × 16 Bit ⇒ 16 Bit Divide (unsigned)	INH	11	11	–	–	–	–	Δ	Δ	Δ	Δ
EDIVS	(Y:D) ÷ (X) ⇒ Y Remainder ⇒ D 32 × 16 Bit ⇒ 16 Bit Divide (signed)	INH	18 14	12	–	–	–	–	Δ	Δ	Δ	Δ
EMACS *sum*	$(M_{(X)}:M_{(X+1)}) \times (M_{(Y)}:M_{(Y+1)}) + (M\sim M+3) \Rightarrow M\sim M+3$ 16 × 16 Bit ⇒ 32 Bit Multiply and Accumulate (signed)	Special	18 12 hh ll	13	–	–	–	–	Δ	Δ	Δ	Δ
EMAXD *opr*	MAX((D), (M:M+1)) ⇒ D MAX of 2 Unsigned 16-Bit Values N, Z, V and C status bits reflect result of internal compare ((D) – (M:M+1))	IDX	18 1A xb	4	–	–	–	–	Δ	Δ	Δ	Δ
		IDX1	18 1A xb ff	4								
		IDX2	18 1A xb ee ff	5								
		[D,IDX]	18 1A xb	7								
		[IDX2]	18 1A xb ee ff	7								
EMAXM *opr*	MAX((D), (M:M+1)) ⇒ M:M+1 MAX of 2 Unsigned 16-Bit Values N, Z, V and C status bits reflect result of internal compare ((D) – (M:M+1))	IDX	18 1E xb	4	–	–	–	–	Δ	Δ	Δ	Δ
		IDX1	18 1E xb ff	5								
		IDX2	18 1E xb ee ff	6								
		[D,IDX]	18 1E xb	7								
		[IDX2]	18 1E xb ee ff	7								
EMIND *opr*	MIN((D), (M:M+1)) ⇒ D MIN of 2 Unsigned 16-Bit Values N, Z, V and C status bits reflect result of internal compare ((D) – (M:M+1))	IDX	18 1B xb	4	–	–	–	–	Δ	Δ	Δ	Δ
		IDX1	18 1B xb ff	4								
		IDX2	18 1B xb ee ff	5								
		[D,IDX]	18 1B xb	7								
		[IDX2]	18 1B xb ee ff	7								
EMINM *opr*	MIN((D), (M:M+1)) ⇒ M:M+1 MIN of 2 Unsigned 16-Bit Values N, Z, V and C status bits reflect result of internal compare ((D) – (M:M+1))	IDX	18 1F xb	4	–	–	–	–	Δ	Δ	Δ	Δ
		IDX1	18 1F xb ff	5								
		IDX2	18 1F xb ee ff	6								
		[D,IDX]	18 1F xb	7								
		[IDX2]	18 1F xb ee ff	7								
EMUL	(D) × (Y) ⇒ Y:D 16 × 16 Bit Multiply (unsigned)	INH	13	3	–	–	–	–	Δ	Δ	–	Δ
EMULS	(D) × (Y) ⇒ Y:D 16 × 16 Bit Multiply (signed)	INH	18 13	3	–	–	–	–	Δ	Δ	–	Δ

Source Form	Operation	Addr. Mode	Machine Coding (hex)	~*	S	X	H	I	N	Z	V	C
EORA *opr*	(A) ⊕ (M) ⇒ A Exclusive-OR A with Memory	IMM DIR EXT IDX IDX1 IDX2 [D,IDX] [IDX2]	88 ii 98 dd B8 hh ll A8 xb A8 xb ff A8 xb ee ff A8 xb A8 xb ee ff	1 3 3 3 3 4 6 6	–	–	–	–	Δ	Δ	0	–
EORB *opr*	(B) ⊕ (M) ⇒ B Exclusive-OR B with Memory	IMM DIR EXT IDX IDX1 IDX2 [D,IDX] [IDX2]	C8 ii D8 dd F8 hh ll E8 xb E8 xb ff E8 xb ee ff E8 xb E8 xb ee ff	1 3 3 3 3 4 6 6	–	–	–	–	Δ	Δ	0	–
ETBL *opr*	(M:M+1)+ [(B)×((M+2:M+3) – (M:M+1))] ⇒ D 16-Bit Table Lookup and Interpolate Initialize B, and index before ETBL. <ea> points at first table entry (M:M+1) and B is fractional part of lookup value (no indirect addr. modes allowed)	IDX	18 3F xb	10	–	–	–	–	Δ	Δ	–	?
EXG *r1, r2*	(r1) ⇔ (r2) (if r1 and r2 same size) *or* $00:(r1) ⇒ r2 (if r1=8-bit; r2=16-bit) *or* ($r1_{low}$) ⇔ (r2) (if r1=16-bit; r2=8-bit) r1 and r2 may be A, B, CCR, D, X, Y, or SP	INH	B7 eb	1	–	–	–	–	–	–	–	–
FDIV	(D) ÷ (X) ⇒ X; r ⇒ D 16 × 16 Bit Fractional Divide	INH	18 11	12	–	–	–	–	–	Δ	Δ	Δ
IBEQ *cntr, rel*	(cntr) + 1⇒ cntr If (cntr) = 0, then Branch else Continue to next instruction Increment Counter and Branch if = 0 (cntr = A, B, D, X, Y, or SP)	REL (9-bit)	04 lb rr	3	–	–	–	–	–	–	–	–
IBNE *cntr, rel*	(cntr) + 1⇒ cntr if (cntr) not = 0, then Branch; else Continue to next instruction Increment Counter and Branch if ≠ 0 (cntr = A, B, D, X, Y, or SP)	REL (9-bit)	04 lb rr	3	–	–	–	–	–	–	–	–
IDIV	(D) ÷ (X) ⇒ X; r ⇒ D 16 × 16 Bit Integer Divide (unsigned)	INH	18 10	12	–	–	–	–	–	Δ	0	Δ
IDIVS	(D) ÷ (X) ⇒ X; r ⇒ D 16 × 16 Bit Integer Divide (signed)	INH	18 15	12	–	–	–	–	Δ	Δ	Δ	Δ

Source Form	Operation	Addr. Mode	Machine Coding (hex)	~*	S	X	H	I	N	Z	V	C
INC *opr*	(M) + \$01 ⇒ M Increment Memory Byte	EXT IDX IDX1 IDX2 [D,IDX] [IDX2]	72 hh ll 62 xb 62 xb ff 62 xb ee ff 62 xb 62 xb ee ff	4 3 4 5 6 6	–	–	–	–	Δ	Δ	Δ	–
INCA INCB	(A) + \$01 ⇒ A Increment Acc. A (B) + \$01 ⇒ B Increment Acc. B	INH INH	42 52	1 1								
INS	(SP) + \$0001 ⇒ SP *Translates to* LEAS 1,SP	IDX	1B 81	2	–	–	–	–	–	–	–	–
INX	(X) + \$0001 ⇒ X Increment Index Register X	INH	08	1	–	–	–	–	–	Δ	–	–
INY	(Y) + \$0001 ⇒ Y Increment Index Register Y	INH	02	1	–	–	–	–	–	Δ	–	–
JMP *opr*	Subroutine address ⇒ PC Jump	EXT IDX IDX1 IDX2 [D,IDX] [IDX2]	06 hh ll 05 xb 05 xb ff 05 xb ee ff 05 xb 05 xb ee ff	3 3 3 4 6 6	–	–	–	–	–	–	–	–
JSR *opr*	(SP) – 2 ⇒ SP; RTN_H:RTN_L ⇒ $M_{(SP)}$:$M_{(SP+1)}$; Subroutine address ⇒ PC Jump to Subroutine	DIR EXT IDX IDX1 IDX2 [D,IDX] [IDX2]	17 dd 16 hh ll 15 xb 15 xb ff 15 xb ee ff 15 xb 15 xb ee ff	4 4 4 4 5 7 7	–	–	–	–	–	–	–	–
LBCC *rel*	Long Branch if Carry Clear (if C = 0)	REL	18 24 qq rr	4/3	–	–	–	–	–	–	–	–
LBCS *rel*	Long Branch if Carry Set (if C = 1)	REL	18 25 qq rr	4/3	–	–	–	–	–	–	–	–
LBEQ *rel*	Long Branch if Equal (if Z = 1)	REL	18 27 qq rr	4/3	–	–	–	–	–	–	–	–
LBGE *rel*	Long Branch Greater Than or Equal (if N ⊕ V = 0) (signed)	REL	18 2C qq rr	4/3	–	–	–	–	–	–	–	–
LBGT *rel*	Long Branch if Greater Than (if Z + (N ⊕ V) = 0) (signed)	REL	18 2E qq rr	4/3	–	–	–	–	–	–	–	–
LBHI *rel*	Long Branch if Higher (if C + Z = 0) (unsigned)	REL	18 22 qq rr	4/3	–	–	–	–	–	–	–	–
LBHS *rel*	Long Branch if Higher or Same (if C = 0) (unsigned) same function as LBCC	REL	18 24 qq rr	4/3	–	–	–	–	–	–	–	–
LBLE *rel*	Long Branch if Less Than or Equal (if Z + (N ⊕ V) = 1) (signed)	REL	18 2F qq rr	4/3	–	–	–	–	–	–	–	–
LBLO *rel*	Long Branch if Lower (if C = 1) (unsigned) *same function as LBCS*	REL	18 25 qq rr	4/3	–	–	–	–	–	–	–	–
LBLS *rel*	Long Branch if Lower or Same (if C + Z = 1) (unsigned)	REL	18 23 qq rr	4/3	–	–	–	–	–	–	–	–
LBLT *rel*	Long Branch if Less Than (if N ⊕ V = 1) (signed)	REL	18 2D qq rr	4/3	–	–	–	–	–	–	–	–
LBMI *rel*	Long Branch if Minus (if N = 1)	REL	18 2B qq rr	4/3	–	–	–	–	–	–	–	–
LBNE *rel*	Long Branch if Not Equal (if Z = 0)	REL	18 26 qq rr	4/3	–	–	–	–	–	–	–	–
LBPL *rel*	Long Branch if Plus (if N = 0)	REL	18 2A qq rr	4/3	–	–	–	–	–	–	–	–
LBRA *rel*	Long Branch Always (if 1=1)	REL	18 20 qq rr	4	–	–	–	–	–	–	–	–

Source Form	Operation	Addr. Mode	Machine Coding (hex)	~*	S	X	H	I	N	Z	V	C
LBRN *rel*	Long Branch Never (if 1 = 0)	REL	18 21 qq rr	3	–	–	–	–	–	–	–	–
LBVC *rel*	Long Branch if Overflow Bit Clear (if V=0)	REL	18 28 qq rr	4/3	–	–	–	–	–	–	–	–
LBVS *rel*	Long Branch if Overflow Bit Set (if V = 1)	REL	18 29 qq rr	4/3	–	–	–	–	–	–	–	–
LDAA *opr*	(M) ⇒ A	IMM	86 ii	1	–	–	–	–	Δ	Δ	0	–
	Load Accumulator A	DIR	96 dd	3								
		EXT	B6 hh ll	3								
		IDX	A6 xb	3								
		IDX1	A6 xb ff	3								
		IDX2	A6 xb ee ff	4								
		[D,IDX]	A6 xb	6								
		[IDX2]	A6 xb ee ff	6								
LDAB *opr*	(M) ⇒ B	IMM	C6 ii	1	–	–	–	–	Δ	Δ	0	–
	Load Accumulator B	DIR	D6 dd	3								
		EXT	F6 hh ll	3								
		IDX	E6 xb	3								
		IDX1	E6 xb ff	3								
		IDX2	E6 xb ee ff	4								
		[D,IDX]	E6 xb	6								
		[IDX2]	E6 xb ee ff	6								
LDD *opr*	(M:M+1) ⇒ A:B	IMM	CC jj kk	2	–	–	–	–	Δ	Δ	0	–
	Load Double Accumulator D (A:B)	DIR	DC dd	3								
		EXT	FC hh ll	3								
		IDX	EC xb	3								
		IDX1	EC xb ff	3								
		IDX2	EC xb ee ff	4								
		[D,IDX]	EC xb	6								
		[IDX2]	EC xb ee ff	6								
LDS *opr*	(M:M+1) ⇒ SP	IMM	CF jj kk	2	–	–	–	–	Δ	Δ	0	–
	Load Stack Pointer	DIR	DF dd	3								
		EXT	FF hh ll	3								
		IDX	EF xb	3								
		IDX1	EF xb ff	3								
		IDX2	EF xb ee ff	4								
		[D,IDX]	EF xb	6								
		[IDX2]	EF xb ee ff	6								
LDX *opr*	(M:M+1) ⇒ X	IMM	CE jj kk	2	–	–	–	–	Δ	Δ	0	–
	Load Index Register X	DIR	DE dd	3								
		EXT	FE hh ll	3								
		IDX	EE xb	3								
		IDX1	EE xb ff	3								
		IDX2	EE xb ee ff	4								
		[D,IDX]	EE xb	6								
		[IDX2]	EE xb ee ff	6								
LDY *opr*	(M:M+1) ⇒ Y	IMM	CD jj kk	2	–	–	–	–	Δ	Δ	0	–
	Load Index Register Y	DIR	DD dd	3								
		EXT	FD hh ll	3								
		IDX	ED xb	3								
		IDX1	ED xb ff	3								
		IDX2	ED xb ee ff	4								
		[D,IDX]	ED xb	6								
		[IDX2]	ED xb ee ff	6								
LEAS *opr*	Effective Address ⇒ SP	IDX	1B xb	2	–	–	–	–	–	–	–	–
	Load Effective Address into SP	IDX1	1B xb ff	2								
		IDX2	1B xb ee ff	2								

Source Form	Operation	Addr. Mode	Machine Coding (hex)	~*	S	X	H	I	N	Z	V	C
LEAX *opr*	Effective Address ⇒ X	IDX	1A xb	2	–	–	–	–	–	–	–	–
	Load Effective Address into X	IDX1	1A xb ff	2								
		IDX2	1A xb ee ff	2								
LEAY *opr*	Effective Address ⇒ Y	IDX	19 xb	2	–	–	–	–	–	–	–	–
	Load Effective Address into Y	IDX1	19 xb ff	2								
		IDX2	19 xb ee ff	2								
LSL *opr*	C ← b7 … b0 ← 0	EXT	78 hh ll	4	–	–	–	–	Δ	Δ	Δ	Δ
		IDX	68 xb	3								
		IDX1	68 xb ff	4								
	Logical Shift Left	IDX2	68 xb ee ff	5								
	same function as ASL	[D,IDX]	68 xb	6								
		[IDX2]	68 xb ee ff	6								
LSLA	Logical Shift Accumulator A to Left	INH	48	1								
LSLB	Logical Shift Accumulator B to Left	INH	58	1								
LSLD	C ← b7 A b0 ← b7 B b0 ← 0	INH	59	1	–	–	–	–	Δ	Δ	Δ	Δ
	Logical Shift Left D Accumulator											
	same function as ASLD											
LSR *opr*	0 → b7 … b0 → C	EXT	74 hh ll	4	–	–	–	–	0	Δ	Δ	Δ
		IDX	64 xb	3								
		IDX1	64 xb ff	4								
	Logical Shift Right	IDX2	64 xb ee ff	5								
		[D,IDX]	64 xb	6								
		[IDX2]	64 xb ee ff	6								
LSRA	Logical Shift Accumulator A to Right	INH	44	1								
LSRB	Logical Shift Accumulator B to Right	INH	54	1								
LSRD	0 → b7 A b0 → b7 B b0 → C	INH	49	1	–	–	–	–	0	Δ	Δ	Δ
	Logical Shift Right D Accumulator											
MAXA	MAX((A), (M)) ⇒ A	IDX	18 18 xb	4	–	–	–	–	Δ	Δ	Δ	Δ
	MAX of 2 Unsigned 8-Bit Values	IDX1	18 18 xb ff	4								
		IDX2	18 18 xb ee ff	5								
	N, Z, V and C status bits reflect result of	[D,IDX]	18 18 xb	7								
	internal compare ((A) – (M)).	[IDX2]	18 18 xb ee ff	7								
MAXM	MAX((A), (M)) ⇒ M	IDX	18 1C xb	4	–	–	–	–	Δ	Δ	Δ	Δ
	MAX of 2 Unsigned 8-Bit Values	IDX1	18 1C xb ff	5								
		IDX2	18 1C xb ee ff	6								
	N, Z, V and C status bits reflect result of	[D,IDX]	18 1C xb	7								
	internal compare ((A) – (M)).	[IDX2]	18 1C xb ee ff	7								
MEM	μ (grade) ⇒ $M_{(Y)}$;	Special	01	5	–	–	?	–	?	?	?	?
	(X) + 4 ⇒ X; (Y) + 1 ⇒ Y; A unchanged											
	if (A) < P1 or (A) > P2 then μ = 0, else											
	μ = MIN[((A) – P1)×S1, (P2 – (A))×S2, $FF]											
	where:											
	A = current crisp input value;											
	X points at 4-byte data structure that describes a trapezoidal membership function (P1, P2, S1, S2);											
	Y points at fuzzy input (RAM location).											
	See instruction details for special cases.											

Source Form	Operation	Addr. Mode	Machine Coding (hex)	~*	S	X	H	I	N	Z	V	C
MINA	MIN((A), (M)) ⇒ A	IDX	18 19 xb	4	–	–	–	–	Δ	Δ	Δ	Δ
	MIN of Two Unsigned 8-Bit Values	IDX1	18 19 xb ff	4								
		IDX2	18 19 xb ee ff	5								
	N, Z, V and C status bits reflect result of	[D,IDX]	18 19 xb	7								
	internal compare ((A) – (M)).	[IDX2]	18 19 xb ee ff	7								
MINM	MIN((A), (M)) ⇒ M	IDX	18 1D xb	4	–	–	–	–	Δ	Δ	Δ	Δ
	MIN of Two Unsigned 8-Bit Values	IDX1	18 1D xb ff	5								
		IDX2	18 1D xb ee ff	6								
	N, Z, V and C status bits reflect result of	[D,IDX]	18 1D xb	7								
	internal compare ((A) – (M)).	[IDX2]	18 1D xb ee ff	7								
MOVB *opr1, opr2*	$(M_1) \Rightarrow M_2$	IMM-EXT	18 0B ii hh ll	4	–	–	–	–	–	–	–	–
	Memory to Memory Byte-Move (8-Bit)	IMM-IDX	18 08 xb ii	4								
		EXT-EXT	18 0C hh ll hh ll	6								
		EXT-IDX	18 09 xb hh ll	5								
		IDX-EXT	18 0D xb hh ll	5								
		IDX-IDX	18 0A xb xb	5								
MOVW *opr1, opr2*	$(M:M+1_1) \Rightarrow M:M+1_2$	IMM-EXT	18 03 jj kk hh ll	5	–	–	–	–	–	–	–	–
	Memory to Memory Word-Move (16-Bit)	IMM-IDX	18 00 xb jj kk	4								
		EXT-EXT	18 04 hh ll hh ll	6								
		EXT-IDX	18 01 xb hh ll	5								
		IDX-EXT	18 05 xb hh ll	5								
		IDX-IDX	18 02 xb xb	5								
MUL	(A) × (B) ⇒ A:B 8 × 8 Unsigned Multiply	INH	12	3	–	–	–	–	–	–	–	Δ
NEG *opr*	0 – (M) ⇒ M *or* $(\overline{M})$ + 1 ⇒ M	EXT	70 hh ll	4	–	–	–	–	Δ	Δ	Δ	Δ
	Two's Complement Negate	IDX	60 xb	3								
		IDX1	60 xb ff	4								
		IDX2	60 xb ee ff	5								
		[D,IDX]	60 xb	6								
		[IDX2]	60 xb ee ff	6								
NEGA	0 – (A) ⇒ A *equivalent to* $(\overline{A})$ + 1 ⇒ B Negate Accumulator A	INH	40	1								
NEGB	0 – (B) ⇒ B *equivalent to* $(\overline{B})$ + 1 ⇒ B Negate Accumulator B	INH	50	1								
NOP	No Operation	INH	A7	1	–	–	–	–	–	–	–	–
ORAA *opr*	(A) + (M) ⇒ A	IMM	8A ii	1	–	–	–	–	Δ	Δ	0	–
	Logical OR A with Memory	DIR	9A dd	3								
		EXT	BA hh ll	3								
		IDX	AA xb	3								
		IDX1	AA xb ff	3								
		IDX2	AA xb ee ff	4								
		[D,IDX]	AA xb	6								
		[IDX2]	AA xb ee ff	6								
ORAB *opr*	(B) + (M) ⇒ B	IMM	CA ii	1	–	–	–	–	Δ	Δ	0	–
	Logical OR B with Memory	DIR	DA dd	3								
		EXT	FA hh ll	3								
		IDX	EA xb	3								
		IDX1	EA xb ff	3								
		IDX2	EA xb ee ff	4								
		[D,IDX]	EA xb	6								
		[IDX2]	EA xb ee ff	6								
ORCC *opr*	(CCR) + M ⇒ CCR Logical OR CCR with Memory	IMM	14 ii	1	⇑	–	⇑	⇑	⇑	⇑	⇑	⇑

Source Form	Operation	Addr. Mode	Machine Coding (hex)	~*	S	X	H	I	N	Z	V	C
PSHA	$(SP) - 1 \Rightarrow SP; (A) \Rightarrow M_{(SP)}$ Push Accumulator A onto Stack	INH	36	2	–	–	–	–	–	–	–	–
PSHB	$(SP) - 1 \Rightarrow SP; (B) \Rightarrow M_{(SP)}$ Push Accumulator B onto Stack	INH	37	2	–	–	–	–	–	–	–	–
PSHC	$(SP) - 1 \Rightarrow SP; (CCR) \Rightarrow M_{(SP)}$ Push CCR onto Stack	INH	39	2	–	–	–	–	–	–	–	–
PSHD	$(SP) - 2 \Rightarrow SP; (A{:}B) \Rightarrow M_{(SP)}{:}M_{(SP+1)}$ Push D Accumulator onto Stack	INH	3B	2	–	–	–	–	–	–	–	–
PSHX	$(SP) - 2 \Rightarrow SP; (X_H{:}X_L) \Rightarrow M_{(SP)}{:}M_{(SP+1)}$ Push Index Register X onto Stack	INH	34	2	–	–	–	–	–	–	–	–
PSHY	$(SP) - 2 \Rightarrow SP; (Y_H{:}Y_L) \Rightarrow M_{(SP)}{:}M_{(SP+1)}$ Push Index Register Y onto Stack	INH	35	2	–	–	–	–	–	–	–	–
PULA	$(M_{(SP)}) \Rightarrow A; (SP) + 1 \Rightarrow SP$ Pull Accumulator A from Stack	INH	32	3	–	–	–	–	–	–	–	–
PULB	$(M_{(SP)}) \Rightarrow B; (SP) + 1 \Rightarrow SP$ Pull Accumulator B from Stack	INH	33	3	–	–	–	–	–	–	–	–
PULC	$(M_{(SP)}) \Rightarrow CCR; (SP) + 1 \Rightarrow SP$ Pull CCR from Stack	INH	38	3	Δ	⇓	Δ	Δ	Δ	Δ	Δ	Δ
PULD	$(M_{(SP)}{:}M_{(SP+1)}) \Rightarrow A{:}B; (SP) + 2 \Rightarrow SP$ Pull D from Stack	INH	3A	3	–	–	–	–	–	–	–	–
PULX	$(M_{(SP)}{:}M_{(SP+1)}) \Rightarrow X_H{:}X_L; (SP) + 2 \Rightarrow SP$ Pull Index Register X from Stack	INH	30	3	–	–	–	–	–	–	–	–
PULY	$(M_{(SP)}{:}M_{(SP+1)}) \Rightarrow Y_H{:}Y_L; (SP) + 2 \Rightarrow SP$ Pull Index Register Y from Stack	INH	31	3	–	–	–	–	–	–	–	–
REV	MIN-MAX rule evaluation Find smallest rule input (MIN). Store to rule outputs unless fuzzy output is already larger (MAX). For rule weights see REVW. Each rule input is an 8-bit offset from the base address in Y. Each rule output is an 8-bit offset from the base address in Y. $FE separates rule inputs from rule outputs. $FF terminates the rule list. REV may be interrupted.	Special	18 3A	3** per rule byte	–	–	–	–	–	–	Δ	–

Source Form	Operation	Addr. Mode	Machine Coding (hex)	~*	S	X	H	I	N	Z	V	C
REVW	MIN-MAX rule evaluation Find smallest rule input (MIN), Store to rule outputs unless fuzzy output is already larger (MAX). Rule weights supported, optional. Each rule input is the 16-bit address of a fuzzy input. Each rule output is the 16-bit address of a fuzzy output. The value $FFFE separates rule inputs from rule outputs. $FFFF terminates the rule list. REVW may be interrupted.	Special	18 3B	3** per rule byte; 5 per wt.	–	–	?	–	?	?	Δ	!
ROL *opr*	C b7 b0 Rotate Memory Left through Carry	EXT IDX IDX1 IDX2 [D,IDX] [IDX2]	75 hh ll 65 xb 65 xb ff 65 xb ee ff 65 xb 65 xb ee ff	4 3 4 5 6 6	–	–	–	–	Δ	Δ	Δ	Δ
ROLA	Rotate A Left through Carry	INH	45	1								
ROLB	Rotate B Left through Carry	INH	55	1								
ROR *opr*	b7 b0 C Rotate Memory Right through Carry	EXT IDX IDX1 IDX2 [D,IDX] [IDX2]	76 hh ll 66 xb 66 xb ff 66 xb ee ff 66 xb 66 xb ee ff	4 3 4 5 6 6	–	–	–	–	Δ	Δ	Δ	Δ
RORA	Rotate A Right through Carry	INH	46	1								
RORB	Rotate B Right through Carry	INH	56	1								
RTC	$(M_{(SP)}) \Rightarrow$ PPAGE; $(SP) + 1 \Rightarrow SP$; $(M_{(SP)}:M_{(SP+1)}) \Rightarrow PC_H:PC_L$; $(SP) + 2 \Rightarrow SP$ Return from Call	INH	0A	6	–	–	–	–	–	–	–	–
RTI	$(M_{(SP)}) \Rightarrow CCR$; $(SP) + 1 \Rightarrow SP$ $(M_{(SP)}:M_{(SP+1)}) \Rightarrow B:A$; $(SP) + 2 \Rightarrow SP$ $(M_{(SP)}:M_{(SP+1)}) \Rightarrow X_H:X_L$; $(SP) + 4 \Rightarrow SP$ $(M_{(SP)}:M_{(SP+1)}) \Rightarrow PC_H:PC_L$; $(SP) - 2 \Rightarrow SP$ $(M_{(SP)}:M_{(SP+1)}) \Rightarrow Y_H:Y_L$; $(SP) + 4 \Rightarrow SP$ Return from Interrupt	INH	0B	8	Δ	⇓	Δ	Δ	Δ	Δ	Δ	Δ
RTS	$(M_{(SP)}:M_{(SP+1)}) \Rightarrow PC_H:PC_L$; $(SP) + 2 \Rightarrow SP$ Return from Subroutine	INH	3D	5	–	–	–	–	–	–	–	–
SBA	$(A) - (B) \Rightarrow A$ Subtract B from A	INH	18 16	2	–	–	–	–	Δ	Δ	Δ	Δ

Source Form	Operation	Addr. Mode	Machine Coding (hex)	~*	S	X	H	I	N	Z	V	C
SBCA *opr*	(A) – (M) – C ⇒ A	IMM	82 ii	1	–	–	–	–	Δ	Δ	Δ	Δ
	Subtract with Borrow from A	DIR	92 dd	3								
		EXT	B2 hh ll	3								
		IDX	A2 xb	3								
		IDX1	A2 xb ff	3								
		IDX2	A2 xb ee ff	4								
		[D,IDX]	A2 xb	6								
		[IDX2]	A2 xb ee ff	6								
SBCB *opr*	(B) – (M) – C ⇒ B	IMM	C2 ii	1	–	–	–	–	Δ	Δ	Δ	Δ
	Subtract with Borrow from B	DIR	D2 dd	3								
		EXT	F2 hh ll	3								
		IDX	E2 xb	3								
		IDX1	E2 xb ff	3								
		IDX2	E2 xb ee ff	4								
		[D,IDX]	E2 xb	6								
		[IDX2]	E2 xb ee ff	6								
SEC	1 ⇒ C *Translates to* ORCC #$01	IMM	14 01	1	–	–	–	–	–	–	–	1
SEI	1 ⇒ I; (inhibit I interrupts) *Translates to* ORCC #$10	IMM	14 10	1	–	–	–	1	–	–	–	–
SEV	1 ⇒ V *Translates to* ORCC #$02	IMM	14 02	1	–	–	–	–	–	–	1	–
SEX *r1, r2*	$00:(r1) ⇒ r2 if r1, bit 7 is 0 *or* $FF:(r1) ⇒ r2 if r1, bit 7 is 1 Sign Extend 8-bit r1 to 16-bit r2 r1 may be A, B, or CCR r2 may be D, X, Y, or SP *Alternate mnemonic for* TFR r1, r2	INH	B7 eb	1	–	–	–	–	–	–	–	–
STAA *opr*	(A) ⇒ M	DIR	5A dd	2	–	–	–	–	Δ	Δ	0	–
	Store Accumulator A to Memory	EXT	7A hh ll	3								
		IDX	6A xb	2								
		IDX1	6A xb ff	3								
		IDX2	6A xb ee ff	3								
		[D,IDX]	6A xb	5								
		[IDX2]	6A xb ee ff	5								
STAB *opr*	(B) ⇒ M	DIR	5B dd	2	–	–	–	–	Δ	Δ	0	–
	Store Accumulator B to Memory	EXT	7B hh ll	3								
		IDX	6B xb	2								
		IDX1	6B xb ff	3								
		IDX2	6B xb ee ff	3								
		[D,IDX]	6B xb	5								
		[IDX2]	6B xb ee ff	5								
STD *opr*	(A) ⇒ M, (B) ⇒ M+1	DIR	5C dd	2	–	–	–	–	Δ	Δ	0	–
	Store Double Accumulator	EXT	7C hh ll	3								
		IDX	6C xb	2								
		IDX1	6C xb ff	3								
		IDX2	6C xb ee ff	3								
		[D,IDX]	6C xb	5								
		[IDX2]	6C xb ee ff	5								

Source Form	Operation	Addr. Mode	Machine Coding (hex)	~*	S	X	H	I	N	Z	V	C
STOP	(SP) – 2 ⇒ SP; RTN_H:RTN_L ⇒ $M_{(SP)}$:$M_{(SP+1)}$; (SP) – 2 ⇒ SP; (Y_H:Y_L) ⇒ $M_{(SP)}$:$M_{(SP+1)}$; (SP) – 2 ⇒ SP; (X_H:X_L) ⇒ $M_{(SP)}$:$M_{(SP+1)}$; (SP) – 2 ⇒ SP; (B:A) ⇒ $M_{(SP)}$:$M_{(SP+1)}$; (SP) – 1 ⇒ SP; (CCR) ⇒ $M_{(SP)}$; STOP All Clocks If S control bit = 1, the STOP instruction is disabled and acts like a two-cycle NOP. Registers stacked to allow quicker recovery by interrupt.	INH	18 3E	9** +5 or +2**	–	–	–	–	–	–	–	–
STS *opr*	(SP_H:SP_L) ⇒ M:M+1 Store Stack Pointer	DIR	5F dd	2	–	–	–	–	Δ	Δ	0	–
		EXT	7F hh ll	3								
		IDX	6F xb	2								
		IDX1	6F xb ff	3								
		IDX2	6F xb ee ff	3								
		[D,IDX]	6F xb	5								
		[IDX2]	6F xb ee ff	5								
STX *opr*	(X_H:X_L) ⇒ M:M+1 Store Index Register X	DIR	5E dd	2	–	–	–	–	Δ	Δ	0	–
		EXT	7E hh ll	3								
		IDX	6E xb	2								
		IDX1	6E xb ff	3								
		IDX2	6E xb ee ff	3								
		[D,IDX]	6E xb	5								
		[IDX2]	6E xb ee ff	5								
STY *opr*	(Y_H:Y_L) ⇒ M:M+1 Store Index Register Y	DIR	5D dd	2	–	–	–	–	Δ	Δ	0	–
		EXT	7D hh ll	3								
		IDX	6D xb	2								
		IDX1	6D xb ff	3								
		IDX2	6D xb ee ff	3								
		[D,IDX]	6D xb	5								
		[IDX2]	6D xb ee ff	5								
SUBA *opr*	(A) – (M) ⇒ A Subtract Memory from Accumulator A	IMM	80 ii	1	–	–	–	–	Δ	Δ	Δ	Δ
		DIR	90 dd	3								
		EXT	B0 hh ll	3								
		IDX	A0 xb	3								
		IDX1	A0 xb ff	3								
		IDX2	A0 xb ee ff	4								
		[D,IDX]	A0 xb	6								
		[IDX2]	A0 xb ee ff	6								
SUBB *opr*	(B) – (M) ⇒ B Subtract Memory from Accumulator B	IMM	C0 ii	1	–	–	–	–	Δ	Δ	Δ	Δ
		DIR	D0 dd	3								
		EXT	F0 hh ll	3								
		IDX	E0 xb	3								
		IDX1	E0 xb ff	3								
		IDX2	E0 xb ee ff	4								
		[D,IDX]	E0 xb	6								
		[IDX2]	E0 xb ee ff	6								

Source Form	Operation	Addr. Mode	Machine Coding (hex)	~*	S	X	H	I	N	Z	V	C
SUBD *opr*	(D) – (M:M+1) ⇒ D Subtract Memory from D (A:B)	IMM DIR EXT IDX IDX1 IDX2 [D,IDX] [IDX2]	83 jj kk 93 dd B3 hh ll A3 xb A3 xb ff A3 xb ee ff A3 xb A3 xb ee ff	2 3 3 3 3 4 6 6	–	–	–	–	Δ	Δ	Δ	Δ
SWI	(SP) – 2 ⇒ SP; RTN_H:RTN_L ⇒ $M_{(SP)}$:$M_{(SP+1)}$; (SP) – 2 ⇒ SP; (Y_H:Y_L) ⇒ $M_{(SP)}$:$M_{(SP+1)}$; (SP) – 2 ⇒ SP; (X_H:X_L) ⇒ $M_{(SP)}$:$M_{(SP+1)}$; (SP) – 2 ⇒ SP; (B:A) ⇒ $M_{(SP)}$:$M_{(SP+1)}$; (SP) – 1 ⇒ SP; (CCR) ⇒ $M_{(SP)}$ 1 ⇒ I; (SWI Vector) ⇒ PC Software Interrupt	INH	3F	9	–	–	–	1	–	–	–	–
TAB	(A) ⇒ B Transfer A to B	INH	18 0E	2	–	–	–	–	Δ	Δ	0	–
TAP	(A) ⇒ CCR *Translates to* TFR A , CCR	INH	B7 02	1	Δ	⇓	Δ	Δ	Δ	Δ	Δ	Δ
TBA	(B) ⇒ A Transfer B to A	INH	18 0F	2	–	–	–	–	Δ	Δ	0	–
TBEQ *cntr, rel*	If (cntr) = 0, then Branch; else Continue to next instruction Test Counter and Branch if Zero (cntr = A, B, D, X,Y, or SP)	REL (9-bit)	04 lb rr	3	–	–	–	–	–	–	–	–
TBL *opr*	(M) + [(B) × ((M+1) – (M))] ⇒ A 8-Bit Table Lookup and Interpolate Initialize B, and index before TBL. <ea> points at first 8-bit table entry (M) and B is fractional part of lookup value. (no indirect addressing modes allowed.)	IDX	18 3D xb	8	–	–	–	–	Δ	Δ	–	?
TBNE *cntr, rel*	If (cntr) not = 0, then Branch; else Continue to next instruction Test Counter and Branch if Not Zero (cntr = A, B, D, X,Y, or SP)	REL (9-bit)	04 lb rr	3	–	–	–	–	–	–	–	–
TFR *r1, r2*	(r1) ⇒ r2 *or* $00:(r1) ⇒ r2 *or* (r1[7:0]) ⇒ r2 Transfer Register to Register r1 and r2 may be A, B, CCR, D, X, Y, or SP	INH	B7 eb	1	– or Δ	– ⇓	– Δ	– Δ	– Δ	– Δ	– Δ	– Δ
TPA	(CCR) ⇒ A *Translates to* TFR CCR , A	INH	B7 20	1	–	–	–	–	–	–	–	–

Source Form	Operation	Addr. Mode	Machine Coding (hex)	~*	S	X	H	I	N	Z	V	C
TRAP	(SP) – 2 ⇒ SP; $RTN_H:RTN_L$ ⇒ $M_{(SP)}:M_{(SP+1)}$; (SP) – 2 ⇒ SP; $(Y_H:Y_L)$ ⇒ $M_{(SP)}:M_{(SP+1)}$; (SP) – 2 ⇒ SP; $(X_H:X_L)$ ⇒ $M_{(SP)}:M_{(SP+1)}$; (SP) – 2 ⇒ SP; (B:A) ⇒ $M_{(SP)}:M_{(SP+1)}$; (SP) – 1 ⇒ SP; (CCR) ⇒ $M_{(SP)}$ 1 ⇒ I; (TRAP Vector) ⇒ PC Unimplemented opcode trap	INH	18 tn tn = $30–$39 or $40–$FF	10	–	–	–	1	–	–	–	–
TST *opr*	(M) – 0 Test Memory for Zero or Minus	EXT IDX IDX1 IDX2 [D,IDX] [IDX2]	F7 hh ll E7 xb E7 xb ff E7 xb ee ff E7 xb E7 xb ee ff	3 3 3 4 6 6	–	–	–	–	Δ	Δ	0	0
TSTA	(A) – 0 Test A for Zero or Minus	INH	97	1								
TSTB	(B) – 0 Test B for Zero or Minus	INH	D7	1								
TSX	(SP) ⇒ X *Translates to* TFR SP,X	INH	B7 75	1	–	–	–	–	–	–	–	–
TSY	(SP) ⇒ Y *Translates to* TFR SP,Y	INH	B7 76	1	–	–	–	–	–	–	–	–
TXS	(X) ⇒ SP *Translates to* TFR X,SP	INH	B7 57	1	–	–	–	–	–	–	–	–
TYS	(Y) ⇒ SP *Translates to* TFR Y,SP	INH	B7 67	1	–	–	–	–	–	–	–	–
WAI	(SP) – 2 ⇒ SP; $RTN_H:RTN_L$ ⇒ $M_{(SP)}:M_{(SP+1)}$; (SP) – 2 ⇒ SP; $(Y_H:Y_L)$ ⇒ $M_{(SP)}:M_{(SP+1)}$; (SP) – 2 ⇒ SP; $(X_H:X_L)$ ⇒ $M_{(SP)}:M_{(SP+1)}$; (SP) – 2 ⇒ SP; (B:A) ⇒ $M_{(SP)}:M_{(SP+1)}$; (SP) – 1 ⇒ SP; (CCR) ⇒ $M_{(SP)}$; WAIT for interrupt	INH	3E	8** (in) + 5 (int)	– or – or –	– – 1	– – –	– 1 1	– – –	– – –	– – –	– – –
WAV	$\sum_{i=1}^{B} S_i F_i \Rightarrow Y{:}D$ $\sum_{i=1}^{B} F_i \Rightarrow X$ Calculate Sum of Products and Sum of Weights for Weighted Average Calculation Initialize B, X, and Y before WAV. B specifies number of elements. X points at first element in S_i list. Y points at first element in F_i list. All S_i and F_i elements are 8-bits. If interrupted, six extra bytes of stack used for intermediate values	Special	18 3C	8** per lable	–	–	?	–	?	Δ	?	?

Source Form	Operation	Addr. Mode	Machine Coding (hex)	~*	S	X	H	I	N	Z	V	C
wavr pseudo-instruction	*see* WAV Resume executing an interrupted WAV instruction (recover intermediate results from stack rather than initializing them to zero)	Special	3C	**	–	–	?	–	?	Δ	?	?
XGDX	(D) ⇔ (X) *Translates to* EXG D, X	INH	B7 C5	1	–	–	–	–	–	–	–	–
XGDY	(D) ⇔ (Y) *Translates to* EXG D, Y	INH	B7 C6	1	–	–	–	–	–	–	–	–

NOTES:

*Each cycle (~) is typically 125 ns for an 8-MHz bus (16-MHz oscillator).

**Refer to detailed instruction descriptions for additional information.

B

68HC812A4 Register Set

(Table used with permission of Motorola, Incorporated)

Address	Bit 7	6	5	4	3	2	1	Bit 0	Name
$0000	PA7	PA6	PA5	PA4	PA3	PA2	PA1	PA0	PORTA[1]
$0001	PB7	PB6	PB5	PB4	PB3	PB2	PB1	PB0	PORTB[1]
$0002	Bit 7	6	5	4	3	2	1	Bit 0	DDRA[1]
$0003	Bit 7	6	5	4	3	2	1	Bit 0	DDRB[1]
$0004	PC7	PC6	PC5	PC4	PC3	PC2	PC1	PC0	PORTC[1]
$0005	PD7	PD6	PD5	PD4	PD3	PD2	PD1	PD0	PORTD[2]
$0006	Bit 7	6	5	4	3	2	1	Bit 0	DDRC[1]
$0007	Bit 7	6	5	4	3	2	1	Bit 0	DDRD[2]
$0008	PE7	PE6	PE5	PE4	PE3	PE2	PE1	PE0	PORTE[3]
$0009	Bit 7	Bit 6	Bit 5	Bit 4	Bit 3	Bit 2	0	0	DDRE[3]
$000A	ARSIE	PLLTE	PIPOE	NECLK	LSTRE	RDWE	0	0	PEAR[4]
$000B	SMODN	MODB	MODA	ESTR	IVIS	0	EMD	EME	MODE[4]
$000C	PUPH	PUPG	PUPF	PUPE	PUPD	PUPC	PUPB	PUPA	PUCR[4]
$000D	RDPJ	RDPH	RDPG	RDPF	RDPE	RDPD	RDPC	RDPAB	RDRIV[4]
$000E	0	0	0	0	0	0	0	0	Reserved[4]
$000F	0	0	0	0	0	0	0	0	Reserved[4]
$0010	RAM15	RAM14	RAM13	RAM12	RAM11	0	0	0	INITRM
$0011	REG15	REG14	REG13	REG12	REG11	0	0	0	INITRG
$0012	EE15	EE14	EE13	EE12	0	0	0	EEON	INITEE
$0013	EWDIR	NDRC	0	0	0	0	0	0	MISC
$0014	RTIE	RSWAI	RSBCK	0	RTBYP	RTR2	RTR1	RTR0	RTICTL
$0015	RTIF	0	0	0	0	0	0	0	RTIFLG
$0016	CME	FCME	FCM	FCOP	DISR	CR2	CR1	CR0	COPCTL
$0017	Bit 7	6	5	4	3	2	1	Bit 0	COPRST
$0018	ITE6	ITE8	ITEA	ITEC	ITEE	ITF0	ITF2	ITF4	ITST0
$0019	ITD6	ITD8	ITDA	ITDC	ITDE	ITE0	ITE2	ITE4	ITST1
$001A	ITC6	ITC8	ITCA	ITCC	ITCE	ITD0	ITD2	ITD4	ITST2
$001B	0	0	0	0	0	ITC0	ITC2	ITC4	ITST3
$001C	0	0	0	0	0	0	0	0	Reserved
$001D	0	0	0	0	0	0	0	0	Reserved
$001E	IRQE	IRQEN	DLY	0	0	0	0	0	INTCR
$001F	1	1	PSEL5	PSEL4	PSEL3	PSEL2	PSEL1	0	HPRIO
$0020	Bit 7	6	5	4	3	2	1	Bit 0	KWIED[5]
$0021	Bit 7	6	5	4	3	2	1	Bit 0	KWIFD[5]
$0022	0	0	0	0	0	0	0	0	Reserved
$0023	0	0	0	0	0	0	0	0	Reserved
$0024	PH7	PH6	PH5	PH4	PH3	PH2	PH1	PH0	PORTH
$0025	Bit 7	6	5	4	3	2	1	Bit 0	DDRH
$0026	Bit 7	6	5	4	3	2	1	Bit 0	KWIEH
$0027	Bit 7	6	5	4	3	2	1	Bit 0	KWIFH
$0028	PJ7	PJ6	PJ5	PJ4	PJ3	PJ2	PJ1	PJ0	PORTJ

Address	Bit 7	6	5	4	3	2	1	Bit 0	Name
$0029	Bit 7	6	5	4	3	2	1	Bit 0	DDRJ
$002A	Bit 7	6	5	4	3	2	1	Bit 0	KWIEJ
$002B	Bit 7	6	5	4	3	2	1	Bit 0	KWIFJ
$002C	Bit 7	6	5	4	3	2	1	Bit 0	KPOLJ
$002D	Bit 7	6	5	4	3	2	1	Bit 0	PUPSJ
$002E	Bit 7	6	5	4	3	2	1	Bit 0	PULEJ
$002F	0	0	0	0	0	0	0	0	Reserved
$0030	0	PF6	PF5	PF4	PF3	PF2	PF1	PF0	PORTF
$0031	0	0	PG5	PG4	PG3	PG2	PG1	PG0	PORTG
$0032	0	Bit 6	5	4	3	2	1	Bit 0	DDRF
$0033	0	0	Bit 5	4	3	2	1	Bit 0	DDRG
$0034	PDA19	PDA18	PDA17	PDA16	PDA15	PDA14	PDA13	PDA12	DPAGE
$0035	PPA21	PPA20	PPA19	PPA18	PPA17	PPA16	PPA15	PPA14	PPAGE
$0036	PEA17	PEA16	PEA15	PEA14	PEA13	PEA12	PEA11	PEA10	EPAGE
$0037	DWEN	PWEN	EWEN	0	0	0	0	0	WINDEF
$0038	0	0	A21E	A20E	A19E	A18E	A17E	A16E	MXAR
$0039	0	0	0	0	0	0	0	0	Reserved
$003A	0	0	0	0	0	0	0	0	Reserved
$003B	0	0	0	0	0	0	0	0	Reserved
$003C	0	CSP1E	CSP0E	CSDE	CS3E	CS2E	CS1E	CS0E	CSCTL0
$003D	0	CSP1FL	CSPA21	CSDHF	CS3EP	0	0	0	CSCTL1
$003E	0	0	SRP1A	SRP1B	SRP0A	SRP0B	STRDA	STRDB	CSSTR0
$003F	STR3A	STR3B	STR2A	STR2B	STR1A	STR1B	STR0A	STR0B	CSSTR1
$0040	0	0	0	0	LDV11	LDV10	LDV9	LDV8	LDV
$0041	LDV7	LDV6	LDV5	LDV4	LDV3	LDV2	LDV1	LDV0	LDV
$0042	0	0	0	0	RDV11	RDV10	RDV9	RDV8	RDV
$0043	RDV7	RDV6	RDV5	RDV4	RDV3	RDV2	RDV1	RDV0	RDV
$0044	0	0	0	0	0	0	0	0	Reserved
$0045	0	0	0	0	0	0	0	0	Reserved
$0046	0	0	0	0	0	0	0	0	Reserved
$0047	LCK	PLLON	PLLS	BCSC	BCSB	BCSA	MCSB	MCSA	CLKCTL
$0048–$005F	0	0	0	0	0	0	0	0	Reserved
$0060	0	0	0	0	0	0	0	0	ATDCTL0
$0061	0	0	0	0	0	0	0	0	ATDCTL1
$0062	ADPU	AFFC	AWAI	0	0	0	ASCIE	ASCIF	ATDCTL2
$0063	0	0	0	0	0	0	FRZ1	FRZ0	ATDCTL3
$0064	0	SMP1	SMP0	PRS4	PRS3	PRS2	PRS1	PRS0	ATDCTL4
$0065	0	S8CM	SCAN	MULT	CD	CC	CB	CA	ATDCTL5
$0066	SCF	0	0	0	0	CC2	CC1	CC0	ATDSTAT
$0067	CCF7	CCF6	CCF5	CCF4	CCF3	CCF2	CCF1	CCF0	ATDSTAT
$0068	SAR9	SAR8	SAR7	SAR6	SAR5	SAR4	SAR3	SAR2	ATDTEST
$0069	SAR1	SAR0	RST	TSTOUT	TST3	TST2	TST1	TST0	ATDTEST
$006A–$006E	0	0	0	0	0	0	0	0	Reserved
$006F	PAD7	PAD6	PAD5	PAD4	PAD3	PAD2	PAD1	PAD0	PORTAD
$0070	Bit 7	6	5	4	3	2	1	Bit 0	ADR0H
$0071	0	0	0	0	0	0	0	0	Reserved
$0072	Bit 7	6	5	4	3	2	1	Bit 0	ADR1H

Address	Bit 7	6	5	4	3	2	1	Bit 0	Name
$0073	0	0	0	0	0	0	0	0	Reserved
$0074	Bit 7	6	5	4	3	2	1	Bit 0	ADR2H
$0075	0	0	0	0	0	0	0	0	Reserved
$0076	Bit 7	6	5	4	3	2	1	Bit 0	ADR3H
$0077	0	0	0	0	0	0	0	0	Reserved
$0078	Bit 7	6	5	4	3	2	1	Bit 0	ADR4H
$0079	0	0	0	0	0	0	0	0	Reserved
$007A	Bit 7	6	5	4	3	2	1	Bit 0	ADR5H
$007B	0	0	0	0	0	0	0	0	Reserved
$007C	Bit 7	6	5	4	3	2	1	Bit 0	ADR6H
$007D	0	0	0	0	0	0	0	0	Reserved
$007E	Bit 7	6	5	4	3	2	1	Bit 0	ADR7H
$007F	0	0	0	0	0	0	0	0	Reserved
$0080	IOS7	IOS6	IOS5	IOS4	IOS3	IOS2	IOS1	IOS0	TIOS
$0081	FOC7	FOC6	FOC5	FOC4	FOC3	FOC2	FOC1	FOC0	CFORC
$0082	OC7M7	OC7M6	OC7M5	OC7M4	OC7M3	OC7M2	OC7M1	OC7M0	OC7M
$0083	OC7D7	OC7D6	OC7D5	OC7D4	OC7D3	OC7D2	OC7D1	OC7D0	OC7D
$0084	Bit 15	14	13	12	11	10	9	Bit 8	TCNT
$0085	Bit 7	6	5	4	3	2	1	Bit 0	TCNT
$0086	TEN	TSWAI	TSBCK	TFFCA	PAOQE	T7QE	T1QE	T0QE	TSCR
$0087	PAOQB	PAOQA	T7QB	T7QA	T1QB	T1QA	T0QB	T0QA	TQCR
$0088	OM7	OL7	OM6	OL6	OM5	OL5	OM4	OL4	TCTL1
$0089	OM3	OL3	OM2	OL2	OM1	OL1	OM0	OL0	TCTL2
$008A	EDG7B	EDG7A	EDG6B	EDG6A	EDG5B	EDG5A	EDG4B	EDG4A	TCTL3
$008B	EDG3B	EDG3A	EDG2B	EDG2A	EDG1B	EDG1A	EDG0B	EDG0A	TCTL4
$008C	C7I	C6I	C5I	C4I	C3I	C2I	C1I	C0I	TMSK1
$008D	TOI	0	TPU	TDRB	TCRE	PR2	PR1	PR0	TMSK2
$008E	C7F	C6F	C5F	C4F	C3F	C2F	C1F	C0F	TFLG1
$008F	TOF	0	0	0	0	0	0	0	TFLG2
$0090	Bit 15	14	13	12	11	10	9	Bit 8	TC0
$0091	Bit 7	6	5	4	3	2	1	Bit 0	TC0
$0092	Bit 15	14	13	12	11	10	9	Bit 8	TC1
$0093	Bit 7	6	5	4	3	2	1	Bit 0	TC1
$0094	Bit 15	14	13	12	11	10	9	Bit 8	TC2
$0095	Bit 7	6	5	4	3	2	1	Bit 0	TC2
$0096	Bit 15	14	13	12	11	10	9	Bit 8	TC3
$0097	Bit 7	6	5	4	3	2	1	Bit 0	TC3
$0098	Bit 15	14	13	12	11	10	9	Bit 8	TC4
$0099	Bit 7	6	5	4	3	2	1	Bit 0	TC4
$009A	Bit 15	14	13	12	11	10	9	Bit 8	TC5
$009B	Bit 7	6	5	4	3	2	1	Bit 0	TC5
$009C	Bit 15	14	13	12	11	10	9	Bit 8	TC6
$009D	Bit 7	6	5	4	3	2	1	Bit 0	TC6
$009E	Bit 15	14	13	12	11	10	9	Bit 8	TC7
$009F	Bit 7	6	5	4	3	2	1	Bit 0	TC7
$00A0	0	PAEN	PAMOD	PEDGE	CLK1	CLK0	PAOVI	PAI	PACTL
$00A1	0	0	0	0	0	0	PAOVF	PAIF	PAFLG
$00A2	Bit 15	14	13	12	11	10	9	Bit 8	PACNT
$00A3	Bit 7	6	5	4	3	2	1	Bit 0	PACNT

Address	Bit 7	6	5	4	3	2	1	Bit 0	Name
$00A4–$00AC	0	0	0	0	0	0	0	0	Reserved
$00AD	0	0	0	0	0	0	TCBYP	PCBYP	TIMTST
$00AE	PT7	PT6	PT5	PT4	PT3	PT2	PT1	PT0	PORTT
$00AF	Bit 7	6	5	4	3	2	1	Bit 0	DDRT
$00B0–$00BF	0	0	0	0	0	0	0	0	Reserved
$00C0	BTST	BSPL	BRLD	SBR12	SBR11	SBR10	SBR9	SBR8	SC0BDH
$00C1	SBR7	SBR6	SBR5	SBR4	SBR3	SBR2	SBR1	SBR0	SC0BDL
$00C2	LOOPS	WOMS	RSRC	M	WAKE	ILT	PE	PT	SC0CR1
$00C3	TIE	TCIE	RIE	ILIE	TE	RE	RWU	SBK	SC0CR2
$00C4	TDRE	TC	RDRF	IDLE	OR	NF	FE	PF	SC0SR1
$00C5	0	0	0	0	0	0	0	RAF	SC0SR2
$00C6	R8	T8	0	0	0	0	0	0	SC0DRH
$00C7	R7T7	R6T6	R5T5	R4T4	R3T3	R2T2	R1T1	R0T0	SC0DRL
$00C8	BTST	BSPL	BRLD	SBR12	SBR11	SBR10	SBR9	SBR8	SC1BDH
$00C9	SBR7	SBR6	SBR5	SBR4	SBR3	SBR2	SBR1	SBR0	SC1BDL
$00CA	LOOPS	WOMS	RSRC	M	WAKE	ILT	PE	PT	SC1CR1
$00CB	TIE	TCIE	RIE	ILIE	TE	RE	RWU	SBK	SC1CR2
$00CC	TDRE	TC	RDRF	IDLE	OR	NF	FE	PF	SC1SR1
$00CD	0	0	0	0	0	0	0	RAF	SC1SR2
$00CE	R8	T8	0	0	0	0	0	0	SC1DRH
$00CF	R7T7	R6T6	R5T5	R4T4	R3T3	R2T2	R1T1	R0T0	SC1DRL
$00D0	SPIE	SPE	SWOM	MSTR	CPOL	CPHA	SSOE	LSBF	SP0CR1
$00D1	SPFQE	SPFQB	SPFQA	0	PUPS	RDS	0	SPC0	SP0CR2
$00D2	0	0	0	0	0	SPR2	SPR1	SPR0	SP0BR
$00D3	SPIF	WCOL	0	MODF	0	0	0	0	SP0SR
$00D4	0	0	0	0	0	0	0	0	Reserved
$00D5	Bit 7	6	5	4	3	2	1	Bit 0	SP0DR
$00D6	PS7	PS6	PS5	PS4	PS3	PS2	PS1	PS0	PORTS
$00D7	Bit 7	6	5	4	3	2	1	Bit 0	DDRS
$00D8–$00DF	0	0	0	0	0	0	0	0	Reserved
$00E0–$00EF	0	0	0	0	0	0	0	0	Reserved
$00F0	1	1	1	1	1	1	PROTLCK	EERC	EEMCR
$00F1	1	BPROT6	BPROT5	BPROT4	BPROT3	BPROT2	BPROT1	BPROT0	EEPROT
$00F2	EEODD	EEVEN	MARG	EECPD	EECPRD	0	EECPM	0	EETST
$00F3	BULKP	0	0	BYTE	ROW	ERASE	EELAT	EEPGM	EEPROG
$00F4–$01FF	0	0	0	0	0	0	0	0	Reserved

1. Port A, port B, port C and data direction registers DDRA, DDRB, and DDRC are not in map in expanded and peripheral modes.
2. Port D and DDRD not in map in wide expanded modes and peripheral mode; also not in map in narrow special expanded mode with EMD set.
3. Port E and DDRE not in map in peripheral mode; also not in map in expanded modes with EME set.
4. Registers also not in map in peripheral mode.
5. Key wake-up associated with port D not in map in wide expanded modes; also not in map in narrow special expanded mode with EMD set.

C

Number Systems and Number Arithmetic

In this appendix, we present three different number systems and the procedure to convert number representations in one number system to the corresponding representations in another system. We also describe the arithmetic operations for one of the three number systems: the binary number system. The number systems of interest are the binary, decimal, and hexadecimal systems. During the coverage of the binary number system, we consider an important number representation scheme called the *2's complement number representation*. This appendix is organized as follows. Section C.1 introduces different number systems, Section C.2 covers binary number arithmetic, and Section C.3 illustrates techniques to convert from one number system to another.

C.1 NUMBER REPRESENTATIONS

A number can be represented in many different ways using different number systems. The most familiar one to us is the decimal number system. We teach our children to add, subtract, multiply, and divide decimal numbers. The decimal number system uses 10 different symbols: 0, 1, 2, 3, 4, 5, 6, 7, 8, and 9. The decimal number system is most natural to us since we have 10 fingers to count. If we had only eight fingers, do you think our civilization would have adopted the decimal number system for use today? Probably not. That means, if we ever find another civilization somewhere in the vast universe and its creatures have some sort of fingers numbering other than 10, chances are that the discovered civilization is using a nondecimal number system. Enough digression.

Different number systems use different numbers of symbols to represent numbers. The binary number system uses only two symbols: 0 and 1. Computers use the binary number system to represent all information. Although the decimal number system is convenient for humans, it is not well suited for machines. The simplest and most convenient number system for electronic machines is the binary number system. Using the binary number system, these machines only need to distinguish two states: on and off.

If 16 symbols are used to represent numbers, we are working with the hexadecimal number system. For the hexadecimal number system, we use 0, 1, 2, 3, 4, 5, 6, 7, 8, 9, A, B, C, D, E, and F to represent numbers. Symbol A in the hexadecimal number system is equivalent to 10 in the decimal number system and symbol B is equivalent to 11 in the decimal number system. Similarly, symbols C, D, E, and F in the hexadecimal system correspond to 12, 13, 14, and 15 in the decimal number system, respectively. That is, each hexadecimal digit is represented by 1 out of 16 different numbers.

The number of symbols we use in a number system is called the *base* of the system. Since the decimal number system has 10 symbols, we say that the base of the decimal number system is 10. A base provides a means to conveniently group numbers together. For example, in the decimal system, 10 ones make 10, 10 tens make 100, 10 one hundreds make 1,000, and so on. We can perform the same task in the binary number system. The base of the binary number system is two. In this system, two ones make two, two twos make four, two fours make eight, two eights make 16, and so forth. Strictly speaking, since there are only two symbols in the binary number system, there are no notions of 2, 4, 8, and 16. Those numbers would be represented as 10 (decimal 2), 100 (decimal 4), 1000 (decimal 8), and 10,000 (decimal 16). Can you try the same exercise with the base for the hexadecimal number system? The base of a system plays a critical role in a number representation as you see shortly.

We consider the topic of number representations in different number systems next. We start this topic with an example. When we tell our kids that 249 days are left until Christmas, they clearly understand from the numerical number that the number of days left before the celebration (or, to them, receiving lots of presents) is two 100s, four 10s, and nine 1s. How do we communicate that with the number 249? Well, we learned as kids to associate numerical values with their positions in a number. That is, when the number (249) was presented to us, we did not say there are nine 100s, four 10s, and two 1s. Instead, we learned the far right number receives unit one (assuming that the decimal point exists to the right of this number), and as we move to its left the value of a numerical number increases by 10-fold. Thus, we associate number 4 with 10s and 2 with 100s. Figure C.1(a) illustrates this example.

The idea of associating positions with proper values is mathematically shown using the base of the number system. Using the base of the decimal number system, we can represent the number 249 as $2 * 10^2 + 4 * 10^1 + 9 * 10^0$, recalling that 10^0 is one. Thus, knowing the base of a number system allows us to properly associate the position of a numerical number with appropriate values or weights.

The example showed that the association of positions and weights are used to represent decimal numbers. How about other number systems—namely, the binary and hexadecimal systems? The idea applies the same way for these systems. Let us consider each number system using the same numerical number.

For the binary number system, recall that we only use symbols 0 and 1 to represent a number. Thus, binary number 10_2 is equivalent to 2 in the decimal number. The subscript 2 in 10_2 denotes that the base of the number is two, indicating a binary number representation. The binary number representation of decimal number 249 is 11111001_2. Section C.3 shows you how this binary number is obtained, given decimal number 249. For now, we want you to focus on the number representation. Using the same analogy we used for the decimal number example, we associate each binary value with its position within the number, as shown in Figure C.1(b). In this example, starting from the rightmost binary digit, we have 1

$$249 = (2 \times 10^2) + (4 \times 10^1) + (9 \times 10^0)$$

(a)

$$11111001 =$$
$$(1 \times 2^7) + (1 \times 2^6) + (1 \times 2^5) +$$
$$(1 \times 2^4) + (1 \times 2^3) + (0 \times 2^2) +$$
$$(0 \times 2^1) + (1 \times 2^0)$$

(b)

$$F9 = (15 \times 16^1) + (9 \times 16^0)$$

(c)

Figure C.1 Number representation for decimal: frame (a) shows the decimal number representation, frame (b) shows the binary number representation, and frame (c) shows the hexadecimal number representation.

one, 0 twos, 0 fours, 1 eight, 1 sixteen, 1 thirty-two, 1 sixty-four, and 1 one hundred twenty-eight. You can verify that the binary number is equivalent to decimal number 249 by adding up the contributions made by each binary value. Using the base, the binary number means $1*2^7+1*2^6+1*2^5+1*2^4+1*2^3+0*2^2+0*2^1+1*2^0$. Again note that the exponent increases from zero by one as we move from the right to the left.

Let us consider now the representation of decimal number 249 in the hexadecimal number system, as shown in Figure C.1(c). The numbers in the hexadecimal number system are represented with 16 different symbols, and base 16_{10} is used to associate positions and hexadecimal digits. Hexadecimal 10_h, where subscript h denotes a hexadecimal representation, now means 16_{10}. The hexadecimal representation of decimal number 249 is $F9_h$. Can you verify the correctness of the number? Recalling that the symbol F is equivalent to decimal number 15, we can convert number $F9_h$ as $15 * 16^1 + 9 * 16^0$. Now that we learned how to represent a number using three different number systems, some examples are in order.

Practice Questions

Question: Represent decimal number 4 using the binary and hexadecimal number systems.

Answer:

Binary Number	$100 = 1 * 2^2 + 0 * 2^1 + 0 * 2^0$
Hexadecimal Number	$4 = 4 * 16^0$

Question: What are the equivalent decimal numbers for the following number representations? (a) 10110_2 and (b) $3DF_h$.

Answer:

$$10110_2 = 1 * 2^4 + 0 * 2^3 + 1 * 2^2 + 1 * 2^1 + 0 * 2^0 = 22_{10}$$

$$3DF_h = 3 * 16^2 + 13 * 16^1 + 15 * 16^0 = 991_{10}$$

C.2 BINARY NUMBER ARITHMETIC

In this section, we illustrate the addition, subtraction, multiplication, and division operations of binary numbers. Computers use both signed (positive and negative) numbers and unsigned (only positive) numbers. To perform the arithmetic operations for both types of numbers, we first need a means to represent both positive and negative numbers. We do that using a binary number representation called the 2's complement number system. We first study the 2's complement number representation. Then we consider each of the four arithmetic operations.

C.2.1 The 2's Complement Number Representation

We saw from the previous section how positive numbers are represented in the binary number system. We tacitly avoided mentioning negative number representations to focus on number representations rather than arithmetic operations in different number systems. In this subsection, we illustrate how computers represent negative numbers in the binary number system. Although we can present the same subject in the hexadecimal number system, we rarely encounter a need to do so since all digital machines use the binary number system to perform any arithmetic operation. The hexadecimal number system only exists to conveniently represent a string of binary numbers, whether a positive or negative number, through a number representation conversion, which is the topic for Section C.3.

We already know that in any number system there are infinite numbers. For a large number, we need many digits to represent the number. To make our case concrete and to make the binary number representation suitable for the 68HC12, we limit the number of numbers we can represent to 256_{10}. This number dictates that we should use eight binary positions usually called *bits*. Why? Suppose you only have a single bit to represent numbers in the binary number system. The only two numbers you can represent are 0 and 1—two different numbers. Now suppose you have two bits to represent numbers. How many different numbers can you represent? They are 00, 01, 10, and 11—four different numbers. That is, you can choose one of two possible numbers for the first binary digit and again one of two possible numbers for the second binary digit. If we enumerate all possible combinations, we end up with the four listed before. Let us make one further observation. The number of possible enumerations is $2 * 2$ for the current example since each bit can hold one of two possible symbols. What if we had three binary digits to represent numbers? You guessed it. The third binary digit can also hold two different symbols, and the number of possible enumeration now is two times the enumeration when we only had two binary digits. Do you grasp the picture? The number of binary digits determines the number of values we can represent in the binary system. More specifically, the number of bits and different values we can represent have the following relationship:

$$2^b = \text{number of different values}$$

Symbol b denotes the number of binary digits we have at our disposal to represent numbers. Do eight digits satisfy our condition to represent 256_{10} different numbers? According to the previous equation, 2^8 certainly gives 256_{10}.

Now that we can denote each binary number using eight binary digits, let us list all possible numbers we can represent:

00000000

00000001

00000010

00000011

...

11111110

11111111

According to the binary representation in Section C.1, the 00000000_2 is 0_{10} and the 11111111 is 255_{10}, making 256_{10} different numbers. To accommodate both positive and negative numbers, we now must split the range of numbers into two equal parts. One simple way to represent both positive and negative numbers is to agree that the most significant digit represents a sign. Recall that the most significant digit is the leftmost one or bit, similar to the most significant decimal digit we use in a decimal number.[1] For the rest of the discussion, we use the terms *bit* and *binary digit* interchangeably. If the seventh digit is used (we start with 0th bit for the rightmost bit) as the sign bit, we have $2^7 = 128$ values we can represent, with the seventh bit being zero and another 128 values with the seventh bit being one. We can agree that if the seventh bit of a number is zero, the number is positive, and the number is negative otherwise. This representation is called the *magnitude number representation*. The representation, however, has a problem in that we have two zeros—a positive zero (00000000) and a negative zero (10000000). The two zeros caused problems with hardware engineers since the idea meant more hardware components to accommodate both zeros. The use of the seventh bit to distinguish positive numbers from negative numbers, however, was a desirable feature for simplifying hardware designs. This led to the number representation used in modern computers—the 2's complement number system.

In the 2's complement number system, we have a single zero represented by 00000000 and uneven positive and negative numbers. The 2's complement number system representation is shown:

$00000001 \Leftarrow 1$

$00000010 \Leftarrow 2$

$00000011 \Leftarrow 3$

...

[1] We call numerical value 9 as the most significant digit of decimal number 925 since the digit corresponds to the physical position associated with the most significant value—namely, 100s.

$$01111111 \Leftarrow 127$$
$$11111111 \Leftarrow -1$$
$$11111110 \Leftarrow -2$$
$$11111101 \Leftarrow -3$$
$$11111100 \Leftarrow -4$$
$$\ldots$$
$$10000001 \Leftarrow -127$$
$$10000000 \Leftarrow -128$$

The range of numbers represented using eight bits is from -128_{10} to 127_{10}. The 2's complement representation not only retained the desired feature of using the most significant bit as the sign bit, but also allowed hardware engineers to easily implement hardware components for the addition and subtraction operations. The use of the seventh bit as the sign of a number is a convenient feature for hardware to distinguish negative numbers from positive numbers since only the most significant bit needs to be tested. The simplification of hardware implementations for binary addition and subtraction operations is obtained by performing both operations using a single hardware module as we show here. We postpone the discussion of this topic to the next subsection.

The name *2's complement* stems from the fact that if we add two numbers of equal magnitudes with opposite signs, we end up with a zero. For example, adding $00000001(1_{10})$ with $11111111(-1_{10})$ gives $00000000(0_{10})$. Take a few other pairs and verify for yourself that the addition of each pair of numbers results in a zero. The only exception to this is $10000000\,(-128_{10})$, which does not have a corresponding positive number counterpart. This special way of representing numbers is the cornerstone for simplifying arithmetic hardware of modern computers.

For positive 2's complement numbers, it is relatively easy to compute the magnitude of a number using the method shown in Section C.1. A straightforward application of the same method does not work for the negative 2's complement numbers. Is there a convenient way to compute magnitudes of a negative number? The answer is to apply two operations in a sequence to the 2's complement negative number. The sequence of operations is based on the simple fact that if we subtract a negative number from zero, we end up with a positive number whose magnitude equals the magnitude of the original negative number. The subtraction from zero operation is carried out by first taking a 1's complement operation, where the 1's complement means to change each current bit to its opposite state. That is, we convert 1 to 0 and 0 to 1 bit by bit for all 8 bits. The second step of adding a binary one is necessary due to the uneven range of number representation of 2's complement numbers. Thus, the sequence of two operations is to take the 1's complement and then add a binary one. Let us look at an example.

Question: Given the number 11110001_2 in the 2's complement form, what is the equivalent decimal value?

Answer: Following our prior discussion, we perform operation 00000000 – 11110001. We perform the operation using the sequence of two separate operations. First, the 1's complement operation produces 00001110_2, and the second addition operation of binary one results 00001111_2. This number can then be converted to its corresponding decimal number using the method presented in Section C.1. Thus, the magnitude of the original number is $1 * 2^3 + 1 * 2^2 + 1 * 2^1 + 1 * 2^0 = 15$ and the decimal equivalent of number 11110001_2 is -15_{10}. We verify the result using a binary subtraction of the two numbers in the next subsection.

The final important question we must ask is: How do we know whether a given binary number is formed using the 2's complement number representation? After all, we have cases where we only deal with positive numbers, such as referring to memory locations, and other cases where we need to consider both positive and negative numbers. The answer to the original question is we do not. A binary number is a binary number, and a computer does not know whether it is a 2's complement signed number or an unsigned number. The responsibility of keeping track of that lies with you—the programmer.

C.2.2 Arithmetic

In this subsection, we discuss the addition, subtraction, multiplication, and division operations of binary numbers. Our discussion of the subject uses a straightforward manner, pointing interested readers to available textbooks for hardware implementation details of these operations. We do so without any apology since one can easily find outstanding coverage of the computer hardware details in many reference books, including the ones shown at the end of this appendix. Besides, we simply do not have room to present all related materials.

Addition and Subtraction Both the addition and subtraction operations of binary numbers follow the same procedures you learned in your elementary school using decimal numbers. The only difference we constantly have to remember is that the base is 2 for binary numbers. Since we know the process, let us apply arithmetic skills we learned during our early school years to add and subtract binary numbers. Our discussion again limits the range of binary numbers to eight bits.

```
 142 ──→   10001110
+ 21 ──→ + 00010101
────      ─────────
 163 ──→   10100011
```

(a) unsigned number interpretation

```
−114 ──→   10100011
+ 21 ──→ + 00010101
────      ─────────
 −93 ──→   10100011
```

(b) 2′s complement signed number interpretation

Figure C.2 An example illustrating the addition operation of binary numbers: (a) the result is interpreted as an unsigned number, and (b) the result is interpreted as a 2's complement signed number.

Suppose we are adding the following two binary numbers.

10001110

00010101

Suppose both numbers are unsigned numbers. The decimal equivalent numbers are then 142_{10} and 21_{10}. Figure C.2(a) shows the steps required to perform the addition. As was the case with decimal numbers, carries from lower bits to higher bits also occur in the addition with base 2.

Now consider that the two binary numbers are formed using the 2's complement number representation. The equivalent decimal numbers are then -114_{10} and 21_{10}. Figure C.2(b) shows the same operation. As alluded to earlier, the hardware performs the identical addition operation oblivious of the 2's complement number representation. It only adds numbers bit by bit while observing carries. The interpretations of the two identical results are quite different as shown in the two frames of the figure.

Let us consider the subtraction operation next. Again, the process is exactly the same as the one we learned with decimal numbers. Let us consider the same two numbers we used for the addition operation example for the binary subtraction operation. Figure C.3(a) shows subtracting 21_{10} from 142_{10}. If necessary, borrows must occur from higher bits to lower bits. As shown, the resulting value 121_{10} is obtained. Figure C.3(b) shows the identical operation, but the same result is interpreted as -135_{10} in the 2's complement number system.

One more example. Let us consider the example used in the previous subsection: $00000000_2 - 11110001_2$. To perform the task, we first need to borrow a bit from an imaginary eighth bit as shown in Figure C.4.

```
   142 ——→   10001110
 − 21  ——→ − 00010101
 ——————    ——————————
   121 ——→   01111001
```

(a) unsigned number interpretation

```
 − 92  ——→   10100100
 − 21  ——→ − 00010101
 ——————    ——————————
 − 113 ——→   10001111
```

(b) 2's complement signed number interpretation

Figure C.3 An example illustrating the subtraction operation of binary numbers: (a) The result is interpreted as an unsigned number, and (b) the result is interpreted as a 2's complement signed number.

The result agrees with the answer obtained in the previous subsection and shows that the 2's complement operation of a number, subtracting a number from zero, is easily performed by first taking the 1's complement of the number followed by addition of binary number one. In the previous subsection, we postponed the discussion of the hardware simplification advantage of the 2's complement number representation. The current topic discussion explains the advantage. The present discussion shows that the easiest way to convert the sign of a number is to take the 2's complement operation of the number. That is applying the sequence of two operations to a signed number to find a number with the opposite sign. Using the same principle, CPUs of modern computers perform the binary subtraction operation by converting a subtrahend to its 2's complement form and adding the transformed number. Thus, CPUs do not require two separate hardware modules to perform additions and subtractions, but a single hardware module to perform

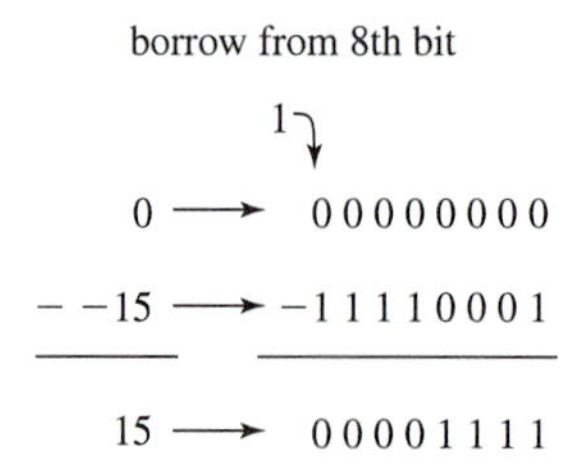

Figure C.4 Another example of illustrating the binary subtraction operation.

both operations. In short, the operation a − b becomes a + (−b) using the 2's complement arithmetic.

Multiplication and Division We can also perform the multiplication and division operations of binary numbers exactly the same way as we learned the operations with decimal numbers. Again, we illustrate both operations using two examples. First, consider performing the multiplication of 00101010_2 with 00000010_2. The corresponding decimal numbers are 42_{10} and 2_{10}. Figure C.5(a) shows the process involved in multiplying the two binary numbers. Note that as we multiply the multiplicand with the multiplier one bit at a time from the right, the value of the subresult shifts to the left by one bit at a time as shown in the figure. Since the second through seventh bits of the multiplier are zeros, these bits do not play any role in producing the result. Once all multiplier bits have been multiplied, the subresults are summed together to produce the final answer.

The division operation is illustrated using dividend $10101110_2(174_{10})$ and divisor $00001000_2(8_{10})$. Again, the process mirrors the one we perform with decimal numbers. We simply ignore the upper five zero bits of the divisor before we perform the division. Figure C.5(b) shows the division operation using the two numbers.

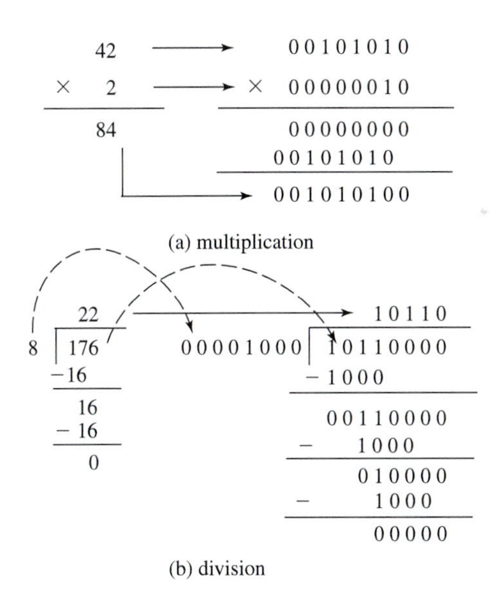

Figure C.5 Two examples showing the multiplication and division operations of binary numbers: (a) multiplying number $00101010_2(42_{10})$ with number $00000010_2(2_{10})$, and (b) dividing number $10101110_2(174_{10})$ by number $000001000_2(8_{10})$.

This subsection showed that the addition, subtraction, multiplication, and division operations of binary numbers follow the exact same procedures used in the decimal number system except that the base of operations is decimal number 2. Similarly, we can perform the arithmetic operations in any other number systems.

C.3 CHANGING THE BASE OF NUMBERS

In this section, we present techniques to convert a number from one number system to another. Again, the number systems of our interest are the binary, decimal, and hexadecimal number systems. The number conversion is important since humans work best with decimal numbers, whereas computers operate with binary numbers. As we see, the hexadecimal number system provides a convenient means to represent binary numbers. To describe the conversion procedure, we take a number from each of the three number systems in turn and show how to change the base to two remaining number systems. We start with a binary number.

The task we want to perform is to generate equivalent decimal and hexadecimal numbers for a given binary number. The process of converting a binary number to a decimal number was seen in Section C.1. We associated each binary bit with its position. For example, given binary number 1101_2, we compute its equivalent decimal number by $1 * 2^3 + 1 * 2^2 + 0 * 2^1 + 1 * 2^0 = 13_{10}$. Similarly, any binary number can be converted to a decimal number by summing each bit's contribution. The conversion to a hexadecimal number requires some insights. The following discussion should provide desired insights. Suppose you want to represent 16 different numbers using binary bits. How many bits would you need for this task? Recall that the number of different patterns a set of bits can form equals the number of different values the same set of bits can represent. As we saw in Section C.1, the different number of patterns is computed by equation 2^b, where b stands for the number of available bits. Coming back to our question, we now can answer that four bits are necessary to represent 16 different values. Notice that each hexadecimal digit can hold 16 different values: 0, 1, 2, 3, 4, 5, 6, 7, 8, 9, A, B, C, D, E, and F. This means that we need four binary bits to represent one hexadecimal digit. Thus, given a binary number, the necessary task is to start from the binary radix point and move to the left as we group four bits as a unit, representing a hexadecimal digit. The binary radix point is the limiting point equivalent to decimal point in the decimal number system. If the last group does not have four bits, the missing bits should be filled with leading zeros from the left. Once we have groups of four bits, we simply need to convert each group to its corresponding hexadecimal digit. Figure C.6 shows how this process is done using an example. The conversion of a four-bit group to a hexadecimal number follows the same step we used for converting a binary number to a decimal number, except now we can represent up to

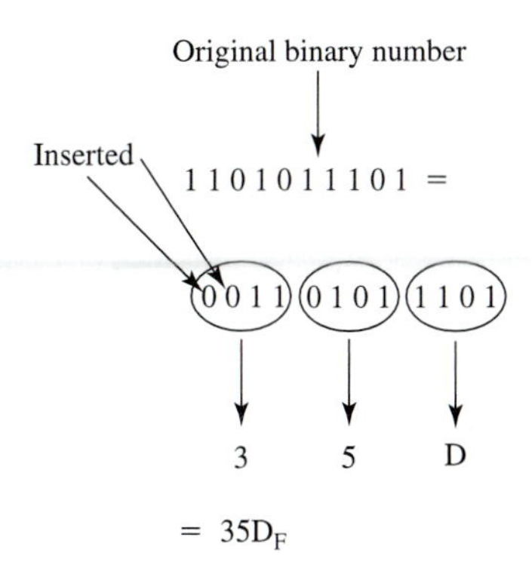

Figure C.6 An example of converting a binary number to a hexadecimal number.

decimal 15. As you become familiar with the conversion process, you learn to associate the 16 different bit patterns with 16 different hexadecimal symbols almost automatically.

In the example, note that the leftmost four-bit group originally did not have four bits. The missing bits of zeros were added before converting the group to a hexadecimal number. We next consider converting a decimal number to binary and hexadecimal numbers. First, let us convert a decimal number to its equivalent binary number. There are two different methods to do the task. You pick the one that appeals to you most. Both methods are shown in Figure C.7 starting with decimal number 249. The first method continuously divides the decimal number with 2 until you cannot do so anymore, keeping track of the remainder. The rationale for this method is that each iteration of division by two represents moving to the left from the binary radix point as we add an additional bit to represent the number. For example, the first division shows that the remainder is 1, which indicates we need to have bit 0 to hold 1, and the quotient is 124, which tells us we can divide the quotient with two again and we require an additional bit to do so. Figure C.7(a) shows the remainders (1 or 0) on the right-hand side for each iteration and the set of corresponding quotients. Once you cannot divide anymore, you can extract the result by gathering up the remainder bits from the bottom to the top. That is, you are gathering bits from the leftmost bit to the rightmost bit.

The second method is similar to the first one by using the values associated with each binary bit. To use this method, you first need to write down decimal values associated with each binary bit, starting from the binary radix point and moving to its left. We continue to generate the bit-associated decimal value while the bit-associated decimal value is less than the original decimal value we want to convert. We then start assigning a value (1 or 0) in bits starting from the left

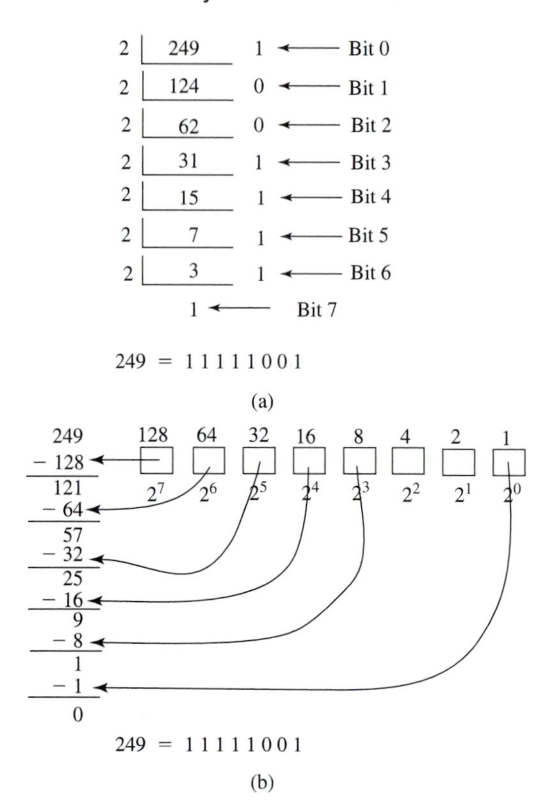

Figure C.7 Illustrations of two different conversion methods. Decimal number 249 is converted to its equivalent binary number by each method.

as we compare the original decimal value with the bit-associated decimal value. Let us look at the example shown in Figure C.7(b). In this example, we need to generate up to decimal value 128, which corresponds to bit 7 starting with bit 0 as the least significant bit. We stopped at the seventh bit since the decimal value to be converted is 249 and the eighth bit is associated with 256, which is greater than the original decimal value. Once the number of necessary bits is found, we start finding the corresponding bit value starting from the leftmost bit, the seventh bit for the current example. Starting with this bit, we consider whether we need the associated decimal value to represent decimal value 249. We certainly do need this bit and the bit must be 1, indicating that we require its contribution. We then move on to the next bit—bit 6. Since bit 7 is contributing to represent decimal 128, the remaining value we need to represent now is 121: 249 − 128. Bit 6 represents 64, which is also required to represent 121. Thus, we also assign 1 to bit 6, acknowledging that this bit is needed to represent decimal value 249. The remaining decimal value we need to represent is 57: 121 − 64. We move on to bit 5, which represents decimal 32. Again we need this number to represent 57, and bit 5 receives 1. Continuing the process, the remaining decimal number to represent is 25: 57−32. Bit 4 contributes 16 and we assign one to this bit. Now the remaining decimal number we need to represent is 9: 25 − 16. Bit 3 is associated with 8, and this bit needs to be 1. The remaining decimal number to represent is 1: 9 − 8. Bit 2 is associated with decimal value 4, but we only need to represent 1. Thus, this bit is set to 0 indicating that we do not need its contribution to represent decimal number 249. Considering bit 1 also shows that the associated decimal number for the bit, 2, is not needed to represent decimal 1. Finally, bit 0 is needed to represent the remaining decimal 1 since the bit-associated number is 1. Combining the bits together, we arrive at answer 11111001_2.

Next, let us consider converting decimal numbers to hexadecimal numbers. The conversion is done using the two methods shown earlier when we converted a decimal number to a binary number. The only difference is to divide with decimal 16 instead of decimal 2 for the first method and generating hexadecimal digit-associated decimal numbers for the second method. The conversions of decimal 249 using both methods are shown in Figure C.8.

Finally, let us consider converting a hexadecimal number to its equivalent binary and decimal numbers. We first study the conversion to binary numbers. To convert a hexadecimal number to its equivalent binary number, we need to perform the reverse task of changing a binary number to a hexadecimal number. That is, we need to represent each hexadecimal digit by a group of four binary bits and

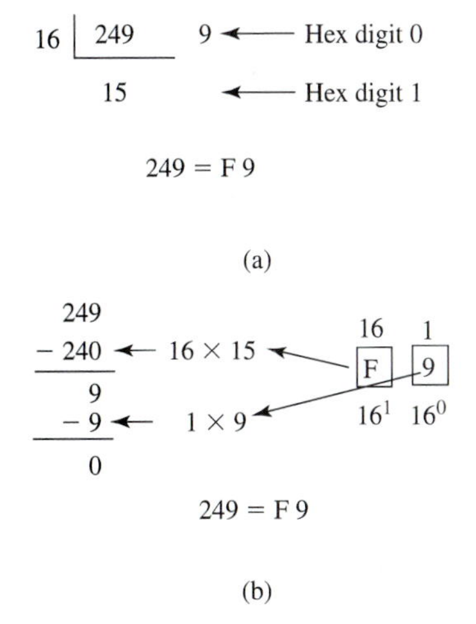

Figure C.8 An example to convert a decimal number to its corresponding hexadecimal number using two different methods.

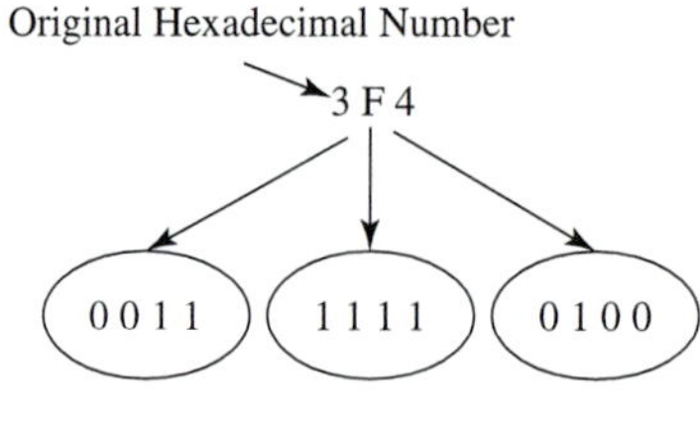

3F4 = 1 1 1 1 1 1 0 1 0 0

(a)

$3\,F\,4 = 3 \times 16^2 + 15 \;\; 16^1 + 4 \text{ x } 16^0 = 1012$

(b)

Figure C.9 An example illustrating the conversion from (a) a hexadecimal number to a binary number, and (b) from a hexadecimal number to a decimal number.

combine together the resulting groups of bits. Figure C.9(a) shows this process using hexadecimal number 3FA.

To convert a hexadecimal number to its equivalent decimal number, you simply need to sum contributions made by each hexadecimal digit, which is identical to the process of converting a binary number to a decimal number. For example, given the hexadecimal number 3FA, we need to perform the following computation:

$$3FA = 3 * 16^2 + 15(F) * 16^1 + 10(A) * 16^0$$

Notice that we converted hexadecimal digit F to decimal number 15 and hexadecimal digit A to decimal number 10 before carrying out the prior computation. In this section, we showed how to convert numbers from one number system to another. The techniques we showed in this section apply to conversions between any two number systems not considered in this appendix.

C.4 SUMMARY AND FURTHER READINGS

In this appendix, we presented number representations in the binary, decimal, and hexadecimal number systems. We showed that an interpretation of a number in any number system is performed by associating the positions of a number with appropriate weights. The appendix also presented the binary number arithmetic along with the 2's complement number representation. The 2's complement number representation provides a convenient means to perform binary arithmetic for negative numbers. Finally, we explained techniques to convert numbers from one number system to another number system in Section C.3. For those interested in the hardware implementation of the binary arithmetic operations discussed in Section C.2, we suggest the following books:

Vincent Heuring and Harry Jordan, *Computer Systems Design and Architecture*, Addison-Wesley, 1997.

David Patterson and John Hennessy, *Computer Organization and Design: The Hardware/Software Interface*, Morgan Kaufmann, 1994.

D

Digital Logic Fundamentals

D.1 OVERVIEW

This appendix contains a brief review of digital logic fundamentals. We cover the basic information of combinational and sequential logic necessary to understand the examples discussed in this text. For a detailed treatment of these topics and other related information, see the excellent digital logic text by John Wakerly ("Digital Design Principle and Practices," Third Edition, Prentice Hall Inc, 2000).

Digital logic components can be subdivided into two different categories: combinational and sequential. These two categories are illustrated in Figure D.1. A combinational logic circuit's output is determined by the current value of its inputs. For example, if we were designing a voting machine for use in a corporate boardroom to automatically determine whether the board members sitting around a conference table voted in the majority on a specific issue, the majority vote (the output) would be determined by the vote (current input) of each board member. As shown in Figure D.1, the output F is a function of the inputs A, B, and C.

Yet a sequential logic circuit's output is not only determined by its current input(s), but also the present state of the circuit. The circuit contains memory components (flip-flops) to store the current state of the sequential logic circuit. It also

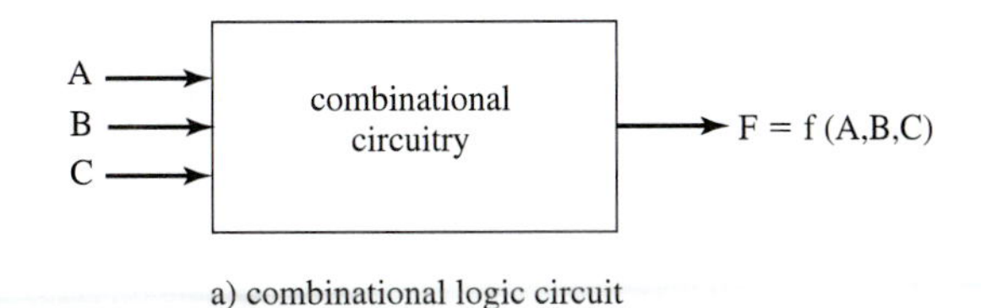

a) combinational logic circuit

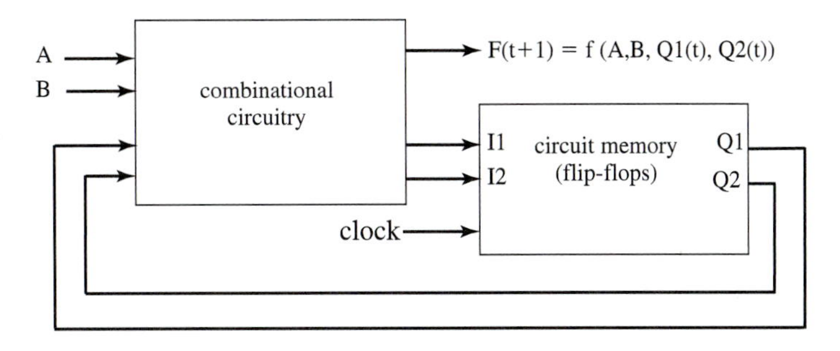

b) sequential logic circuit

Figure D.1 Digital logic fundamentals. (a) A combinational logic circuit's output is determined by the current value of its inputs, (b) A sequential logic circuit's output is determined by its current input(s) and the present state of the circuit.

contains a combinational logic portion to combine the current input(s) with the present state of the circuit to determine the circuit's output and its next state.

An elevator control circuit is a good example of a sequential logic circuit. When someone steps aboard an elevator and pushes the button for the floor that they desire (the input), the elevator control circuit takes into account the floor the elevator is currently on (present state) to determine whether the elevator should move up or down (output) and what floor it should stop at (next state). With this brief introduction to logic circuit categories, let us review each category in more detail.

D.2 BASIC COMBINATIONAL LOGIC

As mentioned previously, a combinational logic circuit's output is determined by the current value of its inputs. The transfer from inputs to outputs does not occur instantaneously. Internally combinational gates consist of several (or more) stages of transistor logic and therefore have a finite propagation delay. Propagation delay is the time delay from input change to output change. Each combinational gate within a given logic family has an associated propagation delay.

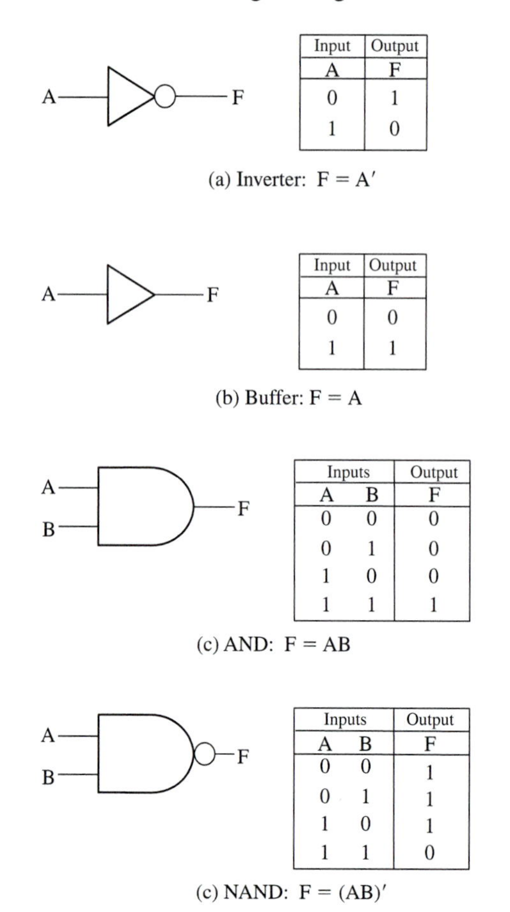

Input	Output
A	F
0	1
1	0

(a) Inverter: $F = A'$

Input	Output
A	F
0	0
1	1

(b) Buffer: $F = A$

Inputs		Output
A	B	F
0	0	0
0	1	0
1	0	0
1	1	1

(c) AND: $F = AB$

Inputs		Output
A	B	F
0	0	1
0	1	1
1	0	1
1	1	0

(c) NAND: $F = (AB)'$

Figure D.2 Combinational logic

Figures D.2 and D.3 are the most common combinational logic gates. These gates may be configured to form more complex devices such as arithmetic logic units (ALUs), multiplexers, demultiplexers/decoders, and so on. We discuss some of these more complex devices in the next section. The analysis and design of combinational circuits is beyond the scope of this brief review. Numerous textbooks dedicated to this topic are widely available. A brief description of the common combinational logic gates follow:

Inverter An inverter is used to change the logic level of the input. A logic high is converted to a logic low at the output and vice versa.

Buffer At first exposure to a buffer, you might wonder what good is a logic device that converts a logic high input to a logic high output and a logic low input

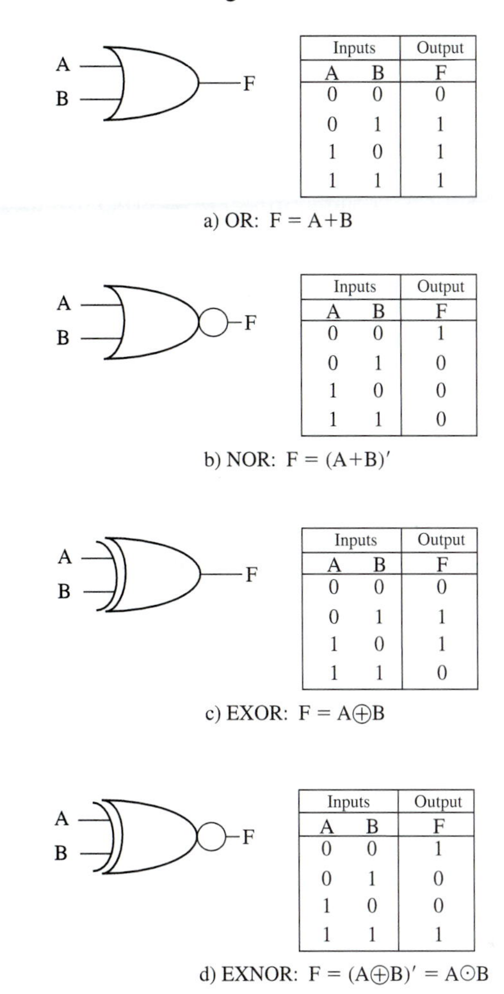

Inputs		Output
A	B	F
0	0	0
0	1	1
1	0	1
1	1	1

a) OR: F = A+B

Inputs		Output
A	B	F
0	0	1
0	1	0
1	0	0
1	1	0

b) NOR: F = (A+B)′

Inputs		Output
A	B	F
0	0	0
0	1	1
1	0	1
1	1	0

c) EXOR: F = $A \oplus B$

Inputs		Output
A	B	F
0	0	1
0	1	0
1	0	0
1	1	1

d) EXNOR: F = $(A \oplus B)' = A \odot B$

Figure D.3 Combinational logic

to a logic low output. The buffer may be used to introduce a desired time delay into a circuit by taking advantage of the gate's propagation delay. The buffer may also be used to extend the fanout capability of a logic signal. Recall from the memory chapter that fanout is the number of input gates that a gate's output may drive (be connected to) and still operate correctly.

AND An "AND" gate provides a logic high output when all of its inputs are logic high.

NAND The "NOT-AND" gate or "NAND" gate is simply an "AND" gate followed by an inverter.

OR An "OR" gate provides a logic high output when one or more of its inputs are at logic high.

NOR The "NOT-OR" gate or "NOR" gate is an "OR" gate followed by an inverter.

EXOR The "Exclusive-OR" gate or "EXOR" provides a logic high output when its inputs are at different logic levels.

EXNOR The "Exclusive-NOR" gate or "EXNOR" is also called the equivalence gate. It provides a logic high output when its inputs are at the same (equivalent) logic level.

D.2.1 Medium-Scale Integration Combinational Circuits

The basic combinational logic components may be assembled into functional units such as arithemetic logic units (ALUs), multiplexers, demultiplexers, magnitude comparators, and so on. These functional units are commonly referred to as medium scale integration (MSI) components since 10s to 100s of fundamental

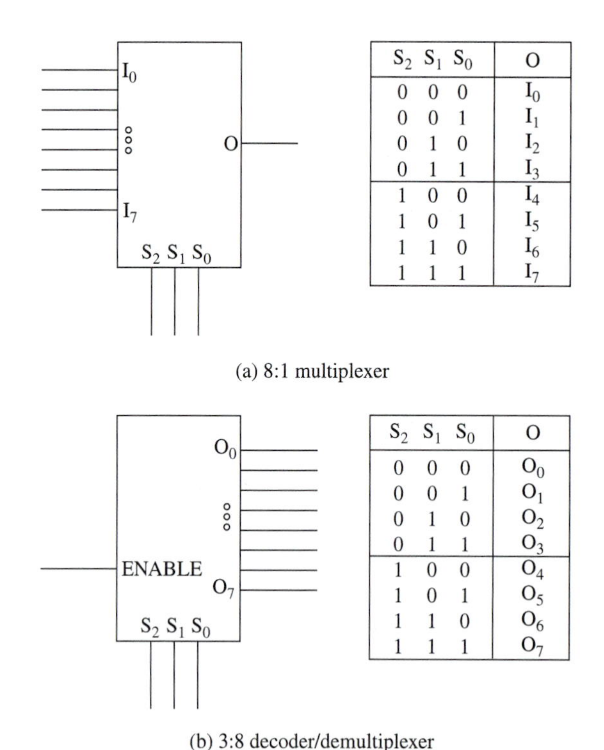

S_2	S_1	S_0	O
0	0	0	I_0
0	0	1	I_1
0	1	0	I_2
0	1	1	I_3
1	0	0	I_4
1	0	1	I_5
1	1	0	I_6
1	1	1	I_7

(a) 8:1 multiplexer

S_2	S_1	S_0	O
0	0	0	O_0
0	0	1	O_1
0	1	0	O_2
0	1	1	O_3
1	0	0	O_4
1	0	1	O_5
1	1	0	O_6
1	1	1	O_7

(b) 3:8 decoder/demultiplexer

Figure D.4 Medium scale integration—combinational logic circuits.

logic components are required to implement them into a single integrated circuit. Space does not permit covering all of the different MSI combinational circuits available. Figure D.4 illustrates some of the MSI combinational logic circuits commonly used in a microprocessor-based system.

Multiplexer A multiplexer may be used for data routing. It has multiple inputs and a single output. An electronic connection is made between a given input and the output by placing the binary value of the input on the select lines S[2:1:0]. For example, to connect input 7 (I_7) to the output O, the binary value 111 is placed on the select lines S[2:1:0].

Decoder/Demultiplexer A decoder/demultiplexer circuit is extensively used in memory address decoding and data routing. A decoder has a one hot code output. That is, only one of its outputs are active at a given time. For example, if 111 is placed on the select lines S[2:1:0], output line O_7 is an active logic high, whereas the other outputs are at an active low logic level.

A decoder may be configured as a data-routing demultiplexer by providing an input signal to the "ENABLE" pin on the decoder. For example, if 111 is placed on the select lines S[2:1:0], output line O_7 is an active logic high when the "ENABLE" pin is high and low when the "ENABLE" pin is low. This has the overall effect of routing the input signal at the "ENABLE" pin to the output pin selected by S[2:1:0].

D.3 SEQUENTIAL LOGIC CIRCUITS

The other category of logic circuits is sequental logic circuits. A sequential logic circuit's output is determined by its current input(s) and the present state of the circuit. The circuit contains memory components (flip-flops) to store the current state of the sequential logic circuit. It also contains a combinational logic portion to combine the current input(s) with the present state of the circuit to determine the circuit's output and its next state. As can be seen from this definition, flip-flops are a key component of a sequential logic circuit.

D.3.1 Flip-Flops

There are many different types of flip-flops: SR, T, D, and JK. We only discuss two of the more common types: the D flip-flop and the JK flip-flop. Both of these flip-flops are illustrated in Figure D.5.

D Flip-Flop The D type flip-flop has a single input designated D and a single output designated Q. For a positive edge-triggered D flip-flop, the D input is

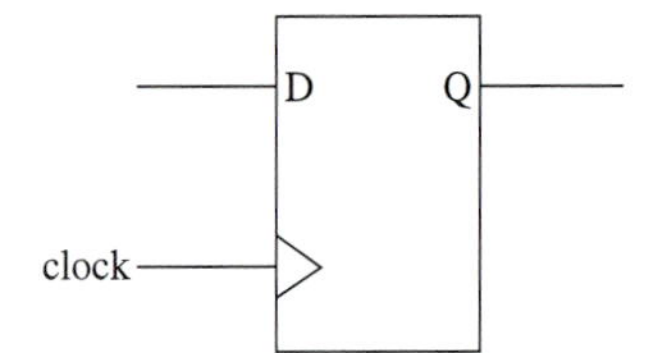

D	Q(t+1)
0	0
1	1

(a) positive edge-triggered synchronous D flip-flop

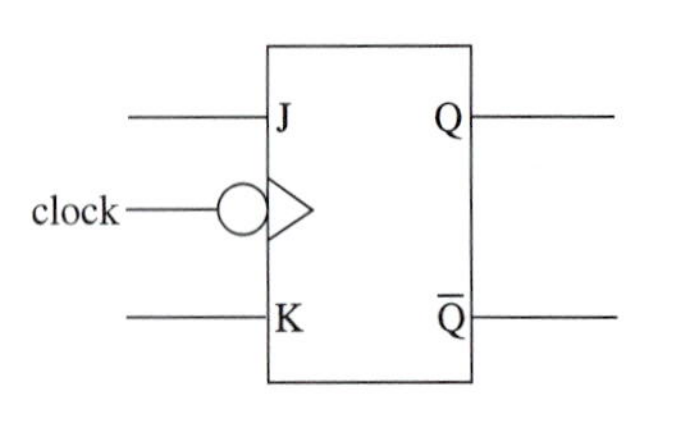

J	K	Q(t)	Q(t+1)
0	0	0	0 (no change)
0	0	1	1 (no change)
0	1	0	0 (reset)
0	1	1	0 (reset)
1	0	0	1 (set)
1	0	1	1 (set)
1	1	0	1 (toggle)
1	1	1	0 (toggle)

(b) negative edge-triggered synchronous J-K flip-flop

Figure D.5 Flip-flops.

transferred and held constant as the Q output on the rising edge of the clock. The action of a positive edge-triggered D flip-flop is illustrated in Figure D.6. The D flip-flop is commonly used to temporarily hold logic values for the microprocessor.

JK Flip-flop The JK edge-triggered flip-flop's operation is slightly more complicated than the D flip-flop. The flip-flop's output after the clock edge, $Q(t+1)$, is determined by the value of the output before the clock edge, $Q(t)$, and the inputs J and K as shown in Figure D.5. For example, if the flip-flop's current output $Q(t)$ is 1 and the J input is 0 and the K input is 1, the output $Q(t+1)$ after the clock edge is logic 0. This is designated as a reset action. The action of a negative edge-triggered JK flip-flop is illustrated in Figure D.6.

D.3.2 MSI Sequential Circuit Components

Flip-flops may be combined with combinational logic components to construct MSI sequential circuit components. In this section, we cover only three of the more common devices: registers, shift registers, and binary counters. These components are illustrated in Figure D.7. As before, the design details of these components are not discussed. The interested reader is referred to Wakerly.

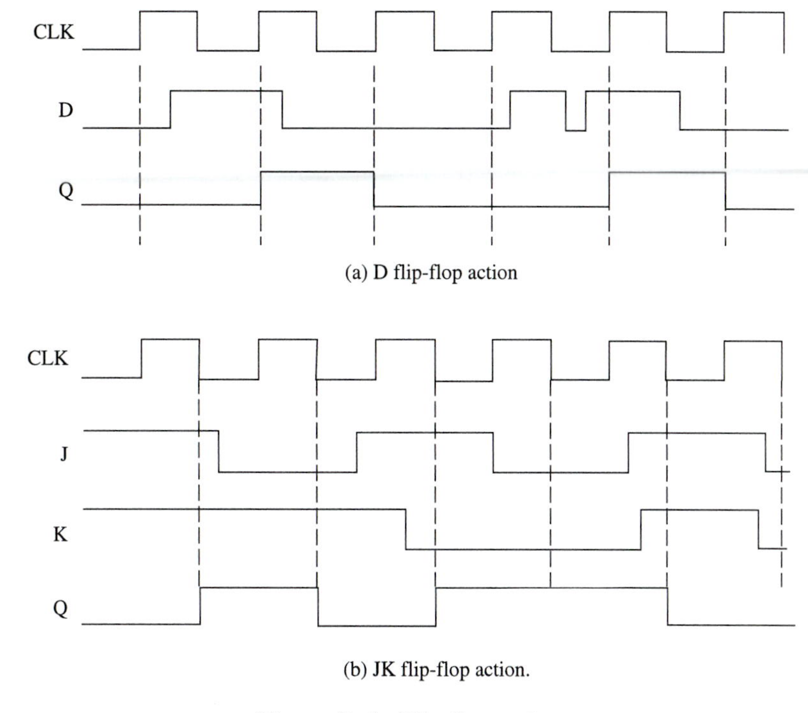

(a) D flip-flop action

(b) JK flip-flop action.

Figure D.6 Flip-flop action.

Registers A register is nothing more than a collection of D flip-flops. Figure D.7 shows a four-bit register. Normally, a register is loaded in parallel by placing an active load signal on the $\overline{load}$ control line. The four bits are loaded in parallel on the next clock edge.

Shift Registers A shift register is a register that has additional circuitry to shift either to the right, left, or both directions. Figure D.7(b) illustrates a four-bit right shift register with parallel load. It is configured with both parallel and serial inputs. If the serial out signal pin is connected to the serial in signal pin, the output from the last bit on the left is connected to the rightmost bit. This circular configuration implements the rotate right function. Each bit is shifted to the right on each incoming clock pulse.

Binary Counters A binary counter increments for every incoming clock pulse. Illustrated in Figure D.7 is a 4-bit binary counter. This counter counts from 0000 to 1111 and then resets to 0000 and continues counting. This counter is also equipped with a parallel load.

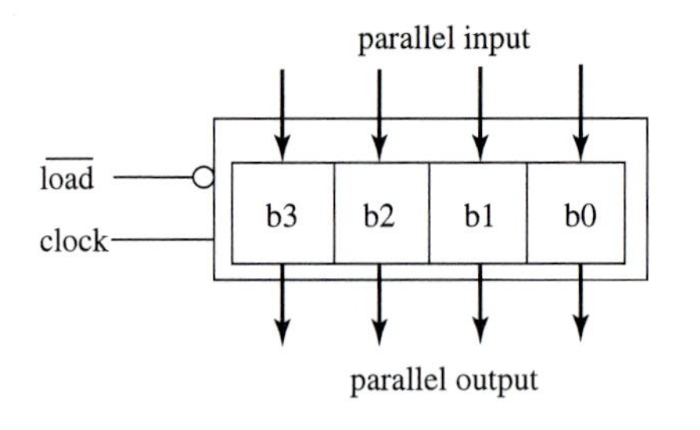

(a) 4-bit register

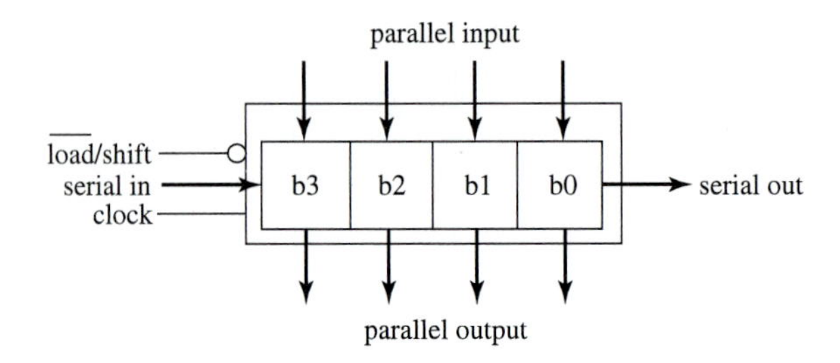

(b) 4-bit right shift register with parallel load

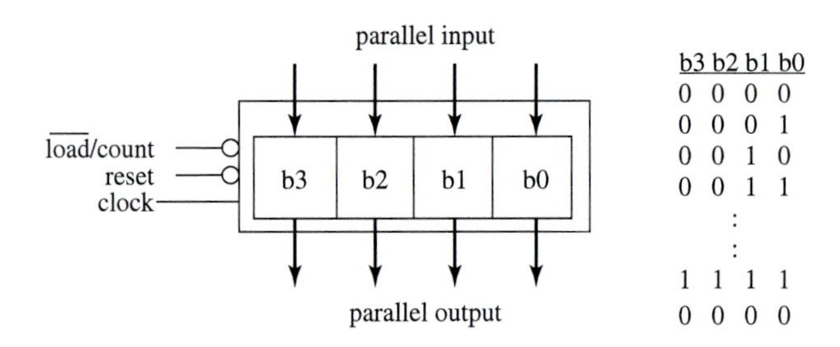

(c) 4-bit binary counter with parallel load

Figure D.7 Medium scale integration—sequential logic circuits.

D.4 SUMMARY

This appendix provided a brief review of logic fundamentals. We saw how logic components may be subdivided into combinational or sequential logic circuits. In each category, we reviewed the fundamental basic components and then saw how they can be combined to form MSI functional units. We limited our discussion to components commonly used in a microprocessor-based system.

E

Mobile Robot and Related Products for the 68HC12

In this appendix, we first provide information to construct your own mobile robot followed by the software and hardware products for the 68HC12 microcontroller. The first section presents engineering diagrams of the mobile robot used at the Air Force Academy. We also include data needed to create all electronic components of the robot in this section. In Section E.2, we list commercial software and hardware products that can be used in conjunction with the 68HC12 microcontroller. The purpose of Section E.2 is not to collect and describe all available products, but to provide the contact information for enough companies who manufacture 68HC12-related products. We do not endorse any particular company, but encourage you to use the information found in this appendix as a starting point to search for the right products for your applications. A large portion of the information of this appendix is extracted from a list of third-vendor products appearing on the Motorola microcontroller web site (*http://www.mcu.motsps.com*). The Motorola site is constantly modified for the up-to-date list of 68HC12 products. The textbook website (*http://www.prenhall.com/pack*) has a direct link to the Motorola's site for your convenience.

E.1 BUILDING YOUR OWN MOBILE ROBOT

In this section, we present the physical dimensions of the components of the mobile robot, which was used throughout the book. If desired, you can use the data provided in this section to create your own mobile robot. The robot contains a circular top plate, a semicircular bottom plate, two motor mount pieces, two DC motors, an IR sensor board, two sets of stability assisting bolts and nuts, two wheels, a connector, and cables to the 68HC812EVB. Figure E.1 displays three different diagrams of the robot seen from three points of view. The three different perspectives provide us a means to completely describe physical appearances of the robot. For example, the top view shows that the IR sensor board is mounted to the front portion of the top plate of the robot and how each sensor is placed to detect walls to the robot's left, center, and right. Similarly, the front view shows the positions of the DC motors and the positional relationship between wheels and motor mounts.

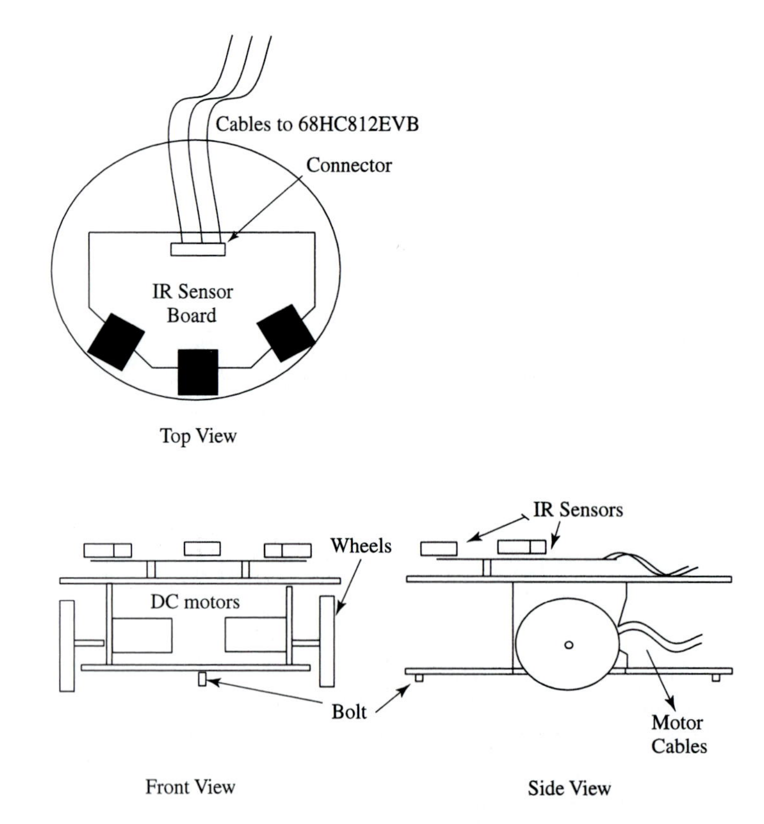

Figure E.1 A diagram of the mobile robot seen from three different perspectives.

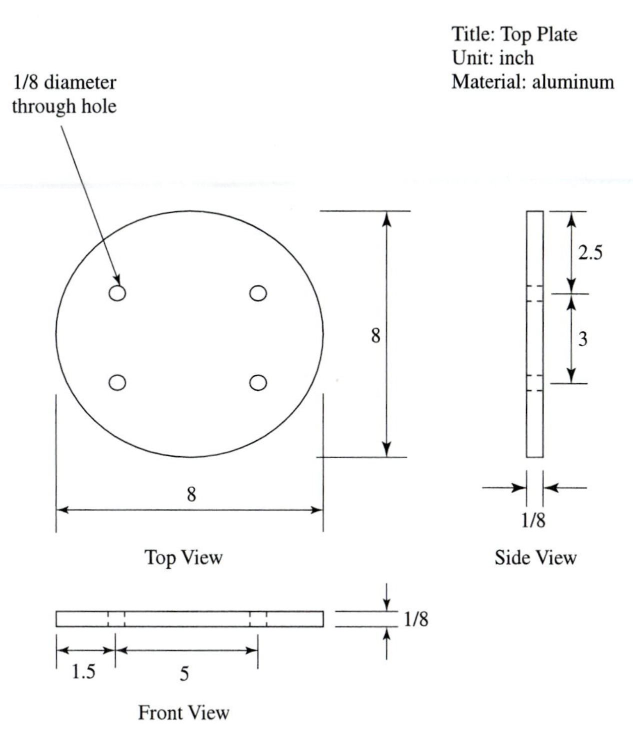

Figure E.2 The top plate of the mobile robot. Three views of the plate is shown with specified dimensions.

The robot body is made of two 8-inch diameter circular aluminum disks. The top plate shown in Figure E.2 houses the IR sensor board. If desired, we can mount the 68HC812EVB for autonomous robot control. Our experience shows that it is prudent to start with the EVB board off the robot connected to the robot using cables during the initial stage of your program development. Once all your programs are tested and you are confident of the correctness of your programs, you can mount the evaluation board on the robot. The bottom plate is shown in Figure E.3. Note that the circular plate has been modified to give rooms for the wheels. Also note that at the front and back of the bottom plate, the robot has holes to place two bolts. These bolts are used to balance the robot (the robot is an unstable system with two ground contact points generated by the two wheels) . For all practical purposes, the plates can be made out of any sturdy material such as plastic or wood.

Two motor mount units are used to fasten DC motors to the robot as shown in Figure E.4. The mount must be tall enough to separate upper and lower decks with enough clearance for wheels. The one used for our robot is $2\frac{3}{4}$ inches tall, 4 inches wide, with an $1\frac{3}{8}$-inch diameter hole for the motor in the center of the

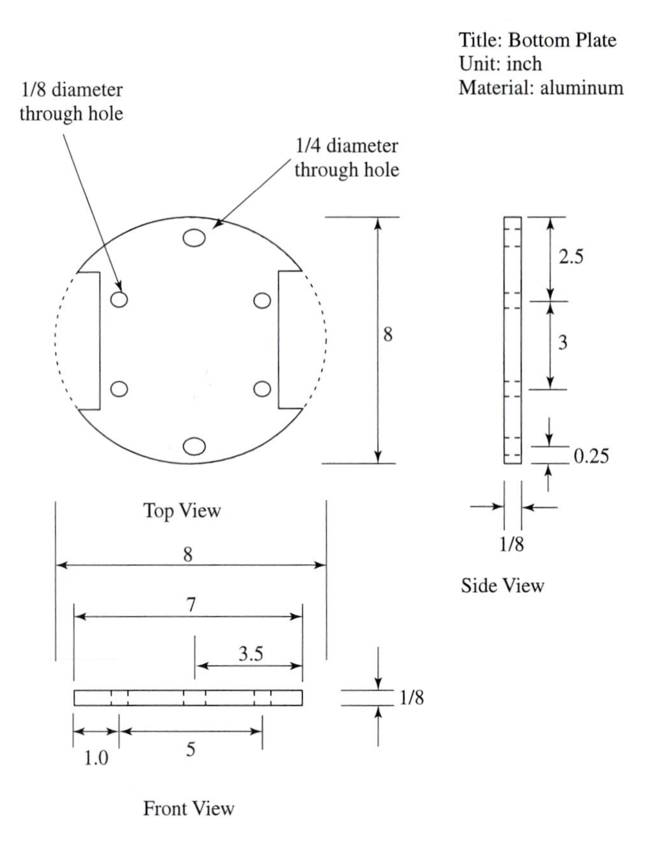

Figure E.3 The figure shows three different views of the bottom plate for the mobile robot.

mount. A setscrew is used to fasten the motor body to the mount, and the motor mount is attached to both the top and bottom plates of the robot. Notice that the motor mount piece has a slight opening at one side of the hole to accommodate easy motor installations.

The wheels on our robot are locally manufactured. The motor shaft is fastened onto the wheel using a setscrew. Alternatively, a locking hub can be used. For a professional looking robot, we recommend purchasing your wheels from a local hobby store or a company named Tower Hobbies. You can find a variety of ready-made wheels. The DC motors we used are two Barber-Colman #FYQF-63310-9 motors that use a 12VDC power source. These motors are available from C&H Sales (stock#DCM9902) for about $15 each (800-325-9465) .

We used a nine-pin connector (five for sensor board, four for motors) to organize cables connecting the robot to the 68HC812EVB. You can get such connectors from DigiKey (part number WM1226 and WM1236) (800-344-4539) .

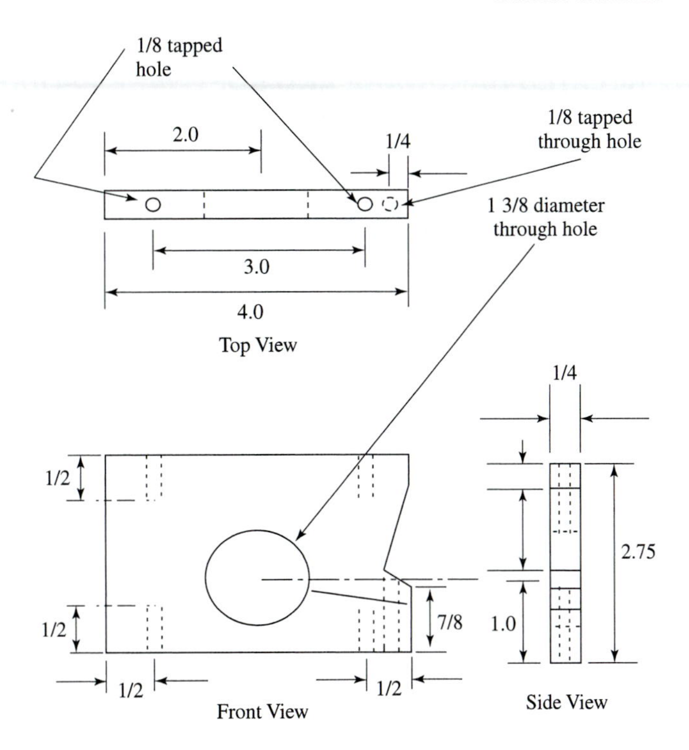

Figure E.4 The motor mount piece is used to tighten a DC motor. Two motor mount pieces (one for each motor) are attached to both the top and bottom plates of the robot.

The sensor board shown in Figure E.1 contains three sensor modules. The board is locally manufactured using a photosensitive PC board and a chemical etching process. Each sensor module is shown in the Chapter 9 Laboratory Application section. For each sensor module, you need a 50 ohm resistor, a 12 M ohm resistor, a 2 M ohm potentiometer, an IR transmitter, and an IR receiver. The hoods for the IR sensors are locally made, but you can use $\frac{1}{4}$-inch shrink tubing to provide the desired directionality of the IR transmitting beam. You can also use a breadboard instead of the sensor board to implement your sensor system. Wire wrapping or soldering on padded prototyping boards are also viable options.

As can be seen in Figure E.1, standoffs are used to raise the sensor board off the top deck. Each standoff is 0.375 inches tall and has 4-40 threads (four standoffs are used). These standoffs are available from Digikey. Finally, for cables, any communication cable such as AWG 22 works. You need nine cables connecting your EVB and the robot.

E.2 68HC12-RELATED HARDWARE AND SOFTWARE PRODUCTS

E.2.1 Hardware

68HC12 Evaluation Boards

- Axiom Manufacturing
  2813 Industrial Lane
  Garland, TX 75041
  (972) 926-9303
  http://www.axman.com
- Elektronikladen Mikrocomputer
  http://www.electronickladen.de
- Hitex Development Tools
  Greschbachstr 12
  76229 Karlsruhe
  Germany
  +49-721-9628-0
  http://www.hitex.de
- Noral
  88 Pleasant St.
  Natick, MA 01760-5634
  (888) 883-3284
  http://www.noral.com
- Newark Electronics (Colorado)
  4725 Paris Street
  Denver, CO 80239-2803
  (303) 373-4540
  http://www.newark.com/edu (National)
  (800) 463-9275 (National)

Flash Memory Programmer

- Hitex Development Tools
  Greschbachstr 12
  76229 Karlsruhe
  Germany
  +49-721-9628-0
  http://www.hitex.de
- HIWARE Metrowerks
  Riehenring 175
  CH-4058
  Basel Switzerland
  +41-61-690-7500
  http://www.hiware.com
- IAR Systems
  One Maritime Plaza, Suite 1770
  San Francisco, CA 94111
  (415) 765-5500
  http://www.iar.com
- Noral
  88 Pleasant St.
  Natick, MA 01760-5634
  (888) 883-3284
  http://www.noral.com
- P & E Microcomputers, Inc.
  710 Commonwealth Ave.
  Boston, MA 02215
  (617) 353-9206
  http://www.pemicro.com

Infrared Emitter and Detector

- Newark Electronics *http://www.newark.com*
- Radio Shack *http://www.radioshack.com*

E.2.2 Software

Development Software

- Archimedes Software, Inc.
  303 Parkplace Center #125
  Kirkland, WA 98033
  (800) 338-1453
  http://www.archimedessoftware.com
- Ashling Microsystems
  1270 Oakmead Parkway, Suite 208
  Sunnyvale, CA 94085
  (408) 732-6490
  http://www.ashling.com
- HIWARE Metrowerks
  Riehenring 175
  CH-4058
  Basel Switzerland
  +41-61-690-7500
  http://www.hiware.com
- IAR Systems
  One Maritime Plaza, Suite 1770
  San Francisco, CA 94111
  (415) 765-5500
  http://www.iar.com
- ImageCraft
  706 Colorado Ave.
  Palo Alto, CA 94303
  (650) 493-9326
  http://www.imagecraft.com
- P & E Microcomputers, Inc.
  710 Commonwealth Ave.
  Boston, MA 02215
  (617) 353-9206
  http://www.pemicro.com

C Compiler/Cross Assembler/Assembler

- Archimedes Software, Inc.
  303 Parkplace Center #125
  Kirkland, WA 98033
  (800) 338-1453
  http://www.archimedessoftware.com
- Ashling Microsystems
  1270 Oakmead Parkway, Suite 208
  Sunnyvale, CA 94085
  (408) 732-6490
  http://www.ashling.com
- Cosmic Software
  400 West Cummings Park, STE 6000
  Woburn, MA 01801-6512
  (781) 932-2556
  http://www.cosmic-software.com
- HIWARE Metrowerks
  Riehenring 175
  CH-4058
  Basel Switzerland
  +41-61-690-7500
  http://www.hiware.com
- IAR Systems
  One Maritime Plaza, Suite 1770
  San Francisco, CA 94111
  (415) 765-5500
  http://www.iar.com
- ImageCraft
  706 Colorado Ave.
  Palo Alto, CA 94303
  (650) 493-9326
  http://www.imagecraft.com

- Metrowerks Corporation
  9801 Metric Blvd., Suite #100
  Austin, TX 78758
  (800) 377-5416
  http://www.metrowerks.com
- P & E Microcomputers, Inc.
  710 Commonwealth Ave.
  Boston, MA 02215
  (617) 353-9206
  http://www.pemicro.com

Emulator/Simulator

- Ashling Microsystems
  1270 Oakmead Parkway, Suite 208
  Sunnyvale, CA 94085
  (408) 732-6490
  http://www.ashling.com
- Avocet Systems, Inc.
  120 Union St.
  P.O. Box 490
  Rockport, Maine 04856
  (800) 448-8500
  http://www.avocetsystems.com
- Cosmic Software
  400 West Cummings Park, STE 6000
  Woburn, MA 01801-6512
  (781) 932-2556
  http://www.cosmic-software.com
- Hitex Development Tools
  Greschbachstr 12
  76229 Karlsruhe
  Germany
  +49-721-9628-0
  http://www.hitex.de

- iSYSTEM
  16776 Bernado Center Drive, Suite 204A
  San Diego, CA 92128
  (858) 385-9100
  http://www.isystem.com
- Nohau Corporation
  51 E Campbell Ave.
  Campbell, CA 95008
  (888) 886-6428
  http://www.nohau.com
- Noral
  88 Pleasant St.
  Natick, MA 01760-5634
  (888) 883-3284
  http://www.noral.com
- P & E Microcomputers, Inc.
  710 Commonwealth Ave.
  Boston, MA 02215
  (617) 353-9206
  http://www.pemicro.com

Background Mode Debugger

- Ashling Microsystems
  1270 Oakmead Parkway, Suite 208
  Sunnyvale, CA 94085
  (408) 732-6490
  http://www.ashling.com
- Avocet Systems, Inc.
  120 Union St.
  P.O. Box 490
  Rockport, Maine 04856
  (800) 448-8500
  http://www.avocetsystems.com

- Cosmic Software
  400 West Cummings Park, STE 6000
  Woburn, MA 01801-6512
  (781) 932-2556
  http://www.cosmic-software.com
- Hitex Development Tools
  Greschbachstr 12
  76229 Karlsruhe
  Germany
  +49-721-9628-0
  http://www.hitex.de
- HIWARE Metrowerks
  Riehenring 175
  CH-4058
  Basel Switzerland
  +41-61-690-7500
  http://www.hiware.com
- IAR Systems
  One Maritime Plaza, Suite 1770
  San Francisco, CA 94111
  (415) 765-5500
  http://www.iar.com
- iSYSTEM
  16776 Bernado Center Drive, Suite 204A
  San Diego, CA 92128
  (858) 385-9100
  http://www.isystem.com
- LAUTERBACH
  4 Mount Royal Ave.
  Marlborough, MA 01752
  (508) 333-6812
  http://www.lauterbach.

- Nohau Corporation
  51 E Campbell Ave.
  Campbell, CA 95008
  (888) 886-6428
  http://www.nohau.com
- Noral
  88 Pleasant St.
  Natick, MA 01760-5634
  (888) 883-3284
  http://www.noral.com
- P & E Microcomputers, Inc.
  710 Commonwealth Ave.
  Boston, MA 02215
  (617) 353-9206
  http://www.pemicro.com

Fuzzy and Neuro Tools

- Inform Software Corp.
  222 South Riverside Plaza, Suite 1410
  Chicago, IL 60606
  (312) 575-0578
  http://www.fuzzytech.com

Index

Software License